Introduction to Cryptography
with Coding Theory

Library of Congress Cataloging-in-Publication Data

Trappe, Wade.
    Introduction to cryptography : with coding theory / Wade Trappe, Lawrence C. Washington.
        p. cm.
    Includes bibliographical references and index.
    ISBN: 0-13-061814-4
    1. Coding Theory. 2. Cryptography.   I. Washington, Lawrence C.
    II. Title
QA268 .T73 2001   2001036652
005.8'2--dc21

Acquisition Editor: *George Lobell*
Editor-in-Chief: *Sally Yagan*
Vice-President/Director of Production and Manufacturing: *David W. Riccardi*
Executive Managing Editor: *Kathleen Schiaparelli*
Senior Managing Editor: *Linda Mihatov Behrens*
Assistant Managing Editor: *Bayani Mendoza de Leon*
Production Editor: *Jeanne Audino*
Manufacturing Buyer: *Alan Fischer*
Manufacturing Manager: *Trudy Pisciotti*
Marketing Manager: *Angela Battle*
Marketing Assistant: *Rachel Beckman*
Editorial Assistant: *Melanie Van Benthuysen*
Art Director: *Jayne Conte*
Cover Designer: *Joseph Sengotta*
Cover Photo: *Toby, 1964. Painting by Victor Vasarely*

Prentice Hall

©2002 by Prentice-Hall, Inc.
Upper Saddle River, New Jersey 07458

Printed in the United States of America

10 9 8 7 6 5 4 3 2 1

ISBN 0-13-061814-4

Pearson Education Ltd., *London*
Pearson Education Australia Pty., Limited, *Sydney*
Pearson Education Singapore, Pte. Ltd
Pearson Education North Asia Ltd., *Hong Kong*
Pearson Education Canada, Ltd., *Toronto*
Pearson Education de Mexico, S.A. de C.V.
Pearson Education—Japan, *Tokyo*
Pearson Education Malaysia, Pte. Ltd.

Introduction to Cryptography
with Coding Theory

Wade Trappe

*Department of Electrical and Computer Engineering and
the Institute for Systems Research
University of Maryland*

Lawrence C. Washington

*Department of Mathematics
University of Maryland*

Prentice
Hall

PRENTICE HALL, Upper Saddle River, NJ 07458

Contents

Preface   **xi**

1 Overview   **1**
   1.1   Secure Communications 2
   1.2   Cryptographic Applications 9

2 Classical Cryptosystems   **12**
   2.1   Shift Ciphers 13
   2.2   Affine Ciphers 14
   2.3   The Vigenère Cipher 16
   2.4   Substitution Ciphers 23
   2.5   Sherlock Holmes 26
   2.6   The Playfair and ADFGX Ciphers 29
   2.7   Block Ciphers 33
   2.8   Binary Numbers and ASCII 37
   2.9   One-Time Pads 38
   2.10   Pseudo-random Bit Generation 40
   2.11   Linear Feedback Shift Register Sequences 42
   2.12   Enigma 49
   2.13   Exercises 54
   2.14   Computer Problems 56

3 Basic Number Theory   **59**
   3.1   Basic Notions 59
   3.2   Solving $ax + by = d$ 65
   3.3   Congruences 66
   3.4   The Chinese Remainder Theorem 72
   3.5   Modular Exponentiation 74
   3.6   Fermat and Euler 75
   3.7   Primitive Roots 79
   3.8   Inverting Matrices Mod n 80
   3.9   Square Roots Mod n 81

3.10 Finite Fields 83
3.11 Exercises 91
3.12 Computer Problems 95

4 The Data Encryption Standard   97
4.1   Introduction 97
4.2   A Simplified DES-Type Algorithm 98
4.3   Differential Cryptanalysis 102
4.4   DES 107
4.5   Modes of Operation 115
4.6   Breaking DES 118
4.7   Password Security 123
4.8   Exercises 125

5 AES: Rijndael   127
5.1   The Basic Algorithm 128
5.2   The Layers 129
5.3   Decryption 133
5.4   Design Considerations 136

6 The RSA Algorithm   137
6.1   The RSA Algorithm 137
6.2   Attacks on RSA 142
6.3   Primality Testing 145
6.4   Factoring 149
6.5   The RSA Challenge 154
6.6   An Application to Treaty Verification 156
6.7   The Public Key Concept 156
6.8   Exercises 159
6.9   Computer Problems 162

7 Discrete Logarithms   165
7.1   Discrete Logarithms 165
7.2   Computing Discrete Logs 166
7.3   Bit Commitment 173
7.4   The ElGamal Public Key Cryptosystem 173
7.5   Exercises 175
7.6   Computer Problems 176

8 Digital Signatures   177
8.1   RSA Signatures 178
8.2   The ElGamal Signature Scheme 179
8.3   Hash Functions 182

8.4 Birthday Attacks 186
8.5 The Digital Signature Algorithm 190
8.6 Exercises 191
8.7 Computer Problems 194

9 E-Commerce and Digital Cash   **196**
9.1 Secure Electronic Transaction 197
9.2 Digital Cash 199
9.3 Exercises 206

10 Secret Sharing Schemes   **208**
10.1 Secret Splitting 208
10.2 Threshold Schemes 209
10.3 Exercises 215
10.4 Computer Problems 217

11 Games   **219**
11.1 Flipping Coins over the Telephone 219
11.2 Poker over the Telephone 221
11.3 Exercises 226

12 Zero-Knowledge Techniques   **228**
12.1 The Basic Setup 228
12.2 Feige-Fiat-Shamir Identification Scheme 231
12.3 Exercises 233

13 Key Establishment Protocols   **236**
13.1 Key Agreement Protocols 237
13.2 Key Pre-distribution 239
13.3 Key Distribution 241
13.4 Public Key Infrastructures (PKI) 246
13.5 Exercises 248

14 Information Theory   **250**
14.1 Probability Review 251
14.2 Entropy 253
14.3 Huffman Codes 258
14.4 Perfect Secrecy 260
14.5 The Entropy of English 263
14.6 Exercises 268

15 Elliptic Curves   **272**

15.1   The Addition Law 272

15.2   Elliptic Curves Mod n 276

15.3   Factoring with Elliptic Curves 280

15.4   Elliptic Curves in Characteristic 2 284

15.5   Elliptic Curve Cryptosystems 287

15.6   Exercises 290

15.7   Computer Problems 293

16 Error Correcting Codes   **295**

16.1   Introduction 295

16.2   Error Correcting Codes 301

16.3   Bounds on General Codes 305

16.4   Linear Codes 311

16.5   Hamming Codes 319

16.6   Golay Codes 320

16.7   Cyclic Codes 329

16.8   BCH Codes 335

16.9   Reed-Solomon Codes 343

16.10 The McEliece Cryptosystem 345

16.11 Other Topics 348

16.12 Exercises 349

16.13 Computer Problems 352

17 Quantum Cryptography   **353**

17.1   A Quantum Experiment 354

17.2   Quantum Key Distribution 357

17.3   Shor's Algorithm 359

17.4   Exercises 370

A Mathematica   **372**

A.1   Getting Started with Mathematica 372

A.2   Some Commands 374

A.3   Examples for Chapter 2 375

A.4   Examples for Chapter 3 382

A.5   Examples for Chapter 6 386

A.6   Examples for Chapter 8 394

A.7   Examples for Chapter 10 395

A.8   Examples for Chapter 11 396

A.9   Examples for Chapter 15 397

B Maple Examples   **403**
  B.1   Getting Started with Maple 403
  B.2   Some Commands 404
  B.3   Examples for Chapter 2 406
  B.4   Examples for Chapter 3 414
  B.5   Examples for Chapter 6 419
  B.6   Examples for Chapter 8 428
  B.7   Examples for Chapter 10 428
  B.8   Examples for Chapter 11 430
  B.9   Examples for Chapter 15 432

C MATLAB Examples   **437**
  C.1   Getting Started with MATLAB 438
  C.2   Examples for Chapter 2 444
  C.3   Examples for Chapter 3 456
  C.4   Examples for Chapter 6 460
  C.5   Examples for Chapter 8 466
  C.6   Examples for Chapter 10 466
  C.7   Examples for Chapter 11 467
  C.8   Examples for Chapter 15 470

D Further Reading   **478**

Bibliography   **479**

Index   **485**

Preface

This book is based on a course in cryptography at the upper level undergraduate and beginning graduate level that has been given at the University of Maryland since 1997. When designing the course, we decided on the following requirements.

- The course should be up-to-date and cover a broad selection of topics from a mathematical point of view.

- The material should be accessible to mathematically mature students having little background in number theory and computer programming.

- There should be examples involving numbers large enough to demonstrate how the algorithms really work.

We wanted to avoid concentrating solely on RSA and discrete logarithms, which would have made the course mostly a number theory course. We also did not want to teach a course on protocols and how to hack into friends' computers. That would have made the course less mathematical than desired.

There are numerous topics in cryptology that can be discussed in an introductory course. We have tried to include many of them. The chapters represent, for the most part, topics that were covered during the different semesters we taught the course. There is certainly more material here than could be treated in most one-semester courses. The first eight chapters represent the core of the material. The choice of which of the remaining chapters are used depends on the level of the students.

The chapters are numbered, thus giving them an ordering. However, except for Chapter 3 on number theory, which pervades the subject, the chapters are fairly independent of each other and can be covered in almost any reasonable order. Although we don't recommend doing so, a daring reader could possibly read Chapters 4 through 17 in reverse order, with only having to look ahead/behind a few times.

The chapters on Information Theory, Elliptic Curves, Quantum Methods, and Error Correcting Codes are somewhat more mathematical than the others. The chapter on Error Correcting Codes was included, at the suggestion of several reviewers, because courses that include introductions to both cryptology and coding theory are fairly common.

Computer examples. Suppose you want to give an example for RSA. You could choose two one-digit primes and pretend to be working with fifty-digit primes, or you could use your favorite software package to do an actual example with large primes. Or perhaps you are working with shift ciphers and are trying to decrypt a message by trying all 26 shifts of the ciphertext. This should also be done on a computer. At the end of the book are appendices containing Computer Examples written in each of Mathematica®, Maple®, and MATLAB® that show how to do such calculations. These languages were chosen because they are user friendly and do not require prior programming experience. Although the course has been taught successfully without computers, these examples are an integral part of the book and should be studied, if at all possible. Not only do they contain numerical examples of how to do certain computations but also they demonstrate important ideas and issues that arise. They were placed at the end of the book because of the logistic and aesthetic problems of including extensive computer examples in three languages at the ends of chapters.

Programs available in each of the three languages can be downloaded from the Web site

www.prenhall.com/washington

In a classroom, all that is needed is a computer (with one of the languages installed) and a projector in order to produce meaningful examples as the lecture is being given. Homework problems (the Computer Problems in various chapters) based on the software allow students to play with examples individually. Of course, students having more programming background could write their own programs instead.

Acknowledgments. Many people helped and provided encouragement during the preparation of this book. First, we would like to thank our students, whose enthusiasm, insights, and suggestions contributed greatly. We are especially grateful to David Bindel, Jason Ernst, Christine Planchak, Haw-ren Fang, Marwan Oweis, Bob Grafton, who provided many corrections and other input. Our colleague Bill Gasarch taught out of the penultimate version of the text. His many excellent comments were extremely helpful. Jonathan Rosenberg and Tim Strobell provided invaluable technical assistance. The reviewers deserve special thanks: David Grant (University of Colorado at Boulder), David M. Pozar (University of Massachusetts, Amherst), Jugal K. Kalita (University of Colorado at Colorado Springs), Anthony Ephremides (University of Maryland, College Park), J. Felipe Voloch (University of Texas at Austin), Agnes Chan (Northeastern University), Daniel F. Warren (Naval Postgraduate School), and one anonymous reviewer. Their suggestions on the exposition and the organization of the topics greatly enhanced the final result. We have enjoyed working with the staff at Prentice Hall, especially the mathematics editor, George Lobell, and the production editor, Jeanne Audino.

The first author would like to thank Nisha Gilra, who provided encouragement and advice; Sheilagh O'Hare for introducing him to the field of cryptography; and K.J. Ray Liu for his support.

The second author thanks Susan Zengerle and Patrick Washington for their patience, help, and encouragement during the writing of this book.

Wade Trappe
wxt@math.umd.edu

Lawrence C. Washington
lcw@math.umd.edu

Chapter 1

Overview of Cryptography and Its Applications

People have always had a fascination with keeping information away from others. As children, many of us had magic decoder rings for exchanging coded messages with our friends and possibly keeping secrets from parents, siblings, or teachers. History is filled with examples where people tried to keep information secret from adversaries. Kings and generals communicated with their troops using basic cryptographic methods to prevent the enemy from learning sensitive military information. In fact, Julius Caesar reportedly used a simple cipher, which has been named after him.

As society has evolved, the need for more sophisticated methods of protecting data has increased. Now, with the information era at hand, the need is more pronounced than ever. As the world becomes more connected, the demand for information and electronic services is growing, and with the increased demand comes increased dependency on electronic systems. Already the exchange of sensitive information, such as credit card numbers, over the Internet is common practice. Protecting data and electronic systems is crucial to our way of living.

The techniques needed to protect data belong to the field of cryptography. Actually, the subject has three names, **cryptography**, **cryptology**, and **cryptanalysis**, which are often used interchangeably. Technically, however, cryptology is the all-inclusive term for the study of communication over nonsecure channels, and related problems. The process of designing systems to do this is called cryptography. Cryptanalysis deals with breaking such systems. Of course, it is essentially impossible to do either cryptography or cryptanalysis without having a good understanding of the methods of both areas.

Often the term **coding theory** is used to describe cryptography; however, this can lead to confusion. Coding theory deals with representing input information symbols by output symbols called code symbols. There are three basic applications that coding theory covers: compression, secrecy, and error correction. Over the past few decades, the term coding theory has become associated predominantly with error correcting codes. Coding theory thus studies communication over noisy channels and how to ensure that the message received is the correct message, as opposed to cryptography, which protects communication over nonsecure channels.

Although error correcting codes are only a secondary focus of this book, we should emphasize that, in any real-world system, error correcting codes are used in conjunction with encryption, since the change of a single bit is enough to destroy the message completely in a well-designed cryptosystem.

Modern cryptography is a field that draws heavily upon mathematics, computer science, and cleverness. This book provides an introduction to the mathematics and protocols needed to make data transmission and electronic systems secure, along with techniques such as electronic signatures and secret sharing.

1.1   Secure Communications

In the basic communication scenario, depicted in Figure 1.1, there are two parties, we'll call them Alice and Bob, who want to communicate with each other. A third party, Eve, is a potential eavesdropper.

When Alice wants to send a message, called the **plaintext**, to Bob, she encrypts it using a method prearranged with Bob. Usually, the encryption method is assumed to be known to Eve; what keeps the message secret is a **key**. When Bob receives the encrypted message, called the **ciphertext**, he changes it back to the plaintext using a decryption key.

Eve could have one of the following goals:

1. Read the message.

2. Find the key and thus read all messages encrypted with that key.

3. Corrupt Alice's message into another message in such a way that Bob will think Alice sent the altered message.

4. Masquerade as Alice, and thus communicate with Bob even though Bob believes he is communicating with Alice.

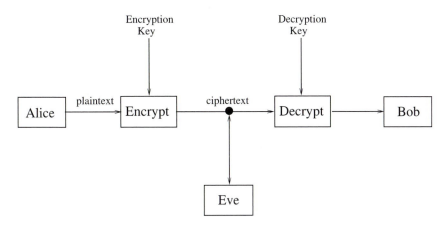

Figure 1.1: The Basic Communication Scenario for Cryptography.

Which case we're in depends on how evil Eve is. Cases (3) and (4) relate to issues of integrity and authentication, respectively. We'll discuss these shortly. A more active and malicious adversary, corresponding to cases (3) and (4), is sometimes called Mallory in the literature. More passive observers (as in cases (1) and (2)) are sometimes named Oscar. We'll generally use only Eve, and assume she is as bad as the situation allows.

Possible Attacks

There are four main types of attack that Eve might be able to use. The differences among these types of attacks are the amounts of information Eve has available to her when trying to determine the key. The four attacks are as follows:

1. **Ciphertext only:** Eve has only a copy of the ciphertext.

2. **Known plaintext:** Eve has a copy of a ciphertext and the corresponding plaintext. For example, suppose Eve intercepts an encrypted press release, then sees the decrypted release the next day. If she can deduce the decryption key, and if Alice doesn't change the key, Eve can read all future messages. Or, if Alice always starts her messages with "Dear Bob," then Eve has a small piece of ciphertext and corresponding plaintext. For many weak cryptosystems, this suffices to find the key. Even for stronger systems such as the German Enigma machine used in World War II, this amount of information has been useful.

3. **Chosen plaintext:** Eve gains temporary access to the encryption machine. She cannot open it to find the key; however, she can encrypt a

large number of suitably chosen plaintexts and try to use the resulting ciphertexts to deduce the key.

4. **Chosen ciphertext:** Eve obtains temporary access to the decryption machine, uses it to "decrypt" several strings of symbols, and tries to use the results to deduce the key.

A chosen plaintext attack could happen as follows. You want to identify an airplane as friend or foe. Send a random message to the plane, which encrypts the message automatically and sends it back. Only a friendly airplane is assumed to have the correct key. Compare the message from the plane with the correctly encrypted message. If they match, the plane is friendly. If not, it's the enemy. However, the enemy can send a large number of chosen messages to one of your planes and look at the resulting ciphertexts. If this allows them to deduce the key, the enemy can equip their planes so they can masquerade as friendly.

An example of a known plaintext attack reportedly happened in World War II in the Sahara Desert. An isolated German outpost every day sent an identical message saying that there was nothing new to report, but of course it was encrypted with the key being used that day. So each day the Allies had a plaintext-ciphertext pair that was extremely useful in determining the key. In fact, during the Sahara campaign, General Montgomery was carefully directed around the outpost so that the transmissions would not be stopped.

One of the most important assumptions in modern cryptography is **Kerckhoffs's Principle:** In assessing the security of a cryptosystem, one should always assume the enemy knows the method being used. This principle was enunciated by Auguste Kerckhoffs in 1883 in his classic treatise *La Cryptographie Militaire*. The enemy can obtain this information in many ways. For example, encryption/decryption machines can be captured and analyzed. Or people can defect or be captured. The security of the system should therefore be based on the key and not on the obscurity of algorithm used. Consequently, we always assume that Eve has knowledge of the algorithm that is used to perform encryption.

Symmetric and Public Key Algorithms

Encryption/decryption methods fall into two categories: **symmetric key** and **public key**. In symmetric key algorithms, the encryption and decryption keys are known to both Alice and Bob. For example, the encryption key is shared and the decryption key is easily calculated from it. In many cases, the encryption key and the decryption key are the same. All of the classical (pre-1970) cryptosystems are symmetric, as are the more recent Data Encryption Standard (DES) and Rijndael (AES).

Public key algorithms were introduced in the 1970s and revolutionized cryptography. Suppose Alice wants to communicate securely with Bob, but they are hundreds of kilometers apart and have not agreed on a key to use. It seems almost impossible for them to do this without first getting together to agree on a key, or using a trusted courier to carry the key from one to the other. Certainly Alice cannot send a message over open channels to tell Bob the key, and then send the ciphertext encrypted with this key. The amazing fact is that this problem has a solution, called public key cryptography. The encryption key is made public, but it is computationally infeasible to find the decryption key without information known only to Bob. The most popular implementation is RSA (see Chapter 6), which is based on the difficulty of factoring large integers. Other versions (see Chapters 7 and 16) are due to ElGamal (based on the discrete log problem) and McEliece (based on error correcting codes).

Here is a nonmathematical way to do public key communication. Bob sends Alice a box and an unlocked padlock. Alice puts her message in the box, locks Bob's lock on it, and sends the box back to Bob. Of course, only Bob can open the box and read the message. The public key methods mentioned previously are mathematical realizations of this idea. Clearly there are questions of authentication that must be dealt with. For example, Eve could intercept the first transmission and substitute her own lock. If she then intercepts the locked box when Alice sends it back to Bob, Eve can unlock her lock and read Alice's message. This is a general problem that must be addressed with any such system.

Public key cryptography represents what is possibly the final step in an interesting historical progression. In the earliest years of cryptography, security depended on keeping the encryption method secret. Later, the method was assumed known, and the security depended on keeping the (symmetric) key private or unknown to adversaries. In public key cryptography, the method and the encryption key are made public, and everyone knows what must be done to find the decryption key. The security rests on the fact (or hope) that this is computationally infeasible. It's rather paradoxical that an increase in the power of cryptographic algorithms over the years has corresponded to an increase in the amount of information given to an adversary about such algorithms.

Public key methods are very powerful, and it might seem that they make the use of symmetric key cryptography obsolete. However, this added flexibility is not free and comes at a computational cost. The amount of computation needed in public key algorithms is typically several orders of magnitude more than the amount of computation needed in algorithms such as DES or Rijndael. The rule of thumb is that public key should not be used for encrypting large quantities of data. For this reason, public key is used in applications where only small amounts of data must be processed (for example, digital signatures and sending keys to be used in symmetric key algorithms).

Within symmetric key cryptography, there are two types of ciphers: stream ciphers and block ciphers. In stream ciphers, the data are fed into the algorithm in small pieces (bits or characters), and the output is produced in corresponding small pieces. In block ciphers, however, a block of input bits is collected and fed into the algorithm all at once, and the output is a block of bits. In Section 2.11 we discuss an example of a stream cipher, namely linear feedback shift registers. Mostly we shall be concerned with block ciphers. In particular, we cover two very significant examples. The first is DES, and the second is Rijndael, which was selected in the year 2000 by the National Institute for Standards and Technology as the replacement for DES. Public key methods such as RSA can also be regarded as block ciphers.

Finally, we mention a historical distinction between different types of encryption, namely **codes** and **ciphers**. In a code, words or certain letter combinations are replaced by codewords (which may be strings of symbols). For example, the British navy in World War I used 03680C, 36276C, and 50302C to represent *shipped at, shipped by*, and *shipped from*, respectively. Codes have the disadvantage that unanticipated words cannot be used. A cipher, on the other hand, does not worry about the linguistic structure of the message but rather encrypts every string of characters, meaningful or not, by some algorithm. A cipher is therefore more versatile than a code. In the early days of cryptography, codes were commonly used, sometimes in conjunction with ciphers. They are still used today; covert operations are often given code names. However, any secret that is to remain secure needs to be encrypted with a cipher. In this book, we'll deal exclusively with ciphers.

Key Length

The security of cryptographic algorithms is a difficult property to measure. Most algorithms employ keys, and the security of the algorithm is related to how difficult it is for an adversary to determine the key. The most obvious approach is to try every possible key and see which ones yield meaningful decryptions. Such a type of attack is called a **brute force attack**. In a brute force attack, the length of the key is directly related to how long it will take to search the entire keyspace. For example, if a key is 16 bits long, then there are $2^{16} = 65536$ possible keys. The DES algorithm has a 56-bit key and thus has $2^{56} \approx 7.2 \times 10^{16}$ possible keys.

In many situations we'll encounter in this book, it will seem that a system can be broken by simply trying all possible keys. However, this is often easier said than done. Suppose you need to try 10^{30} possibilities and you have a computer that can do 10^9 such calculations each second. There are around 3×10^7 seconds in a year, so it would take a little more than 3×10^{13} years to complete the task, longer than the predicted life of the universe.

Longer keys are advantageous but are not guaranteed to make an adversary's task difficult. The algorithm itself also plays a critical role. Some algorithms might be able to be attacked by means other than brute force, and some algorithms just don't make very efficient use of their keys' bits. This is a very important point to keep in mind. Not all 128-bit algorithms are created equal!

For example, one of the easiest cryptosystems to break is the substitution cipher, which we discuss in Section 2.4. The number of possible keys is $26! \approx 4 \times 10^{26}$. In contrast, DES (see Chapter 4) has only $2^{56} \approx 7.2 \times 10^{16}$ keys. But it typically takes over a day on a specially designed computer to find a DES key. The difference is that an attack on a substitution cipher uses the underlying structure of the language, while the attack on DES is by brute force, trying all possible keys.

A brute force attack should be the last resort. A cryptanalyst always hopes to find an attack that is faster. Examples we'll meet are frequency analysis (for the substitution and Vigenère ciphers) and birthday attacks (for discrete logs).

We also warn the reader that just because an algorithm seems secure now, doesn't mean it will remain so. Human ingenuity has led to creative attacks on cryptographic protocols. There are many examples in modern cryptography where an algorithm or protocol was successfully attacked because of a loophole presented by poor implementation, or just because of advances in technology. The DES algorithm, which withstood 20 years of cryptographic scrutiny, ultimately succumbed to attacks by a well-designed parallel computer. Even as you read this book, research in quantum computing is underway, which could dramatically alter the terrain of future cryptographic algorithms.

For example, the security of several systems we'll study depends on the difficulty of factoring large integers, say of around 200 digits. Suppose you want to factor a number n of this size. The method used in elementary school is to divide n by all of the primes up to the square root of n. There are approximately 4×10^{97} primes less than 10^{100}. Trying each one is impossible. The number of electrons in the universe is estimated to be less than 10^{90}. Long before you finish your calculation, you'll get a call from the electric company asking you to stop. Clearly, more sophisticated factoring algorithms must be used, rather than this brute force type of attack. When RSA was invented, there were some good factoring algorithms available, but it was predicted that a 129-digit number such as the RSA challenge number (see Section 6.5) would not be factored within the foreseeable future. However, advances in algorithms and computer architecture have made such factorizations fairly routine (although they still require substantial computing resources), so now numbers of several hundred digits are recommended for security. But if a full-scale quantum computer is ever built, factorizations of even these numbers will be easy, and the whole RSA scheme (along with many other methods) will need to be reconsidered.

A natural question, therefore, is whether there any unbreakable cryptosystems, and why aren't they used all the time?

The answer is yes; there is a system, known as the one-time pad, that is unbreakable. Even a brute force attack will not yield the key. But the unfortunate truth is that the expense of using a one-time pad is enormous. It requires exchanging a key that is as long as the plaintext, and even then the key can only be used once. Therefore, one opts for algorithms that, when implemented correctly with the appropriate key size, are unbreakable in any reasonable amount of time.

An important point when considering key size is that, in many cases, one can mathematically increase security by a slight increase in key size, but this is not always practical. If you are working with chips that can handle words of 64 bits, then an increase in the key size from 64 to 65 bits could mean redesigning your hardware, which could be expensive. Therefore, designing good cryptosystems involves both mathematical and engineering considerations.

Finally, we need a few words about the size of numbers. Your intuition might say that working with a 20-digit number takes twice as long as working with a 10-digit number. That is true in some algorithms. However, if you count up to 10^{10}, you are not even close to 10^{20}; you are only one 10 billionth of the way there. Similarly, a brute force attack against a 60-bit key takes a billion times longer than one against a 30-bit key.

There are two ways to measure the size of numbers: the actual magnitude of the number n, and the number of digits in its decimal representation (we could also use its binary representation), which is approximately $\log_{10}(n)$. The number of single-digit multiplications needed to square a k-digit number n, using the standard algorithm from elementary school, is k^2, or approximately $(\log_{10} n)^2$. The number of divisions needed to factor a number n by dividing by all primes up to the square root of n is around $n^{1/2}$. An algorithm that runs in time a power of $\log n$ is much more desirable than one that runs in time a power of n. In the present example, if we double the number of digits in n, the time it takes to square n increases by a factor of 4, while the time it takes to factor n increases enormously. Of course, there are better algorithms available for both of these operations, but, at present, factorization takes significantly longer than multiplication.

We'll meet algorithms that take time a power of $\log n$ to perform certain calculations (for example, finding greatest common divisors and doing modular exponentiation). There are other computations for which the best known algorithms run only slightly better than a power of n (for example, factoring and finding discrete logarithms). The interplay between the fast algorithms and the slower ones is the basis of several cryptographic algorithms that we'll encounter in this book.

1.2 Cryptographic Applications

Cryptography is not only about encrypting and decrypting messages, it is also about solving real-world problems that require information security. There are four main objectives that arise:

1. **Confidentiality:** Eve should not be able to read Alice's message to Bob. The main tools are encryption and decryption algorithms.

2. **Data Integrity:** Bob wants to be sure that Alice's message has not been altered. For example, transmission errors might occur. Also, an adversary might intercept the transmission and alter it before it reaches the intended recipient. Many cryptographic primitives, such as hash functions, provide methods to detect data manipulation by malicious or accidental adversaries.

3. **Authentication:** Bob wants to be sure that only Alice could have sent the message he received. Under this heading, we also include identification schemes and password protocols (in which case, Bob is the computer). There are actually two types of authentication that arise in cryptography: entity authentication and data-origin authentication. Often the term *identification* is used to specify entity authentication, which is concerned with proving the identity of the parties involved in a communication. Data-origin authentication focuses on tying the information about the origin of the data, such as the creator and time of creation, with the data.

4. **Non-repudiation:** Alice cannot claim she did not send the message. Non-repudiation is particularly important in electronic commerce applications, where it is important that a consumer cannot deny the authorization of a purchase.

Authentication and non-repudiation are closely related concepts, but there is a difference. In a symmetric key cryptosystem, Bob can be sure that a message comes from Alice (or someone who knows Alice's key) since no one else could have encrypted the message that Bob decrypts successfully. Therefore, authentication is automatic. However, he cannot prove to anyone else that Alice sent the message, since he could have sent the message himself. Therefore, non-repudiation is essentially impossible. In a public key cryptosystem, both authentication and non-repudiation can be achieved (see Section 6.7 and Chapter 8).

Much of this book will present specific cryptographic applications, both in the text and as exercises. Here is an overview.

Digital Signatures: One of the most important features of a paper and ink letter is the signature. By signing a document, an individual's identity is tied to the message. The assumption is that it is difficult for another person to forge the signature onto another document. Electronic messages, however, are very easy to copy exactly. How do we prevent an adversary from cutting the signature off one document and attaching it to another electronic document? We shall study cryptographic protocols that allow for electronic messages to be signed in such a way that everyone believes that the signer was the person who signed the document, and such that the signer cannot deny signing the document.

Identification: When logging into a machine or initiating a communication link, a user needs to identify himself or herself. But simply typing in a user name is not sufficient as it does not prove that the user is really who he or she claims to be. Typically a password is used. We shall touch upon various methods for identifying oneself. In the chapter on DES we discuss password files. Later, we present the Feige-Fiat-Shamir identification scheme, which is a zero-knowledge based method for proving identity without revealing a password.

Key Establishment: When large quantities of data need to be encrypted, it is best to use symmetric key encryption algorithms. But how does Alice give the secret key to Bob when she doesn't have the opportunity to meet him personally? There are various ways to do this. One way uses public key cryptography. Another method is the Diffie-Hellman key exchange algorithm. A different approach to this problem is to have a trusted third party give keys to Alice and Bob. Two examples are Blom's key generation scheme and Kerberos, which is a very popular symmetric cryptographic protocol that provides authentication and security in key exchange between users on a network.

Secret Sharing: In Chapter 10, we introduce secret sharing schemes. Suppose that you have a combination to a bank safe, but you don't want to trust any single person with the combination to the safe. Rather, you would like to divide the combination among a group of people, so that at least two of these people must be present in order to open the safe. Secret sharing solves this problem.

E-commerce: How can we carry out secure transactions over open channels such as the Internet, and how can we protect credit card information from fraudulent merchants? We discuss how dual signatures can be used.

Electronic cash: Credit cards and similar devices are convenient but do not provide anonymity. Clearly a form of electronic cash could be useful, at least to some people. However, electronic entities can be copied. We give an example of an electronic cash system that provides anonymity but catches counterfeiters.

Games: How can you flip coins or play poker with people who are not in the same room as you? Dealing the cards, for example, presents a problem. We show how cryptographic ideas can solve these problems.

Chapter 2

Classical Cryptosystems

Methods of making messages unintelligible to adversaries have been important throughout history. In this chapter we shall cover some of the older cryptosystems that were primarily used before the advent of the computer. These cryptosystems are too weak to be of much use today, especially with computers at our disposal, but they give good illustrations of several of the important ideas of cryptology.

First, for these simple cryptosystems, we make some conventions.

- *plaintext* will be written in lower case letters and *CIPHERTEXT* will be written in capital letters (except in the computer problems).

- The letters of the alphabet are assigned numbers as follows:

a	b	c	d	e	f	g	h	i	j	k	l	m	n	o	p
0	1	2	3	4	5	6	7	8	9	10	11	12	13	14	15

q	r	s	t	u	v	w	x	y	z
16	17	18	19	20	21	22	23	24	25

Note that we start with $a = 0$, so z is letter number 25. Because many people are accustomed to a being 1 and z being 26, the present convention can be annoying, but it is standard for the elementary cryptosystems that we'll consider.

- Spaces and punctuation are omitted. This is even more annoying, but it is almost always possible to replace the spaces in the plaintext after decrypting. If spaces were left in, there would be two choices. They could be left as spaces; but this yields so much information on the structure of the message that decryption becomes easier. Or they could be encrypted; but then they would dominate frequency counts (unless the message averages at least eight letters per word), again simplifying decryption.

Note: In this chapter, we'll be using some concepts from number theory, especially modular arithmetic. If you are not familiar with congruences, you should read the first three sections of Chapter 3 before proceeding.

2.1 Shift Ciphers

One of the earliest cryptosystems is often attributed to Julius Caesar. Suppose he wanted to send a plaintext such as

gaul is divided into three parts

but he didn't want Brutus to read it. He shifted each letter by three places, so *a* became *D*, *b* became *E*, *c* became *F*, etc. The end of the alphabet wrapped around to the beginning, so *x* became *A*, *y* became *B*, and *z* became *C*. The ciphertext was then

JDXOLVGLYLGHGLQWRWKUHHSDUWV.

Decryption was accomplished by shifting back by three spaces (and trying to figure out how to put the spaces back in).

We now give the general situation. *If you are not familiar with modular arithmetic, read the first few pages of Chapter 3 before continuing.*

Label the letters as integers from 0 to 25. The key is an integer κ with $0 \leq \kappa \leq 25$. The encryption process is

$$x \mapsto x + \kappa \pmod{26}.$$

Decryption is $x \mapsto x - \kappa \pmod{26}$. For example, Caesar used $\kappa = 3$.

Let's see how the four types of attack work.

1. **Ciphertext only:** Eve has only the ciphertext. Her best strategy is an exhaustive search, since there are only 26 possible keys. If the message is longer than a few letters (we will make this more precise later when we discuss entropy), it is unlikely that there is more than one meaningful message that could be the plaintext. If you don't believe this, try to find some words of four or five letters that are shifts of each other. One such is given in Exercise 1. Another possible

attack, if the message is sufficiently long, is to do a frequency count for the various letters. The letter e occurs most frequently in most English texts. Suppose the letter L appears most frequently in the ciphertext. Since $e = 4$ and $L = 11$, a reasonable guess is that $\kappa = 11 - 4 = 7$. However, for shift ciphers this method takes much longer than an exhaustive search, plus it requires many more letters in the message in order for it to work (anything short, such as this, might not contain a common symbol, thus changing statistical counts).

2. **Known plaintext:** If you know just one letter of the plaintext along with the corresponding letter of ciphertext, you can deduce the key. For example, if you know $t(= 19)$ encrypts to $D(= 3)$, then the key is $\kappa \equiv 3 - 19 \equiv -16 \equiv 10 \pmod{26}$.

3. **Chosen plaintext:** Choose the letter a as the plaintext. The ciphertext gives the key. For example, if the ciphertext is H, then the key is 7.

4. **Chosen ciphertext:** Choose the letter A as ciphertext. The plaintext is the negative of the key. For example, if the plaintext is h, the key is $-7 \equiv 19 \pmod{26}$.

2.2 Affine Ciphers

The shift ciphers may be generalized and slightly strengthened as follows. Choose two integers α and β, with $\gcd(\alpha, 26) = 1$, and consider the function (called an *affine function*)

$$x \mapsto \alpha x + \beta \pmod{26}.$$

For example, let $\alpha = 9$ and $\beta = 2$, so we are working with $9x + 2$. Take a plaintext letter such as $h(= 7)$. It is encrypted to $9 \cdot 7 + 2 \equiv 65 \equiv 13 \pmod{26}$, which is the letter N. Using the same function, we obtain

$$affine \mapsto CVVWPM.$$

How do we decrypt? If we were working with rational numbers rather than mod 26, we would start with $y = 9x + 2$ and solve: $x = \frac{1}{9}(y - 2)$. But $\frac{1}{9}$ needs to be reinterpreted when we work mod 26. Since $\gcd(9, 26) = 1$, there is a multiplicative inverse for 9 (mod 26) (if this last sentence doesn't make sense to you, read Section 3.3 now). In fact, $9 \cdot 3 \equiv 1 \pmod{26}$, so 3 is the desired inverse and can be used in place of $\frac{1}{9}$. We therefore have

$$x \equiv 3(y - 2) \equiv 3y - 6 \equiv 3y + 20 \pmod{26}.$$

Let's try this. The letter $V(= 21)$ is mapped to $3 \cdot 21 + 20 \equiv 83 \equiv 5 \pmod{26}$, which is the letter f. Similarly, we see that the ciphertext *CVVWPM* is decrypted back to *affine*.

Suppose we try to use the function $13x + 4$ as our encryption function. We obtain

$$input \mapsto ERRER.$$

If we alter the input, we obtain

$$alter \mapsto ERRER.$$

Clearly this function leads to errors. It is impossible to decrypt, since several plaintexts yield the same ciphertext. In particular, we note that encryption must be one-to-one, and this fails in the present case.

What goes wrong in this example? If we solve $y = 13x + 4$, we obtain $x = \frac{1}{13}(y - 4)$. But $\frac{1}{13}$ does not exist mod 26 since $\gcd(13, 26) = 13 \neq 1$. More generally, it can be shown that $\alpha x + \beta$ is a one-to-one function mod 26 if and only if $\gcd(\alpha, 26) = 1$. In this case, decryption uses $x \equiv \alpha^* y - \alpha^* \beta \pmod{26}$, where $\alpha \alpha^* \equiv 1 \pmod{26}$. So decryption is also accomplished by an affine function.

The key for this encryption method is the pair (α, β). There are 12 possible choices for α with $\gcd(\alpha, 26) = 1$ and there are 26 choices for β (since we are working mod 26, we only need to consider α and β between 0 and 25). Therefore, there are $12 \cdot 26 = 312$ choices for the key.

Let's look at the possible attacks.

1. **Ciphertext only:** An exhaustive search through all 312 keys would take longer than the corresponding search in the case of the shift cipher; however, it would be very easy to do on a computer. When all possibilities for the key are tried, a fairly short ciphertext, say around 20 characters, will probably correspond to only one meaningful plaintext, thus allowing the determination of the key. It would also be possible to use frequency counts, though this would require much longer texts.

2. **Known plaintext:** With a little luck, knowing two letters of the plaintext and the corresponding letters of the ciphertext suffices to find the key. In any case, the number of possibilities for the key is greatly reduced and a few more letters should yield the key.

   For example, suppose the plaintext starts with *if* and the corresponding ciphertext is *PQ*. In numbers, this means that $8 (= i)$ maps to 15 $(= P)$ and 5 maps to 16. Therefore, we have the equations

   $$8\alpha + \beta \equiv 15 \text{ and } 5\alpha + \beta \equiv 16 \pmod{26}.$$

Subtracting yields $3\alpha \equiv -1 \equiv 25 \pmod{26}$, which has the unique solution $\alpha = 17$. Using the first equation, we find $8 \cdot 17 + \beta \equiv 15 \pmod{26}$, which yields $\beta = 9$.

Suppose instead that the plaintext *go* corresponds to the ciphertext *TH*. We obtain the equations

$$6\alpha + \beta \equiv 19 \text{ and } 14\alpha + \beta \equiv 7 \pmod{26}.$$

Subtracting yields $-8\alpha \equiv 12 \pmod{26}$. Since $\gcd(-8, 26) = 2$, this has two solutions: $\alpha = 5, 18$. The corresponding values of β are both 15 (this is not a coincidence; it will always happen this way). So we have two candidates for the key: $(5, 15)$ and $(18, 15)$. However, $\gcd(18, 26) \neq 1$ so the second is ruled out. Therefore, the key is $(5, 15)$.

The preceding procedure works unless the gcd we get is 13 (or 26). In this case, use another letter of the message, if available.

If we know only one letter of plaintext, we still get a relation between α and β. For example, if we only know that *g* in plaintext corresponds to *T* in ciphertext, then we have $6\alpha + \beta \equiv 19 \pmod{26}$. There are 12 possibilities for α and each gives one corresponding β. Therefore, an exhaustive search through the 12 keys should yield the correct key.

3. **Chosen plaintext:** Choose *ab* as the plaintext. The first character of the ciphertext will be $\alpha \cdot 0 + \beta = \beta$, and the second will be $\alpha + \beta$. Therefore, we can find the key.

4. **Chosen ciphertext:** Choose *AB* as the ciphertext. This yields the decryption function of the form $x = \alpha_1 y + \beta_1$. We could solve for y and obtain the encryption key. But why bother? We have the decryption function, which is what we want.

2.3   The Vigenère Cipher

A variation of the shift cipher was invented back in the sixteenth century. It is often attributed to Vigenère, though Vigenère's encryption methods were more sophisticated. Well into the twentieth century, this cryptosystem was thought by many to be secure, though Babbage and Kasiski had shown how to attack it during the nineteenth century. In the 1920's, Friedman developed additional methods for breaking this and related ciphers.

The key for the encryption is a vector, chosen as follows. First choose a key length, for example, 6. Then choose a vector of this size whose entries are integers from 0 to 25, for example $k = (21, 4, 2, 19, 14, 17)$. Often the key corresponds to a word that is easily remembered. In our case, the word is *vector*. The security of the system depends on the fact that neither the keyword nor its length is known.

To encrypt the message using the k in our example, we take first the letter of the plaintext and shift by 21. Then shift the second letter by 4, the third by 2, and so on. Once we get to the end of the key, we start back at its first entry, so the seventh letter is shifted by 21, the eighth letter by 4, etc. Here is a diagram of the encryption process.

(plaintext)	h	e	r	e	i	s	h	o	w	i	t	w	o	r	k	s
(key)	21	4	2	19	14	17	21	4	2	19	14	17	21	4	2	19
(ciphertext)	C	I	T	X	W	J	C	S	Y	B	H	N	J	V	M	L

A known plaintext attack will succeed if enough characters are known since the key is simply obtained by subtracting the plaintext from the ciphertext mod 26. A chosen plaintext attack using the plaintext *aaaaa . . .* will yield the key immediately, while a chosen ciphertext attack with *AAAAA . . .* yields the negative of the key. But suppose you have only the ciphertext. It was long thought that the method was secure against a ciphertext only attack. However, it is easy to find the key in this case, too.

The cryptanalysis uses the fact that in most English texts the frequencies of letters are not equal. For example, e occurs much more frequently than x. These frequencies have been tabulated in [Beker-Piper] and are provided in Table 2.1.

a	b	c	d	e	f	g	h	i	j
.082	.015	.028	.043	.127	.022	.020	.061	.070	.002

k	l	m	n	o	p	q	r	s	t
.008	.040	.024	.067	.075	.019	.001	.060	.063	.091

u	v	w	x	y	z				
.028	.010	.023	.001	.020	.001				

Table 2.1: Frequencies of Letters in English

Of course, variations can occur, though usually it takes a certain amount of effort to produce them. There is a book *Gadsby* by Ernest Vincent Wright that does not contain the letter e. Even more impressive is the book *La Disparition* by George Perec, written in French, which also does not have a single e (not only are there the usual problems with verbs, etc., but almost all feminine nouns and adjectives must be avoided). There is an English translation by Gilbert Adair, *A Void*, which also does not contain *e*. But generally we can assume that the above gives a rough estimate of what usually happens, as long as we have several hundred characters of text.

If we had a simple shift cipher, then the letter *e*, for example, would always appear as a certain ciphertext letter, which would then have the same frequency as that of *e* in the original text. Therefore, a frequency analysis would probably reveal the key. However, in the preceding example of a Vigenère cipher, the letter *e* appears as both *I* and *X*. If we had used a longer plaintext, *e* would probably have been encrypted as each of *Z*, *I*, *G*, *X*, *S*, and *V*, corresponding to the shifts 21, 4, 2, 19, 14, 17. But the occurrences of *Z* in a ciphertext might not come only from *e*. The letter *v* is also encrypted to *Z* when its position in the text is such that it is shifted by 4. Similarly, *x*, *g*, *l*, and *i* can contribute *Z* to the ciphertext, so the frequency of *Z* is a combination of that of *e*, *v*, *x*, *g*, *l*, and *i* from the plaintext. Therefore, it appears to be much more difficult to deduce anything from a frequency count. In fact, the frequency counts are usually smoothed out and are much closer to $1/26$ for each letter of ciphertext. At least, they should be much closer than the original distribution for English letters.

Here is a more substantial example. The ciphertext is the following:

```
VVHQWVVRHMUSGJGTHKIHTSSEJCHLSFCBGVWCRLRYQTFSVGAHW
KCUHWAUVMERZHMFVVHIPVFHQWCBGELVVHWSOSWMEGWPTGUGLF
DGCIXJCBVPSVWRFWBOIKUHKICGMLWCPCZRLJSHEKGKLXZYVLG
ZVVHOWAADCTGQKEFISGMKOQSLJSUTGKBWMFHOYSJQTWLWCRRT
LKCQSXVVLWUQRHFQVVRWWFSVMJKBKLQHUEFUALXAODRVLCBWQ
WUGDKWUKLXZQIWXZGGOMYJHHWLFOQKWTCIXJSLVEGGVEYGGEI
APUUISFPBTGNWWMUCZRVTWGLRWUGUMNCZVILE
```

The frequencies are as follows:

A	B	C	D	E	F	G	H	I	J	K	L	M
8	5	12	4	15	10	27	16	13	14	17	25	7

N	O	P	Q	R	S	T	U	V	W	X	Y	Z
7	5	9	14	17	24	8	12	22	22	5	8	5

Note that there is no letter whose frequency is significantly larger than the others. As discussed previously, this is because *e*, for example, gets spread among several letters during the encryption process.

How do we decrypt the message? There are two steps: finding the key length and finding the key. In the following, we'll first show how to find the key length and then give one way to find the key. After an explanation of why the method for finding the key works, we give an alternative way to find the key.

Finding the Key Length

Write the ciphertext on a long strip of paper, and again on another long strip. Put one strip above the other, but displaced by a certain number of places (the potential key length). For example, for a displacement of two we have the following:

```
  V V H Q W V V R H M U S G J G
V V H Q W V V R H M U S G J G T H
                            *
```

```
T H K I H T S S E J C H L S F C B
K I H T S S E J C H L S F C B G V
```

```
G V W C R L R Y Q T F S V G A H ···
W C R L R Y Q T F S V G A H W K ···
      *
```

Mark a * each time a letter and the one below it are the same, and count the total number of coincidences. In the text just listed, we have two coincidences so far. If we had continued for the entire ciphertext, we would have counted 14 of them. If we do this for different displacements, we obtain the following data:

displacement:	1	2	3	4	5	6
coincidences:	14	14	16	14	24	12

We have the most coincidences for a shift of 5. As we explain later, this is the best guess for the length of the key. This method works very quickly, even without a computer, and usually yields the key length.

Finding the Key: First Method

Now suppose we have determined the key length to be 5, as in our example. Look at the 1st, 6th, 11th, ... letters and see which letter occurs most frequently. We obtain

A	B	C	D	E	F	G	H	I	J	K	L	M
0	0	7	1	1	2	9	0	1	8	8	0	0

N	O	P	Q	R	S	T	U	V	W	X	Y	Z
3	0	4	5	2	0	3	6	5	1	0	1	0

The most frequent is G, though J, K, C are close behind. However, $J = e$ would mean a shift of 5, hence $C = x$. But this would yield an unusually high frequency for x in the ciphertext. Similarly, $K = e$ would mean $P = j$ and $Q = k$, both of which have too high frequencies. Finally, $C = e$ would require $V = x$, which is unlikely to be the case. Therefore, we decide that $G = e$ and the first element of the key is $2 = c$.

We now look at the 2nd, 7th, 12th, ... letters. We find that G occurs 10 times and S occurs 12 times, and the other letters are far behind. If $G = e$, then $S = q$, which should not occur 12 times in the plaintext. Therefore, $S = e$ and the second element of the key is $14 = o$.

Now look at the 3rd, 8th, 13th, ... letters. The frequencies are

A	B	C	D	E	F	G	H	I	J	K	L	M
0	1	0	3	3	1	3	5	1	0	4	10	0

N	O	P	Q	R	S	T	U	V	W	X	Y	Z
2	1	2	3	5	3	0	2	8	7	1	0	1

The initial guess that $L = e$ runs into problems; for example, $R = k$ and $E = x$ have too high and $A = t$ has too low frequency. Similarly, $V = e$ and $W = e$ do not seem likely. The best choice is $H = e$ and therefore the third key element is $3 = d$.

The 4th, 9th, 14th, ... letters yield $4 = e$ as the fourth element of the key. Finally, the 5th, 10th, 15th, ... letters yield $18 = s$ as the final key element. Our guess for the key is therefore

$$\{2, 14, 3, 4, 18\} = \{c, o, d, e, s\}.$$

As we saw in the case of the 3rd, 8th, 13th, ... letters (this also happened in the 5th, 10th, 15th, ... case), if we take every fifth letter we have a much smaller sample of letters on which we are doing a frequency count. Another letter can overtake e in a short sample. But it is probable that most of the high frequency letters appear with high frequencies, and most of the low ones appear with low frequencies. As in the present case, this is usually sufficient to identify the corresponding entry in the key.

Once a potential key is found, test it by using it to decrypt. It should be easy to tell whether it is correct.

In our example, the key is conjectured to be $(2, 14, 3, 4, 18)$. If we decrypt the ciphertext using this key, we obtain

```
themethodusedforthepreparationandreadingofcodemessagesis
simpleintheextremeandatthesametimeimpossibleoftranslatio
nunlessthekeyisknowntheeasewithwhichthekeymaybechangedis
anotherpointinfavoroftheadoptionofthiscodebythosedesirin
```

gtotransmitimportantmessageswithouttheslightestdangeroft
heirmessagesbeingreadbypoliticalorbusinessrivalsetc

This passage is taken from a short article in *Scientific American, Supplement* LXXXIII (1/27/1917), page 61. A short explanation of the Vigenère cipher is given, and the preceding passage expresses an opinion as to its security.

Before proceeding to a second method for finding the key, we give an explanation of why the procedure given earlier finds the key length.

Put the frequencies of English letters into a vector:

$$\mathbf{A}_0 = (.082, .015, .028, \ldots, .020, .001).$$

Let $\mathbf{A}_i$ be the result of shifting $\mathbf{A}_0$ by i spaces to the right. For example,

$$\mathbf{A}_2 = (.020, .001, .082, .015, \ldots).$$

The dot product of $\mathbf{A}_0$ with itself is

$$\mathbf{A}_0 \cdot \mathbf{A}_0 = (.082)^2 + (.015)^2 + \cdots = .066.$$

Of course, $\mathbf{A}_i \cdot \mathbf{A}_i$ is also equal to .066 since we get the same sum of products, starting with a different term. However, the dot products of $\mathbf{A}_i \cdot \mathbf{A}_j$ are much lower when $i \neq j$, ranging from .031 to .045:

$|i-j|$	0	1	2	3	4	5	6
$\mathbf{A}_i \cdot \mathbf{A}_j$	.066	.039	.032	.034	.044	.033	.036
	7	8	9	10	11	12	13
	.039	.034	.034	.038	.045	.039	.042

The dot product only depends on $|i-j|$. This can be seen as follows. The entries in the vectors are the same as those in $\mathbf{A}_0$, but shifted. In the dot product, the ith entry of $\mathbf{A}_0$ is multiplied by the jth entry, the $(i+1)$st times the $(j+1)$st, etc. So each element is multiplied by the element $j-i$ positions removed from it. Therefore the dot product only depends on the difference $i-j$. However, by reversing the roles of i and j, and noting that $\mathbf{A}_i \cdot \mathbf{A}_j = \mathbf{A}_j \cdot \mathbf{A}_i$, we see that $i-j$ and $j-i$ give the same dot products, so the dot product only depends on $|i-j|$. In the preceding table, we only needed to compute up to $|i-j| = 13$. For example, $i-j = 17$ corresponds to a shift by 17 in one direction, or 9 in the other direction, so $i-j = 9$ will give the same dot product.

The reason $\mathbf{A}_0 \cdot \mathbf{A}_0$ is higher than the other dot products is that the large numbers in the vectors are paired with large numbers and the small ones are paired with small. In the other dot products, the large numbers are paired somewhat randomly with other numbers. This lessens their effect.

Let's assume that the distribution of letters in the plaintext closely matches that of English, as expressed by the vector $\mathbf{A}_0$ above. Look at a random letter in the top strip of ciphertext. It corresponds to a random letter of English shifted by some amount i (corresponding to an element of the key). The letter below it corresponds to a random letter of English shifted by some amount j. The probability that they are both A is the first entry in the vector $\mathbf{A}_i$ times the first entry in the vector $\mathbf{A}_j$. This is because the first entry in the vector $\mathbf{A}_i$ records the probability that a shift of a random letter by i yields the ciphertext letter A, and similarly for $\mathbf{A}_j$. In the same way, the probability that both letters are B is the product of the second entries. The total probability that the two letters in consideration are the same is therefore $\mathbf{A}_i \cdot \mathbf{A}_j$. When $i \neq j$, this is approximately 0.038, but if $i = j$, then the dot product is 0.066.

We are in the situation where $i = j$ exactly when the letters lying one above the other have been shifted by the same amount, namely when the top strip is displaced by an amount equal to the key length (or a multiple of the key length). Therefore we expect more coincidences in this case.

For a displacement of 5 in the preceding ciphertext, we had 326 comparisons and 24 coincidences. By the reasoning just given, we should expect approximately $326 \times 0.066 = 21.5$ coincidences, which is close to the actual value.

Finding the Key: Second Method

Using the preceding ideas, we give another method for determining the key. It seems to work somewhat better than the first method on short samples, though it requires a little more calculation.

We'll continue to work with the preceding example. To find the first element of the key, count the frequencies of the letters in the 1st, 6th, 11th, ... positions, as before, and put them in a vector:

$$\mathbf{V} = (0,0,7,1,1,2,9,0,1,8,8,0,0,3,0,4,5,2,0,3,6,5,1,0,1,0)$$

(the first entry gives the number of occurrences of A, the second gives the number of occurrences of B, etc.). If we divide by 67, which is the total number of letters counted, we obtain a vector

$$\mathbf{W} = (0,\ 0,\ .1045,\ .0149,\ .0149,\ .0299, \ldots, .0149,\ 0)$$

that should approximate one of the vectors $\mathbf{A}_i$, where i is the shift caused by the first element of the key. If we compute $\mathbf{W} \cdot \mathbf{A}_i$ for $0 \leq i \leq 25$, the maximum value should come from the correct value of i. Here are the dot products:

$$.0250, .0391, .0713, .0388, .0275, .0380, .0512, .0301, .0325,$$
$$.0430, .0338, .0299, .0343, .0446, .0356, .0402, .0434, .0502,$$
$$.0392, .0296, .0326, .0392, .0366, .0316, .0488, .0349$$

The largest value is the third, namely .0713, which equals $\mathbf{W} \cdot \mathbf{A}_2$. Therefore, we guess that the first shift is 2, which corresponds to the key letter *c*.

Let's use the same method to find the third element of the key. We calculate a new vector $\mathbf{W}$, using the frequencies for the 3rd, 8th, 13th, ... letters that we tabulated previously:

$$\mathbf{W} = (0, .0152, 0, .0454, .0454, .0152, \ldots, 0, .0152).$$

The dot products $\mathbf{W} \cdot \mathbf{A}_i$ for $0 \le i \le 25$ are

$$.0372, .0267, .0395, .0624, .04741, .0279, .0319, .0504, .0378,$$
$$.0351, .0367, .0395, .0264, .0415, .0427, .0362, .0322, .0457,$$
$$.0526, .0397, .0322, .0299, .0364, .0372, .0352, .0406$$

The largest of these values is the fourth, namely .0624, which equals $\mathbf{W} \cdot \mathbf{A}_3$. Therefore, the best guess is that the first shift is 3, which corresponds to the key letter *d*. The other three elements of the key can be found similarly, again yielding *c, o, d, e, s* as the key.

Notice that largest dot product was significantly larger than the others in both cases, so we didn't have to make several guesses to find the correct one. In this way, the present method is superior to the first method presented; however, the first method is much easier to do by hand.

Why is the present method more accurate than the first one? To obtain the largest dot product, several of the larger values in $\mathbf{W}$ had to match with the larger values in an $\mathbf{A}_i$. In the earlier method, we tried to match only the *e*, then looked at whether the choices for other letters were reasonable. The present method does this all in one step.

2.4 Substitution Ciphers

One of the more popular cryptosystems is the substitution cipher. It is commonly used in the puzzle section of the weekend newspapers, for example. The principle is simple: Each letter in the alphabet is replaced by another (or possibly the same) letter. More precisely, a permutation of the alphabet is chosen and applied to the plaintext. In the puzzle pages, the spaces between the words are usually preserved, which is a big advantage to the solver, since knowledge of word structure becomes very useful. However, to increase security it is better to omit the spaces.

The shift and affine ciphers are examples of substitution ciphers. The Vigenère and Hill ciphers are not, since they permute blocks of letters rather than one letter at a time.

Everyone "knows" that substitution ciphers can be broken by frequency counts. However, the process is more complicated than one might expect.

Consider the following example. Thomas Jefferson has a potentially treasonous message that he wants to send to Ben Franklin. Clearly he does not want the British to read the text if they intercept it, so he encrypts using a substitution cipher. Fortunately, Ben Franklin knows the permutation being used, so he can simply reverse the permutation to obtain the original message (of course, Franklin was quite clever, so perhaps he could have decrypted it without previously knowing the key).

Now suppose we are working for the Government Code and Cypher School in England back in 1776 and are given the following intercepted message to decrypt.

```
LWNSOZBNWVWBAYBNVBSQWVWOHWDIZWRBBNPBPOOUWRPAWXAW
PBWZWMYPOBNPBBNWJPAWWRZSLWZQJBNWIAXAWPBSALIBNXWA
BPIRYRPOIWRPQOWAIENBVBNPBPUSREBNWVVWPAWOIHWOIQWAB
JPRZBNWFYAVYIBSHNPFFIRWVVBNPBBSVWXYAWBNWVWAIENBV
ESDWARUWRBVPAWIRVBIBYBWZPUSREUWRZWAIDIREBNWIATYV
BFSLWAVHASUBNWXSRVWRBSHBNWESDWARWZBNPBLNWRWDWAPR
JHSAUSHESDWARUWRBQWXSUWVZWVBAYXBIDWSHBNWVVWWRZVIB
IVBNWAIENBSHBNWFWSFOWBSPOBWASABSPQSOIVNIBPRZBSIR
VBIBYBWRWLESDWARUWRBOPJIREIBVHSYRZPBISRSRVYXNFAI
RXIFOWVPRZSAEPRIKIREIBVFSLWAVIRVYXNHSAUPVBSVWWUU
SVBOICWOJBSWHHWXBBNWIAVPHWBJPRZNPFFIRWVV
```

A frequency count yields the following (there are 520 letters in the text):

W	B	R	S	I	V	A	P	N	O	$\cdots$
76	64	39	36	36	35	34	32	30	16	$\cdots$

The approximate frequencies of letters in English were given in Section 2.3. We repeat some of the data here in Table 2.2. This allows us to guess with

e	t	a	o	i	n	s	h	r
.127	.091	.082	.075	.070	.067	.063	.061	.060

Table 2.2: Frequencies of Most Common Letters in English

reasonable confidence that W represents e (though B is another possibility).

But what about the other letters? We can guess that B, R, S, I, V, A, P, N, with maybe an exception or two, are probably the same as t, a, o, i, n, s, h, r in some order. But a simple frequency count is not enough to decide which is which. What we need to do now is look at digrams, or pairs of letters. We organize our results in Table 2.3 (we only use the most frequent letters here, though it would be better to include all).

	W	B	R	S	I	V	A	P	N
W	3	4	12	2	4	10	14	3	1
B	4	4	0	11	5	5	2	4	20
R	5	5	0	1	1	5	0	3	0
S	1	0	5	0	1	3	5	2	0
I	1	8	10	1	0	2	3	0	0
V	8	10	0	0	2	2	0	3	1
A	7	3	4	2	5	4	0	1	0
P	0	8	6	0	1	1	4	0	0
N	14	3	0	1	1	1	0	7	0

Table 2.3: Counting Digrams

The entry 1 in the W row and N column means that the combination WN appears 1 time in the text. The entry 14 in the N row and W column means that NW appears 14 times.

We have already decided that $W = e$, but if we had extended the table to include low-frequency letters, we would see that W contacts many of these letters, too, which is another characteristic of e. This helps to confirm our guess.

The vowels a, i, o tend to avoid each other. If we look at the R row, we see that R does not precede S, I, A, N very often. But a look at the R column shows that R follows S, I, A fairly often. So we suspect that R is not one of a, i, o. V and N are out because they would require a, i, or o to precede $W = e$ quite often, which is unlikely. Continuing, we see that the most likely possibilities for a, i, o are S, I, P in some order.

The letter n has the property that around 80% of the letters that precede it are vowels. Since we already have identified W, S, I, P as vowels, we see that R and A are the most likely candidates. We'll have to wait to see which is correct.

The letter h often appears before e and rarely after it. This tells us that $N = h$.

The most common digram is th. Therefore, $B = t$.

Among the frequent letters, r and s remain, and they should equal V and one of A, R. Since r pairs more with vowels and s pairs more with consonants, we see that V must be s and r is represented by either A or R.

The combination rn should appear more than nr, and AR is more frequent than RA, so our guess is that $A = r$ and $R = n$.

We can continue the analysis and determine that $S = o$ (note that to is much more common than ot), $I = i$, and $P = a$ are the most likely choices. We have therefore determined reasonable guesses for 382 of the 520 characters in the text:

```
L   W   N   S   O   Z   B   N   W   V   W   B   A   Y   B   N   V   B   S
    e   h   o           t   h   e   s   e   t   r       t   h   s   t   o


Q   W   V   W   O   H   W   D   I   Z   W   R   B   B   N   P   B   P  ···
    e   s   e       e       i       e   n   t   t   h   a   t   a  ···
```

At this point, knowledge of the language, middle-level frequencies $(l, d, \dots)$, and educated guesses can be used to fill in the remaining letters. For example, in the first line a good guess is that $Y = u$ since then the word *truths* appears. Of course, there is a lot of guesswork, and various hypotheses need to be tested until one works.

Since the preceding should give the spirit of the method, we skip the remaining details. The decrypted message, with spaces (but not punctuation) added, is as follows (the text is from the middle of the Declaration of Independence):

> *we hold these truths to be self evident that all men are created equal that they are endowed by their creator with certain unalienable rights that among these are life liberty and the pursuit of happiness that to secure these rights governments are instituted among men deriving their just powers from the consent of the governed that whenever any form of government becomes destructive of these ends it is the right of the people to alter or to abolish it and to institute new government laying its foundation on such principles and organizing its powers in such form as to seem most likely to effect their safety and happiness*

2.5   Sherlock Holmes

Cryptography has appeared in many places in literature, for example, in the works of Edgar Allen Poe (*The Gold Bug*), William Thackeray (*The History of Henry Esmond*), Jules Verne (*Voyage to the Center of the Earth*), and Agatha Christie (*The Four Suspects*).

Here we give a summary of an enjoyable tale by Arthur Conan Doyle, in which Sherlock Holmes displays his usual cleverness, this time by breaking a ciphersystem. We cannot do the story justice here, so we urge the reader to read *The Adventure of the Dancing Men* in its entirety. The following is a cryptic, and cryptographic, summary of the plot.

Mr. Hilton Cubitt, who has recently married the former Elsie Patrick, mails Sherlock Holmes a letter. In it is a piece of paper with dancing stick figures that he found in his garden at Riding Thorpe Manor:

Two weeks later, Cubitt finds another series of figures written in chalk on his toolhouse door:

Two mornings later another sequence appears:

Three days later, another message appears:

Cubitt gives copies of all of these to Holmes, who spends the next two days making many calculations. Suddenly, Holmes jumps from his chair, clearly having made a breakthrough. He quickly sends a long telegram to someone and then waits, telling Watson that they will probably be going to visit Cubitt the next day. But two days pass with no reply to the telegram, and then a letter arrives from Cubitt with yet another message:

Holmes studies it and says they need to travel to Riding Thorpe Manor as soon as possible. A short time later, a reply to Holmes's telegram arrives, and Holmes indicates that the matter has become even more urgent. When Holmes and Watson arrive at Cubitt's house the next day, they find the police already there. Cubitt has been shot dead. His wife, Elsie, has also

been shot and is in critical condition (although she survives). Holmes asks
several questions, then has someone deliver a note to a Mr. Abe Slaney at
nearby Elrige's Farm. Holmes then explains to Watson and the police how
he decrypted the messages. First, he guessed that the flags on some of the
figures indicated the ends of words. He then noticed that the most common
figure was

so it was likely *E*. This gave the fourth message as *–E–E–*. The possibilities
LEVER, NEVER, SEVER came to mind, but since the message was proba-
bly a one word reply to a previous message, Holmes guessed it was *NEVER*.
Next, Holmes observed that

had the form *E–––E*, which could be *ELSIE*. The third message was then *–
––E ELSIE*. Holmes tried several combinations, finally settling on *COME
ELSIE* as the only viable possibility. The first message therefore was *–M
–ERE ––E SL–NE–*. Holmes guessed that the first letter was *A* and the
third letter as *H*, which gave the message as *AM HERE A–E SLANE–*. It
was reasonable to complete this to *AM HERE ABE SLANEY*. The second
message then was *A– ELRI–ES*. Of course, Holmes correctly guessed that
this must be stating where Slaney was staying. The only letters that seemed
reasonable completed the phrase to *AT ELRIGES*. It was after decrypting
these two messages that Holmes sent a telegram to a friend at the New York
Police Bureau, who sent back the reply that Abe Slaney was "the most
dangerous crook in Chicago." When the final message arrived, Holmes decrypted it to *ELSIE –RE–ARE TO MEET THY GO–*. Since he recognized
the missing letters as *P, P, D*, respectively, Holmes became very concerned
and that's why he decided to make the trip to Riding Thorpe Manor.

When Holmes finishes this explanation, the police urge that they go to
Elrige's and arrest Slaney immediately. However, Holmes suggests that is
unnecessary and that Slaney will arrive shortly. Sure enough, Slaney soon
appears and is handcuffed by the police. While waiting to be taken away,
he confesses to the shooting (it was somewhat in self defense, he claims) and
says that the writing was invented by Elsie Patrick's father for use by his
gang, the Joint, in Chicago. Slaney was engaged to be married to Elsie, but
she escaped from the world of gangsters and fled to London. Slaney finally
traced her location and sent the secret messages. But why did Slaney walk
into the trap that Holmes set? Holmes shows the message he wrote:

From the letters already deduced, we see that this says *COME HERE AT ONCE*. Slaney was sure this message must have been from Elsie since he was certain no one outside of the Joint could write such messages. Therefore, he made the visit that led to his capture.

Comments

What Holmes did was solve a simple substitution cipher, though he did this with very little data. As with most such ciphers, both frequency analysis and a knowledge of the language are very useful. A little luck is nice, too, both in the form of lucky guesses and in the distribution of letters. Note how overwhelmingly *E* was the most common letter. In fact, it appeared 11 times among the 38 characters in the first four messages. This gave Holmes a good start. If Elsie had been Carol and Abe Slaney had been John Smith, the decryption would probably have been more difficult.

Authentication is an important issue in cryptography. If Eve breaks Alice's cryptosystem, then Eve can often masquerade as Alice in communications with Bob. Safeguards against this are important. The judges gave Abe Slaney many years to think about this issue.

The alert reader might have noticed that we cheated a little when decrypting the messages. The same symbol represents the *V* in *NEVER* and the *P*'s in *PREPARE*. This is presumably due to a misprint and has occurred in every printed version of the work, starting with the story's first publication back in 1903. In the original text, the *R* in *NEVER* is written as the *B* in *ABE*, but this is corrected in later editions (however, in some later editions, the first *C* in the message Holmes wrote is given an extra arm and therefore looks like the *M*). If these mistakes had been in the text that Holmes was working with, he would have had a very difficult time decrypting and would have rightly concluded that the Joint needed to use error correction techniques in their transmissions. In fact, some type of error correction should be used in conjunction with almost every cryptographic protocol.

2.6   The Playfair and ADFGX Ciphers

The Playfair and ADFGX ciphers were used in World War I by the British and the Germans, respectively. By modern standards, they are fairly weak systems, but they took real effort to break at the time.

The Playfair system was invented around 1854 by Sir Charles Wheatstone, who named it after his friend, the Baron Playfair of St. Andrews, who worked to convince the government to use it. In addition to being used in World War I, it was used by the British forces in the Boer War.

The key is a word, for example, *playfair*. The repeated letters are removed, to obtain *playfir*, and the remaining letters are used to start a 5×5 matrix. The remaining spaces in the matrix are filled in with the remaining letters in the alphabet, with i and j being treated as one letter:

$$
\begin{array}{ccccc}
p & l & a & y & f \\
i & r & b & c & d \\
e & g & h & k & m \\
n & o & q & s & t \\
u & v & w & x & z
\end{array}
$$

Suppose the plaintext is *meet at the schoolhouse*. Remove spaces and divide the text into groups of two letters. If there is a doubled letter appearing as a group, insert an x and regroup. Add an extra x at the end to complete the last group, if necessary. Our plaintext becomes

me et at th es ch ox ol ho us ex.

Now use the matrix to encrypt each two letter group by the following scheme:

- If the two letters are not in the same row or column, replace each letter by the letter that is in its row and is in the column of the other letter. For example, *et* becomes *MN*, since M is in the same row as e and the same column as t, and N is in the same row as t and the same column as e.

- If the two letters are in the same row, replace each letter with the letter immediately to its right, with the matrix wrapping around from the last column to the first. For example, *me* becomes *EG*.

- If the two letters are in the same column, replace each letter with the letter immediately below it, with the matrix wrapping around from the last row to the first. For example, *ol* becomes *VR*.

The ciphertext in our example is

EG MN FQ QM KN BK SV VR GQ XN KU.

To decrypt, reverse the procedure.

The system succumbs to a frequency attack since the frequencies of the various digrams (two-letter combinations) in English have been tabulated.

Of course, we only have to look for the most common digrams; they should correspond to the most common digrams in English: *th, he, an, in, re, es,* .... Moreover, a slight modification yields results more quickly. For example, both of the digrams *re* and *er* are very common. If the pairs *IG* and *GI* are common in the ciphertext, then a good guess is that *e, i, r, g* form the corners of a rectangle in the matrix. Another weakness is that each plaintext letter has only five possible corresponding ciphertext letters. Also, unless the keyword is long, the last few rows of the matrix are predictable. Observations such as these allow the system to be broken with a ciphertext only attack. For more on its cryptanalysis, see [Gaines].

The ADFGX cipher proceeds as follows. Put the letters of the alphabet into a 5×5 matrix. The letters i and j are treated as one, and the columns of the matrix are labeled with the letters A, D, F, G, X. For example, the matrix could be

	A	D	F	G	X
A	p	g	c	e	n
D	b	q	o	z	r
F	s	l	a	f	t
G	m	d	v	i	w
X	k	u	y	x	h

Each plaintext letter is replaced by the label of its row and column. For example, s becomes FA, and z becomes DG. Suppose the plaintext is

Kaiser Wilhelm.

The result of this initial step is

XA FF GG FA AG DX GX GG FD XX AG FD GA.

So far, this is a disguised substitution cipher. The next step increases the complexity significantly. Choose a keyword, for example, *Rhein*. Label the columns of a matrix by the letters of the keyword and put the result of the initial step into the matrix:

	R	H	E	I	N
	X	A	F	F	G
	G	F	A	A	G
	D	X	G	X	G
	G	F	D	X	X
	A	G	F	D	G
	A				

Now reorder the columns so that the column labels are in alphabetic order:

E	H	I	N	R
F	A	F	G	X
A	F	A	G	G
G	X	X	G	D
D	F	X	X	G
F	G	D	G	A
				A

Finally, the ciphertext is obtained by reading down the columns (omitting the labels) in order:

$$FAGDFAFXFGFAXXDGGGXGXGDGAA.$$

Decryption is easy, as long as you know the keyword. From the length of the keyword and the length of the ciphertext, the length of each column is determined. The letters are placed into columns, which are reordered to match the keyword. The original matrix is then used to recover the plaintext.

The initial matrix and the keyword were changed frequently, making cryptanalysis more difficult, since there was only a limited amount of ciphertext available for any combination. However, the system was successfully attacked by the French cryptanalyst Georges Painvin and the Bureau du Chiffre, who were able to decrypt a substantial number of messages.

Here is one technique that was used. Suppose two different ciphertexts intercepted at approximately the same time agree for the first several characters. A reasonable guess is that the two plaintexts agree for several words. That means that the top few entries of the columns for one are the same as for the other. Search through the ciphertexts and find other places where they agree. These possibly represent the beginnings of the columns. If this is correct, we know the column lengths. Divide the ciphertexts into columns using these lengths. For the first ciphertext, some columns will have one length and others will be one longer. The longer ones represent columns that should be near the beginning; the other columns should be near the end. Repeat for the second ciphertext. If a column is long for both ciphertexts, it is very near the beginning. If it is long for one ciphertext and not for the other, it goes in the middle. If it is short for both, it is near the end. At this point, try the various orderings of the columns, subject to these restrictions. Each ordering corresponds to a potential substitution cipher. Use frequency analysis to try to solve these. One should yield the plaintext, and the initial encryption matrix.

The letters *ADFGX* were chosen because their symbols in Morse code ($\cdot\,-$, $-\cdot\cdot$, $\cdot\cdot-\cdot$, $-\,-\,\cdot$, $-\,\cdot\cdot\,-$) were not easily confused. This was to avoid transmission errors, and represents one of the early attempts to combine error correction with cryptography. Eventually, the *ADFGX* cipher was replaced by the *ADFGVX* cipher, which used a 6×6 initial matrix. This allowed all 26 letters plus 10 digits to be used.

For more on the cryptanalysis of the ADFGX cipher, see [Kahn].

2.7 Block Ciphers

In many of the aforementioned cryptosystems, changing one letter in the plaintext changes exactly one letter in the ciphertext. In the shift, affine, and substitution ciphers, a given letter in the ciphertext always comes from exactly one letter in the plaintext. This greatly facilitates finding the key using frequency analysis. In the Vigenère system, the use of blocks of letters, corresponding to the length of the key, made the frequency analysis more difficult, but still possible, since there was no interaction among the various letters in each block. Block ciphers avoid these problems by encrypting blocks of several letters or numbers simultaneously. A change of one character in a plaintext block should change potentially all the characters in the corresponding ciphertext block.

The Playfair cipher in Section 2.6 is a simple example of a block cipher, since it takes two-letter blocks and encrypts them to two-letter blocks. A change of one letter of a plaintext pair will always change at least one letter, and usually both letters, of the ciphertext pair. However, blocks of two letters are too small to be secure, and frequency analysis, for example, is usually successful.

Many of the modern cryptosystems that will be treated later in this book are block ciphers. For example, DES operates on blocks of 64 bits. AES uses blocks of 128 bits. RSA uses blocks several hundred bits long, depending on the modulus used. All of these block lengths are long enough to be secure against attacks such as frequency analysis.

The standard way of using a block cipher is to convert blocks of plaintext to blocks of ciphertext, independently and one at a time. This is called the electronic codebook (ECB) mode. However, there are ways to use feedback from the blocks of ciphertext in the encryption of subsequent blocks of plaintext. This leads to the cipher block chaining (CBC) mode and cipher feedback (CFB) mode of operation. These are discussed in Section 4.5.

In this section, we discuss the Hill cipher, which is a block cipher invented in 1929 by Lester Hill. It seems never to have been used much in practice. Its significance is that it was perhaps the first time that algebraic methods (linear algebra, modular arithmetic) were used in cryptography in an essential way. As we'll see in later chapters, algebraic methods now occupy a central position in the subject.

Choose an integer n, for example $n = 3$. The key is an $n \times n$ matrix M whose entries are integers mod 26. For example, let

$$M = \begin{pmatrix} 1 & 2 & 3 \\ 4 & 5 & 6 \\ 11 & 9 & 8 \end{pmatrix}.$$

The message is written as a series of row vectors. For example, if the message is *abc*, we change this to the single row vector $(0, 1, 2)$. To encrypt, multiply the vector by the matrix (traditionally, the matrix appears on the right in the multiplication; multiplying on the left would yield a similar theory) and reduce mod 26:

$$(0, 1, 2) \begin{pmatrix} 1 & 2 & 3 \\ 4 & 5 & 6 \\ 11 & 9 & 8 \end{pmatrix} \equiv (0, 23, 22) \pmod{26}.$$

Therefore, the ciphertext is AXW (The fact that the first letter a remained unchanged is a random occurrence; it is not a defect of the method).

In order to decrypt, we need the determinant of M to satisfy

$$\gcd(\det(M),\ 26) = 1.$$

This means that there is a matrix N with integer entries such that $MN \equiv I$ (mod 26), where I is the $n \times n$ identity matrix.

In our example, $\det(M) = -3$. The inverse of M is

$$\frac{-1}{3} \begin{pmatrix} -14 & 11 & -3 \\ 34 & -25 & 6 \\ -19 & 13 & -3 \end{pmatrix}.$$

Since 17 is the inverse of -3 mod 26, we replace $-1/3$ by 17 and reduce mod 26 to obtain

$$N = \begin{pmatrix} 22 & 5 & 1 \\ 6 & 17 & 24 \\ 15 & 13 & 1 \end{pmatrix}.$$

The reader can check that $MN \equiv I \pmod{26}$.

For more on finding inverses of matrices mod n, see Section 3.8.

The decryption is accomplished by multiplying by N, as follows:

$$(0, 23, 22) \begin{pmatrix} 22 & 5 & 1 \\ 6 & 17 & 24 \\ 15 & 13 & 1 \end{pmatrix} \equiv (0, 1, 2) \pmod{26}.$$

In the general method with an $n \times n$ matrix, break the plaintext into blocks of n characters and change each block to a vector of n integers between 0 and 25 using $a = 0, b = 1, \ldots, z = 25$. For example, with the matrix M as above, suppose our plaintext is

blockcipher.

This becomes (we add an x to fill the last space)

$$1 \quad 11 \quad 14 \qquad 2 \quad 10 \quad 2 \qquad 8 \quad 15 \quad 7 \qquad 4 \quad 17 \quad 23.$$

Now multiply each vector by M, reduce the answer mod 26, and change back to letters:

$$(1, 11, 14)M = (199, 183, 181) \equiv (17, \; 1, 25) \quad (\text{mod } 26) = RBZ$$

$$(2, 10, \; 2)M = (\; 64, \; 72, \; 82) \equiv (12, 20, \; 4) \quad (\text{mod } 26) = MUE,$$

etc.

In our case, the ciphertext is

RBZMUEPYONOM.

It is easy to see that changing one letter of plaintext will usually change n letters of ciphertext. For example, if *block* is changed to *clock*, the first three letters of ciphertext change from RBZ to SDC. This makes frequency counts less effective, though they are not impossible when n is small. The frequencies of two-letter combinations, called **digrams**, and three-letter combinations, **trigrams**, have been computed. Beyond that, the number of combinations becomes too large (though tabulating the results for certain common combinations would not be difficult). Also, the frequencies of combinations are so low that it is hard to get meaningful data without a very large amount of text.

Now that we have the ciphertext, how do we decrypt? Simply break the ciphertext into blocks of length n, change each to a vector, and multiply on the right by the inverse matrix N. In our example, we have

$$RBZ = (17, 1, 25) \mapsto (17, 1, 25)N = (755, 427, 66) \equiv (1, 11, 14) = blo,$$

and similarly for the remainder of the ciphertext.

The Hill cipher is difficult to decrypt using only the ciphertext, but it succumbs easily to a known plaintext attack. If we do not know n, we can try various values until we find the right one. So suppose n is known. If we have n of the blocks of plaintext of size n, then we can use the plaintext and the corresponding ciphertext to obtain a matrix equation for M (or for N, which might be more useful). For example, suppose we know that $n = 2$ and we have the plaintext

$$howareyoutoday =$$
$$7 \quad 14 \qquad 22 \quad 0 \qquad 17 \quad 4 \qquad 24 \quad 14 \qquad 20 \quad 19 \qquad 14 \quad 3 \qquad 0 \quad 24$$

corresponding to the ciphertext

$$ZWSENIUSPLJVEU =$$
$$25 \quad 22 \qquad 18 \quad 4 \qquad 13 \quad 8 \qquad 20 \quad 18 \qquad 15 \quad 11 \qquad 9 \quad 21 \qquad 4 \quad 20$$

The first two blocks yield the matrix equation

$$\begin{pmatrix} 7 & 14 \\ 22 & 0 \end{pmatrix} \begin{pmatrix} a & b \\ c & d \end{pmatrix} \equiv \begin{pmatrix} 25 & 22 \\ 18 & 4 \end{pmatrix} \pmod{26}.$$

Unfortunately, the matrix $\begin{pmatrix} 7 & 14 \\ 22 & 0 \end{pmatrix}$ has determinant -308, which is not invertible mod 26 (though this matrix could be used to reduce greatly the number of choices for the encryption matrix). Therefore, we replace the last row of the equation, for example, by the fifth block to obtain

$$\begin{pmatrix} 7 & 14 \\ 20 & 19 \end{pmatrix} \begin{pmatrix} a & b \\ c & d \end{pmatrix} \equiv \begin{pmatrix} 25 & 22 \\ 15 & 11 \end{pmatrix} \pmod{26}.$$

In this case, the matrix $\begin{pmatrix} 7 & 14 \\ 20 & 19 \end{pmatrix}$ is invertible mod 26:

$$\begin{pmatrix} 7 & 14 \\ 20 & 19 \end{pmatrix}^{-1} \equiv \begin{pmatrix} 5 & 10 \\ 18 & 21 \end{pmatrix} \pmod{26}.$$

We obtain

$$M \equiv \begin{pmatrix} 5 & 10 \\ 18 & 21 \end{pmatrix} \begin{pmatrix} 25 & 22 \\ 15 & 11 \end{pmatrix} \equiv \begin{pmatrix} 15 & 12 \\ 11 & 3 \end{pmatrix} \pmod{26}.$$

Because the Hill cipher is vulnerable to this attack, it cannot be regarded as being very strong.

A chosen plaintext attack proceeds by the same strategy, but is a little faster. Again, if you do not know n, try various possibilities until one works. So suppose n is known. Choose the first block of plaintext to be $baaa \cdots = 1000\ldots$, the second to be $abaa \cdots = 0100\ldots$, and continue through the nth block being . . . *aaab* = . . . 0001. The blocks of ciphertext will be the rows of the matrix M.

For a chosen ciphertext attack, use the same strategy as for chosen plaintext, where the choices now represent ciphertext. The resulting plaintext will be the rows of the inverse matrix N.

Claude Shannon, in one of the fundamental papers on the theoretical foundations of cryptography [Shannon1], gave two properties that a good cryptosystem should have to hinder statistical analysis: **diffusion** and **confusion**.

Diffusion means that if we change a character of the plaintext, then several characters of the ciphertext should change, and, similarly, if we change a character of the ciphertext, then several characters of the plaintext should change. We saw that the Hill cipher has this property. This means that frequency statistics of letters, digrams, etc. in the plaintext are diffused over several characters in the ciphertext, which means that much more ciphertext is needed to do a meaningful statistical attack.

Confusion means that the key does not relate in a simple way to the ciphertext. In particular, each character of the ciphertext should depend on several parts of the key. For example, suppose we have a Hill cipher with an $n \times n$ matrix, and suppose we have a plaintext-ciphertext pair of length n^2 with which we are able to solve for the encryption matrix. If we change one character of the ciphertext, one column of the matrix can change completely (see Exercise 12). Of course, it would be more desirable to have the entire key change. When a situation like that happens, the cryptanalyst would probably need to solve for the entire key simultaneously, rather than piece by piece.

The Vigenère and substitution ciphers do not have the properties of diffusion and confusion, which is why they are so susceptible to frequency analysis.

The concepts of diffusion and confusion play a role in any well-designed block cipher. Of course, a disadvantage (which is precisely the cryptographic advantage) of diffusion is error propagation: A small error in the ciphertext becomes a major error in the decrypted message, and usually means the decryption is unreadable.

2.8 Binary Numbers and ASCII

In many situations involving computers, it is more natural to represent data as strings of 0's and 1's, rather than as letters and numbers.

Numbers can be converted to binary (or base 2), if desired, which we'll quickly review. Our standard way of writing numbers is in base 10. For example, 123 means $1 \times 10^2 + 2 \times 10^1 + 3$. Binary uses 2 in place of 10

symbol	!	"	#	$	%	&	'
decimal	33	34	35	36	37	38	39
binary	0100001	0100010	0100011	0100100	0100101	0100110	0100111
(	)	*	+	,	-	.	/
40	41	42	43	44	45	46	47
0101000	0101001	0101010	0101011	0101100	0101101	0101110	0101111
0	1	2	3	4	5	6	7
48	49	50	51	52	53	54	55
0110000	0110001	0110010	0110011	0110100	0110101	0110110	0110111
8	9	:	;	i	=	¿	?
56	57	58	59	60	61	62	63
0111000	0111001	0111010	0111011	0111100	0111101	0111110	0111111
@	A	B	C	D	E	F	G
64	65	66	67	68	69	70	71
1000000	1000001	1000010	1000011	1000100	1000101	1000110	1000111

Table 2.4: ASCII Equivalents of Selected Symbols

and needs only the digits 0 and 1. For example, 110101 in binary represents $2^5 + 2^4 + 2^2 + 1$ (which equals 53 in base 10).

Each 0 or 1 is called a **bit**. A representation that takes 8 bits is called an 8-bit number, or a **byte**. The largest number that 8 bits can represent is 255, and the largest number that 16 bits can represent is 65535.

Often, we want to deal with more than just numbers. In this case, words, symbols, letters, and numbers are given binary representations. There are many possible ways of doing this. One of the standard ways is called ASCII, which stands for American Standard Code for Information Interchange. Each character is represented using 7 bits, allowing for 128 possible characters and symbols to be represented. Eight bit blocks are common for computers to use, and for this reason, each character is often represented using 8 bits. The eighth bit can be used for checking parity to see if an error occurred in transmission, or is often used to extend the list of characters to include symbols such as ü and è .

Table 2.4 gives the ASCII equivalents for some standard symbols. We'll never use them in this book. They are included simply to show how text can be encoded as a sequence of 0's and 1's.

2.9   One-Time Pads

The one-time pad, which is an unbreakable cryptosystem, was developed by Gilbert Vernam and Joseph Mauborgne around 1918. Start by representing the message as a sequence of 0's and 1's. This can be accomplished by writing all numbers in binary, for example, or by using ASCII, as discussed in the previous section. But the message could also be a digitalized video or audio signal.

The key is a random sequence of 0's and 1's of the same length as the message. Once a key is used, it is discarded and never used again. The encryption consists of adding the key to the message mod 2, bit by bit. This process is often called **exclusive or**, and is denoted by XOR. In other words, we use the rules $0 + 0 = 0$, $0 + 1 = 1$, $1 + 1 = 0$. For example, if the message is 00101001 and the key is 10101100, we obtain the ciphertext as follows:

$$\begin{array}{rl} \text{(plaintext)} & 00101001 \\ \text{(key)} + & \underline{10101100} \\ \text{(ciphertext)} & 10000101 \end{array}$$

Decryption uses the same key. Simply add the key onto the ciphertext: $10000101 + 10101100 = 00101001$.

A variation is to leave the plaintext as a sequence of letters. The key is then a random sequence of shifts, each one between 0 and 25. Decryption uses the same key, but subtracts instead of adding the shifts.

This encryption method is completely unbreakable for a ciphertext only attack. For example, suppose the ciphertext is *FIOWPSLQNTISJQL*. The plaintext could be *wewillwinthewar* or it could be *theduckwantsout*. Each one is equally likely, along with all other messages of the same length. Therefore the ciphertext gives no information about the plaintext (except for its length). This will be made more precise when we discuss Shannon's theory of entropy.

If we have a piece of the plaintext, we can find the corresponding piece of the key, but it will tell us nothing about the remainder of the key. In most cases a chosen plaintext or chosen ciphertext attack is not possible. But such an attack would only reveal the part of the key used during the attack, which would not be useful unless this part of the key were to be reused.

How do we implement this system, and where can it be used? The key can be generated in advance. Of course, there is the problem of generating a truly random sequence of 0's and 1's. One way would be to have some people sitting in a room flipping coins, but this would be too slow for most purposes. We could also take a Geiger counter and count how many clicks it makes in a small time period, recording a 0 if this number is even and 1 if it is odd. There are other ways that are faster but not quite as random that can be used in practice (see Section 2.10); but it is easy to see that quickly generating a good key is difficult. Once the key is generated, it can be sent by a trusted courier to the recipient. The message can then be sent when needed. It is reported that the "hot line" between Washington, D.C., and Moscow used one-time pads for secure communications between the leaders of the United States and the U.S.S.R. during the Cold War.

A disadvantage of the one-time pad is that it requires a very long key, which is expensive to produce and expensive to transmit. Once the key is used up, it is dangerous to reuse it for a second message; any knowledge of the first message would give knowledge of the second, for example. Therefore, in most situations, various methods are used in which a small input can generate a reasonably random sequence of 0's and 1's, hence an "approximation" to a one-time pad. The amount of information carried by the courier is then several orders of magnitude smaller than the messages that will be sent. One such method, which is fast but not very secure, is described in the Section 2.11.

A variation of the one-time pad has been developed by Maurer, Rabin, Ding, and others. Suppose it is possible to have a satellite produce and broadcast several random sequences of bits at a rate fast enough that no computer can store more than a very small fraction of the outputs. Alice wants to send a message to Bob. They use a public key method such as RSA (see Chapter 6) to agree on a method of sampling bits from the random bit streams. Alice and Bob then use these bits to generate a key for a one-time pad. By the time Eve has decrypted the public key transmission, the random bits collected by Alice and Bob have disappeared, so Eve cannot decrypt the message. In fact, since the encryption used a one-time pad, she can never decrypt it, so Alice and Bob have achieved everlasting security for their message. Note that bounded storage is an integral assumption for this procedure. The production and the accurate sampling of the bit streams are also important implementation issues.

2.10   Pseudo-random Bit Generation

The one-time pad and many other cryptographic applications require sequences of random bits. Before we can use a cryptographic algorithm, such as DES (Chapter 4) or AES (Chapter 5), it is necessary to generate a sequence of random bits to use as the key.

One way to generate random bits is to use natural randomness that occurs in nature. For example, the thermal noise from a semiconductor resistor is known to be a good source of randomness. However, just as flipping coins to produce random bits would not be practical for cryptographic applications, most natural conditions are not practical due to the inherent slowness in sampling the process and the difficulty of ensuring that an adversary does not observe the process. We would therefore like a method for generating randomness that can be done in software. Most computers have a method for generating random numbers that is readily available to the user. For example, the standard C library contains a function *rand()* that generates pseudo-random numbers between 0 and 65535. This pseudo-random function takes a **seed** as input and produces an output bitstream.

The *rand()* function and many other pseudo-random number generators are based on linear congruential generators. A **linear congruential generator** produces a sequence of numbers $x_1, x_2, \cdots$, where

$$x_n = ax_{n-1} + b \pmod{m}.$$

The number x_0 is the initial seed, while the numbers a, b, and m are parameters that govern the relationship. The use of pseudo-random number generators based on linear congruential generators is suitable for experimental purposes, but is highly discouraged for cryptographic purposes. This is because they are predictable (even if the parameters a, b, and m are not known), in the sense that an eavesdropper can use knowledge of some bits to predict future bits with fairly high probability. In fact, it has been shown that any polynomial congruential generator is cryptographically insecure.

In cryptographic applications, we need a source of bits that is non-predictable. We now discuss two ways to create such non-predictable bits.

The first method uses one-way functions. These are functions $f(x)$ that are easy to compute but for which, given y, it is computationally infeasible to solve $y = f(x)$ for x. Suppose that we have such a one-way function f and a random seed s. Define $x_j = f(s + j)$ for $j = 1, 2, 3, \ldots$. If we let b_j be the least significant bit of x_j, then the sequence $b_0, b_1, \cdots$ will be a pseudo-random sequence of bits. This method of random bit generation is often used, and has proven to be very practical. Two popular choices for the one-way function are DES (Chapter 4) and the Secure Hash Algorithm (Section 8.3). As an example, the cryptographic pseudo-random number generator in the OpenSSL toolkit (used for secure communications over the Internet) is based on SHA.

Another method for generating random bits is to use an intractable problem from number theory. One of the most popular cryptographically secure pseudo-random number generators is the **Blum-Blum-Shub (BBS) pseudo-random bit generator**, also known as the quadratic residue generator. In this scheme, one first generates two large primes p and q that are both congruent to 3 mod 4. We set $n = pq$ and choose a random integer x that is relatively prime to n. To initialize the BBS generator, set the initial seed to $x_0 \equiv x^2 \pmod{n}$. The BBS generator produces a sequence of random bits $b_1, b_2, \cdots$ by

1. $x_j \equiv x_{j-1}^2 \pmod{n}$

2. b_j is the least significant bit of x_j.

Example. Let

$$p = 24672462467892469787 \text{ and } q = 396736894567834589803,$$

$$n = 9788476140853110794168855217413715781961.$$

Take $x = 873245647888478349013$. The initial seed is

$$x_0 \equiv x^2 \pmod{n}$$
$$\equiv 8845298710478780097089917746010122863172.$$

The values for $x_1, x_2, \cdots x_8$ are

$$x_1 \equiv 7118894281131329522745962455498123822408$$
$$x_2 \equiv 3145174608888893164151380152060704518227$$
$$x_3 \equiv 4898007782307156233272233185574899430355$$
$$x_4 \equiv 3935457818935112922347093546189672310389$$
$$x_5 \equiv 6750995115100970489017613031987402446040$$
$$x_6 \equiv 4289914828771740133546190658266515171326$$
$$x_7 \equiv 4431066711454378260890386385593817521668$$
$$x_8 \equiv 7336876124195046397414235333675005372436.$$

Taking the least significant bit of each of these, which is easily done by checking whether the number is odd or even, produces the sequence $b_1, \cdots, b_8 = 0, 1, 1, 1, 0, 0, 0, 0.$ ∎

The Blum-Blum-Shub generator is very likely unpredictable. See [Stinson]. A problem with BBS is that it is can be slow to calculate. One way to improve its speed is to extract the k least significant bits of x_j. As long as $k \leq \log_2 \log_2 n$, this seems to be cryptographically secure.

2.11   Linear Feedback Shift Register Sequences

Note: In this section, all congruences are mod 2.

In many situations involving encryption, there is a trade-off between speed and security. If one wants a very high level of security, speed is often sacrificed, and vice versa. For example, in cable television, many bits of data are being transmitted, so speed of encryption is important. On the other hand, security is not usually as important since there is rarely an economic advantage to mounting an expensive attack on the system.

In this section, we describe a method that can be used when speed is more important than security.

The sequence

$$0100001001011001111100011011101010000101011001111$$

can be described by giving the initial values

$$x_1 \equiv 0,\ x_2 \equiv 1,\ x_3 \equiv 0,\ x_4 \equiv 0,\ x_5 \equiv 0$$

and the linear recurrence relation

$$x_{n+5} \equiv x_n + x_{n+2} \pmod 2.$$

This sequence repeats after 31 terms.

More generally, consider a linear recurrence relation of length m:

$$x_{n+m} \equiv c_0 x_n + c_1 x_{n+1} + \cdots + c_{m-1} x_{n+m-1} \pmod 2,$$

where the coefficients $c_0, c_1, \ldots$ are integers. If we specify the **initial values**

$$x_1, x_2, \ldots, x_m,$$

then all subsequent values of x_n can be computed using the recurrence. The resulting sequence of 0's and 1's can be used as the key for encryption. Namely, write the plaintext as a sequence of 0's and 1's, then add an appropriate number of bits of the key sequence to the plaintext mod 2, bit by bit. For example, if the plaintext is 1011001110001111 and the key sequence is the example given previously, we have

$$
\begin{array}{rl}
\text{(plaintext)} & 1011001110001111 \\
\text{(key) } + & \underline{0100001001011001} \\
\text{(ciphertext)} & 1111000111010110
\end{array}
$$

Decryption is accomplished by adding the key sequence to the ciphertext in exactly the same way.

One advantage of this method is that a key with large period can be generated using very little information. The long period gives an improvement over the Vigenère method, where a short period allowed us to find the key. In the above example, specifying the initial vector $\{0, 1, 0, 0, 0\}$ and the coefficients $\{1, 0, 1, 0, 0\}$ yielded a sequence of period 31, so 10 bits were used to produce 31 bits. It can be shown that the recurrence

$$x_{n+31} \equiv x_n + x_{n+3}$$

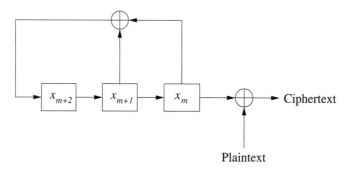

Figure 2.1: A Linear Feedback Shift Register Satisfying $x_{m+3} = x_{m+1} + x_m$.

and any nonzero initial vector will produce a sequence that has period $2^{31} - 1 = 2147483647$. Therefore, 62 bits produce more than two billion bits of key. This is a great advantage over a one-time pad, where the full two billion bits must be sent in advance.

This method can be implemented very easily in hardware using what is known as a **linear feedback shift register** (LFSR) and is very fast. In Figure 2.1 we depict an example of a linear feedback shift register in a simple case. More complicated recurrences are implemented using more registers and more XORs.

For each increment of a counter, the bit in each box is shifted to other boxes as indicated, with $\oplus$ denoting the addition mod 2 of the incoming bits. The output, which is the bit x_m, is added to the next bit of plaintext to produce the ciphertext. The diagram in Figure 2.1 represents the recurrence $x_{m+3} \equiv x_{m+1} + x_m$. Once the initial values x_1, x_2, x_3 are specified, the machine produces the subsequent bits very efficiently.

Unfortunately, the preceding encryption method succumbs easily to a known plaintext attack. More precisely, if we know only a few consecutive bits of plaintext, along with the corresponding bits of ciphertext, we can determine the recurrence relation and therefore compute all subsequent bits of the key. By subtracting (or adding; it's all the same mod 2) the plaintext from the ciphertext mod 2, we obtain the bits of the key. Therefore, for the rest of this discussion, we will ignore the ciphertext and plaintext and assume we have discovered a portion of the key sequence.

For example, suppose we know the initial segment 011010111100 of the sequence 011010111100010011010111 . . ., which has period 15, and suppose we know it is generated by a linear recurrence. How do we determine the coefficients of the recurrence? We do not necessarily know even the length, so we start with length 2 (length 1 would produce a constant sequence). Suppose the recurrence is $x_{n+2} = c_0 x_n + c_1 x_{n+1}$. Let $n = 1$ and $n = 2$ and use the known values $x_1 = 0, x_2 = 1, x_3 = 1, x_4 = 0$. We obtain the equations

$$1 \equiv c_0 \cdot 0 + c_1 \cdot 1 \qquad (n = 1)$$
$$0 \equiv c_0 \cdot 1 + c_1 \cdot 1 \qquad (n = 2).$$

In matrix form, this is

$$\begin{pmatrix} 0 & 1 \\ 1 & 1 \end{pmatrix} \begin{pmatrix} c_0 \\ c_1 \end{pmatrix} \equiv \begin{pmatrix} 1 \\ 0 \end{pmatrix}.$$

The solution is $c_0 = 1, c_1 = 1$, so we guess that the recurrence is $x_{n+2} \equiv x_n + x_{n+1}$. Unfortunately, this is not correct since $x_6 \neq x_4 + x_5$. Therefore, we try length 3. The resulting matrix equation is

$$\begin{pmatrix} 0 & 1 & 1 \\ 1 & 1 & 0 \\ 1 & 0 & 1 \end{pmatrix} \begin{pmatrix} c_0 \\ c_1 \\ c_2 \end{pmatrix} \equiv \begin{pmatrix} 0 \\ 1 \\ 0 \end{pmatrix}.$$

The determinant of the matrix is 0 mod 2; in fact, the equation has no solution. We can see this because every column in the matrix sums to 0 mod 2, while the vector on the right does not.

Now consider length 4. The matrix equation is

$$\begin{pmatrix} 0 & 1 & 1 & 0 \\ 1 & 1 & 0 & 1 \\ 1 & 0 & 1 & 0 \\ 0 & 1 & 0 & 1 \end{pmatrix} \begin{pmatrix} c_0 \\ c_1 \\ c_2 \\ c_3 \end{pmatrix} \equiv \begin{pmatrix} 1 \\ 0 \\ 1 \\ 1 \end{pmatrix}.$$

The solution is $c_0 = 1, c_1 = 1, c_2 = 0, c_3 = 0$. The resulting recurrence is now conjectured to be

$$x_{n+4} \equiv x_n + x_{n+1}.$$

This generates the remaining elements of the piece of key that we already know, so it is our best guess for the recurrence that generates the key sequence. In fact, a quick calculation shows that this is the case, so we have found the recurrence.

The general situation is as follows. To test for a recurrence of length m, we assume we know $x_1, x_2, \ldots, x_{2m}$. The matrix equation is

$$\begin{pmatrix} x_1 & x_2 & \cdots & x_m \\ x_2 & x_3 & \cdots & x_{m+1} \\ \vdots & \vdots & \ddots & \vdots \\ x_m & x_{m+1} & \cdots & x_{2m-1} \end{pmatrix} \begin{pmatrix} c_0 \\ c_1 \\ \vdots \\ c_{m-1} \end{pmatrix} \equiv \begin{pmatrix} x_{m+1} \\ x_{m+2} \\ \vdots \\ x_{2m} \end{pmatrix}.$$

We show later that the matrix is invertible mod 2 if and only if there is no linear recurrence of length less than m that is satisfied by $x_1, x_2, \ldots, x_{2m-1}$.

A strategy for finding the coefficients of the recurrence is now clear. Suppose we know the first 100 bits of the key. For $m = 2, 3, 4, \ldots$, form the $m \times m$ matrix as before and compute its determinant. If several consecutive values of m yield 0 determinants, stop. The last m to yield a nonzero (i.e., 1 mod 2) determinant is probably the length of the recurrence. Solve the matrix equation to get the coefficients $c_0, \ldots, c_{m-1}$. It can then be checked whether the sequence that this recurrence generates matches the sequence of known bits of the key. If not, try larger values of m.

Suppose we don't know the first 100 bits, but rather some other 100 consecutive bits of the key. The same procedure applies, using these bits as the starting point. In fact, once we find the recurrence, we can also work backwards to find the bits preceding the starting point.

Here is an example. Suppose we have the following sequence of 100 bits:

$$1001100100111000110001010001111011001111101010101001$$
$$0110110101100001101110010101111000000100010010000.$$

The first 20 determinants, starting with $m = 1$, are

$$1, 0, 1, 0, 0, 1, 0, 1, 0, 0, 0, 0, 0, 0, 0, 0, 0, 0, 0, 0.$$

A reasonable guess is that $m = 8$ gives the last nonzero determinant. When we solve the matrix equation for the coefficients we get

$$\{c_0, c_1, \ldots, c_7\} = \{1, 0, 1, 0, 1, 1, 1, 1\},$$

so we guess that the recurrence is

$$x_{n+8} \equiv x_n + x_{n+2} + x_{n+4} + x_{n+5} + x_{n+6} + x_{n+7}.$$

This recurrence generates all 100 terms of the original sequence, so we have the correct answer, at least based on the knowledge that we have.

Suppose that the 100 bits were in the middle of some sequence, and we want to know the preceding bits. For example, suppose the sequence starts with x_{17}, so $x_{17} = 1, x_{18} = 0, x_{19} = 0, \ldots$. Write the recurrence as

$$x_n \equiv x_{n+2} + x_{n+4} + x_{n+5} + x_{n+6} + x_{n+7} + x_{n+8}$$

(it might appear that we made some sign errors, but recall that we are working mod 2, so $-x_n \equiv x_n$ and $-x_{n+8} \equiv x_{n+8}$). Letting $n = 16$ yields

$$\begin{aligned} x_{16} &\equiv x_{18} + x_{20} + x_{21} + x_{22} + x_{23} + x_{24} \\ &\equiv 0 + 0 + 0 + 1 + 0 + 1 \equiv 0. \end{aligned}$$

Continuing in this way, we successively determine $x_{15}, x_{14}, \ldots, x_1$.

We now prove the result we promised.

Proposition. *Let*

$$
M = \begin{pmatrix}
x_1 & x_2 & \cdots & x_m \\
x_2 & x_3 & \cdots & x_{m+1} \\
\vdots & \vdots & \ddots & \vdots \\
x_m & x_{m+1} & \cdots & x_{2m-1}
\end{pmatrix}.
$$

If the sequence $x_1, x_2, \ldots, x_{2m-1}$ satisfies a linear recurrence of length less than m, then $\det M \equiv 0$. Conversely, if the sequence $x_1, x_2, \ldots, x_{2m-1}$ satisfies a linear recurrence of length m and $\det M \equiv 0$, then the sequence also satisfies a linear recurrence of length less than m.

Proof. We first make a few remarks on the length of recurrences to explain the last sentence of the proposition. A sequence could satisfy a length 3 relation such as $x_{m+3} \equiv x_{m+2}$. It would clearly then also satisfy shorter relations such as $x_{m+1} = x_m$ (at least for $m \geq 2$). However, there are less obvious ways that a sequence could satisfy a recurrence of length less than expected. For example, consider the relation $x_{n+4} \equiv x_{n+3} + x_{n+1} + x_n$. Suppose the initial values of the sequence are 1, 1, 0, 1. The recurrence allows us to compute subsequent terms: 1, 0, 1, 1, 0, 1, 1, 0, 1, 1, 0, 1.... It is easy to see that the sequence satisfies $x_{n+2} \equiv x_{n+1} + x_n$.

If there is a recurrence of length less than m, then one row of the matrix is a linear combination of other rows. For example, if the recurrence is $x_{n+3} = x_{n+2} + x_n$, then the fourth row is the sum of the first and third rows. Therefore, the determinant is 0 mod 2.

Conversely, suppose the determinant is 0 mod 2. Then there is a nonzero row vector $\bar{b} = (b_0, \ldots, b_{m-1})$ such that $\bar{b}M \equiv 0$. This gives a recurrence relation, but it is not immediately obvious that the recurrence extends all the way to x_{2m-1}. For example, suppose the sum of the first two rows of M equals the third. Then we have $x_{n+2} \equiv x_n + x_{n+1}$ for $n = 1, 2, \ldots m$. We need to extend this all the way to $n = 2m - 3$ to get $x_{2m-1} \equiv x_{2m-3} + x_{2m-2}$. Recall that we are also assuming that there is a recurrence of length m, say $x_{n+m} = c_0 x_{n+1} + \cdots c_{m-1} x_{n+m-1}$ for $0 \leq n < m$. Extend the sequence by defining $x_{2m}, x_{2m+1}, x_{2m+2}, \ldots$ by this recurrence (of course, if the sequence already has terms x_n defined for $n \geq 2m$, these might differ from the temporary values we are using during this proof). We then have a sequence of matrix equations

$$
M_n \begin{pmatrix} c_0 \\ c_1 \\ \vdots \\ c_{m-1} \end{pmatrix} \equiv \begin{pmatrix}
x_{n+1} & x_{n+2} & \cdots & x_{n+m} \\
x_{n+2} & x_{n+3} & \cdots & x_{n+m+1} \\
\vdots & \vdots & \ddots & \vdots \\
x_{n+m} & x_{n+m+1} & \cdots & x_{n+2m-1}
\end{pmatrix} \begin{pmatrix} c_0 \\ c_1 \\ \vdots \\ c_{m-1} \end{pmatrix}
$$

$$\equiv \begin{pmatrix} x_{n+m+1} \\ x_{n+m+2} \\ \vdots \\ x_{n+2m} \end{pmatrix}$$

(where M_n denotes the $m \times m$ matrix in the middle expression). Note that M_0 is the original matrix M. For larger n, it simply expresses the recurrence relation. Recall the vector $\bar{b}$ that satisfies $\bar{b}M \equiv 0$. Let $n = 0$ in the preceding equation and multiply both sides on the left by $\bar{b}$. Since $\bar{b}M_0 \equiv \bar{b}M \equiv 0$, the left yields 0, hence so does the right. This means that $\bar{b} \cdot (x_{m+1}, \ldots, x_{2m}) \equiv 0$.

Now consider the case $n = 1$. What we have just showed is that $\bar{b}$ times the last column of M_1 is 0. But the other columns of M_1 are columns from M_0, so $\bar{b}$ annihilates them, too. Therefore, $\bar{b}M_1 \equiv 0$. The argument just used now implies that $\bar{b}$ times the last column of M_2 is 0. Continuing in this way, we see that $\bar{b}M_n \equiv 0$ for all n.

It is easy to see that this yields a recurrence of length less than m. For example, if $\bar{b} = (1, 1, 1, 0, 0, \ldots)$, then we have $x_{n+2} \equiv x_n + x_{n+1}$ for all n, in particular for $n \leq 2m - 3$ (one might think that the relation should be $x_{n+2} + x_n + x_{n+1} \equiv 0$, but recall that we are working mod 2, so $+$ and $-$ are the same). Also, note that a vector of length m gives a recurrence of length at most $m - 1$ (since the highest nonzero term goes on the other side of the equation). This completes the proof. $\qquad \square$

Finally, we make a few comments about the period of a sequence. Suppose the length of the recurrence is m. Any m consecutive terms of the sequence determine all future elements, and, by reversing the recurrence, all previous values, too. Clearly, if we have m consecutive 0's, then all future values are 0. Also, all previous values are 0. Therefore, we exclude this case from consideration. There are $2^m - 1$ strings of 0's and 1's of length m in which at least one term is nonzero. Therefore, as soon as there are more than $2^m - 1$ terms, some string of length m must occur twice, so the sequence repeats. The period of the sequence is at most $2^m - 1$.

Associated to a recurrence $x_{n+m} \equiv c_0 x_n + c_1 x_{n+1} + \cdots + c_{m-1} x_{n+m-1}$ (mod 2), there is a polynomial

$$f(T) = T^m - c_{m-1}T^{m-1} - \cdots - c_0.$$

If $f(T)$ is irreducible mod 2 (this means that it is not congruent to the product of two lower degree polynomials), then it can be shown that the period divides $2^m - 1$. An interesting case is when $2^m - 1$ is prime (these are called Mersenne primes). If the period isn't 1, that is, if the sequence is not constant, then the period in this special case must be maximal, namely $2^m - 1$. The example where the period is $2^{31} - 1$ is of this type.

Linear feedback shift register sequences have been studied extensively. For example, see [Golomb] or [van der Lubbe].

One way of thwarting the above attack is to use nonlinear recurrences, for example,

$$x_{n+3} \equiv x_{n+2}x_n + x_{n+1}.$$

Generally, these systems are somewhat harder to break. However, we shall not discuss them here.

2.12   Enigma

Mechanical encryption devices known as rotor machines were developed in the 1920s by several people. The best known was designed by Arthur Scherbius and became the famous Enigma machine used by the Germans in World War II.

It was believed to be very secure and several attempts at breaking the system ended in failure. However, a group of three Polish cryptologists, Marian Rejewski, Henryk Zygalski, and Jerzy Różycki, succeeded in breaking early versions of Enigma during the 1930s. Their techniques were passed to the British in 1939, two months before Germany invaded Poland. The British extended the Polish techniques and successfully decrypted German messages throughout World War II.

The fact that Enigma had been broken remained a secret for almost 30 years after the end of the war, partly because the British had sold captured Enigma machines to former colonies and didn't want them to know that the system had been broken.

In the following, we give a brief description of Enigma and then describe an attack developed by Rejewski. For more details, see for example [Kozaczuk]. This book contains appendices by Rejeweski giving details of attacks on Enigma.

A schematic diagram of the machine is presented in Figure 2.2.

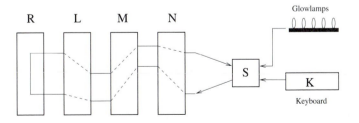

Figure 2.2: A Schematic Diagram of the Enigma Machine.

L, M, N are the rotors. On one side of each rotor are 26 fixed electrical contacts, arranged in a circle. On the other side are 26 spring-loaded contacts, again arranged in a circle so as to touch the fixed contacts of the adjacent rotor. Inside each rotor, the fixed contacts are connected to the spring-loaded contacts in a somewhat random manner. These connections are different in each rotor. Each rotor has 26 possible initial settings.

R is the reversing drum. It has 26 spring-loaded contacts, connected in pairs.

K is the keyboard and is the same as a typewriter keyboard.

S is the plugboard. It has approximately six pairs of plugs that can be used to interchange six pairs of letters.

When a key is pressed, the first rotor N turns $1/26$ of a turn. Then, starting from the key, electricity passes through S, then through the rotors N, M, L. When it reaches the reversing drum R, it is sent back along a different path through L, M, N, then through S. At this point, the electricity lights a bulb corresponding to a letter on the keyboard, which is the letter of the ciphertext.

Since the rotor N rotates before each encryption, this is much more complicated than a substitution cipher. Moreover, the rotors L and M also rotate, but much less often, just like the wheels on an odometer.

Decryption uses exactly the same method. Suppose a sender and receiver have identical machines, both set to the same initial positions. The sender encrypts the message by typing it on the keyboard and recording the sequence of letters indicated by the lamps. This ciphertext is then sent to the receiver, who types the ciphertext into the machine. The sequence of letters appearing in the lamps is the original message. This can be seen as follows. Lamp "a" and key "a" are attached to a wire coming out of the plugboard. Lamp "h" and key "h" are attached to another wire coming out of the plugboard. If the key "a" is pressed and the lamp "h" lights up, then the electrical path through the machine is also connecting lamp "a" to key "h". Therefore, if the "h" key were pressed instead, then the "a" key would light.

Similar reasoning shows that no letter is ever encrypted as itself. This might appear to be a good idea, but actually it is a weakness since it allows a cryptanalyst to discard many possibilities at the start.

The security of the system rests on the keeping secret the initial settings of the rotors, the setting of the plugs on the plugboard, and the internal wiring of the rotors and reversing drum. The settings of the rotors and the plugboard are changed periodically (for example, daily).

We'll assume the internal wiring of the rotors is known. This would be the case if a machine were captured, for example. However, there are ways to deduce this information, given enough ciphertext, and this is what was actually done in some cases.

How many combinations of settings are there? There are 26 initial settings for each of the three rotors. This gives $26^3 = 17576$ possibilities. There are 6 possible orderings of the three rotors. This yields $6 \times 17576 = 105456$ possible ways to initialize the rotors. In later versions of Enigma, there were 5 rotors available, and each day three were chosen. This made 60 possible orderings of the rotors and therefore 1054560 ways to initialize the rotors.

On the plugboard, there are 100391791500 ways of interchanging six pairs of letters.

In all, there seem to be too many possible initializations of the machine to have any hope of breaking the system. Techniques such as frequency analysis fail since the rotations of the rotors change the substitution for each character of the message.

So, how was Enigma attacked? We don't give the whole attack here, but rather show how the initial settings of the rotors were determined in the years around 1937. This attack depended on a weakness in the protocol being used at that time, but it gives the general flavor of how the attacks proceeded in other situations.

Each Enigma operator was given a codebook containing the daily settings to be used for the next month. However, if these settings had been used without modification, then each message sent during a given day would have had its first letter encrypted by the same substitution cipher. The rotor would then have turned and the second letter of each text would have corresponded to another substitution cipher, and this substitution would have been the same for all messages for that day. A frequency analysis on the first letter of each intercepted message during a day would probably allow a decryption of the first letter of each text. A second frequency analysis would decrypt the second letters. Similarly, the remaining letters of the ciphertexts (except for the ends of the longest few ciphertexts) could be decrypted.

To avoid this problem, for each message the operator chose a message key consisting of a sequence of three letters, for example, r, f, u. He then used the daily setting from the codebook to encrypt this message key. But since radio communications were prone to error, he typed in *rfu* twice, therefore encrypting *rfurfu* to obtain a string of six letters. The rotors were then set to positions r, f, and u and the encryption of the actual message began. So the first six letters of the transmitted message were the encrypted message key, and the remainder was the ciphertext. Since each message used a different key, frequency analysis didn't work.

The receiver simply used the daily settings from the codebook to decrypt the first six letters of the message. He then reset the rotors to the positions indicated by the decrypted message key and proceeded to decrypt the message.

The duplication of the key was a great aid to the cryptanalysts. Suppose on some day you intercept several messages, and among them are three that have the following initial six letters:

```
dmqvbn
vonpuy
pucfmq
```

All of these were encrypted with the same daily settings from the codebook. The first encryption corresponds to a permutation of the 26 letters; let's call this permutation A. Before the second letter is encrypted, a rotor turns, so the second letter uses another permutation, call it B. Similarly, there are permutations C, D, E, F for the remaining 4 letters. The strategy is to look at the products AD, BE, and CF.

We need a few conventions and facts about permutations. When we write AD for two permutations A and D, we mean that we apply the permutation A then D (some books use the reverse ordering). The permutation that maps a to b, b to c, and c to a will be denoted as the 3-cycle $(a\,b\,c)$. A similar notation will be used for cycles of other lengths. For example, $(a\,b)$ is the permutation that switches a and b. A permutation can be written as a product of cycles. For example, the permutation

$$(dvpfkxgzyo)(eijmunqlht)(bc)(rw)(a)(s)$$

is the permutation that maps d to v, v to p, t to e, r to w, etc., and fixes a and s. If the cycles are disjoint (meaning that no two cycles have letters in common), then this decomposition into cycles is unique.

Let's look back at the intercepted texts. We don't know the letters of any of the three message keys, but let's call the first message key xyz. Therefore, $xyzxyz$ encrypts to $dmqvbn$. We know that permutation A sends x to d. Also, the fourth permutation D sends x to v. But we know more. Because of the internal wiring of the machine, A actually interchanges x and d and D interchanges x and v. Therefore, the product of the permutations, AD, sends d to v (namely, A sends d to x and then D sends x to v). The unknown x has been eliminated. Similarly, the second intercepted text tells us that AD sends v to p, and the third tells us that AD sends p to f. We have therefore determined that

$$AD = (dvpf \cdots) \cdots .$$

In the same way, the second and fifth letters of the three messages tell us that

$$BE = (oumb \cdots) \cdots$$

and the third and sixth letters tell us that

$$CF = (cqny \cdots) \cdots .$$

With enough data, we can deduce the decompositions of AD, BE, and CF into products of cycles. For example, we might have

$$AD = (dvpfkxgzyo)(eijmunqlht)(bc)(rw)(a)(s)$$
$$BE = (blfqveoum)(hjpswizrn)(axt)(cgy)(d)(k)$$
$$CF = (abviktjgfcqny)(duzrehlxwpsmo).$$

This information depends only on the daily settings of the plugboard and the rotors, not on the message key. Therefore, it relates to every machine used on a given day.

Let's look at the effect of the plugboard. It introduces a permutation S at the beginning of the process and then adds the inverse permutation S^{-1} at the end. We need another fact about permutations: Suppose we take a permutation P and another permutation of the form SPS^{-1} for some permutation S (where S^{-1} denotes the inverse permutation of S; in our case, $S = S^{-1}$) and decompose each into cycles. They will usually not have the same cycles, but the lengths of the cycles in the decompositions will be the same. For example, AD has cycles of length 10, 10, 2, 2, 1, 1. If we decompose $SADS^{-1}$ into cycles for any permutation S, we will again get cycles of lengths 10, 10, 2, 2, 1, 1. Therefore, if the plugboard settings are changed, but the initial positions of the rotors remain the same, then the cycle lengths remain unchanged.

You might have noticed that in the decomposition of AD, BE, and CF into cycles, each cycle length appears an even number of times. This is a general phenomenon. For an explanation, see Appendix E of the aforementioned book by Kozaczuk.

Rejewski and his colleagues compiled a catalog of all 105456 initial settings of the rotors along with the set of cycle lengths for the corresponding three permutations AD, BE, CF. In this way, they could take the ciphertexts for a given day, deduce the cycle lengths, and find the small number of corresponding initial settings for the rotors. Each of these substitutions could be tried individually. The effect of the plugboard (when the correct setting was used) was then merely a substitution cipher, which was easily broken. This method worked until September 1938, when a modified method of transmitting message keys was adopted. Modifications of the above technique were again used to decrypt the messages. The process was also mechanized, using machines called "bombes" to find daily keys, each in around two hours.

These techniques were extended by the British at Bletchley Park during World War II and included building more sophisticated "bombes." These machines, designed by Alan Turing, are often considered to have been the first electronic computers.

2.13   Exercises

1. Caesar wants to arrange a secret meeting with Marc Anthony, either at the Tiber (the river) or at the Coliseum (the arena). He sends the ciphertext *EVIRE*. However, Anthony does not know the key, so he tries all possibilities. Where will he meet Caesar?

2. Encrypt *howareyou* using the affine function $5x + 7 \pmod{26}$. What is the decryption function? Check that it works.

3. Consider an affine cipher (mod 26). You do a chosen plaintext attack using *hahaha*. The ciphertext is *NONONO*. Determine the encryption function.

4. The following ciphertext was encrypted by an affine cipher mod 26:
$$CRWWZ$$
The plaintext starts *ha*. Decrypt the message.

5. Suppose you encrypt using an affine cipher, then encrypt the encryption using another affine cipher (both are working mod 26). Is there any advantage to doing this, rather than using a single affine cipher? Why or why not?

6. Suppose we work mod 27 instead of mod 26 for affine ciphers. How many keys are possible? What if we work mod 29?

7. You want to carry out an affine encryption using the function $\alpha x + \beta$, but you have $\gcd(\alpha, 26) = d > 1$. Show that if $x_1 = x_2 + (26/d)$, then $\alpha x_1 + \beta \equiv \alpha x_2 + \beta \pmod{26}$. This shows that you will not be able to decrypt uniquely in this case.

8. Suppose you have a language with only the 3 letters *a, b, c*, and they occur with frequencies .7, .2, .1, respectively. The following ciphertext was encrypted by the Vigenère method (shifts are mod 3 instead of mod 26, of course):
$$CAAABBCACBCABACAABCCCACA.$$

Show that it is likely that the key length is 2, and determine the most probable key.

9. If **v** and **w** are two vectors in n-dimensional space, $\mathbf{v} \cdot \mathbf{w} = |\mathbf{v}||\mathbf{w}|\cos\theta$, where θ is the angle between the two vectors (measured in the 2-dimensional plane spanned by the two vectors), and $|\mathbf{v}|$ denotes the length of **v**. Use this fact to show that, in the notation of Section 2.3, the dot product $\mathbf{A}_0 \cdot \mathbf{A}_i$ is largest when $i = 0$.

10. The ciphertext *YIFZMA* was encrypted by a Hill cipher with matrix $\begin{pmatrix} 9 & 13 \\ 2 & 3 \end{pmatrix}$. Find the plaintext.

11. The ciphertext text *GEZXDS* was encrypted by a Hill cipher with a 2×2 matrix. The plaintext is *solved*. Find the encryption matrix M.

12. (a) The ciphertext text *ELNI* was encrypted by a Hill cipher with a 2×2 matrix. The plaintext is *dont*. Find the encryption matrix M.
(b) Suppose the ciphertext is *ELNK* and the plaintext is still *dont*. Find the encryption matrix. Note that the second column of the matrix is changed. This shows that the entire second column of the encryption matrix is involved in obtaining the last character of the ciphertext (see the end of Section 2.7).

13. A third-order LFSR sequence starts 001110. Find the next four elements of the sequence.

14. Consider the sequence starting $k_1 = 1, k_2 = 0, k_3 = 1$ and defined by the third-order recursion $k_{n+3} = k_n + k_{n+1} + k_{n+2}$. This sequence can also be given by a second order recursion. Determine this second-order recursion by setting up and solving the appropriate matrix equations.

15. In the mid-1980s, a recruiting advertisement for NSA had 1 followed by one hundred 0's at the top. The text began "You're looking at a 'googol.' Ten raised to the 100th power. One followed by 100 zeroes. Counting 24 hours a day, you would need 120 years to reach a googol. Two lifetimes. It's a number that's impossible to grasp. A number beyond our imagination." How many numbers would you have to count each second in order to reach a googol in 120 years? (Regarding the ad, one guess is that the advertising firm assumed that the time it took to factor a 100-digit number back then was the same as the time it took to count to a googol.)

16. Alice is sending a message to Bob using one of the following cryptosystems. In fact, Alice is bored and her plaintext consists of one letter (known only to her) repeated a few hundred times. Eve knows what system is being used, but not the key, and intercepts the ciphertext. For systems (a) and (b), state how Eve will recognize that the plaintext is one repeated letter and decide whether or not Eve can deduce the key. For system (c), assume Eve guesses that the plaintext is one repeated letter, and show how Eve can

then deduce the key.
(a) Shift cipher
(b) Affine cipher
(c) Vigenère cipher (assume the key is an English word of length of around 8 to 12 letters).

2.14   Computer Problems

1. The following ciphertext was encrypted by a shift cipher:

ycvejqwvhqtdtwvwu

Decrypt. (The ciphertext is stored under the name *ycve*.)

2. The following ciphertext was the output of a shift cipher:

lcllewljazlnnzmvyiylhrmhza

By performing a frequency count, guess the key used in the cipher. Use the computer to test your hypothesis. What is the decrypted plaintext? (The ciphertext is stored under the name *lcll*.)

3. The following ciphertext was encrypted by an affine cipher:

edsgickxhuklzveqzvkxwkzukcvuh

The first two letters of the plaintext are *if*. Decrypt. (The ciphertext is stored under the name *edsg*.)

4. The following ciphertext was encrypted by an affine cipher using the function $3x + b$ for some b:

tcabtiqmfheqqmrmvmtmaq

Decrypt. (The ciphertext is stored under the name *tcab*.)

5. Experiment with the affine cipher $y \equiv mx + n \pmod{26}$ for values of $m > 26$. In particular, determine whether or not these encryptions are the same as ones obtained with $m < 26$.

6. In this problem you are to get your hands dirty doing some programming. Write some code that creates a new alphabet $\{A, C, G, T\}$. For example, this alphabet could correspond to the four nucleotides adenine, cytosine, guanine, and thymine, which are the basic building blocks of DNA and RNA codes.

Associate the letters A, C, G, T with the numbers $0, 1, 2, 3$, respectively.
(a) Using the shift cipher with a shift of 1, encrypt the following sequence of nucleotides which is taken from the beginning of the thirteenth human chromosome:

> *GAATTCGCGGCCGCAATTAACCCTCACTAAAGGGATCT CTAGAACT.*

(b) Write a program that performs affine ciphers on the nucleotide alphabet. What restrictions are there on the affine cipher?

7. The following was encrypted using by the Vigenère method using a key of length at most 6. Decrypt it and decide what is unusual about the plaintext. How did this affect the results?

```
hdsfgvmkoowafweetcmfthskucaqbilgjofmaqlgspvatvxqbiryscpcfr
mvswrvnqlszdmgaoqsakmlupsqforvtwvdfcjzvgsoaoqsacjkbrsevbel
vbksarlscdcaarmnvrysywxqgvellcyluwwveoafgclazowafojdlhssfi
ksepsoywxafowlbfcsocylngqsyzxgjbmlvgrggokgfgmhlmejabsjvgml
nrvqzcrggcrghgeupcyfgtydycjkhqluhgxgzovqswpdvbwsffsenbxapa
sgazmyuhgsfhmftayjxmwznrsofrsoaopgauaaarmftqsmahvqecev
```

(The ciphertext is stored under the name *hdsf*. The plaintext is from *Gadsby* by Ernest Vincent Wright.)

8. The following was encrypted by the Vigenére method. Find the plaintext.

```
ocwyikoooniwugpmxwktzdwgtssayjzwyemdlbnqaaavsuwdvbrflauplo
oubfgqhgcscmgzlatoedcsdeidpbhtmuovpiekifpimfnoamvlpqfxejsm
xmpgkccaykwfzpyuavtelwhrhmwkbbvgtguvtefjlodfefkvpxsgrsorvg
tajbsauhzrzalkwuowhgedefnswmrciwcpaaavogpdnfpktdbalsisurln
psjyeatcuceesohhdarkhwotikbroqrdfmzghgucebvgwcdqxgpbgqwlpb
daylooqdmuhbdqgmyweuik
```

(The ciphertext is stored under the name *ocwy*. The plaintext is from *The Adventure of the Dancing Men* by Sir Arthur Conan Doyle.)

9. The following was encrypted by the Vigenère method. Decrypt it. (The ciphertext is stored under the name *xkju*.)

```
xkjurowmllpxwznpimbvbqjcnowxpcchhvvfvsllfvxhazityxohulxqoja
axelxzxmyjaqfstsrulhhucdskbxknjqidallpqslluhiaqfpbpcidsvcih
whwewthbtxrljnrsncihuvffuxvoukjljswmaqfvjwjsdyljogjxdboxaju
ltucpzmpliwmlubzxvoodybafdskxgqfadshxnxehsaruojaqfpfkndhsaa
fvulluwtaqfrupwjrszxgpfutjqiynrxnyntwmhcukjfbirzsmehhsjshyo
nddzzntzmplilrwnmwmlvuryonthuhabwnvw
```

10. The following is the ciphertext of a Hill cipher

$$\texttt{zirkzwopjjoptfapuhfhadrq}$$

using the matrix

$$\begin{pmatrix} 1 & 2 & 3 & 4 \\ 4 & 3 & 2 & 1 \\ 11 & 2 & 4 & 6 \\ 2 & 9 & 6 & 4 \end{pmatrix}.$$

Decrypt.

11. The following sequence was generated by a linear feedback shift register. Determine the recursion that generated it.
1, 0, 1, 0, 0, 1, 1, 0, 1, 1, 0, 0, 0, 1, 0, 0, 1, 0, 0, 0, 0,
1, 1, 1, 0, 0, 0, 0, 0, 1, 0, 1, 1, 1, 1, 1, 1, 0, 0, 1, 0, 1,
0, 1, 0, 0, 0, 1, 1, 0, 0, 1, 1, 1, 1, 0, 1, 1, 1, 0, 1, 0, 1,
1, 0, 1, 0, 0, 1, 1, 0, 1, 1, 0, 0, 0, 1, 0, 0, 1, 0, 0, 0, 0,
1, 1, 1, 0, 0, 0, 0, 0, 1, 0, 1, 1, 1, 1, 1, 1
(It is stored under the name $L101$.)

12. The following are the first 100 terms of an LFSR output. Find the coefficients of the recurrence.
1, 0, 0, 1, 1, 0, 0, 1, 0, 0, 1, 1, 1, 0, 0, 0, 1, 1, 0, 0, 0,
1, 0, 1, 0, 0, 0, 1, 1, 1, 1, 0, 1, 1, 0, 0, 1, 1, 1, 1, 1, 0,
1, 0, 1, 0, 1, 0, 0, 1, 0, 1, 1, 0, 1, 1, 0, 1, 0, 1, 1, 0, 0,
0, 0, 1, 1, 0, 1, 1, 1, 0, 0, 1, 0, 1, 0, 1, 1, 1, 1, 0, 0, 0,
0, 0, 0, 0, 1, 0, 0, 0, 1, 0, 0, 1, 0, 0, 0, 0
(The sequence is stored under the name $L100$.)

13. The following ciphertext was obtained by XORing an LFSR output with the plaintext.
0, 1, 1, 0, 0, 0, 1, 0, 1, 0, 1, 1, 1, 0, 0, 1, 1, 1, 0, 1, 0,
1, 0, 0, 0, 1, 0, 0, 0, 1, 1, 0, 0, 0, 1, 0, 1, 0, 1, 1, 1, 0,
0, 1, 1, 1, 0, 1, 0, 1
Suppose you know the plaintext starts
1, 0, 0, 1, 0, 0, 1, 0, 0, 1, 0, 0, 1, 0, 0
Find the plaintext. (The ciphertext is stored under the name $L011$.)

Chapter 3

Basic Number Theory

In modern cryptographic systems, the messages are represented by numerical values prior to being encrypted and transmitted. The encryption processes are mathematical operations that turn the input numerical values into output numerical values. Building, analyzing, and attacking these cryptosystems requires mathematical tools. The most important of these is number theory, especially the theory of congruences. This chapter presents the basic tools needed for the rest of the book. More advanced topics such as factoring, discrete logarithms, and elliptic curves, will be treated in later chapters (Chapters 6, 7, and 15, respectively).

3.1   Basic Notions

Divisibility

Number theory is concerned with the properties of the integers. One of the most important is divisibility.

Definition. *Let a and b be integers with $a \neq 0$. We say that a **divides** b, if there is an integer k such that $b = ak$. This is denoted by $a|b$. Another way to express this is that b is a multiple of a.*

Examples. $3|15$, $-15|60$, $7 \nmid 18$ (does not divide).   ■

The following properties of divisibility are useful.

Proposition. *(1) For every $a \neq 0$, $a|0$ and $a|a$. Also, $1|b$ for every b.*
(2) If $a|b$ and $b|c$, then $a|c$.
(3) If $a|b$ and $a|c$, then $a|(sb + tc)$ for all integers s and t.

Proof. (1) Since $0 = a \cdot 0$, we may take $k = 0$ in the definition to obtain $a|0$. Since $a = a \cdot 1$, we take $k = 1$ to prove $a|a$. Since $b = b \cdot 1$, we have $1|b$.
(2) There exist k and ℓ such that $b = ak$ and $c = b\ell$. Therefore, $c = (k\ell)a$, so $a|c$.
(c) Write $b = ak_1$ and $c = ak_2$. Then $sb + tc = a(sk_1 + tk_2)$, so $a|sb + tc$. $\square$

For example, take $a = 2$ in part (2). Then $2|b$ simply means that b is even. The statement in the proposition says that c, which is a multiple of the even number b, must also be even (that is, a multiple of $a = 2$).

Prime Numbers

A number $p > 1$ that is divisible only by 1 and itself is called a **prime number**. The first few primes are $2, 3, 5, 7, 11, 13, 17, \cdots$. An integer $n > 1$ that is not prime is called **composite**, which means that n must expressible as a product ab of integers with $1 < a, b < n$. A fact, known already to Euclid, is that there are infinitely many prime numbers. A more precise statement is the following, proved in 1896.

Prime Number Theorem. *Let $\pi(x)$ be the number of primes less than x. Then*
$$\pi(x) \approx \frac{x}{\ln x},$$
in the sense that the ratio $\pi(x)/(x/\ln x) \to 1$ as $x \to \infty$.

We won't prove this here; its proof would lead us too far away from our cryptographic goals. In various applications, we'll need large primes, say of around 100 digits. We can estimate the number of 100-digit primes as follows:

$$\pi(10^{100}) - \pi(10^{99}) \approx \frac{10^{100}}{\ln 10^{100}} - \frac{10^{99}}{\ln 10^{99}} \approx 3.9 \times 10^{97}.$$

So there are certainly enough such primes. Later, we'll discuss how to find them.

Prime numbers are the building blocks of the integers. Every positive integer has a unique representation as a product of prime numbers raised to different powers. For example, 504 and 1125 have the following factorizations

$$504 = 2^3 3^2 7, \qquad 1125 = 3^2 5^3.$$

Moreover, these factorizations are unique, except for reordering the factors. For example, if we factor 504 into primes, then we will always obtain three factors of 2, two factors of 3, and one factor of 7. Anyone who obtains the prime 41 as a factor has made a mistake.

Theorem. *Every positive integer is a product of primes. This factorization into primes is unique, up to reordering the factors.*

Proof. There is a small technicality that must be dealt with before we begin. When dealing with products, it is convenient to make the convention that an empty product equals 1. This is similar to the convention that $x^0 = 1$. Therefore, the positive integer 1 is a product of primes, namely the empty product. Also, each prime is regarded as a one factor product of primes.

Suppose there exist positive integers that are not products of primes. Let n be the smallest such integer. Then n cannot be 1 (= the empty product), or a prime (= a one factor product), so n must be composite. Therefore, $n = ab$ with $1 < a, b < n$. Since n is the smallest positive integer that is not a product of primes, both a and b are products of primes. But a product of primes times a product of primes is a product of primes, so $n = ab$ is a product of primes. This contradiction shows that the set of integers that are not products of primes must be the empty set. Therefore, every positive integer is a product of primes.

The uniqueness of the factorization is more difficult to prove. We need the following very important property of primes.

Lemma. *If p is a prime and p divides a product of integers ab, then either $p|a$ or $p|b$. More generally, if a prime p divides a product $ab \cdots z$, then p must divide one of the factors $a, b, \ldots, z$.*

For example, when $p = 2$, this says that if a product of two integers is even then one of the two integers must be even. The proof of the lemma will be given at the end of this section, after we discuss the Euclidean algorithm.

Continuing with the proof of the theorem, suppose that an integer n can be written as a product of primes in two different ways:

$$n = p_1^{a_1} p_2^{a_2} \cdots p_s^{a_s} = q_1^{b_1} q_2^{b_2} \cdots q_t^{b_t},$$

where $p_1, \ldots, p_s$ and $q_1, \ldots, q_t$ are primes, and the exponents a_i and b_j are nonzero. If a prime occurs in both factorizations, divide both sides by it to obtain a shorter relation. Continuing in this way, we may assume that none of the primes $p_1, \ldots, p_s$ occur among the q_j's. Take a prime that occurs on the left side, say p_1. Since p_1 divides n, which equals $q_1 q_1 \cdots q_1 q_2 \cdots q_t$, the lemma says that p_1 must divide one of the factors q_j. Since q_j is prime, $p_1 = q_j$. This contradicts the assumption that p_1 does not occur among the q_j's. Therefore, an integer cannot have two distinct factorizations, as claimed. $\square$

Greatest Common Divisor

The **greatest common divisor** of a and b is the largest positive integer dividing both a and b and is denoted by either $gcd(a, b)$ or by (a, b). In this book, we shall use the first notation.

Examples. gcd(6, 4)=2, gcd(5, 7)=1, gcd(24, 60)=12.   ∎

We say that a and b are **relatively prime** if $\gcd(a, b) = 1$. There are two standard ways for finding the gcd:

1. If you can factor a and b into primes, do so. For each prime number, look at the powers that it appears in the factorizations of a and b. Take the smaller of the two. Put these prime powers together to get the gcd. This is easiest to understand by examples:

$$1728 = 2^6 3^2, \quad 135 = 3^3 5, \quad \gcd(1728, 135) = 3^2 = 9$$

$$\gcd(2^5 3^4 7^2, \ 2^2 5^3 7) = 2^2 3^0 5^0 7^1 = 2^2 7 = 28.$$

   Note that if a prime does not appear in a factorization, then it cannot appear in the gcd.

2. Suppose a and b are large numbers, so it might not be easy to factor them. The gcd can be calculated by a procedure known as the **Euclidean algorithm**. It goes back to what everyone learned in grade school: division with remainder. Before giving a formal description of the algorithm, let's see some examples.

Example. Compute gcd(482, 1180).
Solution: Divide 482 into 1180. The quotient is 2 and the remainder is 216. Now divide the remainder 216 into 482. The quotient is 2 and the remainder is 50. Divide the remainder 50 into the previous remainder 216. The quotient is 4 and the remainder is 16. Continue this process of dividing the most recent remainder into the previous one. The last nonzero remainder is the gcd, which is 2 in this case:

$$
\begin{aligned}
1180 &= 2 \cdot 482 + 216 \\
482 &= 2 \cdot 216 + 50 \\
216 &= 4 \cdot 50 + 16 \\
50 &= 3 \cdot 16 + 2 \\
16 &= 8 \cdot 2 + 0.
\end{aligned}
$$

Notice how the numbers are shifted:

$$\text{remainder} \to \text{divisor} \to \text{dividend} \to \text{ignore}.$$

Here is another example:

$$
\begin{aligned}
12345 &= 1 \cdot 11111 + 1234 \\
11111 &= 9 \cdot 1234 + 5 \\
1234 &= 246 \cdot 5 + 4 \\
5 &= 1 \cdot 4 + 1 \\
4 &= 4 \cdot 1 + 0.
\end{aligned}
$$

Therefore, gcd(12345,11111)=1.   ∎

Using these examples as guidelines, we can now give a more formal description of the **Euclidean algorithm**. Suppose that a is greater than b. If not, switch a and b. The first step is to divide a by b, hence represent a in the form

$$a = q_1 b + r_1.$$

If $r_1 = 0$, then b divides a and the greatest common divisor is b. If $r_1 \neq 0$, then continue by representing b in the form

$$b = q_2 r_1 + r_2.$$

Continue in this way until the remainder that is zero, giving the following sequence of steps:

$$
\begin{aligned}
a &= q_1 b + r_1 \\
b &= q_2 r_1 + r_2 \\
r_1 &= q_3 r_2 + r_3 \\
&\;\;\vdots \\
r_{k-2} &= q_k r_{k-1} + r_k \\
r_{k-1} &= q_{k+1} r_k.
\end{aligned}
$$

The conclusion is that

$$\gcd(a, b) = r_k.$$

There are two important aspects to this algorithm:

1. It does not require factorization of the numbers.

2. It is fast.

For a proof that it actually computes the gcd, see Exercise 17.

The Euclidean algorithm allows us to prove the following important result.

Theorem. *Let a and b be two integers, with at least one of a, b nonzero, and let $d = \gcd(a, b)$. Then there exist integers x, y such that $ax + by = d$. In particular, if a and b are relatively prime, then there exist integers x, y with $ax + by = 1$.*

Proof. More generally, we'll show that if r_j is a remainder obtained during the Euclidean algorithm, then there are integers x_j, y_j such that $r_j = ax_j + by_j$. Start with $j = 1$. Taking $x_1 = 1$ and $y_1 = -q_1$, we find that $r_1 = ax_1 + by_1$. Similarly, $r_2 = a(-q_2) + b(1 + q_1 q_2)$. Suppose we have $r_i = ax_i + by_i$ for all $i < j$. Then

$$r_j = r_{j-2} - q_j r_{j-1} = ax_{j-2} + bx_{j-2} - q_j(ax_{j-1} + by_{j-1}).$$

Rearranging yields

$$r_j = a(x_{j-2} - q_j x_{j-1}) + b(x_{j-2} - q_j y_{j-1}).$$

Continuing, we obtain the result for all j, in particular for $j = k$. Since $r_k = \gcd(a, b)$, we are done. $\square$

As a corollary, we deduce the lemma we needed during the proof of the uniqueness of factorization into primes.

Corollary. *If p is a prime and p divides a product of integers ab, then either $p|a$ or $p|b$. More generally, if a prime p divides a product $ab \cdots z$, then p must divide one of the factors $a, b, \ldots, z$.*

Proof. First, let's work with the case $p|ab$. If p divides a, we are done. Now assume $p \nmid a$. We claim $p|b$. Since p is prime, $\gcd(a, p) = 1$ or p. Since $p \nmid a$, the gcd cannot be p. Therefore, $\gcd(a, p) = 1$, so there exist integers x, y with $ax + py = 1$. Multiply by b to obtain $abx + pby = b$. Since $p|ab$ and $p|p$, we have $p|abx + pby$, so $p|b$, as claimed.

If $p|ab \cdots z$, then $p|a$ or $p|b \cdots z$. If $p|a$, we're done. Otherwise, $p|b \cdots z$. We now have a shorter product. Either $p|b$, in which case we're done, or p divides the product of the remaining factors. Continuing in this way, we eventually find that p divides one of the factors of the product. $\square$

The property of primes stated in the corollary holds only for primes. For example, if we know a product ab is divisible by 6, we cannot conclude that a or b is a multiple of 6. The problem is that $6 = 2 \cdot 3$, and the 2 could be in a while the 3 could be in b, as seen in the example $60 = 4 \cdot 15$. More generally, if $n = ab$ is any composite, then $n|ab$ but $n \nmid a$ and $n \nmid b$. Therefore, the primes, and 1, are the only integers with the property of the corollary.

3.2 Solving $ax + by = d$

We did not use the quotients in the Euclidean algorithm. Here is how we can use them. A very basic fact, proved in the last section, is that, given integers a and b, there are integers x and y such that

$$ax + by = \gcd(a, b).$$

How do we find x and y? Suppose we start by dividing a into b, so $b = q_1 a + r_1$, and then proceed as in the Euclidean algorithm. Let the successive quotients be $q_1, q_2, \ldots q_n$, so in the first example of Section 3.1, we have $q_1 = 2, q_2 = 2, q_3 = 4, q_4 = 3, q_5 = 8$. Form the following sequences:

$$x_0 = 0, \; x_1 = 1, \; x_j = -q_{j-1} x_{j-1} + x_{j-2},$$

$$y_0 = 1, \; y_1 = 0, \; y_j = -q_{j-1} y_{j-1} + y_{j-2}.$$

Then

$$a x_n + b y_n = \gcd(a, b).$$

In the first example, we have the following calculation:

$$
\begin{aligned}
x_0 &= \quad 0, \quad x_1 = 1 \\
x_2 &= \quad -2x_1 + x_0 = -2 \\
x_3 &= \quad -2x_2 + x_1 = 5 \\
x_4 &= \quad -4x_3 + x_2 = -22 \\
x_5 &= \quad -3x_4 + x_3 = 71.
\end{aligned}
$$

Similarly, we calculate $y_5 = -29$. An easy calculation shows that

$$482 \cdot 71 + 1180 \cdot (-29) = 2 = \gcd(482, 1180).$$

Notice that we did not use the final quotient. If we had used it, we would have calculated $x_{n+1} = 590$, which is the original number 1180 divided by the gcd, namely 2. Similarly, $y_{n+1} = 241$ is $482/2$.

The preceding method is often called the **extended Euclidean algorithm**. It will be used in the next section for solving certain congruences.

For small numbers, there is another way to find x and y that does not involve as much bookkeeping with subscripts. Let's consider the example $\gcd(12345, 11111) = 1$ from the previous section. We'll use the numbers from that calculation. The idea is to work back through the remainders 1, 4, 5, 1234, and the original numbers 11111 and 12345, and eventually obtain the gcd 1 as a combination of 12345 and 11111. From the line that revealed the gcd, we find

$$1 = 5 - 1 \cdot 4,$$

so we have 1 as a combination of the previous two remainders. Moving up one line, we write the remainder 4 as a combination of 1234 and 5, then substitute into the preceding equation:

$$4 = 1234 - 246 \cdot 5,$$

so

$$1 = 5 - 1 \cdot 4 = 5 - 1 \cdot (1234 - 246 \cdot 5) = 247 \cdot 5 - 1 \cdot 1234.$$

We have now used the last two remainders from the gcd calculation. Write the last unused remainder, namely 5, as a combination of 11111 and 1234, then substitute into the preceding equation:

$$1 = 247 \cdot (11111 - 9 \cdot 1234) - 1 \cdot 1234 = 247 \cdot 11111 - 2224 \cdot 1234.$$

Finally, we substitute for 1234 to obtain

$$1 = 247 \cdot 11111 - 2224 \cdot (12345 - 1 \cdot 11111) = 2471 \cdot 11111 - 2224 \cdot 12345.$$

This yields the gcd 1 as a combination of 12345 and 11111, as desired. As long as the gcd calculation takes only a few steps, this procedure is quite easy to do by hand. But, in general, the previous method is better and adapts well to a computer.

3.3   Congruences

One of the most basic and useful notions in number theory is modular arithmetic, or congruences.

Definition. *Let a, b, n be integers with $n \neq 0$. We say that*

$$a \equiv b \pmod{n}$$

(read: a is **congruent** *to b mod n) if $a - b$ is a multiple (positive or negative) of n.*

Another formulation is that $a \equiv b \pmod{n}$ if a and b differ by a multiple of n. This can be rewritten as $a = b + nk$ for some integer k (positive or negative).

Examples.

$$32 \equiv 7 \pmod{5}, \qquad -12 \equiv 37 \pmod{7}, \qquad 17 \equiv 17 \pmod{13}. \quad \blacksquare$$

Congruence behaves very much like equality. In fact, the notation for congruence was intentionally chosen to resemble the notation for equality.

Proposition. *Let a, b, c, n be integers with $n \neq 0$.*
(1) $a \equiv 0 \pmod{n}$ if and only if $n | a$.
(2) $a \equiv a \pmod{n}$.
(3) $a \equiv b \pmod{n}$ if and only if $b \equiv a \pmod{n}$.
(4) If $a \equiv b$ and $b \equiv c \pmod{n}$, then $a \equiv c \pmod{n}$.

Proof. (1) $a \equiv 0 \pmod{n}$ means that $a = a - 0$ is a multiple of n, which is the same as $n | a$.
(2) $a - a = 0 \cdot n$, so $a \equiv a \pmod{n}$.
(3) If $a \equiv b \pmod{n}$, write $a - b = nk$. Then $b - a = n(-k)$, so $b \equiv a \pmod{n}$. Reversing the roles of a and b gives the reverse implication.
(4) Write $a = b + nk$ and $c = b + n\ell$. Then $a - c = n(k - \ell)$, so $a \equiv c \pmod{n}$. $\square$

Often, we will work with the integers mod n, denoted $\mathbf{Z}_n$. These may be regarded as the set $\{0, 1, 2, \ldots, n - 1\}$, with addition, subtraction, and multiplication mod n. If a is any integer, we may divide a by n and obtain a remainder in this set:

$$a = nq + r \text{ with } 0 \leq r < n.$$

(This is just division with remainder; q is the quotient and r is the remainder.) Then $a \equiv r \pmod{n}$, so every number a is congruent mod n to some integer r with $0 \leq r < n$.

Proposition. *Let a, b, c, d, n be integers with $n \neq 0$, and suppose $a \equiv b \pmod{n}$ and $c \equiv d \pmod{n}$. Then*

$$a + c \equiv b + d, \quad a - c \equiv b - d, \quad ac \equiv bd \pmod{n}.$$

Proof. Write $a = b + nk$ and $c = d + n\ell$, for integers k and ℓ. Then $a + c = b + d + n(k + \ell)$, so $a + c \equiv b + d \pmod{n}$. The proof that $a - c \equiv b - d$ is similar. For multiplication, we have $ac = bd + n(dk + b\ell + nk\ell)$, so $ac \equiv bd$. $\square$

The proposition says you can perform the usual arithmetic operations of addition, subtraction, and multiplication with congruences. You must be careful, however, when trying to perform division, as we'll see.

If we take two numbers and want to multiply them modulo n, we start by multiplying them as integers. If the product is less than n, we stop. If the product is larger than $n - 1$, we divide by n and take the remainder. Addition and subtraction are done similarly. For example, the integers modulo 6 have the following addition table:

+	0	1	2	3	4	5
0	0	1	2	3	4	5
1	1	2	3	4	5	0
2	2	3	4	5	0	1
3	3	4	5	0	1	2
4	4	5	0	1	2	3
5	5	0	1	2	3	4

A table for multiplication mod 6 is

×	0	1	2	3	4	5
0	0	0	0	0	0	0
1	0	1	2	3	4	5
2	0	2	4	0	2	4
3	0	3	0	3	0	3
4	0	4	2	0	4	2
5	0	5	4	3	2	1

Example. Here is an example of how we can do algebra mod n. Consider the following problem: Solve $x + 7 \equiv 3 \pmod{17}$.
Solution: $x \equiv 3 - 7 \equiv -4 \equiv 13 \pmod{17}$.   ∎

There is nothing wrong with negative answers, but usually we write the final answer as an integer from 0 to $n - 1$ when we are working mod n.

Division

Division is much trickier mod n than it is with rational numbers. The general rule is that you can divide by $a \pmod{n}$ when $\gcd(a, n) = 1$.

Proposition. *Let a, b, c, n be integers with $n \neq 0$ and with $\gcd(a, n) = 1$. If $ab \equiv ac \pmod{n}$, then $b \equiv c \pmod{n}$. In other words, if a and n are relatively prime, we can divide both sides of the congruence by a.*

Proof. Since $\gcd(a, n) = 1$, there exist integers x, y such that $ax + ny = 1$. Multiply by $b - c$ to obtain

$$(ab - ac)x + n(b - c)y = b - c.$$

Since $ab - ac$ is a multiple of n, by assumption, and $n(b - c)y$ is also a multiple of n, we find that $b - c$ is a multiple of n. This means that $b \equiv c \pmod{n}$.   □

Example. Solve: $2x + 7 \equiv 3 \pmod{17}$.
Solution: $2x \equiv 3 - 7 \equiv -4$, so $x \equiv -2 \equiv 15 \pmod{17}$. The division by 2 is allowed since gcd(2,17)=1. ∎

Example. Solve: $5x + 6 \equiv 13 \pmod{11}$.
Solution: $5x \equiv 7 \pmod{11}$. Now what do we do? We want to divide by 5, but what does 7/5 mean mod 11? Note that $7 \equiv 18 \equiv 29 \equiv 40 \equiv \cdots$ (mod 11). So $5x \equiv 7$ is the same as $5x \equiv 40$. Now we can divide by 5 and obtain $x \equiv 8 \pmod{11}$ as the answer. Note that $7 \equiv 8 \cdot 5 \pmod{11}$, so 8 acts like 7/5. ∎

The last example can be done another way. Since $5 \cdot 9 \equiv 1 \pmod{11}$, we see that 9 is the multiplicative inverse of 5 (mod 11). Therefore, dividing by 5 can be accomplished by multiplying by 9. If we want to solve $5x \equiv 7$ (mod 11), we multiply both sides by 9 and obtain

$$x \equiv 45x \equiv 63 \equiv 8 \pmod{11}.$$

Proposition. *Suppose* $\gcd(a, n) = 1$. *Let s and t be integers such that $as + nt = 1$ (they can be found using the extended Euclidean algorithm). Then $as \equiv 1 \pmod{n}$, so s is the multiplicative inverse for a (mod n).*

Proof. Since $as - 1 = -nt$, we see that $as - 1$ is a multiple of n. □

The extended Euclidean algorithm is fairly efficient for computing the multiplicative inverse of a by the method stated in the proposition.

Example. Solve $11111x \equiv 4 \pmod{12345}$.
Solution: Referring to the calculation of $\gcd(12345, 11111)$ done earlier, we have quotients $q_1 = 1, q_2 = 9, q_3 = 246, q_4 = 1, q_5 = 4$. Therefore, in the extended Euclidean algorithm, $x_0 = 0, x_1 = 1, x_2 = -1, x_3 = 10, x_4 = -2461, x_5 = 2471$, which tells us that $11111 \cdot 2471 + 12345 \cdot y_5 = 1$, hence

$$11111 \cdot 2471 \equiv 1 \pmod{12345}.$$

Multiplying both sides of the original congruence by 2471 yields

$$x \equiv 9884 \pmod{12345}.$$

In practice, this means that if we are working mod 12345 and we encounter the fraction 4/11111, we can replace it with 9884. This might seem a little strange, but think about what 4/11111 means. It's simply a symbol to represent a quantity that, when multiplied by 11111, yields 4. When we are working mod 12345, the number 9884 also has this property since $11111 \times 9884 \equiv 4 \pmod{12345}$. ∎

Let's summarize some of the discussion:

Finding $a^{-1} \pmod{n}$

1. Use the extended Euclidean algorithm to find integers s and t such that $as + nt = 1$.

2. $a^{-1} \equiv s \pmod{n}$.

Solving $ax \equiv c \pmod{n}$ when $\gcd(a, n) = 1$

(Equivalently, you could be working mod n and encounter a fraction c/a with $\gcd(a, n) = 1$.)

1. Use the extended Euclidean algorithm to find integers s and t such that $as + nt = 1$.

2. The solution is $x \equiv cs \pmod{n}$ (equivalently, replace the fraction c/a with $cs \pmod{n}$).

What if $\gcd(a, n) > 1$?

Occasionally we will need to solve congruences of the form $ax \equiv b \pmod{n}$ when $\gcd(a, n) = d > 1$. The procedure is as follows:

1. If d does not divide b, there is no solution.

2. Assume $d|b$. Consider the new congruence

$$(a/d)x \equiv b/d \pmod{n/d}.$$

   Note that $a/d, b/d, n/d$ are integers and $\gcd(a/d, n/d) = 1$. Solve this congruence by the above procedure to obtain a solution x_0.

3. The solutions of the original congruence $ax \equiv b \pmod{n}$ are

$$x_0, \quad x_0 + (n/d), \quad x_0 + 2(n/d), \ldots, \quad x_0 + (d-1)(n/d) \pmod{n}.$$

Example. Solve $12x \equiv 21 \pmod{39}$.
Solution: $\gcd(12, 39) = 3$, which divides 21. Divide by 3 to obtain the new congruence $4x \equiv 7 \pmod{13}$. A solution $x_0 = 5$ can be obtained by trying a few numbers, or by using the extended Euclidean algorithm. The solutions to the original congruence are $x \equiv 5, 18, 31 \pmod{39}$. ∎

The preceding congruences contained x to the first power. However, nonlinear congruences are also useful. In several places in this book, we will meet equations of the form

$$x^2 \equiv a \pmod{n}.$$

First, consider $x^2 \equiv 1 \pmod 7$. The solutions are $x \equiv 1, 6 \pmod 7$, as we can see by trying the values $0, 1, 2, \ldots, 6$ for x. In general, when p is an odd prime, $x^2 \equiv 1 \pmod p$ has exactly the two solutions $x \equiv \pm 1 \pmod p$ (see Exercise 4).

Now consider $x^2 \equiv 1 \pmod{15}$. If we try the numbers $0, 1, 2, \ldots, 14$ for x, we find that $x = 1, 4, 11, 14$ are solutions. For example, $11^2 \equiv 121 \equiv 1 \pmod{15}$. Therefore, a quadratic congruence for a composite modulus can have more than two solutions, in contrast to the fact that a quadratic equation with real numbers, for example, can have at most two solutions. In Section 3.4, we'll discuss this phenomenon. In Sections 6.4 (factoring), 11.1 (flipping coins), and 12.2 (identification schemes), we'll meet applications of this fact.

Working with Fractions

In many situations, it will be convenient to work with fractions mod n. For example, $1/2 \pmod{12345}$ is easier to write than $6173 \pmod{12345}$ (note that $2 \times 6173 \equiv 1 \pmod{12345}$). The general rule is that a fraction b/a can be used mod n if $\gcd(a, n) = 1$. Of course, it should be remembered that b/a $\pmod n$ really means $a^{-1}b \pmod n$, where a^{-1} denotes the integer mod n that satisfies $a^{-1}a \equiv 1 \pmod n$. But nothing will go wrong if it is treated as a fraction.

Another way to look at this is the following. The symbol "$1/2$" is simply a symbol with exactly one property: If you multiply $1/2$ by 2, you get 1. In all calculations involving the symbol $1/2$, this is the only property that is used. When we are working mod 12345, the number 6173 also has this property, since $6173 \times 2 \equiv 1 \pmod{12345}$. Therefore, $1/2 \pmod{12345}$ and $6713 \pmod{12345}$ may be used interchangeably.

Why can't we use fractions with arbitrary denominators? Of course, we cannot use $1/6 \pmod 6$, since that would mean dividing by $0 \pmod 6$. But even if we try to work with $1/2 \pmod 6$, we run into trouble. For example, $2 \equiv 8 \pmod 6$, but we cannot multiply both sides by $1/2$, since $1 \not\equiv 4$ $\pmod 6$. The problem is that $\gcd(2, 6) = 2 \neq 1$. Since 2 is a factor of 6, we can think of dividing by 2 as "partially dividing by 0." In any case, it is not allowed.

3.4   The Chinese Remainder Theorem

In many situations, it is useful to break a congruence mod n into a system of congruences mod factors of n. Consider the following example. Suppose we know that a number x satisfies $x \equiv 25 \pmod{42}$. This means that we can write $x = 25 + 42k$ for some integer k. Rewriting 42 as $7 \cdot 6$, we obtain $x = 25 + 7(6k)$, which implies that $x \equiv 25 \equiv 4 \pmod 7$. Similarly, since $x = 25 + 6(7k)$, we have $x \equiv 25 \equiv 1 \pmod 6$. Therefore,

$$x \equiv 25 \pmod{42} \Rightarrow \begin{cases} x \equiv 4 \pmod 7 \\ x \equiv 1 \pmod 6. \end{cases}$$

The Chinese remainder theorem shows that this process can be reversed; namely, a system of congruences can be replaced by a single congruence under certain conditions.

Chinese Remainder Theorem. *Suppose* $\gcd(m, n) = 1$. *Given a and b, there exists exactly one solution x (mod mn) to the simultaneous congruences*

$$x \equiv a \pmod m, \qquad x \equiv b \pmod n.$$

Proof. There exist integers s, t such that $ms + nt = 1$. Then $ms \equiv 1 \pmod n$ and $nt \equiv 1 \pmod m$. Let $x = bms + ant$. Then $x \equiv ant \equiv a \pmod m$, and $x \equiv bms \equiv b \pmod n$, as desired. Suppose x_1 is another solution. Then $x \equiv x_1 \pmod m$ and $x \equiv x_1 \pmod n$, so $x - x_1$ is a multiple of both m and n.

Lemma. *Let* m, n *be integers with* $\gcd(m, n) = 1$. *If an integer c is a multiple of both m and n, then c is a multiple of mn.*

Proof. Let $c = mk = n\ell$. Write $ms + nt = 1$ with integers s, t. Multiply by c to obtain $c = cms + cnt = mn\ell s + mnkt = mn(\ell s + kt)$. □

To finish the proof of the theorem, let $c = x - x_1$ in the lemma to find that $x - x_1$ is a multiple of mn. Therefore, $x \equiv x_1 \pmod{mn}$. This means that any two solutions x to the system of congruences are congruent mod mn, as claimed. □

Example. Solve $x \equiv 3 \pmod 7$, $x \equiv 5 \pmod{15}$.
Solution: $x \equiv 80 \pmod{105}$ (note: $105 = 7 \cdot 15$). Since $80 \equiv 3 \pmod 7$ and $80 \equiv 5 \pmod{15}$, 80 is a solution. The theorem guarantees that such a solution exists, and says that it is uniquely determined mod the product mn, which is 105 in the present example. ∎

How does one find the solution? One way, which works with small numbers m and n, is to list the numbers congruent to b (mod n) until you find one that is congruent to a (mod m). For example, the numbers congruent to 5 (mod 15) are

$$5, 20, 35, 50, 65, 80, 95, \ldots.$$

Mod 7, these are $5, 6, 0, 1, 2, 3, 4, \ldots$. Since we want 3 (mod 7), we choose 80.

For slightly larger numbers m and n, making a list would be inefficient. However, a similar idea works. The numbers congruent to b (mod n) are of the form $b + nk$ with k an integer, so we need to solve $b + nk \equiv a$ (mod m). This is the same as

$$nk \equiv a - b \pmod{m}.$$

Since $\gcd(m, n) = 1$ by assumption, there is a multiplicative inverse i for n (mod m). Multiplication by i gives

$$k \equiv (a - b)i \pmod{m}.$$

Substituting back into $x = b + nk$, then reducing mod mn, gives the answer.

Of course, for large numbers, the proof of the theorem gives an efficient method for finding x that is almost the same as the one just given.

Example. Solve $x \equiv 7$ (mod 12345), $\quad x \equiv 3$ (mod 11111).
Solution: First, we know from our calculations in Section 3.3 that the inverse of 11111 (mod 12345) is $i = 2471$. Therefore $k \equiv 2471(7 - 3) \equiv 9884$ (mod 12345). This yields $x = 3 + 11111 \cdot 9884 \equiv 109821127$ (mod $(11111 \cdot 12345)$). ∎

How do you use the Chinese remainder theorem? The main idea is that if you start with a congruence mod a composite number n, you can break it into simultaneous congruences mod each prime power factor of n, then recombine the resulting information to obtain an answer mod n. The advantage is that often it is easier to analyze congruences mod primes or mod prime powers than to work mod composite numbers.

Suppose you want to solve $x^2 \equiv 1$ (mod 35). Note that $35 = 5 \cdot 7$. We have

$$x^2 \equiv 1 \pmod{35} \Leftrightarrow \begin{cases} x^2 \equiv 1 \pmod{7} \\ x^2 \equiv 1 \pmod{5}. \end{cases}$$

Now, $x^2 \equiv 1$ (mod 5) has 2 solutions: $x \equiv \pm 1$ (mod 5). Also, $x^2 \equiv 1$ (mod 7) has 2 solutions: $x \equiv \pm 1$ (mod 7). We can put these together in 4 ways:

$$x \equiv \quad 1 \pmod{5}, \quad x \equiv \quad 1 \pmod{7} \quad \longrightarrow \quad x \equiv 1 \pmod{35},$$

$$x \equiv 1 \quad (\text{mod } 5), \quad x \equiv -1 \quad (\text{mod } 7) \quad \longrightarrow \quad x \equiv 6 \quad (\text{mod } 35),$$

$$x \equiv -1 \quad (\text{mod } 5), \quad x \equiv 1 \quad (\text{mod } 7) \quad \longrightarrow \quad x \equiv 29 \quad (\text{mod } 35),$$

$$x \equiv -1 \quad (\text{mod } 5), \quad x \equiv -1 \quad (\text{mod } 7) \quad \longrightarrow \quad x \equiv 34 \quad (\text{mod } 35).$$

So the solutions of $x^2 \equiv 1 \pmod{35}$ are $x \equiv 1, 6, 29, 34 \pmod{35}$.

In general, if $n = p_1 p_2 \cdots p_r$ is the product of r distinct odd primes, then $x^2 \equiv 1 \pmod{n}$ has 2^r solutions. This is a consequence of the following.

Chinese Remainder Theorem (General Form). *Let $m_1, \ldots, m_k$ be integers with $\gcd(m_i, m_j) = 1$ whenever $i \neq j$. Given integers $a_1, \ldots, a_k$, there exists exactly one solution $x \pmod{m_1 \cdots m_k}$ to the simultaneous congruences*

$$x \equiv a_1 \quad (\text{mod } m_1), \; x \equiv a_2 \quad (\text{mod } m_2), \; \ldots, \; x \equiv a_k \quad (\text{mod } m_k).$$

For example, the theorem guarantees a solution to the simultaneous congruences

$$x \equiv 1 \quad (\text{mod } 11), \qquad x \equiv -1 \quad (\text{mod } 13), \qquad x \equiv 1 \quad (\text{mod } 17).$$

In fact, $x \equiv 1871 \pmod{11 \cdot 13 \cdot 17}$ is the answer.

For a procedure that produces the number x in the theorem, see Exercise 13.

3.5   Modular Exponentiation

Throughout this book, we will be interested in numbers of the form

$$x^a \quad (\text{mod } n).$$

In this and the next couple of sections, we discuss some properties of numbers raised to a power modulo an integer.

Suppose we want to compute $2^{1234} \pmod{789}$. If we first compute 2^{1234}, then reduce mod 789, we'll be working with very large numbers, even though the final answer has only 3 digits. We should therefore perform each multiplication and then calculate the remainder. Calculating the consecutive powers of 2 would require that we perform the modular multiplication 1233 times. This is method is too slow to be practical, especially when the exponent becomes very large. A more efficient way is the following (all congruences will be mod 789).

We start with $2^2 \equiv 4 \pmod{789}$ and repeatedly square both sides to obtain the following congruences:

$$
\begin{aligned}
2^4 &\equiv 4^2 \equiv 16 \\
2^8 &\equiv 16^2 \equiv 256 \\
2^{16} &\equiv 256^2 \equiv 49 \\
2^{32} &\equiv 34 \\
2^{64} &\equiv 367 \\
2^{128} &\equiv 559 \\
2^{256} &\equiv 37 \\
2^{512} &\equiv 580 \\
2^{1024} &\equiv 286.
\end{aligned}
$$

Since $1234 = 1024 + 128 + 64 + 16 + 2$ (this just means that 1234 equals 10011010010 in binary), we have

$$2^{1234} \equiv 286 \cdot 559 \cdot 367 \cdot 49 \cdot 4 \equiv 481 \pmod{789}.$$

Note that we never needed to work with a number larger than 788^2.

The same method works in general. If we want to compute $a^b \pmod{n}$, we can do it with at most $2\log_2(b)$ multiplications mod n, and we never have to work with numbers larger than n^2. This means that exponentiation can be accomplished quickly, and not much memory is needed.

This method is very useful if a, b, n are 100-digit numbers. If we simply computed a^b, then reduced mod n, the computer's memory would overflow: The number a^b has more than 10^{100} digits, which is more digits than there are particles in the universe. However, the computation of $a^b \pmod{n}$ can be accomplished in less than 700 steps by the present method, never using a number of more than 200 digits.

An algorithmic version of this procedure is given in Exercise 12.

3.6   Fermat's Little Theorem and Euler's Theorem

Two of the most basic results in number theory are Fermat's and Euler's theorems. Originally admired for their theoretical value, they have more recently proved to have important cryptographic applications and will be used repeatedly throughout this book.

Fermat's Little Theorem. *If p is a prime and p does not divide a, then*

$$a^{p-1} \equiv 1 \pmod{p}.$$

Proof. Let
$$S = \{1, 2, 3, \ldots, p - 1\}.$$
Consider the map $\psi : S \to S$ defined by $\psi(x) = ax \pmod{p}$. For example, when $p = 7$ and $a = 2$, the map ψ takes a number x, multiplies it by 2, then reduces the result mod 7.

We need to check that if $x \in S$ then $\psi(x)$ is actually in S, that is, $\psi(x) \neq 0$. Suppose $\psi(x) = 0$. Then $ax \equiv 0 \pmod{p}$. Since $\gcd(a, p) = 1$, we can divide this congruence by a to obtain $x \equiv 0 \pmod{p}$, so $x \notin S$. This contradiction means that $\psi(x)$ cannot be 0, hence $\psi(x) \in S$. Now suppose there are $x, y \in S$ with $\psi(x) = \psi(y)$. This means $ax \equiv ay \pmod{p}$. Since $\gcd(a, p) = 1$, we can divide this congruence by a to obtain $x \equiv y \pmod{p}$. We conclude that if x, y are distinct elements of S, then $\psi(x)$ and $\psi(y)$ are distinct. Therefore,

$$\psi(1), \psi(2), \psi(3), \cdots, \psi(p - 1)$$

are distinct elements of S. Since S has only $p - 1$ elements, these must be the elements of S written in a some order. It follows that

$$
\begin{aligned}
1 \cdot 2 \cdot 3 &\cdots (p - 1) \\
&\equiv \psi(1) \cdot \psi(2) \cdot \psi(3) \cdots \psi(p - 1) \\
&\equiv (a \cdot 1)(a \cdot 2)(a \cdot 3) \cdots (a \cdot (p - 1)) \\
&\equiv a^{p-1}(1 \cdot 2 \cdot 3 \cdots (p - 1)) \pmod{p}.
\end{aligned}
$$

Since $\gcd(j, p) = 1$ for $j \in S$, we can divide this congruence by $1, 2, 3, \ldots, p - 1$. What remains is $1 \equiv a^{p-1} \pmod{p}$. $\qquad\square$

Example. $2^{10} = 1024 \equiv 1 \pmod{11}$. From this we can evaluate 2^{53} $\pmod{11}$: Write $2^{53} = (2^{10})^5 2^3 \equiv 1^5 2^3 \equiv 8 \pmod{11}$. Note that when working mod 11, we are essentially working with the exponents mod 10, not mod 11. In other words, from $53 \equiv 3 \pmod{10}$, we deduce $2^{53} \equiv 2^3$ $\pmod{11}$. $\qquad\blacksquare$

Usually, if $2^{n-1} \equiv 1 \pmod{n}$, the number n is prime. However, there are exceptions: $561 = 3 \cdot 11 \cdot 17$ is composite but $2^{560} \equiv 1 \pmod{561}$. We can see this as follows: Since $560 \equiv 0 \pmod{2}$, we have $2^{560} \equiv 2^0 \equiv 1 \pmod{3}$. Similarly, since $560 \equiv 0 \pmod{10}$ and $560 \equiv 0 \pmod{16}$, we can conclude that $2^{560} \equiv 1 \pmod{11}$ and $2^{560} \equiv 1 \pmod{17}$. Putting things together via the Chinese remainder theorem, we find that $2^{560} \equiv 1 \pmod{561}$.

Another such exception is $1729 = 7 \cdot 13 \cdot 19$. However, these exceptions are fairly rare in practice. Therefore, if $2^{n-1} \equiv 1 \pmod{n}$, it is quite likely that n is prime. Of course, if $2^{n-1} \not\equiv 1 \pmod{n}$ then n cannot be prime. Since

2^{n-1} (mod n) can be evaluated very quickly (see Section 3.5), this gives a way to search for prime numbers. Namely, choose a starting point n_0 and successively test each odd number $n \geq n_0$ to see whether $2^{n-1} \equiv 1$ (mod n). If n fails the test, discard it and proceed to the next n. When an n passes the test, use more sophisticated techniques (see Section 6.3) to test n for primality. The advantage is that this procedure is much faster than trying to factor each n, especially since it eliminates many n quickly. Of course, there are ways to speed up the search, for example, by first eliminating any n that has small prime factors.

We'll also need the analog of Fermat's theorem for a composite modulus n. Let $\phi(n)$ be the number of integers $1 \leq a \leq n$ such that $\gcd(a, n) = 1$. For example, if $n = 10$ then there are 4 such integers, namely 1,3,7,9. Therefore, $\phi(10) = 4$. Often ϕ is called **Euler's ϕ-function.**

If p is a prime and $n = p^r$, then we must remove every pth number in order to get the list of a's with $\gcd(a, n) = 1$, which yields

$$\phi(p^r) = (1 - \frac{1}{p})p^r.$$

In particular,

$$\phi(p) = p - 1.$$

More generally, it can be deduced from the Chinese remainder theorem that for any integer n,

$$\phi(n) = n \prod_{p|n} (1 - \frac{1}{p}),$$

where the product is over the distinct primes p dividing n. When $n = pq$ is the product of two distinct primes, this yields

$$\phi(pq) = (p - 1)(q - 1).$$

Examples.

$$\phi(10) = (2 - 1)(5 - 1) = 4,$$

$$\phi(120) = 120(1 - \frac{1}{2})(1 - \frac{1}{3})(1 - \frac{1}{5}) = 32. \qquad \blacksquare$$

Euler's Theorem. *If* $\gcd(a, n) = 1$, *then*

$$a^{\phi(n)} \equiv 1 \pmod{n}.$$

Proof. The proof of this theorem is almost the same as the one given for Fermat's theorem. Let S be the set of integers $1 \leq x \leq n$ with $\gcd(x, n) = 1$. Let $\psi : S \rightarrow S$ be defined by $\psi(x) \equiv ax \pmod{n}$. As in the proof of Fermat's theorem, the numbers $\psi(x)$ for $x \in S$ are the numbers in S written in some order. Therefore

$$\prod_{x \in S} x \equiv \prod_{x \in S} \psi(x) \equiv a^{\phi(n)} \prod_{x \in S} x.$$

Dividing out the factors $x \in S$, we are left with $1 \equiv a^{\phi(n)} \pmod{n}$. $\square$

Note that when $n = p$ is prime, Euler's theorem is the same as Fermat's theorem.

Example. What are the last three digits of 7^{803}?
Solution: Knowing the last three digits is the same as working mod 1000. Since $\phi(1000) = 1000(1 - \frac{1}{2})(1 - \frac{1}{5}) = 400$, we have $7^{803} = (7^{400})^2 7^3 \equiv 7^3 \equiv 343 \pmod{1000}$. Therefore, the last three digits are 343.

In this example, we were able to change the exponent 803 to 3 because $803 \equiv 3 \pmod{\phi(1000)}$. ∎

Example. Compute $2^{43210} \pmod{101}$.
Solution: From Fermat's theorem, we know that $2^{100} \equiv 1 \pmod{101}$. Therefore,
$$2^{43210} \equiv (2^{100})^{432} 2^{10} \equiv 1^{432} 2^{10} \equiv 1024 \equiv 14 \pmod{101}.$$

In this case we were able to change the exponent 43210 to 10 because $43210 \equiv 10 \pmod{100}$. ∎

To summarize, we state the following:

Basic Principle. *Let a, n, x, y be integers with $n \geq 1$ and $\gcd(a, n) = 1$. If $x \equiv y \pmod{\phi(n)}$, then $a^x \equiv a^y \pmod{n}$. In other words, if you want to work mod n, you should work mod $\phi(n)$ in the exponent.*

Proof. Write $x = y + \phi(n)k$. Then

$$a^x = a^{y + \phi(n)k} = a^y (a^{\phi(n)})^k \equiv a^y 1^k \equiv a^y \pmod{n}.$$

This completes the proof. $\square$

This extremely important fact will be used repeatedly in the remainder of the book. Review the preceding examples until you are convinced that the exponents mod $400 = \phi(1000)$ and mod 100 are what count (i.e., don't be one of the many people who mistakenly try to work with the exponents mod 1000 and mod 101 in these examples).

3.7 Primitive Roots

Consider the powers of 3 (mod 7):

$$3^1 \equiv 3, \quad 3^2 \equiv 2, \quad 3^3 \equiv 6, \quad 3^4 \equiv 4, \quad 3^5 \equiv 5, \quad 3^6 \equiv 1.$$

Note that we obtain all the nonzero congruence classes mod 7 as powers of 3. This means that 3 is a primitive root mod 7 (the term *multiplicative generator* might be better, but is not as common). Similarly, every nonzero congruence class mod 13 is a power of 2, so 2 is a primitive root mod 13. However, $3^3 \equiv 1 \pmod{13}$, so only 1, 3, 9 are powers of 3. Therefore 3 is not a primitive root mod 13. The primitive roots mod 13 are 2, 6, 7, 11.

In general, when p is a prime, a **primitive root** mod p is a number whose powers yield every nonzero class mod p. There are $\phi(p-1)$ primitive roots mod p. In particular, there is always at least one. In practice, it is not difficult to find one, at least if the factorization of $p-1$ is known. See Exercise 10.

The following summarizes the main facts we need about primitive roots.

Proposition. *Let g be a primitive root for the prime p.*

1. *If n is an integer, then $g^n \equiv 1 \pmod{p}$ if and only if $n \equiv 0 \pmod{p-1}$.*

2. *If j and k are integers, then $g^j \equiv g^k \pmod{p}$ if and only if $j \equiv k \pmod{p-1}$.*

Proof. If $n \equiv 0 \pmod{p-1}$, then $n = (p-1)m$ for some m. Therefore

$$g^n \equiv (g^m)^{p-1} \equiv 1 \pmod{p}$$

by Fermat's theorem. Conversely, suppose $g^n \equiv 1 \pmod{p}$. We want to show that $p-1$ divides n, so we divide $p-1$ into n and try to show that the remainder is 0. Write

$$n = (p-1)q + r, \quad \text{with } 0 \leq r < p-1$$

(this is just division with quotient q and remainder r). We have

$$1 \equiv g^n \equiv (g^q)^{p-1} g^r \equiv 1 \cdot g^r \equiv g^r \pmod{p}.$$

Suppose $r > 0$. If we consider the powers $g, g^2, \dots$ of $g \pmod{p}$, then we get back to 1 after r steps. Then

$$g^{r+1} \equiv g, \quad g^{r+2} \equiv g^2, \quad \dots$$

so the powers of $g \pmod{p}$ yield only the r numbers $g, g^2, \ldots, 1$. Since $r < p - 1$, not every number mod p can be a power of g. This contradicts the assumption that g is a primitive root.

The only possibility that remains is that $r = 0$. This means that $n = (p-1)r$, so $p - 1$ divides n. This proves part (1).

For part (2), assume that $j \geq k$ (if not, switch j and k). Suppose that $g^j \equiv g^k \pmod{p}$. Dividing both sides by g^k yields $g^{j-k} \equiv 1 \pmod{p}$. By part (1), $j - k \equiv 0 \pmod{p-1}$, so $j \equiv k \pmod{p-1}$. Conversely, if $j \equiv k \pmod{p-1}$, then $j - k \equiv 0 \pmod{p-1}$, so $g^{j-k} \equiv 1 \pmod{p}$, again by part (1). Multiplying by g^k yields the result. $\qquad\qquad\square$

3.8   Inverting Matrices Mod n

Finding the inverse of a matrix mod n can be accomplished by the usual methods for inverting a matrix, as long as we apply the rule given in Section 3.3 for dealing with fractions. The basic fact we need is that a square matrix is invertible mod n if and only if its determinant and n are relatively prime.

We treat only small matrices here, since that is all we need for the examples in this book. In this case, the easiest way is to find the inverse of the matrix is to use rational numbers, then change back to numbers mod n. It is a general fact that the inverse of an integer matrix can always be written as another integer matrix divided by the determinant of the original matrix. Since we are assuming the determinant and n are relatively prime, we can invert the determinant as in Section 3.3.

For example, in the 2×2 case the usual formula is

$$\begin{pmatrix} a & b \\ c & d \end{pmatrix}^{-1} = \frac{1}{ad - bc} \begin{pmatrix} d & -b \\ -c & a \end{pmatrix},$$

so we need to find an inverse for $ad - bc \pmod{n}$.

Example. Suppose we want to invert $\begin{pmatrix} 1 & 2 \\ 3 & 4 \end{pmatrix} \pmod{11}$. Since $ad - bc = -2$, we need the inverse of -2 mod 11. Since $5 \times (-2) \equiv 1 \pmod{11}$, we can replace $-1/2$ by 5 and obtain

$$\begin{pmatrix} 1 & 2 \\ 3 & 4 \end{pmatrix}^{-1} \equiv \frac{-1}{2} \begin{pmatrix} 4 & -2 \\ -3 & 1 \end{pmatrix} \equiv 5 \begin{pmatrix} 4 & -2 \\ -3 & 1 \end{pmatrix} \equiv \begin{pmatrix} 9 & 1 \\ 7 & 5 \end{pmatrix} \pmod{11}.$$

A quick calculation shows that

$$\begin{pmatrix} 1 & 2 \\ 3 & 4 \end{pmatrix} \begin{pmatrix} 9 & 1 \\ 7 & 5 \end{pmatrix} = \begin{pmatrix} 23 & 11 \\ 55 & 23 \end{pmatrix} \equiv \begin{pmatrix} 1 & 0 \\ 0 & 1 \end{pmatrix} \pmod{11}. \qquad \blacksquare$$

Example. Suppose we want the inverse of

$$M = \begin{pmatrix} 1 & 1 & 1 \\ 1 & 2 & 3 \\ 1 & 4 & 9 \end{pmatrix} \quad (\text{mod } 11).$$

The determinant is 2 and the inverse of M in rational numbers is

$$\frac{1}{2} \begin{pmatrix} 6 & -5 & 1 \\ -6 & 8 & -2 \\ 2 & -3 & 1 \end{pmatrix}.$$

(For ways to calculate the inverse of a matrix, look at any book on linear algebra.) We can replace $1/2$ with 6 mod 11 and obtain

$$M^{-1} \equiv \begin{pmatrix} 3 & 3 & 6 \\ 8 & 4 & 10 \\ 1 & 4 & 6 \end{pmatrix} \quad (\text{mod } 11). \qquad \blacksquare$$

Why do we need the determinant and n to be relatively prime? Suppose $MN \equiv I \pmod{n}$, where I is the identity matrix. Then

$$\det(M)\det(N) \equiv \det(MN) \equiv \det(I) \equiv 1 \pmod{n}.$$

Therefore, $\det(M)$ has an inverse mod n, which means that $\det(M)$ and n must be relatively prime.

3.9 Square Roots Mod n

Suppose we are told that $x^2 \equiv 71 \pmod{77}$ has a solution. How do we find one solution, and how do we find all solutions? More generally, consider the problem of finding all solutions of $x^2 \equiv b \pmod{n}$, where $n = pq$ is the product of two primes. We show in the following that this can be done quite easily, once the factorization of n is known. Conversely, if we know all solutions, then it is easy to factor n.

Let's start with the case of square roots mod a prime p. The easiest case is when $p \equiv 3 \pmod{4}$, and this suffices for our purposes. The case when $p \equiv 1 \pmod{4}$ is more difficult. See [Cohen, pp. 31–34].

Proposition. *Let $p \equiv 3 \pmod{4}$ be prime and let y be an integer. Let $x \equiv y^{(p+1)/4} \pmod{p}$.*

1. If y has a square root mod p, then the square roots of y mod p are $\pm x$.

2. If y has no square root mod p, then $-y$ has a square root mod p, and the square roots of $-y$ are $\pm x$.

Proof. If $y \equiv 0 \pmod p$, all the statements are trivial, so assume $y \not\equiv 0 \pmod p$. Fermat's theorem says that $y^{p-1} \equiv 1 \pmod p$. Therefore,

$$x^4 \equiv y^{p+1} \equiv y^2 y^{p-1} \equiv y^2 \pmod p.$$

This implies that $(x^2 + y)(x^2 - y) \equiv 0 \pmod p$, so $x^2 \equiv \pm y \pmod p$. (See Exercise 3(a).) Therefore, at least one of y and $-y$ is a square mod p. Suppose both y and $-y$ are squares mod p, say $y \equiv a^2$ and $-y \equiv b^2$. Then $-1 \equiv (a/b)^2$ (work with fractions mod p as in Section 3.3), which means -1 is a square mod p. This is impossible when $p \equiv 3 \pmod 4$ (see Exercise 15). Therefore, exactly one of y and $-y$ has a square root mod p. If y has a square root mod p then $y \equiv x^2$, and the two square roots of y are $\pm x$. If $-y$ has a square root then $x^2 \equiv -y$. $\qquad\square$

Example. Let's find the square root of 5 mod 11. Since $(p+1)/4 = 3$, we compute $x \equiv 5^3 \equiv 4 \pmod{11}$. Since $4^2 \equiv 5 \pmod{11}$, the square roots of 5 mod 11 are ± 4.

Now let's try to find a square root of 2 mod 11. Since $(p+1)/4 = 3$, we compute $2^3 \equiv 8 \pmod{11}$. But $8^2 \equiv 9 \equiv -2 \pmod{11}$, so we have found a square root of -2 rather than of 2. This is because 2 has no square root mod 11. $\qquad\blacksquare$

We now consider square roots for a composite modulus. Note that

$$x^2 \equiv 71 \pmod{77}$$

means that

$$x^2 \equiv 71 \equiv 1 \pmod 7 \text{ and } x^2 \equiv 71 \equiv 5 \pmod{11}.$$

Therefore,

$$x \equiv \pm 1 \pmod 7 \text{ and } x \equiv \pm 4 \pmod{11}.$$

The Chinese remainder theorem tells us that a congruence mod 7 and a congruence mod 11 can be recombined into a congruence mod 77. For example, if $x \equiv 1 \pmod 7$ and $x \equiv 4 \pmod{11}$, then $x \equiv 15 \pmod{77}$. In this way, we can recombine in four ways to get the solutions

$$x \equiv \pm 15, \quad \pm 29 \pmod{77}.$$

Now let's turn things around. Suppose $n = pq$ is the product of two primes and we know the four solutions $x \equiv \pm a, \pm b$ of $x^2 \equiv y \pmod n$.

From the construction just used above, we know that $a \equiv b \pmod{p}$ and $a \equiv -b \pmod{q}$ (or the same congruences with p and q switched). Therefore, $p|(a-b)$ but $q \nmid (a-b)$. This means that $\gcd(a-b, n) = p$, so we have found a nontrivial factor of n (this is essentially the Basic Principle of Section 6.3).

For example, in the preceding example we know that $15^2 \equiv 29^2 \equiv 71 \pmod{77}$. Therefore, $\gcd(15 - 29, 77) = 7$ gives a nontrivial factor of 77.

Another example of computing square roots mod n is given in the Section 11.1.

Notice that all the operations used above are fast, with the exception of factoring n. In particular, the Chinese remainder theorem calculation can be done quickly. So can the computation of the gcd. The modular exponentiations needed to compute square roots mod p and mod q can be done quickly using successive squaring. Therefore, we can state the following principle:

Suppose $n = pq$ is the product of two primes congruent to 3 mod 4, and suppose y is a number relatively prime to n which has a square root mod n. Then finding the four solutions $x \equiv \pm a, \pm b$ to $x^2 \equiv y \pmod{n}$ is computationally equivalent to factoring n.

In other words, if we can find the solutions, then we can easily factor n; conversely, if we can factor n, we can easily find the solutions.

3.10   Finite Fields

Note: *This section is more advanced than the rest of the chapter. It is included because finite fields are often used in cryptography. In particular, finite fields appear in four places in this book. The finite field $GF(2^8)$ is used in Rijndael (Chapter 5). Finite fields give an explanation of some phenomena that are mentioned in Section 2.11. Finally, finite fields are used in Section 15.4 and in error correcting codes (Chapter 16).*

Many times throughout this book, we work with the integers mod p, where p is a prime. We can add, subtract, and multiply, but what distinguishes working mod p from working mod an arbitrary integer n is that we can divide by any number that is nonzero mod p. For example, if we need to solve $3x \equiv 1 \pmod{5}$, then we divide by 3 to obtain $x \equiv 2 \pmod{5}$. In contrast, if we want to solve $3x \equiv 1 \pmod{6}$, there is no solution since we cannot divide by 3 (mod 6). Loosely speaking, a set that has the operations of addition, multiplication, subtraction, and division by nonzero elements is called a field. We also require that the associative, commutative, and distributive laws hold.

Examples. The basic examples of fields are the real numbers, the complex numbers, the rational numbers, and the integers mod a prime. The set of all integers is not a field since we sometimes cannot divide and obtain an answer in the set (for example, $4/3$ is not an integer). ∎

Example. Here is a field with 4 elements. Consider the set

$$GF(4) = \{0, 1, \omega, \omega^2\},$$

with the following laws:

1. $0 + x = x$ for all x.

2. $x + x = 0$ for all x.

3. $1 \cdot x = x$ for all x.

4. $\omega + 1 = \omega^2$.

5. Addition and multiplication are commutative and associative, and the distributive law $x(y + z) = xy + xz$ holds for all x, y, z.

Since
$$\omega^3 = \omega \cdot \omega^2 = \omega \cdot (1 + \omega) = \omega + \omega^2 = \omega + (1 + \omega) = 1,$$
we see that ω^2 is the multiplicative inverse of ω. Therefore every nonzero element of $GF(4)$ has a multiplicative inverse, and $GF(4)$ is a field with 4 elements. ∎

In general, a **field** is a set containing elements 0 and 1 (with $1 \neq 0$) and satisfying the following:

1. It has a multiplication and addition satisfying (1), (3), (5) in the preceding list.

2. Every element has an additive inverse (for each x, this means there exists an element $-x$ such that $x + (-x) = 0$).

3. Every nonzero element has a multiplicative inverse.

A field is closed under subtraction. To compute $x - y$, simply compute $x + (-y)$.

The set of 2×2 matrices with real entries is not a field for two reasons. First, the multiplication is not commutative. Second, there are nonzero matrices that do not have inverses (and therefore we cannot divide by them). The set of non-negative real numbers is not a field. We can add, multiply, and divide, but sometimes when we subtract the answer is not in the set.

For every power p^n of a prime, there is exactly one finite field with p^n elements, and these are the only finite fields. We'll soon show how to construct them, but first let's point out that if $n > 1$, then the integers mod p^n do not form a field. The congruence $px \equiv 1 \pmod{p^n}$ does not have a solution, so we cannot divide by p, even though $p \not\equiv 0 \pmod{p^n}$. Therefore, we need more complicated constructions to produce fields with p^n elements.

The field with p^n elements is called $GF(p^n)$. The "GF" is for "Galois field," named for the French mathematician Evariste Galois (1811–1832), who did some early work related to fields.

Example, continued. Here is another way to produce the field $GF(4)$. Let $\mathbf{Z}_2[X]$ be the set of polynomials whose coefficients are integers mod 2. For example, $1 + X^3 + X^6$ and X are in this set. Also, the constant polynomials 0 and 1 are in $\mathbf{Z}_2[X]$. We can add, subtract, and multiply in this set, as long as we work with the coefficients mod 2. For example,

$$(X^3 + X + 1)(X + 1) = X^4 + X^3 + X^2 + 1$$

since the term $2X$ disappears mod 2. The important property for our purposes is that we can perform division with remainder, just as with the integers. For example, suppose we divide $X^2 + X + 1$ into $X^4 + X^3 + 1$. We can do this by long division, just as with numbers:

$$
\begin{array}{r}
X^2 + 1 \\
X^2 + X + 1 \enclose{longdiv}{X^4 + X^3 + 1} \\
\underline{X^4 + X^3 + X^2} \\
X^2 + 1 \\
\underline{X^2 + X + 1} \\
X
\end{array}
$$

In words, what we did was to divide by $X^2 + X + 1$ and obtain the X^2 as the first term of the quotient. Then we multiplied this X^2 times $X^2 + X + 1$ to get $X^4 + X^3 + X^2$, which we subtracted from $X^4 + X^3 + 1$, leaving $X^2 + 1$. We divided this $X^2 + 1$ by $X^2 + X + 1$ and obtained the second term of the quotient, namely 1. Multiplying 1 times $X^2 + X + 1$ and subtracting from $X^2 + 1$ left the remainder X. Since the degree of the polynomial X is less than the degree of $X^2 + X + 1$, we stopped. The quotient was $X^2 + 1$ and the remainder was X:

$$X^4 + X^3 + 1 = (X^2 + 1)(X^2 + X + 1) + X.$$

We can write this as

$$X^4 + X^3 + 1 \equiv X \pmod{X^2 + X + 1}.$$

Whenever we divide by $X^2 + X + 1$ we can obtain a remainder that is either 0 or a polynomial of degree at most 1 (if the remainder had degree 2 or more, we could continue dividing). Therefore, we define $\mathbf{Z}_2[X]$ (mod $X^2 + X + 1$) to be the set

$$\{0, 1, X, X + 1\}$$

of polynomials of degree at most 1, since these are the remainders that we obtain when we divide by $X^2 + X + 1$. Addition, subtraction, and multiplication are done mod $X^2 + X + 1$. This is completely analogous to what happens when we work with integers mod n. In the present situation, we say that two polynomials $f(X)$ and $g(X)$ are congruent mod $X^2 + X + 1$, written $f(X) \equiv g(X)$ (mod $X^2 + X + 1$), if $f(X)$ and $g(X)$ have the same remainder when divided by $X^2 + X + 1$. Another way of saying this is that $f(X) - g(X)$ is a multiple of $X^2 + X + 1$. This means that there is a polynomial $h(X)$ such that $f(X) - g(X) = (X^2 + X + 1)h(X)$.

Now let's multiply in $\mathbf{Z}_2[X]$ (mod $X^2 + X + 1$). For example

$$X \cdot X = X^2 \equiv X + 1 \quad (\text{mod } X^2 + X + 1).$$

(It might seem that the right side should be $-X - 1$, but recall that we are working with coefficients mod 2, so $+1$ and -1 are the same.) As another example, we have

$$X^3 \equiv X \cdot X^2 \equiv X \cdot (X + 1) \equiv X^2 + X \equiv 1 \quad (\text{mod } X^2 + X + 1).$$

It is easy to see that we are working with the set $GF(4)$ from before, with X in place of ω. ∎

Working with $\mathbf{Z}_2[X]$ mod a polynomial can be used to produce finite fields. But we cannot work mod an arbitrary polynomial. The polynomial must be irreducible, which means that it doesn't factor into polynomials of lower degree mod 2. For example, $X^2 + 1$, which is irreducible when we are working with real numbers, is not irreducible when the coefficients are taken mod 2 since $X^2 + 1 = (X + 1)(X + 1)$ when we are working mod 2. However, $X^2 + X + 1$ is irreducible: Suppose it factors mod 2 into polynomials of lower degree. The only possible factors mod 2 are X and $X + 1$, and $X^2 + X + 1$ is not a multiple of either of these, even mod 2.

Here is the general procedure for constructing a finite field with p^n elements, where p is prime and $n \geq 1$. We let $\mathbf{Z}_p$ denote the integers mod p.

1. $\mathbf{Z}_p[X]$ is the set of polynomials with coefficients mod p.

2. Choose $P(X)$ to be an irreducible polynomial mod p of degree n.

3. Let $GF(p^n)$ be $\mathbf{Z}_p[X]$ mod $P(X)$. Then $GF(p^n)$ is a field with p^n elements.

The fact that $GF(p^n)$ has p^n elements is easy to see. The possible remainders after dividing by $P(X)$ are the polynomials of the form $a_0 + a_1X + \cdots + a_{n-1}X^{n-1}$, where the coefficients are integers mod p. There are p choices for each coefficient, hence p^n possible remainders.

For each n, there are irreducible polynomials mod p of degree n, so this construction produces fields with p^n elements for each $n \geq 1$. What happens if we do the same construction for two different polynomials $P_1(X)$ and $P_2(X)$, both of degree n? We obtain two fields, call them $GF(p^n)'$ and $GF(p^n)''$. It is possible to show that these are essentially the same field (the technical term is that the two fields are isomorphic), though this is not obvious since multiplication mod $P_1(X)$ is not the same as multiplication mod $P_2(X)$.

Division

We can easily add, subtract, and multiply polynomials in $\mathbf{Z}_p[X]$, but division is a little more subtle. Let's look at an example. The polynomial $X^8 + X^4 + X^3 + X + 1$ is irreducible in $\mathbf{Z}_2[X]$ (although there are faster methods, one way to show it is irreducible is to divide it by all polynomials of smaller degree in $\mathbf{Z}_2[X]$). Consider the field

$$GF(2^8) = \mathbf{Z}_2[X] \quad (\bmod\ X^8 + X^4 + X^3 + X + 1).$$

Since $X^7 + X^6 + X^3 + X + 1$ is not 0, it should have an inverse. The inverse is found using the analog of the extended Euclidean algorithm. First, perform the gcd calculation for $\gcd(X^7 + X^6 + X^3 + X + 1, X^8 + X^4 + X^3 + X + 1)$. The procedure (remainder $\rightarrow$ divisor $\rightarrow$ dividend $\rightarrow$ ignore) is the same as for integers:

$$X^8 + X^4 + X^3 + X + 1 = (X+1)(X^7 + X^6 + X^3 + X + 1) + (X^6 + X^2 + X)$$
$$X^7 + X^6 + X^3 + X + 1 = (X+1)(X^6 + X^2 + X) + 1.$$

The last remainder is 1, which tells us that the "greatest common divisor" of $X^7 + X^6 + X^3 + X + 1$ and $X^8 + X^4 + X^3 + X + 1$ is 1. Of course, this must be the case, since $X^8 + X^4 + X^3 + X + 1$ is irreducible, so its only factors are 1 and itself.

Now work back through the calculation to express 1 as a linear combination of $X^7 + X^6 + X^3 + X + 1$ and $X^8 + X^4 + X^3 + X + 1$ (or use the formulas for the extended Euclidean algorithm). Recall that in each step we take the last unused remainder and replace it by the dividend minus the quotient times the divisor; since we are working mod 2, the minus signs disappear.

$$
\begin{aligned}
1 &= (X^7+X^6+X^3+X+1)+(X+1)(X^6+X^2+X)\\
&= (X^7+X^6+X^3+X+1)\\
&\quad +(X+1)\Big((X^8+X^4+X^3+X+1)+(X+1)(X^7+X^6+X^3+X+1)\Big)\\
&= (1+(X+1)^2)(X^7+X^6+X^3+X+1)+(X+1)(X^8+X^4+X^3+X+1)\\
&= (X^2)(X^7+X^6+X^3+X+1)+(X+1)(X^8+X^4+X^3+X+1).
\end{aligned}
$$

Therefore,

$$
1 = (X^2)(X^7+X^6+X^3+X+1)+(X+1)(X^8+X^4+X^3+X+1).
$$

Reducing mod $X^8 + X^4 + X^3 + X + 1$, we obtain

$$
(X^2)(X^7+X^6+X^3+X+1) \equiv 1 \quad (\mathrm{mod}\ X^8+X^4+X^3+X+1),
$$

which means that X^2 is the multiplicative inverse of $X^7 + X^6 + X^3 + X + 1$. Whenever we need to divide by $X^7 + X^6 + X^3 + X + 1$, we can instead multiply by X^2. This is the analog of what we did when working with the usual integers mod p.

$GF(2^8)$

Later in this book, we shall discuss Rijndael, which uses $GF(2^8)$ (see Chapter 5), so let's look at this field a little more closely. We'll work mod the irreducible polynomial $X^8 + X^4 + X^3 + X + 1$, since that is the one used by Rijndael. However, there are other irreducible polynomials of degree 8, and any one of them would lead to similar calculations. Every element can be represented uniquely as a polynomial

$$
b_7 X^7 + b_6 X^6 + b_5 X^5 + b_4 X^4 + b_3 X^3 + b_2 X^2 + b_1 X + b + 0,
$$

where each b_i is 0 or 1. The 8 bits $b_7 b_6 b_5 b_4 b_3 b_2 b_1 b_0$ represent a byte, so we can represent the elements of $GF(2^8)$ as 8-bit bytes. For example, the polynomial $X^7 + X^6 + X^3 + X + 1$ becomes 11001011. Addition is the XOR of the bits:

$$
(X^7 + X^6 + X^3 + X + 1) + (X^4 + X^3 + 1)
$$
$$
\rightarrow 11001011 \oplus 00011001 = 11010010
$$
$$
\rightarrow X^7 + X^6 + X^4 + X.
$$

Multiplication is more subtle and does not have as easy an interpretation. That is because we are working mod the polynomial $X^8 + X^4 + X^3 + X + 1$, which we can represent by the 9 bits 100011011. First, let's multiply $X^7 + X^6 + X^3 + X + 1$ by X: With polynomials, we calculate

$$
\begin{aligned}
(X^7 + X^6 + X^3 + X + 1)(X) &= X^8 + X^7 + X^4 + X^2 + X \\
&= (X^7 + X^3 + X^2 + 1) + (X^8 + X^4 + X^3 + X + 1) \\
&\equiv X^7 + X^3 + X^2 + 1 \pmod{X^8 + X^4 + X^3 + X + 1}.
\end{aligned}
$$

The same operation with bits becomes

$$
\begin{aligned}
11001011 \rightarrow \quad & 110010110 && \text{(shift left and append a 0)} \\
\rightarrow \quad & 110010110 \oplus 100011011 && \text{(subtract } X^8 + X^4 + X^3 + X + 1) \\
= \quad & 010001101,
\end{aligned}
$$

which corresponds to the preceding answer. In general, we can multiply by X by the following algorithm:

1. Shift left and append a 0 as the last bit.

2. If the first bit is 0, stop.

3. If the first bit is 1, *XOR* with 100011011.

The reason we stop in step 2 is that if the first bit is 0 then the polynomial still has degree less than 8 after we multiply by X, so it does not need to be reduced. To multiply by higher powers of X, multiply by X several times. For example, multiplication by X^3 can be done with three shifts and at most three *XOR*s. Multiplication by an arbitrary polynomial can be accomplished by multiplying by the various powers of X appearing in that polynomial, then adding (i.e., *XOR*ing) the results.

In summary, we see that the fields operations of addition and multiplication in $GF(2^8)$ can be carried out very efficiently. Similar considerations apply to any finite field.

The analogy between the integers mod a prime and polynomials mod an irreducible polynomial is quite remarkable. We summarize in the following.

$$
\begin{aligned}
\text{integers} &\longleftrightarrow \mathbf{Z}_p[X] \\
\text{prime number } q &\longleftrightarrow \text{irreducible } P(X) \text{ of degree } n \\
\mathbf{Z}_q &\longleftrightarrow \mathbf{Z}_p[X] \pmod{P(X)} \\
\text{field with } q \text{ elements} &\longleftrightarrow \text{field with } p^n \text{ elements}
\end{aligned}
$$

Let $GF(p^n)^*$ denote the nonzero elements of $GF(p^n)$. This set, which has $p^n - 1$ elements, is closed under multiplication, just as the integers not congruent to 0 mod p are closed under multiplication. It can be shown that there is a generating polynomial $g(X)$ such that every element in $GF(p^n)^*$ can be expressed as a power of $g(X)$. This also means that the smallest exponent k such that $g(X)^k \equiv 1$ is $p^n - 1$. This is the analog of a primitive root for primes. There are $\phi(p^n - 1)$ such generating polynomials, where ϕ is Euler's function. An interesting situation occurs when $p = 2$ and $2^n - 1$ is prime. In this case, every nonzero polynomial $f(X) \neq 1$ in $GF(2^n)$ is a generating polynomial. [Remark, for those who know some group theory: The set $GF(2^n)^*$ is a group of prime order in this case, so every element except the identity is a generator.]

The **discrete log problem** mod a prime, which we'll discuss in Chapter 7, has an analog for finite fields; namely, given $h(x)$, find an integer k such that $h(X) = g(X)^k$ in $GF(p^n)$. Finding such a k is believed to be very hard in most situations.

LFSR Sequences

We can now explain a phenomenon that is mentioned in Section 2.11 on LFSR sequences.

Start with a recurrence relation, for example,

$$x_{n+4} \equiv x_n + x_{n+1} \pmod{2}.$$

If the initial values are

$$x_0 = 1, x_1 = 1, x_2 = 0, x_3 = 1$$

the sequence is

$$1\ 1\ 0\ 1\ 0\ 1\ 1\ 1\ 1\ 0\ 0\ 0\ 1\ 0\ 0\ 1\ 1\ 0\ 1 \dots.$$

Associated with the recurrence is the polynomial

$$X^4 + X + 1,$$

which in this case is irreducible mod 2. Therefore, $\mathbf{Z}_2[X] \pmod{X^4 + X + 1}$ is the field $GF(16)$ with 16 elements, represented as polynomials of degree at most 3. To the initial values 1 1 0 1, associate the element $1 + X + X^3$ of $GF(16)$. Multiply this by X and reduce mod $X^4 + X + 1$:

$$X(1+X+X^3) = X+X^2+X^4 \equiv X+X^2+(X+1) \equiv 1+X^2 \pmod{X^4+X+1}.$$

The polynomial $1 + X^2$ can be associated with the numbers 1 0 1 0, which are x_1, x_2, x_3, x_4. Now multiply $1 + X + X^3$ by X^2, which is the same as multiplying $1 + X^2$ by X, and again reduce mod $X^4 + X + 1$:

$$X^2(1 + X + X^3) \equiv X(1 + X^2) \equiv X + X^3 \pmod{X^4 + X + 1},$$

which corresponds to 0 1 0 1, namely x_2, x_3, x_4, x_5. Continuing in this way, we see that

$$X^k(1 + X + X^3) \equiv x_k + x_{k+1}X + x_{k+2}X^2 + x_{k+3}X^3 \quad (\text{mod } X^4 + X + 1)$$

(this can be proved by induction). The sequence starts repeating when $x_k = x_0, x_{k+1} = x_1, x_{k+2} = x_2, x_{k+3} = x_3$, which means that

$$X^k(1 + X + X^3) \equiv 1 + X + X^3 \quad (\text{mod } X^4 + X + 1).$$

Dividing by $1 + X + X^3$ yields

$$X^k \equiv 1 \quad (\text{mod } X^4 + X + 1).$$

The smallest positive k when this happens is $k = 15$, so the sequence repeats after 15 terms, as we can see from the preceding list of elements in the sequence. The fact that $X^k \not\equiv 1$ for $k < 15$ means that the powers of X are all distinct, so the powers of X give all 15 nonzero elements of $GF(16)$. Therefore, X is a generating polynomial.

The general situation is similar. For simplicity, assume that

$$x_{n+m} \equiv c_0 x_n + c_1 x_{n+1} + \cdots + c_{m-1} x_{n+m-1} \quad (\text{mod } 2)$$

is a recurrence relation and that the associated polynomial

$$P(X) = X^m + c_{m-1}X^{m-1} + c_{m-2}X^{m-2} + \cdots c_0$$

is irreducible mod 2. Then $\mathbf{Z}_2[X] \pmod{P(X)}$ is the field $GF(2^m)$. For any set of initial values, except all 0's, the sequence will have period k, where k is the smallest positive integer such that $X^k \equiv 1 \pmod{P(X)}$.

As mentioned previously, when $2^m - 1$ is prime, all polynomials (except 0 and 1) are generating polynomials for $GF(2^m)$. In particular, X is a generating polynomial and therefore $k = 2^m - 1$ is the period of the recurrence.

3.11 Exercises

1. (a) Find integers x and y such that $17x + 101y = 1$.
(b) Find $17^{-1} \pmod{101}$.

2. (a) Solve $7d \equiv 1 \pmod{30}$.
(b) Suppose you write a message as a number $m \pmod{31}$. Encrypt m as $m^7 \pmod{31}$. How would you decrypt? (*Hint*: Decryption is done by raising the ciphertext to a power mod 31. Fermat's theorem will be useful.)

3. (a) Let p be prime. Suppose a and b are integers such that $ab \equiv 0$ (mod p). Show that either $a \equiv 0$ or $b \equiv 0$ (mod p).
(b) Show that if a, b, n are integers with $n|ab$ and $\gcd(a, n) = 1$, then $n|b$.

4. Let $p \geq 3$ be prime. Show that the only solutions to $x^2 \equiv 1$ (mod p) are $x \equiv \pm 1$ (mod p). (*Hint:* Apply Exercise 3(a) to $(x+1)(x-1)$.)

5. Suppose $x \equiv 2$ (mod 7) and $x \equiv 3$ (mod 10). What is x congruent to mod 70?

6. A group of people are arranging themselves for a parade. If they line up three to a row, one person is left over. If they line up four to a row, two people are left over, and if they line up five to a row, three people are left over. What is the smallest possible number of people? What is the next smallest number? (*Hint:* Interpret this problem in terms of the Chinese remainder theorem.)

7. Let p be prime. Show that $a^p \equiv a$ (mod p) for all a.

8. (a) Let $p = 7$, 13, or 19. Show that $a^{1728} \equiv 1$ (mod p) for all a with $p \nmid a$.
(b) Let $p = 7$, 13, or 19. Show that $a^{1729} \equiv a$ (mod p) for all a. (*Hint:* Consider the case $p|a$ separately.)
(c) Show that $a^{1729} \equiv a$ (mod 1729) for all a. Composite numbers n such $a^n \equiv a$ (mod n) for all a are called Carmichael numbers. They are rare (561 is another example), but there are infinitely many of them.

9. Let a and $n > 1$ be integers with $\gcd(a, n) = 1$. The **order** of a mod n is the smallest positive integer r such that $a^r \equiv 1$ (mod n). We denote $r = \operatorname{ord}_n(a)$.
(a) Show that $r \leq \phi(n)$.
(b) Show that if $m = rk$ is a multiple of r, then $a^m \equiv 1$ (mod n).
(c) Suppose $a^t \equiv 1$ (mod n). Write $t = qr + s$ with $0 \leq s < r$ (this is just division with remainder). Show that $a^s \equiv 1$ (mod n).
(d) Using the definition of r and the fact that $0 \leq s < r$, show that $s = 0$ and therefore $r|t$. This, combined with part (b), yields the result that $a^t \equiv 1$ (mod n) if and only if $\operatorname{ord}_n(a)|t$.
(e) Show that $\operatorname{ord}_n(a)|\phi(n)$.

10. This exercise will show by example how to use the results of Exercise 9 to prove a number is a primitive root mod a prime p, once we know the factorization of $p - 1$. In particular, we'll show that 7 is a primitive root mod 601. Note that $600 = 2^3 \cdot 3 \cdot 5^2$.

(a) Show that if an integer $r < 600$ divides 600, then it divides at least one of 300, 200, 120 (these numbers are $600/2$, $600/3$, and $600/5$).
(b) Show that if $\text{ord}_{601}(7) < 600$ then it divides one of the numbers 300, 200, 120.
(c) A calculation shows that

$$7^{300} \equiv 600, \quad 7^{200} \equiv 576, \quad 7^{120} \equiv 423 \pmod{601}.$$

Why can we conclude that $\text{ord}_{601}(7)$ does not divide 300, 200, or 120?
(d) Show that 7 is a primitive root mod 601.
(e) In general, suppose p is a prime and $p-1 = q_1^{a_1} \cdots q_s^{a_s}$ is the factorization of $p - 1$ into primes. Describe a procedure to check whether a number g is a primitive root mod p. (Therefore, if we need to find a primitive root mod p, we can simply use this procedure to test the numbers $g = 2, 3, 5, 6, \ldots$ in succession until we find one that is a primitive root.)

11. We want to find an exponent k such that $3^k \equiv 2 \pmod{65537}$.
(a) Observe that $2^{32} = 1 \pmod{65537}$, but $2^{16} \not\equiv 1 \pmod{65537}$. It can be shown that 3 is a primitive root mod 65537, which implies that $3^n \equiv 1 \pmod{65537}$ if and only if $65536 | n$. Use this to show that $2048 | k$ but 4096 does not divide k. (*Hint:* Raise both sides of $3^k \equiv 2$ to the 16th and to the 32nd powers.)
(b) Use the result of part (a) to conclude that there are only 16 possible choices for k that need to be considered. Use this information to determine k. This problem shows that if $p-1$ has a special structure, for example, a power of 2, then this can be used to avoid exhaustive searches. Therefore, such primes are cryptographically weak. See Exercise 7.5 for a reinterpretation of the present problem.

12. (a) Let $x = b_1 b_2 \ldots b_w$ be an integer written in binary (for example, when $x = 1011$, we have $b_1 = 1, b_2 = 0, b_3 = 1, b_4 = 1$). Let y and n be integers. Perform the following procedure:

    1. Start with $k = 1$ and $s_0 = 1$.

    2. If $b_k = 1$, let $r_k \equiv s_k y \pmod{n}$. If $b_k = 0$, let $r_k = s_k$.

    3. Let $s_{k+1} \equiv r_k^2 \pmod{n}$.

    4. If $k = w$, stop. If $k < w$, add 1 to k and go to (2).

Show that $r_w \equiv y^x \pmod{n}$.
(b) Let x, y, and n be positive integers. Show that the following procedure computes $y^x \pmod{n}$.

    1. Start with $a = x, b = 1, c = y$.

2. If a is even, let $a = a/2$, and let $b = b, c \equiv c^2 \pmod{n}$.

3. If a is odd, let $a = a - 1$, and let $b \equiv bc \pmod{n}, c = c$.

4. If $a \neq 0$, go to step 2.

5. Output b.

(*Remark.* This algorithm is similar to the one in part (a), but it uses the binary bits of x in reverse order.)

13. Here is how to construct the x guaranteed by the general form of the Chinese remainder theorem. Suppose $m_1, \ldots, m_k$ are integers with $\gcd(m_i, m_j) = 1$ whenever $i \neq j$. Let $a_1, \ldots, a_k$ be integers. Perform the following procedure:

1. For $i = 1, \ldots, k$, let $z_i = m_1 \cdots m_{i-1} m_{i+1} \cdots m_k$.

2. For $i = 1, \ldots, k$, let $y_i \equiv z_i^{-1} \pmod{m_i}$.

3. Let $x = a_1 y_1 z_1 + \cdots + a_k y_k z_k$.

Show $x \equiv a_i \pmod{m_i}$ for all i.

14. (a) Find all four solutions to $x^2 \equiv 133 \pmod{143}$. (Note that $143 = 11 \cdot 13$.)
(b) Find all solutions to $x^2 \equiv 77 \pmod{143}$. (There are only two solutions in this case. This is because $\gcd(77, 143) \neq 1$.)

15. Let $p \equiv 3 \pmod 4$ be prime. Show that $x^2 \equiv -1 \pmod p$ has no solutions. (*Hint:* Suppose x exists. Raise both sides to the power $(p-1)/2$ and use Fermat's theorem.)

16. Alice designs a cryptosystem as follows (this system is due to Rabin). She chooses two distinct primes p and q (preferably, both p and q are congruent to 3 mod 4) and keeps them secret. She makes $n = pq$ public. When Bob wants to send Alice a message m, he computes $x \equiv m^2 \pmod{n}$ and sends x to Alice. She makes a decryption machine that does the following: When the machine is given a number x, it computes the square roots of x mod n since it knows p and q. There is usually more than one square root. It chooses one at random, and gives it to Alice. When Alice receives x from Bob, she puts it into her machine. If the output from the machine is a meaningful message, she assumes it is the correct message. If it is not meaningful, she puts x into the machine again. She continues until she gets a meaningful message.
(a) Why should Alice expect to get a meaningful message fairly soon?

(b) If Oscar intercepts x (he already knows n), why should it be hard for him to determine the message m?

(c) If Eve breaks into Alice's office and thereby is able to try a few chosen-ciphertext attacks on Alice's decryption machine, how can she determine the factorization of n?

17. This exercise shows that the Euclidean algorithm computes the gcd. Let a, b, q_i, r_i be as in Section 3.1.

(a) Let d be a common divisor of a, b. Show that $d|r_1$, and use this to show that $d|r_2$.

(b) Let d be as in (a). Use induction to show that $d|r_i$ for all i. In particular, $d|r_k$, the last nonzero remainder.

(c) Use induction to show that $r_k|r_i$ for $1 \le i \le k$.

(d) Using the facts that $r_k|r_1$ and $r_k|r_2$, show that $r_k|b$ and then $r_k|a$. Therefore r_k is a common divisor of a, b.

(e) Use (b) to show that $r_k \ge d$ for all common divisors d, and therefore r_k is the greatest common divisor.

18. (a) Show that the only irreducible polynomials in $\mathbf{Z}_2[X]$ of degree at most 2 are X, $X + 1$, and $X^2 + X + 1$.

(b) Show that $X^4 + X + 1$ is irreducible in $\mathbf{Z}_2[X]$. (*Hint:* If it factors, it must have at least one factor of degree at most 2.)

(c) Show that $X^4 \equiv X+1$, $X^8 \equiv X^2+1$, and $X^{16} \equiv X \pmod{X^4+X+1}$.

(d) Show that $X^{15} \equiv 1 \pmod{X^4 + X + 1}$.

19. (a) Show that $X^2 + 1$ is irreducible in $\mathbf{Z}_3[X]$.

(b) Find the multiplicative inverse of $1 + 2X$ in $\mathbf{Z}_3[X] \pmod{X^2 + 1}$.

3.12 Computer Problems

1. Evaluate $\gcd(8765, 23485)$.

2. (a) Find integers x and y with $65537x + 3511y = 1$.

(b) Find integers x and y with $65537x + 3511y = 17$.

3. Find the last five digits of $3^{1234567}$. (*Note:* Don't ask the computer to print $3^{1234567}$. It is too large!)

4. Solve $314x \equiv 271 \pmod{11111}$.

5. Find all solutions to $216x \equiv 66 \pmod{606}$.

6. Find an integer such that when it is divided by 101 the remainder is 17, when it is divided by 201 the remainder is 18, and when it is divided by 301 the remainder is 19.

7. Let $n = 391 = 17 \cdot 23$. Show that $2^{n-1} \not\equiv 1 \pmod{n}$. Find an exponent $j > 0$ such that $2^j \equiv 1 \pmod{n}$.

8. Let $n = 84047 \cdot 65497$. Find x and y with $x^2 \equiv y^2 \pmod{n}$ but $x \not\equiv \pm y \pmod{n}$.

9. Verify that 3 is a primitive root for the prime 65537. (*Hint:* Use the method of Exercise 10.)

10. Let $M = \begin{pmatrix} 1 & 2 & 4 \\ 1 & 5 & 25 \\ 1 & 14 & 196 \end{pmatrix}$.

(a) Find the inverse of $M \pmod{101}$.
(b) For which primes p does M not have an inverse mod p?

11. Find the square roots of 26055 mod the prime 34807.

12. Find all square roots of 1522756 mod 2325781.

13. Try to find a square root of 48382 mod the prime 83987, using the method of Section 3.9. Square your answer to see if it is correct. What number did you find the square root of?

Chapter 4

The Data Encryption Standard

4.1 Introduction

In 1973, the National Bureau of Standards (NBS), later to become the National Institute of Standards and Technology (NIST), issued a public request seeking a cryptographic algorithm to become a national standard. IBM submitted an algorithm called LUCIFER in 1974. The NBS forwarded it to the National Security Agency, which reviewed it and, after some modifications, returned a version that was essentially the Data Encryption Standard (DES) algorithm. In 1975, NBS released DES, as well as a free license for its use, and in 1977 NBS made it the official data encryption standard.

DES has been used extensively in electronic commerce, for example in the banking industry. If two banks want to exchange data, they first use a public key method such as RSA to transmit a key for DES, then they use DES for transmitting the data. It has the advantage of being very fast and reasonably secure.

From 1975 on, there has been controversy surrounding DES. Some regarded the key size as too small. Many were worried about NSA's involvement. For example, had they arranged for it to have a "trapdoor"— in other words, a secret weakness that would allow only them to break the system? It has also been suggested that NSA modified the design to avoid the possibility that IBM had inserted a trapdoor in LUCIFER. In any case, the design decisions remained a mystery for many years.

In 1990, Eli Biham and Adi Shamir showed how their method of differential cryptanalysis could be used to attack DES. The DES algorithm involves 16 rounds; differential cryptanalysis would be more efficient than exhaustively searching all possible keys if the algorithm used at most 15 rounds. This indicated that perhaps the designers of DES had been aware of this type of attack. A few years later, IBM released some details of the design criteria, which showed that indeed they had constructed the system to be resistant to differential cryptanalysis. This cleared up at least some of the mystery surrounding the algorithm.

The DES has lasted for a long time, but is becoming outdated. Brute force searches (see Section 4.6), though expensive, can now break the system. Therefore, NIST replaced it with a new system in the year 2000. However, it is worth studying DES since it represents a popular class of algorithms and it has been one of the most frequently used cryptographic algorithms in history.

The DES is a block cipher; namely, it breaks the plaintext into blocks of 64 bits, and encrypts each block separately. The actual mechanics of how this is done is often called a **Feistel system**, after Horst Feistel, who was part of the IBM team that developed LUCIFER. In the next section, we give a simple algorithm that has many of the characteristics of this type of system, but is small enough to use as an example. In Section 4.3, we show how differential cryptanalysis can be used to attack this simple system. We give the DES algorithm in Section 4.4, and describe ways it is implemented in Section 4.5. Finally, in Section 4.6, we describe recent progress in breaking DES.

For an extensive discussion of block ciphers, see [Schneier].

4.2   A Simplified DES-Type Algorithm

The DES algorithm is rather unwieldy to use for examples, so in the present section we present an algorithm that has many of the same features, but is much smaller. Like DES, the present algorithm is a block cipher. Since the blocks are encrypted separately, we assume throughout the present discussion that the full message consists of only one block.

The message has 12 bits and is written in the form $L_0 R_0$, where L_0 consists of the first 6 bits and R_0 consists of the last 6 bits. The key K has 9 bits. The ith round of the algorithm transforms an input $L_{i-1} R_{i-1}$ to the output $L_i R_i$ using an 8-bit key K_i derived from K.

The main part of the encryption process is a function $f(R_{i-1}, K_i)$ that

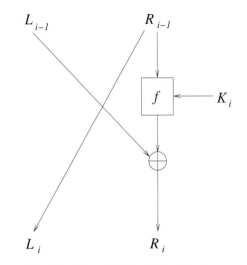

Figure 4.1: One Round of a Feistel System.

takes a 6-bit input R_{i-1} and an 8-bit input K_i and produces a 6-bit output. This will be described later.

The output for the ith round is defined as follows:

$$L_i = R_{i-1} \text{ and } R_i = L_{i-1} \oplus f(R_{i-1}, K_i),$$

where $\oplus$ denotes XOR, namely bit-by-bit addition mod 2. This is depicted in Figure 4.1.

This operation is performed for a certain number of rounds, say n, and produces the ciphertext $L_n R_n$.

How do we decrypt? Start with $L_n R_n$ and switch left and right to obtain $R_n L_n$. (*Note: This switch is built into the DES encryption algorithm, so it is not needed when decrypting DES.*) Now use the same procedure as before, but with the keys K_i used in reverse order $K_n, \ldots, K_1$. Let's see how this works. The first step takes $R_n L_n$ and gives the output

$$[L_n] \quad [R_n \oplus f(L_n, K_n)].$$

We know from the encryption procedure that $L_n = R_{n-1}$ and $R_n = L_{n-1} \oplus f(R_{n-1}, K_n)$. Therefore,

$$[L_n] \quad [R_n \oplus f(L_n, K_n)] = [R_{n-1}] \quad [L_{n-1} \oplus f(R_{n-1}, K_n) \oplus f(L_n, K_n)]$$
$$= [R_{n-1}] \quad [L_{n-1}].$$

The last equality again uses $L_n = R_{n-1}$, so that $f(R_{n-1}, K_n) \oplus f(L_n, K_n)$ is 0. Similarly, the second step of decryption sends $R_{n-1} L_{n-1}$ to $R_{n-2} L_{n-2}$.

Continuing, we see that the decryption process leads us back to R_0L_0.
Switching the left and right halves, we obtain the original plaintext L_0R_0,
as desired.

Note that the decryption process is essentially the same as the encryption
process. We simply need to switch left and right and use the keys K_i in
reverse order. Therefore both the sender and receiver use a common key
and they can use identical machines (though the receiver needs to reverse
left and right inputs).

So far, we have said nothing about the function f. In fact, any f would
work in the above procedures. But some choices of f yield much better
security than others. The type of f used in DES is similar to that which we
describe next. It is built up from a few components.

The first function is an expander. It takes an input of 6 bits and outputs
8 bits. The one we use is given in Figure 4.2.

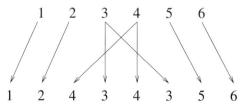

Figure 4.2: The Expander Function.

This means that the first input bit yields the first output bit, the third
input bit yields both the fourth and the sixth output bits, etc. For example,
011001 is expanded to 01010101.

The main components are called S-boxes. We use two:

$$S_1 \quad \begin{bmatrix} 101 & 010 & 001 & 110 & 011 & 100 & 111 & 000 \\ 001 & 100 & 110 & 010 & 000 & 111 & 101 & 011 \end{bmatrix}$$

$$S_2 \quad \begin{bmatrix} 100 & 000 & 110 & 101 & 111 & 001 & 011 & 010 \\ 101 & 011 & 000 & 111 & 110 & 010 & 001 & 100 \end{bmatrix}.$$

The input for an S-box has 4 bits. The first bit specifies which row will
be used: 0 for the first row, 1 for the second. The other 3 bits represent a
binary number that specifies the column: 000 for the first column, 001 for
the second, ..., 111 for the last column. The output for the S-box consists
of the three bits in the specified location. For example, an input of 1010 for
S_1 means we look at the second row, third column, which yields the output
110.

The key K consists of 9 bits. The key K_i for the ith round of encryption
is obtained by using 8 bits of K, starting with the ith bit. For example, if

$K = 010011001$, then $K_4 = 01100101$ (after 5 bits, we reached the end of K, so the last 2 bits were obtained from the beginning of K).

We can now describe $f(R_{i-1}, K_i)$. The input R_{i-1} consists of 6 bits. The expander function is used to expand it to 8 bits. The result is XORed with K_i to produce another 8-bit number. The first 4 bits are sent to S_1, and the last 4 bits are sent to S_2. Each S-box outputs 3 bits, which are concatenated to form a 6-bit number. This is $f(R_{i-1}, K_i)$. We present this in Figure 4.3.

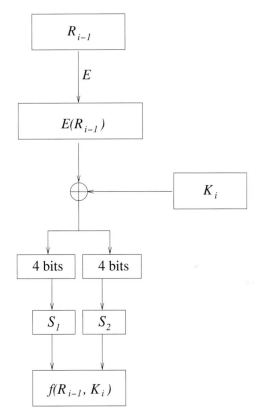

Figure 4.3: The Function $f(R_{i-1}, K_i)$.

For example, suppose $R_{i-1} = 100110$ and $K_i = 01100101$. We have

$$E(100110) \oplus K_i = 10101010 \oplus 01100101 = 11001111.$$

The first 4 bits are sent to S_1 and the last 4 bits are sent to S_2. The second row, fifth column of S_1 contains 000. The second row, last column of S_2 contains 100. Putting these outputs one after the other yields $f(R_{i-1}, K_i) = 000100$.

We can now describe what happens in one round. Suppose the input is

$$L_{i-1}R_{i-1} = 011100100110$$

and $K_i = 01100101$, as previously. This means that $R_{i-1} = 100110$, as in the example just discussed. Therefore $f(R_{i-1}, K_i) = 000100$. This is XORed with $L_{i-1} = 011100$ to yield $R_i = 011000$. Since $L_i = R_{i-1}$, we obtain

$$L_iR_i = 100110011000.$$

The output becomes the input for the next round.

4.3 Differential Cryptanalysis

Differential cryptanalysis was introduced by Biham and Shamir around 1990, though it was probably known much earlier to the designers of DES at IBM and NSA. The idea is to compare the differences in the ciphertexts for suitably chosen pairs of plaintexts and thereby deduce information about the key. Note that the difference of two strings of bits can be found by XORing them. Because the key is introduced by XORing with $E(R_{i-1})$, looking at the XOR of the inputs removes the effect of the key at this stage and hence removes some of the randomness introduced by the key. We'll see that this allows us to deduce information as to what the key could be.

Differential Cryptanalysis for Three Rounds

We eventually want to describe how to attack the above system when it uses four rounds, but we need to start by analyzing three rounds. Therefore, we temporarily start with L_1R_1 instead of L_0R_0.

The situation is now as follows. We have obtained access to a three-round encryption device that uses the preceding procedure. We know all the inner workings of the encryption algorithm such as the S-boxes, but we do not know the key. We want to find the key by a chosen plaintext attack. We use various inputs L_1R_1 and obtain outputs L_4R_4.

We have

$$R_2 = L_1 \oplus f(R_1, K_2)$$

$$L_3 = R_2 = L_1 \oplus f(R_1, K_2)$$

$$R_4 = L_3 \oplus f(R_3, K_4) = L_1 \oplus f(R_1, K_2) \oplus f(R_3, K_4).$$

Suppose we have another message $L_1^*R_1^*$ with $R_1 = R_1^*$. For each i, let $R_i' = R_i \oplus R_i^*$ and $L_i' = L_i \oplus L_i^*$. Then $L_i'R_i'$ is the "difference" (or sum; we are working mod 2) of L_iR_i and $L_i^*R_i^*$. The preceding calculation applied to $L_1^* R_1^*$ yields a formula for R_4^*. Since we have assumed that $R_1 = R_1^*$, we have $f(R_1, K_2) = f(R_1^*, K_2)$. Therefore, $f(R_1, K_2) \oplus f(R_1^*, K_2) = 0$ and

$$R_4' = R_4 \oplus R_4^* = L_1' \oplus f(R_3, K_4) \oplus f(R_3^*, K_4).$$

This may be rearranged to

$$R_4' \oplus L_1' = f(R_3, K_4) \oplus f(R_3^*, K_4).$$

Finally, since $R_3 = L_4$ and $R_3^* = L_4^*$, we obtain

$$R_4' \oplus L_1' = f(L_4, K_4) \oplus f(L_4^*, K_4).$$

Note that if we know the input XOR, namely $L_1' R_1'$, and if we know the outputs $L_4 R_4$ and $L_4^* R_4^*$, then we know everything in this last equation except K_4.

Now let's analyze the inputs to the S-boxes used to calculate $f(L_4, K_4)$ and $f(L_4^*, K_4)$. If we start with L_4, we first expand and then XOR with K_4 to obtain $E(L_4) \oplus K_4$, which are the bits sent to S_1 and S_2. Similarly, L_4^* yields $E(L_4^*) \oplus K_4$. The XOR of these is

$$E(L_4) \oplus E(L_4^*) = E(L_4 \oplus L_4^*) = E(L_4')$$

(the first equality follows easily from the bit-by-bit description of the expansion function). Therefore, we know that

1. the XORs of the inputs to the two S-boxes (namely, the first four and the last four bits of $E(L_4')$);

2. the XORs of the two outputs (namely, the first three and the last three bits of $R_4' \oplus L_1'$).

Let's restrict our attention to S_1. The analysis for S_2 will be similar. It is fairly fast to run through all pairs of 4-bit inputs with a given XOR (there are only 16 of them) and see which ones give a desired output XOR. These can be computed once for all and stored in a table.

For example, suppose we have input XOR equal to 1011 and we are looking for output XOR equal to 100. We can run through the input pairs $(1011,0000)$, $(1010,0001)$, $(1001,0010)$, ..., each of which has XOR equal to 1011, and look at the output XORs. We find that the pairs $(1010,0001)$ and $(0001, 1010)$ both produce output XORs 100. For example, 1010 means we look at the second row, third column of S_1, which is 110. Moreover, 0001 means we look at the first row, second column, which is 010. The output XOR is therefore $110 \oplus 010 = 100$.

We know L_4 and L_4^*. For example, suppose $L_4 = 101110$ and $L_4^* = 000010$. Therefore, $E(L_4) = 10111110$ and $E(L_4^*) = 00000010$, so the inputs to S_1 are $1011 \oplus K_4^L$ and $0000 \oplus K_4^L$, where K_4^L denotes the left 4 bits of K_4. If we know that the output XOR for S_1 is 100, then $(1011 \oplus K_4^L, 0000 \oplus K_4^L)$ must be one of the pairs on the list we just calculated, namely (1010,0001) and (0001, 1010). This means that $K_4^L = 0001$ or 1010.

If we repeat this procedure a few more times, we should be able to eliminate one of the two choices for K_4 and hence determine 4 bits of K. Similarly, using S_2, we find 4 more bits of K. We therefore know 8 of the 9 bits of K. The last bit can be found by trying both possibilities and seeing which one produces the same encryptions as the machine we are attacking.

Here is a summary of the procedure (for notational convenience, we describe it with both S-boxes used simultaneously, though in the examples we work with the S-boxes separately):

1. Look at the list of pairs with input XOR $= E(L_4')$ and output XOR $= R_4' \oplus L_1'$.

2. The pair $\left(E(L_4) \oplus K_4, E(L_4^*) \oplus K_4\right)$ is on this list.

3. Deduce the possibilities for K_4.

4. Repeat until only one possibility for K_4 remains.

Example. We start with

$$L_1 R_1 = 000111011011$$

and the machine encrypts in three rounds using the key $K = 001001101$, though we do not yet know K. We obtain (note that since we are starting with $L_1 R_1$, we start with the shifted key $K_1 = 010011010$)

$$L_4 R_4 = 000011100101.$$

If we start with

$$L_1^* R_1^* = 101110011011$$

(note that $R_1 = R_1^*$), then

$$L_4^* R_4^* = 100100011000.$$

We have $E(L_4) = 00000011$ and $E(L_4^*) = 10101000$. The inputs to S_1 have XOR equal to 1010 and the inputs to S_2 have XOR equal to 1011. The S-boxes have output XOR $R_4' \oplus L_1' = 111101 \oplus 101001 = 010100$, so the output XOR from S_1 is 010 and that from S_2 is 100.

For the pairs $(1001, 0011), (0011, 1001)$, S_1 produces output XOR equal to 010. Since the first member of one of these pairs should be the left four bits of $E(L_4) \oplus K_4 = 0000 \oplus K_4$, the first four bits of K_4 are in $\{1001, 0011\}$. For the pairs $(1100, 0111), (0111, 1100)$, S_2 produces output XOR equal to 100. Since the first member of one of these pairs should be the right four bits of $E(L_4) \oplus K_4 = 0011 \oplus K_4$, the last four bits of K_4 are in $\{1111, 0100\}$.

Now repeat (with the same machine and hence the same key K) and with

$$L_1 R_1 = 010111011011 \text{ and } L_1^* R_1^* = 101110011011.$$

A similar analysis shows that the first four bits of K_4 are in $\{0011, 1000\}$ and the last four bits are in $\{0100, 1011\}$. Combining this with the previous information, we see that the first 4 bits of K_4 are 0011 and the last 4 bits are 0100. Therefore, $K = 00 * 001101$ (recall that K_4 starts with the fourth bit of K.

It remains to find the third bit of K. If we use $K = 000001101$, it encrypts $L_1 R_1$ to 001011101010, which is not $L_4 R_4$, while $K = 001001101$ yields the correct encryption. Therefore, the key is $K = 001001101$. ∎

Differential Cryptanalysis for Four Rounds

Suppose now that we have obtained access to a four-round device. Again, we know all the inner workings of the algorithm except the key, and we want to determine the key. The analysis we used for three rounds still applies, but to extend it to four rounds we need to use more probabilistic techniques.

There is a weakness in the box S_1. If we look at the 16 input pairs with XOR equal to 0011, we discover that 12 of them have output XOR equal to 011. Of course, we expect on the average that two pairs should yield a given output XOR, so the present case is rather extreme. A little variation is to be expected, but we'll see that this large variation makes it easy to find the key.

There is a similar weakness in S_2, though not quite as extreme. Among the 16 input pairs with XOR equal to 1100, there are 8 with output XOR equal to 010.

Suppose now that we start with randomly chosen R_0 and R_0^* such that $R_0' = R_0 \oplus R_0^* = 001100$. This is expanded to $E(001100) = 00111100$. Therefore the input XOR for S_1 is 0011 and the input XOR for S_2 is 1100. With probability 12/16 the output XOR for S_1 will be 011, and with probability 8/16 the output XOR for S_2 will be 010. If we assume the outputs of the two S-boxes are independent, we see that the combined output XOR will be 011010 with probability $(12/16)(8/16) = 3/8$. Because the expansion function sends bits 3 and 4 to both S_1 and S_2, the two boxes cannot be assumed to have independent outputs, but 3/8 should still be a reasonable estimate for what happens.

Now suppose we choose L_0 and L_0^* so that $L_0' = L_0 \oplus L_0^* = 011010$. Recall that in the encryption algorithm the output of the S-boxes is XORed with L_0 to obtain R_1. Suppose the output XOR of the S-boxes is 011010. Then $R_1' = 011010 \oplus L_0' = 000000$. Since $R_1' = R_1 \oplus R_1^*$, it follows that $R_1 = R_1^*$.

Putting everything together, we see that if we start with two randomly chosen messages with XOR equal to $L_0' R_0' = 011010001100$, then there is a probability of around 3/8 that $L_1' R_1' = 001100000000$.

Here's the strategy for finding the key. Try several randomly chosen pairs of inputs with XOR equal to 011010001100. Look at the outputs $L_4 R_4$ and $L_4^* R_4^*$. Assume that $L_1' R_1' = 001100000000$. Then use three-round differential cryptanalysis with $L_1' = 001100$ and the known outputs to deduce a set of possible keys K_4. When $L_1' R_1' = 001100000000$, which should happen around 3/8 of the time, this list of keys will contain K_4, along with some other random keys. The remaining 5/8 of the time, the list should contain random keys. Since there seems to be no reason that any incorrect key should appear frequently, the correct key K_4 will probably appear in the lists of keys more often than the other keys.

Here is an example. Suppose we are attacking a four-round device. We try one hundred random pairs of inputs $L_0 R_0$ and $L_0^* R_0^* = L_0 R_0 \oplus$ 011010001100. The frequencies of possible keys we obtain are in the following table. We find it easier to look at the first four bits and the last four bits of K_4 separately.

First 4 bits	Frequency	First 4 bits	Frequency
0000	12	1000	33
0001	7	1001	40
0010	8	1010	35
0011	15	1011	35
0100	4	1100	59
0101	3	1101	32
0110	4	1110	28
0111	6	1111	39

Last 4 bits	Frequency	Last 4 bits	Frequency
0000	14	1000	8
0001	6	1001	16
0010	42	1010	8
0011	10	1011	18
0100	27	1100	8
0101	10	1101	23
0110	8	1110	6
0111	11	1111	17

It is therefore likely that $K_4 = 11000010$. Therefore the key K is 10*110000.

To determine the remaining bit, we proceed as before. We can compute that 000000000000 is encrypted to 100011001011 using $K = 101110000$ and is encrypted to 001011011010 using $K = 100110000$. If the machine we are attacking encrypts 000000000000 to 100011001011, we conclude that the second key cannot be correct, so the correct key is probably $K = 101110000$.

The preceding attack can be extended to more rounds by extensions of these methods. It might be noticed that we could have obtained the key at least as quickly by simply running through all possibilities for the key. That is certainly true in this simple model. However, in more elaborate systems such as DES, differential cryptanalytic techniques are much more efficient than exhaustive searching through all keys, at least until the number of rounds becomes fairly large. In particular, the reason that DES uses 16 rounds appears to be because differential cryptanalysis is more efficient than exhaustive search until 16 rounds are used.

There is another attack on DES, called **linear cryptanalysis**, that was developed by Mitsuru Matsui [Matsui]. The main ingredient is an approximation of DES by a linear function of the input bits. It is theoretically faster than an exhaustive search for the key and requires around 2^{43} plaintext-ciphertext pairs to find the key. It seems that the designers of DES had not anticipated linear cryptanalysis. For details of the method, see [Matsui].

4.4 DES

A block of ciphertext consists of 64 bits. The key has 56 bits, but is expressed as a 64-bit string. The 8th, 16th, 24th, ..., bits are parity bits, arranged so that each block of 8 bits has an odd number of 1's. This is for error detection purposes. The output of the encryption is a 64-bit ciphertext.

The DES algorithm, depicted in Figure 4.4, starts with a plaintext m of 64 bits, and consists of three stages:

1. The bits of m are permuted by a fixed initial permutation to obtain $m_0 = IP(m)$. Write $m_0 = L_0 R_0$, where L_0 is the first 32 bits of m_0 and R_0 is the last 32 bits.

2. For $1 \leq i \leq 16$, perform the following:

$$
\begin{aligned}
L_i &= R_{i-1} \\
R_i &= L_{i-1} \oplus f(R_{i-1}, K_i),
\end{aligned}
$$

where K_i is a string of 48 bits obtained from the key K and f is a function to be described later.

3. Switch left and right to obtain $R_{16}L_{16}$, then apply the inverse of the initial permutation to get the ciphertext $c = IP^{-1}(R_{16}L_{16})$.

Decryption is performed by exactly the same procedure, except that the keys $K_1, \ldots, K_{16}$ are used in reverse order. The reason this works is the same as for the simplified system described in Section 4.2. Note that the left-right switch in step 3 of the DES algorithm means that we do not have to do the left-right switch that was needed for decryption in Section 4.2.

We now describe the steps in more detail.

The initial permutation, which seems to have no cryptographic significance, but which was perhaps designed to make the algorithm load more efficiently into chips that were available in 1970s, can be described by the Initial Permutation table. This means that the 58th bit of m becomes the 1st bit of m_0, the 50th bit of m becomes the 2nd bit of m_0, etc.

						Initial Permutation									
58	50	42	34	26	18	10	2	60	52	44	36	28	20	12	4
62	54	46	38	30	22	14	6	64	56	48	40	32	24	16	8
57	49	41	33	25	17	9	1	59	51	43	35	27	19	11	3
61	53	45	37	29	21	13	5	63	55	47	39	31	23	15	7

The function $f(R, K_i)$, depicted in Figure 4.5, is described in several steps.

1. First, R is expanded to $E(R)$ by the following table.

				Expansion Permutation							
32	1	2	3	4	5	4	5	6	7	8	9
8	9	10	11	12	13	12	13	14	15	16	17
16	17	18	19	20	21	20	21	22	23	24	25
24	25	26	27	28	29	28	29	30	31	32	1

This means that the first bit of $E(R)$ is the 32nd bit of R, etc. Note that $E(R)$ has 48 bits.

2. Compute $E(R) \oplus K_i$, which has 48 bits, and write it as $B_1 B_2 \cdots B_8$, where each B_j has 6 bits.

3. There are 8 S-boxes $S_1, \ldots, S_8$, given on page 112. B_j is the input for S_j. Write $B_j = b_1 b_2 \cdots b_6$. The row of the S-box is specified by $b_1 b_6$ while $b_2 b_3 b_4 b_5$ determines the column. For example, if $B_3 = 001001$, we look at the row 01, which is the second row (00 gives the first row) and column 0100, which is the 5th column (0100 represents 4 in

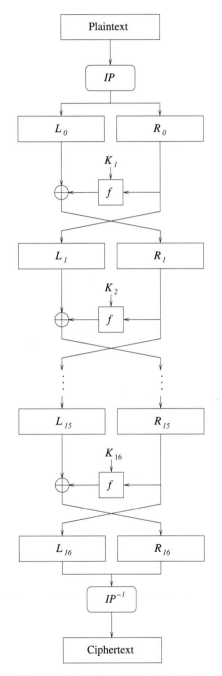

Figure 4.4: The DES Algorithm

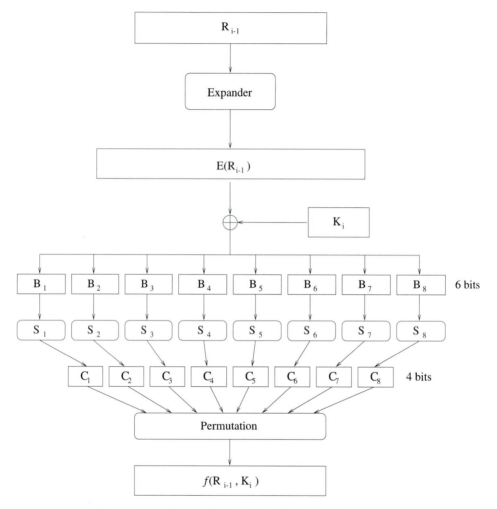

Figure 4.5: The DES Function $f(R_{i-1}, K_i)$.

binary; the first column is numbered 0, so the fifth is labeled 4). The entry in S_3 in this location is 3, which is 3 in binary. Therefore, the output of S_3 is 0011 in this case. In this way, we obtain eight 4-bit outputs $C_1, C_2, \ldots C_8$.

4. The string $C_1 C_2 \cdots C_8$ is permuted according to the following table.

16	7	20	21	29	12	28	17	1	15	23	26	5	18	31	10
2	8	24	14	32	27	3	9	19	13	30	6	22	11	4	25

The resulting 32-bit string is $f(R, K_j)$.

Finally, we describe how to obtain $K_1, \ldots K_{16}$. Recall that we start with a 64-bit K.

1. The parity bits are discarded and the remaining bits are permuted by the following table.

Key Permutation													
57	49	41	33	25	17	9	1	58	50	42	34	26	18
10	2	59	51	43	35	27	19	11	3	60	52	44	36
63	55	47	39	31	23	15	7	62	54	46	38	30	22
14	6	61	53	45	37	29	21	13	5	28	20	12	4

Write the result as $C_0 D_0$, where C_0 and D_0 have 28 bits.

2. For $1 \le i \le 16$, let $C_i = LS_i(C_{i-1})$ and $D_i = LS_i(D_{i-1})$. Here LS_i means shift the input one or two places to the left, according to the following table.

Number of Key Bits Shifted per Round																
Round	1	2	3	4	5	6	7	8	9	10	11	12	13	14	15	16
Shift	1	1	2	2	2	2	2	2	1	2	2	2	2	2	2	1

3. 48 bits are chosen from the 56-bit string $C_i D_i$ according to the following table. The output is K_i.

14	17	11	24	1	5	3	28	15	6	21	10
23	19	12	4	26	8	16	7	27	20	13	2
41	52	31	37	47	55	30	40	51	45	33	48
44	49	39	56	34	53	46	42	50	36	29	32

S-Boxes

S-box 1

14	4	13	1	2	15	11	8	3	10	6	12	5	9	0	7
0	15	7	4	14	2	13	1	10	6	12	11	9	5	3	8
4	1	14	8	13	6	2	11	15	12	9	7	3	10	5	0
15	12	8	2	4	9	1	7	5	11	3	14	10	0	6	13

S-box 2

15	1	8	14	6	11	3	4	9	7	2	13	12	0	5	10
3	13	4	7	15	2	8	14	12	0	1	10	6	9	11	5
0	14	7	11	10	4	13	1	5	8	12	6	9	3	2	15
13	8	10	1	3	15	4	2	11	6	7	12	0	5	14	9

S-box 3

10	0	9	14	6	3	15	5	1	13	12	7	11	4	2	8
13	7	0	9	3	4	6	10	2	8	5	14	12	11	15	1
13	6	4	9	8	15	3	0	11	1	2	12	5	10	14	7
1	10	13	0	6	9	8	7	4	15	14	3	11	5	2	12

S-box 4

7	13	14	3	0	6	9	10	1	2	8	5	11	12	4	15
13	8	11	5	6	15	0	3	4	7	2	12	1	10	14	9
10	6	9	0	12	11	7	13	15	1	3	14	5	2	8	4
3	15	0	6	10	1	13	8	9	4	5	11	12	7	2	14

S-box 5

2	12	4	1	7	10	11	6	8	5	3	15	13	0	14	9
14	11	2	12	4	7	13	1	5	0	15	10	3	9	8	6
4	2	1	11	10	13	7	8	15	9	12	5	6	3	0	14
11	8	12	7	1	14	2	13	6	15	0	9	10	4	5	3

S-box 6

12	1	10	15	9	2	6	8	0	13	3	4	14	7	5	11
10	15	4	2	7	12	9	5	6	1	13	14	0	11	3	8
9	14	15	5	2	8	12	3	7	0	4	10	1	13	11	6
4	3	2	12	9	5	15	10	11	14	1	7	6	0	8	13

S-box 7

4	11	2	14	15	0	8	13	3	12	9	7	5	10	6	1
13	0	11	7	4	9	1	10	14	3	5	12	2	15	8	6
1	4	11	13	12	3	7	14	10	15	6	8	0	5	9	2
6	11	13	8	1	4	10	7	9	5	0	15	14	2	3	12

S-box 8

13	2	8	4	6	15	11	1	10	9	3	14	5	0	12	7
1	15	13	8	10	3	7	4	12	5	6	11	0	14	9	2
7	11	4	1	9	12	14	2	0	6	10	13	15	3	5	8
2	1	14	7	4	10	8	13	15	12	9	0	3	5	6	11

It turns out that each bit of the key is used in approximately 14 of the 16 rounds.

A few remarks are in order. In a good cipher system, each bit of the ciphertext should depend on all bits of the plaintext. The expansion $E(R)$ is designed so that this will happen in only a few rounds. The purpose of the initial permutation is not completely clear. It has no cryptographic purpose. The S-boxes are the heart of the algorithm and provide the security. Their design was somewhat of a mystery until IBM published the following criteria in the early 1990's (for details, see [Coppersmith1]).

1. Each S-box has 6 input bits and 4 output bits. This was the largest that could be put on one chip in 1974.

2. The outputs of the S-boxes should not be close to being linear functions of the inputs (linearity would have made the system much easier to analyze).

3. Each row of an S-box contains all numbers from 0 to 15.

4. If two inputs to an S-box differ by 1 bit, the outputs must differ by 2 bits.

5. If two inputs to an S-box differ in their first 2 bits but have the same last 2 bits, the outputs must be unequal.

6. There are 32 pairs of inputs having a given XOR. For each of these pairs, compute the XOR of the outputs. No more than eight of these output XORs should be the same. This is clearly to avoid an attack via differential cryptanalysis.

7. A criterion similar to (6), but involving three S-boxes.

In the early 1970s, it took several months of searching for a computer to find appropriate S-boxes. Now, such a search could be completed in a very short time.

DES Is Not a Group

One possible way of effectively increasing the key size of DES is to double encrypt. Choose keys K_1 and K_2 and encrypt a plaintext P by $E_{K_2}(E_{K_1}(P))$. Does this increase the security?

Meet-in-the-middle attacks on cryptosystems are discussed in Section 8.4. It is pointed out that, if an attacker has sufficient memory, double encryption provides little extra protection. Moreover, if a cryptosystem is such that double encryption is equivalent to a single encryption, then there is no additional security obtained by double encryption.

In addition, if double encryption is equivalent to single encryption, then the (single encryption) cryptosystem is much less secure than one might guess initially (see Exercise 8.10). If this were true for DES, for example, then exhaustive search through all 2^{56} keys could be replaced by a search of length around 2^{28}, which would be quite easy to do.

For affine ciphers (Section 2.2) and for RSA (Chapter 6), double encrypting with two keys K_1 and K_2 is equivalent to encrypting with a third key K_3. Is the same true for DES? Namely, is there a key K_3 such that $E_{K_3} = E_{K_2}E_{K_1}$? This question is often rephrased in the equivalent form "Is DES a group?" (The reader who is unfamiliar with group theory can ask "Is DES closed under composition?".)

Fortunately, it turns out that DES is not a group. We sketch the proof. For more details, see [Campbell-Wiener]. Let E_0 represent encryption with the key consisting entirely of 0's and let E_1 represent encryption with the key consisting entirely of 1's. These keys are weak for cryptographic purposes (see Exercise 5). Moreover, D. Coppersmith found that applying $E_1 \circ E_0$ repeatedly to certain plaintexts yielded the original plaintext after around 2^{32} iterations. A sequence of encryptions (for some plaintext P)

$$E_1E_0(P), \; E_1E_0(E_1E_0(P)), \; E_1E_0(E_1E_0(E_1E_0(P))), \ldots, (E_1E_0)^n(P) = P,$$

where n is the smallest positive integer such that $(E_1E_0)^n(P) = P$, is called a cycle of length n.

Lemma. *If m is the smallest positive integer such that $(E_1E_0)^m(P) = P$ for all P, and n is the length of a cycle (so $(E_1E_0)^n(P_0) = P_0$ for a particular P_0), then n divides m.*

Proof. Divide n into m, with remainder r. This means that $m = nq + r$ for some integer q, and $0 \le r < n$. Since $(E_1E_0)^n(P_0) = P_0$, encrypting q times with $(E_1E_0)^n$ leaves P_0 unchanged. Therefore,

$$P_0 = (E_1E_0)^m(P_0) = (E_1E_0)^r(E_1E_0)^{nq}(P_0) = (E_1E_0)^r(P_0).$$

Since n is the smallest positive integer such that $(E_1E_0)^n(P_0) = P_0$, and $0 \le r < n$, we must have $r = 0$. This means that $m = nq$, so n divides m. $\qquad\square$

Suppose now that DES is closed under composition. Then $E_1E_0 = E_K$ for some key K. Moreover, $E_K^2, E_K^3, \ldots$ are also represented by DES keys. Since there are only 2^{56} possible keys, we must have $E_K^j = E_K^i$ for some integers i, j with $0 \le i < j \le 2^{56}$ (otherwise we would have $2^{56} + 1$ distinct encryption keys). Decrypt i times: $E_K^{j-i} = D_K^i E_K^j = D_K^i E_K^i$, which is the identity map. Since $0 < j - i \leq 2^{56}$, the smallest positive integer m such that E_K^m is the identity map also satisfies $m \leq 2^{56}$.

Coppersmith found the lengths of the cycles for 33 plaintexts P_0. By the lemma, m is a multiple of these cycle lengths. Therefore, m is greater than or equal to the least common multiple of these cycle lengths, which turned out to be around 10^{277}. But if DES is closed under composition, we showed that $m \leq 2^{56}$. Therefore, DES is not closed under composition.

4.5   Modes of Operation

DES is an example of a block encryption algorithm. A block of plaintext, 64 bits in the case of DES, is encrypted to a block of ciphertext. These algorithms can be run in many different modes. We now examine three of the most popular modes of operation.

Electronic Codebook (ECB)

The natural manner for using a block cipher is to break a long piece of plaintext into appropriate sized blocks of plaintext and process each block separately with the encryption function $E_K()$. This is known as the electronic codebook (ECB) mode of operation. The plaintext P is broken into smaller chunks $P = [P_1, P_2, \cdots, P_L]$ and the ciphertext is

$$C = [C_1, C_2, \cdots, C_L]$$

where $C_j = E_K(P_j)$ is the encryption of P_j using the key K.

There is a natural weakness in the ECB mode of operation that becomes apparent when dealing with long pieces of plaintext. Say an adversary Eve has been observing communication between Alice and Bob for a long enough period of time. If Eve has managed to acquire some plaintext pieces corresponding to the ciphertext pieces that she has observed, she can start to build up a codebook with which she can decipher future communication between Alice and Bob. Eve never needs to calculate the key K; she just looks up a ciphertext message in her codebook and uses the corresponding plaintext (if available) to decipher the message.

This can be a serious problem since many real world messages consist of repeated fragments. E-mail is a prime example. An e-mail between Alice and Bob might start with the following header:

```
Date:  Tue, 29 Feb 2000 13:44:38 -0500 (EST)
```

The ciphertext starts with the encrypted version of the 8 characters "Date: Tu". If Eve finds this piece of ciphertext often occurs on a Tuesday, she

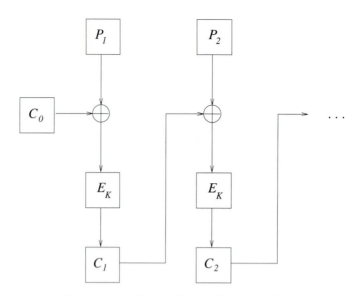

Figure 4.6: Cipher Block Chaining Mode.

might be able to guess, without knowing any of the plaintext, that such messages that are e-mail sent on Tuesdays. With patience and ingenuity, Eve might be able to piece together enough of the message's header and trailer to figure out the context of the message. With even greater patience and computer memory, she might be able to piece together important pieces of the message.

Another problem that arises in ECB mode occurs when Eve tries to modify the encrypted message being sent to Bob. She might be able to extract key portions of the message and use her codebook to construct a false ciphertext message that she can insert in the data stream.

Cipher Block Chaining (CBC)

One method for reducing the problems that occur in ECB mode is to use chaining. Chaining is a feedback mechanism where the encryption of a block depends on the encryption of previous blocks. In particular, encryption proceeds as

$$C_j = E_K(P_j \oplus C_{j-1})$$

while decryption proceeds as

$$P_j = D_K(C_j) \oplus C_{j-1}$$

where C_0 is some chosen initial value and where $D_K()$ is the decryption function.

Thus, in CBC mode, the plaintext is XORed with the previous ciphertext block and the result is encrypted. Figure 4.6 depicts CBC.

Cipher Feedback (CFB)

One of the problems with CBC mode is that a bit error in a plaintext, or in the calculation/storage of a previous ciphertext block, can lead to an error in the calculation of the current ciphertext block. This will affect all subsequent ciphertext blocks. Another drawback of both CBC and ECB methods is that encryption (and hence decryption) cannot begin until a complete block of 8 bytes of data is available.

Cipher feedback mode is a stream mode of operation where one 8-bit piece of message (e.g. a single character) is encrypted without having to wait for an entire block of data to be available. This is useful in interactive computer communications, for example.

The plaintext is broken into 8-bit pieces: $P = [P_1, P_2, \ldots]$ where each P_j has 8 bits, rather than the 64 bits used in ECB and CBC. Encryption proceeds as follows. An initial 64-bit X_1 is chosen. Then for $j = 1, 2, 3, \ldots$, the following is performed:

$$C_j = P_j \oplus L_8(E_K(X_j))$$

$$X_{j+1} = R_{56}(X_j) \parallel C_j$$

where $L_8(X)$ denotes the 8 leftmost bits of X, $R_{56}(X)$ denotes the rightmost 56 bits of X, and $X \parallel Y$ denotes the string obtained by writing X followed by Y.

Decryption is done with the following steps:

$$P_j = C_j \oplus L_8(E_K(X_j))$$

$$X_{j+1} = R_{56}(X_j) \parallel C_j.$$

Let's step through one round of the CFB algorithm. First, we have a 64-bit register that is initialized with X_1. These 64 bits are encrypted using E_K and the leftmost 8 bits of $E_K(X_1)$ are extracted and XORed with the 8-bit P_1 to form C_1. Then C_1 is sent to the recipient. Before working with P_2, the 64-bit register X_1 is updated by extracting the rightmost 56 bits. The 8 bits of C_1 are appended on the right to form $X_2 = R_{56}(X_1) \parallel C_1$. Then P_2 is encrypted by the same process, but using X_2 in place of X_1. After P_2 is encrypted to C_2, the 64-bit register is updated to form

$$X_3 = L_{56}(X_2) \parallel C_2 = L_{48}(X_1) \parallel C_1 \parallel C_2.$$

By the end of the 8th round, the initial X_1 has disappeared from the 64-bit register and $X_9 = C_1\|C_2\|\cdots\|C_8$. The C_j continue to pass through the register, so for example $X_{20} = C_{12}\|C_{13}\|\cdots\|C_{19}$.

Note that CFB encrypts the plaintext in a manner similar to one-time pads or LFSRs. The key K and the numbers X_j are used to produce binary strings that are XORed with the plaintext to produce the ciphertext. This is a much different type of encryption than the ECB and CBC, where the ciphertext is the output of DES.

In practical applications, CFB is useful because it can recover from errors in transmission of the ciphertext. Suppose that the transmitter sends the ciphertext blocks $C_1, C_2, \ldots, C_k, \ldots$, and C_1 is corrupted during transmission, so that the receiver observes $\tilde{C}_1, C_2, \ldots$. Decryption takes $\tilde{C}_1$ and produces a garbled version of P_1 with bit errors in the locations that $\tilde{C}_1$ had bit errors. Now, after decrypting this ciphertext block, the receiver forms an incorrect X_2, which we denote $\tilde{X}_2$. If X_1 was $(*, *, *, *, *, *, *, *)$, then $\tilde{X}_2 = (*, *, *, *, *, *, *, \tilde{C}_1)$. When the receiver gets an uncorrupted C_2 and decrypts, then a completely garbled version of P_2 is produced. When forming X_3, the decrypter actually forms $\tilde{X}_3 = (*, *, *, *, *, *, \tilde{C}_1, C_2)$. The decrypter repeats this process, ultimately getting bad versions of $P_1, P_2, \cdots, P_9$. When the decrypter calculates X_9, the error block has moved to the leftmost block of $\tilde{X}_9$ as $\tilde{X}_9 = (\tilde{C}_1, C_2, \cdots, C_8)$. At the next step, the error will have been flushed from the X_{10} register, and X_{10} and subsequent registers will be uncorrupted.

4.6   Breaking DES

DES was the standard cryptographic system for the last 20 years of the twentieth century. Its history is shrouded in mystery; most particular are the questions regarding the level of involvement the NSA had in strengthening or weakening its security. People have spent countless hours looking for trapdoors and loopholes that the NSA might have installed in the algorithm. Although the true history of DES will probably never be known (at least until a massive declassification of government materials a hundred years in the future), DES has shown strength and ability to endure brute force attacks as well as more sophisticated attacks such as differential cryptanalysis.

Recently, DES has begun to show signs of age. In this section we discuss various efforts to break DES, and we present possible alternatives to DES that will have to be employed in light of the cracking of DES.

From 1975 onward, there have been questions regarding the strength of DES. Many in the academic community complained about the size of the DES keys, claiming that a 56-bit key was insufficient for security. In fact, a few months after the NBS release of DES, Whitfield Diffie and Martin

Hellman published a paper titled "Exhaustive cryptanalysis of the NBS Data Encryption Standard" in which they estimated that a machine could be built for $20 million (in 1977 dollars) that would crack DES in roughly a day. This machine's purpose was specifically to attack DES, which is a point that we will come back to later.

In 1987 DES came under its second five-year review. At this time NBS asked for suggestions whether to accept the standard for another period, to modify the standard, or to dissolve the standard altogether. The discussions regarding DES saw NSA opposing the recertification of DES. The NBS argued at that time that DES was beginning to show signs of weakness, given the current of level of computing power, and proposed doing away with DES entirely and replacing it with a set of NSA-designed algorithms whose inner workings would be known only to NSA and be well protected from reverse engineering techniques. This proposal was turned down, partially due to the fact that several key American industries would be left unprotected while replacement algorithms were put in place. In the end, DES was reapproved as a standard, yet in the process it had been acknowledged that DES was showing signs of weakness.

Five years later, after NBS had been renamed NIST, the next five-year review came around. Despite the weaknesses mentioned in 1987 and the technology advances that had taken place in five years, NIST recertified the DES algorithm in 1992.

In 1993, Michael Wiener, a researcher at Bell-Northern Research, proposed and designed a device that would attack DES more efficiently than ever before. The idea was to use the already well-developed switching technology available to the telephone industry. The year 1996 saw the formulation of three basic approaches for attacking symmetric ciphers such as DES. The first method was to do distributive computation across a vast collection of machines. This had the advantage that it was relatively cheap, and the cost that was involved could be easily distributed over many people. Another approach was to design custom architecture (such as Michael Wiener's idea) for attacking DES. This promised to be more effective, yet also more expensive, and could be considered as the high-end approach. The middle of the line approach involved programmable logic arrays and has received the least attention to date.

In all three of these cases, the most popular approach to attacking DES has been to perform an exhaustive search of the key space. For DES this seems to be reasonable since, as mentioned earlier, more complicated cryptanalytic techniques have failed to show significant improvement over exhaustive search.

The distributive computing approach to breaking DES became very popular, especially with the growing popularity of the Internet. In 1997 the RSA Data Security company issued a challenge to find the key and crack a DES encrypted message. Whoever cracked the message would win a $10,000 prize. Only five months after the announcement of the 1997 DES Challenge, Rocke Verser submitted the winning DES key. What is important about this is that it represents an example where the distributive computing approach had successfully attacked DES. Rocke Verser had implemented a program where thousands of computers spread over the Internet had managed to crack the DES cipher. People volunteered time on their personal (and corporate) machines, running Verser's program under the agreement that Verser would split the winnings 60% to 40% with the owner of the computer that actually found the key. The key was finally found by Michael Sanders. Roughly 25% of the DES keyspace had been searched by that time. The DES Challenge phrase decrypted to "Strong cryptography makes the world a safer place."

In the following year, RSA Data Security issued DES Challenge II. This time the correct key was found by Distributed Computing Technologies, and the message decrypted to "Many hands make light work." The key was found after searching roughly 85% of the possible keys and was done in 39 days. The fact that the winner of the second challenge searched more of the keyspace and performed the task quicker than the first task shows the dramatic effect that a year of advancement in technology can have on cryptanalysis.

In the summer of 1998 the Electronic Frontier Foundation (EFF) developed a project called DES Cracker whose purpose was to reveal the vulnerability of the DES algorithm when confronted with a specialized architecture. The DES Cracker project was founded on a simple principle: The average computer is ill suited for the task of cracking DES. This is a reasonable statement since ordinary computers, by their very nature, are multipurpose machines that are designed to handle generic tasks such as running an operating system or even playing a computer game or two. What the EFF team proposed to do was build specialized hardware that would take advantage of the parallelizable nature of the exhaustive search. The team had a budget of $200,000.

We now describe briefly the architecture that the EFF team's research produced. For more information regarding the EFF Cracker as well as the other tasks their cracker was designed to handle, see [Gilmore].

The EFF DES Cracker consisted of basically three main parts: a personal computer, software, and a large collection of specialized chips. The computer was connected to the array of chips and the software oversaw the tasking of each chip. For the most part, the software didn't interact much with the hardware; it just gave the chips the necessary information to start processing and waited until the chips returned candidate keys. In this sense, the hardware efficiently eliminated a large number of invalid keys and only returned keys that were potentially promising. The software then processed each of the promising candidate keys on its own, checking to see if one of the promising keys was in fact the actual key.

The DES Cracker took a 128-bit (16-byte) sample of ciphertext and broke it into two 64-bit (8-byte) blocks of text. Each chip in the EFF DES Cracker consisted of 24 search units. A search unit was a subset of a chip whose task was to take a key and two 64-bit blocks of ciphertext and attempt to decrypt the first 64-bit block using the key. If the "decrypted" ciphertext looked interesting, then the search unit decrypted the second block and checked to see if that "decrypted" ciphertext was also interesting. If both decrypted texts were interesting then the search unit told the software that the key it checked was promising. If, when the first 64-bit block of ciphertext was decrypted, the decrypted text did not seem interesting enough, then the search unit incremented its key by 1 to form a new key. It then tried this new key, again checking to see if the result was interesting, and proceeded this way as it searched through its allotted region of keyspace.

How did the EFF team define an "interesting" decrypted text? First they assumed that the plaintext satisfied some basic assumption, for example that it was written using letters, numbers, and punctuation. Since the data they were decrypting was text, they knew each byte corresponded to an 8-bit character. Of the 256 possible values that an 8 bit character type represented, only 69 characters were interesting (the uppercase and lowercase alphabet, the numbers, the space, and a few punctuation marks). For a byte to be considered interesting, it had to contain one of these 69 characters, and hence had a 69/256 chance of being interesting. Approximating this ratio to 1/4, and assuming that the decrypted bytes are in fact independent, we see that the chance that an 8 byte block of decrypted text was interesting is $1/4^8 = 1/65536$. Thus only 1/65536 of the keys it examined were considered promising.

This was not enough of a reduction. The software would still spend too much time searching false candidates. In order to narrow down the field of promising key candidates even further, it was necessary to use the second 8-byte block of text. This block was decrypted to see if the result was interesting. Assuming independence between the blocks, we get that only $1/4^{16} = 1/65536^2$ of the keys could be considered promising. This significantly reduced the amount of keyspace that the software had to examine.

Each chip consisted of twenty-four search units, and each search unit was given its own region of the key space that it was responsible for searching. A single 40-MHz chip would have taken roughly 38 years to search the entire key space. To reduce further the amount of time needed to process the keys, the EFF team used 64 chips on a single circuit board, then twelve boards to each chassis, and finally two chassis were connected to the personal computer that oversaw the communication with the software.

The end result was that the DES Cracker consisted of about 1500 chips and could crack DES in roughly 4.5 days on average. The DES Cracker was by no means an optimum model for cracking DES. In particular, each of the chips that it used ran at 40 MHz, which is slow by modern standards. Newer models could certainly be produced in the future that employ chips running at much faster clock cycles.

This development strongly indicates the need for a replacement for DES. There are two main approaches to achieving increased security in the future. The first involves using DES multiple times and leads to the popular method called Triple DES. The second approach is to find a new system that employs a larger key size than 56 bits.

We start by describing the idea behind multiple DES schemes. The idea is to encrypt the same plaintext multiple times using the same algorithm with different keys. **Double DES** encrypts the plaintext by first encrypting with one key and then encrypting again using a different key. Since DES does not form a group (see Section 4.4), one might guess that Double DES should double the key space and thus the key space should consist of 2^{112} keys. This, however, is not true. Merkle and Hellman showed that the double encryption scheme actually has the security level of a 57-bit key. The reduction from 2^{112} to 2^{57} makes use of the **meet-in-the-middle attack** (see Section 8.4).

Since Double DES has a weakness, **Triple DES** is often used. This appears to have a level of security approximately equivalent to a 112-bit key. There are at least two ways that Triple DES can be implemented. One is to choose three keys, K_1, K_2, K_3 and perform $E_{K_1}(E_{K_2}(E_{K_3}(m)))$. The other is to choose two keys, K_1 and K_2, and perform $E_{K_1}(D_{K_2}(E_{K_1}(m)))$. When $K_1 = K_2$, this reduces to single DES. This compatibility is the reason for using D_{K_2} instead of E_{K_2} in the middle; the use of D instead of E gives no extra cryptographic strength. Both versions of Triple DES are resistant to meet-in-the-middle attacks (cf. Exercise 6). However, there are other attacks on the two-key version ([Merkle-Hellman] and [van Oorschot-Wiener]) that indicate possible weaknesses, though they require so much memory as to be impractical.

Another strengthening of DES has been proposed by Rivest. Choose three keys, K_1, K_2, K_3 and perform $K_1 \oplus E_{K_2}(K_3 \oplus m)$. In other words, modify the plaintext by *XOR*ing with K_1, then apply DES with K_2, then *XOR* the result with K_3. This method, known as DESX, has been shown to be fairly secure. See [Kilian-Rogaway].

Another approach is to use one of the new family of encryption algorithms being developed. In 1998 NIST requested comments on 15 algorithms that were candidates to take the place of DES as the new encryption standard, which would be known as the Advanced Encryption Standard (AES). In the year 2000, one of these, Rijndael, was chosen to be the AES. It will be described in the next chapter.

4.7 Password Security

When you log in to a computer and enter your password, the computer checks that your password belongs to you and then grants access. However, it would be quite dangerous to store the passwords in a file in the computer. Someone who obtains that file would then be able to open anyone's account. Making the file available only to the computer administrator might be one solution; but what happens if the administrator makes a copy of the file shortly before changing jobs? The solution is to encrypt the passwords before storing them.

Let $f(x)$ be a **one-way function**. This means that it is easy to compute $f(x)$, but it is very difficult to solve $y = f(x)$ for x. A password x can then be stored as $f(x)$, along with the user's name. When the user logs in, and enters the password x, the computer calculates $f(x)$ and checks that it matches the value of $f(x)$ corresponding to that user. An intruder who obtains the password file will have only the value of $f(x)$ for each user. To log in to the account, the intruder needs to know x, which is hard to compute.

In many systems, the encrypted passwords are stored in a public file. Therefore, anyone with access to the system can obtain this file. Assume the function $f(x)$ is known. Then all the words in a dictionary, and various modifications of these words (writing them backwards, for example) can be fed into $f(x)$. Comparing the results with the password file will often yield the passwords of several users.

This **dictionary attack** can be partially prevented by making the password file not publicly available, but there is still the problem of the departing (or fired) computer administrator. Therefore, other ways of making the information more secure are also needed.

Here is another interesting problem. It might seem desirable that $f(x)$ can be computed very quickly. However, a slightly slower $f(x)$ can slow down a dictionary attack. But slowing down $f(x)$ too much could also cause problems. If $f(x)$ is designed to run in a tenth of a second on a very fast computer, it could take an unacceptable amount of time to login on a slower computer. There doesn't seem to be a completely satisfactory way to resolve this.

One way to hinder a dictionary attack is with what is called **salt**. Each password is randomly padded with an additional 12 bits. These 12 bits are then used to modify the function $f(x)$. The result is stored in the password file, along with the user's name and the values of the 12-bit salt. When a user enters a password x, the computer finds the value of the salt for this user in the file, then uses it in the computation of the modified $f(x)$, which is compared with the value stored in the file.

When salt is used and the words in the dictionary are fed into $f(x)$, they need to be padded with each of the $2^{12} = 4096$ possible values of the salt.

This slows down the computations considerably. Also, suppose an attacker stores the values of $f(x)$ for all the words in the dictionary. This could be done in anticipation of attacking several different password files. With salt, the storage requirements increase dramatically, since each word needs to be stored 4096 times.

The main purpose of salt is to stop attacks that aim at finding a random person's password. In particular, it makes the set of poorly chosen passwords somewhat more secure. Since many people use weak passwords, this is desirable. Salt does not slow down an attack against an individual password (except by preventing use of over-the-counter DES chips). If Eve wants to find Bob's password and has access to the password file, she finds the value of the salt used for Bob and tries a dictionary attack, for example, using only that value of salt. If Bob's password is not in the dictionary, this will fail, and Eve may have to resort to an exhaustive search of all possible passwords.

In many Unix password schemes, the one-way function is based on DES. The first eight characters of the password are converted to 7-bit ASCII (see Section 2.8). These 56 bits become a DES key. If the password is shorter than eight symbols, it is padded with zeros to obtain the 56 bits. The "plaintext" of all zeros is then encrypted using 25 rounds of DES with this key. The output is stored in the password file. The function

$$\text{password} \quad \rightarrow \quad \text{output}$$

is believed to be one-way. Namely, we know the "ciphertext," which is the output, and the "plaintext," which is all zeros. Finding the key, which is the password, amounts to a known plaintext attack on DES, which is generally assumed to be difficult.

In order to increase security, salt is added as follows. A random 12-bit number is generated as the salt. Recall that in DES, the expansion function E takes a 32-bit input R (the right side of the input for the round) and expands it to 48 bits $E(R)$. If the first bit of the salt is 1, the first and 25th bits of $E(R)$ are swapped. If the second bit of the salt is 1, the 2nd and 26th bits of $E(R)$ are swapped. This continues through the 12th bit of the salt. If it is 1, the 12th and 36th bits of $E(R)$ are swapped. When a bit of the salt is 0, it causes no swap. If the salt is all zero, then no swaps occur and we are working with the usual DES. In this way, the salt means that 4096 variations of DES are possible.

One advantage of using salt to modify DES is that someone cannot use high-speed DES chips to compute the one-way function when performing a dictionary attack. Instead, a chip would need to be designed that tries all 4096 modifications of DES caused by the salt; otherwise the attack could be performed with software, which is much slower.

Salt is regarded by many as a temporary measure. As storage space increases and computer speed improves, a factor of 4096 quickly fades. For this reason, several new password schemes are being studied for future implementation.

4.8 Exercises

1. Consider the following DES-like encryption method. Start with a message of $2n$ bits. Divide it into two blocks of length n (a left half and a right half): $M_0 M_1$. The key K consists of k bits, for some integer k. There is a function $f(K, M)$ that takes an input of k bits and n bits and gives an output of n bits. One round of encryption starts with a pair $M_j M_{j+1}$. The output is the pair $M_{j+1} M_{j+2}$, where

$$M_{j+2} = M_j \oplus f(K, M_{j+1}).$$

($\oplus$ means XOR, which is addition mod 2 on each bit). This is done for m rounds, so the ciphertext is $M_m M_{m+1}$.

(a) If you have a machine that does the m-round encryption just described, how would you use the same machine to decrypt the ciphertext $M_m M_{m+1}$ (using the same key K)? Justify your answer.

(b) Suppose K has n bits and $f(K, M) = K \oplus M$, and suppose the encryption process consists of $m = 2$ rounds. If you know only a ciphertext, can you deduce the plaintext and the key? If you know a ciphertext and the corresponding plaintext, can you deduce the key? Justify your answers.

(c) Suppose K has n bits and $f(K, M) = K \oplus M$, and suppose the encryption process consists of $m = 3$ rounds. Why is this system not secure?

2. As described in Section 4.7, a common way of storing passwords on a computer is to use DES with the password as the key to encrypt a fixed plaintext (usually 000 . . . 0). The ciphertext is then stored in the file. When you log in, the procedure is repeated and the ciphertexts are compared. Why is this method more secure than the similar-sounding method of using the password as the plaintext and using a fixed key (for example, 000...0)?

3. Show that the decryption procedures given for the CBC and CFB modes actually perform the desired decryptions.

4. For a string of bits $\mathcal{S}$, let $\overline{\mathcal{S}}$ denote the complementary string obtained by changing all the 1's to 0's and all the 0's to 1's (equivalently, $\overline{\mathcal{S}} = \mathcal{S} \oplus 11111\ldots$). Show that if the DES key K encrypts P to C, then $\overline{K}$ encrypts $\overline{P}$ to $\overline{C}$.

5. (a) Let $K = 111\ldots111$ be the DES key consisting of all 1's. Show that if $E_K(P) = C$, then $E_K(C) = P$, so encryption twice with this key returns the plaintext.

(b) Find another key with the same property as K in part (a).

6. Suppose Triple DES is performed by choosing two keys K_1, K_2 and computing $E_{K_1}(E_{K_2}(E_{K_2}(m)))$ (note that the order of the keys has been modified from the usual two-key version of Triple DES). Show how to attack this modified version with a meet-in-the-middle attack.

Chapter 5

The Advanced Encryption Standard: Rijndael

In 1997, the National Institute of Standards and Technology put out a call for candidates to replace DES. Among the requirements were that the new algorithm should allow key sizes of 128, 192, and 256 bits, it should operate on blocks of 128 input bits, and it should work on a variety of different hardware, for example, 8-bit processors that could be used in smart cards and the 32-bit architecture commonly used in personal computers. Speed and cryptographic strength were also important considerations. In 1998, the cryptographic community was asked to comment on 15 candidate algorithms. Five finalists were chosen: MARS (from IBM), RC6 (from RSA Laboratories), Rijndael (from Joan Daemen and Vincent Rijmen), Serpent (from Ross Anderson, Eli Biham, and Lars Knudsen), and Twofish (from Bruce Schneier, John Kelsey, Doug Whiting, David Wagner, Chris Hall, and Niels Ferguson). Eventually, Rijndael was chosen as the Advanced Encryption Standard. The other four algorithms are also very strong, and it is likely that they will used in many future cryptosystems.

As with other block ciphers, Rijndael can be used in several modes, for example, ECB, CBC, and CFB (see Section 4.5).

Before proceeding to the algorithm, we answer a very basic question: How do you pronounce Rijndael? We quote from their Web page:

If you're Dutch, Flemish, Indonesian, Surinamer or South-

African, it's pronounced like you think it should be. Otherwise, you could pronounce it like "Reign Dahl", "Rain Doll", "Rhine Dahl". We're not picky. As long as you make it sound different from "Region Deal."

5.1   The Basic Algorithm

Rijndael is designed for use with keys of lengths 128, 192, and 256 bits. For simplicity, we'll restrict to 128 bits. First, we give a brief outline of the algorithm, then describe the various components in more detail.

The algorithm consists of 10 rounds. Each round has a round key, derived from the original key. There is also a 0th round key, which is the original key. A round starts with an input of 128 bits and produces an output of 128 bits.

There are four basic steps, called **layers**, that are used to form the rounds:

1. **The ByteSub Transformation:** This non-linear layer is for resistance to differential and linear cryptanalysis attacks.

2. **The ShiftRow Transformation:** This linear mixing step causes diffusion of the bits over multiple rounds.

3. **The MixColumn Transformation:** This layer has a purpose similar to ShiftRow.

4. **AddRoundKey:** The round key is *XOR*ed with the result of the above layer.

A round is then

$$\rightarrow \boxed{ByteSub} \rightarrow \boxed{ShiftRow} \rightarrow \boxed{MixColumn} \rightarrow \boxed{AddRoundKey} \rightarrow .$$

Putting everything together, we obtain the following:

Rijndael Encryption

---

1. ARK, using the 0th round key.
2. Nine rounds of BS, SR, MC, ARK, using round keys 1 to 9.
3. A final round: BS, SR, ARK, using the 10th round key.

The final round uses the ByteSub, ShiftRow, and AddRoundKey steps but omits MixColumn (this omission will be explained in the decryption section).

The 128-bit output is the ciphertext block.

5.2 The Layers

We now describe the steps in more detail. The 128 input bits are grouped into 16 bytes of 8 bits each, call them

$$a_{0,0}, a_{1,0}, a_{2,0}, a_{3,0}, a_{0,1}, a_{1,1}, \ldots, a_{3,3}.$$

These are arranged into a 4×4 matrix

$$\begin{pmatrix} a_{0,0} & a_{0,1} & a_{0,2} & a_{0,3} \\ a_{1,0} & a_{1,1} & a_{1,2} & a_{1,3} \\ a_{2,0} & a_{2,1} & a_{2,2} & a_{2,3} \\ a_{3,0} & a_{3,1} & a_{3,2} & a_{3,3} \end{pmatrix}.$$

In the following, we'll occasionally need to work with the finite field $GF(2^8)$. This is covered in Section 3.10. However, for the present purposes, we only need the following facts. The elements of $GF(2^8)$ are bytes, which consist of 8 bits. They can be added by *XOR*. They can also be multiplied in a certain way (i.e., the product of two bytes is again a byte), but this process is more complicated. Each byte b except the zero byte has a multiplicative inverse; that is, there is a byte b' such that $b \cdot b' = 00000001$. Since we can do arithmetic operations on bytes, we can work with matrices whose entries are bytes.

As a technical point, we note that the model of $GF(2^8)$ depends on a choice of irreducible polynomial of degree 8. The choice for Rijndael is $X^8 + X^4 + X^3 + X + 1$. This is also the polynomial used in the examples in Section 3.10. Other choices for this polynomial would presumably give equally good algorithms.

The ByteSub Transformation

In this step, each of the bytes in the matrix is changed to another byte by Table 5.1, called the S-box.

Write a byte as 8 bits: *abcdefgh*. Look for the entry in the *abcd* row and *efgh* column. (the rows and columns are numbered from 0 to 15). This entry, when converted to binary, is the output. For example, if the input byte is 10001011, we look in row 8 (the ninth row) and column 11 (the twelfth column). The entry is 61, which is 111101 in binary. This is the output of the S-box.

The output of ByteSub is again a 4×4 matrix of bytes, let's call it

$$\begin{pmatrix} b_{0,0} & b_{0,1} & b_{0,2} & b_{0,3} \\ b_{1,0} & b_{1,1} & b_{1,2} & b_{1,3} \\ b_{2,0} & b_{2,1} & b_{2,2} & b_{2,3} \\ b_{3,0} & b_{3,1} & b_{3,2} & b_{3,3} \end{pmatrix}.$$

S-Box															
99	124	119	123	242	107	111	197	48	1	103	43	254	215	171	118
202	130	201	125	250	89	71	240	173	212	162	175	156	164	114	192
183	253	147	38	54	63	247	204	52	165	229	241	113	216	49	21
4	199	35	195	24	150	5	154	7	18	128	226	235	39	178	117
9	131	44	26	27	110	90	160	82	59	214	179	41	227	47	132
83	209	0	237	32	252	177	91	106	203	190	57	74	76	88	207
208	239	170	251	67	77	51	133	69	249	2	127	80	60	159	168
81	163	64	143	146	157	56	245	188	182	218	33	16	255	243	210
205	12	19	236	95	151	68	23	196	167	126	61	100	93	25	115
96	129	79	220	34	42	144	136	70	238	184	20	222	94	11	219
224	50	58	10	73	6	36	92	194	211	172	98	145	149	228	121
231	200	55	109	141	213	78	169	108	86	244	234	101	122	174	8
186	120	37	46	28	166	180	198	232	221	116	31	75	189	139	138
112	62	181	102	72	3	246	14	97	53	87	185	134	193	29	158
225	248	152	17	105	217	142	148	155	30	135	233	206	85	40	223
140	161	137	13	191	230	66	104	65	153	45	15	176	84	187	22

Table 5.1: S-Box for Rijndael

The ShiftRow Transformation

The four rows of the matrix are shifted cyclically to the left by offsets of 0, 1, 2, and 3, to obtain

$$
\begin{pmatrix}
c_{0,0} & c_{0,1} & c_{0,2} & c_{0,3} \\
c_{1,0} & c_{1,1} & c_{1,2} & c_{1,3} \\
c_{2,0} & c_{2,1} & c_{2,2} & c_{2,3} \\
c_{3,0} & c_{3,1} & c_{3,2} & c_{3,3}
\end{pmatrix}
=
\begin{pmatrix}
b_{0,0} & b_{0,1} & b_{0,2} & b_{0,3} \\
b_{1,1} & b_{1,2} & b_{1,3} & b_{1,0} \\
b_{2,2} & b_{2,3} & b_{2,0} & b_{2,1} \\
b_{3,3} & b_{3,0} & b_{3,1} & b_{3,2}
\end{pmatrix}.
$$

The MixColumn Transformation

Regard a byte as an element of $GF(2^8)$, as in Section 3.10. Then the output of the ShiftRow step is a 4×4 matrix $(c_{i,j})$ with entries in $GF(2^8)$. Multiply this by a matrix, again with entries in $GF(2^8)$, to produce the output $(d_{i,j})$, as follows:

$$
\begin{pmatrix}
00000010 & 00000011 & 00000001 & 00000001 \\
00000001 & 00000010 & 00000011 & 00000001 \\
00000001 & 00000001 & 00000010 & 00000011 \\
00000011 & 00000001 & 00000001 & 00000010
\end{pmatrix}
\begin{pmatrix}
c_{0,0} & c_{0,1} & c_{0,2} & c_{0,3} \\
c_{1,0} & c_{1,1} & c_{1,2} & c_{1,3} \\
c_{2,0} & c_{2,1} & c_{2,2} & c_{2,3} \\
c_{3,0} & c_{3,1} & c_{3,2} & c_{3,3}
\end{pmatrix}
$$

$$= \begin{pmatrix} d_{0,0} & d_{0,1} & d_{0,2} & d_{0,3} \\ d_{1,0} & d_{1,1} & d_{1,2} & d_{1,3} \\ d_{2,0} & d_{2,1} & d_{2,2} & d_{2,3} \\ d_{3,0} & d_{3,1} & d_{3,2} & d_{3,3} \end{pmatrix}.$$

The RoundKey Addition

The round key, derived from the key in a way we'll describe later, consists of 128 bits, which are arranged in a 4×4 matrix $(k_{i,j})$ consisting of bytes. This is *XOR*ed with the output of the MixColumn step:

$$\begin{pmatrix} d_{0,0} & d_{0,1} & d_{0,2} & d_{0,3} \\ d_{1,0} & d_{1,1} & d_{1,2} & d_{1,3} \\ d_{2,0} & d_{2,1} & d_{2,2} & d_{2,3} \\ d_{3,0} & d_{3,1} & d_{3,2} & d_{3,3} \end{pmatrix} \oplus \begin{pmatrix} k_{0,0} & k_{0,1} & k_{0,2} & k_{0,3} \\ k_{1,0} & k_{1,1} & k_{1,2} & k_{1,3} \\ k_{2,0} & k_{2,1} & k_{2,2} & k_{2,3} \\ k_{3,0} & k_{3,1} & k_{3,2} & k_{3,3} \end{pmatrix}$$

$$= \begin{pmatrix} e_{0,0} & e_{0,1} & e_{0,2} & e_{0,3} \\ e_{1,0} & e_{1,1} & e_{1,2} & e_{1,3} \\ e_{2,0} & e_{2,1} & e_{2,2} & e_{2,3} \\ e_{3,0} & e_{3,1} & e_{3,2} & e_{3,3} \end{pmatrix}.$$

This is the final output of the round.

The Key Schedule

The original key consists of 128 bits, which are arranged into a 4×4 matrix of bytes. This matrix is expanded by adjoining 40 more columns, as follows. Label the first four columns $W(0), W(1), W(2), W(3)$. The new columns are generated recursively. Suppose columns up through $W(i-1)$ have been defined. If i is not a multiple of 4, then

$$W(i) = W(i-4) \oplus W(i-1).$$

If i is a multiple of 4, then

$$W(i) = W(i-4) \oplus T(W(i-1)),$$

where $T(W(i-1))$ is the transformation of $W(i-1)$ obtained as follows. Let the elements of the column $W(i-1)$ be a, b, c, d. Shift these cyclically to obtain b, c, d, a. Now replace each of these bytes with the corresponding element in the S-box from the ByteSub step, to get 4 bytes e, f, g, h. Finally, compute the round constant

$$r(i) = 00000010^{(i-4)/4}$$

in $GF(2^8)$ (recall that we are in the case where i is a multiple of 4). Then $T(W(i-1))$ is the column vector

$$(e \oplus r(i), f, g, h).$$

In this way, columns $W(4), \ldots, W(43)$ are generated from the initial four columns.

The **round key** for the ith round consists of the columns

$$W(4i), W(4i+1), W(4i+2), W(4i+3).$$

The Construction of the S-Box

Although the S-box is implemented as a lookup table, it has a simple mathematical description. Start with a byte $x_7 x_6 x_5 x_4 x_3 x_2 x_1 x_0$, where each x_i is a binary bit. Compute its inverse in $GF(2^8)$, as in Section 3.10. If the byte is 00000000, there is no inverse, so we use 00000000 in place of its inverse. The resulting byte $y_7 y_6 y_5 y_4 y_3 y_2 y_1 y_0$ represents an 8-dimensional column vector, with the rightmost bit y_0 in the top position. Multiply by a matrix and add the column vector $(1, 1, 0, 0, 0, 1, 1, 0)$ to obtain a vector $(z_0, z_1, z_2, z_3, z_4, z_5, z_6, z_7)$ as follows:

$$
\begin{pmatrix}
1 & 0 & 0 & 0 & 1 & 1 & 1 & 1 \\
1 & 1 & 0 & 0 & 0 & 1 & 1 & 1 \\
1 & 1 & 1 & 0 & 0 & 0 & 1 & 1 \\
1 & 1 & 1 & 1 & 0 & 0 & 0 & 1 \\
1 & 1 & 1 & 1 & 1 & 0 & 0 & 0 \\
0 & 1 & 1 & 1 & 1 & 1 & 0 & 0 \\
0 & 0 & 1 & 1 & 1 & 1 & 1 & 0 \\
0 & 0 & 0 & 1 & 1 & 1 & 1 & 1
\end{pmatrix}
\begin{pmatrix}
y_0 \\ y_1 \\ y_2 \\ y_3 \\ y_4 \\ y_5 \\ y_6 \\ y_7
\end{pmatrix}
+
\begin{pmatrix}
1 \\ 1 \\ 0 \\ 0 \\ 0 \\ 1 \\ 1 \\ 0
\end{pmatrix}
=
\begin{pmatrix}
z_0 \\ z_1 \\ z_2 \\ z_3 \\ z_4 \\ z_5 \\ z_6 \\ z_7
\end{pmatrix}.
$$

The byte $z_7 z_6 z_5 z_4 z_3 z_2 z_1 z_0$ is the entry is the S-box.

For example, start with the byte 11001011. Its inverse in $GF(2^8)$ is 00000100, as we calculated in Section 3.10. We now calculate

$$
\begin{pmatrix}
1 & 0 & 0 & 0 & 1 & 1 & 1 & 1 \\
1 & 1 & 0 & 0 & 0 & 1 & 1 & 1 \\
1 & 1 & 1 & 0 & 0 & 0 & 1 & 1 \\
1 & 1 & 1 & 1 & 0 & 0 & 0 & 1 \\
1 & 1 & 1 & 1 & 1 & 0 & 0 & 0 \\
0 & 1 & 1 & 1 & 1 & 1 & 0 & 0 \\
0 & 0 & 1 & 1 & 1 & 1 & 1 & 0 \\
0 & 0 & 0 & 1 & 1 & 1 & 1 & 1
\end{pmatrix}
\begin{pmatrix}
0 \\ 0 \\ 1 \\ 0 \\ 0 \\ 0 \\ 0 \\ 0
\end{pmatrix}
+
\begin{pmatrix}
1 \\ 1 \\ 0 \\ 0 \\ 0 \\ 1 \\ 1 \\ 0
\end{pmatrix}
=
\begin{pmatrix}
1 \\ 1 \\ 1 \\ 1 \\ 1 \\ 0 \\ 0 \\ 0
\end{pmatrix}.
$$

This yields the byte 00011111. The first 4 bits 1100 represent 12 in binary and the last 4 bits 1011 represent 11 in binary. Subtract 1 from each of these numbers (since the first row and column are numbered 0) and look in the 11th column and 10th row of the S-box. The entry is 31, which in binary is 00011111.

Some of the considerations in the design of the S-box were the following. The map $x \mapsto x^{-1}$ was used to achieve nonlinearity. However, the simplicity of this map could possibility allow certain attacks, so it was combined with multiplication by the matrix and adding the vector, as described previously. The matrix was chosen mostly because of its simple form (note how the rows are shifts of each other). The vector was chosen so that no input ever equals its S-box output or the complement of its S-box output (complementation means changing each 1 to 0 and each 0 to 1).

5.3 Decryption

Each of the steps ByteSub, ShiftRow, MixColumn, and AddRoundKey is invertible:

1. The inverse of ByteSub is another lookup table, called **InvByteSub**.

2. The inverse of ShiftRow is obtained by shifting the rows to the right instead of to the left, yielding **InvByteSub**.

3. The inverse of MixColumn exists because the 4×4 matrix used in Mix-Column is invertible. The transformation **InvMixColumn** is given by multiplication by the matrix

$$\begin{pmatrix} 00001110 & 00001011 & 00001101 & 00001001 \\ 00001001 & 00001110 & 00001011 & 00001101 \\ 00001101 & 00001001 & 00001110 & 00001011 \\ 00001011 & 00001101 & 00001001 & 00001110 \end{pmatrix}.$$

4. AddRoundKey is its own inverse.

The Rijndael encryption consists of the steps (with the obvious abbreviations)

ARK
BS, SR, MC, ARK
...
BS, SR, MC, ARK
BS, SR, ARK.

Recall that MC is missing in the last round.

To decrypt, we need to run through the inverses of these steps in the reverse order. This yields the following preliminary version of decryption:

ARK, ISR, IBS
ARK, IMC, ISR, IBS
. . .
ARK, IMC, ISR, IBS
ARK .

However, we want to rewrite this decryption in order to make it look more like encryption.

Observe that applying BS then SR is the same as first applying SR then BS. This happens because BS acts one byte at a time and SR permutes the bytes. Correspondingly, the order of ISR and IBS can be reversed.

We also want to reverse the order of ARK and IMC, but this is not possible. Instead, we proceed as follows. Applying MC and then ARK to a matrix $(c_{i,j})$ is given as

$$(c_{i,j}) \quad \rightarrow \quad (m_{i,j})(c_{i,j}) \quad \rightarrow \quad (e_{i,j}) = (m_{i,j})(c_{i,j}) \oplus (k_{i,j}),$$

where $(m_{i,j})$ is a the 4×4 matrix in MixColumn and $(k_{i,j})$ is the round key matrix. The inverse is obtained by solving $(e_{i,j}) = (m_{i,j})(c_{i,j}) \oplus (k_{i,j})$ for $(c_{i,j})$ in terms of $(e_{i,j})$, namely, $(c_{i,j}) = (m_{i,j})^{-1}(e_{i,j}) \oplus (m_{i,j})^{-1}(k_{i,j})$. Therefore, the process is

$$(e_{i,j}) \quad \rightarrow \quad (m_{i,j})^{-1}(e_{i,j}) \rightarrow (m_{i,j})^{-1}(e_{i,j}) \oplus (k'_{i,j}),$$

where $(k'_{i,j}) = (m_{i,j})^{-1}(k_{i,j})$. The first arrow is simply InvMixColumn applied to $(e_{i,j})$. If we let **InvAddRoundKey** be *XOR*ing with $(k'_{i,j})$, then we have that the inverse of "MC then ARK" is " IMC then IARK." Therefore, we can replace the steps "ARK then IMC" with the steps "IMC then IARK" in the preceding decryption sequence.

We now see that decryption is given by

ARK, IBS, ISR
IMC, IARK, IBS, ISR
. . .
IMC, IARK, IBS, ISR
ARK .

Regroup the lines to obtain the final version:

Rijndael Decryption

---

1. ARK, using the 10th round key
2. Nine rounds of IBS, ISR, IMC, IARK, using round keys 9 to 1
3. A final round: IBS, ISR, ARK, using the 0th round key

Therefore, the decryption is given by essentially the same structure as encryption, but ByteSub, ShiftRow, and MixColumn are replaced by their inverses, and AddKeyRound is replaced by InvAddKeyRound, except in the initial and final steps. Of course, the round keys are used in the reverse order, so the first ARK uses the 10th round key, and the last ARK uses the 0th round key.

The preceding shows why the MixColumn is omitted in the last round. Suppose it had been left in. Then the encryption would start ARK, BS, SR, MC, ARK, ..., and it would end with ARK, BS, SR, MC, ARK. Therefore, the beginning of the decryption would be (after the reorderings) IMC, IARK, IBS, ISR, ... This means the decryption would have an unnecessary IMC at the beginning. This would have the effect of slowing down the algorithm.

Another way to look at encryption is that there is an initial ARK, then a sequence of alternating half rounds

$$(BS, SR), (MC, ARK), (BS, SR), \ldots, (MC, ARK), (BS, SR),$$

followed by a final ARK. The decryption is ARK, followed by a sequence of alternating half rounds

$$(IBS, ISR), (IMC, IARK), (IBS, ISR), \ldots, (IMC, IARK), (IBS, ISR),$$

followed by a final ARK. From this point of view, we see that a final MC would not fit naturally into any of the half rounds, and it is natural to leave it out.

On 8-bit processors, decryption is not quite as fast as encryption. This is because the entries in the 4×4 matrix for InvMixColumn are more complex than those for MixColumn, and this is enough to make decryption take around 30% longer than encryption for these processors. However, in many applications, decryption is not needed, for example, when CFB mode (see Section 4.5) is used. Therefore, this is not considered to be a significant drawback.

The fact that encryption and decryption are not identical processes leads to the expectation that there are no weak keys, in contrast to DES (see Exercise 4.5) and several other algorithms.

5.4 Design Considerations

The Rijndael algorithm is not a Feistel system (see Sections 4.1 and 4.2). In a Feistel system, half the bits are moved but not changed during each round. In Rijndael, all bits are treated uniformly. This has the effect of diffusing the input bits faster. It can be shown that two rounds are sufficient to obtain full diffusion, namely, each of the 128 output bits depends on each of the 128 input bits.

The S-box was constructed in an explicit and simple algebraic way so as to avoid any suspicions of trapdoors built into the algorithm. The desire was to avoid the mysteries about the S-boxes that haunted DES. The Rijndael S-box is highly nonlinear, since it is based on the mapping $x \mapsto x^{-1}$ in $GF(2^8)$. It is excellent at resisting differential and linear cryptanalysis, as well as more recently studied methods called interpolation attacks.

The ShiftRow step was added to resist two recently developed attacks, namely truncated differentials and the Square attack (Square was a predecessor of Rijndael).

The MixColumn causes diffusion among the bytes. A change in one input byte in this step always results in all four output bytes changing. If two input bytes are changed, at least three output bytes are changed.

The Key Schedule involves nonlinear mixing of the key bits, since it uses the S-box. The mixing is designed to resist attacks where the cryptanalyst knows part of the key and tries to deduce the remaining bits. Also, it aims to ensure that two distinct keys do not have a large number of round keys in common. The round constants are used to eliminate symmetries in the encryption process by making each round different.

The number of rounds was chosen to be 10 because there are attacks that are better than brute force up to six rounds. No known attack beats brute force for seven or more rounds. It was felt that four extra rounds provide a large enough margin of safety. Of course, the number of rounds could easily be increased if needed.

Chapter 6

The RSA Algorithm

6.1   The RSA Algorithm

Alice wants to send a message to Bob, but they have not had previous contact and they do not want to take the time to send a courier with a key. Therefore, all information that Alice sends to Bob will potentially be obtained by the evil observer Eve. However, it is still possible for a message to be sent in such a way that Bob can read it but Eve cannot.

With all the previously discussed methods, this would be impossible. Alice would have to send a key, which Eve would intercept. She could then decrypt all subsequent messages. The possibility of the present scheme, called a **public key cryptosystem**, was first publicly suggested by Diffie and Hellman in their classic paper [Diffie-Hellman]. However, they did not yet have a practical implementation (although they did present an alternative key exchange procedure that works over public channels; see Section 13.1). In the next few years, several methods were proposed. The most successful, based on the idea that factorization of integers into their prime factors is hard, was proposed by Rivest, Shamir, and Adleman in 1977 and is known as the RSA algorithm.

It had long been claimed that government cryptographic agencies had discovered the RSA algorithm several years earlier, but secrecy rules prevented them from releasing any evidence. Finally, in 1997, documents released by CESG, a British cryptographic agency, showed that in 1970, James Ellis had discovered public key cryptography, and in 1973, Clifford Cocks had written an internal document describing a version of the RSA algorithm in which the encryption exponent e (see the discussion that follows) was the same as the modulus n.

Here is how the RSA algorithm works. Bob chooses two distinct large primes p and q and multiplies them together to form

$$n = pq.$$

He also chooses an encryption exponent e such that

$$\gcd(e, (p-1)(q-1)) = 1.$$

He sends the pair (n, e) to Alice but keeps the values of p and q secret. In particular, Alice, who could possibly be an enemy of Bob, never needs to know p and q to send her message to Bob securely. Alice writes her message as a number m. If m is larger than n, she breaks the message into blocks, each of which is less than n. However, for simplicity, let's assume for the moment that $m < n$. Alice computes

$$c \equiv m^e \pmod{n}$$

and sends c to Bob. Since Bob knows p and q, he can compute $(p-1)(q-1)$ and therefore can find the decryption exponent d with

$$de \equiv 1 \pmod{(p-1)(q-1)}.$$

As we'll see later,
$$m \equiv c^d \pmod{n},$$

so Bob can read the message.

We summarize the algorithm in the following table.

The RSA Algorithm

---

1. Bob chooses secret primes p and q and computes $n = pq$.
2. Bob chooses e with $\gcd(e, (p-1)(q-1)) = 1$.
3. Bob computes d with $de \equiv 1 \pmod{(p-1)(q-1)}$.
4. Bob makes n and e public, and keeps p, q, d secret.
5. Alice encrypts m as $c \equiv m^e \pmod{n}$ and sends c to Bob.
6. Bob decrypts by computing $m \equiv c^d \pmod{n}$.

Example. Bob chooses

$$p = 885320963, \quad q = 238855417.$$

Then

$$n = p \cdot q = 211463707796206571.$$

Let the encryption exponent be

$$e = 9007.$$

The values of n and e are sent to Alice.

Alice's message is *cat*. We will depart from our earlier practice of numbering the letters starting with $a = 0$; instead, we start the numbering at $a = 01$ and continue through $z = 26$. In the previous method, if the letter a appeared at the beginning of a message, it would yield a message number m starting with 00, so the a would disappear.

The message is therefore

$$m = 30120.$$

Alice computes

$$c \equiv m^e \equiv 30120^{9007} \equiv 113535859035722866 \pmod{n}.$$

She sends c to Bob.

Since Bob knows p and q, he knows $(p-1)(q-1)$. He uses the extended Euclidean algorithm (see Section 3.2) to compute d such that

$$de \equiv 1 \pmod{(p-1)(q-1)}.$$

The answer is

$$d = 116402471153538991.$$

Bob computes

$$c^d \equiv 113535859035722866^{116402471153538991} \equiv 30120 \pmod{n},$$

so he obtains the original message.   ■

There are several aspects that need to be explained, but perhaps the most important is why $m \equiv c^d \pmod{n}$. Recall Euler's theorem (Section 3.6): If $\gcd(a, n) = 1$, then $a^{\phi(n)} \equiv 1 \pmod{n}$. In our case, $\phi(n) = \phi(pq) = (p-1)(q-1)$. Suppose $\gcd(m, n) = 1$. This is very likely the case; since p and

q are large, m probably has neither as a factor. Since $de \equiv 1 \pmod{\phi(n)}$, we can write $de = 1 + k\phi(n)$ for some integer k. Therefore

$$c^d \equiv (m^e)^d \equiv m^{1+k\phi(n)} \equiv m \cdot (m^{\phi(n)})^k \equiv m \cdot 1^k \equiv m \pmod{n}.$$

We have shown that Bob can recover the message. If $\gcd(m, n) \neq 1$, Bob still recovers the message. See Exercise 13.

What does Eve do? She intercepts n, e, c. She does not know p, q, d. We assume that Eve has no way of factoring n. The obvious way of computing d requires knowing $\phi(n)$. We show later that this is equivalent to knowing p and q. Is there another way? We will show that if Eve can find d, then she can probably factor n. Therefore, it is unlikely that Eve finds d.

Since Eve knows $c \equiv m^e \pmod{n}$, why doesn't she simply take the eth root of c? This works well if we are not working mod n but is very difficult in our case. For example, if you know that $m^3 \equiv 3 \pmod{85}$, you cannot calculate the cube root of 3, namely $1.2599\ldots$, on your calculator and then reduce mod 85. Of course, a case-by-case search would eventually yield $m = 7$, but this method is not feasible for large n.

How does Bob choose p and q? They should be chosen at random, independently of each other. How large depends on the level of security needed, but it seems that they should have at least 100 digits. For reasons that we discuss later, it is perhaps best if they are of slightly different lengths. When we discuss primality testing, we'll see that finding such primes can be done fairly quickly. A few other tests should be done on p and q to make sure they are not bad. For example, if $p - 1$ has only small prime factors, then n is easy to factor by the $p - 1$ method (see Section 6.4), so p should be rejected and replaced with another prime.

Why does Bob require $\gcd(e, (p-1)(q-1)) = 1$? Recall (see Section 3.3) that $de \equiv 1 \pmod{(p-1)(q-1)}$ has a solution d if and only if $\gcd(e, (p-1)(q-1)) = 1$. Therefore, this condition is needed in order for d to exist. The extended Euclidean algorithm can be used to compute d quickly. Since $p - 1$ is even, $e = 2$ cannot be used; one might be tempted to use $e = 3$. However, there are dangers in using small values of e (see Section 6.2 and Computer Problem 14), so something larger is usually recommended. For example, one could let e be a moderately large prime. Then there is no difficulty ensuring that $\gcd(e, (p-1)(q-1)) = 1$.

In the encryption process, Alice calculates $m^e \pmod{n}$. Recall that this can be done fairly quickly and without large memory, for example, by successive squaring. This is definitely an advantage of modular arithmetic: If Alice tried to calculate m^e first, then reduce mod n, it is possible that recording m^e would overflow her computer's memory. Similarly, the decryption process of calculating $c^d \pmod{n}$ can be done efficiently. Therefore, all the operations needed for encryption and decryption can be done quickly (i.e., in time a power of $\log n$). The security is provided by the assumption that n cannot be factored.

We made two claims. We justify them here. Recall that the point of these two claims was that finding $\phi(n)$ or finding the decryption exponent d is essentially as hard as factoring n. Therefore, if factoring is hard, then there should be no fast, clever way of finding d.

Claim 1: Suppose $n = pq$ is the product of two distinct primes. If we know n and $\phi(n)$, then we can quickly find p and q.

Note that

$$n - \phi(n) + 1 = pq - (p - 1)(q - 1) + 1 = p + q.$$

Therefore, we know pq and $p + q$. The roots of the polynomial

$$X^2 - (n - \phi(n) + 1)X + n = X^2 - (p + q)X + pq = (X - p)(X - q)$$

are p and q, but they can also be calculated by the quadratic formula:

$$p, q = \frac{(n - \phi(n) + 1) \pm \sqrt{(n - \phi(n) + 1)^2 - 4n}}{2}.$$

This yields p and q.

For example, suppose $n = 221$ and we know that $\phi(n) = 192$. Consider the quadratic equation

$$X^2 - 30X + 221.$$

The roots are

$$p, q = \frac{30 \pm \sqrt{30^2 - 4 \cdot 221}}{2} = 13, \quad 17.$$

Claim 2: If we know d and e, then we can probably factor n.

In the discussion of factorization methods in Section 6.4, we show that if we have a universal exponent $b > 0$ such that $a^b \equiv 1 \pmod{n}$ for all a with $\gcd(a, n) = 1$, then we can probably factor n. Since $de - 1$ is a multiple of $\phi(n)$, say $de - 1 = k\phi(n)$, we have

$$a^{de-1} \equiv (a^{\phi(n)})^k \equiv 1 \pmod{n}$$

whenever $\gcd(a, n) = 1$. The method for universal exponents can now be applied.

One way the RSA algorithm can be used is when there are several banks, for example, that want to be able to send financial data to each other. If there are several thousand banks, then it is impractical for each pair of banks to have a key for secret communication. A better way is the following. Each bank chooses integers n and e as before. These are then published in a public book. Suppose bank A wants to send data to bank B. Then A looks up B's n and e and uses them to send the message. In practice, the RSA algorithm is not quite fast enough for sending massive amounts of data. Therefore the RSA algorithm is often used to send a key for a faster encryption method such as DES.

6.2   Attacks on RSA

In practice, the RSA algorithm has proven to be effective, as long as it is implemented correctly. We give a few possible implementation mistakes in the Exercises. Here are a few other potential difficulties. Note that a consequence of the following is that we should choose d carefully. One way is to choose d first, then find e with $de \equiv 1 \pmod{\phi(n)}$.

Theorem. *Let $n = pq$, where p and q are primes with $q < p < 2q$. Suppose $d < \frac{1}{3}n^{1/4}$. Given (n, e) such that $de \equiv 1 \pmod{\phi(n)}$, there is an efficient procedure for computing d.*

The method, which uses the continued fraction for e/n, is given in [Wiener]. This result suggests that for good security, p and q should be a slightly different sizes and that d should be large. This is unfortunate since a small d makes decryption faster.

Theorem. *Let $n = pq$ have m digits. If we know the first $m/4$, or the last $m/4$, digits of p, we can efficiently factor n.*

In other words, if p and q have 100 digits, and we know the first 50 digits, or the last 50 digits, of p, then we can factor n. Therefore, if we choose a random starting point to choose our prime p, the method should be such that a large amount of p is not predictable. For example, suppose we take a random 50-digit number N and test numbers of the form $N \cdot 10^{50} + k$, $k = 1, 3, 5, \ldots$, for primality until we find a prime p (which should happen for $k < 1000$). An attacker who knows that this method is used will know 47 of the last 50 digits (they will all be 0 except for the last 3 digits). Trying the method of the theorem for the various values of $k < 1000$ will eventually lead to the factorization of n.

For details of the preceding result, see [Coppersmith2]. A related result is the following.

Theorem. *Suppose (n, e) is an RSA public key and n has m digits. Let d be the decryption exponent. If we have at least the last $m/4$ digits of d, we can efficiently find d in time that is linear in $e \log_2 e$.*

This means that the time to find d is bounded as a function linear in $e \log_2 e$. If e is small, it is therefore quite fast to find d when we know a large part of d. If e is large, perhaps around n, the theorem is no better than a case-by-case search for d. For details, see [Boneh et al.].

For more on these types of attacks on RSA, see [Boneh].

Timing Attacks

Another type of attack on RSA and similar systems was discovered by Paul Kocher in 1995, while he was an undergraduate at Stanford. He showed that it is possible to discover the decryption exponent by carefully timing the computation times for a series of decryptions. Though there are ways to thwart the attack, this development was unsettling. There had been a general feeling of security since the mathematics was well understood. Kocher's attack demonstrated that a system could still have unexpected weaknesses.

Here is how the timing attack works. Suppose Eve is able to observe Bob decrypt several ciphertexts y. She times how long this takes for each y. Knowing each y and the time required for it to be decrypted will allow her to find the decryption exponent d. But first, how could Eve obtain such information? There are several situations where encrypted messages are sent to Bob and his computer automatically decrypts and responds. Measuring the response times suffices for the present purposes.

We need to assume that we know the hardware being used to calculate y^d (mod n). We can use this information to calculate the computation times for various steps that potentially occur in the process.

Let's assume that y^d (mod n) is computed by the algorithm given in Exercise 3.12, which is as follows:

Let $d = b_1 b_2 \ldots b_w$ be written in binary (for example, when $x = 1011$, we have $b_1 = 1, b_2 = 0, b_3 = 1, b_4 = 1$). Let y and n be integers. Perform the following procedure:

1. *Start with $k = 1$ and $s_0 = 1$.*

2. *If $b_k = 1$, let $r_k \equiv s_k y$ (mod n). If $b_k = 0$, let $r_k = s_k$.*

3. *Let $s_{k+1} \equiv r_k^2$ (mod n).*

4. *If $k = w$, stop. If $k < w$, add 1 to k and go to (2).*

Then $r_w \equiv y^d$ (mod n).

Note that the multiplication $s_k y$ occurs only when the bit $b_k = 1$. In many situations, there is a reasonably large variation in how long this multiplication takes. We assume this is the case here.

Before we continue, we need a few facts from probability. Suppose we have a random process that produces real numbers t as outputs. For us, t will be the time it takes for the computer to complete a calculation, given a random input y. The mean is the average value of these outputs. If we record outputs $t_1, \ldots, t_n$, the mean should be approximately $m = (t_1 + \cdots t_n)/n$. The variance for the random process is approximated by

$$\text{Var}(\{t_i\}) = \frac{(t_1 - m)^2 + \cdots + (t_n - m)^2}{n}.$$

The standard deviation is the square root of the variance and gives a measure of how much variation there is in the values of the t_i's.

The important fact we need is that when two random processes are independent, the variance for the sum of their outputs is the sum of the variances of the two processes. For example, we will break the computation done by the computer into two independent processes, which will take times t' and t''. The total time t will be $t' + t''$. Therefore, $\text{Var}(\{t_i\})$ should be approximately $\text{Var}(\{t_i'\}) + \text{Var}(\{t_i''\})$.

Now assume Eve knows ciphertexts $y_1, \ldots, y_n$ and the times that it took to compute each $y_i^d \pmod{n}$. Suppose she knows bits $b_1, \ldots, b_{k-1}$ of the exponent d. Since she knows the hardware being used, she knows how much time was used in calculating $r_1, \ldots, r_{k-1}$ in the preceding algorithm. Therefore she knows, for each y_i, the time t_i that it takes to compute $r_k, \ldots, r_w$.

Eve wants to determine b_k. If $b_k = 1$, a multiplication $s_k y \pmod{n}$ will take place for each ciphertext y_i that is processed. If $b_k = 0$, there is no such multiplication.

Let t_i' be the amount of time it takes the computer to perform the multiplication $s_k y \pmod{n}$, though Eve does not yet know whether this multiplication actually occurs. Let $t_i'' = t_i - t_i'$. Eve computes $\text{Var}(\{t_i\})$ and $\text{Var}(\{t_i''\})$. If $\text{Var}(\{t_i\}) > \text{Var}(\{t_i''\})$, then Eve concludes that $b_k = 1$. If not, $b_k = 0$. After determining b_k, she proceeds in the same manner to find all the bits.

Why does this work? If the multiplication occurs, t_i'' is the amount of time it takes the computer to complete the calculation after the multiplication. It is reasonable to assume t_i' and t_i'' are outputs that are independent of each other. Therefore,

$$\text{Var}(\{t_i\}) \approx \text{Var}(\{t_i'\}) + \text{Var}(\{t_i''\}) > \text{Var}(\{t_i''\}).$$

If the multiplication does not occur, t_i' is the amount of time for an operation unrelated to the computation, so it is reasonable to assume t_i and t_i' are independent. Therefore,

$$\text{Var}(\{t_i''\}) \approx \text{Var}(\{t_i\}) + \text{Var}(\{-t_i'\}) > \text{Var}(\{t_i\}).$$

Note that we couldn't use the mean in place of the variance, since the mean of $\{-t_i\}$ would be negative, so the last inequality would not hold. All that can be deduced from the mean is the total number of nonzero bits in d.

The preceding gives a fairly simple version of the method. In practice, various modifications would be needed, depending on the specific situation. But the general strategy remains the same. For more details, see [Kocher].

6.3 Primality Testing

Suppose we have an integer of 200 digits that we want to test for primality. Why not divide by all the primes less than its square root? There are around 4×10^{97} primes less than 10^{100}. This is significantly more than the number of particles in the universe. Moreover, if the computer can handle 10^9 primes per second, the calculation would take around 10^{81} years. Clearly, better methods are needed. Some of these are discussed in this section.

A very basic idea, one that is behind many factorization methods, is the following.

Basic Principle. *Let n be an integer and suppose there exist integers x and y with $x^2 \equiv y^2 \pmod{n}$, but $x \not\equiv \pm y \pmod{n}$. Then n is composite. Moreover, $\gcd(x - y, n)$ gives a nontrivial factor of n.*

Proof. Let $d = \gcd(x - y, n)$. If $d = n$ then $x \equiv y \pmod{n}$, which is assumed not to happen. Suppose $d = 1$. A basic result on divisibility is that if $a|bc$ and $\gcd(a, b) = 1$, then $a|c$ (See Exercise 3.3). In our case, since n divides $x^2 - y^2 = (x - y)(x + y)$ and $d = 1$, we must have that n divides $x + y$, which contradicts the assumption that $x \not\equiv -y \pmod{n}$. Therefore, $d \neq 1, n$, so d is a nontrivial factor of n. $\square$

Example. Since $12^2 \equiv 2^2 \pmod{35}$, but $12 \not\equiv \pm 2 \pmod{35}$, we know that 35 is composite. Moreover, $\gcd(12 - 2, 35) = 5$ is a nontrivial factor of 35. ∎

It might be surprising, but factorization and primality testing are not the same. It is much easier to prove a number is composite than it is to factor it. There are many large integers that are known to be composite but that have not been factored. How can this be done? We give a simple example. We know by Fermat's theorem that if p is prime, then $2^{p-1} \equiv 1 \pmod{p}$. Let's use this to show 35 is not prime. By successive squaring, we find (congruences are mod 35)

$$2^4 \equiv 16,$$
$$2^8 \equiv 256 \equiv 11$$
$$2^{16} \equiv 121 \equiv 16$$
$$2^{32} \equiv 256 \equiv 11.$$

Therefore,

$$2^{34} \equiv 2^{32} 2^2 \equiv 11 \cdot 4 \equiv 9 \not\equiv 1 \pmod{35}.$$

Fermat's theorem says that 35 cannot be prime, so we have proved 35 to be composite without finding a factor.

This method generalizes as follows.

Miller-Rabin Primality Test. *Let $n > 1$ be an odd integer. Write $n - 1 = 2^k m$ with m odd. Choose a random integer a with $1 < a < n - 1$. Compute $b_0 \equiv a^m \pmod{n}$. If $b_0 \equiv \pm 1 \pmod{n}$, then stop and declare that n is probably prime. Otherwise, let $b_1 \equiv b_0^2 \pmod{n}$. If $b_1 \equiv 1 \pmod{n}$, then n is composite (and $\gcd(b_0 - 1, n)$ gives a nontrivial factor of n). If $b_1 \equiv -1 \pmod{n}$, then stop and declare that n is probably prime. Otherwise, let $b_2 \equiv b_1^2 \pmod{n}$. If $b_2 \equiv 1 \pmod{n}$, then n is composite. If $b_2 \equiv -1 \pmod{n}$, then stop and declare that n is probably prime. Continue in this way until stopping or reaching b_{k-1}. If $b_{k-1} \not\equiv -1 \pmod{n}$, then n is composite.*

Example. Let $n = 561$. Then $n - 1 = 560 = 16 \cdot 35$, so $2^k = 2^4$ and $m = 35$. Let $a = 2$. Then

$$b_0 \equiv 2^{35} \equiv 263 \pmod{561}$$
$$b_1 \equiv b_0^2 \equiv 166 \pmod{561}$$
$$b_2 \equiv b_1^2 \equiv 67 \pmod{561}$$
$$b_3 \equiv b_2^2 \equiv 1 \pmod{561}.$$

Since $b_3 \equiv 1 \pmod{561}$, we conclude that 561 is composite. Moreover, $\gcd(b_2 - 1, 561) = 33$, which is a nontrivial factor of 561. ∎

If n is composite and $a^{n-1} \equiv 1 \pmod{n}$, then we say that n is a pseudoprime for the base a. If a and n are such that n passes the Miller-Rabin test, we say that n is a strong pseudoprime for the base a. We showed in Section 3.6 that $2^{560} \equiv 1 \pmod{561}$, so 561 is a pseudoprime for the base 2. However, the preceding calculation shows that 561 is not a strong pseudoprime for the base 2. For a given base, strong pseudoprimes are much more rare than pseudoprimes.

Up to 10^{10}, there are 455052511 primes. There are 14884 pseudoprimes for the base 2, and 3291 strong pseudoprimes for the base 2. Therefore, calculating 2^{n-1} (mod n) will fail to recognize a composite in this range with probability less than 1 out of 30 thousand, and using the Miller-Rabin test with $a = 2$ will fail with probability less than 1 out of 100 thousand.

It can be shown that the probability that the Miller-Rabin test fails to recognize a composite for a randomly chosen a is at most $1/4$. In fact, it fails much less frequently than this. See [Damgård et al.]. If we repeat the test 10 times, say, with randomly chosen values of a, then we expect that the probability of certifying a composite number as prime is at most $(1/4)^{10} \simeq 10^{-6}$. In practice, using the test for a single a is fairly accurate.

Though strong pseudoprimes are rare, it has been proved that, for any finite set B of bases, there are infinitely many integers that are strong pseudoprimes for all $b \in B$. The first strong pseudoprime for all the bases $b = 2, 3, 5, 7$ is 3215031751. There is a 337-digit number that is a strong pseudoprime for all bases that are primes < 200.

Suppose we need to find a prime of around 100 digits. The prime number theorem asserts that the density of primes around x is approximately $1/\ln x$. When $x = 10^{100}$, this gives a density of around $1/\ln(10^{100}) = 1/230$. Since we can skip the even numbers, this can be raised to $1/115$. Pick a random starting point, and throw out the even numbers (and multiples of other small primes). Test each remaining number in succession by the Miller-Rabin test. This will tend to eliminate all the composites. On average, it will take less than 100 uses of the Miller-Rabin test to find a likely candidate for a prime, so this can be done fairly quickly. If we need to be completely certain that the number in question is prime, there are more sophisticated primality tests that can test a number of 100 digits in a few seconds.

Why does the test work? Suppose, for example, that $b_3 \equiv 1$ (mod n). This means that $b_2^2 \equiv 1^2$ (mod n). Apply the Basic Principle from before. Either $b_2 \equiv \pm 1$ (mod n), or $b_2 \not\equiv \pm 1$ (mod n) and n is composite. In the latter case, $\gcd(b_2 - 1, n)$ gives a nontrivial factor of n. In the former case, the algorithm would have stopped by the previous step. If we reach b_{k-1}, we have computed $b_{k-1} \equiv a^{(n-1)/2}$ (mod n). The square of this is a^{n-1}, which must be 1 (mod n) if n is prime, by Fermat's theorem. Therefore, if n is prime, $b_{k-1} \equiv \pm 1$ (mod n). All other choices mean that n is composite. Moreover, if $b_{k-1} \equiv 1$, then, if we didn't stop at an earlier step, $b_{k-2}^2 \equiv 1^2$ (mod n) with $b_{k-2} \not\equiv \pm 1$ (mod n). This means that n is composite (and we can factor n).

In practice, if n is composite, usually we reach b_{k-1} and it is not ± 1 (mod n). In fact, usually $a^{n-1} \not\equiv 1$ (mod n). This means that Fermat's theorem fails, so n is not prime.

For example, let $n = 299$ and $a = 2$. Since $2^{298} \equiv 140$ (mod 299), Fermat's theorem and also the Miller-Rabin test say that 299 is not prime (without factoring it). The reason this happens is the following. Note that $299 = 13 \times 23$. An easy calculation shows that $2^{12} \equiv 1 \pmod{13}$ and no smaller exponent works. In fact, $2^j \equiv 1 \pmod{13}$ if and only if j is a multiple of 12. Since 298 is not a multiple of 12, we have $2^{298} \not\equiv 1 \pmod{13}$, and therefore also $2^{298} \not\equiv 1 \pmod{299}$. Similarly, $2^j \equiv 1 \pmod{23}$ if and only if j is a multiple of 11, from which we can again deduce that $2^{298} \not\equiv 1 \pmod{299}$. If Fermat's theorem (and the Miller-Rabin test) were to give us the wrong answer in this case, we would have needed $13 \cdot 23 - 1$ to be a multiple of $12 \cdot 11$.

Consider the general case $n = pq$, a product of two primes. For simplicity, consider the case where $p > q$ and suppose $a^k \equiv 1 \pmod{p}$ if and only if $k \equiv 0 \pmod{p-1}$. This means that a is a primitive root mod p; there are $\phi(p-1)$ such $a \bmod p$. Since $0 < q - 1 < p - 1$, we have

$$n - 1 \equiv pq - 1 \equiv q(p-1) + q - 1 \not\equiv 0 \pmod{p-1}.$$

Therefore, $a^{n-1} \not\equiv 1 \pmod{p}$ by our choice of a, which implies that $a^{n-1} \not\equiv 1 \pmod{n}$. Similar reasoning shows that usually $a^{n-1} \not\equiv 1 \pmod{n}$ for many other choices of a, too.

But suppose we are in a case where $a^{n-1} \equiv 1 \pmod{n}$. What happens? Let's look at the example of $n = 561$. Since $561 = 3 \times 11 \times 17$, we consider what is happening to the sequence b_0, b_1, b_2, b_3 mod 3, mod 11, and mod 17:

$$
\begin{array}{llll}
b_0 \equiv -1 & \pmod{3}, & \equiv -1 \pmod{11}, & \equiv 2 \pmod{17} \\
b_1 \equiv 1 & \pmod{3}, & \equiv 1 \pmod{11}, & \equiv 4 \pmod{17} \\
b_2 \equiv 1 & \pmod{3}, & \equiv 1 \pmod{11}, & \equiv -1 \pmod{17} \\
b_3 \equiv 1 & \pmod{3}, & \equiv 1 \pmod{11}, & \equiv 1 \pmod{17}.
\end{array}
$$

Since $b_3 \equiv 1 \pmod{561}$, we have $b_2^2 \equiv b_3 \equiv 1$ mod all three primes. But there is no reason that b_3 is the first time we get $b_i \equiv 1$ mod a particular prime. We already have $b_1 \equiv 1$ mod 3 and mod 11, but we have to wait for b_3 when working mod 17. Therefore, $b_2^2 \equiv b_3 \equiv 1$ mod 3, mod 11, and mod 17, but b_2 is congruent to 1 only mod 3 and mod 11. Therefore, $b_2 - 1$ contains the factors 3 and 11, but not 17. This is why $\gcd(b_2 - 1, 561)$ finds the factor 33 of 561. The reason we could factor 561 by this method is that the sequence $b_0, b_1, \ldots$ reached 1 mod the primes not all at the same time.

More generally, consider the case $n = pq$ (a product of several primes is similar) and suppose $a^{n-1} \equiv 1 \pmod{n}$. As pointed out previously, it is very unlikely that this is the case; but if it does happen, look at what is happening mod p and mod q. It is likely that the sequences $b_i \pmod{p}$ and $b_i \pmod{q}$ reach -1 and then 1 at different times, just as in the example of 561. In this case, we will be have $b_i \equiv -1 \pmod{p}$ but $b_i \equiv 1 \pmod{q}$ for some i; therefore, $b_i^2 \equiv 1 \pmod{n}$ but $b_i \not\equiv \pm 1 \pmod{n}$. Therefore, we'll be able to factor n.

The only way that n can pass the Miller-Rabin test is to have $a^{n-1} \equiv 1$ (mod n) and also to have the sequences b_i (mod p) and b_i (mod q) reach 1 at the same time. This rarely happens.

For more on primality testing and its history, see [Williams].

6.4   Factoring

We now turn to factoring. The basic method of dividing an integer n by all primes $p \le \sqrt{n}$ is much too slow for most purposes. For many years, people have worked on developing more efficient algorithms. We present some of them here. In Chapter 15, we'll also cover a method using elliptic curves, and in Chapter 17, we'll show how a quantum computer, if built, could factor efficiently.

One method, which is also too slow, is usually called the **Fermat factorization** method. The idea is to express n as a difference of two squares: $n = x^2 - y^2$. Then $n = (x+y)(x-y)$ gives a factorization of n. For example, suppose we want to factor $n = 295927$. Compute $n + 1^2$, $n + 2^2$, $n + 3^2$, ..., until we find a square. In this case, $295927 + 3^2 = 295936 = 544^2$. Therefore,
$$295927 = (544 + 3)(544 - 3) = 547 \cdot 541.$$

The Fermat method works well when n is the product of two primes that are very close together. If $n = pq$, it takes $|p - q|/2$ steps to find the factorization. But if p and q are two randomly selected 100-digit primes, it is likely that $|p - q|$ will be very large, probably around 100-digits, too. So Fermat factorization is unlikely to work. Just to be safe, however, the primes for an RSA modulus are often chosen to be of slightly different sizes.

We now turn to more modern methods. On the surface, the Miller-Rabin test looks like it might factor n quite often; but what usually happens is that b_{k-1} is reached without ever having $b_u \equiv \pm 1$ (mod n). The problem is that usually $a^{n-1} \not\equiv 1$ (mod n). Suppose, on the other hand, that we have some exponent r, maybe not $n - 1$, such that $a^r \equiv 1$ (mod n) for all a with $\gcd(a, n) = 1$. Then it is often possible to factor n. We note that such an exponent r must be even (if $n > 2$); since we can take $a \equiv -1$ (mod n), we need $(-1)^r \equiv 1$.

Universal Exponent Factorization Method. *Suppose we have an exponent $r > 0$ such that $a^r \equiv 1$ (mod n) for all a with $\gcd(a, n) = 1$. Write $r = 2^k m$ with m odd. Choose a random a with $1 < a < n - 1$. If $\gcd(a, n) \ne 1$, we have a factor of n, so assume $\gcd(a, n) = 1$. Let $b_0 \equiv a^m$ (mod n), and successively define $b_{u+1} \equiv b_u^2$ (mod n) for $0 \le u \le k - 1$. If $b_0 \equiv 1$ (mod n), then stop and try a different a. If, for some u, we have*

$b_u \equiv -1 \pmod{n}$, *stop and try a different a. If, for some u we have $b_{u+1} \equiv 1$* (mod n) *but $b_u \not\equiv \pm 1 \pmod{n}$, then* $\gcd(b_u - 1, \, n)$ *gives a nontrivial factor of n.*

This looks very similar to the Miller-Rabin test. The difference is that the existence of r guarantees that we have $b_{u+1} \equiv 1 \pmod{n}$ for some u, which doesn't happen as often in the Miller-Rabin situation. Trying a few values of a has a very high probability of factoring n.

Of course, we might ask how we can find an exponent r. Generally, this seems to be very difficult, and this test cannot be used in practice. However, it is useful in showing that knowing the decryption exponent in the RSA algorithm allows us to factor the modulus.

In some situations, we don't know a universal exponent, but we know an exponent r that works for one value of a. Sometimes this allows us to factor n.

Exponent Factorization Method. *Suppose we have an exponent $r > 0$ and an integer a such that $a^r \equiv 1 \pmod{n}$. Write $r = 2^k m$ with m odd. Let $b_0 \equiv a^m \pmod{n}$, and successively define $b_{u+1} \equiv b_u^2 \pmod{n}$ for $0 \le u \le k-1$. If $b_0 \equiv 1 \pmod{n}$, then stop; the procedure has failed to factor n. If, for some u, we have $b_u \equiv -1 \pmod{n}$, stop; the procedure has failed to factor n. If, for some u, we have $b_{u+1} \equiv 1 \pmod{n}$ but $b_u \not\equiv \pm 1 \pmod{n}$, then $\gcd(b_u - 1, \, n)$ gives a nontrivial factor of n.*

Of course, if we take $a = 1$, then any r works. But then $b_0 = 1$, so the method fails. But if a and r are found by some reasonably sensible method, there is a good chance that this method will factor n.

If one of the prime factors of n has a special property, it is sometimes easier to factor n. For example, if p divides n and $p - 1$ has only small prime factors, the following method is effective. It was invented by Pollard in 1974.

The $p-1$ Factoring Algorithm. *Choose an integer $a > 1$. Often $a = 2$ is used. Choose a bound B. Compute $b \equiv a^{B!} \pmod{n}$ as follows. Let $b_1 \equiv a \pmod{n}$ and $b_j \equiv b_{j-1}^j \pmod{n}$. Then $b_B \equiv b \pmod{n}$. Let $d = \gcd(b - 1, \, n)$. If $1 < d < n$, we have found a nontrivial factor of n.*

Suppose p is a prime factor of n such that $p - 1$ has only small prime factors. Then it is likely that $p - 1$ will divide $B!$, say $B! = (p-1)k$. By Fermat's theorem, $b \equiv a^{B!} \equiv (a^{p-1})^k \equiv 1 \pmod{p}$, so p will occur in the greatest common divisor of $b - 1$ and n. If q is another prime factor of n, it is unlikely that $b \equiv 1 \pmod{q}$, unless $q - 1$ also has only small prime factors. If $d = n$, not all is lost. In this case, we have an exponent r (namely

$B!$) and an a such that $a^r \equiv 1 \pmod{n}$. There is a good chance that the above Exponent Factorization Method will factor n. Alternatively, we could choose a smaller value of B and repeat the calculation (this is somewhat similar to what the Exponent Factorization Method is doing).

How do we choose the bound B? If we choose a small B, then the algorithm will run quickly but will have a very small chance of success. If we choose a very large B, then the algorithm will be very slow. The actual value used will depend on the situation at hand.

In the applications, we will use integers that are products of two primes, say $n = pq$, but that are hard to factor. Therefore, we should ensure that $p-1$ has at least one large prime factor. This is easy to accomplish. Suppose we want p to have around 100 digits. Choose a large prime p_0, perhaps around 10^{40}. Look at integers of the form $kp_0 + 1$, with k running through some integers around 10^{60}. Test $kp_0 + 1$ for primality by the Miller-Rabin test, as before. On the average, this should produce a desired value of p in less than 100 steps. Now choose a large prime q_0 and follow the same procedure to obtain q. Then $n = pq$ will be hard to factor by the $p - 1$ method.

The elliptic curve factorization method (see Section 15.3) gives a generalization of the $p - 1$ method. However, it uses some random numbers near $p-1$ and only requires at least one of them to have only small prime factors. This allows the method to detect many more primes p, not just those where $p - 1$ has only small prime factors.

The Quadratic Sieve

Suppose we want to factor $n = 3837523$. Observe the following:

$$
\begin{aligned}
9398^2 &\equiv 5^5 \cdot 19 \pmod{3837523} \\
19095^2 &\equiv 2^2 \cdot 5 \cdot 11 \cdot 13 \cdot 19 \pmod{3837523} \\
1964^2 &\equiv 3^2 \cdot 13^3 \pmod{3837523} \\
17078^2 &\equiv 2^6 \cdot 3^2 \cdot 11 \pmod{3837523}.
\end{aligned}
$$

If we multiply the relations, we obtain

$$
\begin{aligned}
(9398 \cdot 19095 \cdot 1964 \cdot 17078)^2 &\equiv (2^4 \cdot 3^2 \cdot 5^3 \cdot 11 \cdot 13^2 \cdot 19)^2 \\
2230387^2 &\equiv 2586705^2.
\end{aligned}
$$

Since $2230387 \not\equiv \pm 2586705 \pmod{3837523}$, we can factor 3837523 by calculating

$$
\gcd(2230387 - 2586705, 3837523) = 1093.
$$

The other factor is $3837523/1093 = 3511$.

Here is a way of looking at the calculations we just did. First, we generate squares such that when they are reduced mod n =3837523 they can be written as products of small primes (in the present case, primes less than 20). This set of primes is called our **factor base**. We'll discuss how to generate such squares shortly. Each of these squares gives a row in a matrix, where the entries are the exponents of the primes 2, 3, 5, 7, 11, 13, 17, 19. For example, the relation $17078^2 \equiv 2^6 \cdot 3^2 \cdot 11 \pmod{3837523}$ gives the row 6, 2, 0, 0, 1, 0, 0, 0.

In addition to the preceding relations, suppose that we have also found the following relations:

$$
\begin{aligned}
8077^2 &\equiv 2 \cdot 19 \pmod{3837523} \\
3397^2 &\equiv 2^5 \cdot 5 \cdot 13^2 \pmod{3837523} \\
14262^2 &\equiv 5^2 \cdot 7^2 \cdot 13 \pmod{3837523}.
\end{aligned}
$$

We obtain the matrix

	2	3	5	7	11	13	17	19
9398	0	0	5	0	0	0	0	1
19095	2	0	1	0	1	1	0	1
1964	0	2	0	0	0	3	0	0
17078	6	2	0	0	1	0	0	0
8077	1	0	0	0	0	0	0	1
3397	5	0	1	0	0	2	0	0
14262	0	0	2	2	0	1	0	0

Now look for linear dependencies mod 2 among the rows. Here are three of them:

1. 1st + 5th + 6th = $(6,0,6,0,0,2,0,2) \equiv 0 \pmod 2$

2. 1st + 2nd + 3rd + 4th = $(6,4,6,0,2,4,0,2) \equiv 0 \pmod 2$

3. 3rd + 7th = $(0,2,2,2,0,4,0,0) \equiv 0 \pmod 2$

When we have such a dependency, the product of the numbers yields a square. For example, these three yield

1. $(9398 \cdot 8077 \cdot 3397)^2 \equiv 2^6 \cdot 5^6 \cdot 13^2 \cdot 19^2 \equiv (2^3 \cdot 5^3 \cdot 13 \cdot 19)^2$

2. $(9398 \cdot 19095 \cdot 1964 \cdot 17078)^2 \equiv (2^3 \cdot 3^2 \cdot 5^3 \cdot 11 \cdot 13^2 \cdot 19)^2$

3. $(1964 \cdot 14262)^2 \equiv (3 \cdot 5 \cdot 7 \cdot 13^2)^2$

Therefore, we have $x^2 \equiv y^2 \pmod n$ for various values of x and y. If $x \not\equiv \pm y \pmod n$, then $\gcd(x - y, n)$ yields a nontrivial factor of n. If $x \equiv \pm y \pmod n$, then $\gcd(x - y, n) = 1$ or n, so we don't obtain a factorization. In our three examples, we have

1. $3590523^2 \equiv 247000^2$, but $3590523 \equiv -247000 \pmod{3837523}$

2. $2230387^2 \equiv 2586705^2$ and $\gcd(2230387 - 2586705, 3837523) = 1093$

3. $1147907^2 \equiv 17745^2$ and $\gcd(1147907 - 17745, 3837523) = 1093$

We now return to the basic question: How do we find the numbers 9398, 19095, etc.? The idea is to produce squares that are slightly larger than a multiple of n, so they are small mod n. This means that there is a good chance they are products of small primes. An easy way is to look at numbers of the form $[\sqrt{in} + j]$ for small j and for various values of i. Here $[x]$ denotes the greatest integer less than or equal to x. The square of such a number is approximately $in + 2j\sqrt{in} + j^2$, which is approximately $2j\sqrt{in} + j^2$ mod n. As long as i is not too large, this number is fairly small, hence there is a good chance it is a product of small primes.

In the preceding calculation, we have $8077 = [\sqrt{17n} + 1]$ and $9398 = [\sqrt{23n} + 4]$, for example.

The method just used is the basis of many of the best current factorization methods. The main step is to produce congruence relations

$$x^2 \equiv \text{product of small primes.}$$

An improved version of the above method is called the quadratic sieve. A recent method, the number field sieve, uses more sophisticated techniques to produce such relations and is somewhat faster in many situations.

Once we have several congruence relations, they are put into a matrix, as before. If we have more rows than columns in the matrix, we are guaranteed to have a linear dependence relation mod 2 among the rows. This leads to a congruence $x^2 \equiv y^2 \pmod{n}$. Of course, as in the case of 1st + 5th + 6th $\equiv 0 \pmod 2$ considered previously, we might end up with $x \equiv \pm y$, in which case we don't obtain a factorization. But this situation is expected to occur at most half the time. So if we have enough relations— for example, if there are several more rows than columns— then we should have a relation that yields $x^2 \equiv y^2$ with $x \not\equiv \pm y$. In this case $\gcd(x - y, n)$ is a nontrivial factor of n.

In the last half of the twentieth century, there was dramatic progress in factoring. This was partly due to the development of computers and partly due to improved algorithms. A major impetus was provided by the use of factoring in cryptology, especially the RSA algorithm. Table 6.1 gives the factorization records (in terms of the number of decimal digits) for various years.

Year	Number of digits
1964	20
1974	45
1984	71
1994	129
1999	155

Table 6.1: Factorization Records

6.5   The RSA Challenge

When the RSA algorithm was first made public in 1977, the authors made the following challenge.

Let the RSA modulus be

$$n = $$
11438162575788886766923577997614661201021829672124236256256184293570693524573338978305971235639587050589890751475992900268795434541

and let $e = 9007$ be the encryption exponent. The ciphertext is

$$c = $$
96869613754622061477140922254355882905759991124574319874695120930816298225145708356931476622883989628013391990551829945157815154.

Find the message.

The only known way of finding the plaintext is to factor n. In 1977, it was estimated that the then-current factorization methods would take 4×10^{16} years to do this, so the authors felt safe in offering \$100 to anyone who could decipher the message before April 1, 1982. However, techniques have improved, and in 1994, Atkins, Graff, Lenstra, and Leyland succeeded in factoring n.

They used 524339 "small" primes, namely those less than 16333610, plus they allowed factorizations to include up to two "large" primes between 16333610 and 2^{30}. The idea of allowing large primes is the following: If one large prime q appears in two different relations, these can be multiplied to produce a relation with q squared. Multiplying by $q^{-2} \pmod{n}$ yields a relation involving only small primes. In the same way, if there are several relations, each with the same two large primes, a similar process yields a relation with only small primes. The "birthday paradox" (see Section 8.4) implies that there should be several cases where a large prime occurs in more than one relation.

Six hundred people, with a total of 1600 computers working in spare time, found congruence relations of the desired type. These were sent by e-mail to a central machine, which removed repetitions and stored the results in a large matrix. After 7 months, they obtained a matrix with 524339 columns and 569466 rows. Fortunately, the matrix was sparse, in the sense that most of the entries of the matrix were 0's, so it could be stored efficiently. Gaussian elimination reduced the matrix to a nonsparse matrix with 188160 columns and 188614 rows. This took a little less than 12 hours. With another 45 hours of computation, they found 205 dependencies. The first three yielded the trivial factorization of n, but the fourth yielded the factors

$p=$
34905295108476509491478496199038981334177646384933878
43990820577,

$q=$
32769132993266709549961988190834461413177642967992942
539798288533.

Computing $9007^{-1} \pmod{(p-1)(q-1)}$ gave the decryption exponent

$d=$
10669861436857802444286877132892015478070990663393786
28012262244966310631259117744708733401685974623065539
68544513277109053606095.

Calculating $c^d \pmod{n}$ yielded the plaintext message

20080500130107090300231518041900011805001917210501130
91908001519190906180107705,

which, when changed back to letters using $a = 01, b = 02, \ldots,$ blank $= 00,$ yielded

the magic words are squeamish ossifrage

(a squeamish ossifrage is an oversensitive hawk; the message was chosen so that no one could decrypt the message by guessing the plaintext and showing that it encrypted to the ciphertext). For more details of this factorization, see [Atkins et al.].

6.6   An Application to Treaty Verification

Countries A and B have signed a nuclear test ban treaty. Now each wants to make sure the other doesn't test any bombs. How, for example, is country A going to use seismic data to monitor country B? Country A wants to put sensors in B, which then send data back to A. Two problems arise.

1. Country A wants to be sure that Country B doesn't modify the data.

2. Country B wants to look at the message before it's sent to be sure that nothing else, such as espionage data, is being transmitted.

These seemingly contradictory requirements can be met by reversing RSA. First, A chooses $n = pq$ to be the product of two large primes and chooses encryption and decryption exponents e and d. The numbers n and e are given to B, but p, q, and d are kept secret. The sensor (it's buried deep in the ground and is assumed to be tamper proof) collects the data x and uses d to encrypt x to $y \equiv x^d \pmod{n}$. Both x and y are sent first to country B, which checks that $y^e \equiv x \pmod{n}$. If so, it knows that the encrypted message y corresponds to the data x, and forwards the pair x, y to A. Country A then checks that $y^e \equiv x \pmod{n}$, also. If so, A can be sure that the number x has not been modified, since if x is chosen, then solving $y^e \equiv x \pmod{n}$ for y is the same as decrypting the RSA message x, and this is believed to be hard to do. Of course, B could choose a number y first, then let $x \equiv y^e \pmod{n}$, but then x would probably not be a meaningful message, so A would realize that something had been changed.

The preceding method is essentially the RSA signature scheme, which will be studied in Section 8.1.

6.7   The Public Key Concept

In 1976, Diffie and Hellman described the concept of public key cryptography, though at that time no realizations of the concept were publicly known (as mentioned in the introduction to this chapter, Clifford Cocks of the British cryptographic agency CESG had invented a secret version of RSA in 1973). In this section, we give the general theory of public key systems.

There are several implementations of public key cryptography other than RSA. In later chapters we describe two of them. One is due to ElGamal and is based on the difficulty of finding discrete logarithms. The other is due to McEliece and uses error correcting codes. There are also public key systems based on the knapsack problem. We don't cover them in this book; some versions have been broken and they are generally suspected to be weaker than systems such as RSA and ElGamal.

A **public key cryptosystem** is built up of several components. First, there is the set M of possible messages (potential plaintexts and ciphertexts). There is also the set K of "keys." These are not exactly the encryption/decryption keys; in RSA, a key k is a triple (e, d, n) with $ed \equiv 1$ (mod $\phi(n)$). For each key k, there is an encryption function E_k and a decryption function D_k. Usually, E_k and D_k are assumed to map M to M, though it would be possible to have variations that allow the plaintexts and ciphertexts to come from different sets. These components must satisfy the following requirements:

1. $E_k(D_k(m)) = m$ and $D_k(E_k(m)) = m$ for every $m \in M$ and every $k \in K$.

2. For every m and every k, the values of $E_k(m)$ and $D_k(m)$ are easy to compute.

3. For almost every $k \in K$, if someone knows only the function E_k, it is computationally infeasible to find an algorithm to compute D_k.

4. Given $k \in K$, it is easy to find the functions E_k and D_k.

Requirement (1) says that encryption and decryption cancel each other. Requirement (2) is needed; otherwise, efficient encryption and decryption would not be possible. Because of (4), a user can choose a secret random k from K and obtain functions E_k and D_k. Requirement (3) is what makes the system public key. Since it is difficult to determine D_k from E_k, it is possible to publish E_k without compromising the security of the system.

Let's see how RSA satisfies these requirements. The message space can be taken to be all nonnegative integers. As we mentioned previously, a key for RSA is a triple $k = (e, d, n)$. The encryption function is

$$E_k(m) = m^e \pmod{n},$$

where we break m into blocks if $m \geq n$. The decryption function is

$$D_k(m) = m^d \pmod{n},$$

again with m broken into blocks if needed. The functions E_k and D_k are immediately determined from knowledge of k (requirement (4)) and are easy to compute (requirement (2)). They are inverses of each other since $ed \equiv 1$ (mod $\phi(n)$), so (1) is satisfied. If we know E_k, which means we know e and n, then we have seen that it is (probably) computationally infeasible to determine d, hence D_k. Therefore, (3) is (probably) satisfied.

Once a public key system is set up, each user generates a key k and determines E_k and D_k. The encryption function E_k is made public, while

D_k is kept secret. If there is a problem with impostors, a trusted authority can be used to distribute and verify keys.

In a symmetric system, Bob can be sure that a message that decrypts successfully must have come from Alice (who could really be a group of authorized users) or someone who has Alice's key. Only Alice has been given the key, so no one else could produce the ciphertext. However, Alice could deny sending the message since Bob could have simply encrypted the message himself. Therefore, authentication is easy (Bob knows that the message came from Alice, if he didn't forge it himself) but non-repudiation is not (see Section 1.2).

In a public key system, anyone can encrypt a message and send it to Bob, so he will have no idea where it came from. He certainly won't be able to prove it came from Alice. Therefore, more steps are needed for authentication and non-repudiation. However, these goals are easily accomplished as follows.

Alice starts with her message m and computes $E_{k_b}(D_{k_a}(m))$, where k_a is Alice's key and k_b is Bob's key. Then Bob can decrypt using D_{k_b} to obtain $D_{k_a}(m)$. He uses the publicly available E_{k_a} to obtain $E_{k_a}(D_{k_a}(m)) = m$. Bob knows that the message must have come from Alice since no one else could have computed $D_{k_a}(m)$. For the same reason, Alice cannot deny sending the message. Of course, all this assumes that most random "messages" are meaningless, so it is unlikely that a random string of symbols decrypts to a meaningful message unless the string was the encryption of something meaningful.

Concrete versions of these methods of authentication will be discussed in Chapter 8 on digital signatures.

It is possible to use one-way functions with certain properties to construct a public key cryptosystem. Let $f(m)$ be an invertible one-way function. This means $f(x)$ is easy to compute, but, given y, it is computationally infeasible to find the unique value of x such that $y = f(x)$. Now suppose $f(x)$ has a **trapdoor**, which means that there is an easy way to solve $y = f(x)$ for x, but only with some extra information known only to the designer of the function. Moreover, it should be computationally infeasible for someone other than the designer of the function to determine this trapdoor information. If there is a very large family of one-way functions with trapdoors, they can be used to form a public key cryptosystem. Each user generates a function from the family in such a way that only that user knows the trapdoor. The user's function is then published as a public encryption algorithm. When Alice wants to send a message m to Bob, she looks up his function $f_b(x)$ and computes $y = f_b(m)$. Alice sends y to Bob. Since Bob knows the trapdoor for $f_b(x)$, he can solve $y = f_b(m)$ and thus find m.

In RSA, the functions $f(x) = x^e \pmod{n}$, for appropriate n and e, form the family of one-way functions. The trapdoor information is the factorization of n. In the ElGamal system (Section 7.4), the one-way function is obtained from exponentiation modulo a prime, and the trapdoor information is knowledge of a discrete log. In the McEliece system (Section 16.10), the trapdoor information is an efficient way for finding the nearest codeword ("error correction") for certain linear binary codes.

6.8 Exercises

1. The ciphertext 5859 was obtained from the RSA algorithm using $n = 11413$ and $e = 7467$. Using the factorization $11413 = 101 \cdot 113$, find the plaintext.

2. Let p be a large prime. Suppose you encrypt a message x by computing $y \equiv x^e \pmod{p}$ for some (suitably chosen) encryption exponent e. How do you find a decryption exponent d such that $y^d \equiv x \pmod{p}$?

3. Let p be a large prime. Alice wants to send a message m to Bob, where $1 \le m \le p - 1$. Alice and Bob choose integers a and b relatively prime to $p - 1$. Alice computes $c \equiv m^a \pmod{p}$ and sends c to Bob. Bob computes $d \equiv c^b \pmod{p}$ and sends d back to Alice. Since Alice knows a, she finds a_1 such that $aa_1 \equiv 1 \pmod{p - 1}$. Then she computes $e \equiv d^{a_1} \pmod{p}$ and sends e to Bob. Explain what Bob must now do to obtain m, and show that this works.

4. Naive Nelson uses RSA to receive a single ciphertext c, corresponding to the message m. His public modulus is n and his public encryption exponent is e. Since he feels guilty that his system was used only once, he agrees to decrypt any ciphertext that someone sends him, as long as it is not c, and return the answer to that person. Evil Eve sends him the ciphertext $2^e c$ $\pmod{n}$. Show how this allows Eve to find m.

5. In order to increase security, Bob chooses n and two encryption exponents e_1, e_2. He asks Alice to encrypt her message m to him by first computing $c_1 \equiv m^{e_1} \pmod{n}$, then encrypting c_1 to get $c_2 \equiv c_1^{e_2} \pmod{n}$. Alice then sends c_2 to Bob. Does this double encryption increase security over single encryption? Why or why not?

6. Let p and q be distinct odd primes, and let $n = pq$. Suppose that the integer x satisfies $\gcd(x, pq) = 1$.
(a) Show that $x^{\frac{1}{2}\phi(n)} \equiv 1 \pmod{p}$ and $x^{\frac{1}{2}\phi(n)} \equiv 1 \pmod{q}$.
(b) Use (a) to show that $x^{\frac{1}{2}\phi(n)} \equiv 1 \pmod{n}$.

(c) Use (b) to show that if $ed \equiv 1 \pmod{\frac{1}{2}\phi(n)}$ then $x^{ed} \equiv x \pmod{n}$. (This shows that we could work with $\frac{1}{2}\phi(n)$ instead of $\phi(n)$ in RSA.)

7. The exponents $e = 1$ and $e = 2$ should not be used in RSA. Why?

8. Suppose that there are two users on a network. Let their RSA moduli be n_1 and n_2, with n_1 not equal to n_2. If you are told that n_1 and n_2 are not relatively prime, how would you break their systems?

9. You are trying to factor $n = 642401$. Suppose you discover that

$$516107^2 \equiv 7 \pmod{n}$$

and that

$$187722^2 \equiv 2^2 \cdot 7 \pmod{n}.$$

Use this information to factor n.

10. Suppose two users Alice and Bob have the same RSA modulus n and suppose that their encryption exponents e_A and e_B are relatively prime. Charles wants to send the message m to Alice and Bob, so he encrypts to get $c_A \equiv m^{e_A}$ and $c_B \equiv m^{e_B} \pmod{n}$. Show how Eve can find m if she intercepts c_A and c_B.

11. Suppose Alice uses the RSA method as follows. She starts with a message consisting of several letters, and assigns $a = 1, b = 2, \ldots, z = 26$. She then encrypts each letter separately. For example, if her message is *cat*, she calculates $3^e \pmod{n}$, $1^e \pmod{n}$, and $20^e \pmod{n}$. Then she sends the encrypted message to Bob. Explain how Eve can find the message without factoring n. In particular, suppose $n = 8881$ and $e = 13$. Eve intercepts the message

$$4461 \qquad 794 \qquad 2015 \qquad 2015 \qquad 3603.$$

Find the message without factoring 8881.

12. Show that if $x^2 \equiv y^2 \pmod{n}$ and $x \not\equiv \pm y \pmod{n}$, then $\gcd(x+y, n)$ is a nontrivial factor of n.

13. Let $n = pq$ be the product of two distinct primes.
(a) Let m be a multiple of $\phi(n)$. Show that if $\gcd(a, n) = 1$, then $a^m \equiv 1 \pmod{p}$ and $\pmod{q}$.
(b) Suppose m is as in part (a), and let a be arbitrary (possibly $\gcd(a, n) \neq 1$). Show that $a^{m+1} \equiv a \pmod{p}$ and $\pmod{q}$.

(c) Let e and d be encryption and decryption exponents for RSA with modulus n. Show that $a^{ed} \equiv a \pmod{n}$ for all a. This shows that we do not need to assume $\gcd(a, n) = 1$ in order to use RSA.

(d) If p and q are large, why is it likely that $\gcd(a, n) = 1$ for a randomly chosen a?

14. Suppose $n = pqr$ is the product of three distinct primes. How would an RSA-type scheme work in this case? In particular, what relation would e and d satisfy?

Note: There does not seem to be any advantage in using three primes instead of two. The running times of some factorization methods depend on the size of the smallest prime factor. Therefore, if three primes are used, the size of n must be increased in order to achieve the same level of security as obtained with two primes.

15. Let $p = 7919$ and $q = 17389$. Let $e = 66909025$. A calculation shows that $e^2 \equiv 1 \pmod{(p-1)(q-1)}$. Alice decides to encrypt the message $m = 12345$ using RSA with modulus $n = pq$ and exponent e. Since she wants the encryption to be very secure, she encrypts the ciphertext, again using n and e (so she has double encrypted the original plaintext). What is the final ciphertext that she sends? Justify your answer without using a calculator.

16. Suppose you are using RSA (with modulus $n = pq$ and encrypting exponent e), but you decide to restrict your messages to numbers m satisfying $m^{1000} \equiv 1 \pmod{n}$.

(a) Show that if d satisfies $de \equiv 1 \pmod{1000}$, then d works as a decryption exponent for these messages.

(b) Assume that both p and q are congruent to 1 mod 1000. Determine how many messages satisfy $m^{1000} \equiv 1 \pmod{n}$. You may assume and use the fact that $m^{1000} \equiv 1 \pmod{r}$ has 1000 solutions when r is a prime congruent to 1 mod 1000.

17. Suppose Bob's encryption company produces two machines, A and B, both of which are supposed to be implementations of RSA using the same modulus $n = pq$ for some unknown primes p and q. Both machines also use the same encryption exponent e. Each machine receives a message m and outputs a ciphertext that is supposed to be $m^e \pmod{n}$. Machine A always produces the correct output. However, Machine B, because of implementation and hardware errors, always outputs a ciphertext $c \pmod{n}$ such that $c \equiv m^e \pmod{p}$ and $c \equiv m^e + 1 \pmod{q}$. How could you use machines A and B to find p and q? (See Computer Problem 11 for a discussion of how such a situation could arise.)

6.9   Computer Problems

Note: Many of the numbers in the following problems are too large for MATLAB without the assistance of the Maple Kernel.

1. Paul Revere's friend in a tower at M.I.T. says he'll send the message *one* if (the British are coming) by land and *two* if by sea. Since they know that RSA will be invented in the Boston area, they decide that the message should be encrypted using RSA with $n = 712446816787$ and $e = 6551$. Paul Revere receives the ciphertext 273095689186. What was the plaintext?

2. In an RSA cryptosystem, suppose you know $n = 718548065973745507$, $e = 3449$, and $d = 543546506135745129$. Factor n.

3. Choose two 30-digit primes p and q, and an encryption exponent e. Encrypt each of the plaintexts *cat, bat, hat, encyclopedia, antidisestablishmentarianism*. Can you tell from looking at the ciphertexts that the first three plaintexts differ in only one letter or that the last two plaintexts are much longer than the first three?

4. Factor 618240007109027021 by the $p - 1$ method.

5. Factor 8834884587090814646372459890377418962766907 by the $p - 1$ method. (The number is stored as *n1*.)

6. Let $n = 537069139875071$. Suppose you know that

$$85975324443166^2 \equiv 4624361062261^2 \pmod{n}.$$

Factor n.

7. Let $n = 84047 \cdot 65497$. Find x and y with $x^2 \equiv y^2 \pmod{n}$ but $x \not\equiv \pm y \pmod{n}$.

8. (a) Suppose you know that

$$33335^2 \equiv 670705093^2 \pmod{670726081}.$$

Use this information to factor 670726081.
(b) Suppose you know that $3^2 \equiv 670726078^2 \pmod{670726081}$. Why won't this information help you to factor 670726081?

9. Suppose you know that

$$
\begin{aligned}
2^{958230} &\equiv 1488665 \pmod{3837523} \\
2^{1916460} &\equiv 1 \pmod{3837523}.
\end{aligned}
$$

How would you use this information to factor 3837523? Note that the exponent 1916460 is twice the exponent 958230.

10. (a) Suppose the primes p and q used in the RSA algorithm are consecutive primes. How would you factor $n = pq$?
(b) The ciphertext 10787770728 was encrypted using $n = 10993522499$ and $e = 113$. The factors p and q of n were chosen so that $q - p = 2$. Decrypt the message.
(c) The following ciphertext c was encrypted mod n using the exponent e:

$$n = 1524157875019059857018818321508350890378588686212111004433$$

$$e = 9007$$

$$c = 141077461765569500241199505617854673388398574333341423525.$$

The prime factors p and q of n are consecutive primes. Decrypt the message. (n is stored as *naive*, c is stored as *cnaive*.)

11. Let $p = 123456791$, $q = 987654323$, and $e = 127$. Let the message be $m = 14152019010605$.
(a) Compute $m^e \pmod{p}$ and $m^e \pmod{q}$; then use the Chinese remainder theorem to combine these to get $c \equiv m^e \pmod{pq}$.
(b) Change one digit of $m^e \pmod{p}$ (for example, this could be caused by some radiation). Now combine this with $m^e \pmod{q}$ to get an incorrect value f for $m^e \pmod{pq}$. Compute $\gcd(c - f, pq)$. Why does this factor pq? The method of (a) for computing $m^e \pmod{pq}$ is attractive since it does not require as large multiprecision arithmetic as working directly mod pq. However, as part (b) shows, if an attacker can cause an occasional bit to fail, then pq can be factored.

12. Suppose that $p = 76543692179$, $q = 343434343453$, and $e = 457$. The ciphertext $c \equiv m^e \pmod{pq}$ is transmitted, but an error occurs during transmission. The received ciphertext is 2304329328016936947195. The receiver is able to determine that the digits received are correct but that last digit is missing. Determine the missing digit and decrypt the message.

13. Test 38200901201 for primality using the Miller-Rabin test with $a = 2$. Then test using $a = 3$. Note that the first test says that 38200901201 is probably prime, while the second test says that it is composite. A composite number such as 38200901201 that passes the Miller-Rabin test for a number a is called a **strong a-pseudoprime**.

14. (a) Suppose there are three users with pairwise relatively prime moduli n_1, n_2, n_3, but suppose their encryption exponents are all $e = 3$. If the same message is sent to each of them and you intercept the ciphertexts, how can you determine the message (without factoring)?

(b) Suppose

$$n_1 = 2469247531693, \quad n_2 = 11111502225583, \quad n_3 = 44444222221411$$

and the corresponding ciphertexts are

$$359335245251, \quad 10436363975495, \quad 5135984059593.$$

These were all encrypted using $e = 3$. Find the message. (*Hint:* The Chinese remainder theorem will be helpful. So will $x^{1/3}$.)

Chapter 7

Discrete Logarithms

7.1 Discrete Logarithms

In the RSA algorithm, we saw how the difficulty of factoring yields useful cryptosystems. There is another number theory problem, namely discrete logarithms, that has similar applications.

Fix a prime p. Let α and β be nonzero integers mod p and suppose

$$\beta \equiv \alpha^x \pmod{p}.$$

The problem of finding x is called the **discrete logarithm problem**. If n is the smallest positive integer such that $\alpha^n \equiv 1 \pmod{p}$, we may assume $0 \le x < n$, and then we denote

$$x = L_\alpha(\beta)$$

and call it the discrete log of β with respect to α (the prime p is omitted from the notation).

For example, let $p = 11$ and let $\alpha = 2$. Since $2^6 \equiv 9 \pmod{11}$, we have $L_2(9) = 6$. Of course, $2^6 \equiv 2^{16} \equiv 2^{26} \equiv 9 \pmod{11}$, so we could consider taking any one of 6, 16, 26 as the discrete logarithm. But we fix the value by taking the smallest nonnegative value, namely 6. Note that we could have defined the discrete logarithm in this case to be the congruence class 6 mod

165

10. In some ways, this would be more natural, but there are applications where it is convenient to have a number, not just a congruence class.

Often, α is taken to be a primitive root mod p, which means that every β is a power of α (mod p). If α is not a primitive root, then the discrete logarithm will not be defined for certain values of β.

Given a prime p, it is fairly easy to find a primitive root in many cases. See Exercise 3.10.

The discrete log behaves in many ways like the usual logarithm. In particular, if α is a primitive root mod p, then

$$L_\alpha(\beta_1\beta_2) \equiv L_\alpha(\beta_1) + L_\alpha(\beta_2) \pmod{p-1}$$

(see Exercise 3).

When p is small, it is easy to compute discrete logs by exhaustive search through all possible exponents. However, when p is large this is not feasible. We give some ways of attacking discrete log problems later. However, it is believed that discrete logs are hard to compute in general. This assumption is the basis of several cryptosystems.

The size of the largest primes for which discrete logs can be computed has usually been approximately the same size as the size of largest integers that could be factored (both of these refer to computations that would work for arbitrary numbers of these sizes; special choices of integers will succumb to special techniques, and thus discrete log computations and factorizations work for much larger specially chosen numbers). In the year 2001, a discrete log was computed for a 110-digit prime, which was the record at that time. The record factorization up to then was 155 digits.

A function $f(x)$ is called a **one-way function** if $f(x)$ is easy to compute, but, given y, it is computationally infeasible to find x with $f(x) = y$. Modular exponentiation is probably an example of such a function. It is easy to compute α^x (mod p), but solving $\alpha^x \equiv \beta$ for x is probably hard. Multiplication of large primes can also be regarded as a (probable) one-way function: It is easy to multiply primes but difficult to factor the result to recover the primes. One-way functions have many cryptographic uses.

7.2   Computing Discrete Logs

In this section, we present some methods for computing discrete logarithms. Another useful method, the important birthday attack, is discussed in Section 8.4.

For simplicity, take α to be a primitive root mod p, so $p-1$ is the smallest positive exponent n such that $\alpha^n \equiv 1$ (mod p). This implies that

$$\alpha^{m_1} \equiv \alpha^{m_2} \pmod{p} \iff m_1 \equiv m_2 \pmod{p-1}.$$

Assume that

$$\beta \equiv \alpha^x, \quad 0 \le x < p - 1.$$

We want to find x.

First, it's easy to determine $x \pmod 2$. Note that

$$\left(\alpha^{(p-1)/2}\right)^2 \equiv \alpha^{p-1} \equiv 1 \pmod p,$$

so $\alpha^{(p-1)/2} \equiv \pm 1 \pmod p$ (see Exercise 3.4). However, $p - 1$ is assumed to be the smallest exponent to yield $+1$, so we must have

$$\alpha^{(p-1)/2} \equiv -1 \pmod p.$$

Starting with $\beta \equiv \alpha^x \pmod p$, raise both sides to the $(p-1)/2$ power to obtain

$$\beta^{(p-1)/2} \equiv \alpha^{x(p-1)/2} \equiv (-1)^x \pmod p.$$

Therefore, if $\beta^{(p-1)/2} \equiv +1$, then x is even; otherwise, x is odd.

Example. Suppose we want to solve $2^x \equiv 9 \pmod{11}$. Since

$$\beta^{(p-1)/2} \equiv 9^5 \equiv 1 \pmod{11},$$

we must have x even. In fact, $x = 6$, as we saw previously. ∎

The Pohlig-Hellman Algorithm

The preceding idea was extended by Pohlig and Hellman to give an algorithm to compute discrete logs when $p - 1$ has only small prime factors. Suppose

$$p - 1 = \prod_i q_i^{r_i}$$

is the factorization of $p - 1$ into primes. Let q^r be one of the factors. We'll compute $L_\alpha(\beta) \pmod{q^r}$. If this can be done for each $q_i^{r_i}$, the answers can be recombined using the Chinese remainder theorem to find the discrete logarithm.

Write

$$x = x_0 + x_1 q + x_2 q^2 + \cdots \text{ with } 0 \le x_i \le q - 1.$$

We'll determine the coefficients $x_0, x_1, \ldots x_{r-1}$ successively, and thus obtain $x \bmod q^r$. Note that

$$\begin{aligned} x\left(\frac{p-1}{q}\right) &= x_0\left(\frac{p-1}{q}\right) + (p-1)(x_1 + x_2 q + x_3 q^2 + \cdots) \\ &= x_0\left(\frac{p-1}{q}\right) + (p-1)n, \end{aligned}$$

where n is an integer. Starting with $\beta \equiv \alpha^x$, raise both sides to the $(p-1)/q$ power to obtain

$$\beta^{(p-1)/q} \equiv \alpha^{x(p-1)/q} \equiv \alpha^{x_0(p-1)/q}(\alpha^{p-1})^n \equiv \alpha^{x_0(p-1)/q} \pmod{p}.$$

The last congruence is a consequence of Fermat's theorem: $\alpha^{p-1} \equiv 1 \pmod{p}$. To find x_0, simply look at the powers

$$\alpha^{k(p-1)/q} \pmod{p}, \quad k = 0, 1, 2, \ldots, q-1,$$

until one of them yields $\beta^{(p-1)/q}$. Then $x_0 = k$. Note that since $\alpha^{m_1} \equiv \alpha^{m_2} \iff m_1 \equiv m_2 \pmod{p-1}$, and since the exponents $k(p-1)/q$ are distinct mod $p-1$, there is a unique k that yields the answer.

An extension of this idea yields the remaining coefficients. Assume $q^2 | p - 1$. Let

$$\beta_1 \equiv \beta\alpha^{-x_0} \equiv \alpha^{q(x_1 + x_2 q + \cdots)} \pmod{p}.$$

Raise both sides to the $(p-1)/q^2$ power to obtain

$$\begin{aligned} \beta_1^{(p-1)/q^2} &\equiv \alpha^{(p-1)(x_1 + x_2 q + \cdots)/q} \\ &\equiv \alpha^{x_1(p-1)/q}(\alpha^{p-1})^{x_2 + x_3 q + \cdots} \\ &\equiv \alpha^{x_1(p-1)/q} \pmod{p}. \end{aligned}$$

The last congruence follows by applying Fermat's theorem. We couldn't calculate $\beta_1^{(p-1)/q^2}$ as $(\beta_1^{p-1})^{1/q^2}$ since fractional exponents cause problems. Note that every exponent we have used is an integer.

To find x_1, simply look at the powers

$$\alpha^{k(p-1)/q} \pmod{p}, \quad k = 0, 1, 2, \ldots, q-1,$$

until one of them yields $\beta_1^{(p-1)/q^2}$. Then $x_1 = k$.

If $q^3 | p-1$, let $\beta_2 \equiv \beta_1\alpha^{-x_1 q}$ and raise both sides to the $(p-1)/q^3$ power to obtain x_2. In this way, we can continue until we find that q^{r+1} doesn't divide $p-1$. Since we cannot use fractional exponents, we must stop. But we have determined $x_0, x_1, \ldots, x_{r-1}$, so we know $x \bmod q^r$.

Repeat the procedure for all the prime factors of $p-1$. This yields x mod $q_i^{r_i}$ for all i. The Chinese remainder theorem allows us to combine these into a congruence for $x \bmod p-1$. Since $0 \le x < p-1$, this determines x.

Example. Let $p = 41$, $\alpha = 7$, and $\beta = 12$. We want to solve

$$7^x \equiv 12 \pmod{41}.$$

Note that
$$41 - 1 = 2^3 \cdot 5.$$

First, let $q = 2$ and let's find $x \mod 2^3$. Write $x \equiv x_0 + 2x_1 + 4x_2 \pmod 8$. To start,
$$\beta^{(p-1)/2} \equiv 12^{20} \equiv 40 \equiv -1 \pmod{41},$$

and
$$\alpha^{(p-1)/2} \equiv 7^{20} \equiv -1 \pmod{41}.$$

Since
$$\beta^{(p-1)/2} \equiv (\alpha^{(p-1)/2})^{x_0} \pmod{41},$$

we have $x_0 = 1$. Next,
$$\beta_1 \equiv \beta\alpha^{-x_0} \equiv 12 \cdot 7^{-1} \equiv 31 \pmod{41}.$$

Also,
$$\beta_1^{(p-1)/2^2} \equiv 31^{10} \equiv 1 \pmod{41}.$$

Since
$$\beta_1^{(p-1)/2^2} \equiv (\alpha^{(p-1)/2})^{x_1} \pmod{41},$$

we have $x_1 = 0$. Continuing, we have
$$\beta_2 \equiv \beta_1\alpha^{-2x_1} \equiv 31 \cdot 7^0 \equiv 31 \pmod{41},$$

and
$$\beta_2^{(p-1)/q^3} \equiv 31^5 \equiv -1 \equiv (\alpha^{(p-1)/2})^{x_2} \pmod{41}.$$

Therefore $x_2 = 1$. We have obtained
$$x \equiv x_0 + 2x_1 + 4x_2 \equiv 1 + 4 \equiv 5 \pmod 8.$$

Now, let $q = 5$ and let's find $x \mod 5$. We have
$$\beta^{(p-1)/5} \equiv 12^8 \equiv 18 \pmod{41}$$

and
$$\alpha^{(p-1)/q} \equiv 7^8 \equiv 37 \pmod{41}.$$

Trying the possible values of k yields
$$37^0 \equiv 1, \quad 37^1 \equiv 37, \quad 37^2 \equiv 16, \quad 37^3 \equiv 18, \quad 37^4 \equiv 10 \pmod{41}.$$

Therefore, 37^3 gives the desired answer, so $x \equiv 3 \pmod 5$.

Since $x \equiv 5 \pmod 8$ and $x \equiv 3 \pmod 5$, we combine these to obtain $x \equiv 13 \pmod{40}$, so $x = 13$. A quick calculation checks that $7^{13} \equiv 12 \pmod{41}$, as desired. ∎

As long as the primes q involved in the preceding algorithm are reasonably small, the calculations can be done quickly. However, when q is large, calculating the numbers $\alpha^{k(p-1)/q}$ for $k = 0, 1, 2, \ldots, q-1$ becomes infeasible, so the algorithm no longer is practical. This means that if we want a discrete logarithm to be hard, we should make sure that $p-1$ has a large prime factor.

Note that even if $p - 1 = tq$ has a large prime factor q, the algorithm can determine discrete logs mod t if t is composed of small prime factors. For this reason, often β is chosen to be a power of α^t. Then the discrete log is automatically 0 mod t, so the discrete log hides only mod q information, which the algorithm cannot find. If the discrete log x represents a secret (or better, t times a secret), this means that an attacker does not obtain partial information by determining x mod t, since there is no information hidden this way. This idea is used in the Digital Signature Algorithm, which we discuss in Chapter 8.

The Index Calculus

The idea is similar to the quadratic sieve method of factoring. Again, we are trying to solve $\beta \equiv \alpha^x \pmod{p}$, where p is a large prime and α is a primitive root.

First, there is a precomputation step. Let B be a bound and let p_1, p_2, $\ldots$, p_m be the primes less than B. This set of primes is called our **factor base**. Compute $\alpha^k \pmod{p}$ for several values of k. For each such number, try to write it as a product of the primes less than B. If this is not the case, discard α^k. However, if $\alpha^k \equiv \prod p_i^{a_i} \pmod{p}$, then

$$k \equiv \sum a_i L_\alpha(p_i) \pmod{p-1}.$$

When we obtain enough such relations, we can solve for $L_\alpha(p_i)$ for each i.

Now, for random integers r, compute $\beta\alpha^r \pmod{p}$. For each such number, try to write it as a product of primes less than B. If we succeed, we have $\beta\alpha^r \equiv \prod p_i^{b_i} \pmod{p}$, which means

$$L_\alpha(\beta) \equiv -r + \sum b_i L_\alpha(p_i) \pmod{p-1}.$$

This algorithm is effective if p is of moderate size. This means that p should be chosen to have at least 200 digits, maybe more, if the discrete log problem is to be hard.

Example. Let $p = 131$ and $\alpha = 2$. Let $B = 10$, so we are working with the primes 2,3,5,7. A calculation yields the following:

$$2^1 \equiv 2 \pmod{131}$$
$$2^8 \equiv 5^3 \pmod{131}$$
$$2^{12} \equiv 5 \cdot 7 \pmod{131}$$
$$2^{14} \equiv 3^2 \pmod{131}$$
$$2^{34} \equiv 3 \cdot 5^2 \pmod{131}.$$

Therefore,

$$1 \equiv L_2(2) \pmod{130}$$
$$8 \equiv 3L_2(5) \pmod{130}$$
$$12 \equiv L_2(5) + L_2(7) \pmod{130}$$
$$14 \equiv 2L_2(3) \pmod{130}$$
$$34 \equiv L_2(3) + 2L_2(5) \pmod{130}.$$

The second congruence yields $L_2(5) \equiv 46 \pmod{130}$. Substituting this into the third congruence yields $L_2(7) \equiv -34 \equiv 96 \pmod{130}$. The fourth congruence only yields the value of $L_2(3) \pmod{65}$ since $\gcd(2, 130) \neq 1$. This gives two choices for $L_2(3) \pmod{130}$. Of course, we could try them and see which works. Or we could use the fifth congruence to obtain $L_2(3) \equiv 72 \pmod{130}$. This finishes the precomputation step.

Suppose now that we want to find $L_2(37)$. Trying a few randomly chosen exponents yields $37 \cdot 2^{43} \equiv 3 \cdot 5 \cdot 7 \pmod{131}$, so

$$L_2(37) \equiv -43 + L_2(3) + L_2(5) + L_2(7) \equiv 41 \pmod{130}.$$

Therefore, $L_2(37) = 41$.   ∎

Of course, once the precomputation has been done, it can be reused for computing several discrete logs for the same prime p.

Computing Discrete Logs Mod 4

When $p \equiv 1 \pmod 4$, the Pohlig-Hellman algorithm computes discrete logs mod 4 quite quickly. What happens when $p \equiv 3 \pmod 4$? The Pohlig-Hellman algorithm won't work, since it would require us to raise numbers to the $(p-1)/4$ power, which would yield the ambiguity of a fractional exponent. The surprising fact is that if we have an algorithm that quickly computes discrete logs mod 4 for a prime $p \equiv 3 \pmod 4$, then we can use it to compute discrete logs mod p quickly. Therefore, it is unlikely that such an algorithm exists.

There is a philosophical reason that we should not expect such an algorithm. A natural point of view is that the discrete log should be regarded as a number mod $p - 1$. Therefore, we should be able to obtain information on the discrete log only modulo the power of 2 that appears in $p - 1$. When $p \equiv 3 \pmod 4$, this means that asking questions about discrete logs mod 4 is somewhat unnatural. The question is possible only because we normalized the discrete log to be an integer between 0 and $p - 2$. For example, $2^6 \equiv 2^{16} \equiv 9 \pmod{11}$. We defined $L_2(9)$ to be 6 in this case; if we had allowed it also to be 16, we would have two values for $L_2(9)$, namely 6 and 16, that are not congruent mod 4. Therefore, from this point of view, we shouldn't even be asking about $L_2(9) \mod 4$.

We need the following lemma, which is similar to the method for computing square roots mod a prime $p \equiv 3 \pmod 4$ (see Section 3.9).

Lemma. *Let $p \equiv 3 \pmod 4$ be prime, let $r \geq 2$, and let y be an integer. Suppose α and γ are two nonzero numbers mod p such that $\gamma \equiv \alpha^{2^r y} \pmod p$. Then*

$$\gamma^{(p+1)/4} \equiv \alpha^{2^{r-1}y} \pmod p.$$

Proof.

$$\gamma^{(p+1)/4} \equiv \alpha^{(p+1)2^{r-2}y} \equiv \alpha^{2^{r-1}y}(\alpha^{p-1})^{2^{r-2}y} \equiv \alpha^{2^{r-1}y} \pmod p.$$

The final congruence is because of Fermat's theorem.   □

Fix the prime $p \equiv 3 \pmod 4$ and let α be a primitive root. Assume we have a machine that, given an input β, gives the output $L_\alpha(\beta) \mod 4$. As we saw previously, it is easy to compute $L_\alpha(\beta) \mod 2$. So the new information supplied by the machine is really only the second bit of the discrete log.

Now assume $\alpha^x \equiv \beta \pmod p$ let $x = x_0 + 2x_1 + 4x_2 + \cdots + 2^n x_n$ be the binary expansion of x. Using the $L_\alpha(\beta) \pmod 4$ machine, we determine x_0 and x_1. Suppose we have determined $x_0, x_1, \ldots, x_{r-1}$ with $r \geq 2$. Let

$$\beta_r \equiv \beta\alpha^{-(x_0 + \cdots + 2^{r-1}x_{r-1})} \equiv \alpha^{2^r(x_r + 2x_{r+1} + \cdots)}.$$

Using the lemma $r - 1$ times, we find

$$\beta_r^{((p+1)/4)^{r-1}} \equiv \alpha^{2(x_r + 2x_{r+1} + \cdots)} \pmod p.$$

Applying the $L_\alpha \pmod 4$ machine to this equation yields the value of x_r. Proceeding inductively, we obtain all the values $x_0, x_1, \ldots, x_n$. This determines x, as desired.

It is possible to make this algorithm more efficient. See, for example, [Stinson, page 175].

In conclusion, if we believe that finding discrete logs for $p \equiv 3 \pmod 4$ is hard, then so is computing such discrete logs mod 4.

7.3   Bit Commitment

Alice claims that she has a method to predict the outcome of football games. She wants to sell her method to Bob. Bob asks her to prove her method works by predicting the results of the games that will be played this weekend. "No way," says Alice. "Then you will simply make your bets and not pay me. If you want me to prove my system works, why don't I show you my predictions for last week's games?" Clearly there is a problem here. We'll show how to resolve it.

Here's the setup. Alice wants to send a bit b, which is either 0 or 1, to Bob. There are two requirements.

1. Bob cannot determine the value of the bit without Alice's help.

2. Alice cannot change the bit once she sends it.

One way is for Alice to put the bit in a box, put her lock on it, and send it to Bob. When Bob wants the value of the bit, Alice removes the lock and Bob opens the box. We want to implement this mathematically in such a way that Alice and Bob do not have to be in the same room when the bit is revealed.

Here is a solution. Alice and Bob agree on a large prime $p \equiv 3 \pmod 4$ and a primitive root α. Alice chooses a random number $x < p - 1$ whose second bit x_1 is b. She sends $\beta \equiv \alpha^x \pmod p$ to Bob. We assume that Bob cannot compute discrete logs for p. As pointed out in the last section, this means that he cannot compute discrete logs mod 4. In particular, he cannot determine the value of $b = x_1$. When Bob wants to know the value of b, Alice sends him the full value of x, and by looking at $x \mod 4$, he finds b. Alice cannot send a value of x different than the one already used, since Bob checks that $\beta \equiv \alpha^x \pmod p$, and this equation has a unique solution $x < p - 1$.

Back to football: For each game, Alice sends $b = 1$ if she predicts the team will win, $b = 0$ if she predicts it will lose. After the game has been played, Alice reveals the bit to Bob, who can see whether her predictions were correct. In this way, Bob cannot profit from the information by receiving it before the game, and Alice cannot change her predictions once the game has been played.

7.4   The ElGamal Public Key Cryptosystem

In Chapter 6, we studied a public key cryptosystem whose security is based on the difficulty of factoring. It is also possible to design a system whose security relies on the difficulty of computing discrete logarithms. This was done by ElGamal in 1985. This system does not quite fit the definition of a public key cryptosystem given at the end of Chapter 6, since the set of possible plaintexts (integers mod p) is not the same as the set of possible ciphertexts (pairs of integers (r, t) mod p). However, this technical point will not concern us.

Alice wants to send a message m to Bob. Bob chooses a large prime p and a primitive root α. Assume m is an integer with $0 \leq m < p$. If m is larger, break it into smaller blocks. Bob also chooses a secret integer a and computes $\beta \equiv \alpha^a \pmod{p}$. The information (p, α, β) is made public and is Bob's public key. Alice does the following:

1. Downloads (p, α, β)

2. Chooses a secret random integer k and computes $r \equiv \alpha^k \pmod{p}$

3. Computes $t \equiv \beta^k m \pmod{p}$

4. Sends the pair (r, t) to Alice

Bob decrypts by computing

$$tr^{-a} \equiv m \pmod{p}.$$

This works because

$$tr^{-a} \equiv \beta^k m (\alpha^k)^{-a} \equiv (\alpha^a)^k m \alpha^{-ak} \equiv m \pmod{p}.$$

If Eve determines a, then she can also decrypt by the same procedure that Bob uses. Therefore, it is important for Bob to keep a secret. The numbers α and β are public, and $\beta \equiv \alpha^a \pmod{p}$. The difficulty of computing discrete logs is what keeps a secure.

Since k is a random integer, β^k will be a random nonzero integer mod p. Therefore, $t \equiv \beta^k m \pmod{p}$ is m multiplied by a random integer, and t is random mod p (unless $m = 0$, which should be avoided, of course). Therefore, t gives Eve no information about m. Knowing r does not seem to give Eve enough additional information.

The integer k is difficult to determine from r, since this is again a discrete logarithm problem. However, if Eve finds k, she can then calculate $t\beta^{-k}$, which is m.

It is important that a different random k be used for each message. Suppose Alice encrypts messages m_1 and m_2 for Bob and uses the same value k for each message. Then r will be the same for both messages, so the ciphertexts will be (r, t_1) and (r, t_2). If Eve finds out the plaintext m_1, she can also determine m_2, as follows. Note that

$$t_1/m_1 \equiv \beta^k \equiv t_2/m_2 \pmod{p}.$$

Since Eve knows t_1 and t_2, she computes $m_2 \equiv t_2 m_1 / t_1 \pmod{p}$.

In Chapter 15, we'll meet an analog of the ElGamal method that uses elliptic curves.

7.5 Exercises

1. Let $p = 13$. Compute $L_2(3)$.

2. Let $p = 19$. Then 2 is a primitive root. Use the Pohlig-Hellman method to compute $L_2(14)$.

3. (a) Let α be a primitive root mod p. Show that

$$L_\alpha(\beta_1 \beta_2) \equiv L_\alpha(\beta_1) + L_\alpha(\beta_2) \pmod{p-1}.$$

(*Hint:* You need the proposition in Section 3.7.)
(b) More generally, let α be arbitrary. Show that

$$L_\alpha(\beta_1 \beta_2) \equiv L_\alpha(\beta_1) + L_\alpha(\beta_2) \pmod{\mathrm{ord}_p(\alpha)},$$

where $\mathrm{ord}_p(\alpha)$ is defined in Exercise 3.9.

4. (a) Suppose you have a random 500-digit prime p. Suppose some people want to store passwords, written as numbers. If x is the password, then the number $2^x \pmod{p}$ is stored in a file. When y is given as a password, the number $2^y \pmod{p}$ is compared with the entry for the user in the file. Suppose someone gains access to the file. Why is it hard to deduce the passwords?
(b) Suppose p is instead chosen to be a five-digit prime. Why would the system in part (a) not be secure?

5. Let's reconsider Exercise 3.11 from the point of view of the Pohlig-Hellman algorithm. The only prime q is 2. For k as in 3.11, write $k = x_0 + 2x_1 + \cdots + 2^{15} x_{15}$.
(a) Show that the Pohlig-Hellman algorithm yields

$$x_0 = x_1 = \cdots = x_{10} = 0$$

and

$$2 = \beta = \beta_1 = \cdots = \beta_{11}.$$

(b) Use the Pohlig-Hellman algorithm to compute k.

7.6   Computer Problems

1. Let $p = 53047$. Verify that $L_3(8576) = 1234$.

2. Let $p = 3989$.
(a) Show that $L_2(3925) = 2000$ and $L_2(1046) = 3000$.
(b) Compute $L_2(3925 \cdot 1046)$. (*Note:* The answer should be less than 3988.)

3. Let $p = 31$. Evaluate $L_3(24)$.

4. Let $p = 1201$. Use the Pohlig-Hellman algorithm to find $L_{11}(2)$.

Chapter 8

Digital Signatures

For years, people have been using various types of signatures to associate their identities to documents. In the middle ages, a nobleman sealed a document with a wax imprint of his insignia. The assumption was that the noble was the only person able to reproduce the insignia. In modern transactions, credit card slips are signed. The salesperson is supposed to verify the signature by comparing with the signature on the card. With the development of electronic commerce and electronic documents, these methods no longer suffice.

For example, suppose you want to sign an electronic document. Why can't you simply digitize your signature and append it to the document? Anyone who has access to it can simply remove the signature and add it to something else, for example, a check for a large amount of money. With classical signatures, this would require cutting the signature off the document, or photocopying it, and pasting it on the check. This would rarely pass for an acceptable signature. However, such an electronic forgery is quite easy and cannot be distinguished from the original.

Therefore, we require that digital signatures cannot be separated from the message and attached to another. That is, the signature is not only tied to the signer but also to the message that is being signed. Also, the digital signature needs to be easily verified by other parties. Digital signature schemes therefore consist of two distinct steps: the signing process, and the verification process.

In the following, we first present two signature schemes. We then make some elementary remarks about hash functions and discuss the Digital Signature Standard. We also discuss the important "birthday attacks" on discrete logarithms and signature schemes.

8.1   RSA Signatures

Bob has a document that Alice agrees to sign. They do the following:

1. Alice generates two large primes p, q, and computes $n = pq$. She chooses e_A such that $1 < e_A < \phi(n)$ with $\gcd(e_A, \phi(n)) = 1$, and calculates d_A such that $e_A d_A \equiv 1 \pmod{\phi(n)}$. Alice publishes (e_A, n) and keeps private d_A, p, q.

2. Alice's signature is
$$y \equiv m^{d_A} \pmod{n}.$$

3. The pair (m, y) is then made public.

Bob can then verify that Alice really signed the message by doing the following:

1. Download Alice's (e_A, n).

2. Calculate $z \equiv y^{e_A} \pmod{n}$. If $z = m$, then Bob accepts the signature as valid; otherwise the signature is not valid.

Suppose Eve wants to attach Alice's signature to another message m_1. She cannot simply use the pair (m_1, y), since $y^{e_A} \not\equiv m_1 \pmod{n}$. Therefore she needs y_1 with $y_1^{e_A} \equiv m_1 \pmod{n}$. This is the same problem as decrypting an RSA "ciphertext" m_1 to obtain the "plaintext" y_1. This is believed to be hard to do.

Another possibility is that Eve chooses y_1 first, then lets the message be $m_1 \equiv y_1^{e_A} \pmod{n}$. It does not appear that Alice can deny having signed the message m_1 under the present scheme. However, it is very unlikely that m_1 will be a meaningful message. It will probably be a random sequence of characters, and not a message committing her to give Eve millions of dollars. Therefore, Alice's claim that it has been forged will be believable.

There is a variation on this procedure that allows Alice to sign a document without knowing its contents. Suppose Bob has made an important discovery. He wants to record publicly what he has done (so he will have priority when it comes time to award Nobel prizes), but he does not want anyone else to know the details (so he can make a lot of money from his invention). Bob and Alice do the following. The message to be signed is m.

1. Alice chooses an RSA modulus n ($n = pq$, the product of two large primes), an encryption exponent e, and decryption exponent d. She makes n and e public while keeping p, q, d private. In fact, she can erase p, q, d from her computer's memory at the end of the signing procedure.

2. Bob chooses a random integer k (mod n) with $\gcd(k, n) = 1$ and computes $t \equiv k^e m$ (mod n). He sends t to Alice.

3. Alice signs t by computing $s \equiv t^d$ (mod n). She returns s to Bob.

4. Bob computes s/k (mod n). This is the signed message m^d.

Let's show that s/k is the signed message: Note that $k^{ed} \equiv (k^e)^d \equiv k$ (mod n), since this is simply the encryption, then decryption, of k in the RSA scheme. Therefore,

$$s/k \equiv t^d/k \equiv k^{ed}m^d/k \equiv m^d \pmod{n},$$

which is the signed message.

The choice of k is random, so k^e (mod n) is the RSA encryption of a random number, and hence random. Therefore, $k^e m$ (mod n) gives essentially no information about m (however, it would not hide a message such as $m = 0$). In this way, Alice knows nothing about the message she is signing.

Once the signing procedure is finished, Bob has the same signed message as he would have obtained via the standard signing procedure.

There are several potential dangers with this protocol. For example, Bob could have Alice sign a promise to pay him a million dollars. Safeguards are needed to prevent such problems. We will not discuss these here.

Schemes such as these, called **blind signatures**, have been developed by David Chaum, who has several patents on them.

8.2 The ElGamal Signature Scheme

The ElGamal encryption method from Section 7.4 can be modified to give a signature scheme. One feature that is different from RSA is that, with the ElGamal method, there are many different signatures that are valid for a given message.

Suppose Alice wants to sign a message. To start, she chooses a large prime p and a primitive root α. Alice next chooses a secret integer a such that $1 \leq a \leq p - 2$. and calculates $\beta \equiv \alpha^a$ (mod p). The values of p, α, and β are made public. The security of the system will be in the fact that a is kept private. It is difficult for an adversary to determine a from (p, α, β) since the discrete log problem is considered difficult.

In order for Alice to sign a message m, she does the following:

1. Selects a secret random k such that $\gcd(k, p-1) = 1$

2. Computes $r \equiv \alpha^k \pmod{p}$

3. Computes $s \equiv k^{-1}(m - ar) \pmod{p-1}$

The signed message is the triple (m, r, s).

Bob can verify the signature as follows:

1. Download Alice's public key (p, α, β).

2. Compute $v_1 \equiv \beta^r r^s \pmod{p}$, and $v_2 \equiv \alpha^m \pmod{p}$.

3. The signature is declared valid if and only if $v_1 \equiv v_2 \pmod{p}$.

We now show that the verification procedure works. Assume the signature is valid. Since $s \equiv k^{-1}(m - ar) \pmod{p-1}$, we have $sk \equiv m - ar \pmod{p-1}$, so $m \equiv sk + ar \pmod{p-1}$. Therefore (recall that a congruence mod $p-1$ in the exponent yields an overall congruence mod p),

$$v_2 \equiv \alpha^m \equiv \alpha^{sk+ar} \equiv (\alpha^a)^r (\alpha^k)^s \equiv \beta^r r^s \equiv v_1 \pmod{p}.$$

Suppose Eve discovers the value of a. Then she can perform the signing procedure and produce Alice's signature on any desired document. Therefore, it is very important that a remain secret.

If Eve has another message m, she cannot compute the corresponding s since she doesn't know a. Suppose she tries to bypass this step by choosing an s that satisfies the verification equation. This means she needs s to satisfy

$$\beta^r r^s \equiv \alpha^m \pmod{p}.$$

This can be rearranged to $r^s \equiv \beta^{-r} \alpha^m \pmod{p}$, which is a discrete logarithm problem. Therefore, it should be hard to find an appropriate s. If s is chosen first, the equation for r is similar to a discrete log problem, but more complicated. It is generally assumed that it is also difficult to solve. It is not known whether there is a way to choose r and s simultaneously, though this seems to be unlikely. Therefore, the signature scheme appears to be secure, as long as discrete logs mod p are difficult to compute (for example, $p-1$ should not be a product of small primes; see Section 7.2).

Suppose Alice wants to sign a second document. She must choose a new random value of k. Suppose instead that she uses the same k for messages m_1 and m_2. Then the same value of r is used in both signatures, so Eve will see that k has been used twice. The s values are different, call them s_1 and s_2. Eve knows that

$$s_1 k - m_1 \equiv -ar \equiv s_2 k - m_2 \pmod{p-1}.$$

Therefore,
$$(s_1 - s_2)k \equiv m_1 - m_2 \pmod{p-1}.$$

Let $d = \gcd(s_1 - s_2, p - 1)$. There are d solutions to the congruence, and they can be found by the procedure given in Section 3.3. Usually d is small, so there are not very many possible values of k. Eve computes α^k for each possible k until she gets the value r. She now knows k. Eve now solves

$$ar \equiv m_1 - ks_1 \pmod{p-1}$$

for a. There are $\gcd(r, p - 1)$ possibilities. Eve computes α^a for each one until she obtains β, at which point she has found a. She now has completely broken the system and can reproduce Alice's signatures at will.

Example. Alice wants to sign the message $m_1 = 151405$ (which corresponds to *one*, if we let $01 = a, 02 = b, \ldots$). She chooses $p = 225119$. Then $\alpha = 11$ is a primitive root. She has a secret number a. She computes $\beta \equiv \alpha^a \equiv 18191 \pmod{p}$. To sign the message, she chooses a random number k and keeps it secret. She computes $r \equiv \alpha^k \equiv 164130 \pmod{p}$. Then she computes

$$s_1 \equiv k^{-1}(m_1 - ar) \equiv 130777 \pmod{p-1}.$$

The signed message is the triple $(151405, 164130, 130777)$.

Now suppose Alice also signs the message $m_2 = 202315$ (which is *two*) and produces the signed message $(202315, 164130, 164899)$. Immediately, Eve recognizes that Alice used the same value of k, since the value of r is the same in both signatures. She therefore writes the congruence

$$-34122k \equiv (s_1 - s_2)k \equiv m_1 - m_2 \equiv -50910 \pmod{p-1}.$$

Since $\gcd(-34122, p - 1) = 2$, there are two solutions, which can be found by the method described in Section 3.3. Divide the congruence by 2:

$$-17061k \equiv -25455 \pmod{(p-1)/2}.$$

This has the solution $k \equiv 239 \pmod{(p-1)/2}$, so there are two values of k $\pmod{p}$, namely 239 and $239 + (p-1)/2 = 112798$. Calculate

$$\alpha^{239} \equiv 164130, \quad \alpha^{112798} \equiv 59924 \pmod{p}.$$

Since the first is the correct value of r, Eve concludes that $k = 239$. She now rewrites $s_1 k \equiv m_1 - ar \pmod{p-1}$ to obtain

$$164130a \equiv ra \equiv m_1 - s_1 k \equiv 187104 \pmod{p-1}.$$

Since $\gcd(164130, p-1) = 2$, there are two solutions, namely $a = 28862$ and $a = 141421$, which can be found by the method of Section 3.3. Eve computes

$$\alpha^{28862} \equiv 206928, \quad \alpha^{141421} \equiv 18191 \pmod{p}.$$

Since the second value is β, she has found that $a = 141421$.

Now that Eve knows a, she can forge Alice's signature on any document.

∎

The ElGamal signature scheme is an example of a **signature with appendix**. The message is not easily recovered from the signature (r, s). The message m must be included in the verification procedure. This is in contrast to the RSA signature scheme, which is a **message recovery scheme**. In this case, the message is readily obtained from the signature y. Therefore, only y needs to be sent since anyone can deduce m as $y^{e_A} \pmod{n}$. It is unlikely that a random y will yield a meaningful message m, so there is little danger that someone can successfully replace a valid message with a forged message by changing y.

8.3   Hash Functions

In the two signature schemes just discussed, the signature is at least as long as the message. This is a disadvantage when the message is long. To remedy the situation, a hash function is used. The signature scheme is then applied to the hash of the message, rather than to the message itself.

A **cryptographic hash function** h takes as input a message of arbitrary length and produces as output a **message digest** of fixed length, for example 160 bits as depicted in Figure 8.1. Certain properties should be satisfied:

1. Given a message m, the message digest $h(m)$ can be calculated very quickly.

2. Given a message digest y, it is computationally infeasible to find an m with $h(m) = y$ (in other words, h is a **one-way**, or **preimage resistant**, function).

3. It is computationally infeasible to find messages m_1 and m_2 with $h(m_1) = h(m_2)$ (this condition is requiring h to be **strongly collision-free**).

Note that since the set of possible messages is much larger than the set of possible message digests, there should always be many examples of messages m_1 and m_2 with $h(m_1) = h(m_2)$. The requirement (3) says that it should

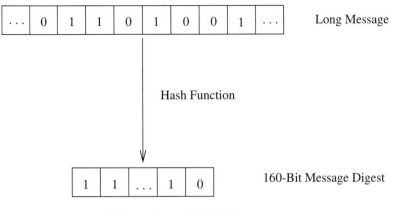

Figure 8.1: A Hash Function.

be hard to find examples. In particular, if Bob produces a message m and its hash $h(m)$, Alice wants to be reasonably certain that Bob does not know another message m' with $h(m') = h(m)$, even if both m and m' are allowed to be random strings of symbols.

Example. Let n be a large integer. Let $h(m) = m \pmod{n}$ be regarded as an integer between 0 and $n-1$. This function clearly satisfies (1). However, (2) and (3) fail: Given y, let $m = y$. Then $h(m) = y$. So h is not one-way. Similarly, choose any two values m_1 and m_2 that are congruent mod n. Then $h(m_1) = h(m_2)$, so h is not strongly collision-free. ∎

Example. The following example, sometimes called the discrete log hash function, is due to Chaum, van Heijst, and Pfitzmann. It satisfies (2) and (3) but is much too slow to be used in practice. However, it demonstrates the basic idea of a hash function.

First we select a large prime number p such that $q = (p-1)/2$ is also prime (see Exercise 8). We now choose two primitive roots α and β for p. Since α is a primitive root, there exists a such that $\alpha^a \equiv \beta \pmod{p}$. However, we assume that a is not known (finding a, if not given it in advance, involves solving a discrete log problem, which we assume is hard).

The hash function h will map integers mod q^2 to integers mod p. Therefore the message digest contains approximately half as many bits as the message. This is not as drastic a reduction in size as usually required in practice, but it suffices for our purposes.

Write $m = x_0 + x_1 q$ with $0 \le x_0, x_1 \le q - 1$. Then

$$h(m) \equiv \alpha^{x_0} \beta^{x_1} \pmod{p}.$$

The following shows that the function h is probably strongly collision-free.

Proposition. *If we know messages $m \neq m'$ with $h(m) = h(m')$, then we can determine the discrete logarithm $a = L_{\alpha}(\beta)$.*

Proof. Write $m = x_0 + x_1 q$ and $m' = x_0' + x_1' q$. Suppose

$$\alpha^{x_0} \beta^{x_1} \equiv \alpha^{x_0'} \beta^{x_1'} \pmod{p}.$$

Using the fact that $\beta \equiv \alpha^a \pmod{p}$, we rewrite this as

$$\alpha^{a(x_1 - x_1') - (x_0' - x_0)} \equiv 1 \pmod{p}.$$

Since α is a primitive root mod p, we know that $\alpha^k \equiv 1 \pmod{p}$ if and only if $k \equiv 0 \pmod{p-1}$. In our case, this means that

$$a(x_1 - x_1') \equiv x_0' - x_0 \pmod{p-1}.$$

Let $d = \gcd(x_1 - x_1', p - 1)$. There are exactly d solutions to the preceding congruence (see Section 3.3), and they can be found quickly. By the choice of p, the only factors of $p - 1$ are $1, 2, q, p - 1$. Since $0 \leq x_1, x_1' \leq q - 1$, it follows that $-(q - 1) \leq x_1 - x_1' \leq q - 1$. Therefore, if $x_1 - x_1' \neq 0$, then it is a nonzero multiple of d of absolute value less than q. This means that $d \neq q, p - 1$, so $d = 1$ or 2. Therefore there are at most 2 possibilities for a. Calculate α^a for each possibility; only one of them will yield β. Therefore, we obtain a, as desired.

On the other hand, if $x_1 - x_1' = 0$, then the preceding yields $x_0' - x_0 \equiv 0 \pmod{p-1}$. Since $-(q - 1) \leq x_0' - x_0 \leq q - 1$, we must have $x_0' = x_0$. Therefore, $m = m'$, contrary to our assumption. $\square$

Suppose now that we have a function g that starts with a message digest y and quickly finds an m with $h(m) = y$. In this case, it is easy to find $m_1 \neq m_2$ with $h(m_1) = h(m_2)$: Choose a random m and compute $y = h(m)$, then compute $g(y)$. Since h maps q^2 messages to $p - 1 = 2q$ message digests, there are many messages m' with $h(m') = h(m)$. It is therefore not very likely that $m' = m$. If it is, try another random m. Soon, we should find a collision, that is, messages $m_1 \neq m_2$ with $h(m_1) = h(m_2)$. The preceding proposition shows that we can then solve a discrete log problem. Therefore, it is unlikely that such a function g exists.

As we mentioned earlier, this hash function is good for illustrative purposes but is impractical because of its slow nature. Although it can be computed efficiently via repeated squaring, it turns out that even repeated squaring is too slow for practical applications. In applications such as electronic commerce, the extra time required to perform the multiplications in software is prohibitive. There are several professional strength hash functions available. For example, there is the popular MD family due to Rivest. In particular, MD4 and its stronger version MD5 are widely used and produce 128-bit message digest for messages of arbitrary length. Another alternative is NIST's Secure Hash Algorithm (SHA), which yields a 160-bit message digest. A description of these algorithms here would not be very enlightening. For details of these and other hash functions, see [Stinson], [Schneier], and [Menezes et al.].

Hashing, Signing, and Applications

One useful application of hash functions is to make signature schemes more efficient. The hash function h is made public. Starting with a message m, Alice calculates the hash $h(m)$. This output $h(m)$ is significantly smaller, and hence signing the hash may be done more quickly than signing the entire message. Alice calculates the signed message $sig(h(m))$ for the hash function and uses it as the signature of the message. The pair $(m, sig(h(m)))$ now conveys basically the same knowledge as the original signature scheme did. It has the advantages that it is faster to create (under the reasonable assumption that the hash operation is quick) and requires less resources for transmission or storage.

Is this method secure? Suppose Eve has possession of Alice's signed message $(m, sig(h(m))$. She has another message m' to which she wants to add Alice's signature. This means that she needs $sig(h(m')) = sig(h(m))$; in particular, she needs $h(m') = h(m)$. If the hash function is one-way, Eve will find it hard to find any such m'. The chance that her desired m' will work is very small. Moreover, since we require our hash function to be strongly collision-free, it is unlikely that Eve can find two messages $m_1 \neq m_2$ with the same signatures. Of course, if she did, she could have Alice sign m_1, then transfer her signature to m_2. But Alice would get suspicious since m_1 (and m_2) would very likely be meaningless messages.

In the next section, however, we'll see how Eve can trick Alice if the size of the message digest is too small (and we'll see that the hash function will not be strongly collision-free, either).

Hash functions may also be employed as a check on data integrity. The question of data integrity comes up in basically two scenarios. The first is when the data (encrypted or not) are being transmitted to another person and a noisy communication channel introduces errors to the data. The second occurs when an observer rearranges the transmission in some manner before it gets to the receiver. Either way, the data have become corrupted.

For example, suppose Alice sends Bob long messages about financial transactions with Eve and encrypts them in blocks. Perhaps Eve deduces that the tenth block of each message lists the amount of money that is to be deposited to Eve's account. She could easily substitute the tenth block from one message into another and increase the deposit.

In another situation, Alice might send Bob a message consisting of several blocks of data, but one of the blocks is lost during transmission. Bob might not ever realize that the block is missing.

Here is how hash functions can be used. Say we send $(m, h(m))$ over the communications channel and it is received as (M, H). To check whether errors might have occurred, the recipient computes $h(M)$ and sees whether it equals H. If any errors occurred, it is likely that $h(M) \neq H$, because of the collision-free properties of h.

8.4   Birthday Attacks

If there are 23 people in a room, the probability is slightly more than 50% that two of them have the same birthday. If there are 30, the probability is around 70%. This might seem surprising; it is called the *birthday paradox*. Let's see why it's true. We'll ignore leap years and assume that all birthdays are equally likely (if not, the probabilities given would be slightly higher).

Consider the case of 23 people. We'll compute the probability that they all have different birthdays. Line them up in a row. The first person uses up one day, so the second person has probability $(1 - 1/365)$ of having a different birthday. There are two days removed for the third person, so the probability is $(1 - 2/365)$ that the third birthday differs from the first two. Therefore, the probability of all three people having different birthdays is $(1 - 1/365)(1 - 2/365)$. Continuing in this way, we see that the probability that all 23 people have different birthdays is

$$\left(1 - \frac{1}{365}\right)\left(1 - \frac{2}{365}\right) \cdots \left(1 - \frac{22}{365}\right) = .493$$

Therefore, the probability of at least two having the same birthday is

$$1 - .493 = .507$$

One way to understand the preceding calculation intuitively is to consider the case of 40 people. If the first 30 have a match, we're done, so suppose the first 30 have different birthdays. Now we have to choose the last 10 birthdays. Since 30 birthdays are already chosen, we have approximately a 10% chance that a randomly chosen birthday will match one of the first 30. And we are choosing 10 birthdays. Therefore, it shouldn't be too surprising that we get a match. In fact, the probability is 89% that there is a match among 40 people.

More generally, suppose we have n objects, where n is large. There are r people, and each chooses an object (with replacement, so several people could choose the same one). If $r \approx 1.177\sqrt{n}$, then the probability is 50% that at least two people choose the same object. If $r \approx \sqrt{2\lambda n}$, then the probability is $1 - e^{-\lambda}$ that there is a match. (Note that this is only an approximation that holds for large n; for small n it is better to use the above product and obtain an exact answer.)

The applications of these ideas to cryptology require a slightly different setup. Suppose there are two rooms, each with 30 people. What is the probability that someone in the first room has the same birthday as someone in the second room? More generally, suppose there are n objects and there are two groups of r people. Each person from each group selects an object (with replacement). What is the probability that someone from the first group chooses the same object as someone from the second group? Again, if $r \approx \sqrt{\lambda n}$, then the probability is $1 - e^{-\lambda}$ that there is a match. The probability of exactly i matches is $\lambda^i e^{-\lambda}/i!$. An analysis of this problem, with generalizations, is given in [Girault et al.].

Birthday Attacks on Signature Schemes

Alice is going to sign a document electronically by using one of the signature schemes to sign the hash of the document. Suppose the hash function produces an output of 50 bits. She is worried that Fred will try to trick her into signing an additional contract, perhaps for swamp land in Florida, but she feels safe because the chance of a fraudulent contract having the same hash as the correct document is 1 out of 2^{50}, which is approximately 1 out of 10^{15}. Fred can try several fraudulent contracts, but it is very unlikely that he can find one that has the right hash. Fred, however, has studied the birthday problem and does the following. He finds 30 places where he can make a slight change in the document: adding a space at the end of a line, changing a wording slightly, etc. At each place, he has two choices: Make the small change or leave the original. Therefore, he can produce 2^{30} documents that are essentially identical with the original. Surely, Alice will not object to any of these versions. Now, Fred computes the hash of each of the 2^{30} versions and stores them. Similarly, he makes 2^{30} versions of the fraudulent contract and stores their hashes. Consider the generalized birthday problem with $r = 2^{30}$ and $n = 2^{50}$. We have $r = \sqrt{\lambda n}$ with $\lambda = 2^{10} = 1024$. Therefore, the probability is around $1 - e^{-1024} \approx 1$ that a version of the good document has the same hash as a version of the fraudulent contract. Fred finds the match and asks Alice to sign the good version. He plans to append her signature to the fraudulent contract, too. Since they have the same hash, the signature would be valid for the fraudulent one, so Fred could claim that Alice agreed to buy the swamp land. But Alice is an English teacher and insists on removing a comma from one sentence. Then she signs the document, which has a completely different hash from the document Fred asked her to sign. Fred is foiled again. He now is faced with the prospect of trying to find a fraudulent contract that has the same hash as this new version of the good document. This is essentially impossible.

What Fred did is called the birthday attack. Its practical implication is that you should probably use a hash function with output twice as long as what you believe to be necessary, since the birthday attack effectively halves the number of bits. What Alice did is the recommended way to foil the birthday attack on signature schemes. Before signing an electronic document, make a slight change.

A Birthday Attack on Discrete Logarithms

Suppose we are working with a large prime p and want to evaluate $L_\alpha(\beta)$. In other words, we want to solve $\alpha^x \equiv \beta \pmod p$. We can do this with high probability by a birthday attack.

Make two lists, both of length around $\sqrt{p}$:

1. The first list contains numbers $\alpha^k \pmod p$ for approximately $\sqrt{p}$ randomly chosen values of k.

2. The second list contains numbers $\beta\alpha^{-\ell} \pmod p$ for approximately $\sqrt{p}$ randomly chosen values of ℓ.

There is a good chance that there is a match between some element on the first list and some element on the second list. If so, we have

$$\alpha^k \equiv \beta\alpha^{-\ell}, \text{ hence } \alpha^{k+\ell} \equiv \beta \pmod p.$$

Therefore, $x \equiv k + \ell \pmod{p-1}$ is the desired discrete logarithm.

Meet-in-the-Middle Attacks on Double Encryption

The following is similar to the birthday attacks, but its method of finding a match is deterministic rather than probabilistic. This means that it is guaranteed to find one, rather than only having a very high probability of producing a match. However, the second step, namely removing extraneous matches, is probabilistic.

Alice and Bob are using an encryption method. The encryption functions are called E_k, and the decryption functions are called D_k, where k is a key. We assume that if someone knows k, then he also knows E_k and D_k (so Alice and Bob could be using one of the classical, nonpublic key systems). They have a great idea. Instead of encrypting once, they use two keys k_1 and k_2 and encrypt twice. Starting with a plaintext message m, the ciphertext is $c = E_{k_2}(E_{k_1}(m))$. To decrypt, simply compute $m = D_{k_1}(D_{k_2}(c))$. Eve will need to discover both k_1 and k_2 to decrypt their messages.

Does this provide greater security? For many cryptosystems, applying two encryptions is the same as using an encryption for some other key. For example, the composition of two affine functions is still an affine function (see Exercise 2.5). Similarly, using two RSA encryptions (with the same n) with exponents e_1 and e_2 corresponds to doing a single encryption with exponent $e_1 e_2$. In these cases, double encryption offers no advantage. However, there are systems, such as DES (see Section 4.4) where the composition of two encryptions is not simply encryption with another key. For these, double encryption might seem to offer a much higher level of security. However, the following attack shows that this is not really the case, as long as we have a computer with a lot of memory.

Assume Eve has intercepted a message m and a doubly encrypted ciphertext $c = E_{k_2}(E_{k_1}(m))$. She wants to find k_1 and k_2. She first computes and stores $E_k(m)$ for all possible keys k. She then computes $D_k(c)$ for all possible keys k. Finally, she compares the two lists. This is similar to the birthday attack, except that she knows there will be at least one match, since the correct pair of keys will be one of them. If there are several matches, she takes another plaintext-ciphertext pair and determines which of the pairs she has found will encrypt the plaintext to the ciphertext. This should greatly reduce the list. If there is still more than one pair remaining, she continues until only one pair remains (or she decides that two or more pairs give the same double encryption function). Eve now has the desired pair k_1, k_2.

If Eve has only one plaintext-ciphertext pair, she still has reduced the set of possible key pairs to a short list. If she intercepts a future transmission, she can try each of these possibilities and obtain a very short list of meaningful plaintexts.

If there are N possible keys, Eve needs to compute and store N values $D_k(m)$. She then needs to compute another N numbers $D_k(c)$ and compare them with the stored list. But these $2N$ computations (plus the comparisons) are much less than the N^2 computations required for searching through all key pairs k_1, k_2.

This meet-in-the-middle procedure takes slightly longer than the exhaustive search through all keys for single encryption. It also takes a lot of memory to store the first list. However, the conclusion is that double encryption does not significantly raise the level of security in most situations.

Similarly, we could use triple encryption, using triples of keys. A similar attack brings the level of security down to at most what one might naively expect from double encryption, namely squaring the possible number of keys.

8.5   The Digital Signature Algorithm

The National Institute of Standards and Technology proposed the Digital Signature Algorithm (DSA) in 1991 and adopted it as a standard in 1994. Just like the ElGamal method, DSA is a digital signature scheme with appendix. Also, like other schemes, it is usually a message digest that is signed. In this case, the hash function produces a 160-bit output. We will assume in the following that our data message m has already been hashed. Therefore, we are trying to sign a 160-bit message.

The generation of keys for DSA proceeds as follows. First, there is an initialization phase:

1. Alice finds a prime q that is 160 bits long and chooses a prime p that satisfies $q|p-1$ (see Exercise 8). The discrete log problem should be hard for this choice of p. (In the initial version, p had 512 bits. Later versions of the algorithm allow for longer primes.)

2. Let g be a primitive root mod p and let $\alpha \equiv g^{(p-1)/q} \pmod{p}$. Then $\alpha^q \equiv 1 \pmod{p}$.

3. Alice chooses a secret a such that $1 \leq a < q-1$ and calculates $\beta \equiv \alpha^a \pmod{p}$.

4. Alice publishes (p, q, α, β) and keeps a secret.

Alice signs a message m by the following procedure:

1. Select a random, secret integer k such that $0 < k < q-1$.

2. Compute $r = (\alpha^k \pmod{p}) \pmod{q}$.

3. Compute $s \equiv k^{-1}(m + ar) \pmod{q}$.

4. Alice's signature for m is (r, s), which she sends to Bob along with m.

For Bob to verify, he must

1. Download Alice's public information (p, q, α, β).

2. Compute $u_1 \equiv s^{-1}m \pmod{q}$, and $u_2 \equiv s^{-1}r \pmod{q}$.

3. Compute $v = (\alpha^{u_1}\beta^{u_2} \pmod{p}) \pmod{q}$.

4. Accept the signature if and only if $v = r$.

We show that the verification works. By the definition of s, we have

$$m \equiv (-ar + ks) \pmod{q},$$

which implies

$$s^{-1}m \equiv (-ars^{-1} + k) \pmod{q}.$$

Therefore,

$$\begin{aligned} k &\equiv s^{-1}m + ars^{-1} \pmod{q} \\ &\equiv u_1 + au_2 \pmod{q}. \end{aligned}$$

So $\alpha^k = \alpha^{u_1+au_2} = (\alpha^{u_1}\beta^{u_2} \pmod{p}) \pmod{q}$. Thus $v = r$.

As in the ElGamal scheme, the integer a must be kept secret. Anyone who has knowledge of a can sign any desired document. Also, if the same value of k is used twice, it is possible to find a by the same procedure as before.

In contrast to the ElGamal scheme, the integer r does not carry full information about k. Knowing r allows us to find only the mod q value. There are approximately $2^{512-160} = 2^{342}$ numbers mod p that reduce to a given number mod q.

What is the advantage of having $\alpha^q \equiv 1 \pmod{p}$ rather than using a primitive root? Recall the Pohlig-Hellman attack for solving the discrete log problem. It could find information mod small prime factors of $p - 1$, but it was useless mod large prime factors, such as q. In the ElGamal scheme, an attacker could determine $a \pmod{2^t}$, where 2^t is the largest power of 2 dividing $p - 1$. This would not come close to finding a, but the general philosophy is that many little pieces of information collectively can often be useful. The DSA avoids this problem by removing all but the mod q information for a.

In the ElGamal scheme, three modular exponentiations are needed in the verification step. This step is modified for the DSA so that only two modular exponentiations are needed. Since modular exponentiation is one of the slower parts of the computation, this change speeds up the verification, which can be important if many signatures need to be verified in a short time.

8.6 Exercises

1. Show that if someone discovers the value of k used in the ElGamal signature scheme, then a can also be determined.

2. Suppose that (x, γ, δ) is a message signed with the ElGamal signature scheme. Choose h with $\gcd(h, p - 1) = 1$ and let $\gamma_1 \equiv \gamma^h \pmod{p}$. Let

$\delta_1 \equiv \delta\gamma_1 h^{-1}\gamma^{-1} \pmod{p-1}$.
(a) Find a message x_1 for which $(x_1, \gamma_1, \delta_1)$ is a valid signature.
(b) This method allows Eve to forge a signature on the message x_1. Why is it unlikely that this causes problems?

3. Let $p = 11$, $q = 5$, $\alpha = 3$, and $k = 3$. Show that $(\alpha^k \pmod{p}) \pmod{q} \neq (\alpha^k \pmod{q}) \pmod{p}$. This shows that the order of operations in the DSA is important.

4. Let p be a prime and let α be an integer with $p \nmid \alpha$. Let $h(x) \equiv \alpha^x \pmod{p}$. Explain why $h(x)$ is not a good cryptographic hash function.

5. There are many variations to the ElGamal digital signature scheme that can be obtained by altering the signing equation $s \equiv k^{-1}(m - ar) \pmod{p-1}$. Here are some variations.
(a) Consider the signing equation $s \equiv a^{-1}(m - kr) \pmod{p-1}$. Show that the verification $\alpha^m \equiv (\alpha^a)^s r^r \pmod{p}$ is a valid verification procedure.
(b) Consider the signing equation $s \equiv \alpha m + kr \pmod{p-1}$. Show that the verification $\alpha^s \equiv (\alpha^a)^m r^r \pmod{p}$ is a valid verification procedure.
(c) Consider the signing equation $s \equiv ar + km \pmod{p-1}$. Show that the verification $\alpha^s = (\alpha^a)^r r^m \pmod{p}$ is a valid verification procedure.

6. The ElGamal signature scheme presented is weak to a type of attack known as existential forgery. Here is the basic existential forgery attack. Choose u, v be such that $\gcd(v, p-1) = 1$. Compute $r \equiv \beta^v \alpha^u \pmod{p}$ and $s \equiv -rv^{-1} \pmod{p-1}$.
(a) Prove the claim that the pair (r, s) is a valid signature for the message $m = su \pmod{p-1}$ (of course, it is likely that m is not a meaningful message).
(b) Suppose a hash function h is used and the signature must be valid for $h(m)$ instead of for m (so we need to have $h(m) = su$). Explain how this scheme protects against existential forgery. That is, explain why it is hard to produce a forged, signed message by the this procedure.

7. Alice wants to sign a document using the ElGamal signature scheme. Suppose her random number generator is broken, so she uses $k = a$ in the signature scheme. How will Eve notice this and how can Eve determine the values of k and a (and thus break the system)?

8. (a) In several cryptographic protocols, one needs to choose a prime p such that $q = (p-1)/2$ is also prime. One way to do this is to choose a prime q at random and then test $2q + 1$ for primality. Suppose q is chosen to have approximately 100 decimal digits. Assume $2q + 1$ is a random odd integer of 100 digits. (This is not quite accurate, since $2q + 1$ cannot be congruent to 1 mod 3, for example. But the assumption is good enough for a rough estimate.) Show that the probability that $2q + 1$ is prime is approximately $1/115$ (use the prime number theorem, as in Section 6.3). This means that with approximately 115 random choices for the prime q, you should be able to find a suitable prime p.

(b) In a version of the Digital Signature Algorithm, Alice needs a 160-bit prime q and a 512-bit prime p such that $q|p - 1$. Suppose Alice chooses a random 160-bit prime q and a random 352-bit even number k such that $qk+1$ has 512 bits. Show that the probability that $qk+1$ is prime is approximately $1/177$. This means that Alice can find a suitable q and p fairly quickly.

9. Consider the following variation of the ElGamal signature scheme. Alice chooses a large prime p and a primitive root α. She also chooses a function $f(x)$ that, given an integer x with $0 \le x < p$, returns an integer $f(x)$ with $0 \le f(x) < p-1$. (For example, $f(x) = x^7 - 3x + 2 \pmod{p-1}$ for $0 \le x < p$ is one such function.) She chooses a secret integer a and computes $\beta \equiv \alpha^a \pmod{p}$. The numbers p, α, β and the function $f(x)$ are made public.

Alice wants to sign a message m:

1. Alice chooses a random integer k with $\gcd(k, p - 1) = 1$

2. She computes $r \equiv \alpha^k \pmod{p}$

3. She computes $s \equiv k^{-1}(m - f(r)a) \pmod{p - 1}$.

The signed message is (m, r, s).

Bob verifies the signature as follows:

1. He computes $v_1 \equiv \beta^{f(r)} r^s \pmod{p}$.

2. He computes $v_2 \equiv \alpha^m \pmod{p}$.

3. If $v_1 \equiv v_2 \pmod{p}$, he declares the signature to be valid.

(a) Show that if all procedures are followed correctly, then the verification equation is true.

(b) Suppose Alice is lazy and chooses the constant function satisfying $f(x) = 0$ for all x. Show that Eve can forge a valid signature on every message m_1 (for example, give a value of k and of r and s that will give a valid signature for the message m_1).

10. Let E_K and D_K denote encryption and decryption for some cryptosystem with the key K, so if m is the plaintext, then $E_K(m) = c$ is the ciphertext and $D_K(c) = m$. Assume that if K and L are two keys, then it

is easy to find (and there exists) a key K_1 such that $E_L(E_K(m)) = E_{K_1}(m)$
for all m. Suppose you know a plaintext-ciphertext pair (m_0, c_0).
(a) Show how to use a birthday attack to obtain a key K_0 such that $E_{K_0}(m_0) = c_0$.
(b) Suppose that K_1, as before, exists, but it is not easy to find. Show how
to use a meet-in-the-middle attack to find a decryption function (but you
might not find the decryption key).

8.7   Computer Problems

1. Suppose we use the ElGamal signature scheme with $p = 65539$, $\alpha = 2$,
$\beta = 33384$. We send two signed messages (m, r, s):

$$(809, 18357, 1042) \ (= \text{hi}) \text{ and}$$

$$(22505, 18357, 26272) \ (= \text{bye}).$$

(a) Show that the same value of k was used for each signature.
(b) Use this fact to find this value of k and to find the value of a such that
$\beta \equiv \alpha^a \pmod{p}$.

2. (The numbers in this problem are too large for MATLAB without the
assistance of the Maple Kernel.) Alice and Bob have the following RSA
parameters:

$$n_A = 171024704183616109700818066925197841516671277, \quad e_A = 1571$$

$$n_B = 839073542734369359260871355939062622747633109, \quad e_B = 87697.$$

Bob knows that

$$p_B = 9876345767697834568934613, \quad q_B = 84957894578934573457345793$$

(where $n_B = p_B q_B$). Alice signs a document and sends the document and
signature (m, s) (where $s \equiv m^{d_A} \pmod{n_A}$) to Bob. To keep the contents
of the document secret, she encrypts using Bob's public key. Bob receives
the encrypted signature pair $(m_1, s_1) \equiv (m^{e_B}, s^{e_B}) \pmod{n_B}$, where

$$m_1 = 148237652324987123445124187130930$$

$$s_1 = 431761216284654413401124186720665063.$$

Find the message m and verify that it came from Alice. (The signed pair
is stored as *sigpairm1, sigpairs1*. The numbers n_A, n_B, p_A, p_B are stored as
signa, signb, sigpa, sigpb.)

3. (The numbers in this problem are too large for MATLAB without the assistance of the Maple Kernel.) In problem 2, suppose that Bob had primes $p_B = 7865712896579$ and $q_B = 8495789457893457345793$. Assuming the same encryption exponents, explain why Bob is unable to verify Alice's signature when she sends him the pair (m_2, s_2) with

$$m_2 = 148237652324987123445124187171130930,$$

$$s_2 = 43176121628465441340112418672065063.$$

What modifications need to be made for the procedure to work? (The signed pair is stored as *sigpairm2, sigpairs2*.)

4. (a) If there are 30 people in a classroom, what is the probability that at least two have the same birthday?
(b) How many people should there be in a classroom in order to have a 99% chance that at least two have the same birthday?
(c) How many people should there be in a classroom in order to have 100% probability that at least two have the same birthday?

5. In a family of four, what is the probability that no two people have birthdays in the same month? (Assume all months have equal probabilities.)

6. A professor posts the grades for a class using the last four digits of the Social Security number of each student. In a class of 200 students, what is the probability that at least two students have the same four digits?

Chapter 9

E-Commerce and Digital Cash

As communication technologies, such as the Internet and wireless networks, have advanced, new avenues of commerce have become available. This great potential to reach more customers has led to great potential for theft and fraud. Transmitting credit card and purchase information over nonprotected channels can lead to unwanted parties invading customer privacy and stealing vital credit information. Securing the information necessary to conduct electronic commerce is therefore very important.

In this chapter, we look at two examples of how cryptography can be used in electronic business transactions. The first example is the Secure Electronic Transaction™ (SET) protocol, which was created to standardize the exchange of credit card information for electronic transactions. In addition to providing security and privacy, it aims at preventing alterations of purchase orders and forgery of credit card information. The second example is a model of digital cash, which emulates the behavior of money using digital data. When making a purchase using coin and paper cash, the consumer is ensured that his or her identity is not disclosed to the vendor. In an electronic system, files, instead of coins, are exchanged for products and services. One goal is anonymity. Since electronic files are easily copied, if we guarantee anonymity, then measures must also be taken to prevent counterfeiting. In Section 9.2, we'll show how to achieve both goals in an electronic cash system.

9.1 Secure Electronic Transaction

Every time someone places an order in an electronic transactions over the Internet, large quantities of information are transmitted. These data must be protected from unwanted eavesdroppers in order to ensure the customer's privacy and prevent credit fraud. Requirements for a good electronic commerce system include the following:

1. **Authenticity:** Participants in a transaction cannot be impersonated and signatures cannot be forged.

2. **Integrity:** Documents such as purchase orders and payment instructions cannot be altered.

3. **Privacy:** The details of a transaction should be kept as secure as possible.

4. **Security:** Sensitive account information such as credit card numbers must be protected.

All of these requirements should be satisfied, even over public communication channels such as the Internet.

In 1996, the credit card companies MasterCard and Visa called for the establishment of standards for electronic commerce. The result, whose development involved several companies, is called the SET, or Secure Electronic Transaction^{TM} protocol. It starts with the existing credit card system and allows people to use it securely over open channels.

The SET protocol is fairly complex, involving, for example, issuing certificates by a trusted authority in order to certify that the cardholder and merchant are legitimate, and specifying how payment requests are to be made. In the following we'll discuss one aspect of the whole protocol, namely the use of dual signatures.

There are several possible variations on the following. For example, in order to improve speed, a fast symmetric key system can be used in conjunction with the public key system. If there is a lot of information to be transmitted, a randomly chosen symmetric key plus the hash of the long message can be sent via the public key system, while the long message itself is sent via the faster symmetric system. However, we'll restrict our attention to the simplest case where only public key methods are used.

Suppose Alice wants to buy a book entitled *How to Use Other People's Credit Card Numbers to Defraud Banks*, which she has seen advertised on the Internet. For obvious reasons, she feels uneasy about sending the publisher her credit card information, and she certainly does not want the bank that issued her card to know what she is buying. A similar situation applies to many transactions. The bank does not need to know what the customer is ordering, and for security reasons the merchant should not know the card number. However, these two pieces of information need to be linked in some way. Otherwise the merchant could attach the payment information to another order. **Dual signatures** solve this problem.

The three participants in the following will be the Cardholder (namely, the purchaser), the Merchant, and the Bank (which authorizes the use of the credit card).

The Cardholder has two pieces of information:

- GSO = Goods and Services Order, which consists of the cardholder's and merchant's names, the quantities of each item ordered, the prices, etc.

- PI = Payment Instructions, including the merchant's name, the credit card number, the total price, etc.

The system uses a public hash function; let's call it H. Also, a public key cryptosystem such as RSA is used, and the Cardholder and the Bank have their own public and private keys. Let E_C, E_M, and E_B denote the (public) encryption functions for the Cardholder, the Merchant, and the Bank, and let D_C, D_M, and D_B be the (private) decryption functions.

The Cardholder performs the following procedures:

1. Calculates $GSOMD = H(E_M(GSO))$, which is the message digest, or hash, of an encryption of GSO.

2. Calculates $PIMD = H(E_B(PI))$, which is the message digest of an encryption of PI.

3. Concatenates $GSOMD$ and $PIMD$ to obtain $PIMD\|GSOMD$, then computes the hash of the result to obtain the payment-order message digest $POMD = H(PIMD\|GSOMD)$.

4. Signs $POMD$ by computing $DS = D_C(POMD)$. This is the Dual Signature.

5. Sends $E_M(GSO)$, DS, $PIMD$, and $E_B(PI)$ to the Merchant.

The Merchant then does the following:

1. Calculates $H(E_M(GSO))$ (which should equal $GSOMD$).

2. Calculates $H(PIMD\|H(E_M(GSO)))$ and $E_C(DS)$. If they are equal, then the Merchant has verified the Cardholder's signature, and is therefore convinced that the order is from the Cardholder.

3. Computes $D_M(E_M(GSO))$ to obtain GSO.

4. Sends $GSOMD$, $E_B(PI)$, and DS to the Bank.

The Bank now performs the following:

1. Computes $H(E_B(PI))$ (which should equal $PIMD$).

2. Concatenates $H(E_B(PI))$ and $GSOMD$.

3. Computes $H(H(E_B(PI))\|GSOMD)$ and $E_C(DS)$. If they are equal, the Bank has verified the Cardholder's signature.

4. Computes $D_B(E_B(PI))$, obtaining the payment instructions PI.

5. Returns an encrypted (with E_M) digitally signed authorization to the Merchant, guaranteeing payment.

The Merchant completes the procedure as follows:

1. Returns an encrypted (with E_C) digitally signed receipt to the Cardholder, indicating that the transaction has been completed.

The Merchant only sees the encrypted form $E_B(PI)$ of the payment instructions, and so does not see the credit card number. It would be infeasible for the Merchant or the Bank to modify any of the information regarding the order because the hash function is used to compute DS.

The Bank only sees the message digest of the Goods and Services Order, and so has no idea what is being ordered.

The requirements of integrity, privacy, and security are met by this procedure. In actual implementations, several more steps are required in order to protect authenticity. For example, it must be guaranteed that the public keys being used actually belong to the participants as claimed, not to impostors. Certificates from a trusted authority are used for this purpose.

9.2 Digital Cash

Suppose Congressman Bill Passer is receiving large donations from his friend Phil Pockets. For obvious reasons, he would like to hide this fact, pretending instead that the money comes mostly from people such as Vera Goode. Or perhaps Phil does not want Bill to know he's the source of the money. If Phil pays by check, well-placed sources in the bank can expose him. Similarly, Congressman Passer cannot receive payments via credit card. The only anonymous payment scheme seems to be cash.

But now suppose Passer has remained in office for many terms and we are nearing the end of the twenty-first century. All commerce is carried out electronically. Is it possible to have electronic cash? Several problems arise. For example, near the beginning of the twenty-first century, photocopying money was possible, though a careful recipient could discern differences between the copy and the original. Copies of electronic information, however, are indistinguishable from the original. Therefore, someone who has a valid electronic coin could make several copies. Some method is needed to prevent such double spending. One idea would be for a central bank to have records of every coin and who has each one. But if coins are recorded as they are spent, anonymity is compromised. Occasionally, communications with a central bank could fail temporarily, so it is also desirable for the person receiving the coin to be able to verify the coin as legitimate without contacting the bank during each transaction.

T. Okamoto and K. Ohta [Okamoto-Ohta] list six properties a digital cash system should have:

1. The cash can be sent securely through computer networks.

2. The cash cannot be copied and reused.

3. The spender of the cash can remain anonymous. If the coin is spent legitimately, neither the recipient nor the bank can identify the spender.

4. The transaction can be done *offline*, meaning no communication with the central bank is needed during the transaction.

5. The cash can be transferred to others.

6. A piece of cash can be divided into smaller amounts.

Okamoto and Ohta give a system that satisfies all these requirements. Several systems satisfying some of them have been devised by David Chaum. In the following, we describe a system that satisfies 1 through 4, due to S. Brands [Brands].

The reader will surely notice that the system is much more complicated than the centuries old system of actual coins. This is because, as we mentioned previously, electronic objects can be reproduced at essentially no cost, in contrast to physical cash, which has usually been rather difficult to counterfeit. Therefore, steps are needed to catch electronic cash counterfeiters. But this means that something like a user's signature needs to be attached to an electronic coin. How, then, can anonymity be preserved? The solution uses "restricted blind signatures." This process contributes much of the complexity to the scheme.

Participants

Participants are the Bank, the Spender, and the Merchant.

Initialization

Initialization is done once and for all by some central authority. Choose a large prime p such that $q = (p-1)/2$ is also prime (see Exercise 8.8). Let g be the square of a primitive root mod p. This implies that $g^{k_1} \equiv g^{k_2}$ (mod p) $\iff k_1 \equiv k_2$ (mod q). Two secret random exponents are chosen, and g_1 and g_2 are defined to be g raised to these exponents mod p. These exponents are then discarded (storing them serves no useful purpose, and if a hacker discovers them, then the system is compromised). The numbers

$$g, \quad g_1, \quad g_2$$

are made public. Also, two public hash functions are chosen. The first, H, takes a 5-tuple of integers as input and outputs an integer mod q. The second, H_0, takes a 4-tuple of integers as input and outputs an integer mod q.

The Bank

The bank chooses its secret identity number x and computes

$$h \equiv g^x, \quad h_1 \equiv g_1^x, \quad h_2 \equiv g_2^x \pmod{p}.$$

The numbers h, h_1, and h_2 are made public and identify the bank.

The Spender

The Spender chooses a secret identity number u and computes the account number

$$I \equiv g_1^u \pmod{p}.$$

The number I is sent to the Bank, which stores I along with information identifying the Spender (e.g., name, address, etc.). However, the Spender does not send u to the bank. The Bank sends

$$z' \equiv (Ig_2)^x \pmod{p}$$

to the Spender.

The Merchant

The Merchant chooses an identification number M and registers it with the bank.

Creating a Coin

The Spender contacts the bank, asking for a coin. The bank requires proof of identity, just as when someone is withdrawing classical cash from an account. All coins in the present scheme have the same value. A coin will be represented by a 6-tuple of numbers

$$(A, B, z, a, b, r).$$

This may seem overly complicated, but we'll see that most of this effort is needed to preserve anonymity and at the same time prevent double spending.

Here is how the numbers are constructed.

1. The Bank chooses a random number w (a different number for each coin), computes

$$g_w \equiv g^w \text{ and } \beta \equiv (Ig_2)^w \pmod{p},$$

   and sends g_w and β to the Spender.

2. The Spender chooses a secret random 5-tuple of integers

$$(s, x_1, x_2, \alpha_1, \alpha_2).$$

3. The Spender computes

$$A \equiv (Ig_2)^s, \quad B \equiv g_1^{x_1} g_2^{x_2}, \quad z \equiv z'^s,$$
$$a \equiv g_w^{\alpha_1} g^{\alpha_2}, \quad b \equiv \beta^{s\alpha_1} A^{\alpha_2} \pmod{p}.$$

   Coins with $A = 1$ are not allowed. This can happen in only two ways. One is when $s \equiv 0 \pmod{q}$, so we require $s \not\equiv 0$. The other is when $Ig_2 \equiv 1 \pmod{p}$, which means the Spender has solved a discrete logarithm problem by a lucky choice of u. The prime p should be chosen so large that this has essentially no chance of happening.

4. The Spender computes

$$c \equiv \alpha_1^{-1} H(A, B, z, a, b) \pmod{q}$$

   and sends c to the Bank. Here H is the public hash function mentioned earlier.

5. The Bank computes $c_1 \equiv cx + w \pmod{q}$ and sends c_1 to the Spender.

6. The Spender computes

$$r \equiv \alpha_1 c_1 + \alpha_2 \pmod{q}.$$

The coin (A, B, z, a, b, r) is now complete. The amount of the coin is deducted from the Spender's bank account.

The procedure, which is quite fast, is repeated each time a Spender wants a coin. A new random number w should be chosen by the Bank for each transaction. Similarly, each spender should choose a new 5-tuple $(s, x_1, x_2, \alpha_1, \alpha_2)$ for each coin.

Spending the Coin

The Spender gives the coin (A, B, z, a, b, r) to the Merchant. The following procedure is then performed:

1. The Merchant checks whether

$$g^r \equiv a\, h^{H(A,B,z,a,b)} \quad A^r \equiv z^{H(A,B,z,a,b)} b \pmod{p}.$$

If this is the case, the Merchant knows that the coin is valid. However, more steps are required to prevent double spending.

2. The Merchant computes

$$d = H_0(A, B, M, t),$$

where H_0 is the hash function chosen in the initialization phase and t is a number representing the date and time of the transaction. The number t is included so that different transactions will have different values of d. The Merchant sends d to the Spender.

3. The Spender computes

$$r_1 \equiv dus + x_1, \quad r_2 \equiv ds + x_2 \pmod{q},$$

where u is the Spender's secret number, and s, x_1, x_2 are part of the secret random 5-tuple chosen earlier. The Spender sends r_1 and r_2 to the Merchant.

4. The Merchant checks whether

$$g_1^{r_1} g_2^{r_2} \equiv A^d B \pmod{p}.$$

If this congruence holds, the Merchant accepts the coin. Otherwise, the Merchant rejects it.

The Merchant Deposits the Coin in the Bank

A few days after receiving the coin, the Merchant wants to deposit it in the Bank. The Merchant submits the coin (A, B, z, a, b, r) plus the triple (r_1, r_2, d). The Bank performs the following:

1. The Bank checks that the coin (A, B, z, a, b, r) has not been previously deposited. If it hasn't been, then the next step is performed. If it has been previously deposited, the Bank skips to the Fraud Control procedures discussed in the next subsection.

2. The Bank checks that

$$g^r \equiv a\, h^{H(A,B,z,a,b)} \quad A^r \equiv z^{H(A,B,z,a,b)}b, \text{ and } g_1^{r_1}g_2^{r_2} \equiv A^d B \pmod{p}.$$

   If so, the coin is valid and the Merchant's account is credited.

Fraud Control

There are several possible ways for someone to try to cheat. Here is how they are dealt with.

1. The Spender spends the coin twice, once with the Merchant, and once with someone we'll call the Vendor. The Merchant submits the coin along with the triple (r_1, r_2, d). The Vendor submits the coin along with the triple (r_1', r_2', d'). An easy calculation shows that

$$r_1 - r_1' \equiv us(d - d'), \quad r_2 - r_2' \equiv s(d - d') \pmod{q}.$$

   Dividing yields $u \equiv (r_1 - r_1')(r_2 - r_2')^{-1} \pmod{q}$. The Bank computes $I \equiv g_1^u \pmod{p}$ and identifies the Spender. Since the Bank cannot discover u otherwise, it has proof (at least beyond a reasonable doubt) that double spending has occurred. The Spender is then sent to jail (if the jury believes that the discrete logarithm problem is hard).

2. The Merchant tries submitting the coin twice, once with the legitimate triple (r_1, r_2, d) and once with a forged triple (r_1', r_2', d'). This is essentially impossible for the Merchant to do, since it is very difficult for the Merchant to produce numbers such that

$$g_1^{r_1'}g_2^{r_2'} \equiv A^{d'} B \pmod{p}.$$

3. Someone tries to make an unauthorized coin. This requires finding numbers such that $g^r \equiv a\, h^{H(A,B,z,a,b)}$ and $A^r \equiv z^{H(A,B,z,a,b)}b$. This is probably hard to do. For example, starting with A, B, z, a, b, then

trying to find r, requires solving a discrete logarithm problem just to make the first equation work. Note that the Spender is foiled in attempts to produce a second coin using a new 5-tuple since the values of x is known only to the Bank. Therefore, finding the correct value of r is very difficult.

4. Eve L. Dewar, an evil merchant, receives a coin from the Spender and deposits it in the bank, but also tries to spend the coin with the Merchant. Eve gives the coin to the Merchant, who computes d', which very likely is not equal to d. Eve does not know u, x_1, x_2, s, but she must choose r_1' and r_2' such that $g_1^{r_1'} g_2^{r_2'} \equiv A^{d'} B \pmod{p}$. This again is a type of discrete logarithm problem. Why can't Eve simply use the r_1, r_2 that she already knows? Since $d' \neq d$, the Merchant would find that $g_1^{r_1} g_2^{r_2} \not\equiv A^{d'} B$.

5. Someone working in the Bank tries to forge a coin. This person has essentially the same information as Eve, plus the identification number I. It is possible to make a coin that satisfies $g^r \equiv a \, h^{H(A,B,z,a,b)}$. However, since the Spender has kept u secret, the person in the bank will not be able to produce a suitable r_1. Of course, if $s = 0$ were allowed, this would be possible; this is one reason $A = 1$ is not allowed.

6. Someone steals the coin from the Spender and tries to spend it. The first verification equation is still satisfied, but the thief does not know u and therefore will not be able to produce r_1, r_2 such that $g_1^{r_1} g_2^{r_2} \equiv A^{d'} B$.

7. Eve L. Dewar, the evil merchant, steals the coin and (r_1, r_2, d) from the Merchant before they are submitted to the Bank. Unless the bank requires merchants to keep records of the time and date of each transaction, and therefore be able to reproduce the inputs that produced d, Eve's theft will be successful. This of course is a flaw of ordinary cash, too.

Anonymity

During the entire transaction with the Merchant, the Spender never needs to provide any identification. This is the same as for purchases made with conventional cash. Also, note that the Bank never sees the values of A, B, z, a, b, r for the coin until it is deposited by the Merchant. In fact, the Bank provides only the number w and the number c_1, and has seen only c. However, the coin still contains information that identifies the Spender in the case of double spending. Is it possible for the Merchant or the Bank to extract the Spender's identity from knowledge of the coin (A, B, z, a, b, r) and the triple (r_1, r_2, d)? Since the Bank also knows the identification number I, it suffices to consider the case where the Bank is trying to identify the Spender. Since s, x_1, x_2 are secret random numbers known only to the Spender, A and B are random numbers. In particular, A is a random power of g and cannot be used to deduce I. The number z is simply $A^x \pmod{p}$, and so does not provide any help beyond what is known from A. Since a and b introduce two new secret random exponents α_1, α_2, they are again random numbers from the viewpoint of everyone except the Spender.

At this point, there are five numbers, A, B, z, a, b, that look like random powers of g to everyone except the Spender. However, when $c \equiv \alpha_1^{-1} H(A, B, z, a, b) \pmod{q}$ is sent to the Bank, the Bank might try to compute the value of H and thus deduce α_1. But the Bank has not seen the coin and so cannot compute H. The Bank could try to keep a list of all values c it has received, along with values of H for every coin that is deposited, and then try all combinations to find α_1. But it is easily seen that, in a system with millions of coins, the number of possible values of α_1 is too large for this to be practical. Therefore, it is unlikely that knowledge of c, hence of b, will help the Bank identify the Spender.

The numbers α_1 and α_2 provide what Brands calls a **restricted blind signature** for the coin. Namely, using the coin once does not allow identification of the signer (namely, the Spender), but using it twice does (and the Spender is sent to jail, as pointed out previously).

To see the effect of the restricted blind signature, suppose α_1 is essentially removed from the process by taking $\alpha_1 = 1$. Then the Bank could keep a list of values of c, along with the person corresponding to each c. When a coin is deposited, the value of H would then be computed and compared with the list. Probably there would be only one person for a given c, so the Bank could identify the Spender.

9.3   Exercises

1. Show that a valid coin satisfies the verification equations

$$g^r \equiv a\, h^{H(A,B,z,a,b)}, \quad A^r \equiv z^{H(A,B,z,a,b,r)} b, \text{ and } g_1^{r_1} g_2^{r_2} \equiv A^d B \pmod{p}.$$

2. A hacker discovers the Bank's secret number x. Show how coins can be produced and spent without having an account at the bank.

3. The numbers g_1 and g_2 are powers of g, but the exponents are supposed to be hard to find. Suppose we take $g_1 = g_2$.

(a) Show that if the Spender replaces r_1, r_2 with r_1', r_2' such that $r_1 + r_2 = r_1' + r_2'$, then the verification equations still work.

(b) Show how the Spender can double spend without being identified.

4. Suppose the coin is represented only as (A, B, a, r), for example by ignoring z and r, taking the hash function H to be a function of only A, B, a, and ignoring the verification equation $A^r \equiv z^H r$. Show that the Spender can change the value of u to any desired number (without informing the Bank), compute a new value of I, and produce a coin that will pass the two remaining verification equations.

5. If the Spender double spends, once with the Merchant and once with the Vendor, why is it very likely that $r_2 - r_2' \not\equiv 0 \pmod{q}$ (where r_2, r_2' are as in the discussion of Fraud Control)?

Chapter 10

Secret Sharing Schemes

Imagine, if you will, that you have made billions of dollars from Internet stocks and you wish to leave your estate to relatives. Your money is locked up in a safe whose combination only you know. You don't want to give the combination to each of your seven children because they are less than trustworthy. You would like to divide it among them in such a way that three of them have to get together to reconstruct the real combination. That way, someone who wants some of the inheritance must somehow cooperate with two other children. In this chapter we show how to solve this type of problem.

10.1   Secret Splitting

The first situation that we present is the simplest. Consider the case where you have a message M, represented as an integer, that you would like to split between two people Alice and Bob in such a way that neither of them alone can reconstruct the message M. A solution to this problem readily lends itself: Give Alice a random integer r and give Bob $M - r$. In order to reconstruct the message M, Alice and Bob simply add their pieces together.

A few technical problems arise from the fact that it is impossible to choose a random integer in a way that all integers are equally likely (the sum of the infinitely many equal probabilities, one for each integer, cannot equal 1). Therefore, we choose an integer n larger than all possible messages

M that might occur and regard M and r as numbers mod n. Then there is no problem choosing r as a random integer mod n; simply assign each integer mod n the probability $1/n$.

Now let us examine the case where we would like to split the secret among three people, Alice, Bob, and Charles. Using the previous idea, we choose two random numbers r and s mod n and give $M - r - s \pmod{n}$ to Alice, r to Bob, and s to Charles. To reconstruct the message M, Alice, Bob, and Charles simply add their respective numbers.

For the more general case, if we wish to split the secret M among m people, then we must choose $m - 1$ random numbers $r_1, \ldots, r_{m-1}$ mod n and give them to $m - 1$ of the people, and $M - \sum_{k=1}^{m-1} r_k \pmod{n}$ to the remaining person.

10.2   Threshold Schemes

In the previous section, we showed how to split a secret among m people so that all m were needed in order to reconstruct the secret. In this section we present methods that allow a subset of the people to reconstruct the secret.

It has been reported that the control of nuclear weapons in Russia employed a safety mechanism where two out of three important people were needed in order to launch missiles. This idea is not uncommon. It's in fact a plot device that is often employed in spy movies. One can imagine a control panel with three slots for keys and the missile launch protocol requiring that two of the three keys be inserted and turned at the same time in order to launch missiles to eradicate the earth.

Why not just use the secret splitting scheme of the previous section? Suppose some country is about to attack the enemy of the week, and the secret is split among three officials. A secret splitting method would need all three in order to reconstruct the key needed for the launch codes. This might not be possible; one of the three might be away on a diplomatic mission making peace with the previous week's opponent or might simply refuse because of a difference of opinion.

Definition. *Let t, w be positive integers with $t \leq w$. A (t, w)-**threshold scheme** is a method of sharing a message M among a set of w participants such that any subset consisting of t participants can reconstruct the message M, but no subset of smaller size can reconstruct M.*

The (t, w)-threshold schemes are key building blocks for more general sharing schemes, some of which will be explored in the Exercises for this chapter. We will describe two methods for constructing a (t, w)-threshold scheme.

The first method was invented in 1979 by Shamir and is known as the **Shamir threshold scheme** or the Lagrange interpolation scheme. It is based upon some natural extensions of ideas that we learned in high school algebra, namely that two points are needed to determine a line, three points to determine a quadratic, and so on.

Choose a prime p, which must be larger then all possible messages and also larger than the number w of participants. All computations will be carried out mod p. The prime replaces the integer n of Section 10.1. If a composite number were to be used instead, the matrices we obtain might not have inverses.

The message M is represented as a number mod p, and we want to split it among w people in such a way that t of them are needed to reconstruct the message. The first thing we do is randomly select $t - 1$ integers mod p, call them $s_1, s_2, \cdots s_{t-1}$. Then the polynomial

$$s(x) \equiv M + s_1 x + \cdots + s_{t-1} x^{t-1} \pmod{p}$$

is a polynomial such that $s(0) \equiv M \pmod{p}$. Now, for the w participants, we select distinct integers $x_1, \ldots, x_w \pmod{p}$ and give each person a pair (x_i, y_i) with $y_i \equiv s(x_i) \pmod{p}$. For example, $1, 2, \ldots, w$ is a reasonable choice for the x's, so we give out the pairs $(1, s(1)), \ldots, (w, s(w))$, one to each person. The prime p is known to all, but the polynomial $s(x)$ is kept secret.

Now suppose t people get together and share their pairs. For simplicity of notation, we assume the pairs are $(x_1, y_1), \cdots, (x_t, y_t)$. They want to recover the message M.

We begin with a linear system approach. Suppose we have a polynomial $s(x)$ of degree $t - 1$ that we would like to reconstruct from the points $(x_1, y_1), \cdots, (x_t, y_t)$, where $y_k = s(x_k)$. This means that

$$y_k \equiv M + s_1 x_k^1 + \cdots + s_{t-1} x_k^{t-1} \pmod{p}, \quad 1 \le k \le t.$$

If we denote $s_0 = M$, then we may rewrite this as

$$\begin{pmatrix} 1 & x_1 & \cdots & x_1^{t-1} \\ 1 & x_2 & \cdots & x_2^{t-1} \\ \vdots & \vdots & \ddots & \vdots \\ 1 & x_t & \cdots & x_t^{t-1} \end{pmatrix} \begin{pmatrix} s_0 \\ s_1 \\ \vdots \\ s_t \end{pmatrix} \equiv \begin{pmatrix} y_1 \\ y_2 \\ \vdots \\ y_t \end{pmatrix} \pmod{p}.$$

The matrix, let's call it V, is what is known as a Vandermonde matrix. We know that this system has a unique solution mod p if the determinant of the matrix V is nonzero mod p (see Section 3.8). It can be shown that the determinant is

$$\det V = \prod_{1 \le j < k \le t} (x_k - x_j),$$

which is zero mod p only when two of the x_i's coincide mod p (this is where we need p to be prime; see Exercise 3.3). Thus, as long as we have distinct x_k's, the system has a unique solution.

We now describe an alternative approach that leads to a formula for the reconstruction of the polynomial and hence for the secret message. Our goal is to reconstruct a polynomial $s(x)$ given that we know t of its values (x_k, y_k). First, let

$$l_k(x) = \prod_{\substack{i=1 \\ i \neq k}}^{t} \frac{x - x_i}{x_k - x_i} \quad (\text{mod } p).$$

Here, we work with fractions mod p as described in Section 3.3. Then

$$l_k(x_j) \equiv \begin{cases} 1 \text{ when } k = j \\ 0 \text{ when } k \neq j. \end{cases}$$

This is because $l_k(x_k)$ is a product of factors $(x_k - x_i)/(x_k - x_i)$, all of which are 1. When $k \neq j$, the product for $l_k(x_j)$ contains the factor $(x_j - x_j)/(x_k - x_j)$, which is 0.

The **Lagrange interpolation polynomial**

$$p(x) = \sum_{k=1}^{t} y_k l_k(x)$$

satisfies the requirement $p(x_j) = y_j$ for $1 \leq k \leq t$. For example,

$$p(x_1) = y_1 l_1(x_1) + y_2 l_2(x_2) + \cdots \equiv y_1 \cdot 1 + y_2 \cdot 0 + \cdots \equiv y_1 \quad (\text{mod } p).$$

We know from the previous approach with the Vandermonde matrix that the polynomial $s(x)$ is the only one of degree $t-1$ that takes on the specified values. Therefore, $p(x) = s(x)$.

Now, to reconstruct the secret message all we have to do is calculate $p(x)$ and evaluate it at $x = 0$. This gives us the formula

$$M \equiv \sum_{k=1}^{t} y_k \prod_{\substack{j=1 \\ j \neq k}}^{t} \frac{-x_j}{x_k - x_j} \quad (\text{mod } p).$$

Example. Let's construct a (3, 8)-threshold scheme, so we have 8 people and we want any 3 to be able to determine the secret, while two people cannot determine any information about the message.

Suppose the secret is the number $M = 190503180520$ (which corresponds to the word "secret"). Choose a prime p, for example, $p = 1234567890133$ (we need a prime at least as large as the secret, but there is no advantage in using primes much larger than the maximum size of the secret). Choose random numbers s_1 and s_2 mod p and form the polynomial

$$s(x) = M + s_1 x + s_2 x^2.$$

For example, let's work with

$$s(x) = 190503180520 + 482943028839x + 1206749628665x^2.$$

We now give the eight people pairs $(x, s(x))$. There is no need to choose the values of x randomly, so we simply use $x = 1, 2, \ldots, 8$. Therefore, we distribute the following pairs, one to each person:

$$(1, 645627947891)$$
$$(2, 1045116192326)$$
$$(3, 154400023692)$$
$$(4, 442615222255)$$
$$(5, 675193897882)$$
$$(6, 852136050573)$$
$$(7, 973441680328)$$
$$(8, 1039110787147) .$$

Suppose persons 2, 3, and 7 want to collaborate to determine the secret. Let's use the Lagrange interpolating polynomial. They calculate that the following polynomial passes through their three points:

$$20705602144728/5 - 1986192751427x + (1095476582793/5)x^2.$$

At this point they realize that they should have been working mod p. But

$$740740734080 \times 5 \equiv 1 \pmod{p},$$

so they replace $1/5$ by 740740734080, as in Section 3.3, and reduce mod p to obtain

$$190503180520 + 482943028839x + 1206749628665x^2.$$

This is, of course, the original polynomial $s(x)$. All they care about is the constant term 190503180520, which is the secret. (The last part of the preceding calculations could have been shortened slightly, since they only needed the constant term, not the whole polynomial.)

Similarly, any three people could reconstruct the polynomial and obtain the secret.

If persons 2, 3, and 7 chose the linear system approach instead, they would need to solve the following:

$$\begin{pmatrix} 1 & 2 & 4 \\ 1 & 3 & 9 \\ 1 & 7 & 49 \end{pmatrix} \begin{pmatrix} M \\ s_1 \\ s_2 \end{pmatrix} \equiv \begin{pmatrix} 1045116192326 \\ 154400023692 \\ 973441680328 \end{pmatrix} \pmod{1234567890133}.$$

This yields

$$(M, s_1, s_2) \equiv (190503180520, 482943028839, 1206749628665),$$

so they again recover the polynomial and the message.

What happens if only two people get together? Do they obtain any information? For example, suppose that persons 4 and 6 share their points (4, 442615222255) and (6, 852136050573) with each other. Let c be any possible secret. There is a unique quadratic polynomial $ax^2 + bx + c$ passing through the points $(0, c)$, $(4, 442615222255)$, and $(6, 852136050573)$. Therefore, any secret can still occur.

Similarly, they cannot guess the share held, for example, by person 7: Any point $(7, y_7)$ yields a unique secret c, and any secret c yields a polynomial $ax^2 + bx + c$, which corresponds to $y_7 = 49a + 7b + c$. Therefore, every value of y_7 can occur, and each corresponds to a secret. So persons 4 and 6 don't obtain any additional information about which secrets are more likely when they have only their own two points.

Similarly, if we use a polynomial of degree $t - 1$, there is no way that $t-1$ persons can obtain information about the message with only their data. Therefore, t people are required to obtain the message. ∎

There are other methods that can be used for secret sharing. We now describe one due to Blakley, also from 1979. Suppose there are several people and we want to arrange that any three can find the secret, but no two can. Choose a prime p and let x_0 be the secret. Choose y_0, z_0 randomly mod p. We therefore have a point $Q = (x_0, y_0, z_0)$ in three-dimensional space mod p. Each person is given the equation of a plane passing through Q. This is accomplished as follows. Choose a, b randomly mod p and then set $c \equiv z_0 - ax_0 - by_0 \pmod{p}$. The plane is then

$$z = ax + by + c.$$

This is done for each person. Usually, three planes will intersect in a point, which must be Q. Two planes will intersect in a line, so usually no information can obtained concerning the secret x_0 (but see Exercise 11).

Note that only one coordinate should be used to carry the secret. If the secret had instead been distributed among all three coordinates x_0, y_0, z_0, then there might be only one meaningful message corresponding to a point on a line that is the intersection of two persons' planes.

The three persons who want to deduce the secret can proceed as follows. They have three equations

$$a_i x + b_i y - z \equiv -c_i \pmod{p}, \quad 1 \le i \le 3,$$

which yield the matrix equation

$$\begin{pmatrix} a_1 & b_1 & -1 \\ a_2 & b_2 & -1 \\ a_3 & b_3 & -1 \end{pmatrix} \begin{pmatrix} x_0 \\ y_0 \\ z_0 \end{pmatrix} \equiv \begin{pmatrix} -c_1 \\ -c_2 \\ -c_3 \end{pmatrix}.$$

As long as the determinant of this matrix is nonzero mod p, the matrix can be inverted mod p and the secret x_0 can be found (of course, in practice, one would tend to solve this by row operations rather than by inverting the matrix).

Example. Let $p = 73$. Suppose we give A, B, C, D, E the following planes:

$$A : z = 4x + 19y + 68$$

$$B : z = 52x + 27y + 10$$

$$C : z = 36x + 65y + 18$$

$$D : z = 57x + 12y + 16$$

$$E : z = 34x + 19y + 49.$$

If A, B, C want to recover the secret, they solve

$$\begin{pmatrix} 4 & 19 & -1 \\ 52 & 27 & -1 \\ 36 & 65 & -1 \end{pmatrix} \begin{pmatrix} x_0 \\ y_0 \\ z_0 \end{pmatrix} \equiv \begin{pmatrix} -68 \\ -10 \\ -18 \end{pmatrix} \pmod{73}.$$

The solution is $(x_0, y_0, z_0) = (42, 29, 57)$, so the secret is $x_0 = 42$. Similarly, any three of A, B, C, D, E can cooperate to recover x_0. ∎

By using $(t-1)$-dimensional hyperplanes in t-dimensional space, we can use the same method to create a (t, w)-threshold scheme for any values of t and w.

As long as p is reasonably large, it is very likely that the matrix is invertible, though this is not guaranteed. It would not be hard to arrange ways to choose a, b, c so that the matrix is always invertible. Essentially, this is what happens in the Shamir method. The matrix equations for both methods are similar, and the Shamir method could be regarded as a special case of the Blakley method. But since the Shamir method yields a Vandermonde matrix, the equations can always be solved. The other advantage of the Shamir method is that it requires less information to be carried by each person: (x, y) versus $(a, b, c, \dots)$.

We now return to the Shamir method and consider variations of the basic situation. By giving certain persons more shares, it is possible to make some people more important than others. For example, suppose we have a system in which eight shares are required to obtain the secret, and suppose the boss is given four shares, her daughters are given two shares, and the other employees are each given one share. Then the boss and two of her daughters can obtain the secret, or three daughters and two regular employees, for example.

Here is a more complicated situation. Suppose two companies A and B share a bank vault. They want a system where four employees from A and three from B are needed in order to obtain the secret combination. Clearly it won't work if we simply supply shares that are all for the same secret, since one company could simply use enough partial secrets from its employees that the other company's shares would not be needed. The following is a solution that works. Write the secret s as the sum of two numbers $s \equiv c_A + c_B$ (mod p). Now make c_A into a secret shared among the employees of A as the constant term of a polynomial of degree 3. Similarly, let c_B be the constant term of a polynomial of degree 2 and use this to distribute shares of c_B among the employees of B. If four employees of A and three employees of B get together, then those from A determine c_A and those from B determine c_B. Then they add c_A and c_B to get s.

Note that A does not obtain any information about the secret s by itself since $c_A + x \equiv s$ (mod p) has a unique solution x for every s, so every possible value of s corresponds to a possible value of c_B. Therefore, knowing c_A does not help A to find the secret; A also needs to know c_B.

10.3 Exercises

1. Suppose you have a secret, namely 5. You want to set up a system where four persons A, B, C, D are given shares of the secret in such a way that any two of them can determine the secret, but no one alone can determine the secret. Describe how this can be done. In particular, list the actual pieces of information (i.e., numbers) that you could give to each person to accomplish this.

2. You set up a (2, 30) Shamir threshold scheme, working mod the prime 101. Two of the shares are (1,13) and (3,12). Another person received the share $(2, *)$, but the part denoted by $*$ is unreadable. What is the correct value of $*$?

3. In a $(3, 5)$ Shamir secret sharing scheme with modulus $p = 17$, the following were given to Alice, Bob, and Charles: $(1, 8)$, $(3, 10)$, $(5, 11)$. Calculate the corresponding Lagrange interpolating polynomial, and identify the secret.

4. In a Shamir secret sharing scheme, the secret is the constant term of a degree 4 polynomial mod the prime 1093. Suppose three people have the secrets $(2, 197)$, $(4, 874)$, and $(13, 547)$. How many possibilities are there for the secret?

5. Mark doesn't like mods, so he wants to implement a $(2, 30)$ Shamir secret sharing scheme without them. His secret is M (a positive integer) and he gives person i the share $(i, M + si)$ for a positive integer s that he randomly chooses. Bob receives the share $(20, 97)$. Describe how Bob can narrow down the possibilities for M and determine what values of M are possible.

6. A key distributor uses a $(2, 20)$-threshold scheme to distribute a combination to an electronic safe to 20 participants.
(a) What is the smallest number of participants needed to open the safe, given that one unknown participant is a cheater who will reveal a random share?
(b) If they are only allowed to try one combination (if they are wrong the electronic safe shuts down permanently), then how many participants are necessary to open the safe? (*Note:* This one is a little subtle. A majority vote actually works with four people, but you need to show that a tie cannot occur.)

7. A certain military office consists of one general, two colonels, and five desk clerks. They have control of a powerful missile, but don't want the missile launched unless the general decides to launch it, or the two colonels decide to launch it, or the five desk clerks decide to launch it, or one colonel and three desk clerks decide to launch it. Describe how you would do this with a secret sharing scheme. (*Hint:* Try distributing the shares of a $(10, 30)$ Shamir scheme.)

8. Suppose there are four people in a room, exactly one of whom is a foreign agent. The other three people have been given pairs corresponding to a Shamir secret sharing scheme in which any two people can determine the secret. The foreign agent has randomly chosen a pair. The people and pairs are as follows. All the numbers are mod 11.

$$A : (1, 4) \quad B : (3, 7) \quad C : (5, 1) \quad D : (7, 2).$$

Determine who the foreign agent is and what the message is.

9. Consider the following situation: Government A, Government B, and Government C are hostile to each other, but the common threat of Antarctica looms over them. They each send a delegation consisting of 10 members to an international summit to consider the threat that Antarctica's penguins pose to world security. They decide to keep a watchful eye on their tuxedoed rivals. However, they also decide that if the birds get too rowdy, then they will launch a full-force attack on Antarctica. Using secret sharing techniques, describe how they can arrange to share the launch codes so that it is necessary that three members from delegation A, four members from delegation B, and two members from C cooperate to reconstruct the launch codes.

10. This problem explores what is known as the Newton form of the interpolant. In the Shamir method, we presented two methods for calculating the interpolating polynomial. The system of equations approach is difficult to solve and easy to evaluate, while with the Lagrange approach it is quite simple to determine the interpolating polynomial but becomes a labor to evaluate. The Newton form of the interpolating polynomial comes from choosing $1, x - x_1, (x - x_1)(x - x_2), \cdots, (x - x_1)(x - x_2) \cdots (x - x_t)$ as a basis. The interpolating polynomial is then $p(x) = c_0 + c_1(x - x_1) + c_2(x - x_1)(x - x_2) + \cdots + c_t(x - x_1)(x - x_2) \cdots (x - x_t)$. Show that we can solve for the coefficients c_k by solving a system $Nc = y$. What special properties do you observe in the matrix N? Why does this make the system easier to solve?

11. In a Blakley $(3, w)$ scheme, suppose persons A and B are given the planes $z = 2x + 3y + 13$ and $z = 5x + 3y + 1$. Show that they can recover the secret without a third person.

10.4 Computer Problems

1. Alice, Bob, and Charles have each received shares of a secret that was split using the secret splitting scheme described in Section 10.1. Suppose that $n = 2110763$. Alice is given the share $M - r - s = 1008369$, Bob is given the share $r = 593647$, and Charles is given the share $s = 631870$. Determine the secret M.

2. For a Shamir (4,7) secret sharing scheme, take $p = 8737$ and let the shares be

$$(1, 214), (2, 7543), (3, 6912), (4, 8223), (5, 3904), (6, 3857), (7, 510).$$

Take a set of four shares and find the secret. Now take another set of four shares and verify that the secret obtained is the same.

3. Alice, Bob, Charles, and Dorothy use a (2, 4) Shamir secret sharing scheme using the prime $p = 984583$. Suppose that Alice gets the share (38, 358910), Bob gets the share (3876, 9612), Charles gets the share (23112, 28774), and Dorothy gets the share (432, 178067). One of these shares was incorrectly received. Determine which one is incorrect, and find the secret.

Chapter 11

Games

11.1 Flipping Coins over the Telephone

Alice is living in Anchorage and Bob is living in Baltimore. A friend, not realizing that they are no longer together, leaves them a car in his will. How do they decide who gets the car? Bob phones Alice and says he'll flip a coin. Alice chooses "Tails" but Bob says "Sorry, it was Heads." So Bob gets the car.

For some reason, Alice suspects Bob might not have been honest. (Actually, he told the truth; as soon as she called tails, he pulled out his specially made two-headed penny so he wouldn't have to lie.) She resolves that the next time this happens, she'll use a different method. So she goes to her local cryptologist, who tells her the following method.

Alice chooses two large random primes p and q, both congruent to 3 mod 4. She keeps them secret but sends the product $n = pq$ to Bob. Then Bob chooses a random integer x and computes $y \equiv x^2 \pmod{n}$. He keeps x secret but sends y to Alice. Alice knows that y has a square root mod n (if it doesn't, her calculations will reveal this fact, in which case she accuses Bob of cheating), so she uses her knowledge of p and q to find the four square roots $\pm a$, $\pm b$ of $y \pmod{n}$ (see Section 3.9). One of these will be x, but she doesn't know which one. She chooses one at random (this is the "flip"), say b, and sends it to Bob. If $b \equiv \pm x \pmod{n}$, Bob tells Alice that she wins. If

$b \not\equiv \pm x \pmod{n}$, Bob wins.

Alice		**Bob**
$n = pq$	$\longrightarrow$	n
y	$\longleftarrow$	$y \equiv x^2$
$a^2 \equiv b^2 \equiv y$	$\longrightarrow$	b
Alice wins	$\longleftarrow$	$b \equiv \pm x$
or		or
Bob wins	$\longleftarrow$	$b \not\equiv \pm x$

But, asks Alice, how can I be sure Bob doesn't cheat? If Alice sends b to Bob and $x \equiv \pm a \pmod{n}$, then Bob knows all four square roots of y $\pmod{n}$, so he can factor n. In particular, $\gcd(x - b, n)$ gives a nontrivial factor of n. Therefore, if it is computationally infeasible to factor n, the only way Bob could produce the factors p and q would be when his value of x is not plus or minus the value Alice sends. If Alice sends Bob $\pm x$, Bob has no more information than he had when Alice sent him the number n. Therefore, he should not be able to produce p and q in this case. So Alice can check that Bob didn't cheat by asking Bob for the factorization of n.

What if Alice tries to cheat by sending Bob a random number rather than a square root of y? This would surely prevent Bob from factoring n. Bob can guard against this by checking that the square of the number Alice sends is congruent to y.

Suppose Alice tries to deceive Bob by sending a product of three primes. Of course, Bob could ask Alice for the factorization of n at the end of the game; if Alice produces two factors, they can be quickly checked for primality. But Bob shouldn't worry about this possibility. When n is the product of three distinct primes, there are eight square roots of y. Therefore, up to sign there are four choices of numbers for Alice to send. Each of the three wrong choices will allow Bob to find a nontrivial factor of n. So Alice would decrease her chances of winning to only one in four. Therefore, she should not try this.

There is one flaw in this procedure. Suppose Bob decides he wants to lose. He can then claim his value of x was exactly the value that Alice sent him. Alice cannot dispute this since the only information she has is the square of Bob's number, which is congruent to the square of her number. There are other procedures that can prevent Bob from trying to lose, but we will not discuss them here.

Finally, we should mention that it is not difficult to find primes p and q that are congruent to 3 mod 4. The density of primes congruent to 1 mod 4 is the same as the density of primes that are 3 mod 4. Therefore, find a random prime p. If it is not 3 mod 4, try another. This process should succeed quickly. We can find q similarly.

Example. Alice chooses

$$p = 2038074743 \text{ and } q = 1190494759.$$

She sends

$$n = pq = 2426317299991771937$$

to Bob. Bob takes

$$x = 1414213562373095048$$

(this isn't as random as it looks; but Bob thinks the decimal expansions of square roots look random) and computes

$$y \equiv x^2 \equiv 363278601055491705 \pmod{n},$$

which he sends to Alice.

Alice computes

$$y^{(p+1)/4} \equiv 1701899961 \pmod{p} \text{ and } y^{(q+1)/4} \equiv 325656728 \pmod{q}.$$

Therefore, she knows that

$$x \equiv \pm 1701899961 \pmod{p} \text{ and } x \equiv \pm 325656728 \pmod{q}.$$

The Chinese remainder theorem puts these together in four ways to yield

$$x \equiv \pm 1012103737618676889 \text{ or } \pm 937850352623334103 \pmod{n}.$$

Suppose Alice sends 1012103737618676889 to Bob. This is $-x \pmod{n}$, so Bob declares Alice the winner.

Suppose instead that Alice sends 937850352623334103 to Bob. Then Bob claims victory. By computing

$$\gcd(1414213562373095048 - 937850352623334103, n) = 1190494759,$$

he can prove that he won. ∎

11.2 Poker over the Telephone

Alice and Bob quickly tire of flipping coins over the telephone and decide to try poker. Bob pulls out his deck of cards, shuffles, and deals two hands, one for Alice and one for himself. Now what does he do? Alice won't let him read the cards to her. Also, she suggests that he might not be playing with a full deck. Arguments ensue. But then someone suggests that they each choose their own cards. The betting is fast and furious. After several hundred coins (they remain unused from the coin-flipping protocol) have been wagered, Alice and Bob discover that they each have a royal flush. Each claims the other must have cheated. Fortunately, their favorite cryptologist can help.

Here is the method she suggests, in nonmathematical terms. Bob takes 52 identical boxes, puts a card in each box, and puts a lock on each one. He dumps the boxes in a bag and sends them to Alice. She chooses five boxes, puts her locks on them, and sends them back to Bob. He takes his locks off and sends the five boxes back to Alice, who takes her locks off and finds her five cards. Then she chooses five more boxes and sends them back to Bob. He takes off his locks and gets his five cards. Now suppose Alice wants to replace three cards. She puts three cards in a discard box, puts on her lock, and sends the box to Bob. She then chooses three boxes from the remaining 42 card boxes, puts on her locks, and sends them to Bob. Bob removes his locks and sends them back to Alice, who removes her locks and gets the cards. If Bob wants to replace two cards, he puts them in another discard box, puts on his lock, and sends the box to Alice. She chooses two card boxes and sends them to Bob. He removes his locks and gets his cards. They then compare hands to see who wins. We'll assume Alice wins.

After the hand has been played, Bob wants to check that Alice put three cards in her discard box since he wants to be sure she wasn't playing with eight cards. He puts his lock on the box and sends the box to Alice, who takes her lock off. Since Bob's lock is still on the box, she can't change the contents. She sends the box back to Bob, who removes the lock and finds the three cards that Alice discarded (this differs from standard poker in that Bob sees the actual cards discarded; in a standard game, Bob only sees that Alice discards three cards and doesn't need to look at them afterward). Similarly, Alice can check that Bob discarded two cards.

Bob can check that Alice played with the hand that was dealt by asking her to send her cards to him. Alice cannot change her hand since all the remaining cards still have Bob's locks on them (and Bob can't open them since Alice has them in her possession).

Of course, various problems arise if Alice or Bob unjustly accuses the other of cheating. But, ignoring such complications, we see that Alice and Bob can now play poker. However, the postage for sending 52 boxes back and forth is starting to cut into Alice's profits. So she goes back to her cryptologist and asks for a mathematical implementation. The following is the method.

Alice and Bob agree on a large prime p. Alice chooses a secret integer α with $\gcd(\alpha, p-1) = 1$, and Bob chooses a secret integer β with $\gcd(\beta, p-1) = 1$. Alice computes α' such that $\alpha\alpha' \equiv 1 \pmod{p-1}$ and Bob computes β' with $\beta\beta' \equiv 1 \pmod{p-1}$. A different α and β are used for each hand. A different p could be used for each hand also.

Note that $c^{\alpha\alpha'} \equiv c \pmod{p}$, and similarly for β. This can be seen as follows: $\alpha\alpha' \equiv 1 \pmod{p-1}$, so $\alpha\alpha' = 1 + (p-1)k$ for some integer k. Therefore, when $c \not\equiv 0 \pmod{p}$

$$c^{\alpha\alpha'} \equiv c \cdot \left(c^{p-1}\right)^k \equiv c \cdot 1^k \equiv c \pmod{p}.$$

Trivially, we also have $c^{\alpha\alpha'} \equiv c \pmod{p}$ when $c \equiv 0 \pmod{p}$.

The 52 cards are changed to 52 distinct numbers $c_1, \ldots, c_{52} \pmod{p}$ via some prearranged scheme. Bob computes $b_i \equiv c_i^\beta \pmod{p}$ for $1 \le i \le 52$, randomly permutes these numbers, and sends them to Alice. Alice chooses five numbers $b_{i_1}, \cdots, b_{i_5}$, computes $b_{i_j}^\alpha \pmod{p}$ for $1 \le j \le 5$, and sends these numbers to Bob. Bob takes off his lock by raising these numbers to the β' power and sends them to Alice, who removes her lock by raising to the α' power. This gives Alice her hand.

Alice then chooses five more of the numbers b_i and sends them back to Bob, who removes his locks by raising the numbers to the β' power. This gives him his hand. The rest of the game proceeds in this fashion.

It seems to be quite difficult for Alice to deduce Bob's cards. She could guess which encrypted card b_i corresponds to a fixed unencrypted card c_j. This means Alice would need to solve equations of the form $c_j^\beta \equiv b_i \pmod{p}$ for b. Doing this for the 52 choices for b_i would give at most 52 choices for β. The correct exponent β could then be determined by choosing another card $c_{j'}$ and trying the various possibilities for β to see which ones give the encrypted values that are on the list of encrypted cards. But these equations that Alice needs to solve are discrete logarithm problems, which are generally assumed to be difficult when p is large (see Chapter 7).

Example. Let's consider a simplified game where there are only five cards: ten, jack, queen, king, ace. Each player is dealt one card. The winner is the one with the higher card. Change the cards to numbers using $a = 01, b = 02, \ldots$, so we have the following:

Ten	Jack	Queen	King	Ace
200514	10010311	1721050514	11091407	10305

Let the prime be $p = 2396271991$. Alice chooses her secret $\alpha = 1234567$ and Bob chooses his secret $\beta = 7654321$. Alice computes $\alpha' = 402406273$ and Bob computes $\beta' = 200508901$. This can be done via the extended Euclidean algorithm. Just to be sure, Alice checks that $\alpha\alpha' \equiv 1 \pmod{p-1}$, and Bob does a similar calculation with β and β'.

Bob now calculates (congruences are mod p)

$$200514^\beta \equiv 914012224$$
$$10010311^\beta \equiv 1507298770$$
$$1721050514^\beta \equiv 74390103$$
$$11091407^\beta \equiv 2337996540$$
$$10305^\beta \equiv 1112225809.$$

He shuffles these numbers and sends them to Alice:

1507298770,   1112225809,   2337996540,   914012224,   74390103.

Since Alice does not know β, it is unlikely she can deduce which card is which without a lot of computation.

Alice now chooses her card by choosing one of these numbers— for example, the fourth— raises it to the power α, and sends it to Bob:

$$914012224^\alpha \equiv 1230896099 \pmod{p}.$$

Bob takes off his lock by raising this to the power β' and sends it back to Alice:

$$1230896099^{\beta'} \equiv 1700536007 \pmod{p}.$$

Alice now removes her lock by raising this to the power α':

$$1700536007^{\alpha'} \equiv 200514 \pmod{p}.$$

Her card is therefore the ten.

Now Alice chooses Bob's card by simply choosing one of the original cards she received— for example, 1507298770— and sending it back to Bob. Bob computes

$$1507298770^{\beta'} \equiv 10010311 \pmod{p}.$$

Therefore, his card is the jack.

This accomplishes the desired dealing of the cards. Alice and Bob now compare cards and Bob wins. To prevent cheating, Alice and Bob then reveal their secret exponents α and β. Suppose Alice tries to claim she has the king. Bob can quickly compute α' and show that the card he sent to Alice was the ten. ∎

How to Cheat

No game of poker would be complete without at least the possibility of cheating. Here's how to do it here.

Bob goes to his local number theorist, who tells him about quadratic residues. A number r (mod p) is called a **quadratic residue** mod p if the congruence $x^2 \equiv r$ (mod p) has a solution; in other words, r is a square mod p. A nonresidue n is an integer such that $x^2 \equiv n$ (mod p) has no solution.

There is an easy way to decide whether or not a number $z \not\equiv 0$ (mod p) is a quadratic residue or nonresidue:

$$z^{(p-1)/2} \equiv \begin{cases} +1 & (\text{mod } p) \quad \text{if } z \text{ is a quadratic residue} \\ -1 & (\text{mod } p) \quad \text{if } z \text{ is a quadratic nonresidue} \end{cases}$$

(see Exercise 1). This determination can also be done using the Legendre or Jacobi symbol plus quadratic reciprocity.

Recall that we needed $\gcd(\alpha, p-1) = 1$ and $\gcd(\beta, p-1) = 1$. Therefore, α and β are odd. A card c is encrypted to c^β, and

$$\left(c^\beta\right)^{(p-1)/2} \equiv \left(c^{(p-1)/2}\right)^\beta \equiv c^{(p-1)/2} \quad (\text{mod } p),$$

since $(\pm 1)^{\text{odd}} \equiv \pm 1$ (with the same choice of signs on both sides of the congruence). Therefore, c is a quadratic residue mod p if and only if c^β is a quadratic residue. The corresponding statement also applies to the α and $\alpha\beta$ power of the cards.

When Alice sends Bob the five cards that will make up her hand, Bob quickly checks these cards to see which are residues quadratic and which are nonresidues. This means that there are two sets R and N, and for each of Alice's cards, he knows whether the card is in R or N. This gives him a slight advantage. For example, suppose he needs to know whether or not she has the Queen of Hearts and he determines that it is in N. If she has only one N card, the chances are low that she has the card. In this way, Bob obtains a slight advantage and starts winning.

Alice quickly consults her local cryptologist, who fortunately knows about quadratic residues, too. Now when Alice chooses Bob's hand, she arranges that all of his cards are in R, for example. Then she knows that his hand is chosen from 26 cards rather than 52. This is better than the partial information that Bob has and is useful enough that she gains an advantage over Bob. Finally, Alice gets very bold. She sneakily chooses the prime p so that the Ace, King, Queen, Jack, and Ten of Spades are the only quadratic residues. When she chooses Bob's hand, she gives him five nonresidues. She chooses the five residues for herself. Bob, who has been computing residues and nonresidues on each hand, has already been getting suspicious since his cards have all been residues or all been nonresidues for several hands. But now he sees before the hand is played that she has chosen a royal flush for herself. He accuses her of cheating, arguments ensue, and they go back to coin flipping.

Example. Let's return to the simplified example. The choice of prime p was not random. In fact,

$$200514^{(p-1)/2} \equiv 1$$
$$10010311^{(p-1)/2} \equiv 1$$
$$1721050514^{(p-1)/2} \equiv 1$$
$$11091407^{(p-1)/2} \equiv 1$$
$$10305^{(p-1)/2} \equiv -1,$$

so only the ace is a nonresidue, while all the remaining cards are quadratic residues.

When Alice is choosing her hand, she computes

$$1507298770^{(p-1)/2} \equiv 1$$
$$1112225809^{(p-1)/2} \equiv -1$$
$$2337996540^{(p-1)/2} \equiv 1$$
$$914012224^{(p-1)/2} \equiv 1$$
$$74390103^{(p-1)/2} \equiv 1.$$

This tells her that the ace is 1112225809. She raises it to the power α', then sends it to Bob. He raises it to the power β' and sends it back to Alice, who raises it to the power α'. Of course, she finds that her card is the ace. ∎

For more on playing poker over the telephone, see [Fortune-Merritt].

11.3   Exercises

1. Let g be a primitive root for the prime p. This means that the numbers $1, g, g^2, g^3, \ldots, g^{p-1}$ (mod p) yield all nonzero congruence classes mod p.
(a) Let i be fixed and suppose $x^2 \equiv g^i$ (mod p) has a solution x. Show that i must be even. (*Hint:* Write $x \equiv g^j$ for some j. Now use the fact that $g^k \equiv g^l$ (mod p) if and only if $k \equiv l$ (mod $p-1$).) This shows that the nonzero squares mod p are exactly $1, g^2, g^4, g^6, \ldots$ (mod p), and therefore $g, g^3, g^5, \ldots$ are the quadratic nonresidues mod p.
(b) Using the definition of primitive root, show that $g^{(p-1)/2} \not\equiv 1$ (mod p).
(c) Use Exercise 3.4 to show that $g^{(p-1)/2} \equiv -1$ (mod p).
(d) Let $x \not\equiv 0$ (mod p). Show that $x^{(p-1)/2} \equiv 1$ (mod p) if x is a quadratic residue and $x^{(p-1)/2} \equiv -1$ (mod p) if x is a quadratic nonresidue mod p.

2. In the coin flipping protocol with $n = pq$, suppose Bob sends a number y such that neither y nor $-y$ has a square root mod n.

(a) Show that y cannot be a square both mod p and mod q. Similarly, $-y$ cannot be a square mod both primes.

(b) Suppose y is not a square mod q. Show that $-y$ is a square mod q.

(c) Show that y is a square mod one of the primes and $-y$ is a square mod the other.

(d) Benevolent Alice decides to correct Bob's "mistake." Suppose y is a square mod p and $-y$ is a square mod q. Alice calculates a number b such that $b^2 \equiv y \pmod{p}$ and $b^2 \equiv -y \pmod{q}$ and sends b to Bob (there are two pairs of choices for b). Show how Bob can use this information to factor n, hence claim victory.

3. (a) Let p be an odd prime. Show that if $x \equiv -x \pmod{p}$, then $x \equiv 0 \pmod{p}$.

(b) Let p be an odd prime. Suppose $x, y \not\equiv 0 \pmod{p}$ and $x^2 \equiv y^2 \pmod{p^2}$. Show that $x \equiv \pm y \pmod{p^2}$ (*Hint*: Look at the proof of the Basic Principle in Section 6.3.)

(c) Suppose Alice cheats when flipping coins by choosing $p = q$. Show that Bob always loses in the sense that Alice always returns $\pm x$. Therefore, it is wise for Bob to ask for the two primes at the end of the game.

Chapter 12

Zero-Knowledge Techniques

12.1 The Basic Setup

A few years ago, it was reported that some thieves set up a fake automatic teller machine at a shopping mall. When a person inserted a bank card and typed in an identification number, the machine recorded the information but responded with the message that it could not accept the card. The thieves then made counterfeit bank cards and went to legitimate teller machines and withdrew cash, using the identification numbers they had obtained.

How can this be avoided? There are several situations where someone reveals a secret identification number or password in order to complete a transaction. Anyone who obtains this secret number, plus some (almost public) identification information (for example, the information on a bank card), can masquerade as this person. What is needed is a way to use the secret number without giving any information that can be reused by an eavesdropper. This is where zero-knowledge techniques come in.

The basic challenge-response protocol is best illustrated by an example due to Quisquater, Guillou, and Berson [Quisquater et al.]. Suppose there is a tunnel with a door, as in Figure 12.1. Peggy (the prover) wants to prove to Victor (the verifier) that she can go through the door without giving any information to Victor about how she does it (or even which direction she can pass through the door). They proceed as follows. Peggy enters the tunnel

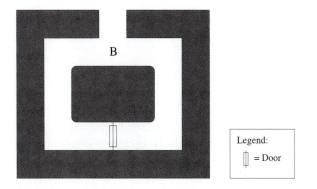

Figure 12.1: The Tunnel Used in the Zero-Knowledge Protocol.

and goes down either the left side or the right side of the tunnel. Victor waits outside for a minute, then comes in and stands at point B. He calls out "Left" or "Right" to Peggy. Peggy then comes to point B by the left or right tunnel, as requested. This entire protocol is repeated several times, until Victor is satisfied. Of course, in each round, Peggy randomly chooses which side she will go down, and Victor randomly chooses which side he will request.

Since Peggy must choose to go down the left or right side before she knows what Victor will say, she has only a 50% chance of fooling Victor if she doesn't know how to go through the door. Therefore, if Peggy comes out the correct side for each of 10 repetitions, there is only one chance in $2^{10} = 1024$ that Peggy doesn't know how to go through the door. At this point, Victor is probably convinced, though he could try a few more times just to be sure.

Suppose Eve is watching the proceedings on a video monitor set up at B. She will not be able to use anything she sees to convince Victor or anyone else that she, too, can go through the door. Moreover, she might not even be convinced that Peggy can go through the door. After all, Peggy and Victor could have planned the sequence of rights and lefts ahead of time. By this reasoning, there is no useful information that Victor obtains that can be transmitted to anyone.

Note that there is never a proof, in a strict mathematical sense, that Peggy can go through the door. But there is overwhelming evidence, obtained through a series of challenges and responses. This is a feature of zero-knowledge "proofs."

There are several mathematical versions of this procedure, but we'll concentrate on one of them. Let $n = pq$ be the product of two large primes. Let y be a square mod n with $\gcd(y, n) = 1$. Recall that finding square roots mod n is hard; in fact, finding square roots mod n is equivalent to factoring

n (see Section 3.9). However, Peggy claims to know a square root s of y. Victor wants to verify this, but Peggy does not want to reveal s. Here is the method:

1. Peggy chooses two random numbers r_1 and r_2 with

$$r_1 r_2 \equiv s \pmod{n}$$

   (of course, she chooses r_1 at random with $\gcd(r_1, n) = 1$ and lets $r_2 \equiv sr_1^{-1}$, or she could similarly choose r_2 first). She computes

$$x_1 \equiv r_1^2, \quad x_2 \equiv r_2^2 \pmod{n}$$

   and sends x_1 and x_2 to Victor.

2. Victor checks that $x_1 x_2 \equiv y \pmod{n}$, then chooses either x_1 or x_2 and asks Peggy to supply a square root of it. He checks that it is an actual square root.

3. The first two steps are repeated several times, until Victor is convinced.

Of course, if Peggy knows s, the procedure proceeds without problems. But what if Peggy doesn't know a square root of y? She can still send Victor two numbers x_1 and x_2 with $x_1 x_2 \equiv y$. If she knows a square root of x_1 and a square root of x_2, then she knows a square root of $y \equiv x_1 x_2$. Therefore, for at least one of them, she does not know a square root. At least half the time, Victor is going to ask her for a square root she doesn't know. Since computing square roots is hard, she is not able to produce the desired answer, and therefore Victor finds out that she doesn't know s.

Suppose, however, that Peggy predicts correctly that Victor will ask for a square root of x_2. Then she chooses a random r_2, computes $x_2 \equiv r_2^2$ (mod n), and lets $x_1 \equiv yx_2^{-1}$ (mod n). She sends x_1 and x_2 to Victor, and everything works. This method gives Peggy a 50% chance of fooling Victor on any given round, but it requires her to guess which number Victor will request each time. As soon as she fails, Victor will find out that she doesn't know s.

If Victor verifies that Peggy knows a square root, does he obtain any information that can be used by someone else? No, since in any step he is only learning the square root of a random square, not a square root of y. Of course, if Peggy uses the same random numbers more than once, he could find out the square roots of both x_1 and x_2 and hence a square root of y. So Peggy should be careful in her choice of random numbers.

Suppose Eve is listening. She also will only learn square roots of random numbers. If she tries to use the same sequence of random numbers to masquerade as Peggy, she needs to be asked for the square roots of exactly the same sequence of x_1's and x_2's. If Victor asks for a square root of an x_1 in place of an x_2 at one step, for example, Eve will not be able to supply it.

12.2 The Feige-Fiat-Shamir Identification Scheme

The preceding protocol requires several communications between Peggy and Victor. The Feige-Fiat-Shamir method reduces this number and uses a type of parallel verification. This then is used as the basis of an identification scheme.

Again, let $n = pq$ be the product of two large primes. Peggy has secret numbers $s_1, \ldots, s_k$. Let $v_i \equiv s_i^{-2} \pmod{n}$ (we assume $\gcd(s_i, n) = 1$). The numbers v_i are sent to Victor. Victor will try to verify that Peggy knows the numbers $s_1, \ldots, s_k$. Peggy and Victor proceed as follows:

1. Peggy chooses a random integer r, computes $x \equiv r^2 \pmod{n}$ and sends x to Victor.

2. Victor chooses numbers $b_1, \ldots, b_k$ with each $b_i \in \{0, 1\}$. He sends these to Peggy.

3. Peggy computes $y \equiv r s_1^{b_1} s_2^{b_2} \cdots s_k^{b_k} \pmod{n}$ and sends y to Victor.

4. Victor checks that $x \equiv y^2 v_1^{b_1} v_2^{b_2} \cdots v_k^{b_k} \pmod{n}$.

5. Steps 1 through 4 are repeated several times (each time with a different r).

Consider the case $k = 1$. Then Peggy is asked for either r or rs_1. These are two random numbers whose quotient is a square root of v_1. Therefore, this is essentially the same idea as the simplified scheme discussed previously, with quotients instead of products.

Now let's analyze the case of larger k. Suppose, for example, that Victor sends $b_1 = 1, b_2 = 1, b_4 = 1$, and all other $b_i = 0$. Then Peggy must produce $y \equiv rs_1 s_2 s_4$, which is a square root of $xv_1 v_2 v_4$. In fact, in each round, Victor is asking for a square root of a number of the form $xv_{i_1} v_{i_2} \cdots v_{i_j}$. Peggy can supply a square root if she knows $r, s_{i_1}, \ldots, s_{i_j}$. If she doesn't, she will have a hard time computing a square root.

If Peggy doesn't know any of the numbers $s_1, \ldots, s_k$ (the likely scenario also if someone other than Peggy is pretending to be Peggy), she could guess the string of bits that Victor will send. Suppose she guesses correctly, before she sends x. She lets y be a random number and declares $x \equiv y^2 v_1^{b_1} v_2^{b_2} \cdots v_k^{b_k} \pmod{n}$. When Victor sends the string of bits, Peggy sends back the value of y. Of course, the verification congruence is satisfied. But if Peggy guesses incorrectly, she will need to modify her choice of y, which means she will need some square roots of v_i's.

For example, suppose Peggy is able to supply the correct response when $b_1 = 1, b_2 = 1, b_4 = 1$, and all other $b_i = 0$. This could be accomplished by guessing the bits and using the preceding method of choosing x. However, suppose Victor sends $b_1 = 1, b_3 = 1$, and all other $b_i = 0$. Then Peggy will be ready to supply a square root of $x v_1 v_2 v_4$ but will be asked to supply a square root of $x v_1 v_3$. This, combined with what she knows, is equivalent to knowing a square root of $v_2^{-1} v_3 v_4^{-1}$, which she is not able to compute. In an extreme case, Victor could send all bits equal to 0, which means Peggy must supply a square root of x. With Peggy's guess as before, this means she would know a square root of $v_1 v_2 v_4$. In summary, if Peggy's guess is not correct, she will need to know the square root of a nonempty product of v_i's, which she cannot compute. Therefore, there are 2^k possible strings of bits that Victor can send, and only one will allow Peggy to fool Victor. In one iteration of the protocol, the chances are only one in 2^k that Victor will be fooled. If the procedure is repeated t times, the chances are 1 in 2^{kt} that Victor is fooled. Recommended values are $k = 5$ and $t = 4$. Note that this gives the same probability as 20 iterations of the earlier scheme, so the present procedure is more efficient in terms of communication between Peggy and Victor. Of course, Victor has not obtained as strong a verification that Peggy knows, for example, s_1, but he is very certain that Eve is not masquerading as Peggy, since Eve should not know any of the s_i's.

The preceding can be used to design an identification scheme. Let I be a string that includes Peggy's name, birth date, and any other information deemed appropriate. Let H be a public hash function. A trusted authority Arthur (the bank, a passport agency, ...) chooses $n = pq$ to be the product of two large primes. Arthur computes $H(I\|j)$ for some small values of j, where $I\|j$ means j is appended to I. Using his knowledge of p, q, he can determine which of these numbers $H(I\|j)$ have square roots mod n and calculate a square root for each such number. This yields numbers $v_1 = H(I\|j_1), \ldots, v_k = H(I\|j_k)$ and square roots $s_1, \ldots, s_k$. The numbers $I, n, j_1, \ldots, j_k$ are made public. Arthur gives the numbers $s_1, \ldots, s_k$ to Peggy, who keeps them secret. The prime numbers p, q are discarded once the square roots are calculated. Likewise, Arthur does not need to store $s_1, \ldots, s_k$ once they are given to Peggy. These two facts add to the security, since someone who breaks into Arthur's computer cannot compromise Peggy's security. Moreover, a different n can be used for each person, so it is hard to compromise the security of more than one individual at a time.

Note that since half the numbers mod p and half the numbers mod q have square roots, the Chinese remainder theorem implies that $1/4$ of the numbers mod n have square roots. Therefore, each $H(I\|j)$ has a $1/4$ probability of having a square root mod n. This means that Arthur should be able to produce the necessary numbers $j_1, \ldots, j_k$ quickly.

Peggy goes to an automatic teller machine, for example. The machine reads I from Peggy's card. It downloads $n, j_1, \ldots, j_k$ from a database and calculates $v_i = H(I||j_i)$ for $1 \leq i \leq k$. It then performs the preceding procedure to verify that Peggy knows $s_1, \ldots, s_k$. After a few iterations, the machine is convinced that the person is Peggy and allows her to withdraw cash. A naive implementation would require a lot of typing on Peggy's part, but at least Eve won't get Peggy's secret numbers. A better implementation would use chips embedded in the card and store some information in such a way that it cannot be extracted.

If Eve obtains the communications used in the transaction, she cannot determine Peggy's secret numbers. In fact, because of the zero-knowledge nature of the protocol, Eve obtains no information on the secret numbers $s_1, \ldots, s_k$ that can be reused in future transactions.

12.3   Exercises

1. Consider the diagram of tunnels in Figure 12.2. Suppose each of the four doors to the central chamber is locked so that a key is needed to enter, but no key is needed to exit. Peggy claims she has the key to one of the doors. Devise a zero-knowledge protocol in which Peggy proves to Victor that she can enter the central chamber. Victor should obtain no knowledge of which door Peggy can unlock.

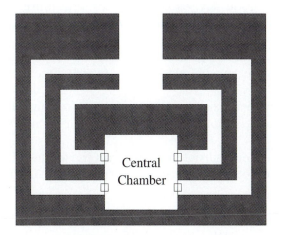

Figure 12.2: Diagram for Exercise 1.

2. Suppose p is a large prime, α is a primitive root, and $\beta \equiv \alpha^a \pmod{p}$. The numbers p, α, β are public. Peggy wants to prove to Victor that she knows a without revealing it. They do the following:

1. Peggy chooses a random number r (mod $p - 1$).

2. Peggy computes $h_1 \equiv \alpha^r$ (mod p) and $h_2 \equiv \alpha^{a-r}$ (mod p) and sends h_1, h_2 to Victor.

3. Victor chooses $i = 1$ or $i = 2$ asks Peggy to send either $r_1 = r$ or $r_2 = a - r$ (mod $p - 1$).

4. Victor checks that $h_1 h_2 \equiv \beta$ (mod p) and that $h_i \equiv \alpha^{r_i}$ (mod p).

5. They repeat this procedure several times.

(a) Suppose Peggy does not know a. Why will she sometimes be unable to produce numbers that convince Victor?

(b) If they repeat the procedure t times, and Peggy does not know a, what is the probability that Peggy can convince Victor that she knows a?

(c) Suppose naive Nelson tries a variant. He wants to convince Victor that he knows a, so he chooses a random r as before, but does not send h_1, h_2. Victor asks for r_i and Nelson sends it. They do this several times. Why is Victor not convinced of anything? What is the essential difference between Nelson's scheme and Peggy's scheme that causes this?

3. Naive Nelson thinks he understands zero-knowledge protocols. He wants to prove to Victor that he knows the factorization of n (which equals pq for two large primes p and q) without revealing this factorization to Victor or anyone else. Nelson devises the following procedure: Victor chooses a random integer x mod n, computes $y \equiv x^2$ (mod n), and sends y to Nelson. Nelson computes a square root s of y mod n and sends s to Victor. Victor checks that $s^2 \equiv y$ (mod n). Victor repeats this 20 times.

(a) Describe how Nelson computes s. You may assume that p and q are $\equiv 3$ (mod 4).

(b) Explain how Victor can use this procedure to have a high probability of finding the factorization of n. (Therefore, this is not a zero-knowledge protocol.)

(c) Suppose Eve is eavesdropping and hears the values of each y and s. Is it likely that Eve obtains any useful information? (Assume no value of y repeats.)

4. Exercise 2 gave a zero-knowledge proof that Peggy knows a discrete logarithm. Here is another method. Suppose p is a large prime, α is a primitive root, and $\beta \equiv \alpha^a$ (mod p). The numbers p, α, β are public. Peggy wants to prove to Victor that she knows a without revealing it. They do the following:

1. Alice chooses a random integer k with $1 \le k < p - 1$, computes $\gamma \equiv \alpha^k$ (mod p), and sends γ to Victor.

2. Victor chooses a random integer r with $1 \leq r < p - 1$ and sends r to Peggy.

3. Peggy computes $y \equiv k - ar \pmod{p-1}$ and sends y to Victor.

4. Victor checks whether $\gamma \equiv \alpha^y \beta^r \pmod{p}$. If so, he believes that Peggy knows a.

(a) Show that the verification equation holds if the procedure is followed correctly.
(b) Does Victor obtain any information that will allow him to compute a?
(c) Suppose Eve finds out the values of γ, r, and y. Will she be able to determine a?
(d) Suppose Peggy repeats the procedure with the same value of k, but Victor uses a different values r_1 and r_2. How can Eve, who has listened to all communications between Victor and Peggy, determine a?

The preceding procedure is the basis for the **Schnorr identification scheme**. Victor could be a bank and a could be Peggy's personal identification number. The bank stores β, and Peggy must prove she knows a to access her account. Alternatively, Victor could be a central computer and Peggy could be logging on to the computer through nonsecure telephone lines. Peggy's password is a, and the central computer stores β.

In the Schnorr scheme, p is usually chosen so that $p-1$ has a large prime factor q, and α, instead of being a primitive root, is taken to satisfy $\alpha^q \equiv 1 \pmod{p}$. The congruence defining y is then taken mod q. Moreover, r is taken to satisfy $1 \leq r \leq 2^t$ for some t, for example, $t = 40$.

Chapter 13

Key Establishment Protocols

So far in this book we have discussed various cryptographic concepts and focused on developing algorithms for secure communication. But a cryptographic algorithm is only as strong as the security of its keys. If Alice were to announce to the whole world her key before starting a DES session with Bob, then anyone could eavesdrop. Such a scenario is absurd, of course. But it represents an extreme version of a very important issue: If Alice and Bob are unable to meet in order to exchange their keys, can they still decide on a key without compromising future communication?

In this chapter we address the important topic of protocols for establishing keys. In particular, we consider the fundamental problem of sharing secret information for the establishment of keys for symmetric cryptography. By symmetric cryptography, we mean a system such as DES where both the sender and the recipient use the same key. This is in contrast to public key methods such as RSA, where the sender has one key (the encryption exponent) and the receiver has another (the decryption exponent).

In key establishment protocols, there is a sequence of steps that take place between Alice and Bob so that they can share some secret information needed in the establishment of a key. Since public key cryptography methods employ public encryption keys that are stored on public databases, one might think that public key cryptography provides an easy solution to this problem. This is partially true. The main downside to public key cryptography is that even the best public key cryptosystems are computationally slow when compared with the best symmetric key methods. RSA, for example, requires exponentiation, which is not as fast as the mixing of bits that takes place in DES. Therefore, sometimes RSA is used to transmit a DES key that will then be used for transmitting vast amounts of data. However, a central server that needs to communicate with many clients in short time intervals sometimes needs key establishment methods that are faster than current versions of public key algorithms. Therefore, in this and in various other situations, we need to consider other means for the exchange and establishment of keys for symmetric encryption algorithms.

There are two basic types of key establishment. In **key agreement** protocols, neither party knows the key in advance; it is determined as a result of their interaction. In **key distribution** protocols, one party has decided on a key and transmits it to the other party.

13.1   Key Agreement Protocols

Key agreement is a type of protocol whereby a key is established by exchanging information between two parties Alice and Bob. Each party derives the key as a function of the information that is exchanged.

It turns out that key agreement protocols are best done using asymmetric (public key) cryptography. We will present a famous protocol due to Diffie-Hellman that provides the establishment of a key with two message transfers. As we discuss later, it does not provide authentication, and in order to fix this shortcoming we may make use of digital signature schemes. This more sophisticated protocol is called the **Station-to-Station (STS)** protocol.

Diffie-Hellman Key Exchange

Alice and Bob want to establish a key for communicating. The Diffie-Hellman scheme for accomplishing this is as follows:

1. Either Alice or Bob selects a large, secure prime number p and a primitive root $\alpha \pmod{p}$. Both p and α can be made public.

2. Alice chooses a secret random x with $1 \leq x \leq p - 2$, and Bob selects a secret random y with $1 \leq y \leq p - 2$.

3. Alice sends $\alpha^x \pmod{p}$ to Bob, and Bob sends $\alpha^y \pmod{p}$ to Alice.

4. Using the messages that they each have received, they can each calculate the session key K. Alice calculates K by $K \equiv (\alpha^y)^x \pmod{p}$, and Bob calculates K by $K \equiv (\alpha^x)^y \pmod{p}$.

The Intruder-in-the-Middle Attack

Eve, who has recently learned the difference between a knight and a rook, claims that she can play two chess grandmasters simultaneously and either win one game or draw both games. The strategy is simple. She waits for the first grandmaster to move, then makes the identical move against the second grandmaster. When the second grandmaster responds, Eve makes that play against the first grandmaster. Continuing in this way, Eve cannot lose both games (unless she runs into time trouble because of the slight delay in transferring the moves).

A similar strategy, called the **intruder-in-the-middle attack**, can be used against the Diffie-Hellman scheme just given. It proceeds as follows:

1. Eve chooses an exponent z.

2. Eve intercepts α^x and α^y.

3. Eve sends α^z to Alice and to Bob (Alice believes she is receiving α^x and Bob believes he is receiving α^y).

4. Eve computes $K_{AO} \equiv (\alpha^x)^z \pmod{p}$ and $K_{OB} \equiv (\alpha^x)^z \pmod{p}$. Alice, not realizing that Eve is in the middle, also computes K_{AO}, and Bob computes K_{OB}.

5. When Alice sends a message to Bob, encrypted with K_{AO}, Eve intercepts it, deciphers it, encrypts it with K_{OB}, and sends it to Bob. Bob decrypts with K_{OB} and obtains the message. Bob has no reason to believe the communication was insecure. Meanwhile, Eve is reading the juicy gossip that she has obtained.

The Station-to-Station (STS) Protocol

To avoid the intruder-in-the-middle attack, it is desirable to have a procedure that authenticates Alice's and Bob's identities to each other while the key is being formed. A protocol that can do this is known as an **authenticated key agreement protocol**.

The standard solution uses digital signatures. Each user U has a digital signature function sig_U with verification algorithm ver_U. For example, sig_U could produce an RSA or ElGamal signature, and ver_U checks that it is a valid signature for U. The verification algorithms are compiled and made public by the trusted authority Trent, who certifies that ver_U is actually the verification algorithm for U, and not for Eve.

Suppose now that Alice and Bob want to establish a key to use in an encryption function E_K. They proceed as in the Diffie-Hellman key exchange, but with the added feature of digital signatures:

1. They choose a large prime p and a primitive root α.

2. Alice chooses a random x and Bob chooses a random y.

3. Alice computes $\alpha^x \pmod{p}$, and Bob computes $\alpha^y \pmod{p}$.

4. Alice sends α^x to Bob.

5. Bob computes $K \equiv (\alpha^x)^y \pmod{p}$.

6. Bob sends α^y and $E_K(sig_B(\alpha^y, \alpha^x))$ to Alice.

7. Alice computes $K \equiv (\alpha^y)^x \pmod{p}$.

8. Alice decrypts $E_K(sig_B(\alpha^y, \alpha^x))$ to obtain $sig_B(\alpha^y, \alpha^x)$.

9. Alice asks Trent to verify that ver_B is Bob's verification algorithm.

10. Alice uses ver_B to verify Bob's signature.

11. Alice sends $E_K(sig_A(\alpha^x, \alpha^y))$ to Bob.

12. Bob decrypts, asks Trent to verify that ver_A is Alice's verification algorithm, and then uses ver_A to verify Alice's signature.

An enhanced version of this, due to Diffie, van Oorschot, and Wiener, is known as the Station-to-Station protocol. Note that Alice and Bob are also certain that they are using the same key K, since it is very unlikely that an incorrect key would give a decryption that is a valid signature.

13.2   Key Pre-distribution

In the simplest version of this protocol, if Alice wants to communicate with Bob, the keys or key schedules (lists describing which keys to use at which times) are decided upon in advance and somehow this information is sent securely from one to the other. For example, this method was used by the German navy in World War II. However, the British were able to use codebooks from captured ships to find daily keys and thus read messages.

There are some obvious limitations and drawbacks to pre-distribution. First, it requires two parties, Alice and Bob, to have met or to have established a secure channel between them in the first place. Second, once Alice and Bob have met and exchanged information, there is nothing they can do, other than meeting again, to change the key information in case it gets compromised.

Here is a general, slightly modified, situation. First, we require a trusted authority whom we call Trent. For every pair of users, call them (A, B),

Trent produces a random key K_{AB} that will be used as a key for a symmetric encryption method (hence $K_{BA} = K_{AB}$). It is assumed that Trent is powerful and has established a secure channel to each of the users. He distributes all the keys that he has determined to his users. Thus, if Trent is responsible for n users, each user will be receiving $n - 1$ keys to store, and Trent must send $n(n - 1)/2$ keys securely. If n is large, this could be a problem. The storage that each user requires is also a problem.

One method for reducing the amount of information that must be sent from the trusted authority is the **Blom key pre-distribution scheme**. Start with a network of n users, and let p be a large prime $p \geq n$. Everyone has knowledge of the prime p. The protocol is now the following:

1. Each user U in the network is assigned a distinct public number r_U $(\bmod\ p)$.

2. Trent chooses three secret random numbers a, b, and c mod p.

3. For each user U, Trent calculates the numbers

$$a_U \equiv a + br_U \quad (\bmod\ p) \quad b_U \equiv b + cr_U \quad (\bmod\ p)$$

   and sends them via his secure channel to U.

4. Each user U forms the linear polynomial

$$g_U(x) = a_U + b_U x.$$

5. If Alice (A) wants to communicate with Bob (B), then Alice computes $K_{AB} = g_A(r_B)$, while Bob computes $K_{BA} = g_B(r_A)$.

6. It can be shown that $K_{AB} = K_{BA}$ (Exercise 2). Alice and Bob communicate via a symmetric encryption system, for example, DES, using the key (or a key derived from) K_{AB}.

Example. Consider a network consisting of three users Alice, Bob, and Charlie. Let $p = 23$, and let

$$r_A = 11, \quad r_B = 3, \quad r_C = 2.$$

Suppose Trent chooses the numbers $a = 8$, $b = 3$, $c = 1$. The corresponding linear polynomials are given by

$$g_A(x) = 18 + 14x, \quad g_B(x) = 17 + 6x, \quad g_C(x) = 14 + 5x.$$

It is now possible to calculate the keys that this scheme would generate:

$$K_{AB} = g_A(r_B) = 14, \quad K_{AC} = g_A(r_C) = 0, \quad K_{BC} = g_B(r_C) = 6.$$

It is easy to check that $K_{AB} = K_{BA}$, etc., in this example. ∎

If the two users Eve and Oscar conspire, they can determine a, b, and c, and therefore find all numbers a_A, b_A for all users. They proceed as follows. They know the numbers a_E, b_E, a_O, b_O. The defining equations for the last three of these numbers can be written in matrix form as

$$\begin{pmatrix} 0 & 1 & r_E \\ 1 & r_O & 0 \\ 0 & 1 & r_O \end{pmatrix} \begin{pmatrix} a \\ b \\ c \end{pmatrix} \equiv \begin{pmatrix} b_E \\ a_O \\ b_O \end{pmatrix} \pmod{p}.$$

The determinant of the last three rows of the matrix is $r_E - r_O$. Since the numbers r_A were chosen to be distinct mod p, the determinant is nonzero mod p and therefore the system has a unique solution a, b, c.

Without Eve's help, Oscar has only a 2×3 matrix to work with and therefore cannot find a, b, c. In fact, suppose he wants to calculate the key K_{AB} being used by Alice and Bob. Since $K_{AB} \equiv a + b(r_A + r_B) + c(r_A r_B)$ (see Exercise 2), Oscar has the matrix equation

$$\begin{pmatrix} 1 & r_A + r_B & r_A r_B \\ 1 & r_O & 0 \\ 0 & 1 & r_O \end{pmatrix} \begin{pmatrix} a \\ b \\ c \end{pmatrix} \equiv \begin{pmatrix} K_{AB} \\ a_O \\ b_O \end{pmatrix} \pmod{p}.$$

The matrix has determinant $(r_O - r_A)(r_O - r_B) \not\equiv 0 \pmod{p}$. Therefore, there is a solution a, b, c for every possible value of K_{AB}. This means that Oscar obtains no information about K_{AB}.

For each $k \geq 1$, there are Blom schemes that are secure against coalitions of at most k users, but which succumb to conspiracies of $k + 1$ users. See [Blom].

13.3 Key Distribution

Key pre-distribution protocols have the shortcoming that their keys are predetermined and that there is no easy method to change the key after a certain amount of time. When using the same key for long periods of time, one runs a risk that the key will become compromised. The more data that are transmitted, the more data there are with which to build statistical attacks.

In this section we discuss a class of key establishment protocols known as **transport protocols**. In this scenario, either Alice will decide on a key and transmit it to Bob, or our trusted authority Trent will act as a key server. In the first case, Alice will have to employ some secure protocol in order to give the key to Bob. In the second scenario, when Alice wishes to communicate with Bob, she requests a key from Trent that is good for a single session, and Trent sends this session key to both Alice and Bob via some secure protocol.

Shamir's Three-Pass Protocol

Alice wishes to transfer a secret key K to Bob via communication on a public channel. First, Alice chooses a large prime number p that is secure (i.e., such that the discrete log problem is hard mod p) as well as being large enough to represent the key K. For example, if Alice were trying to send a 56-bit DES key, she would need a prime number that is at least 56 bits long. However, for security purposes, she would want to choose a prime significantly longer than 56 bits. Alice publishes p so that Bob (or anyone else) can download it. Bob downloads p. Alice and Bob now do the following:

1. Alice selects a random number a with $\gcd(a, p-1) = 1$ and Bob selects a random number b with $\gcd(b, p-1) = 1$. We will denote by a^{-1} and b^{-1} the inverses of a and b mod $p - 1$.

2. Alice sends $K_1 \equiv K^a \pmod{p}$ to Bob.

3. Bob sends $K_2 \equiv K_1^b \pmod{p}$ to Alice.

4. Alice sends $K_3 \equiv K_2^{a^{-1}} \pmod{p}$ to Bob.

5. Bob computes $K \equiv K_3^{b^{-1}} \pmod{p}$.

At the end of this protocol, both Alice and Bob have the key K. The security lies in the difficulty of the discrete logarithm problem. However, without some added safeguards, the procedure is not secure against an intruder-in-the-middle attack.

Kerberos

Kerberos (named for the three-headed dog that guarded the entrance to Hades) is a real-world implementation of a symmetric cryptography protocol whose purpose is to provide strong levels of authentication and security in key exchange between users in a network. Here we use the term *users* loosely, as a user might be an individual, or it might be a program requesting communication with another program. Kerberos grew out of a larger development project at M.I.T. known as Project Athena. The purpose of Athena was to integrate a huge network of computer workstations into the curriculum of the undergraduate student body at M.I.T., allowing students to be able to access their files easily from anywhere on the network. As one might guess, such a development quickly raised questions about network security. In particular, communication across a public network such as Athena is very insecure and it is easily possible to observe data flowing across a network and look for interesting bits of information such as passwords and other types of information that one would wish to remain private. Kerberos was developed in order to address such security issues. In the following, we present the basic Kerberos model and describe what it is and what it attempts to do. For more thorough descriptions, see [Schneier].

Kerberos is based on a client/server architecture. A client is either a user or some software that has some task that it seeks to accomplish. For example, a client might wish to send e-mail, print documents, or mount devices. Servers are larger entities whose function is to provide services to the clients. As an example, on the Internet and World Wide Web there is a concept of a domain name server (DNS), which provides names or addresses to clients such as e-mail programs or Internet browsers.

The basic Kerberos model has the following participants:

- Cliff: a client

- Serge: a server

- Trent: a trusted authority

- Grant: a ticket-granting server

The trusted authority is also known as an authentication server. To begin, Cliff and Serge have no secret key information shared between them, and it is the purpose of Kerberos to give each of them information securely. A result of the Kerberos protocol is that Serge will have verified Cliff's identity (he wouldn't want to have a conversation with a fake Cliff, would he?), and a session key will be established.

The protocol, depicted in Figure 13.1, begins with Cliff requesting a ticket for Ticket-Granting Service from Trent. Since Trent is the powerful trusted authority, he has a database of password information for all the clients (for this reason, Trent is also sometimes referred to as the Kerberos server). Trent returns a ticket that is encrypted with the client's secret password information. Cliff would now like to use the service that Serge provides, but before he can do this, he must be allowed to talk to Serge. Cliff presents his ticket to Grant, the ticket-granting server. Grant takes this ticket, and if everything is OK (recall that the ticket has some information identifying Cliff), then Grant gives a new ticket to Cliff that will allow Cliff

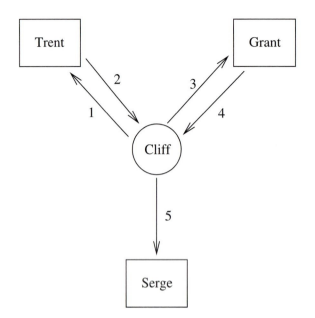

Figure 13.1: Kerberos.

to make use of Serge's service (and only Serge's service; this ticket will not be valid with Sarah, a different server). Cliff now has a service ticket, which he can present to Serge. He sends Serge the service ticket as well as an authentication credential. Serge checks the ticket with the authentication credential to make sure it is valid. If this final exchange checks out, then Serge will provide the service to Cliff.

The Kerberos protocol is a formal version of protocols we use in everyday life (for example cashing a check at a bank, or getting on a ride at a fair).

We now look at Kerberos in more detail. Kerberos makes use of a symmetric encryption algorithm. In Version V, Kerberos makes use of DES operating in CBC mode; however, any symmetric encryption algorithm would suffice.

1. Cliff to Trent: Cliff sends a message to Trent that contains his name and the name of the ticket-granting server that he will use (in this case Grant).

2. Trent to Cliff: Trent looks up Cliff's name in his database. If he finds it, he generates a session key K_{CG} that will be used between Cliff and Grant. Trent also has a secret key K_C with which he can communicate with Cliff, so he uses this to encrypt the Cliff-Grant session key:

$$T = e_{K_C}(K_{CG}).$$

In addition, Trent creates a Ticket Granting Ticket (TGT), which will allow Cliff to authenticate himself to Grant. This ticket is encrypted using Grant's personal key K_G (which Trent also has):

$$TGT =$$

Grant's name$\|e_{K_G}$(Cliff's name, Cliff's Address, Timestamp1, K_{CG}).

Here $\|$ is used to denote concatenation. The ticket that Cliff receives is the concatenation of these two subtickets:

$$\text{Ticket} = T\|TGT.$$

3. Cliff to Grant: Cliff can extract K_{CG} using the key K_C, which he shares with Trent. Using K_{CG}, Cliff can now communicate securely with Grant. Cliff now creates an authenticator, which will consist of his name, his address, and a timestamp. He encrypts this using K_{CG} to get

$$\text{Auth}_{CG} = e_{K_{CG}}(\text{Cliff's name, Cliff's address, Timestamp2}).$$

Cliff now sends Auth$_{CG}$ as well as TGT to Grant so that Grant can administer a service ticket.

4. Grant to Cliff: Grant now has Auth$_{CG}$ and TGT. Part of TGT was encrypted using Grant's secret key, so Grant can extract this portion and can decrypt it. Thus he can recover Cliff's name, Cliff's address, Timestamp1, as well as K_{CG}. Grant can now use K_{CG} to decrypt Auth$_{CG}$ in order to verify the authenticity of Cliff's request. That is, $d_{K_{CG}}$ (Auth$_{CG}$) will provide another copy of Cliff's name, Cliff's address, and a different timestamp. If the two versions of Cliff's name and address match, and if Timestamp1 and Timestamp2 are sufficiently close to each other, then Grant will declare Cliff valid. Now that Cliff is approved by Grant, Grant will generate a session key K_{CS} for Cliff to communicate with Serge and will also return a service ticket. Grant has a secret key K_S which he shares with Serge. The service ticket is

$$\text{ServTicket} =$$

$$e_{K_S} (\text{Cliff's name, Cliff's address, Timestamp3, ExpirationTime}, K_{CS}).$$

Here ExpirationTime is a quantity that describes the length of validity for this service ticket. The session key is encrypted using a session key between Cliff and Grant:

$$e_{K_{CG}} (K_{CS}).$$

Grant sends ServTicket and $e_{K_{CG}} (K_{CS})$ to Cliff.

5. Cliff to Serge: Cliff is now ready to start making use of Serge's services. He starts by decrypting $e_{K_{CG}}(K_{CS})$ in order to get the session key K_{CS} that he will use while communicating with Serge. He creates an authenticator to use with Serge:

$$\text{Auth}_{CS} = e_{K_{CS}}(\text{Cliff's name, Cliff's address, Timestamp4}).$$

Cliff now sends Serge Auth$_{CS}$ as well as ServTicket. Serge can decrypt ServTicket and extract from this the session key K_{CS} that he is to use with Cliff. Using this session key, he can decrypt Auth$_{CS}$ and verify that Cliff is who he says he is, and that Timestamp4 is within ExpirationTime of Timestamp3. If Timestamp4 is not within ExpirationTime of Timestamp3, then Cliff's ticket is stale and Serge rejects his request for service. Otherwise, Cliff and Serge may make use of K_{CS} to perform their exchange.

13.4   Public Key Infrastructures (PKI)

Public key cryptography is a powerful tool that allows for authentication, key distribution, and non-repudiation. In these applications, the public key is published, but when you access public keys, what assurance do you have that Alice's public key actually belongs to Alice? Perhaps Eve has substituted her own public key in place of Alice's. Unless confidence exists in how the keys were generated, and in their authenticity and validity, the benefits of public key cryptography are minimal.

In order for public key cryptography to be useful in commercial applications, it is necessary to have an infrastructure that keeps track of public keys. A public key infrastructure, or PKI for short, is a framework consisting of policies defining the rules under which the cryptographic systems operate and procedures for generating and publishing keys and certificates.

All PKIs consist of certification and validation operations. Certification binds a public key to an entity, such as a user or a piece of information. Validation guarantees that certificates are valid.

A **certificate** is a quantity of information that has been signed by its publisher, who is commonly referred to as the **certification authority (CA)**. There are many types of certificates. Two popular ones are identity certificates and credential certificates. Identity certificates contain an entity's identity information, such as an e-mail address, and a list of public keys for the entity. Credential certificates contain information describing access rights. In either case, the data are typically encrypted using the CA's private key.

Suppose we have a PKI, and the CA publishes identity certificates for Alice and Bob. If Alice knows the CA's public key, then she can take the encrypted identity certificate for Bob that has been published and extract Bob's identity information as well as a list of public keys needed to communicate securely with Bob. The difference between this scenario and the conventional public key scenario is that Bob doesn't publish his keys, but instead the trust relationship is placed between Alice and the publisher. Alice might not trust Bob as much as she might trust a CA such as the government or the phone company. The concept of trust is critical to PKIs and is perhaps one of the most important properties of a PKI.

It is unlikely that a single entity could ever keep track of and issue every Internet user's public keys. Instead, PKIs often consist of multiple CAs that are allowed to certify each other and the certificates they issue. Thus, Bob might be associated with a different CA than Alice, and when requesting Bob's identity certificate, Alice might only trust it if her CA trusts Bob's CA. On large networks like the Internet, there may be many CAs between Alice and Bob, and it becomes necessary for each of the CAs between her and Bob to trust each other.

In addition, most PKIs have varying levels of trust, allowing some CAs to certify other CAs with varying degrees of trust. It is possible that CAs may only trust other CAs to perform specific tasks. For example, Alice's CA may only trust Bob's CA to certify Bob and not certify other CAs, while Alice's CA may trust Dave's CA to certify other CAs. Trust relationships can become very elaborate, and, as these relationships become more complex, it becomes more difficult to determine to what degree Alice will trust a certificate that she receives.

Here are two examples of PKIs that are used in practice.

Pretty Good Privacy (PGP) is a program that was originally created by Phil Zimmerman to encrypt and sign e-mail messages. It uses a combination of public key and private key cryptography to achieve this. Each user maintains a keyring, which consists of the public keys of people with whom the user exchanges e-mail. In order for Alice to protect her keyring from tampering, she signs the keys in her keyring using her private key.

The PGP program allows users to exchange keyrings. When Alice receives Bob's keyring, she gives it one of four different trust levels:

- Complete trust: Alice completely trusts Bob and she will trust any key that has been signed using Bob's key.

- Partial trust: Alice has some confidence in Bob but does not completely trust him. Before she trusts a key that has been signed by Bob, she requires that the key has been signed by other individuals.

- No trust: Alice does not trust Bob and therefore does not trust Bob's certification of any keys that have been signed using his key.

- Unknown: Alice is unsure whether she should trust Bob. Typically this is treated the same as no trust.

As users share keyrings, a **web of trust** is built between the users. It is possible that Alice will eventually trust someone that she has never met. The simplicity of PGP has made it popular for applications such as secure e-mail. However, for e-commerce applications more sophisticated PKIs are needed.

X.509 is one such PKI. It is an international standard that is designed to provide authentication for directory services on large computer networks. Because of its origin as a standard for the International Organization for Standardization and for the International Telecommunication Union, many products have been created based on it. For example, X.509 is used in Visa and Mastercard's Secure Electronic Transaction standard.

One of the building blocks of the X.509 certificate is a naming convention to identify the user and issuer of the certificate. In Version 1 and Version 2 of X.509, the standard used a naming convention known as X.500. Version 3 of X.509 allows for alternative naming conventions. In addition, X.509 certificates contain fields that specify which version of X.509 the certificate conforms to, a validity period that describes the times for which the certificate is valid, and the user's public key information. Version 3 X.509 certificates allow the CA to include a list of trust policies within the certificate. These trust policies can inform the user for what purpose the certified key can be used and can state for what group of users a particular CA can certify certificates.

Because the X.509 certificate contains fields describing trust policies, it is more powerful than PGP and can be used in applications requiring more specific levels of certification. For example, with X.509 it is possible to designate that a public key is suitable only for secure e-mail applications and not suitable for e-commerce applications.

13.5   Exercises

1. In a network of three users, A, B, and C, we would like to use the Blom scheme to establish session keys between pairs of users. Let $p = 31$ and let

$$r_A = 11 \quad r_B = 3 \quad r_C = 2.$$

Suppose Trent chooses the numbers

$$a = 8 \quad b = 3 \quad c1 = 1.$$

Calculate the session keys.

2. (a) Show that in the Blom scheme, $K_{AB} \equiv a + b(r_A + r_B) + cr_Ar_B$ (mod p).
(b) Show that $K_{AB} = K_{BA}$.
(c) Another way to view the Blom scheme is by using a polynomial in two variables. Define the polynomial $f(x, y) = a + b(x + y) + cxy$ (mod p). Express the key K_{AB} in terms of f.

3. You (U) and I (I) are evil users on a network that uses the Blom scheme for key establishment with $k = 1$. We have decided to get together to figure out the other session keys on the network. In particular, suppose $p = 31$ and $r_U = 9, r_I = 2$. We have received $a_U = 18, b_U = 29, a_I = 24, b_I = 13$ from Trent, the trusted authority. Calculate a, b, and c.

4. Here is another version of the intruder-in-the-middle attack. It has the "advantage" that Eve does not have to intercept and retransmit all the messages between Bob and Alice. Suppose Eve discovers that $p = Mq + 1$, where q is prime and M is small. Eve intercepts α^x and α^y as before. She sends Bob $(\alpha^x)^q$ (mod p) and sends Alice $(\alpha^y)^q$ (mod p).
(a) Show that Alice and Bob each calculate the same key.
(b) Show that there are only M possible values for K, so Eve may find K by exhaustive search.

5. Bob, Ted, Carol, and Alice want to agree on a common key (cryptographic key, that is). They publicly choose a large prime p and a primitive root α. They privately choose random numbers b, t, c, a, respectively. Describe a protocol that allows them to compute $K \equiv \alpha^{btca}$ (mod p) securely (ignore intruder-in-the-middle attacks).

6. Suppose naive Nelson tries to implement an analog of the Diffie-Hellman key exchange as follows. Nelson wants to send the key K to Heidi. He chooses a one-time pad key K_N and XORs it with K. He sends $M_1 = K_N \oplus K$ to Heidi. She XORs what she receives with her one-time pad key K_H to get $M_2 = M_1 \oplus K_H$. Heidi sends M_2 to Nelson, who computes $M_3 = M_2 \oplus K_N$. Nelson sends M_3 to Heidi, who recovers K as $M_3 \oplus K_3$.
(a) Show that $K = M_3 \oplus K_3$.
(b) Suppose Eve intercepts M_1, M_2, M_3. How can she recover K?

Chapter 14

Information Theory

In this chapter we introduce the theoretical concepts behind the security of a cryptosystem. The basic question is the following: If Eve observes a piece of ciphertext, does she gain any new information about the encryption key that she did not already have? To address this issue, we need a mathematical definition for what information is. This involves probability and the use of a very important measure called entropy.

Many of the ideas in this chapter originated with Claude Shannon in the late 1940s.

Before we start, let's consider an example. Roll a standard six-sided die. Let A be the event that the number of dots is odd, and let B be the event that the number of dots is at least 3. If someone tells you that the roll belongs to the event $A \cap B$, then you know that there are only two possibilities for what the roll is. In this sense, $A \cap B$ tells you more about the value of the roll than just the event A, or just the event B. In this sense, the information contained in the event $A \cap B$ is larger than the information just in A or just in B.

The idea of information is closely linked with the idea of uncertainty. Going back to the example of the die, if you are told that the event $A \cap B$ happened, you become less uncertain about what the value of the roll was than if you are simply told that event A occurred. Thus the information increased while the uncertainty decreased. Entropy provides a measure of the increase in information or the decrease in uncertainty provided by the outcome of an experiment.

14.1   Probability Review

In this section we briefly introduce the concepts from probability needed for what follows. An understanding of probability and the various identities that arise is essential for the development of entropy.

Consider an experiment X with possible outcomes in a set $\mathcal{X}$. For example, X could be flipping a coin and $\mathcal{X} = \{\text{heads, tails}\}$. We assume each outcome is assigned a probability. In the present example, $p(X = \text{heads}) = 1/2$ and $p(X = \text{tails}) = 1/2$. Often, the outcome X of an experiment is called a **random variable**.

In general, for each $x \in \mathcal{X}$, denote the probability that $X = x$ by

$$p_X(x) = p_x = p(X = x).$$

Note that $\sum_{x \in \mathcal{X}} p_x = 1$. If $A \subseteq \mathcal{X}$, let

$$p(A) = \sum_{x \in A} p_x,$$

which is the probability that X takes a value in A.

Often one performs an experiment where one is measuring several different events. These events may or may not be related, but they may be lumped together to form a new random event. For example, if we have two random events X and Y with possible outcomes $\mathcal{X}$ and $\mathcal{Y}$, respectively, then we may create a new random event $Z = (X, Y)$ that groups the two events together. In this case, the new event Z has a set of possible outcomes $\mathcal{Z} = \mathcal{X} \times \mathcal{Y}$, and Z is sometimes called a joint random variable.

Example. Draw a card from a standard deck. Let X be the suit of the card, so $\mathcal{X} = \{\text{clubs, diamonds, hearts, spades}\}$. Let Y be the value of the card, so $\mathcal{Y} = \{\text{two, three, } \ldots, \text{ ace}\}$. Then $\mathcal{Z}$ gives the 52 possibilities for the card. Note that if $x \in \mathcal{X}$ and $y \in \mathcal{Y}$, then $p((X, Y) = (x, y)) = p(X = x, Y = y)$ is simply the probability that the card drawn has suit x and value y. Since all cards are equally probable, this probability is $1/52$, which is the probability that $X = x$ (namely $1/4$) times the probability that $Y = y$ (namely $1/13$). As we discuss later, this means X and Y are independent. ∎

Example. Roll a die. Suppose we are interested in two things: whether the number of dots is odd and whether the number is at least 2. Let $X = 0$ if the number of dots is even and $X = 1$ if the number of dots is odd. Let $Y = 0$ if the number of dots is less than 2 and $Y = 1$ if the number of dots is at least 2. Then $Z = (X, Y)$ gives us the results of both experiments together. Note that the probability that the number of dots is odd and less than 2 is $p(Z = (1, 0)) = 1/6$. This is not equal to $p(X = 0) \cdot p(Y = 0)$, which is

$(1/2)(1/6) = 1/12$. This means that X and Y are not independent. As we'll see, this is closely related to the fact that knowing X gives us information about Y.   ∎

We denote

$$p_{X,Y}(x,y) = p(X = x, Y = y).$$

Note that we can recover the probability that $X = x$ as

$$p_X(x) = \sum_{y \in \mathcal{Y}} p_{X,Y}(x,y).$$

We say that two events X and Y are **independent** if

$$p_{X,Y}(x,y) = p_X(x)p_Y(y)$$

for all $x \in \mathcal{X}$ and all $y \in \mathcal{Y}$. In the preceding example, the suit of a card and the value of the card were independent.

We are also interested in the probabilities for Y given that $X = x$ has occurred. If $p_X(x) > 0$, define the **conditional probability** of $Y = y$ given that $X = x$ to be

$$p_Y(y|x) = \frac{p_{X,Y}(x,y)}{p_X(x)}.$$

One way to think of this is that we have restricted to the set where $X = x$. This has total probability $p_X(x) = \sum_y p_{X,Y}(x,y)$. The fraction of this sum that comes from $Y = y$ is $p_Y(y|x)$.

Note that X and Y are independent if and only if

$$p_Y(y|x) = p_Y(y)$$

for all x, y. In other words, the probability of y is unaffected by what happens with X.

There is a nice way to go from the conditional probability of Y given X to the conditional probability of X given Y.

Bayes's Theorem. *If $p_X(x) > 0$ and $p_Y(y) > 0$, then*

$$p_X(x|y) = \frac{p_X(x)p_Y(y|x)}{p_Y(y)}.$$

The proof consists of simply writing the conditional probabilities in terms of their definitions.

14.2 Entropy

Roll a six-sided die and a ten-sided die. Which outcome has more uncertainty? If you make a guess at the outcome of each roll, you are more likely to be wrong with the ten-sided die than with the six-sided die. Therefore, the ten-sided die has more uncertainty. Similarly, compare a fair coin toss in which heads and tails are equally likely with a coin toss in which heads occur 90% of the time. Which is has more uncertainty? The fair coin toss does, again because there is more randomness in its possibilities.

In our definition of uncertainty, we want to make sure that two random variables X and Y that have same probability distribution have the same uncertainty. In order to do this, the measure of uncertainty must only be a function of the probability distributions and not of the names chosen for the outcomes.

We demand that the measure of uncertainty satisfy the following properties:

1. To each set of nonnegative numbers $p_1, \ldots, p_n$ with $p_1 + \cdots + p_n = 1$, the uncertainty is given by a number $H(p_1, \ldots, p_n)$.

2. H should be a continuous function of the probability distribution, so a small change in the probability distribution should not drastically change the uncertainty.

3. $H(\frac{1}{n}, \ldots, \frac{1}{n}) \leq H(\frac{1}{n+1}, \ldots, \frac{1}{n+1})$ for all $n > 0$. In other words, in situations where all outcomes are equally likely, the uncertainty increases when there are more possible outcomes.

4. If $0 < q < 1$, then

$$H(p_1, \ldots, qp_j, (1-q)p_j, \ldots, p_n) = H(p_1, \ldots, p_j, \ldots, p_n) + p_j H(q, 1-q).$$

What this means is that if the jth outcome is broken into two suboutcomes, with probabilities qp_j and $(1-q)p_j$, then the entropy is increased by the uncertainty caused by the choice between the two suboutcomes, multiplied by the probability p_j that we are in this case to begin with. For example, if we roll a six-sided die, we can record two outcomes: *even* and *odd*. This has uncertainty $H(\frac{1}{2}, \frac{1}{2})$. Now suppose we break the outcome *even* into the suboutcomes 2 and $\{4, 6\}$. Then we have three possible outcomes: 2, $\{4, 6\}$, and *odd*. We have

$$H(\frac{1}{6}, \frac{1}{3}, \frac{1}{2}) = H(\frac{1}{2}, \frac{1}{2}) + \frac{1}{2} H(\frac{2}{3}, \frac{1}{3}).$$

The first term is the uncertainty caused by *even* versus *odd*. The second term is the uncertainty added by splitting *even* into two suboutcomes.

From these basic assumptions, Shannon [Shannon2] showed the following.

Theorem. *Let $H(X)$ be a function satisfying properties (1)–(4) above. In other words, for each random variable X with outcomes $\mathcal{X} = \{x_1, \ldots, x_n\}$ having probabilities $p_1, \ldots, p_n$, the function H assigns a number $H(X)$ subject to the conditions (1)–(4). Then H must be of the form*

$$H(p_1, \cdots, p_n) = -\lambda \sum_k p_k \log_2 p_k,$$

where λ is a positive constant and where the sum is taken over those k such that $p_k > 0$.

Because of the theorem, we define the **entropy** of the variable X to be

$$H(X) = -\sum_{x \in \mathcal{X}} p(x) \log_2 p(x).$$

The entropy $H(X)$ is a measure of the uncertainty in the outcome of X.

The observant reader might notice that there are problems when we have elements $x \in \mathcal{X}$ that have probability 0. In this case we define $0 \log_2 0 = 0$, which is justified by looking at the limit of $x \log_2 x$ as $x \to 0$. It is typical convention that the logarithm is taken base 2, in which case entropy is measured in bits. From now on we will drop the subscript in the logarithm and assume that we are taking the log base 2. The entropy of X may also be interpreted as the expected value of $-\log_2 p(X)$ (recall that $E[g(X)] = \sum_x g(x)p(x)$).

We now look at some examples.

Example. Consider a fair coin toss. There are two outcomes, each with probability 1/2. The entropy of this random event is

$$-(\frac{1}{2} \log_2 \frac{1}{2} + \frac{1}{2} \log_2 \frac{1}{2}) = 1 \text{ bit.} \qquad \blacksquare$$

Example. Consider a nonfair coin toss X with probability p of getting heads and probability $1 - p$ of getting tails (where $0 < p < 1$). The entropy of this event is

$$H(X) = -p \log_2 p - (1 - p) \log_2(1 - p).$$

If one considers $H(X)$ as a function of p, one sees that the entropy is a maximum when $p = \frac{1}{2}$. $\qquad \blacksquare$

Example. Consider an n-sided fair die. There are n outcomes, each with probability $1/n$. The entropy is

$$-\frac{1}{n}\log_2(1/n) - \cdots - \frac{1}{n}\log_2(1/n) = \log_2(n).$$ ∎

There is a relationship between entropy and the number of yes-no questions needed to determine accurately the outcome of a random event. If one considers a totally nonfair coin toss where $p(1) = 1$, then $H(X) = 0$. This result can be interpreted as not requiring any questions to determine what the value of the event was. If someone rolls a four-sided die, then it takes two yes-no questions to find out the outcome. For example, is the number less than 3? Is the number odd?

A slightly more subtle example is obtained by flipping two coins. Let X be the number of heads, so the possible outcomes are $\{0, 1, 2\}$. The probabilities are $1/4$, $1/2$, $1/4$ and the entropy is

$$-\frac{1}{4}\log_2(1/4) - \frac{1}{2}\log_2(1/2) - \frac{1}{4}\log_2(1/4) = \frac{3}{2}.$$

Note that we can average $3/2$ questions to determine the outcome. For example, the first question could be "Is there exactly one head?" Half of the time, this will suffice to determine the outcome. The other half of the time a second question is needed, for example, "Are there two heads?" So the average number of questions equals the entropy.

Another way of looking at $H(X)$ is that it measures the number of bits of information that we obtain when we are given the outcome of X. For example, suppose the outcome of X is a random 4-bit number, where each possibility has probability $1/16$. As computed previously, the entropy is $H(X) = 4$, which says we have received 4 bits of information when we are told the value of X.

In a similar vein, entropy relates to the minimal amount of bits necessary to represent an event on a computer (which is a binary device). See Section 14.3. There is no sense recording events whose outcomes can be predicted with 100% certainty; it would be a waste of space. In storing information, one wants to code just the uncertain parts because that is where the real information is.

If we have two random variables X and Y, the joint entropy $H(X, Y)$ is defined as

$$H(X, Y) = -\sum_{x \in \mathcal{X}} \sum_{y \in \mathcal{Y}} p_{X,Y}(x, y) \log_2 p_{X,Y}(x, y).$$

This is just the entropy of the joint random variable $Z = (X, Y)$ discussed in Section 14.1.

In a cryptosystem, we might want to know the uncertainty in a key, given knowledge of the ciphertext. This leads us to the concept of **conditional entropy**, which is the amount of uncertainty in Y, given X. It is defined to be

$$
\begin{aligned}
H(Y|X) \quad &= \quad \sum_x p_X(x) H(Y|X = x) \\
&= -\sum_x p_X(x) \left(\sum_y p_Y(y|x) \log_2 p_Y(y|x) \right) \\
&= -\sum_x \sum_y p_{X,Y}(x, y) \log_2 p_Y(y|x).
\end{aligned}
$$

The last equality follows from the relationship $p_{X,Y}(x, y) = p_Y(y|x) p_X(x)$. The quantity $H(Y|X = x)$ is the uncertainty in Y given the information that $X = x$. It is defined in terms of conditional probabilities by the expression in parentheses on the second line. We calculate $H(Y|X)$ by forming a weighted sum of these uncertainties to get the total uncertainty in Y given that we know the value of X.

Remark. The preceding definition of conditional entropy uses the weighted average, over the various $x \in \mathcal{X}$, of the entropy of Y given $X = x$. Note that $H(Y|X) \neq -\sum_{x,y} p_Y(y|x) \log_2(p_Y(y|x))$. This sum does not have properties that information or uncertainty should have. For example, if X and Y are independent, then this definition would imply that the uncertainty of Y given X is greater than the uncertainty of Y (see Exercise 15). This clearly should not be the case.

We now derive an important tool, the chain rule for entropies. It will be useful in Section 14.4.

Theorem (Chain Rule). $H(X, Y) = H(X) + H(Y|X)$.

Proof.

$$
\begin{aligned}
H(X, Y) \quad &= -\sum_{x \in \mathcal{X}} \sum_{y \in \mathcal{Y}} p_{X,Y}(x, y) \log_2 p_{X,Y}(x, y) \\
&= -\sum_{x \in \mathcal{X}} \sum_{y \in \mathcal{Y}} p_{X,Y}(x, y) \log_2 p_X(x) p_Y(y|x)
\end{aligned}
$$

$$= -\sum_{x \in \mathcal{X}} \sum_{y \in \mathcal{Y}} p_{X,Y}(x,y) \log_2 p_X(x) - \sum_{x \in \mathcal{X}} \sum_{y \in \mathcal{Y}} p_{X,Y}(x,y) \log_2 p_Y(y|x)$$

$$= -\left(\sum_x \log_2 p_X(x) \sum_y p_{X,Y}(x,y) \right) + H(Y|X)$$

$$= -\sum_x p_X(x) \log_2 p_X(x) + H(Y|X) \quad \left(\text{since } \sum_y p_{X,Y}(x,y) = p_X(x)\right)$$

$$= H(X) + H(Y|X).$$

$\square$

What does the chain rule tell us? It says that the uncertainty of the joint event (X, Y) is equal to the uncertainty of event X + uncertainty of event Y given that event X has happened.

We now state three more results about entropy.

Theorem.

1. $H(X) \le \log_2 |\mathcal{X}|$, where $|\mathcal{X}|$ denotes the number of elements in $\mathcal{X}$. We have equality if and only if all elements of $\mathcal{X}$ are equally likely.

2. $H(X, Y) \le H(X) + H(Y)$.

3. *(Conditioning reduces entropy)* $H(Y|X) \le H(Y)$, with equality if and only if X and Y are independent.

The first result states that you are most uncertain when the probability distribution is uniform. Referring back to the example of the nonfair coin flip, the entropy was maximum for $p = \frac{1}{2}$. This extends to events with more possible outcomes. For a proof of (1), see [Welsh, p. 5].

The second result says that the information contained in the pair (X, Y) is at most the information contained in X plus the information contained in Y. The reason for the inequality is that possibly the information supplied by X and Y overlap (which is when X and Y are not independent). For a proof of (2), see [Stinson].

The third result is one of the most important results in information theory. Its interpretation is very simple. It says that the uncertainty one has in a random event Y given that event X occurred is less than the uncertainty in event Y alone. That is, X can only tell you information about event Y; it can't make you any more uncertain about Y.

The third result is an easy corollary of the second plus the chain rule:

$$H(X) + H(Y|X) = H(X, Y) \le H(X) + H(Y).$$

14.3   Huffman Codes

Information theory originated in the late 1940s from the seminal papers by Claude Shannon. One of the primary motivations behind Shannon's mathematical theory of information was the problem of finding a more compact way of representing data. In short, he was concerned with the problem of compression. In this section we shall briefly touch on the relationship between entropy and compression and introduce Huffman codes as a method for more succinctly representing data.

For more on how to compress data, see [Cover-Thomas] or [Nelson-Gailly].

Example. Suppose we have an alphabet with four letters a, b, c, d, and suppose these letters appear in a text with frequencies as follows.

a	b	c	d
.5	.3	.1	.1

We could represent a as the binary string 00, b as 01, c as 10, and d as 11. This means that the message would average 2 bits per letter. However, suppose we represent a as 1, b as 01, c as 001, and d as 000. Then the average number of bits per letter is

$$(1)(.5) + (2)(.3) + (3)(.1) + (3)(.1) = 1.7$$

(the number of bits for a times the frequency of a, plus the number of bits for b times the frequency of b, etc.). This encoding of the letters is therefore more efficient. ∎

In general, we have a random variable with outputs in a set $\mathcal{X}$. We want to represent the outputs in binary in an efficient way; namely, the average number of bits per output should be as small as possible.

An early example of such a procedure is Morse code, which represents letters as sequences of dots and dashes and was developed to send messages by telegraph. Morse asked printers which letters were used most, and made the more frequent letters have smaller representations. For example, e is represented as $\cdot$ and t as $-$. But x is $- \cdot \cdot -$ and z is $- - \cdot \cdot$.

A more recent method was developed by Huffman. The idea is to list all the outputs and their probabilities. The smallest two are assigned 1 and 0 and then combined to form an output with a larger probability. The same procedure is then applied to the new list, assigning 1 and 0 to the two smallest, then combining them to form a new list. This procedure is continued until there is only one output remaining. The binary strings are then obtained by reading backwards through the procedure, recording the bits that have been assigned to a given output and to combinations containing it. This is best explained by an example.

Suppose we have outputs a, b, c, d with probabilities $.5, .3, .1, .1$, as in the preceding example. The diagram in Figure 14.1 gives the procedure.

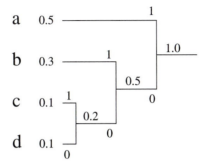

Figure 14.1: An Example of Huffman Encoding.

Note that when there were two choices for the lowest, we made a random choice for which one received 0 and which one received 1. Tracing backwards through the table, we see that a only received a 1, b received 01, c received 001, and d received 000. These are exactly the assignments made previously that gave a low number of bits per letter.

A useful feature of Huffman encoding is that it is possible to read a message one letter at a time. For example, the string 011000 can only be read as *bad*; moreover, as soon as we have read the first two bits 01, we know that the first letter is b.

Suppose instead that we wrote the bits assigned to letters in reverse order, so b is 10 and c is 001. Then the message 101000 cannot be determined until all bits have been read, since it potentially could start with *bb* or *ba*.

Even worse, suppose we had assigned 0 to a instead of 1. Then the messages *aaa* and *d* would be the same. It is possible to show that Huffman encoding avoids these two problems.

The average number of bits per output is closely related to the entropy.

Theorem. *Let L be the average number of bits per output for Huffman encoding for the random variable X. Then*

$$H(X) \leq L < H(X) + 1.$$

This result agrees with the interpretation that the entropy measures how many bits of information is contained in the output of X. We omit the proof. In our example, the entropy is

$$H(X) = -\big(.5\log_2(.5) + .3\log_2(.3) + .1\log(.1) + .1\log(.1)\big) \approx 1.685\,.$$

14.4   Perfect Secrecy

Intuitively, the one-time pad provides perfect secrecy. Entropy allows us to state this in mathematical terms.

Suppose we have a cipher system with possible plaintexts $\mathcal{P}$, ciphertexts $\mathcal{C}$, and keys $\mathcal{K}$. Each plaintext in $\mathcal{P}$ has a certain probability of occurring; some are more likely than others. The choice of a key in $\mathcal{K}$ is always assumed to be independent of the choice of plaintext. The possible ciphertexts in $\mathcal{C}$ have various probabilities, depending on the probabilities for $\mathcal{P}$ and $\mathcal{K}$.

If Eve intercepts a ciphertext, how much information does she obtain for the key? In other words, what is $H(K|C)$? Initially, the uncertainty in the key was $H(K)$. Has the knowledge of the ciphertext decreased the uncertainty?

Example. Suppose we have three possible plaintexts: a, b, c with probabilities .5, .3, .2 and two keys k_1, k_2 with probabilities .5 and .5. Suppose the possible ciphertexts are U, V, W. Let e_k be the encryption function for the key k. Suppose

$$e_{k_1}(a) = U, \; e_{k_1}(b) = V, \; e_{k_1}(c) = W$$
$$e_{k_2}(a) = U, \; e_{k_2}(b) = W, \; e_{k_2}(c) = V.$$

Let $p_P(a)$ denote the probability that the plaintext is a, etc. The probability that the ciphertext is U is

$$
\begin{aligned}
p_C(U) &= p_K(k_1)p_P(a) + p_K(k_2)p_P(a) \\
&= (.5)(.5) + (.5)(.5) = .50.
\end{aligned}
$$

Similarly, we calculate $p_C(V) = .25$ and $p_C(W) = .25$.

Suppose someone intercepts a ciphertext. This gives some information on the plaintext. For example, if the ciphertext is U, then it can be deduced immediately that the plaintext was a. If the ciphertext is V, the plaintext was either b or c.

We can even say more: The probability that a ciphertext is V is .25, so the conditional probability that the plaintext was b, given that the ciphertext is V is

$$p(b|V) = \frac{p_{(P,C)}(b,V)}{p_C(V)} = \frac{p_{(P,K)}(b,k_1)}{p_C(V)} = \frac{(.3)(.5)}{.25} = .6.$$

Similarly, $p(c|V) = .4$ and $p(a|V) = 0$. We can also calculate

$$p(a|W) = 0, \quad p(b|W) = .6, \quad p(c|W) = .4.$$

Note that the original probabilities of the plaintexts were .5, .3, and .2; knowledge of the ciphertext allows us to revise the probabilities. Therefore, the ciphertext gives us information about the plaintext. We can quantify this via the concept of conditional entropy. First, the entropy of the plaintext is

$$H(P) = -\left(.5 \log_2(.5) + .3 \log_2(.3) + .2 \log_2(.2)\right) = 1.485.$$

The conditional entropy of P given C is

$$H(P|C) = -\sum_{x \in \{a,b,c\}} \sum_{Y \in \{U,V,W\}} p(Y)p(x|Y) \log_2(p(x|Y)) = .485.$$

Therefore, in the present example, the uncertainty for the plaintext decreases when the ciphertext is known. ∎

On the other hand, we suspect that for the one-time pad the ciphertext yields no information about the plaintext that was not known before. In other words, the uncertainty for the plaintext should equal the uncertainty for the plaintext given the ciphertext. This leads us to the following definition and theorem.

Definition. *A cryptosystem has* **perfect secrecy** *if $H(P|C) = H(P)$.*

Theorem. *The one-time pad has perfect secrecy.*

Proof. Recall that the basic setup is the following: There is an alphabet with Z letters (for example, Z could be 2 or 26). The possible plaintexts consist of strings of characters of length L. The ciphertexts are strings of characters of length L. There are Z^L keys, each consisting of a sequence of length L denoting the various shifts to be used. The keys are chosen randomly, so each occurs with probability $1/Z^L$.

Let $c \in \mathcal{C}$ be a possible ciphertext. As before, we calculate the probability that c occurs:

$$p_C(c) = \sum_{\substack{x \in \mathcal{P},\, k \in \mathcal{K} \\ e_k(x) = c}} p_P(x) p_K(k).$$

Here $e_k(x)$ denotes the ciphertext obtained by encrypting x using the key k. The sum is over those pairs x, k such that k encrypts x to c. Note that we have used the independence of P and K to write joint probability $p_{(P,K)}(x, k)$ as the product of the individual probabilities.

In the one-time pad, every key has equal probability $1/Z^L$, so we can replace $p_K(k)$ in the above sum by $1/Z^L$. We obtain

$$p_C(c) = \frac{1}{Z^L} \sum_{\substack{x \in \mathcal{P},\, k \in \mathcal{K} \\ e_k(x) = c}} p_P(x).$$

We now use another important feature of the one-time pad: For each plaintext x and each ciphertext c, there is exactly one key k such that $e_k(x) = c$. Therefore, every $x \in \mathcal{P}$ occurs exactly once in the preceding sum, so we have $Z^{-L} \sum_{x \in \mathcal{P}} p_P(x)$. But the sum of the probabilities of all possible plaintexts is 1, so we obtain

$$p_C(c) = \frac{1}{Z^L}.$$

This confirms what we already suspected: Every ciphertext occurs with equal probability.

Now let's calculate some entropies. Since K and C each have equal probabilities for all Z^L possibilities, we have

$$H(K) = H(C) = \log_2(Z^L).$$

We now calculate $H(P, K, C)$ in two different ways. Since knowing (P, K, C) is the same as knowing (P, K), we have

$$H(P, K, C) = H(P, K) = H(P) + H(K).$$

The last equality is because P and K are independent. Also, knowing (P, K, C) is the same as knowing (P, C) since C and P determine K for the one-time pad. Therefore,

$$H(P, K, C) = H(P, C) = H(P|C) + H(C).$$

The last equality is the chain rule. Equating the two expressions, and using the fact that $H(K) = H(C)$, we obtain $H(P|C) = H(P)$. This proves that the one-time pad has perfect secrecy.   □

The preceding proof yields the following more general result. Let $\#\mathcal{K}$ denote the number of possible keys, etc.

Theorem. *Consider a cryptosystem such that*

1. *Every key has probability $1/\#\mathcal{K}$.*

2. *For each $x \in \mathcal{P}$ and $c \in \mathcal{C}$ there is exactly one $k \in \mathcal{K}$ such that $e_k(x) = c$.*

Then this cryptosystem has perfect secrecy.

It is easy to deduce from condition (2) that $\#\mathcal{C} = \#\mathcal{K}$. Conversely, it can be shown that if $\#\mathcal{P} = \#\mathcal{C} = \#\mathcal{K}$ and the system has perfect secrecy, then (1) and (2) hold (see [Stinson, Theorem 2.4]).

It is natural to ask how the preceding concepts apply to RSA. The possibly surprising answer is that $H(P|C) = 0$; namely, the ciphertext determines the plaintext. The reason is that entropy does not take into account computation time. The fact that it might take billions of years to factor n is irrelevant. What counts is that all the information needed to recover the plaintext is contained in the knowledge of n, e, and c.

The more relevant concept for RSA is the computational complexity of breaking the system.

14.5 The Entropy of English

In an English text, how much information is obtained per letter? If we had a random sequence of letters, each appearing with probability 1/26, then the entropy would be $\log_2(26) = 4.70$; so each letter would contain 4.7 bits of information. If we include spaces, we get $\log_2(27) = 4.75$. But the letters are not equally likely: a has frequency .082, b has frequency .015, etc. (see Section 2.3). Therefore, we consider

$$-\left(.082 \log_2 .082 + .015 \log_2 .015 + \cdots\right) = 4.18.$$

However, this doesn't tell the whole story. Suppose we have the sequence of letters *we are studyin*. There is very little uncertainty as to what the last letter is; it is easy to guess that it is g. Similarly, if we see the letter q, it is extremely likely that the next letter is u. Therefore, the existing letters often give information about the next letter, which means that there is not as much additional information carried by that letter. This says that the entropy calculated previously is still too high. If we use tables of the frequencies of the $26^2 = 676$ digrams (a digram is a two-letter combination), we can calculate the conditional entropy of one letter, given the preceding letter, to be 3.56. Using trigram frequencies, we find that the conditional entropy of a letter, given the preceding two letters, is approximately 3.3. This means that, on the average, if we know two consecutive letters in a text, the following letter carries 3.3 bits of additional information. Therefore, if we have a long text, we should expect to be able to compress it at least by a factor of around $3.3/4.7 = .7$.

Let L represent the letters of English. Let L^N denote the N-gram combinations. Define the entropy of English to be

$$H_{\text{English}} = \lim_{N \to \infty} \frac{H(L^N)}{N},$$

where $H(L^N)$ denotes the entropy of N-grams. This gives the average amount of information per letter in a long text, and it also represents the average amount of uncertainty in guessing the next letter, if we already know a lot of the text. If the letters were all independent of each other, so the probability of the digram qu equaled the probability of q times the probability of u, then we would have $H(L^N) = N \cdot H(L)$, and the limit would be $H(L)$, which is the entropy for one-letter frequencies. But the interactions of letters, as noticed in the frequencies for digrams and trigrams, lower the value of $H(L^N)$.

How do we compute $H(L^N)$? Calculating 100-gram frequencies is impossible. Even tabulating the most common of them and getting an approximation would be difficult. Shannon proposed the following idea.

Suppose we have a machine that is an optimal predictor, in the sense that, given a long string of text, it can calculate the probabilities for the letter that will occur next. It then guesses the letter with highest probability. If correct, it notes the letter and writes down a 1. If incorrect, it guesses the second most likely letter. If correct, it writes down a 2, etc. In this way, we obtain a sequence of numbers. For example, consider the text *itissunnytoday*. Suppose the predictor says that t is the most likely for the 1st letter, and it is wrong; it's second guess is i, which is correct, so we write the i and put 2 below it. The predictor then predicts that t is the next letter, which is correct. We put 1 beneath the t. Continuing, suppose it finds i on its 1st guess, etc. We obtain a situation like the following:

$$
\begin{array}{cccccccccccccc}
i & t & i & s & s & u & n & n & y & t & o & d & a & y \\
2 & 1 & 1 & 1 & 4 & 3 & 2 & 1 & 4 & 1 & 1 & 1 & 1 & 1
\end{array}
$$

Using the prediction machine, we can reconstruct the text. The prediction machine says that its second guess for the first letter will be i, so we know the 1st letter is i. The predictor says that its first guess for the next letter is t, so we know that's next. The first guess for the next is i, etc.

What this means is that if we have a machine for predicting, we can change a text into a string of numbers without losing any information, because we can reconstruct the text. Of course, we could attempt to write a computer program to do the predicting, but Shannon suggested that the best predictor is a person who speaks English. Of course, a person is unlikely to be as deterministic as a machine, and repeating the experiment (assuming the person forgets the text from the first time) might not yield an identical result. So reconstructing the text might present a slight difficulty. But it is still a reasonable assumption that a person approximates an optimal predictor.

Given a sequence of integers corresponding to a text, we can count the frequency of each number. Let

$$q_i = \text{ frequency of the number } i.$$

Since the text and the sequence of numbers can be reconstructed from each other, their entropies must be the same. The largest the entropy can be for the sequence of numbers is when these numbers are independent. In this case, the entropy is $-\sum_{i=1}^{26} q_i \log_2(q_i)$. However, the numbers are probably not independent. For example, if there are a couple consecutive 1's, then perhaps the predictor has guessed the rest of the word, which means that there will be a few more 1's. However, we get an upper bound for the entropy, which is usually better than the one we obtain using frequencies of letters. Moreover, Shannon also found a lower bound for the entropy. His results are

$$\sum_{1=1}^{26} i(q_i - q_{i+1}) \log_2(i) \leq H_{\text{English}} \leq -\sum_{i=1}^{26} q_i \log_2(q_i).$$

Actually, these are only approximate upper and lower bounds, since there is experimental error, and we are really considering a limit as $N \to \infty$.

These results allow an experimental estimation of the entropy of English. Alice chooses a text and Bob guesses the first letter, continuing until the correct guess is made. Alice records the number of guesses. Bob then tries to guess the second letter, and the number of guesses is again recorded. Continuing in this way, Bob tries to guess each letter. When he is correct, Alice tells him and records the number of guesses. Shannon gave Table 14.1 as a typical result of an experiment. Note that he included spaces, but ignored punctuation, so he had 27 possibilities: There are 102 symbols. There are seventy-nine 1's, eight 2's, three 3's, etc. This gives

$$q_1 = 79/102, \quad q_2 = 8/102, \quad q_3 = 3/102, \quad q_4 = q_5 = 2/102,$$
$$q_6 = 3/102, \quad q_7 = q_8 = q_{11} = q_{15} = q_{17} = 1/102.$$

The upper bound for the entropy is therefore

$$-\left(\frac{79}{102} \log_2 \frac{79}{102} + \cdots + \frac{1}{102} \log_2 \frac{1}{102}\right) \approx 1.42.$$

Note that since we are using $0 \log_2 0 = 0$, the terms with $q_i = 0$ can be omitted. The lower bound is

$$1 \cdot \left(\frac{79}{102} - \frac{8}{102}\right) \log_2(1) + 2 \cdot \left(\frac{8}{102} - \frac{3}{102}\right) \log_2(2) + \cdots \approx .72.$$

A reasonable estimate is therefore that the entropy of English is near 1, maybe slightly more than 1.

If we want to send a long English text, we could write each letter (and the space) as a string of 5 bits. This would mean that a text of length

```
t  h  e  r  e     i  s     n  o     r  e  v  e  r  s  e
1  1  1  5  1  1  2  1  1  2  1  1  15 1  17 1  1  1  2  1

o  n     a     m  o  t  o  r  c  y  c  l  e     a
3  2  1  2  2  7  1  1  1  4  1  1  1  1  1  3  1

f  r  i  e  n  d     o  f     m  i  n  e     f  o  u  n  d
8  6  1  3  1  1  1  1  1  1  1  1  1  1  6  2  1  1  1  1

t  h  i  s     o  u  t     r  a  t  h  e  r
1  1  2  1  1  1  1  1  4  1  1  1  1  1  1

d  r  a  m  a  t  i  c  a  l  l  y     t  h  e
11 5  1  1  1  1  1  1  1  1  1  1  6  1  1  1

o  t  h  e  r     d  a  y
1  1  1  1  1  1  1  1  1  1
```

Table 14.1: Shannon's Experiment on the Entropy of English.

102, such as the preceding, would require 510 bits. It would be necessary to use something like this method if the letters were independent and equally likely. However, suppose we do a Huffman encoding of the message $1, 1, 1, 5, 1, 1, 2, \ldots$ from Table 14.1. Let

$$1 \leftrightarrow 1 \quad 2 \leftrightarrow 110 \quad 3 \leftrightarrow 1010 \quad 4 \leftrightarrow 0100$$
$$5 \leftrightarrow 11100 \quad 6 \leftrightarrow 0010 \quad 7 \leftrightarrow 01100 \quad 8 \leftrightarrow 11000$$
$$11 \leftrightarrow 01000 \quad 15 \leftrightarrow 10000 \quad 17 \leftrightarrow 100000.$$

All other numbers up to 27 can be represented by various combinations of 6 or more bits. To send the message requires

$$79 \cdot 1 + 8 \cdot 3 + 3 \cdot 4 + 2 \cdot 4 + \cdots + 1 \cdot 6 = 171 \text{ bits,}$$

which is 1.68 bits per letter.

Note that 5 bits per letter is only slightly more than the "random" entropy 4.75, and 1.68 bits per letter is slightly more than our estimate of the entropy of English. These agree with the result that entropy differs from the average length of a Huffman encoding by at most 1.

One way to look at the preceding entropy calculations is to say that English is around 75% redundant. Namely, if we send a long message in standard written English, compared to the optimally compressed text, the ratio is approximately 4 to 1 (that is, the random entropy 4.75 divided by the entropy of English, which is around 1). In our example, we were close, obtaining a ratio near 3 to 1 (namely 4.75/1.68).

Define the **redundancy** of English to be

$$R = 1 - \frac{H_{\text{English}}}{\log_2(26)}.$$

Then R is approximately 0.75, which is the 75% redundancy mentioned previously.

Unicity Distance

Suppose we have a ciphertext. How many keys will decrypt it to something meaningful? If the text is long enough, we suspect that there is a unique key and a unique corresponding plaintext. The unicity distance n_0 for a cryptosystem is the length of ciphertext at which one expects that there is a unique meaningful plaintext. A rough estimate for the unicity distance is

$$n_0 = \frac{\log_2 |K|}{R \log_2 |L|},$$

where $|K|$ is the number of possible keys, $|L|$ is the number of letters or symbols, and R is the redundancy (see [Stinson]). We'll take $R = .75$ (whether we include spaces in our language or not; the difference is small).

For example, consider the substitution cipher, which has 26! keys. We have

$$n_0 = \frac{\log_2 26!}{.75 \log_2 26} \approx 25.1.$$

This means that if a ciphertext has length 25 or more, we expect that usually there is only one possible meaningful plaintext. Of course, if we have a ciphertext of length 25, there are probably several letters that have not appeared. Therefore, there could be several possible keys, all of which decrypt the ciphertext to the same plaintext.

As another example, consider the affine cipher. There are 312 keys, so

$$n_0 = \frac{\log_2 312}{.75 \log_2 26} \approx 2.35.$$

This should be regarded as only a very rough approximation. Clearly it should take a few more letters to get a unique decryption. But the estimate of 2.35 indicates that very few letters suffice to yield a unique decryption in most cases for the affine cipher.

Finally, consider the one-time pad for a message of length N. The encryption is a separate shift mod 26 for each letter, so there are 26^N keys. We obtain the estimate

$$n_0 \approx \frac{\log_2 26^N}{.75 \log_2 26} = 1.33N.$$

In this case, it says we need more letters than the entire ciphertext to get a unique decryption. This reflects the fact that all plaintexts are possible for any ciphertext.

14.6   Exercises

1. Let X_1 and X_2 be two independent tosses of a fair coin. Find the entropy $H(X_1)$ and the joint entropy $H(X_1, X_2)$. Why is $H(X_1, X_2) = H(X_1) + H(X_2)$?

2. Consider an unfair coin where the two outcomes, heads and tails, have probabilities $p(heads) = p$ and $p(tails) = 1 - p$.
(a) If the coin is flipped two times, what are the possible outcomes along with their respective probabilities?
(b) Show that the entropy in part (a) is $-2p \log_2(p) - 2(1 - p) \log_2(1 - p)$. How could this have been predicted without calculating the probabilities in part (a)?

3. A random variable X takes the values $1, 2, \cdots, n, \cdots$ with probabilities $\frac{1}{2}, \frac{1}{2^2}, \cdots, \frac{1}{2^n}, \cdots$. Calculate the entropy $H(X)$.

4. Let X be a random variable taking on integer values. The probability is $1/2$ that X is in the range $[0, 2^8 - 1]$, with all such values being equally likely, and the probability is $1/2$ that the value is in the range $[2^8, 2^{32} - 1]$, with all such values being equally likely. Compute $H(X)$.

5. Let X be a random event taking on the values $-2, -1, 0, 1, 2$, all with positive probability. What is the general inequality/equality between $H(X)$ and $H(Y)$, where Y is the following?
(a) $Y = 2^X$
(b) $Y = X^2$

6. (a) In this problem we explore the relationship between the entropy of a random variable X and the entropy of a function $f(X)$ of the random variable. The following is a short proof that shows $H(f(X)) \leq H(X)$. Explain what principles are used in each of the steps.

$$H(X, f(X)) = H(X) + H(f(X)|X) = H(X),$$

$$H(X, f(X)) = H(f(X)) + H(X|f(X)) \geq H(f(X)).$$

(b) Letting X take on the values ± 1 and letting $f(x) = x^2$, show that it is possible to have $H(f(X)) < H(X)$.

(c) In part (a), show that you have equality if and only if f is a one-to-one function (more precisely, f is one-to-one on the set of outputs of X that have nonzero probability).

(d) The preceding results can be used to study the behavior of the run length coding of a sequence. Run length coding is a technique that is commonly used in data compression. Suppose that $X_1, X_2, \cdots, X_n$ are random variables that take the values 0 or 1. This sequence of random variables can be thought of as representing the output of a binary source. The run length coding of $X_1, X_2, \cdots, X_n$ is a sequence $\mathbf{L} = (L_1, L_2, \cdots, L_k)$ that represents the lengths of consecutive symbols with the same value. For example, the sequence 110000100111 has a run length sequence of $\mathbf{L} = (2, 4, 1, 2, 3)$. Observe that $\mathbf{L}$ is a function of $X_1, X_2, \cdots, X_n$. Show that $\mathbf{L}$ and X_1 uniquely determine $X_1, X_2, \cdots, X_n$. Do $\mathbf{L}$ and X_n determine $X_1, X_2, \cdots, X_n$? Using these observation and the preceding results, compare $H(X_1, X_2, \cdots, X_n)$, $H(\mathbf{L})$, and $H(\mathbf{L}, X_1)$.

7. A bag contains five red balls, three white balls, and two black balls that are identical to each other in every manner except color.

(a) Choose two balls from the bag with replacement. What is the entropy of this experiment?

(b) What is the entropy of choosing two balls without replacement? (*Note*: In both parts, the order matters; i.e., red then white is not the same as white then red).

8. We often run into situations where we have a sequence of n random events. For example, a piece of text is a long sequence of letters. We are concerned with the rate of growth of the joint entropy as n increases. Define the entropy rate of a sequence $\mathbf{X} = \{X_k\}$ of random events as

$$H_\infty(\mathbf{X}) = \lim_{n \to \infty} \frac{1}{n} H(X_1, X_2, \cdots X_n).$$

(a) A very crude model for a language is to assume that subsequent letters in a piece of text are independent and come from identical probability distributions. Using this, show that the entropy rate equals $H(X_1)$.

(b) In general, there is dependence among the random variables. Assume that $X_1, X_2, \cdots X_n$ have the same probability distribution but are somehow dependent on each other (for example, if I give you the letters TH you can guess that the next letter is E). Show that

$$H(X_1, X_2, \cdots X_n) \le \sum_k H(X_k)$$

and thus that

$$H_\infty(\mathbf{X}) \le H(X_1)$$

(if the limit defining H_∞ exists).

9. Suppose we have a cryptosystem with only two possible plaintexts. The plaintext a occurs with probability 1/3 and b occurs with probability 2/3. There are two keys, k_1 and k_2, and each is used with probability 1/2. Key k_1 encrypts a to A and b to B. Key k_2 encrypts a to B and b to A.
(a) Calculate $H(P)$, the entropy for the plaintext.
(b) Calculate $H(P|C)$, the conditional entropy for the plaintext given the ciphertext. (*Optional hint:* This can be done with no additional calculation by matching up this system with another well-known system.)

10. Consider a cryptosystem $\{P, K, C\}$.
(a) Explain why $H(P, K) = H(C, P, K) = H(P) + H(K)$.
(b) Suppose the system has perfect secrecy. Show that

$$H(C, P) = H(C) + H(P)$$

and

$$H(C) = H(K) - H(K|C, P).$$

(c) Suppose the system has perfect secrecy and, for each pair of plaintext and ciphertext, there is at most one corresponding key that does the encryption. Show that $H(C) = H(K)$.

11. Prove that for a cryptosystem $\{P, K, C\}$ we have

$$H(C|P) = H(P, K, C) - H(P) - H(K|C, P) = H(K) - H(K|C, P).$$

12. Consider a Shamir secret sharing scheme where any 5 people of a set of 20 can determine the secret K, but no fewer can do so. Let $H(K)$ be the entropy of the choice of K, and let $H(K|S_1)$ be the conditional entropy of K, given the information supplied to the first person. What are the relative sizes of $H(K)$ and $H(K|S_1)$? (Larger, smaller, equal?)

13. Let X be a random event taking on the values $1, 2, 3, \ldots, 36$, all with equal probability.
(a) What is the entropy $H(X)$?
(b) Let $Y = X^{36} \pmod{37}$. What is $H(Y)$?

14. Let $p_i \geq 0$ for $1 \leq i \leq n$. Show that the maximum of $-\sum_i p_i \log_2 p_i$, subject to the constraint $\sum_i p_i = 1$, occurs when $p_1 = \cdots = p_n$. (*Hint:* Lagrange multipliers could be useful in this problem.)

15. (a) Suppose we define $\tilde{H}(Y|X) = -\sum_{x,y} p_Y(y|x) \log_2 p_Y(y|x)$. Show that if X and Y are independent, and X has $|\mathcal{X}|$ possible outputs, then $\tilde{H}(Y|X) = |\mathcal{X}| H(Y) \geq H(Y)$.
(b) Use (a) to show that $\tilde{H}(Y|X)$ is not a good description of the uncertainty of Y given X.

Chapter 15

Elliptic Curves

In the mid-1980s, Miller and Koblitz introduced elliptic curves into cryptography, and Lenstra showed how to use elliptic curves to factor integers. Since that time, elliptic curves have played an increasingly important role in many cryptographic situations. One of their advantages is that they seem to offer a level of security comparable to classical cryptosystems that use much larger key sizes. For example, it is estimated in [Blake et al.] that certain conventional systems with a 4096-bit key size can be replaced by 313-bit elliptic curve systems. Using much shorter numbers can represent a considerable savings in hardware implementations.

In this chapter, we present some of the highlights. For more details on elliptic curves and their cryptologic uses, see [Blake et al.].

15.1   The Addition Law

An elliptic curve E is the graph of an equation

$$E: \quad y^2 = x^3 + ax + b,$$

where a, b are in whatever is the appropriate set (rational numbers, complex numbers, integers mod n, etc.). We also include a **"point at infinity,"** denoted ∞, which is most easily regarded as sitting at the top of the y-axis. It can be treated rigorously in the context of projective geometry, but this intuitive notion suffices for what we need. The bottom of the y-axis is

272

identified with the top, so ∞ also sits at the bottom of the y-axis. When we are working with real numbers, the graph E has one of two possible forms, depending on whether the cubic polynomial in x has one real root or three real roots. For example, the graphs of $y^2 = x(x+1)(x-1)$ and $y^2 = x^3 + 73$ are the following:

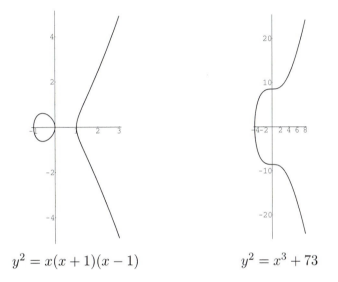

$$y^2 = x(x+1)(x-1) \qquad\qquad y^2 = x^3 + 73$$

We assume that the cubic polynomial $x^3 + ax + b$ has no multiple roots. This means we exclude, for example, the graph of $y^2 = x^2(x-1)$. Such curves will be discussed in Section 15.3.

Historical point: Elliptic curves are not ellipses. They received their name from their relation to *elliptic integrals* such as

$$\int_{z_1}^{z_2} \frac{dx}{\sqrt{x^3 + ax + b}} \quad \text{and} \quad \int_{z_1}^{z_2} \frac{x\,dx}{\sqrt{x^3 + ax + b}}$$

that arise in the computation of the arc length of ellipses.

Technical point: For most situations, equations of the form $y^2 = x^3 + ax + b$ suffice for elliptic curves. However, sometimes it is necessary to consider elliptic curves given by equations of the form

$$y^2 + a_1 xy + a_3 y = x^3 + a_2 x^2 + a_4 x + a_6,$$

where $a_1, \ldots, a_6$ are constants. If we are working mod p, where $p > 3$ is prime, or if we are working with real, rational, or complex numbers, then simple changes of variables transform the present equation into the form $y^2 = x^3 + ax + b$. However, if we are working mod 2 or mod 3, or with a finite field of characteristic 2 or 3 (that is, 1+1=0 or 1+1+1=0), then we need to use the more general form. Elliptic curves over fields of characteristic 2 will be mentioned briefly in Section 15.4.

Given two points P_1 and P_2 on E, we can obtain a third point P_3 on E as follows (see Figure 15.1): Draw the line L through P_1 and P_2 (if $P_1 = P_2$, take the tangent line to E at P_1). The line L intersects E in a third point Q. Reflect Q through the x-axis (i.e., change y to $-y$) to get P_3. Define a law of addition on E by

$$P_1 + P_2 = P_3.$$

Note that this is not the same as adding points in the plane.

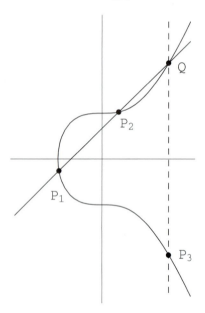

Figure 15.1: Adding Points on an Elliptic Curve.

Example. Suppose E is defined by $y^2 = x^3 + 73$. Let $P_1 = (2, 9)$ and $P_2 = (3, 10)$. The line L through P_1 and P_2 is $y = x+7$. Substituting into the equation for E yields $(x+7)^2 = x^3 + 73$, which yields $x^3 - x^2 - 14x + 24 = 0$. Since L intersects E in P_1 and P_2, we already know two roots, namely $x = 2$ and $x = 3$. Moreover, the sum of the three roots is minus the coefficient of x^2 (Exercise 1) and therefore equals 1. So the third point of intersection has $x = -4$. Since $y = x + 7$, we have $y = 3$, and $Q = (-4, 3)$. Therefore, $P_3 = (-4, -3)$.

Now suppose we want to add P_3 to itself. The slope of the tangent line to E at P_3 is obtained by implicitly differentiating the equation for E:

$$2y \, dy = 3x^2 \, dx, \quad \text{so} \quad \frac{dy}{dx} = \frac{3x^2}{2y} = -8,$$

where we have substituted $(x, y) = (-4, -3)$ from P_3. In this case, the line L is $y = -8(x + 4) - 3$. Substituting into the equation for E yields $(-8(x + 4) - 3)^2 = x^3 + 73$, hence $x^3 - (-8)^2 x^2 + \ldots = 0$. The sum of the three roots is 64 (= minus the coefficient of x^2). Because the line L is tangent to E, it follows that $x = -4$ is a double root. We see that the third root is $64 - 2(-4) = 72$. The corresponding value of y (use the equation of L) is -611. Changing y to $-y$ yields

$$P_3 + P_3 = (72, 611). \qquad\qquad\qquad \blacksquare$$

What happens if we try to compute $P + \infty$? A line through ∞ and P is vertical. It intersects E in $P = (x, y)$ and also in $(x, -y)$. When we reflect $(x, -y)$ across the x-axis, we get back $P = (x, y)$. Therefore,

$$P + \infty = P.$$

We can also subtract points. First, observe that the line through (x, y) and $(x, -y)$ is vertical, so the third point of intersection with E is ∞. The reflection across the x-axis is still ∞ (that's what we meant when we said ∞ sits at the top and at the bottom of the y-axis). Therefore,

$$(x, y) + (x, -y) = \infty.$$

Since ∞ plays the role of an additive identity (as does 0 in addition), we define

$$-(x, y) = (x, -y).$$

To subtract points $P - Q$, simply add P and $-Q$.

Another way to express the addition law is to say that

$$P + Q + R = \infty \iff P, Q, R \text{ are collinear.}$$

(see Exercise 7).

For computations, we can ignore the geometrical interpretation and work only with formulas, which are as follows:

Addition Law. *Let E be given by $y^2 = x^3 + ax + b$ and let*

$$P_1 = (x_1, y_2), \quad P_2 = (x_2, y_2).$$

Then

$$P_1 + P_2 = P_3 = (x_3, y_3),$$

where

$$x_3 = m^2 - x_1 - x_2$$
$$y_3 = m(x_1 - x_3) - y_1$$

and

$$m = \begin{cases} (y_2 - y_1)/(x_2 - x_1) & \text{if } P_1 \neq P_2 \\ (3x_1^2 + a)/(2y_1) & \text{if } P_1 = P_2. \end{cases}$$

If the slope m is infinite, then $P_3 = \infty$. There is one additional law: $\infty + P = P$ for all points P.

It can be shown that the addition law is associative:

$$(P + Q) + R = P + (Q + R).$$

It is also commutative:

$$P + Q = Q + P.$$

When adding several points, it therefore doesn't matter in what order the points are added nor how they are grouped together. In technical terms, we have found that the points of E form an abelian group. The point ∞ is the identity element of this group.

15.2   Elliptic Curves Mod n

If n is an integer, we can work with elliptic curves mod n using the aforementioned ideas. For example, consider

$$E : y^2 \equiv x^3 + 2x + 3 \pmod{5}.$$

The points on E are the pairs (x, y) mod 5 that satisfy the equation, along with the point at infinity. These can be listed as follows. The possibilities for x mod 5 are 0, 1, 2, 3, 4. Substitute each of these into the equation and find the values of y that solve the equation:

$$x \equiv 0 \Rightarrow y^2 \equiv 3 \quad (\text{mod } 5) \Rightarrow \text{no solutions}$$
$$x \equiv 1 \Rightarrow y^2 \equiv 6 \equiv 1 \quad (\text{mod } 5) \Rightarrow y \equiv 1, 4 \quad (\text{mod } 5)$$
$$x \equiv 2 \Rightarrow y^2 \equiv 15 \equiv 0 \quad (\text{mod } 5) \Rightarrow y \equiv 0 \quad (\text{mod } 5)$$
$$x \equiv 3 \Rightarrow y^2 \equiv 36 \equiv 1 \quad (\text{mod } 5) \Rightarrow y \equiv 1, 4 \quad (\text{mod } 5)$$
$$x \equiv 4 \Rightarrow y^2 \equiv 75 \equiv 0 \quad (\text{mod } 5) \Rightarrow y \equiv 0 \quad (\text{mod } 5)$$
$$x = \infty \Rightarrow y = \infty.$$

Therefore, the points on E are $(1, 1), (1, 4), (2, 0), (3, 1), (3, 4), (4, 0), (\infty, \infty)$.

The addition of points on an elliptic curve mod n is done via the same formulas as given previously, except that a rational number a/b must be treated as ab^{-1}, where $b^{-1}b \equiv 1 \pmod{n}$. This requires that $\gcd(b, n) = 1$ and is the key to using elliptic curves for factorization.

Example. Let's compute $(1, 4) + (3, 1)$ on the curve just considered. The slope is

$$m \equiv \frac{1 - 4}{3 - 1} \equiv 1 \quad (\text{mod } 5).$$

Therefore,

$$x_3 \equiv m^2 - x_1 - x_2 \equiv 1^2 - 1 - 3 \equiv 2 \quad (\text{mod } 5)$$
$$y_3 \equiv m(x_1 - x_3) - y_1 \equiv 1(1 - 2) - 4 \equiv 0 \quad (\text{mod } 5).$$

This means that

$$(1, 4) + (3, 1) = (2, 0). \qquad \blacksquare$$

Example. Here is a somewhat larger example. Let $n = 2773$. Let

$$E : y^2 \equiv x^3 + 4x + 4 \quad (\text{mod } 2773), \text{ and } P = (1, 3).$$

Let's compute $2P = P + P$. To get the slope of the tangent line, we differentiate implicitly and evaluate at $(1, 3)$:

$$2y \, dy = (3x^2 + 4) \, dx \Rightarrow \frac{dy}{dx} = \frac{7}{6}.$$

But we are working mod 2773. Using the extended Euclidean algorithm (see Section 3.2), we find that $2311 \cdot 6 \equiv 1 \pmod{2773}$, so we can replace $1/6$ by 2311. Therefore,

$$m \equiv \frac{7}{6} \equiv 7 \times 2311 \equiv 2312 \quad (\text{mod } 2773).$$

The formulas yield

$$x_3 \equiv 2312^2 - 1 - 1 \equiv 1771 \pmod{2773}$$
$$y_3 \equiv 2312(1 - 1771) - 3 \equiv 705 \pmod{2773}.$$

The final answer is
$$2P = P + P = (1771, 705). \qquad \blacksquare$$

Number of Points Mod p

Let $E : y^2 \equiv x^3 + ax + b \pmod{p}$ be an elliptic curve, where $p \geq 5$ is prime. We can list the points on E by letting $x = 0, 1, \ldots, p - 1$ and seeing when $x^3 + ax + b$ is a square mod p. Since half of the nonzero numbers are squares mod p, we expect that $x^3 + ax + b$ will be a square approximately half the time. When it is a nonzero square, there are two square roots: y and $-y$. Therefore, approximately half the time we get two values of y and half the time we get no y. Therefore, we expect around p points. Including the point ∞, we expect a total of approximately $p + 1$ points. In the 1930s, H. Hasse made this estimate more precise.

Hasse's Theorem. *Suppose $E \pmod{p}$ has N points. Then*

$$|N - p - 1| < 2\sqrt{p}.$$

The proof of this theorem is well beyond the scope of this book. It can also be shown that whenever N and p satisfy the inequality of the theorem, there is an elliptic curve E mod p with exactly N points.

If p is large, say around 10^{20}, it is infeasible to count the points on an elliptic curve by listing them. More sophisticated algorithms have been developed by Schoof, Atkin, Elkies, and others to deal with this problem.

Discrete Logarithms on Elliptic Curves

Recall the classical discrete logarithm problem: We know that $x \equiv g^k \pmod{p}$ for some k, and we want to find k. There is an elliptic curve version: Suppose we have points A, B on an elliptic curve E and we know that $B = kA \, (= A + A + \cdots + A)$ for some integer k. We want to find k. This might not look like a logarithm problem, but it is clearly the analog of the classical discrete logarithm problem. Therefore, it is called the **discrete logarithm problem** for elliptic curves.

There is no good general attack on the discrete logarithm problem for elliptic curves. There is an analog of the Pohlig-Hellman attack that works in some situations. Let E be an elliptic curve mod a prime p and let n

be the smallest integer such that $nA = \infty$. If n has only small prime factors, then it is possible to calculate the discrete logarithm k mod the prime powers dividing n and then use the Chinese remainder theorem to find k (see Exercise 12). The Pohlig-Hellman attack can be thwarted by choosing E and A so that n has a large prime factor.

There is no replacement for the index calculus attack described in Section 7.2. This is because there is no good analog of "small." You might try to use points with small coordinates in place of the "small primes," but this doesn't work. When you factor a number by dividing off the prime factors one by one, the quotients get smaller and smaller until you finish. On an elliptic curve, you could have a point with fairly small coordinates, subtract off a small point, and end up with a point with large coordinates (see Computer Problem 5). So there is no good way to know when you are making progress toward expressing a point in terms of the factor base of small points.

The birthday attack on discrete logarithms works for elliptic curves (Exercise 6), though it requires too much memory to be practical in most situations. For other attacks, see [Blake et al.].

Representing Plaintext

In most cryptographic systems, we must have a method for mapping our original message into a numerical value upon which we can perform mathematical operations. In order to use elliptic curves, we need a method for mapping a message onto a point on an elliptic curve. Elliptic curve cryptosystems then use elliptic curve operations on that point to yield a new point that will serve as the ciphertext.

The problem of encoding plaintext messages as points on an elliptic curve is not as simple as it was in the conventional case. In particular, there is no known polynomial time, deterministic algorithm for writing down points on an arbitrary elliptic curve $E \pmod{p}$. However, there are fast probabilistic methods for finding points, and these can be used for encoding messages. These methods have the property that with small probability they will fail to produce a point. By appropriately choosing parameters, this probability can be made arbitrarily small, say on the order of $1/2^{30}$.

Here is one method, due to Koblitz. The idea is the following. Let $E : y^2 \equiv x^3 + ax + b \pmod{p}$ be the elliptic curve. The message m (already represented as a number) will be embedded in the x-coordinate of a point. However, the probability is only about $1/2$ that $m^3 + am + b$ is a square mod p. Therefore, we adjoin a few bits at the end of m and adjust them until we get a number x such that $x^3 + ax + b$ is a square mod p.

More precisely, let K be a large integer so that a failure rate of $1/2^K$ is acceptable when trying to encode a message as a point. Assume that m

satisfies $(m + 1)K < p$. The message m will be represented by a number $x = mK + j$, where $0 \leq j < K$. For $j = 0, 1, \ldots, K - 1$, compute $x^3 + ax + b$ and try to calculate the square root of $x^3 + ax + b \pmod{p}$. For example, if $p \equiv 3 \pmod 4$, the method of Section 3.9 can be used. If there is a square root y, then we take $P_m = (x, y)$; otherwise, we increment j by one and try again with the new x. We repeat this until either we find a square root or $j = K$. If j ever equals K, then we fail to map a message to a point. Since $x^3 + ax + b$ is a square approximately half of the time, we have about a $1/2^K$ chance of failure.

In order to recover the message from the point $P_m = (x, y)$ we simply calculate m by

$$m = [x/K],$$

where $[x/K]$ denotes the greatest integer less than or equal to x/K.

Example. Let $p = 179$ and suppose that our elliptic curve is $y^2 = x^3 + 2x + 7$. If we are satisfied with a failure rate of $1/2^{10}$, then we may take $K = 10$. Since we need $mK + K < 179$, we need $0 \leq m \leq 16$. Suppose our message is $m = 5$. We consider x of the form $mK + j = 50 + j$. The possible choices for x are $50, 51, \ldots, 59$. For $x = 51$ we get $x^3 + 2x + 7 \equiv 121 \pmod{179}$, and $11^2 \equiv 121 \pmod{179}$. Thus, we represent the message $m = 5$ by the point $P_m = (51, 11)$. The message m can be recovered by $m = [51/10] = 5$. ∎

15.3 Factoring with Elliptic Curves

Suppose $n = pq$ is a number we wish to factor. Choose a random elliptic curve mod n and a point on the curve. In practice, one chooses several (around 14 for numbers around 50 digits; more for larger integers) curves with points and runs the algorithm in parallel.

How do we choose the curve? First, choose a point P and a coefficient a. Then choose b so that P lies on the curve $y^2 = x^3 + ax + b$. This is much more efficient than choosing a and b and then trying to find a point.

For example, let $n = 2773$. Take $P = (1, 3)$ and $a = 4$. Since we want $3^2 \equiv 1^3 + 4 \cdot 1 + b$, we take $b = 4$. Therefore, our curve is

$$E : \quad y^2 \equiv x^3 + 4x + 4 \pmod{2773}.$$

We calculated $2P = (1771, 705)$ in a previous example. Note that during the calculation, we needed to find $6^{-1} \pmod{2773}$. This required that $\gcd(6, 2773) = 1$ and used the extended Euclidean algorithm, which was essentially a gcd calculation.

Now let's calculate $3P = 2P + P$. The line through the points $2P = (1771, 705)$ and $P = (1, 3)$ has slope $702/1770$. When we try to invert 1770 mod 2773, we find that gcd(1770,2773)=59, so we cannot do this. So what do we do? Our original goal was to factor 2773, so we don't need to do anything more. We have found the factor 59, which yields the factorization $2773 = 59 \cdot 47$.

Here's what happened. Using the Chinese remainder theorem, we can regard E as a pair of elliptic curves, one mod 59 and the other mod 47. It turns out that $3P = \infty$ (mod 59), while $4P = \infty$ (mod 47). Therefore, when we tried to compute $3P$, we had a slope that was infinite mod 59 but finite mod 47. In other words, we had a denominator that was 0 mod 59 but nonzero mod 47. Taking the gcd allowed us to isolate the factor 59.

The same type of idea is the basis for many factoring algorithms. If $n = pq$, you cannot separate p and q as long as they behave identically. But if you can find something that makes them behave slightly differently, then they can be found. In the example, the multiples of P reached ∞ faster mod 59 than mod 47. Since in general the primes p and q should act fairly independently of each other, one would expect that for most curves E (mod pq) and points P, the multiples of P would reach ∞ mod p and mod q at different times. This will cause the gcd to find either p or q.

Usually, it takes several more steps than 3 or 4 to reach ∞ mod p or mod q. In practice, one multiplies P by a large number with many small prime factors, for example, 10000!. This can be done via successive doubling (the additive analog of successive squaring; see Exercise 10). The hope is that this multiple of P is ∞ either mod p or mod q. This is very much the analog of the $p - 1$ method of factoring. However, recall that the $p - 1$ method (see Section 6.4) usually doesn't work when $p - 1$ has a large prime factor. The same type of problem could occur in the elliptic curve method just outlined when the number m such that mP equals ∞ has a large prime factor. If this happens (so the method fails to produce a factor after a while), we simply change to a new curve E. This curve will be independent of the previous curve and the value of m such that $mP = \infty$ should have essentially no relation to the previous m. After several tries (or if several curves are treated in parallel), a good curve is often found, and the number $n = pq$ is factored. In contrast, if the $p - 1$ method fails, there is nothing that can be changed other than using a different factorization method.

Example. We want to factor $n = 455839$. Choose

$$E : y^2 \equiv x^3 + 5x - 5, \quad P = (1, 1).$$

Suppose we try to compute $10!P$. There are many ways to do this. One is to compute $2!P, 3!P = 3(2!P), 4!P = 4(3!P), \ldots$. If we do this, everything is fine through $7!P$, but $8!P$ requires inverting 599 (mod n). Since gcd(599, n) = 599, we can factor n as 599×761.

Let's examine this more closely. A computation shows that E (mod 599) has $640 = 2^7 \times 5$ points and E (mod 761) has $777 = 3 \times 7 \times 37$ points. Moreover, 640 is the smallest positive m such that $mP = \infty$ on E (mod 599), and 777 is the smallest positive m such that $mP = \infty$ on E (mod 761). Since 8! is a multiple of 640, it is easy to see that $8!P = \infty$ on E (mod 599), as we calculated. Since 8! is not a multiple of 777, it follows that $8!P \neq \infty$ on E (mod 761). Recall that we obtain ∞ when we divide by 0, so calculating $8!P$ asked us to divide by 0 (mod 599). This is why we found the factor 599. ∎

In general, consider an elliptic curve E (mod p) for some prime p. The smallest positive m such that $mP = \infty$ on this curve divides the number N of points on E (mod p) (if you know group theory, you'll recognize this as a corollary of Lagrange's theorem), so $NP = \infty$. Quite often, m will be N or a large divisor of N. In any case, if N is a product of small primes, then $B!$ will be a multiple of N for a reasonably small value of B. Therefore, $B!P = \infty$.

A number that has only small prime factors is called **smooth**. More precisely, if all the prime factors of an integer are less than or equal to B, then it is called **B-smooth**. This concept played a role in the quadratic sieve (Section 6.4), the $p-1$ factoring method (Section 6.4), and the index calculus attack on discrete logarithms (Section 7.2).

Recall from Hasse's theorem that N is an integer near p. It is possible to show that the density of smooth integers is large enough (we'll leave *small* and *large* undefined here) that if we choose a random elliptic curve E (mod p), then there is a reasonable chance that the number N is smooth. This means that the elliptic curve factorization method should find p for this choice of the curve. If we try several curves E (mod n), where $n = pq$, then it is likely that at least one of the curves E (mod p) or E (mod q) will have its number of points being smooth.

In summary, the advantage of the elliptic curve factorization method over the $p-1$ method is the following. The $p-1$ method requires that $p-1$ is smooth. The elliptic curve method requires only that there are enough smooth numbers near p so that at least one of some randomly chosen integers near p is smooth. This means that elliptic curve factorization succeeds much more often than the $p-1$ method.

The elliptic curve method seems to be best suited for factoring numbers of medium size, say around 40 or 50 digits. These numbers are no longer used for the security of factoring-based systems such as RSA, but it is sometimes useful in other situations to have a fast factorization method for such numbers. For larger numbers, the quadratic sieve and number field sieve are superior (see Section 6.4).

Degenerate Curves

In practice, the case where the cubic polynomial $x^3 + ax + b$ has multiple roots does not arise. But what happens if it does? Does the factorization algorithm still work? The discriminant $4a^3 + 27b^2$ is zero if and only if there is a multiple root (this is the cubic analog of the fact that $ax^2 + bx + c$ has a double root if and only if $b^2 - 4ac = 0$). Since we are working mod $n = pq$, the result says that there is a multiple root mod n if and only if the discriminant is 0 mod n. Since n is composite, there is also the intermediate case where the gcd of n and the discriminant is neither 1 nor n. But this gives a nontrivial factor of n, so we can stop immediately in this case.

Example. Let's look at an example:

$$y^2 = x^3 - 3x + 2 = (x-1)^2(x+2).$$

Given a point $P = (x, y)$ on this curve, we associate the number

$$(y + \sqrt{3}(x-1))/(y - \sqrt{3}(x-1)).$$

It can be shown that adding the points on the curve corresponds to multiplying the corresponding numbers. The formulas still work, as long as we don't use the point $(1, 0)$. Where does this come from? The two lines tangent to the curve at $(1, 0)$ are $y + \sqrt{3}(x-1) = 0$ and $y - \sqrt{3}(x-1) = 0$. This number is simply the ratio of these two expressions.

Since we need to work mod n, we give an example mod 143. We choose 143 since 3 is a square mod 143; in fact, $82^2 \equiv 3 \pmod{143}$. If this were not the case, things would become more technical with this curve. We could easily rectify the situation by choosing a new curve.

Consider the point $P = (-1, 2)$ on $y^2 = x^3 - 3x + 2 \pmod{143}$. Look at its multiples:

$$P = (-1, 2), \quad 2P = (2, 141), \quad 3P = (112, 101), \quad 4P = (10, 20).$$

When trying to compute $5P$, we find the factor 11 of 143.

Recall that we are assigning numbers to each point on the curve, other than $(1,1)$. Since we are working mod 143, we use 82 in place of $\sqrt{3}$. Therefore, the number corresponding to $(-1, 2)$ is $(2 + 82(-1 - 1))/(2 - 82(-1 - 1)) = 80 \pmod{143}$. We can compute the numbers for all the points above:

$$P \leftrightarrow 80, \quad 2P \leftrightarrow 108, \quad 3P \leftrightarrow 60, \quad 4P \leftrightarrow 81.$$

Let's compare with the powers of 80 mod 143:

$$80^1 \equiv 80, \quad 80^2 \equiv 108, \quad 80^3 \equiv 60, \quad 80^4 \equiv 81, \quad 80^5 \equiv 45.$$

We get the same numbers. This is simply the fact mentioned previously that the addition of points on the curve corresponds to multiplication of the corresponding numbers. Moreover, note that $45 \equiv 1 \pmod{11}$, but not mod 13. This corresponds to the fact that 5 times the point $(-1, 2)$ is ∞ mod 11 but not mod 13. Note that 1 is the multiplicative identity for multiplication mod 11, while ∞ is the additive identity for addition on the curve.

It is easy to see from the preceding that factorization using the curve $y^2 = x^3 - 3x + 2$ is essentially the same as using the classical $p-1$ factorization method (see Section 6.4).   ∎

In the preceding example, the cubic equation had a double root. An even worse possibility is the cubic having a triple root. Consider the curve

$$y^2 = x^3.$$

To a point $(x, y) \neq (0, 0)$ on this curve, associate the number x/y. Let's start with the point $P = (1, 1)$ and compute its multiples:

$$P = (1, 1), \quad 2P = (\frac{1}{4}, \frac{1}{8}), \quad 3P = (\frac{1}{9}, \frac{1}{27}), \dots, \quad mP = (\frac{1}{m^2}, \frac{1}{m^3}).$$

Note that the corresponding numbers x/y are $1, 2, 3, \dots, m$. Adding the points on the curve corresponds to adding the numbers x/y.

If we are using the curve $y^2 = x^3$ to factor n, we need to change the points mP to integers mod n, which requires finding inverses for m^2 and m^3 mod n. This is done by the extended Euclidean algorithm, which is essentially a gcd computation. We find a factor of n when $\gcd(m, n) \neq 1$. Therefore, this method is essentially the same as computing in succession $\gcd(2, n), \gcd(3, n), \gcd(4, n), \dots$ until a factor is found. This is a slow version of trial division, the oldest factorization technique known. Of course, in the elliptic curve factorization algorithm, a large multiple $(B!)P$ of P is usually computed. This is equivalent to factoring by computing $\gcd(B!, n)$, a method that is often used to test for prime factors up to B.

In summary, we see that the $p-1$ method and trial division are included in the elliptic curve factorization algorithm if we allow degenerate curves.

15.4   Elliptic Curves in Characteristic 2

Many applications use elliptic curves mod 2, or elliptic curves defined over the finite fields $GF(2^n)$ (these are described in Section 3.10). This is often because mod 2 adapts well to computers.

If we're working mod 2, the equations for elliptic curves need to be modified slightly. There are many reasons for this. For example, the derivative of y^2 is $2yy' = 0$, since 2 is the same as 0. This means that the tangent lines we compute are vertical, so $2P = \infty$ for all points P. A more sophisticated explanation is that the curve $y^2 \equiv x^3 + ax + b \pmod{2}$ has singularities (points where the partial derivatives with respect to x and y simultaneously vanish).

The equations we need are of the form

$$E : y^2 + a_1 xy + a_3 y = x^3 + a_2 x^2 + a_4 x + a_6,$$

where $a_1, \ldots, a_6$ are constants. The addition law is slightly more complicated. We still have three points adding to infinity if and only if they lie on a line. Also, the lines through ∞ are vertical. But, as we'll see in the following example, finding $-P$ from P is not as the same as before.

Example. Let $E : y^2 + y \equiv x^3 + x \pmod{2}$. As before, we can list the points on E:

$$(0,0), \quad (0,1), \quad (1,0), \quad (1,1), \quad \infty.$$

Let's compute $(0,0) + (1,1)$. The line through these two points is $y = x$. Substituting into the equation for E yields $x^2 + x \equiv x^3 + x$, which can rewritten as $x^2(x+1) \equiv 0$. The roots are $x = 0, 0, 1 \pmod{2}$. Therefore, the third point of intersection also has $x = 0$. Since it lies on the line $y = x$, it must be $(0,0)$. (This might be puzzling. What is happening is that the line is tangent to E at $(0,0)$ and also intersects E in the point $(1,1)$.) As before, we now have

$$(0,0) + (0,0) + (1,1) = \infty.$$

To get $(0,0) + (1,1)$ we need to compute $\infty - (0,0)$. This means we need to find P such that $P + (0,0) = \infty$. A line through ∞ is still a vertical line. In this case, we need one through $(0,0)$, so we take $x = 0$. This intersects E in the point $P = (0,1)$. We conclude that $(0,0) + (0,1) = \infty$. Putting everything together, we see that

$$(0,0) + (1,1) = (0,1). \qquad \blacksquare$$

In most applications, elliptic curves mod 2 are not large enough. Therefore, elliptic curves over finite fields are used. For an introduction to finite fields, see Section 3.10. However, in the present section, we only need the field $GF(4)$, which we now describe.

Let

$$GF(4) = \{0, 1, \omega, \omega^2\},$$

with the following laws:

1. $0 + x = x$ for all x.

2. $x + x = 0$ for all x.

3. $1 \cdot x = x$ for all x.

4. $1 + \omega = \omega^2$.

5. Addition and multiplication are commutative and associative, and the distributive law holds: $x(y + z) = xy + xz$ for all x, y, z.

Since
$$\omega^3 = \omega \cdot \omega^2 = \omega \cdot (1 + \omega) = \omega + \omega^2 = \omega + (1 + \omega) = 1,$$

we see that ω^2 is the multiplicative inverse of ω. Therefore, every nonzero element of $GF(4)$ has a multiplicative inverse.

Elliptic curves with coefficients in finite fields are treated just like elliptic curves with integer coefficients.

Example. Consider
$$E : y^2 + xy = x^3 + \omega,$$

where $\omega \in GF(4)$ is as before. Let's list the points of E with coordinates in $GF(4)$:

$$x = 0 \Rightarrow y^2 = \omega \Rightarrow y = \omega^2$$
$$x = 1 \Rightarrow y^2 + y = 1 + \omega = \omega^2 \Rightarrow \text{ no solutions}$$
$$x = \omega \Rightarrow y^2 + \omega y = 0 \Rightarrow y = 1, \omega^2$$
$$x = \omega^2 \Rightarrow y^2 + \omega^2 y = 1 + \omega = \omega^2 \Rightarrow \text{ no solutions}$$
$$x = \infty \Rightarrow y = \infty.$$

The points on E are therefore

$$(0, \omega^2), \quad (\omega, 1), \quad (\omega, \omega^2), \quad \infty.$$

Let's compute $(0, \omega^2) + (\omega, \omega^2)$. The line through these two points is $y = \omega^2$. Substitute this into the equation for E:

$$\omega^4 + \omega^2 x = x^3 + \omega,$$

which becomes $x^3 + \omega^2 x = 0$. This has the roots $x = 0, \omega, \omega$. The third point of intersection of the line and E is therefore (ω, ω^2), so

$$(0, \omega^2) + (\omega, \omega^2) + (\omega, \omega^2) = \infty.$$

We need $-(\omega, \omega^2)$, namely the point P with $P + (\omega, \omega^2) = \infty$. The vertical line $x = \omega$ intersects E in $P = (\omega, 1)$, so

$$(0, \omega^2) + (\omega, \omega^2) = (\omega, 1). \qquad \blacksquare$$

For cryptographic purposes, elliptic curves are used over fields $GF(2^n)$ with n large, say at least 150.

15.5 Elliptic Curve Cryptosystems

Elliptic curves versions exist for many cryptosystems, in particular those involving discrete logarithms. An advantage of elliptic curves over working with integers mod p is the following. In the integers, it is possible to use the factorization into primes (especially small primes) to attack the discrete logarithm problem. This is known as the index calculus and is described in Section 7.2. There seems to be no good analog of this method for elliptic curves. Therefore, it is possible to use smaller primes, or smaller finite fields, with elliptic curves and achieve a level of security comparable to that for much larger integers mod p. This allows great savings in hardware implementations, for example.

In the following, we describe three elliptic curve versions of classical algorithms. As we'll see, there is a general procedure for changing a classical system based on discrete logarithms into one using elliptic curves:

1. Change modular multiplication to addition of points on an elliptic curve.

2. Change modular exponentiation to multiplying a point on an elliptic curve by an integer.

Of course, the second situation above is really a special case of the first, since exponentiation consists of multiplying a number by itself several times, and multiplying a point by an integer is adding the point to itself several times.

An Elliptic Curve ElGamal Cryptosystem

We recall the non-elliptic curve version. Alice wants to send a message x to Bob, so Bob chooses a large prime p and an integer $\alpha \mod p$. He also chooses a secret integer a and computes $\beta \equiv \alpha^a \pmod{p}$. Bob makes p, α, β public and keeps a secret. Alice chooses a random k and computes y_1 and y_2, where

$$y_1 \equiv \alpha^k \text{ and } y_2 \equiv x\beta^k \pmod{p}.$$

She sends (y_1, y_2) to Bob, who then decrypts by calculating

$$x \equiv y_2 y_1^{-a} \pmod{p}.$$

Now we describe the elliptic curve version. Bob chooses an elliptic curve $E \pmod{p}$, where p is a large prime. He chooses a point α on E and a secret integer a. He computes

$$\beta = a\alpha \quad (= \alpha + \alpha + \cdots + \alpha).$$

The points α and β are made public, while a is kept secret. Alice expresses her message as a point x on E (see Section 15.2). She chooses a random integer k, computes

$$y_1 = k\alpha \text{ and } y_2 = x + k\beta,$$

and sends the pair y_1, y_2 to Bob. Bob decrypts by calculating

$$x = y_2 - ay_1.$$

A more workable version of this system is due to Menezes and Vanstone. It is described in [Stinson, p. 189].

Example. We must first generate a curve. Let's use the prime $p = 8831$, the point $G = (x, y) = (4, 11)$, and $a = 3$. To make G lie on the curve $y^2 \equiv x^3 + ax + b \pmod{p}$, we take $b = 45$. Alice has a message, represented as a point $P_m = (5, 1743)$, that she wishes to send to Bob. Here is how she does it.

Bob has chosen a random number $a_B = 3$ and has published the point $a_B G = (413, 1808)$.

Alice downloads this and chooses a random number $k = 8$. She sends Bob $kG = (5415, 6321)$ and $P_m + k(a_B G) = (6626, 3576)$. He first calculates $a_B(kG) = 3(5415, 6321) = (673, 146)$. He now subtracts this from $(6626, 3576)$:

$$(6626, 3576) - (673, 146) = (6626, 3576) + (673, -146) = (5, 1743).$$

Note that we subtracted points by using the rule $P - Q = P + (-Q)$ from Section 15.1. ∎

Elliptic Curve Diffie-Hellman Key Exchange

Alice and Bob want to exchange a key. In order to do so, they agree on a public basepoint G on an elliptic curve $E : y^2 \equiv x^3 + ax + b \pmod{p}$. Let's choose $p = 7211$ and $a = 1$ and $G = (3, 5)$. This gives us $b = 7206$. Alice chooses N_A randomly and Bob chooses N_B randomly. Let's suppose

$N_A = 12$ and $N_B = 23$. They keep these private to themselves but publish $N_A G$ and $N_B G$. In our case, we have

$$N_A G = (1794, 6375) \text{ and } N_B G = (3861, 1242).$$

Alice now takes $N_B G$ and multiplies by N_A to get the key:

$$N_A(N_B G) = 12(3861, 1242) = (1472, 2098).$$

Similarly, Bob takes $N_A G$ and multiplies by N_B to get the key:

$$N_B(N_A G) = 23(1794, 6375) = (1472, 2098).$$

Notice that they have the same key.

ElGamal Digital Signatures

There is an elliptic curve analog of the procedure described in Section 8.2. A few modifications are needed to account for the fact that we are working with both integers and points on an elliptic curve.

Alice wants to sign a message m (which might actually be the hash of a long message). We assume m is an integer. She fixes an elliptic curve $E \pmod{p}$, where p is a large prime, and a point A on E. The number of points n on E is calculated (see Exercise 8). We assume $0 \le m < n$ (if not, choose a larger p). Alice also chooses a private integer a and computes $B = aA$. The prime p, the curve E, the integer n, and the points A and B are made public. To sign the message, Alice does the following:

1. Chooses a random integer k with $1 \le k < n$ and $\gcd(k, n) = 1$, and computes $R = kA = (x, y)$

2. Computes $s \equiv k^{-1}(m - ax) \pmod{n}$

3. Sends the signed message (m, R, s) to Alice

Note that R is a point on E, and m and s are integers.

Bob verifies the signature as follows:

1. Downloads Alice's public information p, E, n, A, B

2. Computes $V_1 = xB + sR$ and $V_2 = mA$

3. Declares the signature valid if $V_1 = V_2$

The verification procedure works because

$$V_1 = xB + sR = xaA + k^{-1}(m - ax)(kA) = xaA + (m - ax)A = mA = V_2.$$

There is a subtle point that should be mentioned. We have used k^{-1} in this verification equation as the integer mod n satisfying $k^{-1}k \equiv 1 \pmod{n}$. Therefore $k^{-1}k$ is not 1, but rather an integer congruent to 1 mod n. So $k^{-1}k = 1 + tn$ for some integer t. It can be shown that $nA = \infty$. Therefore,

$$k^{-1}kA = (1 + tn)A = A + t(nA) = A + t\infty = A.$$

This shows that k^{-1} and k cancel each other in the verification equation, as we implicitly assumed above.

The classical ElGamal scheme and the present elliptic curve version are analogs of each other. The integers mod p are replaced with the elliptic curve E, and the number $p - 1$ becomes n. Note that the calculations in the classical scheme work with integers that are nonzero mod p, and there are $p - 1$ such congruence classes. The elliptic curve version works with points on the elliptic curve that are multiples of A, and the number of such points is a divisor of n.

The use of the x-coordinate of R in the elliptic version is somewhat arbitrary. Any method of assigning integers to points on the curve would work. Using the x-coordinate is an easy choice. Similarly, in the classical ElGamal scheme, the use of the integer r in the mod $p - 1$ equation for s might seem a little unnatural, since r was originally defined mod p. However, any method of assigning integers to the integers mod p would work. The use of r itself is an easy choice (see Exercise 8.9).

There is an elliptic curve version of the Digital Signature Algorithm that is similar to the preceding (Exercise 11).

15.6   Exercises

1. Let $x^3 + a_2x^2 + a_1x + a_0$ be a cubic polynomial with roots r_1, r_2, r_3. Show that $r_1 + r_2 + r_3 = -a_2$.

2. (a) List the points on the elliptic curve $E: \quad y^2 \equiv x^3 - 2 \pmod{7}$.
(b) Find the sum $(3, 2) + (6, 5)$ on E.
(c) Find the sum $(3, 2) + (3, 2)$ on E.

3. Factor $n = 11413$ by the elliptic curve method by choosing a random elliptic curve and a random point (if it doesn't work, try another).

4. Suppose you want to factor a composite integer n by using the elliptic curve method. You start with the curve $y^2 = x^3 - 4x \pmod{n}$ and the point $(2, 0)$. Why will this not yield the factorization of n?

5. Devise an analog of the procedure in Exercise 7.4(a) that uses elliptic curves.

6. Show how to use a birthday attack (see Section 8.4) to attack the discrete log problem on elliptic curves.

7. Show that if P, Q, R are points on an elliptic curve, then

$$P + Q + R = \infty \iff P, Q, R \text{ are collinear.}$$

8. Let P be a point on the elliptic curve $E \bmod n$.
(a) Show that there are only finitely many points on E, so P has only finitely many distinct multiples.
(b) Show that there are integers i, j with $i > j$ such that $iP = jP$. Conclude that $(i - j)P = \infty$.
(c) The smallest positive integer k such that $kP = \infty$ is called the **order** of P. Let m be an integer such that $mP = \infty$. Show that k divides m. (*Hint:* Imitate the proof of Exercise 3.9(c, d).)
(d) (for those who know some group theory) Use Lagrange's theorem from group theory to show that the number of points on E is a multiple of the order of P. (Combined with Hasse's theorem, this gives a way of finding the number of points on E. See Computer Problems 1 and 4.)

9. Let P be a point on the elliptic curve $E \bmod n$. Suppose you know a positive integer k such that $kP = \infty$. You want to prove (or disprove) that k is the order of P.
(a) Show that if $(k/p)P = \infty$ for some prime factor p of k, then k is not the order of P.
(b) Suppose $m|k$ and $1 \le m < k$. Show that $m|(k/p)$ for some prime divisor p of k.
(c) Suppose that $(k/p)P \ne \infty$ for each prime factor of k. Use Exercise 8(c) to show that the order of P is k. (Compare with Exercise 3.10. For an example, see Computer Problem 4.)

10. (a) Let $x = b_1 b_2 \dots b_w$ be an integer written in binary. Let P be a point on the elliptic curve E. Perform the following procedure:

    1. Start with $k = 1$ and $S_0 = \infty$.

    2. If $b_k = 1$, let $R_k = S_k + P$. If $b_k = 0$, let $R_k = S_k$.

3. Let $S_{k+1} = 2R_k$.

4. If $k = w$, stop. If $k < w$, add 1 to k and go to (2).

Show that $R_w = xP$. (Compare with Exercise 3.12(a).)
(b) Let x, be a positive integer and let P be a point on an elliptic curve. Show that the following procedure computes xP.

1. Start with $a = x, B = \infty, C = P$.

2. If a is even, let $a = a/2$, and let $B = B, C = 2C$.

3. If a is odd, let $a = a - 1$, and let $B = B + C, C = C$.

4. If $a \neq 0$, go to step 2.

5. Output B.

(Compare with Exercise 3.12(b).)

11. Here is an elliptic curve version of the Digital Signature Algorithm. Alice wants to sign a message m, which is an integer. She chooses a prime p, an elliptic curve E (mod p). The number of points n on E is computed and a large prime factor q of n is found. A point $A(\neq \infty)$ is chosen such that $qA = \infty$. (In fact, n is not needed. Choose a point A' on E and find an integer m with $mA' = \infty$. There are ways of doing this, though it is not easy. Let q be a large prime factor of m, if it exists, and let $A = (m/q)A'$. Then $qA = \infty$.) It is assumed that $0 \leq m < q$. Alice chooses her secret integer a and computes $B = aA$. The public information is p, E, q, A, B. Alice does the following:

1. Chooses a random integer k with $1 \leq k < q$ and computes $R = kA = (x, y)$

2. Computes $s \equiv k^{-1}(m + ax) \pmod{q}$

3. Sends the signed message (m, R, s) to Bob

Bob verifies the signature as follows:

1. Computes $u_1 \equiv s^{-1}m \pmod{q}$ and $u_2 \equiv s^{-1}x \pmod{q}$

2. Computes $V = u_1 A + u_2 B$

3. Declares the signature valid if $V = R$

(a) Show that the verification equation holds for a correctly signed message. Where is the fact that $qA = \infty$ used (see the "subtle point" mentioned in the ElGamal scheme in Section 15.5)?
(b) Why does $k^{-1} \pmod{q}$ exist?
(c) If q is large, why is there very little chance that s^{-1} does not exist mod q? How do we recognize the case when it doesn't exist? (Of course, in this case, Alice should start over by choosing a new k.)
(d) How many computations "(large integer)×(point on E)" are made in the verification process here? How many are made in the verification process for the elliptic ElGamal scheme described in the text (see the end of Section 8.5)?

12. Let A and B be points on an elliptic curve and suppose $B = kA$ for some integer k. Suppose also that $2^n A = \infty$ for some integer n, but $T = 2^{n-1}A \neq \infty$.
(a) Show that if $k \equiv k' \pmod{2^n}$, then $B = k'A$. Therefore, we may assume that $0 \leq k < 2^n$.
(b) Let j be an integer. Show that $jT = \infty$ when j is even and $jT \neq \infty$ when j is odd.
(c) Write $k = x_0 + 2x_1 + 4x_2 + \cdots + 2^{m-1}x_{m-1}$, where each x_i is 0 or 1 (binary expansion of k). Show that $x_0 = 0$ if and only if $2^{n-1}B = \infty$.
(d) Suppose that for some $m < n$ we know $x_0, \ldots, x_{m-1}$. Let $Q_m = B - (x_0 + \cdots + 2^{m-1}x_{m-1})A$. Show that $2^{n-m-1}Q_m = \infty$ if and only if $x_m = 0$. This allows us to find x_m. Continuing in this way, we obtain $x_0, \ldots, x_{n-1}$, and therefore we can compute k. This technique can be extended to the case where $sA = \infty$, where s is an integer with only small prime factors. This is the analog of the Pohlig-Hellman algorithm (see Section 7.2).

15.7 Computer Problems

1. Let E be the elliptic curve $y^2 \equiv x^3 + 2x + 3 \pmod{19}$.
(a) Find the sum $(1, 5) + (9, 3)$.
(b) Find the sum $(9, 3) + (9, -3)$.
(c) Using the result of part (b), find the difference $(1, 5) - (9, 3)$.
(d) Find an integer k such that $k(1, 5) = (9, 3)$.
(e) Show that $(1, 5)$ has exactly 20 distinct multiples, including ∞.
(f) Using (e) and Exercise 8(d), show that the number of points on E is a multiple of 20. Use Hasse's theorem to show that E has exactly 20 points.

2. You want to represent the message 12345 as a point (x, y) on the curve $y^2 \equiv x^3 + 7x + 11 \pmod{593899}$. Write $x = 12345\_$ and find a value of the missing last digit of x such that there is a point on the curve with this x-coordinate.

3. (a) Factor 3900353 using elliptic curves.
(b) Try to factor 3900353 using the $p-1$ method of Section 6.4. Using the knowledge of the prime factors obtained from part (a), explain why the $p-1$ method does not work well for this problem.

4. Let $P = (2,3)$ be a point on the elliptic curve $y^2 \equiv x^3 - 10x + 21$ (mod 557).
(a) Show that $189P = \infty$, but $63P \neq \infty$ and $27P \neq \infty$.
(b) Use Exercise 9 to show that P has order 189.
(c) Use Exercise 8(d) and Hasse's theorem to show that the elliptic curve has 567 points.

5. Compute the difference $(5,9) - (1,1)$ on the elliptic curve $y^2 \equiv x^3 - 11x + 11$ (mod 593899). Note that the answer involves large integers, even though the original points have small coordinates.

Chapter 16

Error Correcting Codes

In a good cryptographic system, changing one bit in the ciphertext changes enough bits in the corresponding plaintext to make it unreadable. Therefore, we need a way of detecting and correcting errors that could occur when ciphertext is transmitted.

Many noncryptographic situations also require error correction, for example, fax machines, computer hard drives, CD players, and anything that works with digitally represented data. Error correcting codes solve this problem.

Though coding theory (communication over noisy channels) is technically not part of cryptology (communication over nonsecure channels), in Section 16.10 we describe how error correcting codes can be used to construct a public key cryptosystem.

16.1 Introduction

All communication channels contain some degree of noise, namely interference caused by various sources such as neighboring channels, electric impulses, deterioration of the equipment, etc. This noise can interfere with data transmission. Just as holding a conversation in a noisy room becomes more difficult as the noise becomes louder, so too does data transmission become more difficult as the communication channel becomes noisier. In order to hold a conversation in a loud room, you either raise your voice, or you are forced to repeat yourself. The second method is the one that will concern us; namely, we need to add some redundancy to the transmission in order for the recipient to be able to reconstruct the message. In the following, we give several examples of techniques that can be used. In each case, the symbols in the original message are replaced by *codewords* that have some redundancy built into them.

Example 1. (repetition codes)

Consider an alphabet $\{A, B, C, D\}$. We want to send a letter across a noisy channel that has a probability $p = 0.1$ of error. If we want to send C, for example, then there is a 90% chance that the symbol received is C. This leaves too large a chance of error. Instead, we repeat the symbol three times, thus sending CCC. Suppose an error occurs and the received word is CBC. We take the symbol that occurs most frequently as the message, namely C. The probability of the correct message being found is the probability that all three letters are correct plus the probability that exactly one of the three letters is wrong:

$$(0.9)^3 + 3(0.9)^2(0.1) = 0.972,$$

which leaves a significantly smaller chance of error.

Two of the most important concepts for codes are error detection and error correction. If there are at most two errors, this repetition code allows us to detect that errors have occurred. If the received message is CBC, then there could be either one error from CCC or two errors from BBB; we cannot tell which. If at most one error has occurred, then we can correct the error and deduce that the message was CCC. Note that if we used only two repetitions instead of three, we could detect the existence of one error, but we could not correct it (did CB come from BB or CC?).

This example was chosen to point out that error correcting codes can use arbitrary sets of symbols. Typically, however, the symbols that are used are mathematical numbers such as integers mod a prime or binary strings. For example, we can replace the letters A, B, C, D by 2-bit strings: 00, 01, 10, 11. The preceding procedure (repeating three times) then gives us the codewords

$$000000, \ 010101, \ 101010, \ 111111. \qquad \blacksquare$$

Example 2. (parity check)

Suppose we want to send a message of 7 bits. Add an eighth bit so that the number of nonzero bits is even. For example, the message 0110010 becomes 01100101, and the message 1100110 becomes 11001100. An error of one bit during transmission is immediately discovered since the message received will have an odd number of nonzero bits. However, it is impossible to tell which bit is incorrect, since an error in any bit could have yielded the odd number of nonzero bits. When an error is detected, the best thing to do is resend the message. ∎

Example 3. (two-dimensional parity code)

The parity check code of the previous example can be used to design a code that can correct an error of one bit. The two-dimensional parity code arranges the data into a two-dimensional array, and then parity bits are computed along each row and column.

To demonstrate the code, suppose we want to encode the 20 data bits 10011011001100101011. We arrange the bits into a 4×5 matrix

$$
\begin{matrix}
1 & 0 & 0 & 1 & 1 \\
0 & 1 & 1 & 0 & 0 \\
1 & 1 & 0 & 0 & 1 \\
0 & 1 & 0 & 1 & 1
\end{matrix}
$$

and calculate the parity bits along the rows and columns. We define the last bit in the lower right corner of the extended matrix by calculating the parity of the parity bits that were calculated along the columns. This results in the 5×6 matrix

$$
\begin{matrix}
1 & 0 & 0 & 1 & 1 & 1 \\
0 & 1 & 1 & 0 & 0 & 0 \\
1 & 1 & 0 & 0 & 1 & 1 \\
0 & 1 & 0 & 1 & 1 & 1 \\
0 & 1 & 1 & 0 & 1 & 1
\end{matrix}
$$

Suppose that this extended matrix of bits is transmitted and that a bit error occurs at the bit in the third row and fourth column. The receiver arranges the received bits into a 5×6 matrix and obtains

$$
\begin{matrix}
1 & 0 & 0 & 1 & 1 & 1 \\
0 & 1 & 1 & 0 & 0 & 0 \\
1 & 1 & 0 & 1 & 1 & 1 \\
0 & 1 & 0 & 1 & 1 & 1 \\
0 & 1 & 1 & 0 & 1 & 1
\end{matrix}
$$

The parities of the third row and fourth column are odd, so this locates the error as occurring at the third row and fourth column.

If two errors occur, this code can detect their existence. For example, if bit errors occur at the second and third bits of the second row, then the parity checks of the second and third columns will indicate the existence of two bit errors. However, in this case it is not possible to correct the errors, since there are several possible locations for them. For example, if the second and third bits of the fifth row were incorrect instead, then the

parity checks would be the same as when these errors occurred in the second
row. ∎

Example 4. (Hamming [7, 4] code)

The original message consists of blocks of 4 binary bits. These are replaced by codewords, which are blocks of 7 bits, by multiplying on the right
by the matrix

$$G = \begin{pmatrix} 1 & 0 & 0 & 0 & 1 & 1 & 0 \\ 0 & 1 & 0 & 0 & 1 & 0 & 1 \\ 0 & 0 & 1 & 0 & 0 & 1 & 1 \\ 0 & 0 & 0 & 1 & 1 & 1 & 1 \end{pmatrix}.$$

For example, the message 1100 becomes

$$(1, 1, 0, 0) \begin{pmatrix} 1 & 0 & 0 & 0 & 1 & 1 & 0 \\ 0 & 1 & 0 & 0 & 1 & 0 & 1 \\ 0 & 0 & 1 & 0 & 0 & 1 & 1 \\ 0 & 0 & 0 & 1 & 1 & 1 & 1 \end{pmatrix} \equiv (1, 1, 0, 0, 0, 1, 1) \pmod 2.$$

Since the first four columns of G are the identity matrix, the first four entries
of the output are the original message. The remaining 3 bits provide the
redundancy that allows error detection and correction. In fact, as we'll see,
we can easily correct an error if it affects only one of the seven bits in a
codeword.

Suppose, for example, that the codeword 1100011 is sent but is received
as 1100001. How do we detect and correct the error? Write G in the form
$[I_4, P]$, where P is a 4×3 matrix. Form the matrix $H = [P^T, I_3]$, where P^T
is the transpose of P. Multiply the message received times the transpose of
H:

$$(1, 1, 0, 0, 0, 0, 1) \begin{pmatrix} 1 & 1 & 0 & 1 & 1 & 0 & 0 \\ 1 & 0 & 1 & 1 & 0 & 1 & 0 \\ 0 & 1 & 1 & 1 & 0 & 0 & 1 \end{pmatrix}^T$$

$$\equiv (1, 1, 0, 0, 0, 0, 1) \begin{pmatrix} 1 & 1 & 0 \\ 1 & 0 & 1 \\ 0 & 1 & 1 \\ 1 & 1 & 1 \\ 1 & 0 & 0 \\ 0 & 1 & 0 \\ 0 & 0 & 1 \end{pmatrix} \equiv (0, 1, 0) \pmod 2.$$

This is the 6th row of H^T, which means there was an error in the 6th bit
of the message received. Therefore, the correct codeword was 1100011. The
first 4 bits give the original message 1100. If there had been no errors,
the result of multiplying by H^T would have been (0, 0, 0), so we would have

recognized that no correction was needed. This rather mysterious procedure will be explained when we discuss Hamming codes in Section 16.5. For the moment, note that it allows us to correct errors of one bit fairly efficiently.

The Hamming [7, 4] code is a significant improvement over the repetition code. In the Hamming code, if we want to send 4 bits of information, we transmit 7 bits. Up to two errors can be detected and up to one error can be corrected. For a repetition code to achieve this level of error detection and correction, we need to transmit 12 bits in order to send a 4-bit message. Later, we'll express this mathematically by saying that the code rate of this Hamming code is 4/7, while the code rate of the repetition code is 4/12=1/3. Generally, a higher code rate is better, as long as not too much error correcting capability is lost. For example, sending a 4-bit message as itself has a code rate of 1 but is unsatisfactory in most situations since there is no error correction capability. ∎

Example 5. (ISBN code)

The International Standard Book Number (ISBN) provides another example of an error detecting code. The ISBN is a 10-digit codeword that is assigned to each book when it is published. For example, this book has ISBN number $0 - 13 - 061814 - 4$. The first digit represents the language that is used; 0 indicates English. The next two digits represent the publisher. For example, 13 is associated with the publisher (Prentice Hall) of the book you are currently reading. The next six numbers correspond to a book identity number that is assigned by the publisher. The tenth digit is chosen so that the ISBN number $a_1 a_2 \cdots a_{10}$ satisfies

$$\sum_{j=1}^{10} j a_j \equiv 0 \pmod{11}.$$

Notice that the equation is done modulo 11. The first 9 numbers $a_1 a_2 \cdots a_9$ are taken from $\{0, 1, \cdots 9\}$ but a_{10} may be 10, in which case it is represented by the symbol X.

Suppose that the ISBN number $a_1 a_2 \cdots a_{10}$ is sent over a noisy channel, or is written on a book order form, and is received as $x_1 x_2 \cdots x_{10}$. The ISBN code can detect a single error, or a double error that occurs due to the transposition of the digits. To accomplish this, the receiver calculates the weighted checksum

$$S = \sum_{j=1}^{10} j x_j \pmod{11}.$$

If $S \equiv 0 \pmod{11}$, then we do not detect any errors, though there is a small chance that an error occurred and was undetected. Otherwise, we have detected an error. However, we cannot correct it (see Exercise 2).

If $x_1x_2 \cdots x_{10}$ is the same as $a_1a_2 \cdots a_{10}$ except in one place x_k, we may write $x_k = a_k + e$ where $e \neq 0$. Calculating S gives

$$S = \sum_{j=1}^{10} ja_j + ke \equiv ke \pmod{11}.$$

Thus, if a single error occurs we can detect it. The other type of error that can be *reliably* detected is when a_k and a_l have been transposed. This is one of the most common errors that occur when someone is copying numbers. In this case $x_l = a_k$ and $x_k = a_l$. Calculating S gives

$$
\begin{aligned}
S = \sum_{j=1}^{10} jx_j &= \sum_{j=1}^{10} ja_j + (k-l)a_l + (l-k)a_k \pmod{11} \\
&\equiv (k-l)(a_l - a_k) \pmod{11}
\end{aligned}
$$

If $a_l \neq a_k$, then the checksum is not equal to 0, and an error is detected. $\blacksquare$

Example 6. (Hadamard code)

This code was used by the *Mariner* spacecraft in 1969 as it sent pictures back to Earth. There are 64 codewords; 32 are represented by the rows of the 32×32 matrix

$$H = \begin{pmatrix} 1 & 1 & 1 & 1 & \cdots & 1 \\ 1 & -1 & 1 & -1 & \cdots & -1 \\ \vdots & \vdots & \vdots & \vdots & \ddots & \vdots \\ 1 & -1 & -1 & 1 & \cdots & -1 \end{pmatrix}.$$

The matrix is constructed as follows. Number the rows and columns from 0 to 31. To obtain the entry h_{ij} in the ith row and jth column, write $i = a_4a_3a_2a_1a_0$ and $j = b_4b_3b_2b_1b_0$ in binary. Then

$$h_{ij} = (-1)^{a_0b_0 + a_1b_1 + \cdots + a_4b_4}.$$

For example, when $i = 31$ and $j = 3$, we have $i = 11111$ and $j = 00011$. Therefore, $h_{31,3} = (-1)^2 = 1$.

The other 32 codewords are obtained by using the rows of $-H$. Note that the dot product of any two rows of H is 0, unless the two rows are equal, in which case the dot product is 32.

When *Mariner* sent a picture, each pixel had a darkness given by a 6-bit number. This was changed to one of the 64 codewords and transmitted. A received message (that is, a string of 1's and -1's of length 32) can be decoded (that is, corrected to a codeword) as follows. Take the dot product of the message with each row of H. If the message is correct, it will have dot product 0 with all rows except one, and it will have dot product ± 32 with that row. If the dot product is 32, the codeword is that row of H. If it is -32, the codeword is the corresponding row of $-H$. If the message has one error, the dot products will all be ± 2, except for one, which will be ± 30. This again gives the correct row of H or $-H$. If there are two errors, the dot products will all be $0, \pm 2, \pm 4$, except for one, which will be $\pm 32, \pm 30$, or ± 28. Continuing, we see that if there are 7 errors, all the dot products will be between -14 and 14, except for one between -30 and -16 or between 16 and 30, which yields the correct codeword. With 8 or more errors, the dot products start overlapping, so correction is not possible. However, detection is possible for up to 15 errors, since it takes 16 errors to change one codeword to another.

This code has a relatively low code rate of 6/32, since it uses 32 bits to send a 6-bit message. However, this is balanced by a high error correction rate. Since the messages from *Mariner* were fairly weak, the potential for errors was high, so high error correction capability was needed. The other option would have been to increase the strength of the signal and use a code with a higher code rate and less error correction. The transmission would have taken less time and therefore potentially have used less energy. However, in this case, it turned out that using a weaker signal more than offset the loss in speed. This issue (technically known as **coding gain**) is an important engineering consideration in the choice of which code to use in a given application. ∎

16.2 Error Correcting Codes

A sender starts with a message and **encodes** it to obtain codewords consisting of sequences of symbols. These are transmitted over a noisy channel, depicted in Figure 16.1, to the receiver. Often the sequences of symbols that are received contain errors and therefore might not be codewords. The receiver must **decode**, which means correct the errors in order to change what is received back to codewords and then recover the original message.

The symbols used to construct the codewords belong to an alphabet. When the alphabet consists of the binary bits 0 and 1, the code is called a **binary code**. A code that uses sequences of 3 symbols, often represented as integers mod 3, is called a **ternary code**. In general, a code that uses an alphabet consisting of q symbols is called a **q-ary code**.

Definition. *Let $\mathcal{A}$ be an alphabet and let $\mathcal{A}^n$ denote the set of n-tuples of elements of $\mathcal{A}$. A **code of length n** is a nonempty subset of $\mathcal{A}^n$.*

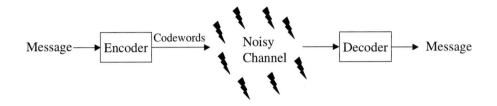

Figure 16.1: Encoding and Decoding.

The n-tuples that make up a code are called **codewords**, or code vectors. For example, in a binary repetition code where each symbol is repeated three times, the alphabet is the set $\mathcal{A} = \{0, 1\}$ and the code is the set $\{(0, 0, 0), (1, 1, 1)\} \subset \mathcal{A}^3$.

Strictly speaking, the codes in the definition are called **block codes**. Other codes exist where the codewords can have varying lengths. These will be mentioned briefly at the end of this chapter, but otherwise we focus only on block codes.

For a code that is a random subset of $\mathcal{A}^n$, decoding could be a time-consuming procedure. Therefore, most useful codes are subsets of $\mathcal{A}^n$ satisfying additional conditions. The most common is to require that $\mathcal{A}$ be a finite field, so that $\mathcal{A}^n$ is a vector space, and require that the code be a subspace of this vector space. Such codes are called *linear* and will be discussed in Section 16.4.

For the rest of this section, however, we work with arbitrary, possibly nonlinear, codes. We always assume that our codewords are n-dimensional vectors.

In order to decode, it will be useful to put a measure on how close two vectors are to each other. This is provided by the Hamming distance. Let u, v be two vectors in $\mathcal{A}^n$. The **Hamming distance** $d(u, v)$ is the number of places where the two vectors differ. For example, if we use binary vectors and have the vectors $u = (1, 0, 1, 0, 1, 0, 1, 0)$ and $v = (1, 0, 1, 1, 1, 0, 0, 0)$, then u and v differ in two places (the 4th and the 7th) so $d(u, v) = 2$. As another example, suppose we are working with the usual English alphabet. Then $d(fourth, eighth) = 4$ since the two strings differ in four places.

The importance of the Hamming distance $d(u, v)$ is that it measures the minimum number of "errors" needed for u to be changed to v. The following gives some of its basic properties.

Proposition. *$d(u,v)$ is a metric on $\mathcal{A}^n$, which means that it satisfies*

1. *$d(u,v) \geq 0$, and $d(u,v) = 0$ if and only if $u = v$*

2. *$d(u,v) = d(v,u)$ for all u,v*

3. *$d(u,v) \leq d(u,w) + d(w,v)$ for all u,v,w.*

The third property is often called the triangle inequality.

Proof. (1) $d(u,v) = 0$ is exactly the same as saying that u and v differ in no places, which means that $u = v$. Part (2) is obvious. For part (3), observe that if u and v differ in a place, then either u and w differ at that place, or v and w differ at that place, or both. Therefore, the number of places where u and v differ is less than or equal to the number of places where u and w differ, plus the number of places where v and w differ. □

For a code C, one can calculate the Hamming distance between any two distinct codewords. Out of this table of distances, there is a minimum value $d(C)$, which is called the **minimum distance** of C. In other words,

$$d(C) = \min\{d(u,v)|u,v \in C, u \neq v\}.$$

The minimum distance of C is very important number, since it gives the smallest number of errors needed to change one codeword into another.

When a codeword is transmitted over a noisy channel, errors are introduced into some of the entries of the vector. We correct these errors by finding the codeword whose Hamming distance from the received vector is as small as possible. In other words, we change the received vector to a codeword by changing the fewest places possible. This is called **nearest neighbor decoding**.

We say that a code can **detect** up to s errors if changing a codeword in at most s places cannot change it to another codeword. The code can **correct** up to t errors if, whenever changes are made at t of fewer places in a codeword c, then the closest codeword is still c. This definition says nothing about an efficient algorithm for correcting the errors. It simply requires that nearest neighbor decoding gives the correct answer when there are at most t errors. An important result from the theory of error correcting codes is the following.

Theorem. *1. A code C can detect up to s errors if $d(C) \geq s+1$.*
2. A code C can correct up to t errors if $d(C) \geq 2t+1$.

Proof. (1) Suppose that $d(C) \geq s+1$. If a codeword c is sent and s or fewer errors occur, then the received message r cannot be a different codeword. Hence, an error is detected.

(2) Suppose that $d(C) \geq 2t+1$. Assume that the codeword c is sent and the received word r has t or fewer errors, i.e. $d(c,r) \leq t$. If c_1 is any other codeword besides c, we claim that $d(c_1,r) \geq t+1$. To see this, suppose that $d(c_1,r) \leq t$. Then, by applying the triangle inequality, we have

$$2t+1 \leq d(C) \leq d(c,c_1) \leq d(c,r) + d(c_1,r) \leq t+t = 2t.$$

This is a contradiction, so $d(c_1,r) \geq t+1$. Since r has t or fewer errors, nearest neighbor decoding successfully decodes r to c. □

How does one find the nearest neighbor? One way is to calculate the distance between the received message r and each of the codewords, then select the codeword with the smallest Hamming distance. In practice, this is impractical for large codes. In general, the problem of decoding is challenging, and considerable research effort is devoted to looking for fast decoding algorithms. In later sections, we'll discuss a few decoding techniques that have been developed for special classes of codes.

Before continuing, it is convenient to introduce some notation.

Notation. A code of length n, with M codewords, and with minimum distance $d = d(C)$, is called an $(\mathbf{n}, \mathbf{M}, \mathbf{d})$ **code**.

When we discuss linear codes, we'll have a similar notation, namely, an $[n,k,d]$ code. Note that this latter notation uses square brackets, while the present one uses curved parentheses. (These two similar notations cause less confusion than one might expect!)

The binary repetition code $\{(0,0,0),(1,1,1)\}$ is a $(3,2,3)$ code. The Hadamard code of Example 6, Section 16.1, is a $(32,64,16)$ code (it could correct up to 7 errors because $16 \geq 2 \cdot 7 + 1$).

If we have a q-ary (n,M,d) code, then we define the **code rate**, or **information rate**, R by

$$R = \frac{\log_q M}{n}.$$

For example, for the Hadamard code, $R = \log_2(64)/32 = 6/32$. The code rate represents the ratio of the number of input data symbols to the number of transmitted code symbols. It is an important parameter to consider when implementing real-world systems, as it represents what fraction of the bandwidth is being used to transmit actual data. The code rate was mentioned in Examples 4 and 6 in Section 16.1. A few limitations on the code rate will be discussed in Section 16.3.

Given a code, it is possible to construct other codes that are essentially the same. Suppose that we have a codeword c that is expressed as $c = (c_1, c_1, \cdots, c_n)$. Then we may define a positional permutation of c by permuting the order of the entries of c. For example, the new vector $c' = (c_2, c_3, c_1)$ is a positional permutation of $c = (c_1, c_2, c_3)$. Another type of operation that can be done is a symbol permutation. Suppose that we have a permutation of the q-ary symbols. Then we may fix a position and apply this permutation of symbols to that fixed position for every codeword. For example, suppose that we have the following permutation of the ternary symbols $\{0 \rightarrow 2, 1 \rightarrow 0, 2 \rightarrow 1\}$, and that we have the following codewords: $(0, 1, 2)$, $(0, 2, 1)$, and $(2, 0, 1)$. Then applying the permutation to the second position of all of the codewords gives the following vectors: $(0, 0, 2)$, $(0, 1, 1)$ and $(2, 2, 1)$.

Formally, we say that two codes are **equivalent** if one code can be obtained from the other by a series of the following operations:

1. Permuting the positions of the code

2. Permuting the symbols appearing in a fixed position of all codewords

It is easy to see that all codes equivalent to an (n, M, d) code are also (n, M, d) codes. However, for certain choices of n, M, d, there can be several inequivalent (n, M, d) codes.

16.3 Bounds on General Codes

We have shown that an (n, M, d) code can correct t errors if $d \geq 2t + 1$. Hence, we would like the minimum distance d to be large so that we can correct as many errors as possible. But we also would like for M to be large so that the code rate R will be as close to 1 as possible. This would allow us to use bandwidth efficiently when transmitting messages over noisy channels. Unfortunately, increasing d tends to increase n or decrease M.

In this section, we study the restrictions on n, M, and d without worrying about practical aspects such as whether the codes with good parameters have efficient decoding algorithms. It is still useful to have results such as the ones we'll discuss since they give us some idea of how good an actual code is, compared to the theoretical limits.

First, we treat upper bounds for M in terms of n and d. Then we show that there exist codes with M larger than certain lower bounds. Finally, we see how some of our examples compare with these bounds.

Upper Bounds

Our first result was given by R. Singleton in 1964 and is known as the **Singleton bound**.

Theorem. *Let C be a q-ary (n, M, d) code. Then*

$$M \leq q^{n-d+1}.$$

Proof. For a codeword $c = (a_1, \ldots, a_n)$, let $c' = (a_d, \ldots, a_n)$. If $c_1 \neq c_2$ are two codewords, then they differ in at least d places. Since c'_1 and c'_2 are obtained by removing $d - 1$ entries from c_1 and c_2, they must differ in at least one place, so $c'_1 \neq c'_2$. Therefore, the number M of codewords c equals the number of vectors c' obtained in this way. There are at most q^{n-d+1} vectors c' since there are $n - d + 1$ positions in these vectors. This implies that $M \leq q^{n-d+1}$, as desired. $\square$

Corollary. *The code rate of a q-ary (n, M, d) code is at most $1 - \frac{d-1}{n}$.*

Proof. The corollary follows immediately from the definition of code rate.
                                                                           $\square$

The corollary implies that if the **relative minimum distance** d/n is large, the code rate is forced to be small.

A code that satisfies the Singleton bound with equality is called an **MDS code** (maximum distance separable). The Singleton bound can be rewritten as $q^d \leq q^{n+1}/M$, so an MDS code has the largest possible value of d for a given n and M. The Reed-Solomon codes (Section 16.9) are an important class of MDS codes.

Before deriving another upper bound, we need to introduce a geometric interpretation that is useful in error correction. A **Hamming sphere** of radius t centered at a codeword c is denoted by $B(c, t)$ and is defined to be all vectors that are at most a Hamming distance of t from the codeword c. That is, a vector u belongs to the Hamming sphere $B(c, t)$ if $d(c, u) \leq t$. We calculate the number of vectors in $B(c, t)$ in the following lemma.

Lemma. *A sphere $B(c, t)$ in n-dimensional q-ary space has*

$$\binom{n}{0} + \binom{n}{1}(q-1) + \binom{n}{2}(q-1)^2 + \cdots + \binom{n}{r}(q-1)^r$$

elements.

Proof. First we calculate the number of vectors that are a distance 1 from c. These vectors are the ones that differ from c in exactly one location. There are n possible locations and $q - 1$ ways to make an entry different. Thus the number of vectors that have a Hamming distance of 1 from c is $n(q - 1)$. Now let's calculate the number of vectors that have Hamming distance m from c. There are $\binom{n}{m}$ ways in which we can choose m locations to differ from the values of c. For each of these m locations, there are $q - 1$ choices for symbols different from the corresponding symbol from c. Hence, there are

$$\binom{n}{m}(q - 1)^m$$

vectors that have a Hamming distance of m from c. Including the vector c itself, and using the identity $\binom{n}{0} = 1$, we get the result:

$$\binom{n}{0} + \binom{n}{1}(q - 1) + \binom{n}{2}(q - 1)^2 + \cdots + \binom{n}{r}(q - 1)^r.$$

$\square$

We may now state the **Hamming bound**, which is also called the **sphere packing bound**.

Theorem. *Let C be a q-ary (n, M, d) code with $d \geq 2t + 1$. Then*

$$M \leq \frac{q^n}{\sum_{j=0}^{t} \binom{n}{j}(q - 1)^j}.$$

Proof. Around each codeword c we place a Hamming sphere of radius t. Since the minimum distance of the code is $d \geq 2t + 1$, these spheres do not overlap. The total number of vectors in all of the Hamming spheres cannot be greater than q^n. Thus, we get

(number of codewords) × (number of elements per sphere)

$$= M \sum_{j=0}^{t} \binom{n}{j}(q - 1)^j \leq q^n.$$

This yields the desired inequality for M. $\square$

An (n, M, d) code with $d = 2t + 1$ that satisfies the Hamming bound with equality is called a **perfect code**. A perfect t-error correcting code is one such that the M Hamming spheres of radius t with centers at the codewords cover the entire space of q-ary n-tuples. The Hamming codes (Section 16.5) and the Golay code $\mathcal{G}_{23}$ (Section 16.6) are perfect. Other examples of perfect codes are the trivial $(n, q^n, 1)$ code obtained by taking all n-tuples, and the binary repetition codes of odd length (Exercise 15).

Perfect codes have been studied a lot, and they are interesting from many viewpoints. The complete list of perfect codes is now known. It includes the preceding examples, plus a ternary $[11, 6, 5]$ code constructed by Golay. We leave the reader a caveat. With a name like perfect codes, one might assume that perfect codes are the best error correcting codes. This, however, is not true, as there are error correcting codes, such as Reed-Solomon codes, that are not perfect codes yet have better error correcting capabilities for certain situations than perfect codes.

Lower Bounds

One of the problems central to the theory of error correcting codes is to find the largest code of a given length and given minimum distance d. This leads to the following definition.

Definition. *Let the alphabet $\mathcal{A}$ have q elements. Given n and d with $d \leq n$, the largest M such that an (n, M, d) code exists is denoted $A_q(n, d)$.*

We can always find at least one (n, M, d) code: Fix an element a_0 of $\mathcal{A}$. Let C be the set of all vectors $(a, a, \ldots, a, a_0, \ldots, a_0)$ (with d copies of a and $n - d$ copies of a_0) with $a \in \mathcal{A}$. There are q such vectors, and they are at distance d from each other, so we have an (n, q, d) code. This gives the trivial lower bound $A_q(n, d) \geq q$. We'll obtain much better bounds later.

It is easy to see that $A_q(n, 1) = q^n$: When a code has minimum distance $d = 1$, we can take the code to be all q-ary n-tuples. At the other extreme, $A_q(n, n) = q$ (Exercise 7).

The following lower bound, known as the **Gilbert-Varshamov bound,** was discovered in the 1950s.

Theorem. *Given n, d with $n \geq d$, there exists a q-ary (n, M, d) code with*

$$M \geq \frac{q^n}{\sum_{j=0}^{d-1} \binom{n}{j}(q-1)^j}.$$

This means that

$$A_q(n, d) \geq \frac{q^n}{\sum_{j=0}^{d-1} \binom{n}{j}(q-1)^j}.$$

Proof. Start with a vector c_1 and remove all vectors in $\mathcal{A}^n$ (where $\mathcal{A}$ is an alphabet with q symbols) that are in a Hamming sphere of radius $d - 1$

about that vector. Now choose another vector c_2 from those that remain. Since all vectors with distance at most $d - 1$ from c_1 have been removed, $d(c_2, c_1) \geq d$. Now remove all vectors that have distance at most $d - 1$ from c_2, and choose c_3 from those that remain. We cannot have $d(c_3, c_1) \leq d - 1$ or $d(c_3, c_2) \leq d - 1$, since all vectors satisfying these inequalities have been removed. Therefore, $d(c_3, c_i) \geq d$ for $i = 1, 2$. Continuing in this way, choose $c_4, c_5, \ldots$, until there are no more vectors.

The selection of a vector removes at most

$$\sum_{j=0}^{d-1} \binom{n}{j} (q-1)^j$$

vectors from the space. If we have chosen M vectors $c_1, \ldots, c_M$, then we have removed at most

$$M \sum_{j=1}^{d-1} \binom{n}{j} (q-1)^j$$

vectors, by the preceding lemma. We can continue until all q^n vectors are removed, which means we can continue at least until

$$M \sum_{j=1}^{d-1} \binom{n}{j} (q-1)^j \geq q^n.$$

Therefore, there exists a code $\{c_1, \ldots, c_M\}$ with M satisfying the preceding inequality.

Since $A_q(n, d)$ is the largest such M, it also satisfies the inequality.

There is one minor technicality that should be mentioned. We actually have constructed an (n, M, e) code with $e \geq d$. However, by modifying a few entries of c_2 if necessary, we can arrange that $d(c_2, c_1) = d$. The remaining vectors are then chosen by the above procedure. This produces a code where the minimal distance is exactly d. $\qquad\square$

If we want to send codewords with n bits over a noisy channel, and there is a probability p that any given bit will be corrupted, then we expect the number of errors to be approximately pn when n is large. Therefore, we need an (n, M, d) code with $d > 2pn$. We therefore need to consider (n, M, d) codes with $d/n \approx x > 0$, for some given $x > 0$. How does this affect M and the code rate?

Here is what happens. Fix q and choose x with $0 < x < 1 - 1/q$. The **asymptotic Gilbert-Varshamov bound** says that there is a sequence of

q-ary (n, M, d) codes with $n \to \infty$ and $d/n \to x$ such that the code rate approaches a limit $\geq H_q(x)$, where

$$H_q(x) = 1 - x \log_q(q - 1) + x \log_q(x) + (1 - x) \log_q(1 - x).$$

The graph of $H_2(x)$ is as in Figure 16.2. Of course, we would like to have

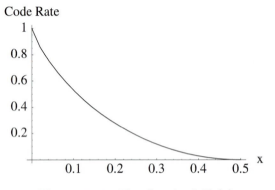

Figure 16.2: The Graph of $H_2(x)$

codes with high error correction (that is, high x), and with high code rate ($= k/n$). The asymptotic result says that there are codes with error correction and code rate good enough to lie arbitrarily close to, or above, the graph.

The existence of certain sequences of codes having code rate limit strictly larger than $H_q(x)$ (for certain x and q) was proved in 1982 by Tsfasman, Vladut, and Zink using Goppa codes arising from algebraic geometry.

Examples

Consider the binary repetition code C of length 3 with the two vectors $(0, 0, 0)$ and $(1, 1, 1)$. It is a $(3, 2, 3)$ code. The Singleton bound say that $2 = M \leq 2$, so C is an MDS code. The Hamming bound says that

$$2 = M \leq \frac{2^3}{\binom{3}{0} + \binom{3}{1}} = 2,$$

so C is also perfect. The Gilbert-Varshamov bound says that there exists a $(3, M, 3)$ binary code with

$$M \geq \frac{2^3}{\binom{3}{0} + \binom{3}{1} + \binom{3}{2}} = \frac{8}{7},$$

which means $M \geq 2$.

The Hamming $[7, 4]$ code has $M = 16$ and $d = 3$, so it is a $(7, 16, 3)$ code. The Singleton bound says that $16 = M \leq 2^4$, so it is an MDS code. The Hamming bound says that

$$16 = M \leq \frac{2^7}{\binom{7}{0} + \binom{7}{1}} = 16,$$

so the code is perfect. The Gilbert-Varshamov bound says that there exists a $(7, M, 3)$ code with

$$M \geq \frac{2^7}{\binom{7}{0} + \binom{7}{1} + \binom{7}{2}} = \frac{128}{29} \approx 4.4,$$

so the Hamming code is much better than this lower bound. Codes that have efficient error correction algorithms and also exceed the Gilbert-Varshamov bound are currently relatively rare.

The Hadamard code from Section 16.1 is a binary (because there are two symbols) $(32, 64, 16)$ code. The Singleton bound says that $64 = M \leq 2^{17}$, so it is not very sharp in this case. The Hamming bound says that

$$64 = M \leq \frac{2^{32}}{\sum_{j=0}^{7} \binom{32}{j}} \approx 951.3.$$

The Gilbert-Varshamov bound says there exists a binary $(32, M, 16)$ code with

$$M \geq \frac{2^{32}}{\sum_{j=0}^{15} \binom{32}{j}} \approx 2.3.$$

16.4 Linear Codes

When you are having a conversation with a friend over a cellular phone, your voice is turned into digital data that has an error correcting code applied to it before it is sent. When your friend receives the data, the errors in transmission must be accounted for by decoding the error correcting code. Only after decoding are the data turned into sound that represents your voice.

The amount of delay it takes for a packet of data to be decoded is critical in such an application. If it took several seconds, then the delay would become aggravating and make holding a conversation difficult.

The problem of efficiently decoding a code is therefore of critical importance. In order to decode quickly, it is helpful to have some form of structure in the code rather than taking the code to be a random subset of $\mathcal{A}^n$. This is one of the primary reasons for studying linear codes. For the remainder of this chapter, we restrict our attention to linear codes.

Henceforth, the alphabet $\mathcal{A}$ will be a finite field $\mathbf{F}$. For an introduction to finite fields, see Section 3.10. For much of what we do, the reader can assume that $\mathbf{F}$ is $\mathbf{Z}_2 = \{0, 1\}$ = the integers mod 2, in which case we are working with binary vectors. Another concrete example of a finite field is $\mathbf{Z}_p$ = the integers mod a prime p. For other examples, see Section 3.10. In particular, as is pointed out there, $\mathbf{F}$ must be one of the finite fields $GF(q)$; but the present notation is more compact. Since we are working with arbitrary finite fields, we'll use "=" instead of "≡" in our equations. If you want to think of $\mathbf{F}$ as being $\mathbf{Z}_2$, just replace all equalities between elements of $\mathbf{F}$ with congruences mod 2.

The set of n-dimensional vectors with entries in $\mathbf{F}$ is denoted by $\mathbf{F}^n$. They form a vector space over $\mathbf{F}$. Recall that a subspace of $\mathbf{F}^n$ is a nonempty subset S that is closed under linear combinations, which means that if s_1, s_2 are in S and a_1, a_2 are in $\mathbf{F}$, then $a_1 s_1 + a_2 s_2 \in S$. By taking $a_1 = a_2 = 0$, for example, we see that $(0, 0, , \ldots, 0) \in S$.

Definition. *A* **linear code** *of dimension k and length n over a field* $\mathbf{F}$ *is a k-dimensional subspace of* $\mathbf{F}^n$. *Such a code is called an* **[n, k]** *code. If the minimum distance of the code is d, then the code is called an* **[n, k, d]** **code**.

When $\mathbf{F} = \mathbf{Z}_2$, the definition can be given more simply. A binary code of length n and dimension k is a set of 2^k binary n-tuples (the codewords) such that the sum of any two codewords is always a codeword.

Many of the codes we have met are linear codes. For example, the binary repetition code $\{(0, 0, 0), (1, 1, 1)\}$ is a 1-dimensional subspace of $\mathbf{Z}_2^3$. The parity check code from Example 2 in Section 16.1 is a linear code of dimension 7 and length 8. It consists of those binary vectors of length 8 such that the sum of the entries is 0 mod 2. It is not hard to show that the set of such vectors forms a subspace. The vectors

$$(1, 0, 0, 0, 0, 0, 0, 1), (0, 1, 0, 0, 0, 0, 0, 1), \ldots, (0, 0, 0, 0, 0, 0, 1, 1)$$

form a basis of this subspace. Since there are seven basis vectors, the subspace is 7-dimensional.

The Hamming [7, 4] code from Example 4 of Section 16.1 is a linear code of dimension 4 and length 7. Every codeword is a linear combination of the four rows of the matrix G. Since these four rows span the code and are linearly independent, they form a basis.

The ISBN code (Example 5 of Section 16.1) is not linear. It consists of a set of 10-dimensional vectors with entries in $\mathbf{Z}_{11}$. However, it is not closed under linear combinations since X is not allowed as one of the first nine entries.

Let C be a linear code of dimension k over a field $\mathbf{F}$. If $\mathbf{F}$ has q elements, then C has q^k elements. This may be seen as follows. There is a basis of C with k elements; call them $v_1, \ldots, v_k$. Every element of C can be written uniquely in the form $a_1 v_1 + \cdots + a_k v_k$, with $a_1, \ldots, a_k \in \mathbf{F}$. There are q choices for each a_i and there are k numbers a_i. This means there are q^k elements of C, as claimed. Therefore, an $[n, k, d]$ linear code is an (n, q^k, d) code in the notation of Section 16.2.

For an arbitrary, possibly nonlinear, code, computing the minimum distance could require computing $d(u, v)$ for every pair of codewords. For a linear code, the computation is much easier. Define the **Hamming weight** $wt(u)$ of a vector u to be the number of nonzero places in u. It equals $d(u, 0)$, where 0 denotes the vector $(0, 0, \ldots, 0)$.

Proposition. *Let C be a linear code. Then $d(C)$ equals the smallest Hamming weight of all nonzero code vectors: $d(C) = \min\{wt(u) \mid 0 \neq u \in C\}$.*

Proof. Since $wt(u) = d(u, 0)$ is the distance between two codewords, we have $wt(u) \geq d(C)$ for all codewords u. It remains to show that there is a codeword with weight equal to $d(C)$. Note that $d(v, w) = wt(v - w)$ for any two vectors v, w. This is because an entry of $v - w$ is nonzero, and hence gets counted in $wt(v - w)$, if and only if v and w differ in that entry. Choose v and w to be distinct codewords such that $d(v, w) = d(C)$. Then $wt(v - w) = d(C)$, so the minimum weight of the nonzero codewords equals $d(C)$. $\square$

To construct a linear $[n, k]$ code, we have to construct a k-dimensional subspace of $\mathbf{F}^n$. The easiest way to do this is to choose k linearly independent vectors and take their span. This can be done by choosing a $k \times n$ **generating matrix** G of rank k, with entries in $\mathbf{F}$. The set of vectors of the form vG, where v runs through all row vectors in $\mathbf{F}^k$, then gives the subspace.

For our purposes, we'll usually take $G = [I_k, P]$, where I_k is the $k \times k$ identity matrix and P is a $k \times (n - k)$ matrix. The rows of G are the basis for a k-dimensional subspace of the space of all vectors of length n. This subspace is our linear code C. In other words, every codeword is uniquely expressible as a linear combination of rows of G. If we use a matrix $G = [I_k, P]$ to construct a code, the first k columns determine the codewords. The remaining $n - k$ columns provide the redundancy.

The code in the second half of Example 1, Section 16.1, has

$$G = \begin{pmatrix} 1 & 0 & 1 & 0 & 1 & 0 \\ 0 & 1 & 0 & 1 & 0 & 1 \end{pmatrix}.$$

The codewords 101010 and 010101 appear as rows in the matrix and the codeword 111111 is the sum of these two rows. This is a $[6, 2]$ code.

The code in Example 2 has

$$G = \begin{pmatrix} 1 & 0 & 0 & 0 & 0 & 0 & 0 & 1 \\ 0 & 1 & 0 & 0 & 0 & 0 & 0 & 1 \\ 0 & 0 & 1 & 0 & 0 & 0 & 0 & 1 \\ 0 & 0 & 0 & 1 & 0 & 0 & 0 & 1 \\ 0 & 0 & 0 & 0 & 1 & 0 & 0 & 1 \\ 0 & 0 & 0 & 0 & 0 & 1 & 0 & 1 \\ 0 & 0 & 0 & 0 & 0 & 0 & 1 & 1 \end{pmatrix}.$$

For example, the codeword 11001001 is the sum mod 2 of the 1st, 2nd, and 5th rows, hence is obtained by multiplying $(1, 1, 0, 0, 1, 0, 0)$ times G. This is an $[8, 7]$ code.

In Example 4, the matrix G is given in the description of the code. As you can guess from its name, it is a $[7, 4]$ code.

As mentioned previously, we could start with any $k \times n$ matrix of rank k. Its rows would generate an $[n, k]$ code. However, row and column operations can be used to transform the matrix to the form of G we are using, so we usually do not work with the more general situation. A code described by a matrix $G = [I_k, P]$ as before is said to be **systematic**. In this case, the first k bits are the **information symbols** and the last $n - k$ symbols are the **check symbols**.

Suppose we have $G = [I_k, P]$ as the generating matrix for a code C. Let

$$H = [-P^T, I_{n-k}],$$

where P^T is the transpose of P. In Example 4 of Section 16.1, this is the matrix that was used to correct errors. For Example 2, we have $H = [1, 1, 1, 1, 1, 1, 1, 1]$. Note that in this case a binary string v is a codeword if and only if the number of nonzero bits is even, which is the same as saying that its dot product with H is zero. This can be rewritten as $vH^T = 0$, where H^T is the transpose of H.

More generally, suppose we have a linear code $C \subset \mathbf{F}^n$. A matrix H is called a **parity check matrix** for C if H has the property that a vector $v \in \mathbf{F}^n$ is in C if and only if $vH^T = 0$. We have the following useful result.

Theorem. *If $G = [I_k, P]$ is the generating matrix for a code C, then $H = [-P^T, I_{n-k}]$ is a parity check matrix for C.*

Proof. Consider the ith row of G, which has the form

$$v_i = (0, \ldots, 1, \ldots, 0, p_{i,1}, \ldots, p_{i,n-k}),$$

where the 1 is in the ith position. This is a vector of the code C. The jth column of H^T is the vector

$$(-p_{1,j}, \ldots, -p_{n-k,j}, 0, \ldots, 1, \ldots, 0),$$

where the 1 is in the $(n - k + j)$th position. To obtain the jth element of $v_i H^T$, take the dot product of these two vectors, which yields

$$1 \cdot (-p_{i,j}) + p_{i,j} \cdot 1 = 0.$$

Therefore, H^T annihilates every row v_i of G. Since every element of C is a sum of rows of G, we find that $v H^T = 0$ for all $v \in C$.

Recall the following fact from linear algebra: The left null space of an $m \times n$ matrix of rank r has dimension $n - r$. Since H^T contains I_{n-k} as a submatrix, it has rank $n - k$. Therefore its left null space has dimension k. But we have just proved that C is contained in this null space. Since C also has dimension k, it must equal the null space, which is what the theorem claims. □

We now have a way of detecting errors: If v is received during a transmission and $v H^T \neq 0$, then there is an error. If $v H^T = 0$, we cannot conclude that there is no error, but we do know that v is a codeword. Since it is more likely that no errors occurred than enough errors occurred to change one codeword into another codeword, the best guess is that an error did not occur.

We can also use a parity check matrix to make the task of decoding easier. First, let's look at an example.

Example. Let C be the binary linear code with generator matrix

$$G = \begin{pmatrix} 1 & 0 & 1 & 1 \\ 0 & 1 & 1 & 0 \end{pmatrix}.$$

We are going to make a table of all binary vectors of length 4 according to the following procedure. First, list the four elements of the code in the first row, starting with $(0, 0, 0, 0, 0)$. Then, among the 12 remaining vectors, choose one of smallest weight (there might be several choices). Add this vector to the first row to obtain the second row. From the remaining 8 vectors, again choose one with smallest weight and add it to the first row to obtain the third row. Finally, choose a vector with smallest weight from the remaining four vectors, add it to the first row, and obtain the fourth row. We obtain the following:

$$
\begin{array}{llll}
(0,0,0,0) & (1,0,1,1) & (0,1,1,0) & (1,1,0,1) \\
(1,0,0,0) & (0,0,1,1) & (1,1,1,0) & (0,1,0,1) \\
(0,1,0,0) & (1,1,1,1) & (0,0,1,0) & (1,0,0,1) \\
(0,0,0,1) & (1,0,1,0) & (0,1,1,1) & (1,1,0,0)
\end{array}
$$

This can be used as a decoding table. When we receive a vector, find it in the table. Decode by changing the vector to the one at the top of its column. The error that is removed is first element of its row. For example, suppose we receive $(0, 1, 0, 1)$. It is the last element of the second row. Decode it to $(1, 1, 0, 1)$, which means removing the error $(1, 0, 0, 0)$. In this small example, this is not exactly the same as nearest neighbor decoding, since $(0, 0, 1, 0)$ decodes as $(0, 1, 1, 0)$ when it has an equally close neighbor $(0, 0, 0, 0)$. The problem is that the minimum distance of the code is 2, so general error correction is not possible. However, if we use a code that can correct up to t errors, this procedure correctly decodes all vectors that are distance at most t from a codeword.

In a large example, finding the vector in the table can be tedious. In fact, writing the table can be rather difficult (that's why we used such a small example). This is where a parity check matrix H comes to the rescue.

The first vector v in a row is called the **coset leader**. Let r be any vector in the same row as v. Then $r = v + c$ for some codeword c, since this is how the table was constructed. Therefore

$$rH^T = vH^T + cH^T = vH^T,$$

since $cH^T = 0$ by the definition of a parity check matrix. The vector $S(r) = rH^T$ is called the **syndrome** of r. What we have shown is that two vectors in the same row have the same syndrome. Replace the preceding table with the following much smaller table.

Coset Leader	Syndrome
(0, 0, 0, 0)	(0, 0)
(1, 0, 0, 0)	(1, 1)
(0, 1, 0, 0)	(1, 0)
(0, 0, 0, 1)	(0, 1)

This table may be used for decoding as follows. For a received vector r, calculate its syndrome $S(r) = rH^T$. Find this syndrome on the list and subtract the corresponding coset leader from r. This gives the same decoding as above. For example, if $r = (0, 1, 0, 1)$, then

$$S(r) = (0, 1, 0, 1) \begin{pmatrix} 1 & 1 \\ 1 & 0 \\ 1 & 0 \\ 0 & 1 \end{pmatrix} = (1, 1).$$

This is the syndrome for the second row. Subtract the coset leader $(1, 0, 0, 0)$ from r to obtain the codeword $(1, 1, 0, 1)$. ∎

We now consider the general situation. The method of the example leads us to two definitions.

Definition. *Let C be a linear code and let u be an n-dimensional vector. The set $u + C$ given by*

$$u + C = \{u + c \mid c \in C\}$$

is called a **coset** *of C.*

It is easy to see that if $v \in u + C$, then the sets $v + C$ and $u + C$ are the same (Exercise 9).

Definition. *A vector having minimum Hamming weight in a coset is called a* **coset leader**.

The **syndrome** of a vector u is defined to be $S(u) = uH^T$. The following lemma allows us to determine the cosets easily.

Lemma. *Two vectors u and v belong to the same coset if and only if they have the same syndrome.*

Proof. Two vectors u and v to belong to the same coset if an only if their difference belongs to the code C, that is $u - v \in C$. This happens if and only if $(u - v)H^T = 0$, which is equivalent to $S(u) = uH^T = vH^T = S(v)$. $\square$

Decoding can be achieved by building a syndrome lookup table, which consists of the coset leaders and their corresponding syndromes. With a syndrome lookup table, we can decode with the following steps:

1. For a received vector r calculate its syndrome $S(r) = rH^T$.

2. Next find the coset leader with the same syndrome as $S(r)$. Call the coset leader c_0.

3. Decode r as $r - c_0$.

Syndrome decoding requires significantly fewer steps than searching for the nearest codeword to a received vector. However, for large codes it is still too inefficient to be practical. In general, the problem of finding the nearest neighbor in a general linear code is hard; in fact, it is what is known as an NP-complete problem. However, for certain special types of codes, efficient decoding is possible. We treat some examples in the next few sections.

Dual Codes

The vector space $\mathbf{F}^n$ has a dot product, defined in the usual way:

$$(a_1, \ldots, a_n) \cdot (b_0, \ldots, b_n) = a_0 b_0 + \cdots + a_n b_n.$$

For example, if $\mathbf{F} = \mathbf{Z}_2$, then

$$(0, 1, 0, 1, 1, 1) \cdot (0, 1, 0, 1, 1, 1) = 0,$$

so we find the possibly surprising fact that the dot product of a nonzero vector with itself can sometimes be 0, in contrast to the situation with real numbers. Therefore, the dot product does not tell us the length of a vector. But it is still a useful concept.

If C is a linear $[n, k]$ code, define the **dual code**

$$C^\perp = \{u \in \mathbf{F}^n \mid u \cdot c = 0 \text{ for all } c \in C\}.$$

Proposition. *If C is a linear $[n, k]$ code with generating matrix $G = [I_k, P]$, then $C^\perp$ is a linear $[n, n-k]$ code with generating matrix $H = [-P^T, I_{n-k}]$. Moreover, G is a parity check matrix for $C^\perp$.*

Proof. Since every element of C is a linear combination of the rows of G, a vector u is in $C^\perp$ if and only if $uG^T = 0$. This means that $C^\perp$ is the left null space of G^T. Also, we see that G is a parity check matrix for $C^\perp$. Since G has rank k, so does G^T. The left null space of G^T therefore has dimension $n - k$, so $C^\perp$ has dimension $n - k$. Because H is a parity check matrix for C, and the rows of G are in C, we have $GH^T = 0$. Taking the transpose of this relation, and recalling that transpose reverses order $((AB)^T = B^T A^T)$, we find $HG^T = 0$. This means that the rows of H are in the left null space of G^T; therefore, in $C^\perp$. Since H has rank $n - k$, the span of its rows has dimension $n - k$, which is the same as the dimension of $C^\perp$. It follows that the rows of H span $C^\perp$, so H is a generating matrix for $C^\perp$. $\qquad\square$

A code C is called **self-dual** is $C = C^\perp$. The Golay code $\mathcal{G}_{24}$ of Section 16.6 is an important example of a self-dual code.

Example. Let $C = \{(0, 0, 0), (1, 1, 1)\}$ be the binary repetition code. Since $u \cdot (0, 0, 0) = 0$ for every u, a vector u is in $C^\perp$ if and only if $u \cdot (1, 1, 1) = 0$. This means that $C^\perp$ is a parity check code: $(a_1, a_2, a_3) \in C^\perp$ if and only if $a_1 + a_2 + a_3 = 0$. ∎

Example. Let C be the binary code with generating matrix

$$G = \begin{pmatrix} 1 & 0 & 0 & 1 \\ 0 & 1 & 1 & 0 \end{pmatrix}.$$

The proposition says that $C^\perp$ has generating matrix

$$H = \begin{pmatrix} 0 & 1 & 1 & 0 \\ 1 & 0 & 0 & 1 \end{pmatrix}.$$

This is G with the rows switched, so the rows of G and the rows of H generate the same subspace. Therefore, $C = C^\perp$, which says that C is self-dual. ∎

16.5 Hamming Codes

The Hamming codes are an important class of single error correcting codes that can easily encode and decode. They were originally used in controlling errors in long-distance telephone calls. Binary Hamming codes have the following parameters:

1. Code length: $n = 2^m - 1$

2. Dimension: $k = 2^m - m - 1$

3. Minimum distance: $d = 3$

The easiest way to describe a Hamming code is through its parity check matrix. For a binary Hamming code of length $n = 2^m - 1$, first construct an $m \times n$ matrix whose columns are all nonzero binary m-tuples. For example, for a $[7, 4]$ binary Hamming code we take $m = 3$, so $n = 7$ and $k = 4$, and start with

$$\begin{pmatrix} 1 & 0 & 1 & 0 & 1 & 0 & 1 \\ 0 & 1 & 1 & 0 & 0 & 1 & 1 \\ 0 & 0 & 0 & 1 & 1 & 1 & 1 \end{pmatrix}.$$

In order to obtain a parity check matrix for a code in systematic form, we move the appropriate columns to the end so that the matrix ends with the $m \times m$ identity matrix. The order of the other columns is irrelevant. The result is the parity check matrix H for a Hamming $[n, k]$ code. In our example, we move the 4th, 2nd, and 1st columns to the end to obtain

$$H = \begin{pmatrix} 1 & 1 & 0 & 1 & 1 & 0 & 0 \\ 1 & 0 & 1 & 1 & 0 & 1 & 0 \\ 0 & 1 & 1 & 1 & 0 & 0 & 1 \end{pmatrix},$$

which is the matrix H from Example 3.

We can easily calculate a generator matrix G from the parity check matrix H. Since Hamming codes are single error correcting codes, the syndrome method for decoding can be simplified. In particular, the error vector e is allowed to have weight at most 1, and therefore will be zero or will have all zeros except for a single 1 in the jth position.

The Hamming decoding algorithm, which corrects up to one bit error, is as follows:

1. Compute the syndrome $s = yH^T$ for the received vector y. If $s = 0$, then there are no errors. Return the received vector and exit.

2. Otherwise, determine the position j of the column of H that is the transpose of the syndrome.

3. Change the jth bit in the received word, and output the resulting code.

As long as there is at most one bit error in the received vector, the result will be the codeword that was sent.

Example. The $[15, 11]$ binary Hamming code has parity check matrix

$$\begin{pmatrix} 0 & 0 & 0 & 0 & 1 & 1 & 1 & 1 & 1 & 1 & 1 & 1 & 0 & 0 & 0 \\ 1 & 1 & 1 & 0 & 0 & 0 & 0 & 1 & 1 & 1 & 1 & 0 & 1 & 0 & 0 \\ 0 & 1 & 1 & 1 & 0 & 1 & 1 & 0 & 0 & 1 & 1 & 0 & 0 & 1 & 0 \\ 1 & 0 & 1 & 1 & 1 & 0 & 1 & 0 & 1 & 0 & 1 & 0 & 0 & 0 & 1 \end{pmatrix}.$$

Assume the received vector is

$$y = (0, 0, 0, 0, 1, 0, 0, 0, 0, 0, 1, 1, 0, 0, 1)).$$

The syndrome $s = yH^T$ is calculated to be $s = (1, 1, 1, 1)$. Notice that s is the transpose of the 11th column of H, so we change the 11th bit of y to get the decoded word as

$$(1, 0, 0, 1, 0, 0, 0, 0, 1, 0, 0, 0, 0, 0, 0).$$

Since the first 11 bits give the information, the original message was

$$(1, 0, 0, 1, 0, 0, 0, 0, 1, 0, 0). \qquad\qquad \blacksquare$$

16.6   Golay Codes

Two of the most famous binary codes are the Golay codes $\mathcal{G}_{23}$ and $\mathcal{G}_{24}$. The $[24, 12, 8]$ extended Golay code $\mathcal{G}_{24}$ was used by the *Voyager I* and *Voyager II* spacecrafts during 1979-1981 to provide error correction for transmission back to Earth of color pictures of Jupiter and Saturn. The (non-extended)

Golay code $\mathcal{G}_{23}$, which is a [23, 12, 7] code, is closely related to $\mathcal{G}_{23}$. We shall construct $\mathcal{G}_{24}$ first, then modify it to obtain $\mathcal{G}_{23}$. There are many other ways to construct the Golay codes. See [MacWilliams-Sloane].

The generating matrix for $\mathcal{G}_{24}$ is the 12×24 matrix $G =$

$$
\begin{pmatrix}
1 & 0 & 0 & 0 & 0 & 0 & 0 & 0 & 0 & 0 & 0 & 0 & 1 & 1 & 1 & 0 & 1 & 1 & 1 & 0 & 0 & 0 & 1 & 0 \\
0 & 1 & 0 & 0 & 0 & 0 & 0 & 0 & 0 & 0 & 0 & 0 & 1 & 0 & 1 & 1 & 0 & 1 & 1 & 1 & 0 & 0 & 0 & 1 \\
0 & 0 & 1 & 0 & 0 & 0 & 0 & 0 & 0 & 0 & 0 & 0 & 1 & 1 & 0 & 1 & 1 & 0 & 1 & 1 & 1 & 0 & 0 & 0 \\
0 & 0 & 0 & 1 & 0 & 0 & 0 & 0 & 0 & 0 & 0 & 0 & 1 & 0 & 1 & 0 & 1 & 1 & 0 & 1 & 1 & 1 & 0 & 0 \\
0 & 0 & 0 & 0 & 1 & 0 & 0 & 0 & 0 & 0 & 0 & 0 & 1 & 0 & 0 & 1 & 0 & 1 & 1 & 0 & 1 & 1 & 1 & 0 \\
0 & 0 & 0 & 0 & 0 & 1 & 0 & 0 & 0 & 0 & 0 & 0 & 1 & 0 & 0 & 0 & 1 & 0 & 1 & 1 & 0 & 1 & 1 & 1 \\
0 & 0 & 0 & 0 & 0 & 0 & 1 & 0 & 0 & 0 & 0 & 0 & 1 & 1 & 0 & 0 & 0 & 1 & 0 & 1 & 1 & 0 & 1 & 1 \\
0 & 0 & 0 & 0 & 0 & 0 & 0 & 1 & 0 & 0 & 0 & 0 & 1 & 1 & 1 & 0 & 0 & 0 & 1 & 0 & 1 & 1 & 0 & 1 \\
0 & 0 & 0 & 0 & 0 & 0 & 0 & 0 & 1 & 0 & 0 & 0 & 1 & 1 & 1 & 1 & 0 & 0 & 0 & 1 & 0 & 1 & 1 & 0 \\
0 & 0 & 0 & 0 & 0 & 0 & 0 & 0 & 0 & 1 & 0 & 0 & 1 & 0 & 1 & 1 & 1 & 0 & 0 & 0 & 1 & 0 & 1 & 1 \\
0 & 0 & 0 & 0 & 0 & 0 & 0 & 0 & 0 & 0 & 1 & 0 & 1 & 1 & 0 & 1 & 1 & 1 & 0 & 0 & 0 & 1 & 0 & 1 \\
0 & 0 & 0 & 0 & 0 & 0 & 0 & 0 & 0 & 0 & 0 & 1 & 0 & 1 & 1 & 1 & 1 & 1 & 1 & 1 & 1 & 1 & 1 & 1 \\
\end{pmatrix}
$$

All entries of G are integers mod 2. The first 12 columns of G are the 12×12 identity matrix. The last 11 columns are obtained as follows. The squares mod 11 are 0, 1, 3, 4, 5, 9 (for example, $4^2 \equiv 3$ and $7^2 \equiv 5$). Take the vector $(x_0, \ldots, x_{10}) = (1, 1, 0, 1, 1, 1, 0, 0, 0, 1, 0)$, with a 1 in positions 0, 1, 3, 4, 5, 9. This gives the last 11 entries in the first row of G. The last 11 elements of the other rows, except the last, are obtained by cyclically permuting the entries in this vector. (*Note:* The entries are integers mod 2, not mod 11. The squares mod 11 are used only to determine which positions receive a 1.) The 13th column and the 12th row are included because they can be; they increase k and d and help give the code some of its nice properties. The basic properties of $\mathcal{G}_{24}$ are given in the following theorem.

Theorem. $\mathcal{G}_{24}$ *is a self-dual [24, 12, 8] binary code. The weights of all vectors in $\mathcal{G}_{24}$ are multiples of 4.*

Proof. The rows in G have length 24. Since the 12×12 identity matrix is contained in G, the 12 rows of G are linearly independent. Therefore, $\mathcal{G}_{24}$ has dimension 12, so it is a $[24, 12, d]$ code for some d. The main work will be to show that $d = 8$. Along the way, we'll show that $\mathcal{G}_{24}$ is self-dual and that the weights of its codewords are 0 (mod 4).

Of course, it would be possible to have a computer list all $2^{12} = 4096$ elements of $\mathcal{G}_{24}$ and their weights. We would then verify the claims of the theorem. However, we prefer to give a more theoretical proof.

Let r_1 be the first row of G and let $r \neq r_1$ be any of the other first 11 rows. An easy check shows that r_1 and r have exactly four 1's in common, and each has four 1's that are matched with 0's in the other vector. In the sum $r_1 + r$, the four common 1's cancel mod 2, and the remaining four 1's from each row give a total of eight 1's in the sum. Therefore, $r_1 + r$ has weight 8. Also, the dot product $r_1 \cdot r$ receives contributions only from the common 1's, so $r_1 \cdot r = 1 \cdot 1 + 1 \cdot 1 + 1 \cdot 1 + 1 \cdot 1 = 4 \equiv 0 \pmod{2}$.

Now let u and v be any two distinct rows of G, other than the last row. The first 12 entries and the last 11 entries of v are cyclic permutations of the corresponding parts of u and also of the corresponding parts of the first row. Since a permutation of the entries does not change the weights of vectors or the value of dot products, the preceding calculation of $r_1 + r$ and $r_1 \cdot r$ applies to u and v. Therefore

1. $wt(u + v) = 8$

2. $u \cdot v \equiv 0 \pmod{2}$.

Any easy check shows that (1) and (2) also hold if u or v is the last row of G, so we see that (1) and (2) hold for any two distinct rows u, v of G. Also, each row of G has an even number of 1's, so (2) holds even when $u = v$.

Now let c_1 and c_2 be arbitrary elements of $\mathcal{G}_{24}$. Then c_1 and c_2 are linear combinations of rows of G, so $c_1 \cdot c_2$ is a linear combination of numbers of the form $u \cdot v$ for various rows u and v of G. Each of these dot products is 0 mod 2, so $r_1 \cdot r_2 \equiv 0 \pmod{2}$. This implies that $C \subseteq C^\perp$. Since C is a 12-dimensional subspace of 24-dimensional space, $C^\perp$ has dimension $24 - 12 = 12$. Therefore, C and $C^\perp$ have the same dimension, and one is contained in the other. Therefore, $C = C^\perp$, which says that C is self-dual.

Observe that the weight of each row of G is a multiple of 4. The following lemma will be used to show that every element of $\mathcal{G}_{24}$ has weight that is a multiple of 4.

Lemma. *Let v_1 and v_2 be binary vectors of the same length. Then*

$$wt(v_1 + v_2) = wt(v_1) + wt(v_2) - 2[v_1 \cdot v_2],$$

where the notation $[v_1 \cdot v_2]$ means that the dot product is regarded as a usual integer, not mod 2 (for example, $[(1, 0, 1, 1) \cdot (1, 1, 1, 1)] = 3$, rather than 1).

Proof. The nonzero entries of $v_1 + v_2$ occur when exactly one of the vectors v_1, v_2 has an entry 1 and the other has a 0 as its corresponding entry. When both vectors have a 1, these numbers add to 0 mod 2 in the sum. Note that $wt(v_1) + wt(v_2)$ counts the total number of 1's in v_1 and v_2 and therefore includes these 1's that canceled each other. The contributions to $[v_1 \cdot v_2]$ are caused exactly by these 1's that are common to the two vectors. So there are $[v_1 \cdot v_2]$ entries in v_1 and the same number in v_2 that are included in $wt(v_1) + wt(v_2)$, but do not contribute to $wt(v_1 + v_2)$. Putting everything together yields the equation in the lemma. $\qquad\square$

We now return to the proof of the theorem. Consider a vector g in $\mathcal{G}_{24}$. It can be written as a sum $g \equiv u_1 + \cdots + u_k \pmod{2}$, where $u_1, \ldots, u_k$ are distinct rows of G. We'll prove that $wt(g) \equiv 0 \pmod{4}$ by induction on k. Looking at G, we see that the weights of all rows of G are multiples of 4, so the case $k = 1$ is true. Suppose, by induction, that all vectors that can be expressed as a sum of $k - 1$ rows of G have weight $\equiv 0 \pmod{4}$. In particular, $u = u_1 + \cdots + u_{k-1}$ has weight a multiple of 4. By the lemma,

$$wt(g) = wt(u + u_k) = wt(u) + wt(u_k) - 2[u \cdot u_k] \equiv 0 + 0 - 2[u \cdot u_k] \pmod{4}.$$

But $u \cdot u_k \equiv 0 \pmod{2}$, as we proved. Therefore, $2[u \cdot u_k] \equiv 0 \pmod{4}$. We have proved that $wt(g) \equiv 0 \pmod{4}$ whenever g is a sum of k rows. By induction, all sums of rows of G have weight $\equiv 0 \pmod{4}$. This proves that all weights of $\mathcal{G}_{24}$ are multiples of 4.

Finally, we prove that the minimum weight in $\mathcal{G}_{24}$ is 8. This is true for the rows of G, but we also must show it for sums of rows of G. Since the weights of codewords are multiples of 4, we must show that there is no codeword of weight 4, since the weights must then be at least 8. In fact, 8 is then the minimum, because the first row of G, for example, has weight 8.

We need the following lemma.

Lemma. *The rows of the 12×12 matrix B formed from the last 12 columns of G are linearly independent mod 2. The rows of the 11×11 matrix A formed from the last 11 elements of the first 11 rows of G are linearly dependent mod 2. The only linear dependence relation is that the sum of all 11 rows of A is 0 mod 2.*

Proof. Since $\mathcal{G}_{24}$ is self-dual, the dot product of any two rows of G is 0. This means that the matrix product $G\,G^T = 0$. Since $G = [I|B]$ (that is, I followed by the matrix B), this may be rewritten as

$$I^2 + B\,B^T = 0,$$

which implies that $B^{-1} = B^T$ (we're working mod 2, so the minus signs disappear). This means that B is invertible, so the rows are linearly independent.

The sum of the rows of A is 0 mod 2, so this is a dependence relation. Let $v_1 = (1, \ldots, 1)^T$ be an 11-dimensional column vector. Then $Av_1 = 0$, which is just another way of saying that the sum of the rows is 0. Suppose v_2 is a nonzero 11-dimensional column vector such that $Av_2 = 0$. Extend v_1 and v_2 to 12-dimensional vectors v_1', v_2' by adjoining a 0 at the top of each column vector. Let r_{12} be the bottom row of B. Then

$$Bv_i' = (0, \ldots, 0, r_{12} \cdot v_i')^T.$$

This equation follows from the fact that $Av_i = 0$. Note that multiplying a matrix times a vector consists of taking the dot products of the rows of the matrix with the vector.

Since B is invertible and $v_i' \neq 0$, we have $Bv_i' \neq 0$, so $r_1 \cdot v_i' \neq 0$ Since we are working mod 2, the dot product must equal 1. Therefore,

$$B(v_1' + v_2') = (0, \ldots, 0, r_1 \cdot v_1' + r_1 \cdot v_2')^T = (0, \ldots, 0, 1 + 1)^T = 0.$$

Since B is invertible, we must have $v_1' + v_2' = 0$, so $v_1' = v_2'$ (we are working mod 2). Ignoring the top entries in v_1' and v_2', we obtain $v_2 = (1, \ldots, 1)$. Therefore, the only nonzero vector in the null space of A is v_1. Since the vectors in the null space of a matrix give the linear dependencies among the rows of the matrix, we conclude that the only dependency among the rows of A is that the sum of the rows is 0. This proves the lemma. $\square$

Suppose g is a codeword in $\mathcal{G}_{24}$. If g is, for example, the sum of the 2nd, 3rd, and 7th rows, then g will have 1's in the 2nd, 3rd, and 7th positions, because the first 12 columns of G form an identity matrix. In this way, we see that if g is the sum of k rows of G, then $wt(g) \geq k$. Suppose now that $wt(g) = 4$. Then g is the sum of at most 4 rows of G. Clearly, g cannot be a single row of G, since each row has weight at least 8. If g is the sum of two rows, we proved that $wt(g)$ is 8. If $g = r_1 + r_2 + r_3$ is the sum of 3 rows of G, then there are two possibilities.

(1) First, suppose that the last row of G is not one of the rows in the sum. Then three 1's are used from the 13th column, so a 1 appears in the 13th position of g. The 1's from the first 12 positions (one for each of the rows r_1, r_2, r_3) contribute three more 1's to g. Since $wt(g) = 4$, we have accounted for all four 1's in g. Therefore, the last 11 entries of g are 0. By the preceding lemma, a sum of only three rows of the matrix A cannot be 0. Therefore, this case is impossible.

(2) Second, suppose that the last row of G appears in the sum for g, say $g = r_1 + r_2 + r_3$ with $r_3 =$ the last row of G. Then the last 11 entries

of g are formed from the sum of two rows of A (from r_1 and r_2) plus the vector $(1, 1, \ldots, 1)$ from r_3. Recall that the weight of the sum of two distinct rows of G is 8. There is a contribution of 2 to this weight from the first 13 columns. Therefore, looking at the last 11 columns, we see that the sum of two distinct rows of A has weight 6. Adding a vector mod 2 to the vector $(1, 1, \ldots, 1)$ changes all the 1's to 0's and all the 0's to 1's. Therefore, the weight of the last 11 entries of g is 5. Since $wt(g) = 4$, this is impossible, so this case also cannot occur.

Finally, if g is the sum of four rows of G, then the first 12 entries of g have four 1's. Therefore, the last 12 entries of g are all 0. By the lemma, a sum of 4 rows of B cannot be 0, so we have a contradiction. This completes the proof that there is no codeword of weight 4.

Since the weights are multiples of 4, the smallest possibility for the weight is 8. As we pointed out previously, there are codewords of weight 8, so we have proved that the minimum weight of $\mathcal{G}_{24}$ is 8. Therefore $\mathcal{G}_{24}$ is a [24,12,8] code, as claimed. This completes the proof of the theorem. $\qquad\square$

The (non-extended) Golay code $\mathcal{G}_{23}$ is obtained by deleting the last entry of each codeword in $\mathcal{G}_{24}$.

Theorem. *$\mathcal{G}_{23}$ is a linear [23,12,7] code.*

Proof. Clearly each codeword has length 23. Also, the set of vectors in $\mathcal{G}_{23}$ is easily seen to be closed under addition (if v_1, v_2 are vectors of length 24, then the first 23 entries of $v_1 + v_2$ are computed from the first 23 entries of v_1 and v_2) and $\mathcal{G}_{23}$ forms a binary vector space. The generating matrix G' for $\mathcal{G}_{23}$ is obtained by removing the last column of the matrix G for $\mathcal{G}_{24}$. Since G' contains the 12×12 identity matrix, the rows of G' are linearly independent, and hence span a 12-dimensional vector space. If g' is a codeword in $\mathcal{G}_{23}$, then g' can be obtained by removing the last entry of some element g of $\mathcal{G}_{24}$. If $g' \neq 0$, then $g \neq 0$, so $wt(g) \geq 8$. Since g' has one entry fewer than g, we have $wt(g') \geq 7$. This completes the proof. $\qquad\square$

Decoding $\mathcal{G}_{24}$

Suppose a message is encoded using $\mathcal{G}_{24}$ and the received message contains at most 3 errors. In the following, we show a way to correct these errors.

Let G be the 12×24 generating matrix for $\mathcal{G}_{24}$. Write G in the form

$$G = [I, B] = (c_1, \cdots, c_{24}),$$

where I is the 12×12 identity matrix, B consists of the last 12 columns of G, and $c_1, \ldots, c_{24}$ are column vectors. Note that $c_1, \ldots, c_{12}$ are the standard basis elements for 12-dimensional space. Write

$$B^T = (b_1, \ldots, b_{12}),$$

where $b_1, \ldots, b_{12}$ are column vectors. This means that $b_1^T, \ldots, b_{12}^T$ are the rows of B.

Suppose the received message is $r = c + e$, where c is a codeword from $\mathcal{G}_{24}$ and

$$e = (e_1, \ldots, e_{24})$$

is the error vector. We assume $wt(e) \le 3$.

The algorithm is as follows. The justification is given below.

1. Let $s = rG^T$ be the syndrome.

2. Compute the row vectors $s, sB, s + c_j^T, 13 \le j \le 24$, and $sB + b_j^T, 1 \le j \le 12$.

3. If $wt(s) \le 3$, then the nonzero entries of s correspond to the nonzero entries of e.

4. If $wt(sB) \le 3$, then there is a nonzero entry in the kth position of sB exactly when the $(k + 12)$th entry of e is nonzero.

5. If $wt(s + c_j^T) \le 2$ for some j with $13 \le j \le 24$, then $e_j = 1$ and the nonzero entries of $s + c_j^T$ are in the positions of the other nonzero entries of the error vector e.

6. If $wt(sB + b_j^T) \le 2$ for some j with $1 \le j \le 12$, then $e_j = 1$. If there is a nonzero entry for this $sB + b_j^T$ in position k (there are at most two such k), then $e_{12+k} = 1$.

Example. The sender starts with the message

$$m = (1, 1, 0, 0, 0, 0, 0, 0, 0, 0, 1, 0).$$

The codeword is computed as

$$mG = (1, 1, 0, 0, 0, 0, 0, 0, 0, 0, 1, 0, 1, 0, 0, 0, 0, 1, 0, 1, 0, 1, 1, 0)$$

and sent to us. Suppose we receive the message as

$$r = (1, 1, 0, 1, 0, 0, 0, 0, 0, 0, 1, 0, 1, 0, 0, 0, 0, 1, 0, 0, 0, 0, 1, 0).$$

A calculation shows that

$$s = (0, 1, 1, 1, 1, 0, 1, 1, 0, 0, 1, 0)$$

and

$$sB = (1, 0, 1, 0, 1, 1, 0, 0, 1, 0, 0, 0).$$

Neither of these has weight at most 3, so we compute $s + c_j^T, 13 \le j \le 24$ and $sB + b_j^T, 1 \le j \le 12$. We find that

$$sB + b_4^T = (0, 0, 0, 0, 0, 0, 0, 1, 0, 1, 0, 0).$$

This means that there is an error in position 4 (corresponding to the choice b_4) and in positions 20 (= 12 + 8) and 22(= 12 + 10) (corresponding to the nonzero entries in positions 8 and 10 of $sB + b_4^T$). We therefore compute

$$c = r + (0, 0, 0, 1, 0, 0, 0, 0, 0, 0, 0, 0, 0, 0, 0, 0, 0, 0, 0, 1, 0, 1, 0, 0)$$
$$= (1, 1, 0, 0, 0, 0, 0, 0, 0, 0, 1, 0, 1, 0, 0, 0, 0, 1, 0, 1, 0, 1, 1, 0).$$

Moreover, since G is in systematic form, we recover the original message from the first 12 entries:

$$m = (1, 1, 0, 0, 0, 0, 0, 0, 0, 0, 1, 0). \qquad \blacksquare$$

We now justify the algorithm and show that if $wt(e) \le 3$, then at least one of the preceding cases occurs.

Since $\mathcal{G}_{24}$ is self-dual, the dot product of a row of G with any codeword c is 0. This means that $cG^T = 0$. In our case, we have $r = c + e$, so

$$s = rG^T = cG^T + eG^T = eG^T = e_1 c_1^T + \cdots + e_{24} c_{24}^T.$$

This last equality just expresses the fact that the vector $e = (e_1, \ldots, e_{24})$ times the matrix G^T equals e_1 times the first row c_1^T of G^T, plus e_2 times the second row of G^T, etc. Also,

$$sB = eG^T B = e \begin{bmatrix} I \\ B^T \end{bmatrix} B = e \begin{bmatrix} B \\ I \end{bmatrix},$$

since $B^T = B^{-1}$ (proved in the preceding lemma). We have

$$\begin{bmatrix} B \\ I \end{bmatrix} = [B^T, I]^T = (b_1, \ldots, b_{12}, c_1, \ldots, c_{12}).$$

Therefore,

$$sB = e(b_1, \ldots, b_{12}, c_1, \ldots, c_{12})^T = e_1 b_1^T + \cdots + e_{24} c_{12}^T.$$

If $wt(e) \leq 3$, then either $wt((e_1, \ldots, e_{12})) \leq 1$ or $wt((e_{13}, \ldots, e_{24})) \leq 1$, since otherwise there would be too many nonzero entries in e. We therefore consider the following four cases.

1. $wt((e_1, \ldots, e_{12})) = 0$. Then

    $$sB = e_{13} c_1^T + \cdots + e_{24} c_{12}^T = (e_{13}, \ldots, e_{24}).$$

    Therefore, $wt(sB) \leq 3$ and we can determine the errors as in step (4) of the algorithm.

2. $wt((e_1, \ldots, e_{12})) = 1$. Then $e_j = 1$ for exactly one j with $1 \leq j \leq 12$, so

    $$sB = b_j^T + e_{13} c_1^T + \cdots + e_{24} c_{12}^T.$$

    Therefore,

    $$sB + b_j^T = e_{13} c_1^T + \cdots + e_{24} c_{12}^T = (e_{13}, \ldots, e_{24}).$$

    The vector $(e_{13}, \ldots, e_{24})$ has at most two nonzero entries, so we are in step (6) of the algorithm.

    The choice of j is uniquely determined by sB. Suppose $wt(sB + b_k^T) \leq 2$ for some $k \neq j$. Then

    $$wt(b_k^T + b_j^T) = wt(sB + b_k^T + sB + b_j^T)$$

    $$\leq wt(sB + b_k^T) + wt(sB + b_j^T) \leq 2 + 2 = 4$$

    (see Exercise 6). However, we showed in the proof of the theorem about $\mathcal{G}_{24}$ that the weight of the sum of any two distinct rows of G has weight 8, from which it follows that the sum of any two distinct rows of B has weight 6. Therefore, $wt(b_k^T + b_j^T) = 6$. This contradiction shows that b_k cannot exist, so b_j is unique.

3. $wt((e_{13}, \ldots, e_{24})) = 0$. In this case,

    $$s = e_1 c_1^T + \cdots + e_{12} c_{12}^T = (e_1, \ldots, e_{12}).$$

    We have $wt(s) \leq 3$, so we are in step (3) of the algorithm.

4. $wt((e_{13}, \ldots, e_{24})) = 1$. In this case, $e_j = 1$ for some j with $13 \le j \le 24$. Therefore,

$$s = e_1 c_1^T + \cdots + e_{12} c_{12}^T + c_j^T,$$

and we obtain

$$s + c_j^T = e_1 c_1^T + \cdots + e_{12} c_{12}^T = (e_1, \ldots, e_{12}).$$

There are at most two nonzero entries in $(e_1, \ldots, e_{12})$, so we are in step (5) of the algorithm.

As in (2), the choice of c_j is uniquely determined by s.

In each of these cases, we obtain a vector, let's call it e', with at most three nonzero entries. To correct the errors, we add (or subtract; we are working mod 2) e' to the received vector r to get $c' = r + e'$. How do we know this is the vector that was sent? By the choice of e', we have

$$e' G^T = s,$$

so

$$c' G^T = r G^T + e' G^T = s + s = 0.$$

Since $\mathcal{G}_{24}$ is self-dual, G is a parity check matrix for $\mathcal{G}_{24}$. Since $c' G^T = 0$, we conclude that c' is a codeword. We obtained c' by correcting at most three errors in r. Since we assumed there were at most three errors, and since the minimum weight of $\mathcal{G}_{24}$ is 8, this must be the correct decoding. So the algorithm actually corrects the errors, as claimed.

The preceding algorithm requires several steps. We need to compute the weights of 26 vectors. Why not just look at the various possibilities for 3 errors and see which correction yields a codeword? There are $\binom{24}{0} + \binom{24}{1} + \binom{24}{2} + \binom{24}{3} = 2325$ possibilities for the locations of at most three errors, so this could be done on a computer. However, the preceding decoding algorithm is faster.

16.7 Cyclic Codes

Cyclic codes are a very important class of codes. In the next two sections, we'll meet two of the most useful examples of these codes. In this section, we describe the general framework.

A code C is called **cyclic** if

$$(c_1, c_2, \ldots, c_n) \in C \text{ implies } (c_n, c_1, c_2, \ldots, c_{n-1}) \in C.$$

For example, if $(1, 1, 0, 1)$ is in a cyclic code, then so is $(1, 1, 1, 0)$. Applying the definition two more times, we see that $(0, 1, 1, 1)$ and $(1, 0, 1, 1)$ are also codewords, so all cyclic permutations of the codeword are codewords. This might seem to be a strange condition for a code to satisfy. After all, it would seem to be rather irrelevant that, for a given codeword, all of its cyclic shifts are still codewords. The point is that cyclic codes have a lot of structure, which makes them easier to study. In the case of BCH codes (see Section 16.8), this structure yields an efficient decoding algorithm.

Let's start with an example. Consider the binary matrix

$$G = \begin{pmatrix} 1 & 0 & 1 & 1 & 1 & 0 & 0 \\ 0 & 1 & 0 & 1 & 1 & 1 & 0 \\ 0 & 0 & 1 & 0 & 1 & 1 & 1 \end{pmatrix}.$$

The rows of G generate a 3-dimensional subspace of 7-dimensional binary space. In fact, in this case, the cyclic shifts of the first row give all the nonzero codewords:

$$G = \{(0,0,0,0,0,0,0), (1,0,1,1,1,0,0), (0,1,0,1,1,1,0), (0,0,1,0,1,1,1),$$
$$(1,0,0,1,0,1,1), (1,1,0,0,1,0,1), (1,1,1,0,0,1,0), ((0,1,1,1,0,0,1)\}.$$

Clearly the minimum weight is 4, so we have a cyclic [7, 3, 4] code.

We now show an algebraic way to obtain this code. Let $\mathbf{Z}_2[X]$ denote polynomials in X with coefficients mod 2, and let $\mathbf{Z}_2[X]/(X^7 - 1)$ denote these polynomials mod $(X^7 - 1)$. For a detailed description of what this means, see Section 3.10. For the present, it suffices to say that working mod $X^7 - 1$ means we are working with polynomials of degree less than 7. Whenever we have a polynomial of degree 7 or higher, we divide by $X^7 - 1$ and take the remainder.

Let $g(X) = 1 + X^2 + X^3 + X^4$. Consider all products

$$g(X)f(X) = a_0 + a_1 X + \cdots + a_6 X^6$$

with $f(X)$ of degree ≤ 2. Write the coefficients of the product as a vector $(a_0, \ldots, a_6)$. For example, $g(X) \cdot 1$ yields $(1,0,1,1,1,0,0)$, which is the top row of G. Similarly, $g(X)X$ yields the second row of G and $g(X)X^2$ yields the third row of G. Also, $g(X)(1 + X^2)$ yields $(1,0,0,1,0,1,1)$, which is the sum of the first and third rows of G. In this way, we obtain all the codewords of our code.

We obtained this code by considering products $g(X)f(X)$ with $\deg(f) \leq 2$. We could also work with $f(X)$ of arbitrary degree and obtain the same code, as long as we work mod (X^7-1). Note that $g(X)(X^3+X^2+1) = X^7-1$ (mod 2). Divide $X^3 + X^2 + 1$ into $f(X)$:

$$f(X) = (X^3 + X^2 + 1)q(X) + f_1(X),$$

with $\deg(f_1) \leq 2$. Then

$$g(X)f(X) = g(X)(X^3 + X^2 + 1)q(X) + g(X)f_1(X)$$
$$= (X^7 - 1)q(X) + g(X)f_1(X) \equiv g(X)f_1(X) \mod (X^7 - 1).$$

Therefore $g(X)f_1(X)$ gives the same codeword as $g(X)f(X)$, so we may restrict to working with polynomials of degree at most two, as claimed.

Why is the code cyclic? Start with the vector for $g(X)$. The vectors for $g(X)X$ and $g(X)X^2$ are cyclic shifts of the one for $g(X)$ by one place and by two places, respectively. What happens if we multiply by X^3? We obtain a polynomial of degree 7, so we divide by $X^7 - 1$ and take the remainder:

$$g(X)X^3 = X^3 + X^5 + X^6 + X^7 = (X^7 - 1)(1) + (1 + X^3 + X^5 + X^6).$$

The remainder yields the vector $(1,0,0,1,0,1,1)$. This is the cyclic shift by three places of the vector for $g(X)$.

A similar calculation for $j = 4, 5, 6$ shows that the vector for $g(X)X^j$ yields the shift by j places of the vector for $g(X)$. In fact, this is a general phenomenon. If $q(X) = a_0 + a_1X + \cdots + a_6X^6$ is a polynomial, then

$$q(X)X = a_0X + a_1X^2 + \cdots + a_6X^7$$
$$= a_6(X^7 - 1) + a_6 + a_0X + a_1X^2 + \cdots + a_5X^6.$$

The remainder is $a_6 + a_0X + a_1X^2 + \cdots + a_5X^6$, which corresponds to the vector $(a_6, a_0, \ldots, a_5)$. Therefore, multiplying by X and reducing mod $X^7 - 1$ corresponds to a cyclic shift by one place of the corresponding vector. Repeating this j times shows that multiplying by X^j corresponds to shifting by j places.

We now describe the general situation. Let $\mathbf{F}$ be a finite field. For a treatment of finite fields, see Section 3.10. For the present purposes, you may think of $\mathbf{F}$ as being the integers mod p, where p is a prime number, since this is an example of a finite field. For example, you could take $\mathbf{F} = \mathbf{Z}_2 = \{0, 1\}$, the integers mod 2. Let $\mathbf{F}[X]$ denote polynomials in X with coefficients in $\mathbf{F}$. Choose a positive integer n. We'll work in $\mathbf{F}[X]/(X^n - 1)$, which denotes the elements of $\mathbf{F}[X]$ mod $(X^n - 1)$. This means we're working with polynomials of degree less than n. Whenever we encounter a polynomial of degree $\geq n$, we divide by $X^n - 1$ and take the remainder. Let $g(X)$ be a polynomial in $\mathbf{F}[X]$. Consider the set of polynomials

$$m(X) = g(X)f(X) \mod (X^n - 1),$$

where $f(X)$ runs through all polynomials in $\mathbf{F}[X]$ (we only need to consider $f(X)$ with degree less than n, since higher-degree polynomials can be reduced mod $X^n - 1$). Write

$$m(X) = a_0 + a_1X + \cdots + a_{n-1}X^{n-1}.$$

The coefficients give us the n-dimensional vector $(a_0, \ldots, a_{n-1})$. The set of all such coefficients forms a subspace C of n-dimensional space $\mathbf{F}^n$. Then C is a code.

If $m(X) = g(X)f(X) \mod (X^n - 1)$ is any such polynomial, and $s(X)$ is another polynomial, then $m(X)s(X) = g(X)f(X)s(X) \mod (X^n - 1)$ is the multiple of $g(X)$ by the polynomial $f(X)s(X)$. Therefore, it yields an element of the code C. In particular, multiplication by X and reducing mod $X^n - 1$ corresponds to a codeword that is a cyclic shift of the original codeword, as above. Therefore, C is cyclic.

The following theorem gives the general description of cyclic codes.

Theorem. *Let C be a cyclic code of length n over a finite field $\mathbf{F}$. To each codeword $(a_0, \ldots, a_{n-1}) \in C$, associate the polynomial $a_0 + a_1 X + \cdots + a_{n-1}X^{n-1}$ in $\mathbf{F}[X]$. Among all the nonzero polynomials obtained from C in this way, let $g(X)$ have the smallest degree. By dividing by its highest coefficient, we may assume that the highest nonzero coefficient of $g(X)$ is 1. The polynomial $g(X)$ is called the* **generating polynomial** *for C. Then*

1. *$g(X)$ is uniquely determined by C.*

2. *$g(X)$ is a divisor of $X^n - 1$.*

3. *C is exactly the set of coefficients of the polynomials of the form $g(X)f(X)$ with $\deg(f) \leq n - 1 - \deg(g)$.*

4. *Write $X^n - 1 = g(X)h(X)$. Then $m(X) \in \mathbf{F}[X]/(X^n - 1)$ corresponds to an element of C if and only if $h(X)m(X) \equiv 0 \mod (X^n - 1)$.*

Proof. (1) If $g_1(X)$ is another such polynomial, then $g(X)$ and $g_1(X)$ have the same degree and have highest nonzero coefficient equal to 1. Therefore, $g(X) - g_1(X)$ has lower degree and still corresponds to a codeword, since C is closed under subtraction. Since $g(X)$ had the smallest degree among nonzero polynomials corresponding to codewords, $g(X) - g_1(X)$ must be 0, which means that $g_1(X) = g(X)$. Therefore $g(X)$ is unique.

(2) Divide $g(X)$ into $X^n - 1$:

$$X^n - 1 = g(X)h(X) + r(X)$$

for some polynomials $h(X)$ and $r(X)$, with $\deg(r) < \deg(g)$. This means that

$$-r(X) \equiv g(X)h(X) \mod (X^n - 1).$$

As explained previously, multiplying $g(X)$ by powers of X corresponds to cyclic shifts of the codeword associated to $g(X)$. Since C is assumed to be cyclic, the polynomials $g(X)X^j \mod (X^n - 1)$ for $j = 0, 1, 2, \dots$ therefore correspond to codewords; call them $c_0, c_1, c_2, \dots$. Write $h(X) = b_0 + b_1 X + \cdots + b_k X^k$. Then $g(X)h(X)$ corresponds to the linear combination

$$b_0 c_0 + b_1 c_1 + \cdots + b_k c_k.$$

Since each b_i is in $\mathbf{F}$ and each c_i is in C, we have a linear combination of elements of C. But C is a vector subspace of n-dimensional space $\mathbf{F}^n$. Therefore this linear combination is in C. This means that $r(X)$, which is $g(X)h(X) \mod (X^n - 1)$, corresponds to a codeword. But $\deg(r) < \deg(g)$, which is the minimal degree of a polynomial corresponding to a nonzero codeword in C. Therefore $r(X) = 0$. Consequently $X^n - 1 = g(X)h(X)$, so $g(X)$ is a divisor of $X^n - 1$.

(3) Let $m(X)$ correspond to an element of C. Divide $g(X)$ into $m(X)$:

$$m(X) = g(X)f(X) + r_1(X),$$

with $\deg(r_1(X)) < \deg(g(X))$. As before, $g(X)f(X) \mod (X^n - 1)$ corresponds to a codeword. Also, $m(X)$ corresponds to a codeword, by assumption. Therefore $m(X) - g(X)f(X) \mod (X^n - 1)$ corresponds to the difference of these codewords, which is a codeword. But this polynomial is just $r_1(X) = r_1(X) \mod (X^n - 1)$. As before, this polynomial has degree less than $\deg(g(X))$, so $r_1(X) = 0$. Therefore, $m(X) = g(X)f(X)$. Since $\deg(m) \le n - 1$, we must have $\deg((f) \le n - 1 - \deg(g)$. Conversely, as explained in the proof of (2), since C is cyclic, any such polynomial of the form $g(X)f(X)$ yields a codeword. Therefore these polynomials yield exactly the elements of C.

(4) Write $X^n - 1 = g(X)h(X)$, which can be done by (2). Suppose $m(X)$ corresponds to an element of C. Then $m(X) = g(X)f(X)$, by (4), so

$$h(X)m(X) = h(X)g(X)f(X) = (X^n - 1)f(X) \equiv 0 \mod (X^n - 1).$$

Conversely, suppose $m(X)$ is a polynomial such that $h(X)m(X) \equiv 0 \mod (X^n - 1)$. Write $h(X)m(X) = (X^n - 1)q(X) = h(X)g(X)q(X)$, for some polynomial $q(X)$. Dividing by $h(X)$ yields $m(X) = g(X)q(X)$, which is a multiple of $g(X)$, and hence corresponds to a codeword. This completes the proof of the theorem. $\square$

Let $g(X) = a_0 + a_1 X + \cdots + a_{k-1} X^{k-1} + X^k$ be as in the theorem. By part (3) of the theorem, every element of C corresponds to a polynomial of the form $g(X)f(X)$, with $\deg(f(X)) \le n - 1 - k$. This means that each such $f(X)$ is a linear combination of the monomials $1, X, X^2, \dots, X^{n-1-k}$.

It follows that the codewords of C are linear combinations of the codewords corresponding to the polynomials

$$g(X),\ g(X)X,\ g(X)X^2,\ldots,\ g(X)X^{n-1-k}.$$

But these are the vectors

$$(a_0,\ldots,a_k,0,0,\ldots),(0,a_0,\ldots,a_k,0,\ldots),\ldots,(0,\ldots,0,a_0,\ldots,a_k).$$

Therefore, a generating matrix for C can be given by

$$G = \begin{pmatrix} a_0 & a_1 & \cdots & a_k & 0 & 0 & \cdots \\ 0 & a_0 & a_1 & \cdots & a_k & 0 & \cdots \\ \vdots & \vdots & \vdots & \vdots & \vdots & \vdots & \vdots \\ 0 & \cdots & 0 & a_0 & a_1 & \cdots & a_k \end{pmatrix}.$$

We can use part (5) of the theorem to obtain a parity check matrix for C. Let $h(X) = b_0 + b_1 X + \cdots + b_l X^l$ be as in the theorem (where $l = n - k$). We'll prove that the $k \times n$ matrix

$$H = \begin{pmatrix} b_l & b_{l-1} & \cdots & b_0 & 0 & 0 & \cdots \\ 0 & b_l & b_{l-1} & \cdots & b_0 & 0 & \cdots \\ \vdots & \vdots & \vdots & \vdots & \vdots & \vdots & \vdots \\ 0 & \cdots & 0 & b_l & b_{l-1} & \cdots & b_0 \end{pmatrix}$$

is a parity check matrix for C. Note that the order of the coefficients of $h(X)$ is reversed. Recall that H is a parity check matrix for C means that $Hc^T = 0$ if and only if $c \in C$.

Proposition. *H is a parity check matrix for C.*

Proof. First observe that since $g(X)$ has 1 as its highest nonzero coefficient, and since $g(X)h(X) = X^n - 1$, the highest nonzero coefficient b_l of $h(X)$ must also be 1. Therefore, H is in row echelon form and consequently its rows are linearly independent. Since H has k rows, it has rank k. The right null space of H therefore has dimension $n - k$.

Let $m(X) = c_0 + c_1 X + \cdots + c_{n-1} X^{n-1}$. We know from part (5) that $(c_0, c_1, \ldots, c_{n-1}) \in C$ if and only if $h(X)m(X) \equiv 0 \mod (X^n - 1)$.

Choose j with $l \le j \le n - 1$ and look at the coefficient of X^j in the product $h(X)m(X)$. It equals

$$b_0 c_j + b_1 c_{j-1} + \cdots + b_{l-1} c_{j-l+1} + b_l c_{j-l}.$$

There is a technical point to mention: Since we are looking at $h(X)m(X)$ mod $(X^n - 1)$, we need to worry about a contribution from the term X^{n+j} (since $X^{n+j} \equiv X^n X^j \equiv 1 \cdot X^j$, the monomial X^{n+j} reduces to X^j). However, the highest-degree term in the product $h(X)m(X)$ before reducing mod $X^n - 1$ is $c_{n-1}X^{l+n-1}$. Since $l \le j$, we have $l + n - 1 < j + n$. Therefore, there is no term with X^{n+j} to worry about.

When we multiply H times $(c_0, c_1, \ldots, c_{n-1})^T$, we obtain a vector whose first entry is

$$b_l c_0 + b_{l-1} c_1 + \cdots + b_0 c_l.$$

More generally, the ith entry (where $1 \le i \le k$) is

$$b_l c_{i-1} + b_{l-1} c_i + \cdots + b_0 c_{l+i-1}.$$

This is the coefficient of X^{l+i-1} in the product $h(X)m(X) \mod (X^n - 1)$.

If $(c_0, c_1, \ldots, c_{n-1})$ is in C, then $h(X)m(X) \equiv 0 \mod (X^n - 1)$, so all these coefficients are 0. Therefore, H times $(c_0, c_1, \ldots, c_{n-1})^T$ is the 0 vector, so the transposes of the vectors of C are contained in the right null space of H. Since both C and the null space have dimension k, we must have equality. This proves that $c \in C$ if and only if $Hc^T = 0$, which means that H is a parity check matrix for C. $\qquad\square$

Example. In the example at the beginning of this section, we had $n = 7$ and $g(X) = X^4 + X^3 + X^2 + 1$. We have $g(X)(X^3 + X^2 + 1) = X^7 - 1$, so $h(X) = X^3 + X^2 + 1$. The parity check matrix is

$$H = \begin{pmatrix} 1 & 1 & 0 & 1 & 0 & 0 & 0 \\ 0 & 1 & 1 & 0 & 1 & 0 & 0 \\ 0 & 0 & 1 & 1 & 0 & 1 & 0 \\ 0 & 0 & 0 & 1 & 1 & 0 & 1 \end{pmatrix}.$$

$\blacksquare$

The parity check matrix gives a way of detecting errors, but correcting errors for general cyclic codes is generally quite difficult. In the next section, we describe a class of cyclic codes for which a good decoding algorithm exists.

16.8   BCH Codes

BCH codes are a class of cyclic codes. They were discovered around 1959 by R. C. Bose and D. K. Ray-Chaudhuri and independently by A. Hocquenghem. One reason they are important is that there exist good decoding algorithms (see, for example, [Gallager] or [Wicker]). BCH codes are used in satellites. The special BCH codes called Reed-Solomon codes (see Section 16.9) have numerous applications.

Before describing BCH codes, we need a fact about finite fields. Let $\mathbf{F}$ be a finite field with q elements. From Section 3.10, we know that $q = p^m$ is a power of a prime number p. Let n be a positive integer not divisible by p. Then it can be proved that there exists a finite field $\mathbf{F}'$ containing $\mathbf{F}$ such that $\mathbf{F}'$ contains a primitive nth root of unity α. This means that $\alpha^n = 1$, but $\alpha^k \neq 1$ for $1 \leq k < n$.

For example, if $\mathbf{F} = \mathbf{Z}_2$, the integers mod 2, and $n = 3$, we may take $\mathbf{F}' = GF(4)$. The element ω in the description of $GF(4)$ in Section 3.10 is a primitive 3rd root of unity. More generally, a primitive nth root of unity exists in a finite field $\mathbf{F}'$ with q' elements if and only if $n | q' - 1$.

The reason we need the auxiliary field $\mathbf{F}'$ is that several of the calculations we perform need to be carried out in this larger field. In the following, when we use an nth root of unity α, we'll implicitly assume that we're calculating in some field $\mathbf{F}'$ that contains α. The results of the calculations, however, will give results about codes over the smaller field $\mathbf{F}$.

The following result, often called the **BCH bound**, gives an estimate for the minimum weight of a cyclic code.

Theorem. *Let C be a cyclic $[n, k, d]$ code over a finite field $\mathbf{F}$, where $\mathbf{F}$ has $q = p^m$ elements. Assume $p \nmid n$. Let $g(X)$ be the generating polynomial for C. Let α be a primitive nth root of unity and suppose that for some integers ℓ and δ,*

$$g(\alpha^\ell) = g(\alpha^{\ell+1}) = \cdots = g(\alpha^{\ell+\delta}) = 0.$$

Then $d \geq \delta + 2$.

Proof. Suppose $(c_0, c_1, \ldots, c_{n-1}) \in C$ has weight w with $1 \leq w < \delta + 2$. We want to obtain a contradiction. Let $m(X) = c_0 + c_1 X + \cdots + c_{n-1} X^{n-1}$. We know that $m(X)$ is a multiple of $g(X)$, so

$$m(\alpha^\ell) = m(\alpha^{\ell+1}) = \cdots = m(\alpha^{\ell+\delta}) = 0.$$

Let $c_{i_1}, c_{i_2}, \ldots, c_{i_w}$ be the nonzero coefficients of $m(X)$, so

$$m(X) = c_{i_1} X^{i_1} + c_{i_2} X^{i_2} + \cdots + c_{i_w} X^{i_w}.$$

The fact that $m(\alpha^j) = 0$ for $l \leq j \leq \ell + w - 1$ (note that $w - 1 \leq \delta$) can be rewritten as

$$
\begin{pmatrix}
\alpha^{\ell i_1} & \cdots & \alpha^{\ell i_w} \\
\alpha^{(\ell+1)i_1} & \cdots & \alpha^{(\ell+1)i_w} \\
\vdots & \ddots & \vdots \\
\alpha^{(\ell+w-1)i_1} & \cdots & \alpha^{(\ell+w-1)i_w}
\end{pmatrix}
\begin{pmatrix}
c_{i_1} \\
c_{i_2} \\
\vdots \\
c_{i_w}
\end{pmatrix}
=
\begin{pmatrix}
0 \\
0 \\
\vdots \\
0
\end{pmatrix}.
$$

We claim that the determinant of the matrix is nonzero. We need the following evaluation of the Vandermonde determinant. The proof can be found in most books on linear algebra.

Proposition.

$$\det \begin{pmatrix} 1 & 1 & \cdots & 1 \\ x_1 & x_2 & \cdots & x_n \\ x_1^2 & x_2^2 & \cdots & x_n^2 \\ \vdots & \vdots & \ddots & \vdots \\ x_1^{n-1} & x_2^{n-1} & \cdots & x_n^{n-1} \end{pmatrix} = \prod_{1 \le i < j \le n} (x_j - x_i)$$

(the product is over all pairs of integers (i, j) with $1 \le i < j \le n$). In particular, if $x_1, \ldots, x_n$ are pairwise distinct, the determinant is nonzero.

In our matrix, we can factor $\alpha^{\ell i_1}$ from the first column, $\alpha^{\ell i_2}$ from the second column, etc., to obtain

$$\det \begin{pmatrix} \alpha^{\ell i_1} & \cdots & \alpha^{\ell i_w} \\ \alpha^{(\ell+1)i_1} & \cdots & \alpha^{(\ell+1)i_w} \\ \vdots & \ddots & \vdots \\ \alpha^{(\ell+w-1)i_1} & \cdots & \alpha^{(\ell+w-1)i_w} \end{pmatrix}$$

$$= \alpha^{\ell i_1 + \cdots + \ell i_w} \det \begin{pmatrix} 1 & \cdots & 1 \\ \alpha^{i_1} & \cdots & \alpha^{i_w} \\ \vdots & \ddots & \vdots \\ \alpha^{(w-1)i_1} & \cdots & \alpha^{(w-1)i_w} \end{pmatrix}.$$

Since $\alpha^{i_1}, \cdots, \alpha^{i_w}$ are pairwise distinct, the determinant is nonzero. Why are these numbers distinct? Suppose $\alpha^{i_j} = \alpha^{i_k}$. We may assume $i_j \le i_k$. We have $0 \le i_j \le i_k < n$. Therefore, $0 \le i_k - i_j < n$. Note that $\alpha^{i_k - i_j} = 1$. Since α is a primitive nth root of unity, $\alpha^i \ne 1$ for $1 \le i < n$. Therefore, $i_k - i_j = 0$, so $i_j = i_k$. This means that the numbers $\alpha^{i_1}, \cdots, \alpha^{i_w}$ are pairwise distinct, as claimed.

Since the determinant is nonzero, the matrix is nonsingular. This implies that $(c_{i_1}, \ldots, c_{i_w}) = 0$, contradicting the fact that these were the nonzero c_i's. Therefore all nonzero codewords have weight at least $\delta + 2$. This completes the proof of the theorem. $\qquad \square$

Example. Let $\mathbf{F} = \mathbf{Z}_2 =$ the integers mod 2, and let $n = 3$. Let $g(X) = X^2 + X + 1$. Then

$$C = \{(0, 0, 0), (1, 1, 1)\},$$

which is a binary repetition code. Let ω be a primitive 3rd root of unity, as in the description of $GF(4)$ in Section 3.10. Then $g(\omega) = g(\omega^2) = 0$. In the theorem, we can therefore take $\ell = 1$ and $\delta = 1$. We find that the minimal weight of C is at least 3. In this case, the bound is sharp, since the minimal weight of C is exactly 3.   ∎

Example. Let $\mathbf{F}$ be any finite field and let n be any positive integer. Let $g(X) = X - 1$. Then $g(1) = 0$, so we may take $\ell = 0$ and $\delta = 0$. We conclude that the minimum weight of the code generated by $g(X)$ is at least 2 (actually, the theorem assumes that $p \nmid n$, but this assumption is not needed for this special case where $\ell = \delta = 0$). We have seen this code before. If $(c_0, \ldots, c_{n-1})$ is a vector, and $m(X) = c_0 + \cdots + c_{n-1}X^{n-1}$ is the associated polynomial, then $m(X)$ is a multiple of $X - 1$ exactly when $m(1) = 0$. This means that $c_0 + \cdots + c_{n-1} = 0$. So a vector is a codeword if and only if the sum of its entries is 0. When $\mathbf{F} = \mathbf{Z}_2$, this is the parity check code, and for other finite fields it is a generalization of the parity check code. The fact that its minimal weight is 2 is easy to see directly: If a codeword has a nonzero entry, then it must contain another nonzero entry to cancel it and make the sum of the entries be 0. Therefore, each nonzero codeword has at least two nonzero entries, and hence has weight at least 2. The vector $(1, -1, 0, \ldots)$ is a codeword and has weight 2, so the minimal weight is exactly 2.   ∎

Example. Let's return to the example of a binary cyclic code of length 7 from Section 16.7. We have $\mathbf{F} = \mathbf{Z}_2$, and $g(X) = 1 + X^2 + X^3 + X^4$. We can factor $g(X) = (X-1)(X^3 + X + 1)$. Let α be a root of $X^3 + X + 1$. Then α is a primitive 7th root of unity (see Exercise 18), and we are working in $GF(8)$. Since $\mathbf{Z}_2 \subset GF(8)$, we have $2 = 1 + 1 = 0$ and $-1 = 1$. Therefore, $\alpha^3 = \alpha + 1$. Squaring yields $\alpha^6 = \alpha^2 + 2\alpha + 1 = \alpha^2 + 1$. Therefore, $(\alpha^2)^3 + (\alpha^2) + 1 = 0$. This means that $g(\alpha^2) = 0$, so

$$g(1) = g(\alpha) = g(\alpha^2) = 0.$$

In the theorem, we can take $\ell = 0$ and $\delta = 2$. Therefore, the minimal weight in the code is at least 4 (in fact, it is exactly 4).   ∎

To define the BCH codes, we need some more notation. We are going to construct codes of length n over a finite field $\mathbf{F}$. Factor $X^n - 1$ into irreducible factors over $\mathbf{F}$:

$$X^n - 1 = f_1(X)f_2(X) \cdots f_r(X),$$

where each $f_i(X)$ is a polynomial with coefficients in $\mathbf{F}$, and each $f_i(X)$ cannot be factored into lower degree polynomials with coefficients in $\mathbf{F}$. We may assume that the highest nonzero coefficient of each $f_i(X)$ is 1. Let α be a primitive nth root of unity. Then $\alpha^0, \alpha^1, \alpha^2, \ldots, \alpha^{n-1}$ are roots of $X^n - 1$. This means that

$$X^n - 1 = (X - 1)(X - \alpha)(X - \alpha^2) \cdots (X - \alpha^{n-1}).$$

Therefore each $f_i(X)$ is a product of some of these factors $(X - \alpha^j)$, and each α^j is a root of exactly one of the polynomials $f_i(X)$. For each j, let $q_j(X)$ be the polynomial $f_i(X)$ such that $f_i(\alpha^j) = 0$. This gives us polynomials $q_0(X), q_1(X), \ldots q_{n-1}(X)$. Of course, usually these polynomials are not all distinct, since a polynomial $f_i(X)$ that has two different powers α^j, α^k as roots will serve as both $q_j(X)$ and $q_k(X)$ (see the examples given later in this section).

A **BCH code of designed distance d** is a code with generating polynomial

$$g(X) = \text{least common multiple of } q_{k+1}(X), q_{k+2}(X), \ldots, q_{k+d-1}(X)$$

for some integer k.

Theorem. *A BCH code of designed distance d has minimum weight at least d.*

Proof. Since $q_j(X)$ divides $g(X)$ for $k + 1 \leq j \leq k + d - 1$, and $q_j(\alpha^j) = 0$, we have

$$g(\alpha^{k+1}) = g(\alpha^{k+2}) = \cdots = g(\alpha^{k+d-1}) = 0.$$

The BCH bound (with $\ell = k + 1$ and $\delta = d - 2$) implies that the code has minimum weight at least $d = \delta + 2$. $\square$

Example. Let $\mathbf{F} = \mathbf{Z}_2$, and let $n = 7$. Then

$$X^7 - 1 = (X - 1)(X^3 + X^2 + 1)(X^3 + X + 1).$$

Let α be a root of $X^3 + X + 1$. Then α is a primitive 7th root of unity, as in the previous example. Moreover, in that example, we showed that α^2 is also a root of $X^3 + X + 1$. In fact, we actually showed that the square of a root of $X^3 + X + 1$ is also a root, so we have that $\alpha^4 = (\alpha^2)^2$ is also a root of $X^3 + X + 1$. (We could square this again, but $\alpha^8 = \alpha$, so we are back to where we started.) Therefore, $\alpha, \alpha^2, \alpha^4$ are the roots of $X^3 + X + 1$, so

$$X^3 + X + 1 = (X - \alpha)(X - \alpha^2)(X - \alpha^4).$$

The remaining powers of α must be roots of $X^3 + X^2 + 1$, so

$$X^3 + X^2 + 1 = (X - \alpha^3)(X - \alpha^5)(X - \alpha^6).$$

Therefore,

$$q_0(X) = X - 1, \quad q_1(X) = q_2(X) = q_4(X) = X^3 + X + 1,$$

$$q_3(X) = q_5(X) = q_6(X) = X^3 + X^2 + 1.$$

If we take $k = -1$ and $d = 3$, then

$$g(X) = \operatorname{lcm}(q_0(X), q_1(X))$$

$$= (X - 1)(X^3 + X + 1) = X^4 + X^3 + X^2 + 1.$$

We obtain the cyclic $[7, 3, 4]$ code discussed in Section 16.7. The theorem says that the minimum weight is at least 3. In this case, we can do a little better. If we take $k = -1$ and $d = 4$, then we have a generating polynomial $g_1(X)$ with

$$g_1(X) = \operatorname{lcm}(q_0(X), q_1(X), q_2(X)) = g(X).$$

This is because $q_2(X) = q_1(X)$, so the least common multiple doesn't change when $q_2(X)$ is included. The theorem now tells us that the minimum weight of the code is at least 4. As we have seen before, the minimum weight is exactly 4. ∎

Example (continued). Let's continue with the previous example, but take $k = 0$ and $d = 7$. Then

$$g(X) = \operatorname{lcm}(q_1(X), \ldots, q_6(X)) = (X^3 + X + 1)(X^3 + X^2 + 1)$$

$$= X^6 + X^5 + X^4 + X^3 + X^2 + X + 1.$$

We obtain the repetition code with only two codewords:

$$\{(0, 0, 0, 0, 0, 0, 0), (1, 1, 1, 1, 1, 1, 1)\}.$$

The theorem says that the minimum distance is at least 7. In fact it is exactly 7. ∎

Example. Let $\mathbf{F} = \mathbf{Z}_5 = \{0, 1, 2, 3, 4\}$ = the integers mod 5. Let $n = 4$. Then

$$X^4 - 1 = (X - 1)(X - 2)(X - 3)(X - 4)$$

(this is an equality, or congruence if you prefer, in $\mathbf{Z}_5$). Let $\alpha = 2$. We have $2^4 = 1$, but $2^j \neq 1$ for $1 \leq j < 4$. Therefore, 2 is a primitive 4th root of unity in $\mathbf{Z}_5$. We have $2^0 = 1$, $2^2 = 4$, $2^3 = 3$ (these are just congruences mod 5). Therefore,

$$q_0(X) = X - 1, \quad q_1(X) = X - 2, \quad q_2(X) = X - 4, \quad q_3(X) = X - 3.$$

In the theorem, let $k = 0, d = 3$. Then

$$g(X) = \text{lcm}\,(q_1(X), q_2(X)) = (X - 2)(X - 4)$$
$$= X^2 - 6X + 8 = X^2 + 4X + 3.$$

We obtain a cyclic $[4, 2]$ code over $\mathbf{Z}_5$ with generating matrix

$$\begin{pmatrix} 3 & 4 & 1 & 0 \\ 0 & 3 & 4 & 1 \end{pmatrix}.$$

The theorem says that the minimum weight is at least 3. Since the first row of the matrix is a codeword of weight 3, the minimum weight is exactly 3. This code is an example of a Reed-Solomon code, which will be discussed in the next section. ∎

Decoding BCH Codes

One of the reason BCH codes are useful is that there are good decoding algorithms. One of the best known is due to Berlekamp and Massey (see [Gallager] or [Wicker]). In following, we won't give the algorithm, but, in order to give the spirit of some of the ideas that are involved, we show a way to correct one error in a BCH code with designed distance $d \geq 3$.

Let C be a BCH code of designed distance $d \geq 3$. Then C is a cyclic code, say of length n, with generating polynomial $g(X)$. There is a primitive nth root of unity α such that

$$g(\alpha^{k+1}) = g(\alpha^{k+2}) = 0$$

for some integer k.

Let

$$H = \begin{pmatrix} 1 & \alpha^{k+1} & \alpha^{2(k+1)} & \cdots & \alpha^{(n-1)(k+1)} \\ 1 & \alpha^{k+2} & \alpha^{2(k+2)} & \cdots & \alpha^{(n-1)(k+2)} \end{pmatrix}.$$

If $c = (c_0, \ldots, c_{n-1})$ is a codeword, then the polynomial $m(X) = c_0 + c_1 X + \cdots + c_{n-1} X^{n-1}$ is a multiple of $g(X)$, so

$$m(\alpha^{k+1}) = m(\alpha^{k+2}) = 0.$$

This may be rewritten in terms of H:

$$cH^T = (c_0, c_1, \ldots, c_{n-1}) \begin{pmatrix} 1 & 1 \\ \alpha^{k+1} & \alpha^{k+2} \\ \alpha^{2(k+1)} & \alpha^{2(k+2)} \\ \vdots & \vdots \\ \alpha^{(n-1)(k+1)} & \alpha^{(n-1)(k+2)} \end{pmatrix} = 0.$$

H is not necessarily a parity check matrix for C, since there might be non-codewords that are also in the null space of H. However, as we shall see, H can correct an error.

Suppose the vector $r = c + e$ is received, where c is a codeword and $e = (e_0, \ldots, e_{n-1})$ is an error vector. We assume that at most one entry of e is nonzero.

Here is the algorithm for correcting one error.

1. Write $rH^T = (s_1, s_2)$.

2. If $s_1 = 0$, there is no error (or there is more than one error), so we're done.

3. If $s_1 \neq 0$, compute s_2/s_1. This will be a power α^{j-1} of α. The error is in the jth position. If we are working over the finite field $\mathbf{Z}_2$, we are done, since then $e_j = 1$. But for other finite fields, there are several choices for the value of e_j.

4. Compute $e_j = s_1/\alpha^{(j-1)(k+1)}$. This is the jth entry of the error vector e. The other entries of e are 0.

5. Subtract the error vector e from the received vector r to obtain the correct codeword c.

Example. Let's look at the BCH code over $\mathbf{Z}_2$ of length 7 and designed distance 7 considered previously. It is the binary repetition code of length 7 and has two codewords: $(0,0,0,0,0,0,0), (1,1,1,1,1,1,1)$. The algorithm corrects one error. Suppose the received vector is $r = (1,1,1,1,0,1,1)$. As before, let α be a root of $X^3 + X + 1$. Then α is a primitive 7th root of unity.

Before proceeding, we need to deduce a few facts about computing with powers of α. We have $\alpha^3 = \alpha + 1$. Multiplying this relation by powers of α yields

$$\alpha^4 = \alpha^2 + \alpha,$$
$$\alpha^5 = \alpha^3 + \alpha^2 = \alpha^2 + \alpha + 1,$$
$$\alpha^6 = \alpha^3 + \alpha^2 + \alpha = (\alpha + 1) + \alpha^2 + \alpha = \alpha^2 + 1.$$

Also, the fact that $\alpha^j = \alpha^{j \pmod 7}$ is useful.

We now can compute

$$rH^T = (1,1,1,1,0,1,1) \begin{pmatrix} 1 & 1 \\ \alpha & \alpha^2 \\ \alpha^2 & \alpha^4 \\ \vdots & \vdots \\ \alpha^6 & \alpha^{12} \end{pmatrix}$$

$$= (\ 1 + \alpha + \alpha^2 + \alpha^3 + \alpha^5 + \alpha^6,\ \ 1 + \alpha^2 + \alpha^4 + \alpha^6 + \alpha^{10} + \alpha^{12}\ )$$

$$= (\ \alpha + \alpha^2,\ \ \alpha\ ).$$

The sum in the first entry, for example, can be evaluated as follows:

$$1 + \alpha + \alpha^2 + \alpha^3 + \alpha^5 + \alpha^6 = 1 + \alpha + \alpha^2 + (1+\alpha) + (\alpha^2 + \alpha + 1) + (\alpha^2 + 1) = \alpha + \alpha^2.$$

Therefore, $s_1 = \alpha + \alpha^2$ and $s_2 = \alpha$. We need to calculate s_2/s_1. Since $s_1 = \alpha + \alpha^2 = \alpha^4$, we have

$$s_2/s_1 = \alpha/\alpha^4 = \alpha^{-3} = \alpha^4.$$

Therefore, $j - 1 = 4$, so the error is in position $j = 5$. The 5th entry of the error vector is $s_1/\alpha^4 = 1$, so the error vector is $(0,0,0,0,1,0,0)$. The corrected message is
$$r - e = (1,1,1,1,1,1,1).$$ ∎

Here is why the algorithm works. Since $cH^T = 0$, we have

$$rH^T = cH^T = eH^T = eH^T = (s_1, s_2).$$

If $e = (0,0,\ldots,e_j,0,\ldots)$ with $e_j \neq 0$, then the definition of H gives

$$s_1 = e_j\alpha^{(j-1)(k+1)}, \quad s_2 = e_j\alpha^{(j-1)(k+2)}.$$

Therefore, $s_2/s_1 = \alpha^{j-1}$. Also, $s_1/\alpha^{(j-1)(k+1)} = e_j$, as claimed.

16.9 Reed-Solomon Codes

The Reed-Solomon codes, constructed in 1960, are an example of BCH codes. Because they work well for certain types of errors, they have been used in spacecraft communications and in compact discs.

Let **F** be a finite field with q elements and let $n = q - 1$. A basic fact from the theory of finite fields is that **F** contains a primitive nth root of unity α. Choose d with $1 \leq d < n$ and let

$$g(X) = (X - \alpha)(X - \alpha^2) \cdots (X - \alpha^{d-1}).$$

This is a polynomial with coefficients in **F**. It generates a BCH code C over **F** of length n, called a **Reed-Solomon code**.

Since $g(\alpha) = \cdots = g(\alpha^{d-1}) = 0$, the BCH bound implies that the minimum distance for C is at least d. Since $g(X)$ is a polynomial of degree

$d - 1$, it has at most d nonzero coefficients. Therefore the codeword corresponding to the coefficients of $g(X)$ is a codeword of weight at most d. It follows that the minimum weight for C is exactly d. The dimension of C is $n - 1 - \deg(g) = n - 1 - d$. Therefore a Reed-Solomon code is a cyclic $[n, n - 1 - d, d]$ code.

The codewords in C correspond to the polynomials

$$g(X)f(X) \text{ with } \deg(f) \le n - d.$$

There are q^{n-d+1} such polynomials $f(X)$ since there are q choices for each of the $n - d + 1$ coefficients of $f(X)$, and thus there are q^{n-d+1} codewords in C. Therefore, a Reed-Solomon code is a MDS code, namely, one that makes the Singleton bound (Section 16.3) an equality.

Example. Let $\mathbf{F} = \mathbf{Z}_7 = \{0, 1, 2, \ldots, 6\}$, the integers mod 7. Then $q = 7$ and $n = q - 1 = 6$. A primitive 6th root of unity α in $\mathbf{F}$ is the same as a primitive root mod 7 (see Section 3.7). We may take $\alpha = 3$. Choose $d = 4$. Then

$$g(X) = (X - 3)(X - 3^2)(X - 3^3) = X^3 + 3X^2 + X + 6.$$

The code has generating matrix

$$G = \begin{pmatrix} 6 & 1 & 3 & 1 & 0 & 0 \\ 0 & 6 & 1 & 3 & 1 & 0 \\ 0 & 0 & 6 & 1 & 3 & 1 \end{pmatrix}.$$

There are $7^3 = 343$ codewords in the code, obtained by taking all linear combinations mod 7 of the three rows of G. The minimum weight of the code is 4. ∎

Example. Let $\mathbf{F} = GF(4) = \{0, 1, \omega, \omega^2\}$, which was introduced in Section 3.10. Then $\mathbf{F}$ has 4 elements, $n = q - 1 = 3$, and $\alpha = \omega$. Choose $d = 2$, so

$$g(X) = (X - \omega).$$

The matrix

$$G = \begin{pmatrix} \omega & 1 & 0 \\ 0 & \omega & 1 \end{pmatrix}$$

is a generating matrix for the code. The code contains all 16 linear combinations of the two rows of G, for example,

$$\omega \cdot (\omega, 1, 0) + 1 \cdot (0, \omega, 1) = (\omega^2, 0, 1).$$

The minimum weight of the code is 2. ∎

In many applications, errors are not randomly distributed. Instead, they occur in bursts. For example, in a CD, a scratch introduces errors in many adjacent bits. A burst of solar energy could have a similar effect on communications from a spacecraft. Reed-Solomon codes are useful in such situations.

For example, suppose we take $\mathbf{F} = GF(2^8)$. The elements of $\mathbf{F}$ are represented as bytes of eight bits each, as in Section 3.10. We have $n = 2^8 - 1 = 255$. Let $d = 33$. The codewords are then vectors consisting of 255 bytes. There are 222 information bytes and 33 check bytes. These codewords are sent as strings of $8 \times 255 = 2040$ binary bits. Disturbances in the transmission will corrupt some of these bits. However, in the case of bursts, these bits will often be in a small region of the transmitted string. If, for example, the corrupted bits all lie within a string of 121 ($= 15 \times 8 + 1$) consecutive bits, there can be errors in at most 16 bytes. Therefore, these errors can be corrected (because $16 < d/2$). On the other hand, if there were 121 bit errors randomly distributed through the string of 2040 bits, numerous bytes would be corrupted, and correct decoding would not be possible. Therefore, the choice of code depends on the type of errors that are expected.

16.10 The McEliece Cryptosystem

In this book, we have mostly described cryptographic systems that are based on number theoretic principles. There are many other cryptosystems that are based on other complex problems. Here we present one based on the difficulty of finding the nearest codeword for a linear binary code.

The idea is simple. Suppose you have a binary string of length 1024 that has 50 errors. There are $\binom{1024}{50} \approx 3 \times 10^{85}$ possible locations for these errors, so an exhaustive search that tries all possibilities is infeasible. Suppose, however, that you have an efficient decoding algorithm that is unknown to anyone else. Then only you can correct these errors and find the corrected string. McEliece showed how to use this to obtain a public key cryptosystem.

Bob chooses G to be the generating matrix for an (n, k) linear error correcting code C with $d(C) = d$. He chooses S to be a $k \times k$ matrix that is invertible mod 2 and lets P be an $n \times n$ permutation matrix, which means that P has exactly one 1 in every row and in every column, with all the other entries being 0. Define

$$G_1 = SGP.$$

The matrix G_1 is the public key for the cryptosystem. Bob keeps S, G, P secret.

In order for Alice to send Bob a message x, she generates a random binary string e of length n that has weight t. She forms the ciphertext by computing

$$y \equiv xG_1 + e \pmod 2.$$

Bob decrypts y as follows:

1. Calculate $y_1 \equiv yP^{-1}$. (Since P is a permutation matrix, $e_1 = eP^{-1}$ is still a binary string of weight t. We have $y_1 \equiv xSG + e_1$.)

2. Apply the error decoder for the code C to y_1 to correct the "error" and obtain the codeword x_1 closest to y_1.

3. Compute x_0 such that $x_0 G \equiv x_1$ (in the examples we have considered, x_0 is simply the first k bits of x_1).

4. Compute $x \equiv x_0 S^{-1}$.

The security of the system lies in the difficulty of decoding y_1 to obtain x_1. There is a little security built into the system by S; however, once a decoding algorithm is known for the code generated by GP, a chosen plaintext attack allows one to solve for the matrix S (as in the Hill cipher).

To make decoding difficult, $d(C)$ should be chosen to be large. McEliece suggested using a $[1024, 512, 101]$ Goppa code. The **Goppa codes** have parameters of the form $n = 2^m, d = 2t + 1, k = n - mt$. For example, taking $m = 10$ and $t = 50$ yields the $[1024, 524, 101]$ code just mentioned. It can correct up to 50 errors. For given values of m and t, there are in fact many inequivalent Goppa codes with these parameters. We will not discuss these codes here except to mention that they have an efficient decoding algorithm and therefore can be used to correct errors quickly.

Example. Consider the matrix

$$G = \begin{pmatrix} 1 & 0 & 0 & 0 & 1 & 1 & 0 \\ 0 & 1 & 0 & 0 & 1 & 0 & 1 \\ 0 & 0 & 1 & 0 & 0 & 1 & 1 \\ 0 & 0 & 0 & 1 & 1 & 1 & 1 \end{pmatrix},$$

which is the generator matrix for the $[7, 4]$ Hamming code. Suppose Alice wishes to send a message

$$m = (1, 0, 1, 1)$$

to Bob. In order to do so, Bob must create an invertible matrix S and a random permutation matrix P that he will keep secret. If Bob chooses

$$S = \begin{pmatrix} 1 & 0 & 0 & 1 \\ 1 & 1 & 0 & 1 \\ 0 & 1 & 0 & 1 \\ 1 & 1 & 1 & 0 \end{pmatrix}$$

and

$$P = \begin{pmatrix} 0 & 0 & 1 & 0 & 0 & 0 & 0 \\ 1 & 0 & 0 & 0 & 0 & 0 & 0 \\ 0 & 0 & 0 & 0 & 1 & 0 & 0 \\ 0 & 0 & 0 & 0 & 0 & 1 & 0 \\ 0 & 0 & 0 & 0 & 0 & 0 & 1 \\ 0 & 1 & 0 & 0 & 0 & 0 & 0 \\ 0 & 0 & 0 & 1 & 0 & 0 & 0 \end{pmatrix}.$$

Using these, Bob generates the public encryption matrix

$$G_1 = \begin{pmatrix} 0 & 0 & 1 & 1 & 0 & 1 & 0 \\ 1 & 0 & 1 & 0 & 0 & 1 & 1 \\ 1 & 1 & 0 & 0 & 0 & 1 & 0 \\ 1 & 0 & 1 & 0 & 1 & 0 & 0 \end{pmatrix}.$$

In order to encrypt, Alice generates her own random error vector e and calculates the ciphertext $y = xG_1 + e$. In the case of a Hamming code the error vector has weight 1. Suppose Alice chooses

$$e = (0, 1, 0, 0, 0, 0, 0).$$

Then

$$y = (0, 0, 0, 1, 1, 0, 0).$$

Bob decrypts by first calculating

$$y_1 = yP^{-1} = (0, 0, 1, 0, 0, 0, 1).$$

Calculating the syndrome of y_1 by applying the parity check matrix H and changing the corresponding bit yields

$$x_1 = (0, 0, 1, 0, 0, 1, 1).$$

Bob next forms a vector x_0 such that $x_0G = x_1$, which can be done by extracting the first four components of x_1, that is,

$$x_0 = (0, 0, 1, 0).$$

Bob decrypts by calculating

$$x = x_0S^{-1} = (1, 0, 1, 1),$$

which is the original plaintext message. ∎

The McEliece system seems to be reasonably secure. For a discussion of its security, see [Chabaud]. A disadvantage of the system compared to RSA, for example, is that the size of the public key G_1 is rather large.

16.11   Other Topics

The field of error correcting codes is a vast subject that is explored by both the mathematical community and the engineering community. In this chapter we have only touched upon a select handful of the concepts of this field. There are many other areas of error correcting codes that we have not discussed.

Perhaps most notable of these is the study of convolutional codes. In this chapter we have entirely focused on block codes, where typically the data are segmented into blocks of a fixed length k and mapped into codewords of a fixed length n. However, in many applications, the data are produced in a continuous fashion, and it is better to map the stream of data into a stream of coded symbols. For example, such codes have the advantage of not requiring the delay needed to observe an entire block of symbols before encoding or decoding.

Another topic that is very important in the study of error correcting codes is that of efficient decoding. In the case of linear codes, we presented syndrome decoding, which is more efficient than performing a search for the nearest codeword. However, for large linear codes, syndrome decoding is still too inefficient to be practical. When BCH and Reed-Solomon codes were introduced, the decoding schemes that were originally presented were impractical for decoding more than a few errors. Later, Berlekamp and Massey provided an efficient approach to decoding BCH and Reed-Solomon codes. There is still a lot of research being done on this topic. We direct the reader to the books [Lin-Costello], [Wicker], [Gallager], and [Berlekamp] for further discussion on the subject of decoding.

We have also focused entirely on bit or symbol errors. However, in modern computer networks, the types of errors that occur are not simply bit or symbol errors but also the complete loss of segments of data. For example, on the Internet, data are transferred over the network in chunks called packets. Due to congestion at various locations on the network, such as routers and switches, packets might be dropped and never reach their intended recipient. In this case, the recipient might notify the sender, requesting a packet to be resent. Protocols such as the Transmission Control Protocol (TCP) provide mechanisms for retransmitting lost packets.

When performing cryptography, it is critical to use a combination of many different types of error control techniques to assure reliable delivery of encrypted messages; otherwise, the receiver might not be able decrypt the messages that were sent.

Finally, we mention that coding theory has strong connections with various problems in mathematics such as finding dense packings of high-dimensional spheres. For more on this, see [Thompson].

16.12 Exercises

1. Two codewords were sent using the Hamming $[7, 4]$ code and were received as 0100111 and 0101010. Each one contains at most one error. Correct the errors. Also, determine the 4-bit messages that were multiplied by the matrix G to obtain the codewords.

2. An ISBN number is incorrectly written as 0-13-116093-8. Show that this is not a correct ISBN number. Find two different valid ISBN numbers such that an error in one digit would give this number. This shows that ISBN cannot correct errors.

3. The following is a parity check matrix for a binary $[n, k]$ code C:

$$\begin{pmatrix} 1 & 1 & 1 & 0 & 0 \\ 1 & 0 & 0 & 1 & 0 \\ 0 & 1 & 0 & 0 & 1 \end{pmatrix}.$$

(a) Find n and k.
(b) Find the generator matrix for C.
(c) List the codewords in C.
(d) What is the code rate for C?

4. Let $C = \{(0, 0, 0), (1, 1, 1)\}$ be a binary repetition code.
(a) Find a parity check matrix for C.
(b) List the cosets and coset leaders for C.
(c) Find the syndrome for each coset.
(d) Use the syndrome decoding method to decode the message $(1, 1, 0)$.

5. Let C be the binary code $\{(0, 0, 0), (1, 1, 0), (1, 0, 1), (0, 1, 1)\}$.
(a) Show that C is not linear.
(b) What is $d(C)$? (Since C is not linear, this cannot be found by calculating the minimum weight.)
(c) Show that C satisfies the Singleton bound with equality.

6. Show that the weight function (on $\mathbf{F}^n$) satisfies the triangle inequality: $wt(u + v) \leq wt(u) + wt(v)$.

7. Show that $A_q(n, n) = q$, where $A_q(n, d)$ is the function defined in Section 16.3.

8. Let C be the repetition code of length n. Show that $C^{\perp}$ is the parity check code of length n. (This is true for arbitrary $\mathbf{F}$.)

9. Let C be a linear code and let $u+C$ and $v+C$ be cosets of C. Show that $u+C=v+C$ if and only if $u-v\in C$. (*Hint*: To show $u+C=v+C$, it suffices to show that $u+c\in v+C$ for every $c\in C$, and that $v+c\in u+C$ for every $c\in C$. To show the opposite implication, use the fact that $u\in u+C$.)

10. Show that if C is a self-dual $[n,k,d]$ code, then n must be even.

11. Show that $g(X)=1+X+X^2+\cdots+X^{n-1}$ is the generating polynomial for the $[n,1]$ repetition code. (This is true for arbitrary $\mathbf{F}$.)

12. Let $g(X)=1+X+X^3$ be a polynomial with coefficients in $\mathbf{Z}_2$.
(a) Show that $g(X)$ is a factor of X^7-1 in $\mathbf{Z}_2[X]$.
(b) The polynomial $g(X)$ is the generating polynomial for a cyclic code $[7,4]$ code C. Find the generating matrix for C.
(c) Find a parity check matrix H for C.
(d) Show that $G'H^T=0$, where

$$G'=\begin{pmatrix} 1 & 1 & 0 & 1 & 0 & 0 & 0 \\ 0 & 1 & 1 & 0 & 1 & 0 & 0 \\ 0 & 0 & 1 & 1 & 0 & 1 & 0 \\ 0 & 1 & 1 & 1 & 0 & 0 & 1 \end{pmatrix}.$$

(e) Show that the rows of G' generate C.
(f) Show that a permutation of the columns of G' gives the generating matrix for the Hamming $[7,4]$ code, and therefore these two codes are equivalent.

13. Let C be the cyclic binary code of length 4 with generating polynomial $g(X)=X^2+1$. Which of the following polynomials correspond to elements of C?

$$f_1(X)=1+X+X^3,\quad f_2(X)=1+X+X^2+X^3,\quad f_3(X)=X^2+X^3.$$

14. Let $g(X)$ be the generating polynomial for a cyclic code C of length n, and let $g(X)h(X)=X^n-1$. Write $h(X)=b_0+b_1X+\cdots+X^\ell$. Show that the dual code $C^\perp$ is cyclic with generating polynomial $\tilde{h}_r(X)=(1/b_0)(1+b_{\ell-1}X+\cdots+b_1X^{\ell-1}+b_0X^\ell)$. (The factor $1/b_0$ is included to make the highest nonzero coefficient be 1.)

15. (a) Let C be a binary repetition code of odd length n (that is, C contains two vectors, one with all 0's and one with all 1's). Show that C is perfect. (*Hint*: Show that every vector lies in exactly one of the two spheres of radius $(n-1)/2$.)
(b) Use (a) to show that if n is odd then $\sum_{j=0}^{(n-1)/2}\binom{n}{j}=2^{n-1}$. (This can also

be proved by applying the binomial theorem to $(1+1)^n$, and then observing that we're using half of the terms.)

16. Let $2 \leq d \leq n$ and let $V_q(n, d-1)$ denote the number of points in a Hamming sphere of radius $d-1$. The proof of the Gilbert-Varshamov bound constructs an (n, M, d) code with $M \geq q^n / V_q(n, d-1)$. However, this code is probably not linear. This exercise will construct a linear $[n, k, d]$ code, where k is the smallest integer satisfying $q^k \geq q^{n-1} / V_q(n, d-1)$.
(a) Show that there exists an $[n, 1, d]$ code C_1.
(b) Suppose $q^{j-1} < q^n / V_q(n, d-1)$ and that we have constructed an $[n, j-1, d]$ code C_{j-1} in $\mathbf{F}^n$ (where $\mathbf{F}$ is the finite field with q elements). Show that there is a vector v with $d(v, c) \geq d$ for all $c \in C_{j-1}$.
(c) Let C_j be the subspace spanned by v and C_{j-1}. Show that C_j has dimension j and that every element of C_j can be written in the form $av + c$ with $a \in \mathbf{F}$ and $c \in C$.
(d) Let $av + c$ be a nonzero element of C_j. Show that $wt(av + c) = wt(v + a^{-1}c) = d(v, -a^{-1}v) \geq d$.
(e) Show that C_j is an $[n, j, d]$ code. Continuing by induction, we obtain the desired code C_k.
(f) Here is a technical point. We have actually constructed an $[n, k, e]$ code with $e \geq d$. Show that by possibly modifying v in step (b), we may arrange that $d(v, c) = d$ for some $c \in C_{j-1}$, so we obtain an $[n, k, d]$ code.

17. Show that the Golay code $\mathcal{G}_{23}$ is perfect.

18. Let α be a root of the polynomial $X^3 + X + 1 \in \mathbf{Z}_2[X]$.
(a) Using the fact that $X^3 + X + 1$ divides $X^7 - 1$, show that $\alpha^7 = 1$.
(b) Show that $\alpha \neq 1$.
(c) Suppose that $\alpha^j = 1$ with $1 \leq j < 7$. Then $\gcd(j, 7) = 1$, so there exist integers a, b with $ja + 7b = 1$. Use this to show that $\alpha^1 = 1$, which is a contradiction. This shows that α is a primitive 7th root of unity.

19. Let C be the binary code generated by the polynomial $g(X) = 1 + X^2 + X^3 + X^4$. As in Section 16.8, $g(1) = g(\alpha) = 0$, where α is a root of $X^3 + X + 1$. Suppose the message $(1, 0, 1, 1, 0, 1, 1)$ is received. It has one error. Use the procedure from Section 16.8 to correct the error.

20. Let $C \subset \mathbf{F}^n$ be a cyclic code of length n with generating polynomial $g(X)$. Assume $C \neq \mathbf{F}^n$.
(a) Show that $\deg(g) \geq 1$.
(b) Write $X^n - 1 = g(X)h(X)$. Let α be a primitive nth root of unity. Show that at least one of $1, \alpha, \alpha^2, \ldots, \alpha^{n-1}$ is a root of $h(X)$. (You may use the fact that $h(X)$ cannot have more than $\deg(h)$ roots.)
(c) Show that $d(C) \geq 2$.

16.13   Computer Problems

1. Three codewords from the Golay code $\mathcal{G}_{24}$ are sent and you receive the vectors

$$(0,1,0,0,0,0,1,1,0,1,0,1,1,0,1,1,0,1,0,0,0,0,1,1),$$

$$(0,0,1,0,1,0,1,0,1,0,1,0,0,1,0,0,1,1,1,0,1,1,0,0),$$

$$(1,1,1,0,1,1,1,1,1,1,1,1,1,1,1,0,1,1,1,1,1,1,1,1).$$

Correct the errors. (The Golay matrix is stored as *golay* and the matrix B is stored as *golayb*.)

2. An 11-bit message is multiplied by the generating matrix for the Hamming [15, 11] code and the resulting codeword is sent. The vector

$$(0,1,1,0,0,0,1,1,0,0,0,1,0,1,0)$$

is received. Assuming there is at most one error, correct it and determine the original 11-bit message. (The parity check matrix for the Hamming [15, 11] code is stored as *hammingpc*.)

Chapter 17

Quantum Techniques in Cryptography

Quantum computing is a new area of research that has only recently started to blossom. Quantum computing and quantum cryptography were born out of the study of how quantum mechanical principles might be used in performing computations. The Nobel Laureate Richard Feynman observed in 1982 that certain quantum mechanical phenomena could not be simulated efficiently on a classical computer. He suggested that the situation could perhaps be reversed by using quantum mechanics to do computations that are impossible on classical computers. Feynman didn't present any examples of such devices, and only recently has there been progress in constructing even small versions.

In 1994 the field of quantum computing had a significant breakthrough when Peter Shor of AT&T Research Labs introduced a quantum algorithm that can factor integers in (probabilistic) polynomial time (if a suitable quantum computer is ever built). This was a dramatic breakthrough as it presented one of the first examples of a scenario in which quantum techniques might significantly outperform classical computing techniques.

In this chapter we introduce a couple of examples from the area of quantum computing and quantum cryptography. By no means is this chapter a thorough treatment of this young field, for even as we write this chapter significant breakthroughs are being made at NIST and other places, and the field likely will continue to advance rapidly.

There are many books and expository articles being written on quantum computing. One readable account is [Rieffel-Polak].

17.1   A Quantum Experiment

Quantum mechanics is a difficult subject to explain to nonphysicists since it deals with concepts where our everyday experiences aren't applicable. In particular, the scale at which quantum mechanical phenomena take place is on the atomic level, which is something that can't be observed without special equipment. There are a few examples, however, that are accessible to us, and we now present one such example and use it to develop the mathematical formulation needed to describe some quantum computing protocols.

Since quantum mechanics is a particle-level physics, we need particles that we are able to observe. Photons are the particles that make up light and are therefore observable (similar demonstrations using other particles, such as electrons, can be performed but require more sophisticated equipment).

In order to understand this experiment better, we recommend that you try it at home. Start by acquiring a powerful light source (such as a strong flashlight or a laser pointer) and three Polaroid filters from a camera supply store.

Label the three filters A, B, and C. Rotate them so that they have the following polarizations: horizontal, 45°, and vertically, respectively (we will explain polarization in more detail after the experiment). Shine the light at the wall and insert filter A between the light source and the wall as in Figure 17.1. The photons coming out of the filter will have horizontal polarization. Now insert filter C as in Figure 17.2. Since filter C has vertical polarization, it filters out all of the horizontally polarized photons from filter A. Notice that no light arrives at the wall after this step, the two filters have removed all of the light components. Now for the final (and most bizarre) step, insert filter B in between filter A and C. You should observe that there is now light arriving at the wall, as depicted in Figure 17.3. This is puzzling, since filter A and C were enough to remove all of the light, yet the addition of a third filter allows for light to reach the wall.

In order to explain this demonstration, we need to discuss the concept of polarization of light.

Light is an example of an electromagnetic wave, meaning that it consists of an electric field that travels orthogonally to a corresponding magnetic field. In order to visualize this, consider the light traveling along the x-axis. Now imagine, for example, that the electric field is a wavelike function that lies in the xz-plane. Then the corresponding magnetic field would be a wavelike function in the xy-plane. For such a scenario, the light is referred

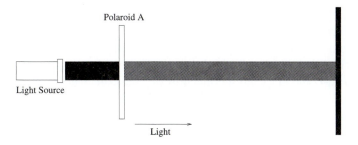

Figure 17.1: The Photon Experiment with Only Filter A Inserted.

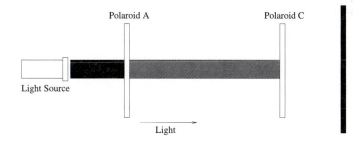

Figure 17.2: The Photon Experiment with Filters A and C Inserted.

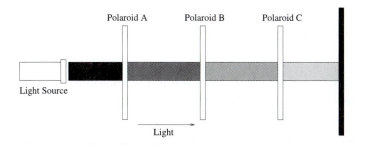

Figure 17.3: The Photon Experiment after All Filters Have Been Inserted.

to as vertically polarized. In general, polarization refers to the direction in which the electric field lies. There is no constraint on this direction.

We will represent a photon's polarization by a unit vector in the two-dimensional complex vector space (however, for our present purposes, real numbers suffice). This vector space has a dot product given by $(a, b) \cdot (c, d) = a\bar{c} + b\bar{d}$, where $\bar{c}$ and $\bar{d}$ denote the complex conjugates of c and d. The square of the length of a vector (a, b) is then $(a, b) \cdot (a, b) = |a|^2 + |b|^2$. Choose a basis for this vector space, which we shall denote $| \uparrow \rangle$ and $| \rightarrow \rangle$. We are choosing to use the ket (the second half of "bracket") notation from physics to represent vectors. We can think of $| \uparrow \rangle$ as being the vertical direction and $| \rightarrow \rangle$ as being horizontal. Therefore, an arbitrary polarization may be represented as $a| \uparrow \rangle + b| \rightarrow \rangle$, where a and b are complex numbers. Since we are working with unit vectors, the following property holds: $|a|^2 + |b|^2 = 1$. We could just have well chosen a different orthogonal basis, for example, one corresponding to a $45°$ rotation: $| \diagdown \rangle$ and $| \diagup \rangle$.

The Polaroid filters perform a measurement of the polarity of the photon. There are two possible outcomes: Either the photon is aligned with the filter, or it is perpendicular to the direction of the filter. If the vector $a| \uparrow \rangle + b| \rightarrow \rangle$ is measured by a vertical filter, then the probability that the photon has vertical polarity after passing through the filter is $|a|^2$. The probability that it will have horizontal polarity is $|b|^2$.

Similarly, suppose we measure a vertically aligned photon with respect to a $45°$ filter. Since

$$| \uparrow \rangle = \frac{1}{\sqrt{2}} | \diagdown \rangle + \frac{1}{\sqrt{2}} | \diagup \rangle,$$

the probability that the photon passes through the filter (which means that it is measured as being aligned at $45°$) is $(1/\sqrt{2})^2 = 1/2$. Similarly, the probability that it doesn't pass through the filter (which means that it is measured at $-45°$) is also $1/2$.

One of the basic principles of quantum mechanics is that such a measurement forces the photon into a definite state. After being measured, the state of the photon will be changed to the result of the measurement. Therefore, if we measured the state of $a| \uparrow \rangle + b| \rightarrow \rangle$ as $| \rightarrow \rangle$, then, from that moment on, the photon will have the state $| \rightarrow \rangle$. If we then measure this photon with a $| \rightarrow \rangle$ filter, we will always observe that the photon is in the $| \rightarrow \rangle$ state; however, if we measure with a $| \uparrow \rangle$ filter, we will never observe that the photon is in the $| \uparrow \rangle$ state.

Let's now explain the interpretation of the experiment. The original light was emitted with random polarization, meaning that the probability of a photon being emitted at state $a_1| \uparrow \rangle + b_1| \rightarrow \rangle$ is equal to the probability of it being emitted at state $a_2| \uparrow \rangle + b_2| \rightarrow \rangle$. Only half of the photons being emitted will pass through the $| \rightarrow \rangle$ filter, and all of these photons will have their state changed to $| \rightarrow \rangle$ (the remaining half are absorbed or reflected and are changed to $| \uparrow \rangle$). When we place the vertical filter after the horizontal filter, the photons, which are in state $| \rightarrow \rangle$, will be stopped.

When we insert filter B in the middle, it corresponds to measuring with respect to $| \nearrow \rangle$, and hence those photons that had $| \rightarrow \rangle$ polarity will come out having $| \nearrow \rangle$ polarity with probability 1/2. Therefore, there has been a 4 : 1 reduction in the amount of photons passing through up to filter B. Now the $| \nearrow \rangle$ photons pass through the $| \uparrow \rangle$ filter with probability 1/2 also, and so the total intensity of light arriving at the wall is 1/8th the original intensity.

17.2 Quantum Key Distribution

Now that we have set up some of the ideas behind quantum mechanics, we can use them to describe a technique for distributing bits through a quantum channel. These bits can be used to establish a key that can be used for communicating across a classical channel, or any other shared secret.

We begin by describing a quantum bit. Start with a two-dimensional complex vector space. Choose a pair of orthogonal vectors of length 1; call them $|0\rangle$ and $|1\rangle$. For example, these two vectors could be either of the two pairs of orthogonal vectors used in the previous section. A **quantum bit**, also known as a **qubit**, is a unit vector in this vector space. For the purposes of the present discussion, we can think of a qubit as a polarized photon. We have chosen $|0\rangle$ and $|1\rangle$ as notation to conveniently represent the 0 and 1 bits, respectively. The other qubits are linear combinations of these two bits.

Since a qubit is a unit vector, it can be represented as $a|0\rangle + b|1\rangle$, where a and b are complex numbers such that $|a|^2 + |b|^2 = 1$. Just as in the case for photons from the preceding section, we can measure this qubit with respect to the basis $|0\rangle, |1\rangle$. The probability that we observe it in the $|0\rangle$ state is $|a|^2$.

Let us now examine how Alice and Bob can communicate with each other in order to establish a message. They will need two things: a quantum channel and a classical channel. A quantum channel is one through which they can exchange polarized photons that are isolated from interactions with the environment (that is, the environment doesn't alter the photons). The classical channel will be used to send ordinary messages to each other. We assume that the evil observer Eve can observe what is being sent on the classical channel and that she can observe and resend photons on the quantum channel.

Alice starts the establishment of a message by sending a sequence of bits to Bob. They are encoded using a randomly chosen basis for each bit as follows. There are two bases: $B_1 = \{|\uparrow\rangle, |\rightarrow\rangle\}$ and $B_2 = \{|\searrow\rangle, |\nearrow\rangle\}$. If Alice chooses B_1, then she encodes 0 as $|\uparrow\rangle$ and 1 as $|\rightarrow\rangle$, while if she chooses B_2 then she encodes 0 and 1 using the two elements of B_2.

Each time Alice sends a photon, Bob randomly chooses to measure with respect to either basis B_1 or B_2. Therefore, for each photon, he obtains an element of that choice of basis as the result of his measurement. Bob records the measurements he has made and keeps them secret. He then tells Alice the basis with which he measured each photon. Alice responds to Bob by telling him which bases were the correct bases for the polarity of the photons that she sent. They keep the bits that used the same bases and discard the other bits. Since two bases were used, Alice and Bob will agree on roughly half of the amount of bits that Alice sent. They can then use these bits as the key for a conventional cryptographic system.

Example. Suppose Alice wants to send the bits $0, 1, 1, 1, 0, 0, 1, 0$. She randomly chooses the bases $B_1, B_2, B_1, B_1, B_2, B_2, B_1, B_2$. Therefore, she sends the qubits (photons)

$$|\uparrow\rangle, |\nearrow\rangle, |\rightarrow\rangle, |\rightarrow\rangle, |\searrow\rangle, |\searrow\rangle, |\rightarrow\rangle, |\searrow\rangle$$

to Bob. He chooses the bases $B_2, B_2, B_2, B_1, B_2, B_1, B_1, B_2$. He measures the qubits that Alice sent and also tells Alice which bases he used. Alice tells him that the 2nd, 4th, 5th, 7th, and 8th match her choices. These yielded measurements

$$|\nearrow\rangle, |\rightarrow\rangle, |\searrow\rangle, |\rightarrow\rangle, |\searrow\rangle$$

for Bob, and they correspond to the bits $1, 1, 0, 1, 0$. Therefore, both Alice and Bob have the same string $1, 1, 0, 1, 0$. They use 11010 as a key for future communication (for example, if they obtained a longer string, they could use the first 56 characters for a DES key). ∎

The security behind quantum key distribution is based upon the laws of quantum mechanics and the fundamental principle that following a measurement of a particle, that particle's state will be altered. Since an eavesdropper Eve must perform measurements in order to observe the photon transmissions between Alice and Bob, Eve will introduce errors in the data that Alice and Bob agreed upon.

Let's see how this happens. Suppose Eve measures the states of the photons transmitted by Alice and allows these measured photons to proceed onto Bob. Since these photons were measured by Eve, they will have the state that Eve observed. Eve will use the wrong basis half of the time when performing the measurement. When Bob performs his measurements, if he uses the correct basis there will be a 25% chance that he will have measured the wrong value.

Let's examine this last statement in more detail. Suppose that Alice sends a photon corresponding to $| \rightarrow \rangle$ and that Bob uses the same basis B_1 as Alice. If Eve uses B_1, then the photon is passed through correctly and then Bob measures the photon correctly. However, if Eve used B_2, then she will measure $| \nearrow \rangle$ and $| \searrow \rangle$ equally likely. The photons that pass to Bob will have one of these orientations and he will therefore half the time measure them correctly as $| \rightarrow \rangle$ and half the time incorrectly. Combining the two possible choices of basis that Eve has causes Bob to have a 25% chance of measuring the incorrect value.

Thus, any eavesdropping introduces a higher error rate in the communication between Alice and Bob. If Alice and Bob test their data for discrepancies over the conventional channel (for example, they could send parity bits), they will detect any eavesdropping.

Actual implementations of this technique have been used to establish keys over a distance of 24 km using conventional fiber optical cables [Hughes et al.].

17.3   Shor's Algorithm

Quantum computers are not yet a reality. The current versions can only handle a few qubits. But, if the great technical problems can be overcome and large quantum computers are built, the effect on cryptography will be enormous. In this section we give a brief glimpse at how a quantum computer could factor large integers, using an algorithm developed by Peter Shor. We avoid discussing quantum mechanics and ask the reader to believe that a quantum computer should be able to do all the operations we describe, and do them quickly. For more details, see, for example, [Ekert-Josza] or [Rieffel-Polak].

What is a quantum computer and what does it do? First, let's look at what a classical computer does. It takes a binary input, for example, 100010, and gives a binary output, perhaps 0101. If it has several inputs, it has to work on them individually. A quantum computer takes as input a certain number of qubits and outputs some qubits. The main difference is that the input and output qubits can be linear combinations of certain basic states. The quantum computer operates on all basic states in this linear combination simultaneously. In effect, a quantum computer is a massively parallel machine.

For example, think of the basic state $|100\rangle$ as representing three particles, the first in orientation 1 and the last two in orientation 0 (with respect to some basis that will implicitly be fixed throughout the discussion). The quantum computer can take $|100\rangle$ and produce some output. However, it can also take as input a normalized (that is, of length 1) linear combination of basic quantum states such as

$$\frac{1}{\sqrt{3}}\left(|100\rangle + |011\rangle + |110\rangle\right)$$

and produce an output just as quickly as it did when working with a basic state. After all, the computer could not know whether a quantum state is one of the basic states, or a linear combination of them, without making a measurement. But such a measurement would alter the input. It is this ability to work with a linear combination of states simultaneously that makes a quantum computer potentially very powerful.

Suppose we have a function $f(x)$ that can be evaluated for an input x by a classical computer. The classical computer asks for an input and produces an output. A quantum computer, on the other hand, can accept as input a sum

$$\frac{1}{C}\sum_x |x\rangle$$

(C is a normalization factor) of all possible input states and produce the output

$$\frac{1}{C}\sum_x |x, f(x)\rangle,$$

where $|x, f(x)\rangle$ is a longer sequence of qubits, representing both x and the value of $f(x)$. (*Technical point:* It might be notationally better to input $(1/C)\sum |x, 00\cdots\rangle$ in order to have some particles to change to $f(x)$. For simplicity, we will not do this.) So we can obtain a list of all the values of $f(x)$. This looks great, but there is a problem. If you make a measurement, you force the quantum state into the result of the measurement. You get $|x_0, f(x_0)\rangle$ for some randomly chosen x_0, and the other states in the output are destroyed. So, if you are going to look at the list of values of $f(x)$, you'd better do it carefully, since you get only one chance. In particular, you probably want to apply some transformation to the output in order to put it into a more desirable form. The skill in programming a quantum computer is in designing the computation so that the outputs you want to examine appear with much higher probability than the others. This is what is done in Shor's factorization algorithm.

Factoring

We want to factor n. The strategy is as follows. Recall that if we can find (nontrivial) a and r with $a^r \equiv 1 \pmod{n}$, then we have a good chance of factoring n (see the exponent factorization method in Section 6.4). Choose a random a and consider the sequence $1, a, a^2, a^3, \ldots$ (mod n). If $a^r \equiv 1$ (mod n), then this sequence will repeat every r terms since $a^{j+r} \equiv a^j a^r \equiv a^j$ (mod n). If we can measure the period of this sequence (or a multiple of the period), we will have an r such that $a^r \equiv 1$ (mod n). We therefore want to design our quantum computer so that when we make a measurement on the output, we'll have a high chance of obtaining the period.

The Discrete Fourier Transform

We need a technique for finding the period of a periodic sequence. Classically, Fourier transforms can be used for this purpose, and they can be used in the present situation, too. Suppose we have a sequence

$$a_0, a_1, \ldots, a_{2^m-1}$$

of length 2^m, for some integer m. Define the Fourier transform to be

$$F(x) = \frac{1}{\sqrt{2^m}} \sum_{c=0}^{2^m-1} e^{\frac{2\pi i c x}{2^m}} a_c,$$

where $0 \le x < 2^m$.

For example, consider the sequence

$$1, 3, 7, 2, 1, 3, 7, 2$$

of length 8 and period 4. The length divided by the period is the frequency, namely 2, which is how many times the sequence repeats. The Fourier transform takes the values

$$
\begin{aligned}
F(0) &= 26/\sqrt{8}, & F(2) &= (-12 + 2i)/\sqrt{8}, \\
F(4) &= 6/\sqrt{8}, & F(6) &= (-12 - 2i)/\sqrt{8},
\end{aligned}
$$

$$F(1) = F(3) = F(5) = F(7) = 0.$$

For example, letting $\zeta = e^{2\pi i/8}$, we find that

$$\sqrt{8}F(1) = 1 + 3\zeta + 7\zeta^2 + 2\zeta^3 + \zeta^4 + 3\zeta^5 + 7\zeta^6 + 2\zeta^7.$$

Since $\zeta^4 = -1$, the terms cancel and we obtain $F(1) = 0$. The nonzero values of F occur at multiples of 2, which is the frequency.

Let's consider another example: $2, 1, 2, 1, 2, 1, 2, 1$. The Fourier transform is

$$F(0) = 12/\sqrt{8}, \quad F(4) = 4/\sqrt{8},$$

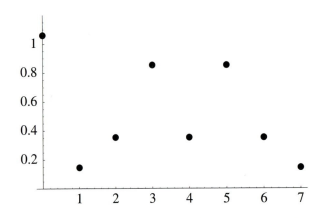

Figure 17.4: The Absolute Value of a Discrete Fourier Transform

$$F(1) = F(2) = F(3) = F(5) = F(6) = F(7) = 0.$$

Here the nonzero values of F are again at the multiples of the frequency.

In general, if the period is a divisor of 2^m, then all the nonzero values of F will occur at multiples of the frequency (however, a multiple of the frequency could still yield 0). See Exercise 2.

Suppose now that the period isn't a divisor of 2^m. Let's look at an example. Consider the sequence $1, 0, 0, 1, 0, 0, 1, 0$. It has length 8 and almost has period 3 and frequency 3, but we stopped the sequence before it had a chance to complete the last period. In Figure 17.4, we graph the absolute value of its Fourier transform (these are real numbers, hence easier to graph than the complex values of the Fourier transform). Note that there are peaks at 0, 3, and 5. If we continued $F(x)$ to larger values of x we would get peaks at $8, 11, 13, 16, \ldots$. The peaks are spaced at an average distance of $8/3$. Dividing the length of the sequence by the average distance yields a period of $8/(8/3) = 3$, which agrees with our intuition.

The fact that there is a peak at 0 is not very surprising. The formula for the Fourier transform shows that the value at 0 is simply the sum of the elements in the sequence divided by the square root of the length of the sequence.

Let's look at one more example: $1, 0, 0, 0, 0, 1, 0, 0, 0, 0 \ 1, 0, 0, 0, 0, 1$. This sequence has 16 terms. Our intuition might say that the period is around 5 and the frequency is slightly more than 3. Figure 17.5 shows the graph of the absolute value of its Fourier transform. Again, the peaks are spaced around 3 apart, so we can say that the frequency is around 3. The period of the original sequence is therefore around 5, which agrees with our intuition.

In the first two examples, the period was a divisor of the length (namely,

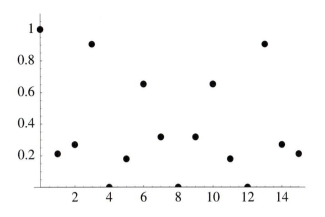

Figure 17.5: The Absolute Value of a Discrete Fourier Transform

8) of the sequence. We obtained nonzero values of the Fourier transform only at multiples of the frequency. In these last two examples, the period was not a divisor of the length (8 or 16) of the sequence. This introduced some "noise" into the situation. We had peaks at approximate multiples of the frequency and values close to 0 away from these peaks.

The conclusion is that the peaks of the Fourier transform tell us approximately the frequency, and therefore the period, of a sequence. This will be useful in Shor's algorithm.

Shor's Algorithm

Choose m so that $n^2 \leq 2^m < 2n^2$. We start with m qubits, all in state 0:

$$|000000000\rangle.$$

As in the previous section, by changing axes, we can transform the first bit to a linear combination of $|0\rangle$ and $|1\rangle$, which gives us

$$\frac{1}{\sqrt{2}}\big(|000000000\rangle + |100000000\rangle\big).$$

We then successively do a similar transformation to the second bit, the third bit, up through the mth bit, to obtain the quantum state

$$\frac{1}{\sqrt{2^m}}\big(|000000000\rangle + |00000001\rangle + |000000010\rangle + \cdots + |111111111\rangle\big).$$

Thus all possible states of the m qubits are superimposed in this sum. For simplicity of notation, we replace each string of 0s and 1s with its decimal equivalent, so we write

$$\frac{1}{\sqrt{2^m}}\left(|0\rangle + |1\rangle + |2\rangle + \cdots + |2^m - 1\rangle\right).$$

Choose a random number a with $1 < a < n$. We may assume $\gcd(a, n) = 1$; otherwise, we have a factor of n. The quantum computer computes the function $f(x) = a^x \pmod{n}$ for this quantum state to obtain

$$\frac{1}{\sqrt{2^m}}\left(|0, a^0\rangle + |1, a^1\rangle + |2, a^2\rangle + \cdots + |2^m - 1, a^{2^m-1}\rangle\right)$$

(for ease of notation, a^x is used to denote $a^x \pmod{n}$). This gives a list of all the values of a^x. However, so far we are not any better off than with a classical computer. If we measure the state of the system, we obtain a basic state $|x_0, a^{x_0}\rangle$ for some randomly chosen x_0. We cannot even specify which x_0 we want to use. Moreover, the system is forced into this state, obliterating all the other values of a^x that have been computed. Therefore, we do not want to measure the whole system. Instead, we measure the value of the second half. Each basic piece of the system is of the form $|x, a^x\rangle$, where x represents m bits and a^x is represented by $m/2$ bits (since $a^x \pmod{n} < n < 2^{m/2}$). If we measure these last $m/2$ bits, we obtain some number $u \pmod{n}$, and the whole system is forced into a combination of those states of the form $|x, u\rangle$ with $a^x \equiv u \pmod{n}$:

$$\frac{1}{C} \sum_{\substack{0 \le x < 2^m \\ a^x \equiv u \pmod{n}}} |x, u\rangle,$$

where C is whatever factor is needed to make the vector have length 1 (in fact, C is the square root of the number of terms in the sum).

Example. At this point, it is probably worthwhile to have an example. Let $n = 21$. (This example might seem simple, but it is larger than quantum computers can currently handle!) Since $21^2 < 2^9 < 2 \cdot 21^2$, we have $m = 9$. Let's choose $a = 11$, so we compute the values of $11^x \pmod{21}$ to obtain

$$\frac{1}{\sqrt{512}}\Big(|0, 1\rangle + |1, 11\rangle + |2, 16\rangle + |3, 8\rangle + |4, 4\rangle + |5, 2\rangle + |6, 1\rangle + |7, 11\rangle +$$

$$|8, 16\rangle + |9, 8\rangle + |10, 4\rangle + |11, 2\rangle + |12, 1\rangle + |13, 11\rangle + |14, 16\rangle +$$

$$|15, 8\rangle + |16, 4\rangle + |17, 2\rangle + |18, 1\rangle + |19, 11\rangle + |20, 16\rangle + \cdots$$

$$+|508, 4\rangle + |509, 2\rangle + |510, 1\rangle + |511, 11\rangle\Big).$$

Suppose we measure the second part and obtain 2. This means we have extracted all the terms of the form $|x, 2\rangle$ to obtain

$$\frac{1}{\sqrt{85}}\big(|5, 2\rangle + |11, 2\rangle + |17, 2\rangle + |23, 2\rangle + \cdots + |497, 2\rangle + |503, 2\rangle + |509, 2\rangle\big).$$

For notational convenience, and since it will no longer be needed, we drop the second part to obtain

$$\frac{1}{\sqrt{85}}\big(|5\rangle + |11\rangle + |17\rangle + |23\rangle + \cdots + |497\rangle + |503\rangle + |509\rangle\big).$$

If we now measured this system, we would simply obtain a number x such that $11^x \equiv 2 \pmod{21}$. This would not be useful. ∎

Suppose we could take two measurements. Then we would have two numbers x and y with $11^x \equiv 11^y \pmod{21}$. This would yield $11^{x-y} \equiv 1 \pmod{21}$. By the exponent factorization method (see Section 6.4), this would give us a good chance of being able to factor 21. However, we cannot take two independent measurements. The first measurement puts the system into the output state, so the second measurement would simply give the same answer as the first.

Not all is lost. Note that in our example, the numbers in our state are periodic mod 6. In general, the values of $a^x \pmod{n}$ are periodic with period r, with $a^r \equiv 1 \pmod{n}$. So suppose we are able to make a measurement that yields the period. We then have a situation where $a^r \equiv 1 \pmod{n}$, so we can hope to factor n by the method from Section 6.4 mentioned above.

The **quantum Fourier transform** is exactly the tool we need. It measures frequencies, which can be used to find the period. If r happens to be a divisor of 2^m, then the frequencies we obtain are multiples of a fundamental frequency f_0, and $r f_0 = 2^m$ In general, r is not a divisor of 2^m, so there will be some dominant frequencies, and they will be approximate multiples of a fundamental frequency f_0 with $r f_0 \approx 2^m$. See the example below.

The quantum Fourier transform is defined on a basic state $|x\rangle$ (with $0 \le x < 2^m$) by

$$QFT(|x\rangle) = \frac{1}{\sqrt{2^m}} \sum_{c=0}^{2^m - 1} e^{\frac{2\pi i c x}{2^m}} |c\rangle.$$

It extends to a linear combination of states by linearity:

$$QFT\big(a_1 |x_1\rangle + \cdots + a_t |x_t\rangle\big) = a_1 QFT(|x_1\rangle) + \cdots + a_t QFT(|x_t\rangle).$$

We can therefore apply QFT to our quantum state.

In our example, we compute

$$QFT\left(\frac{1}{\sqrt{85}}\left(|5\rangle + |11\rangle + |17\rangle + |23\rangle + \cdots + |497\rangle + |503\rangle + |509\rangle\right)\right)$$

and obtain a sum

$$\frac{1}{\sqrt{85}}\sum_{c=0}^{511} g(c)\,|c\rangle$$

for some numbers $g(c)$.

The number $g(c)$ is given by

$$g(c) = \frac{1}{\sqrt{512}} \sum_{\substack{0 \le x < 512 \\ x \equiv 5 \pmod 6}} e^{\frac{2\pi i c x}{512}},$$

which is the discrete Fourier transform of the sequence

$$0,0,0,0,0,1,0,0,0,0,0,1,\ldots,0,0,0,0,0,1,0,0.$$

Therefore, the peaks of the graph of the absolute value of g should correspond to the frequency of the sequence, which should be around $512/6 \approx 85$. The graph in Figure 17.6 is a plot of $|g|$.

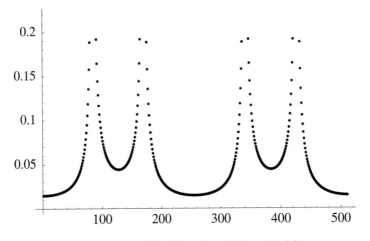

Figure 17.6: The Absolute Value of $g(c)$.

There are sharp peaks at $c = 0$, 85, 171, 256, 341, 427 (the ones at 0 and 256 do not show up on the graph since they are centered at one value; see below). These are the dominant frequencies mentioned previously. The values of g near the peak at $c = 341$ are

338	339	340	341	342	343	344	345
0.305	0.439	0.773	3.111	1.567	0.631	0.398	0.291

The behavior near $c = 85$, 171, and 427 is similar. At $c = 0$ and 256, we have $g(0) = 3.756$, while all the nearby values of c have $g(c) \approx 0.015$.

The peaks are approximately at multiples the fundamental frequency $f_0 = 85$. Of course, we don't really know this yet, since we haven't made any measurements.

Now we measure the quantum state of this Fourier transform. Recall that if we start with a linear combination of states $a_1|x_1\rangle + \cdots + a_t|x_t\rangle$ normalized such that $\sum |a_j|^2 = 1$, then the probability of of obtaining $|x_k\rangle$ is $|a_k|^2$. More generally, if we don't assume $\sum |a_j|^2 = 1$, the probability is

$$|a_k|^2 / \sum |a_j|^2.$$

In our example,

$$3.111^2 / \sum |a_j|^2 \approx .114,$$

so if we sample the Fourier transform, the probability is around $4 \times .114 = .456$ that we obtain one of $c = 85$, 171, 341, 427. Let's suppose this is the case; say we get $c = 427$. We know, or at least expect, that 427 is approximately a multiple of the frequency f_0 that we're looking for:

$$427 \approx j f_0$$

for some j. Since $r f_0 \approx 2^m = 512$, we divide to obtain

$$\frac{427}{512} \approx \frac{j}{r}.$$

Note that $427/512 \approx .834 \approx 5/6$. Since we must have $r \leq \phi(21) < 21$, a reasonable guess is that $r = 6$ (see the following discussion of continued fractions).

In general, Shor showed that there is a high chance of obtaining a value of $c/2^m$ with

$$\left| \frac{c}{2^m} - \frac{j}{r} \right| < \frac{1}{2^{m+1}} < \frac{1}{2n^2},$$

for some j. The method of continued fractions will find the unique (see Exercise 3) value of j/r with $r < n$ satisfying this inequality.

In our example, we take $r = 6$ and check that $a^r = 11^6 \equiv 1 \pmod{21}$.

We want to use the exponent factorization method of Section 6.4 to factor 21. Recall that this method writes $r = 2^k m$ with m odd, and then computes $b_0 \equiv a^m \pmod{n}$. We then successively square b_0 to get $b_1, b_2, \ldots$, until we reach 1 $\pmod{n}$. If b_u is the last $b_i \not\equiv 1 \pmod{n}$, we compute $\gcd(b_u - 1, n)$ to get a factor (possibly trivial) of n.

In our example, we write $6 = 2 \cdot 3$ (a power of 2 times an odd number) and compute (in the notation of Section 6.4)

$$
\begin{aligned}
b_0 &\equiv 11^3 &\equiv 8 &\pmod{21} \\
b_1 &\equiv 11^6 &\equiv 1 &\pmod{21} \\
\gcd(b_0 - 1, 21) &= \gcd(7, 21) = 7,
\end{aligned}
$$

so we obtain $21 = 7 \cdot 3$.

In general, once we have a candidate for r, we check that $a^r \equiv 1 \pmod{n}$. If not, we were unlucky, so we start over with a new a and form a new sequence of quantum states. If $a^r \equiv 1 \pmod{n}$, then we use the exponent factorization method from Section 6.4. If this fails to factor n, start over with a new a. It is very likely that, in a few attempts, a factorization of n will be found.

Continued Fractions

Finally, we show how to find the fraction j/r using the method of continued fractions. We know that $r \leq \phi(n) < n$, so we are trying to approximate a number (such as $427/512$) by a rational number j/r with $r < n$.

First, consider the problem of finding a rational number with small denominator close to a real number x. For example, suppose we want to approximate π. Of course, we could use $314/100 = 157/50$, but we can be more accurate and use a smaller denominator by using $22/7$. So the problem is to get the best approximation using denominators smaller than some bound.

The general procedure for a real number x is the following. Let $[x]$ denote the greatest integer less than or equal to x. Let $a_0 = [x]$ and $x_0 = x$. Then define

$$
x_{i+1} = \frac{1}{x_i - a_i}, \qquad a_{i+1} = [x_{i+1}].
$$

Here's how to proceed for π. We have $[\pi] = 3$. Then $x_1 = 1/(\pi - 3) \approx 7.06251$ and $a_1 = [x_1] = 7$. Next $x_2 = 1/(x_1 - a_1) \approx 15.9966$, and $a_2 = 15$. Continuing, we have $x_3 = 1/(x_2 - a_2) \approx 1.00342$, $a_3 = 1$, and $x_4 = 1/(x_3 - a_3) \approx 292.6$, so $a_4 = 292$. This yields the expansion

$$
\pi = 3 + \cfrac{1}{7 + \cfrac{1}{15 + \cfrac{1}{1 + \cfrac{1}{292 + \cdots}}}}.
$$

If we stop after a few levels of this continued fraction, we obtain the approximations

$$
3, \quad 3 + \frac{1}{7} = \frac{22}{7}, \quad \frac{333}{106}, \quad \frac{355}{113}, \quad \cdots .
$$

The last approximation is very accurate:

$$\pi = 3.14159265\ldots, \text{ and } \quad 355/113 = 3.14159292\ldots.$$

This procedure can be carried out for any real number x and produces a sequence of rational numbers $r_1/s_1, r_2/s_2, \ldots$. Each rational number r_k/s_k that it produces gives a better approximation to x than any other rational number with denominator less than the next denominator s_{k+1}. For example, 22/7 is the best approximation to π among all rational numbers with denominator less than 106.

Now let's apply the procedure to 427/512. We have

$$\frac{427}{512} = 0 + \cfrac{1}{1 + \cfrac{1}{5 + \cfrac{1}{4 + \frac{1}{2}}}}.$$

This yields the numbers

$$0, \quad 1, \quad \frac{5}{6}, \quad \frac{211}{253}, \quad \frac{427}{512}.$$

Since we know the period is less than $n = 21$, the best guess is the last denominator less than n, namely $r = 6$.

In general, we compute the continued fraction expansion of $c/2^m$, where c is the result of the measurement. Then we compute the approximations, as before. The last denominator less than n is the candidate for r.

Final Words

The capabilities of quantum computers and quantum algorithms are of significant importance to economic and government institutions. Many secrets are protected by cryptographic protocols. Quantum cryptography's potential for breaking these secrets as well as its potential for protecting future secrets has caused this new research field to grow rapidly over the past few years.

Although the first full-scale quantum computer is probably many years off, and there are still many who are skeptical of its possibility, quantum cryptography has already succeeded in transmitting secure messages over a distance of greater than 24 km, and quantum computers have been built that can handle a (very) small number of qubits. Quantum computation and cryptography have already changed the manner in which computer scientists and engineers perceive the capabilities and limits of the computer. Quantum computing has rapidly become a popular interdisciplinary research area, and promises to offer many exciting new results in the future.

17.4   Exercises

1. Consider the sequence $2^0, 2^1, 2^2, \ldots$ (mod 15).
(a) What is the period of this sequence?
(b) Suppose you want to use Shor's algorithm to factor $n = 15$. What value of m would you take?
(c) Suppose the measurement in Shor's algorithm yields $c = 192$. What value do you obtain for r? Does this agree with part (a)?
(d) Use the value of r from part (c) to factor 15.

2. (a) Let $0 < s \le m$. Fix an integer c_0 with $0 \le c_0 < 2^s$. Show that

$$\sum_{\substack{0 \le c < 2^m \\ c \equiv c_0 \pmod{2^s}}} e^{\frac{2\pi i c x}{2^m}} = 0$$

if $x \not\equiv 0 \pmod{2^{m-s}}$ and $= 2^{m-s}$ if $x \equiv 0 \pmod{2^{m-s}}$. (*Hint:* Write $c = c_0 + j2^s$ with $0 \le j < 2^{m-s}$, factor $e^{2\pi i x c_0/2^m}$ off the sum, and recognize what's left as a geometric sum.)
(b) Suppose $a_0, a_1, \ldots, a_{2^m-1}$ is a sequence of length 2^m such that $a_k = a_{k+j2^s}$ for all j, k. Show that the Fourier transform $F(x)$ of this sequence is 0 whenever $x \not\equiv 0 \pmod{2^{m-s}}$.
  This shows that if the period of a sequence is a divisor of 2^m then all the nonzero values of F occur at multiples of the frequency (namely, 2^{m-s}).

3. (a) Suppose j/r and j_1/r_1 are two distinct rational numbers, with $0 < r < n$ and $0 < r_1 < n$. Show that

$$\left| \frac{j_1}{r_1} - \frac{j}{r} \right| > \frac{1}{n^2}.$$

(b) Suppose, as in Shor's algorithm, that we have

$$\left| \frac{c}{2^m} - \frac{j}{r} \right| < \frac{1}{2n^2} \text{ and } \left| \frac{c}{2^m} - \frac{j_1}{r_1} \right| < \frac{1}{2n^2}.$$

Show that $j/r = j_1/r_1$.

4. (a) Compute the continued fraction of $12345/11111$. Compare with computation of $\gcd(12345, 11111)$ in Section 3.1.
(b) In general, show that the quotients in the Euclidean algorithm for $\gcd(a, b)$ are exactly the numbers $a_0, a_1, \ldots$ that appear in the continued fraction of a/b.

5. (a) Compute several steps of the continued fractions of $\sqrt{3}$ and $\sqrt{7}$. Do you notice any patterns? (It can be shown that the a_i's in the continued fraction of every irrational number of the form $a + b\sqrt{d}$ with a, b, d rational and $d > 0$ eventually become periodic.)

(b) Compute several steps of the continued fraction expansion of e. Do you notice any patterns? (On the other hand, the continued fraction expansion of π seems to be fairly random.)

Appendix A

Mathematica Examples

These computer examples are written in Mathematica. If you have Mathematica available, you should try some of them on your computer. If Mathematica is not available, it is still possible to read the examples. They provide examples for several of the concepts of this book. For information on getting started with Mathematica, see Section A.1. To download a Mathematica notebook that contains these commands, go to

http://www.prenhall.com/washington

A.1 Getting Started with Mathematica

1. Download the Mathematica notebook math.nb that you find using the links starting at *http://www.prenhall.com/washington*

2. Open Mathematica, and then open math.nb using the menu options under File on the command bar at the top of the Mathematica window. (Perhaps this is done automatically when you download it; it depends on your computer settings.)

3. With math.nb in the foreground, click (left button) on Kernel on the command bar. A menu will appear. Its first line will read Evaluation. Move the arrow so it is on this line. A submenu will appear. Move the arrow down to the line Evaluate Notebook and click (left button). This evaluates the notebook and loads the necessary functions. Ignore any warning messages about spelling. They occur because a few functions have similar names.

4. Go to the command bar at the top and click on File. Move the arrow down to New and click. A new notebook will appear on top of math.nb. However, all the commands of math.nb will still be working.

5. If you want to give the new notebook a name, use the File command and scroll down to Save As.... Then save under some name with a .nb at the end.

6. You are now ready to use Mathematica. If you want to try something easy, type 1+2*3+4^5 and then press the Shift and Enter keys simultaneously. Or, if your keyboard has a number pad with Enter, probably on the right side of the keyboard, you can press that (without the Shift). The result 1031 should appear (it's $1 + 2 \cdot 3 + 4^5$).

7. Turn to the Computer Examples Section A.3. Try typing in some of the commands there. The outputs should be the same as that in the examples. Remember to press Shift Enter (or the numeric Enter) to make Mathematica evaluate an expression.

8. If you want to delete part of your notebook, simply move the arrow to the blue line at the right edge of the window and click the left button. The highlighted part can be deleted by clicking on Edit on the top command bar, then clicking on Cut on the menu that appears.

9. Save your notebook by clicking on File on the command bar, then clicking on Save on the menu that appears.

10. Print your notebook by clicking on File on the command bar, then clicking on Print on the menu that appears. (You will see the advantage of opening a new notebook in Step 4; if you didn't open one, then all the commands in math.nb will also be printed.)

11. If you make a mistake in typing in a command and get an error message, you can edit the command and hit Shift Enter to try again. You don't need to retype everything.

12. If a program seems to be running for a very long time, you can sometimes stop it by clicking on Kernel and Abort Evaluation. If this doesn't work, there is always the Off button on the computer.

13. Look at the commands available through the command bar at the top. For example, Format then Style allows you to change the type font on any cell that has been highlighted (by clicking on its blue bar on the right side).

14. If you are looking for help or a command to do something, try the Help command. The Master Index leads to a lot of useful information. Note that the commands that are built into Mathematica always start with capital letters. The commands that are coming from math.nb start with small letters and will not be found in the Help Index.

15. Some of the number theory and plotting commands require that special packages be loaded (for example, see Example 7 for Chapter 3). These are automatically loaded when the notebook from the Web site is evaluated. If the commands are used independently of that notebook, don't forget to load the packages. One way to identify which packages are needed is to look up the commands in the Master Index.

A.2   Some Commands

The following are some Mathematica commands that are used in the Computer Examples. The commands that start with capital letters, such as **EulerPhi**, are built into Mathematica. The ones that start with small letters, such as **addell**, have been written specially for this text and are in the Mathematica notebook available at

http://www.prenhall.com/washington

addell[{x,y}, {u,v}, a, b, n] finds the sum of the points $\{x, y\}$ and $\{u, v\}$ on the elliptic curve $y^2 \equiv x^3 + ax + b \pmod{n}$.

affinecrypt[txt,m,n] affine encryption of txt using $mx + n$.

allshifts[txt] gives all 26 shifts of txt.

ChineseRemainderTheorem[{a,b,...},{m,n,...}] gives a solution to the simultaneous congruences $x \equiv a \pmod{m}, x \equiv b \pmod{n}, \dots$.

choose[txt,m,n] lists the characters in txt in positions congruent to m (mod n).

coinc[txt,n] the number of matches between txt and txt shifted by n.

corr[v] the dot product of the vector v with the 26 shifts of the alphabet frequency vector.

EulerPhi[n] computes $\phi(n)$ (don't try very large values of n).

ExtendedGCD[m,n] computes the gcd of m and n along with a solution of $mx + ny = $ gcd.

FactorInteger[n] factors n.

frequency[txt] lists the number of occurrences of each letter a through z in txt.

GCD[m,n] is the gcd of m and n.

Inverse[M] finds the inverse of the matrix M.

lfsr[c,k,n] the sequence of n bits produced by the recurrence that has coefficients given by the vector c. The initial values of the bits are given by the vector k.

lfsrlength[v,n] tests the vector v of bits to see if it is generated by a recurrence of length at most n.

lfsrsolve[v,n] given a guess n for the length of the recurrence that generates the binary vector v, it computes the coefficients of the recurrence.

Max[v] is the largest element of the vector v.

Mod[a,n] is the value of a (mod n).

    multell[{x,y}, m, a, b, n] computes m times the point $\{x, y\}$ on the elliptic curve $y^2 \equiv x^3 + ax + b \pmod{n}$.

    multsell[{x,y}, m, a, b, n] lists the first m multiples of the point $\{x, y\}$ on the elliptic curve $y^2 \equiv x^3 + ax + b \pmod{n}$.

    NextPrime[x] gives the next prime $> x$ (the NumberTheoryFunctions package must be loaded).

    num2text0[n] changes a number n to letters. The successive pairs of digits must each be at most 25; a is 00, z is 25.

    num2text[n] changes a number n to letters. The successive pairs of digits must each be at most 26; *space* is 00, a is 01, z is 26.

    PowerMod[a,b,n] computes $a^b \pmod{n}$.

    PrimitiveRoot[p] finds a primitive root for the prime p.

    shift[txt,n] shifts txt by n.

    txt2num0[txt] changes txt to numbers, with $a = 00, \ldots, z = 25$.

    txt2num[txt] changes txt to numbers, with *space*=00, $a = 01, \ldots, z = 26$.

    vigenere[txt,v] gives the Vigenère encryption of txt using the vector v.

    vigvec[txt,m,n] gives the frequencies of the letters a through z in positions congruent to $n \pmod{m}$.

A.3   Examples for Chapter 2

Example 1. A shift cipher was used to obtain the ciphertext **kddmu**. Decrypt it by trying all possibilities.

In[1]:= **allshifts["kddkmu"]**

```
kddkmu
leelnv
mffmow
nggnpx
ohhoqy
piiprz
qjjqsa
rkkrtb
sllsuc
tmmtvd
unnuwe
voovxf
wppwyg
xqqxzh
yrryai
```

```
zsszbj
attack
buubdl
cvvcem
dwwdfn
exxego
fyyfhp
gzzgiq
haahjr
ibbiks
jccjlt
```

As you can see, *attack* is the only word that occurs on this list, so that was the plaintext.

Example 2. Encrypt the plaintext message *cleopatra* using the affine function $7x + 8$:

In[2]:=**affinecrypt["cleopatra", 7, 8]**

Out[2]=whkcjilxi

Example 3. The ciphertext *mzdvezc* was encrypted using the affine function $5x + 12$. Decrypt it.

Solution: First, solve $y \equiv 5x + 12 \pmod{26}$ for x to obtain $x \equiv 5^{-1}(y - 12)$. We need to find the inverse of 5 (mod 26):

In[3]:= **PowerMod[5, -1, 26]**

Out[3]= 21

Therefore, $x \equiv 21(y - 12) \equiv 21y - 12 \cdot 21$. To change $-12 \cdot 21$ to standard form:

In[4]:= **Mod[-12*21, 26]**

Out[4]= 8

Therefore, the decryption function is $x \equiv 21y + 8$. To decrypt the message:

In[5]:= **affinecrypt["mzdvezc", 21, 8]**

Out[5]= anthony

In case you were wondering, the plaintext was encrypted as follows:

In[6]:= **affinecrypt["anthony", 5, 12]**

Out[6]= mzdvezc

Example 4. Here is the example of a Vigenère cipher from the text. Let's see how to produce the data that was used in Section 2.3 to decrypt it. For convenience, we've already stored the ciphertext under the name *vvhq*.

In[7]:= **vvhq**

Out[7]=

vvhqwvvrhmusgjgthkihtssejchlsfcbgvwcrlryqtfsvgahwkcuhwauglq
hnslrljshbltspisprdxljsveeghlqwkasskuwepwqtwvspgoelkcqyfnsv
wljsniqkgnrgybwlwgoviokhkazkqkxzgyhcecmeiujoqkwfwvefqhkijrc
lrlkbienqfrjljsdhgrhlsfqtwlauqrhwdmwlgusgikkflryvcwvspgpmlk
assjvoqxeggveyggzmljcxxljsvpaivwikvrdrygfrjljslveggveyggeia
puuisfpbtgnwwmuczrvtwglrwugumnczvile

Find the frequencies of the letters in the ciphertext:

In[8]:= **frequency[vvhq]**

Out[8]=
{{a, 8}, {b, 5}, {c, 12}, {d, 4}, {e, 15}, {f, 10}, {g, 27},
{h, 16}, {i, 13}, {j, 14}, {k, 17}, {l, 25}, {m, 7}, {n, 7},
{o, 5}, {p, 9}, {q, 14}, {r, 17}, {s, 24}, {t, 8}, {u, 12},
{v, 22}, {w, 22}, {x, 5}, {y, 8}, {z, 5}}

Let's compute the coincidences for shifts of 1, 2, 3, 4, 5, 6:

In[9]:= **coinc[vvhq, 1]**

Out[9]= 14

In[10]:= **coinc[vvhq, 2]**

Out[10]= 14

In[11]:= **coinc[vvhq, 3]**

Out[11]= 16

In[12]:= **coinc[vvhq, 4]**

Out[12]= 14

In[13]:= **coinc[vvhq, 5]**

Out[13]= 24

In[14]:= **coinc[vvhq, 6]**

Out[14]= 12

We conclude that the key length is probably 5. Let's look at the 1st, 6th, 11th, ... letters (namely, the letters in positions congruent to 1 mod 5):

In[15]:= **choose[vvhq, 5, 1]**

Out[15]=
vvuttcccqgcunjtpjgkuqpknjkygkkgcjfqrkqjrqudukvpkvggjjivgjggp
fncwuce

In[16]:= **frequency[%]**

Out[16]= {{a, 0}, {b, 0}, {c, 7}, {d, 1}, {e, 1}, {f, 2},
{g, 9}, {h, 0}, {i, 1}, {j, 8}, {k, 8}, {l, 0}, {m, 0}, {n, 3},
{o, 0}, {p, 4}, {q, 5}, {r, 2}, {s, 0}, {t, 3}, {u, 6}, {v, 5},
{w, 1}, {x, 0}, {y, 1}, {z, 0}}

To express this as a vector of frequencies:

In[17]:= **vigvec[vvhq, 5, 1]**

Out[17]= {0, 0, 0.104478, 0.0149254, 0.0149254, 0.0298507,
0.134328, 0, 0.0149254, 0.119403, 0.119403, 0, 0, 0.0447761,
0, 0.0597015, 0.0746269, 0.0298507, 0, 0.0447761, 0.0895522,
0.0746269, 0.0149254, 0, 0.0149254, 0}

The dot products of this vector with the shifts of the alphabet frequency
vector are computed as follows:

In[18]:= **corr[%]**

Out[18]=
{0.0250149, 0.0391045, 0.0713284, 0.0388209, 0.0274925,
0.0380149, 0.051209, 0.0301493, 0.0324776, 0.0430299,
0.0337761, 0.0298507, 0.0342687, 0.0445672, 0.0355522,
0.0402239, 0.0434328, 0.0501791, 0.0391791, 0.0295821,
0.0326269, 0.0391791, 0.0365522, 0.0316119, 0.0488358,
0.0349403}

The third entry is the maximum, but sometimes the largest entry is hard to
locate. One way to find it is

In[19]:= **Max[%]**

Out[19]= 0.0713284

Now it is easy to look through the list and find this number (it usually
occurs only once). Since it occurs in the third position, the first shift for
this Vigenère cipher is by 2, corresponding to the letter *c*. A procedure
similar to the one just used (using *vigvec[vvhq, 5,2]*,..., *vigvec[vvhq,5,5]*)
shows that the other shifts are probably 14, 3, 4, 18. Let's check that we
have the correct key by decrypting.

In[20]:= **vigenere[vvhq, -{2, 14, 3, 4, 18}]**

Out[20]=

themethodusedforthepreparationandreadingofcodemessagesissim
pleintheextremeandatthesametimeimpossibleoftranslationunles
sthekeyisknowntheeasewithwhichthekeymaybechangedisanotherpo
intinfavoroftheadoptionofthiscodebythosedesiringtotransmiti
mportantmessageswithouttheslightestdangeroftheirmessagesbei
ngreadbypoliticalorbusinessrivalsetc

For the record, the plaintext was originally encrypted by the command

In[21]:= **vigenere[%, {2, 14, 3, 4, 18}]**

Out[21]=

vvhqwvvrhmusgjgthkihtssejchlsfcbgvwcrlryqtfsvgahwkcuhwauglq
hnslrljshbltspisprdxljsveeghlqwkasskuwepwqtwvspgoelkcqyfnsv
wljsniqkgnrgybwlwgoviokhkazkqkxzgyhcecmeiujoqkwfwvefqhkijrc
lrlkbienqfrjljsdhgrhlsfqtwlauqrhwdmwlgusgikkflryvcwvspgpmlk
assjvoqxeggveyggzmljcxxljsvpaivwikvrdrygfrjljslveggveyggeia
puuisfpbtgnwwmuczrvtwglrwugumnczvile

Example 5. The ciphertext

$$22, 09, 00, 12, 03, 01, 10, 03, 04, 08, 01, 17$$

was encrypted using a Hill cipher with matrix

$$\begin{pmatrix} 1 & 2 & 3 \\ 4 & 5 & 6 \\ 7 & 8 & 10 \end{pmatrix}.$$

Decrypt it.

Solution: A matrix $\begin{pmatrix} a & b \\ c & d \end{pmatrix}$ is entered as $\{\{a, b\}, \{c, d\}\}$. Type $M.N$ to multiply matrices M and N. Type $v.M$ to multiply a vector v on the right by a matrix M.

First, we need to invert the matrix mod 26:

In[22]:= **Inverse[{{ 1,2,3},{ 4,5,6},{7,8,10}}]**

Out[22]= $\{\{-\frac{2}{3}, -\frac{4}{3}, 1\}, \{\frac{2}{3}, \frac{11}{3}, -2\}, \{1, -2, 1\}\}$

Since we are working mod 26, we can't stop with numbers like 2/3. We need to get rid of the denominators and reduce mod 26. To do so, we multiply by 3 to extract the numerators of the fractions, then multiply by the inverse of 3 mod 26 to put the "denominators" back in (see Section 3.3):

In[23]:= **%*3**

Out[23]= {{-2, -4, 3}, {-2, 11, -6}, {3, -6, 3}}

In[24]:= **Mod[PowerMod[3, -1, 26]*%, 26]**

Out[24]= {{8,16,1}, {8,21,24}, {1,24,1}}

This is the inverse of the matrix mod 26. We can check this as follows:

In[25]:= **Mod[%.{{1, 2, 3}, {4, 5, 6}, {7, 8, 10}}, 26]**

Out[25]= {{1, 0, 0}, {0, 1, 0}, {0, 0, 1}}

To decrypt, we break the ciphertext into blocks of three numbers and multiply each block on the right by the inverse matrix we just calculated:

In[26]:= **Mod[{22, 09, 00}.%%, 26]**

Out[26]= {14, 21, 4}

In[27]:= **Mod[{12, 03, 01}.%%%, 26]**

Out[27]= {17, 19, 7}

In[28]:= **Mod[{10, 03, 04}.%%%%, 26]**

Out[28]= {4, 7, 8}

In[29]:= **Mod[{08, 01, 17}.%%%%%, 26]**

Out[29]= {11, 11, 23}

Therefore, the plaintext is 14, 21, 4, 17, 19, 7, 4, 7, 8, 11, 11, 23. This can be changed back to letters:

In[30]:= **alph0[142104171907040708111123]**

Out[30]= overthehillx

Note that the final x was appended to the plaintext in order to complete a block of three letters.

Example 6. Compute the first 50 terms of the recurrence

$$x_{n+5} \equiv x_n + x_{n+2} \pmod{2}.$$

The initial values are $0, 1, 0, 0, 0$.

    Solution: The vector of coefficients is $\{1, 0, 1, 0, 0\}$. The initial vector is $\{0, 1, 0, 0, 0\}$. Type

In[31]:= **lfsr[{1, 0, 1, 0, 0}, {0, 1, 0, 0, 0}, 50]**

Out[31]= {0, 1, 0, 0, 0, 0, 1, 0, 0, 1, 0, 1, 1, 0, 0, 1, 1, 1, 1, 1, 0, 0, 0, 1, 1, 0, 1, 1, 1, 0, 1, 0, 1, 0, 0, 0, 0, 1, 0, 0, 1, 0, 1, 1, 0, 0, 1, 1, 1, 1}

Example 7. Suppose the first 20 terms of an LFSR sequence are 1, 0, 1, 0, 1, 1, 1, 0, 0, 0, 0, 1, 1, 1, 0, 1, 0, 1, 0, 1. Find a recurrence that generates this sequence.

Solution: First, we find the length of the recurrence. The command *lfsrlength[v, n]* calculates the determinants mod 2 of the first n matrices that appear in the procedure in Section 2.11:

In[32]:=
lfsrlength[{1, 0, 1, 0, 1, 1, 1, 0, 0, 0, 0, 1, 1, 1, 0, 1, 0, 1, 0, 1}, 10]

    {1, 1}
    {2, 1}
    {3, 0}
    {4, 1}
    {5, 0}
    {6, 1}
    {7, 0}
    {8, 0}
    {9, 0}
    {10, 0}

The last nonzero determinant is the sixth one, so we guess that the recurrence has length 6. To find the coefficients:

In[33]:= **lfsrsolve[{1, 0, 1, 0, 1, 1, 1, 0, 0, 0, 0, 1, 1, 1, 0, 1, 0, 1, 0, 1}, 6]**

Out[33]= {1, 0, 1, 1, 1, 0}

This gives the recurrence as

$$x_{n+6} \equiv x_n + x_{n+2} + x_{n+3} + x_{n+4} \pmod 2.$$

Example 8. The ciphertext 0, 1, 1, 0, 1, 0, 1, 0, 1, 0, 0, 1, 1, 0, 0, 0, 1, 0, 1, 0, 1, 0, 1, 0, 1, 0, 1, 0, 1, 0, 0, 1, 0, 0, 0, 1, 0, 1, 1, 0 was produced by adding the output of a LFSR onto the plaintext mod 2 (i.e., XOR the plaintext with the LFSR output). Suppose you know that the plaintext starts 1, 1, 1, 1, 1, 1, 0, 0, 0, 0, 0, 0, 1, 1, 1, 0, 0. Find the rest of the plaintext.

Solution: XOR the ciphertext with the known part of the plaintext to obtain the beginning of the LFSR output:

In[34]:= **Mod[{1, 1, 1, 1, 1, 1, 0, 0, 0, 0, 0, 0, 1, 1, 1, 0, 0} + {0, 1, 1, 0, 1, 0, 1, 0, 1, 0, 0, 1, 1, 0, 0, 0, 1}, 2]**

Out[34]= {1, 0, 0, 1, 0, 1, 1, 0, 1, 0, 0, 1, 0, 1, 1, 0, 1}

This is the beginning of the LFSR output. Now let's find the length of the recurrence:

In[35]:= **lfsrlength[%, 8]**

      {1, 1}
      {2, 0}
      {3, 1}
      {4, 0}
      {5, 1}
      {6, 0}
      {7, 0}
      {8, 0}

We guess the length is 5. To find the coefficients of the recurrence:

In[36]:= **lfsrsolve[%%, 5]**

Out[36]= {1, 1, 0, 0, 1}

Now we can generate the full output of the LFSR using the coefficients we just found plus the first five terms of the LFSR output:

In[37]:= **lfsr[{1, 1, 0, 0, 1}, {1, 0, 0, 1, 0}, 40]**

Out[37]= {1, 0, 0, 1, 0, 1, 1, 0, 1, 0, 0, 1, 0, 1, 1, 0, 1,
0, 0, 1, 0, 1, 1, 0, 1, 0, 0, 1, 0, 1, 1, 0, 1, 0, 0, 1,
0, 1, 1, 0}

When we XOR the LFSR output with the ciphertext, we get back the plaintext:

In[38]:= **Mod[% + {0, 1, 1, 0, 1, 0, 1, 0, 1, 0, 0, 1, 1, 0, 0, 0, 1, 0, 1,
0, 1, 0, 1, 0, 1, 0, 1, 0, 0, 1, 0, 0, 0, 1, 0, 1, 1, 0}, 2]**

Out[38]= {1, 1, 1, 1, 1, 1, 0, 0, 0, 0, 0, 0, 1, 1, 1, 0, 0,
0, 1, 1, 1, 1, 0, 0, 0, 0, 1, 1, 1, 1, 1, 1, 1, 0, 0, 0,
0, 0, 0, 0}

This is the plaintext.

A.4   Examples for Chapter 3

Example 1. Find gcd(23456, 987654).

In[1]:= **GCD[23456, 987654]**

Out[1]= 2

Example 2. Solve $23456x + 987654y = 2$ in integers x, y.

In[2]:= **ExtendedGCD[23456, 987654]**

Out[2]= {2, {-3158, 75}}

This means that 2 is the gcd and $23456 \cdot (-3158) + 987654 \cdot 75 = 2$.

Example 3. Compute $234 \cdot 456 \pmod{789}$.

In[3]:= **Mod[234*456, 789]**

Out[3]= 189

Example 4. Compute $234567^{876543} \pmod{565656565}$.

In[4]:= **PowerMod[234567, 876543, 565656565]**

Out[4]= 473011223

Example 5. Find the multiplicative inverse of $87878787 \pmod{9191919191}$.

In[5]:= **PowerMod[87878787, -1, 9191919191]**

Out[5]= 7079995354

Example 6. Solve $7654x \equiv 2389 \pmod{65537}$.

Solution: Here is one way:

In[6]:=
**Solve[{7654*x == 2389, Modulus == 65537}, x,
Mode -> Modular]**

Out[6]= {{Modulus -> 65537, x -> 43626}}

Here is another way. It corresponds to the method in Section 3.3. We calculate 7654^{-1} and then multiply it by 2389:

In[7]:= **PowerMod[7654, -1, 65537]**

Out[7]= 54637

In[8]:= **Mod[%*2389, 65537]**

Out[8]= 43626

Example 7. Find x with

$$x \equiv 2 \pmod{78}, x \equiv 5 \pmod{97}, x \equiv 1 \pmod{119}.$$

Solution: First, we need to load a number theory package:

In[9]:=<<NumberTheory'NumberTheoryFunctions'

Now we can solve the problem:

In[10]:= **ChineseRemainderTheorem[{2, 5, 1}, {78, 97, 119}]**

Out[10]= 647480

We can check the answer:

In[11]:= **Mod[647480, {78, 97, 119}]**

Out[11]= {2, 5, 1}

Example 8. Factor 123450 into primes.

In[12]:= **FactorInteger[123450]**

Out[12]= {{2, 1}, {3, 1}, {5, 2}, {823, 1}}

This means that $123450 = 2^1 3^1 5^2 823^1$.

Example 9. Evaluate $\phi(12345)$.

In[13]:= **EulerPhi[12345]**

Out[13]= 6576

Example 10. Find a primitive root for the prime 65537.

Solution: This also requires loading the number theory package (which we have already done). Then type

In[14]:= **PrimitiveRoot[65537]**

Out[14]= 3

Therefore, 3 is a primitive root for 65537.

Example 11. Find the inverse of the matrix $\begin{pmatrix} 13 & 12 & 35 \\ 41 & 53 & 62 \\ 71 & 68 & 10 \end{pmatrix}$ (mod 999).

Solution: First, invert the matrix without the mod:

In[15]:= **Inverse[{{13, 12, 35}, {41, 53, 62}, {71, 68, 10}}]**

Out[15]= {{ $\frac{3686}{34139}$, $-\frac{2260}{34139}$, $\frac{1111}{34139}$ }, { $-\frac{3992}{34139}$, $\frac{2355}{34139}$, $-\frac{629}{34139}$ },
{ $\frac{975}{34139}$, $\frac{32}{34139}$, $-\frac{197}{34139}$ }}

We need to clear the 34139 out of the denominator, so we evaluate 1/34139 mod 999:

In[16]:= **PowerMod[34139, -1, 999]**

Out[16]= 410

Since $410 \cdot 34139 \equiv 1 \pmod{999}$, we multiply the inverse matrix by $410 \cdot 34139$ and reduce mod 999 in order to remove the denominators without changing anything mod 999:

In[17]:= **Mod[410*34139*%%, 999]**

Out[17]= {{772, 472, 965}, {641, 516, 851}, {150, 133, 149}}

Therefore, the inverse matrix mod 999 is $\begin{pmatrix} 772 & 472 & 965 \\ 641 & 516 & 851 \\ 150 & 133 & 149 \end{pmatrix}$.

In many cases, it is possible to determine by inspection the common denominator that must be removed. When this is not the case, note that the determinant of the original matrix will always work as a common denominator.

Example 12. Find a square root of 26951623672 mod the prime $p = 98573007539$.

Solution: Since $p \equiv 3 \pmod{4}$, we can use the Proposition of Section 3.9:

In[18]:=**PowerMod[26951623672, (98573007539 + 1)/4, 98573007539]**

Out[18]= 98338017685

The other square root is minus this one:

In[19]:=**Mod[-%, 98573007539]**

Out[19]= 234989854

Example 13. Let $n = 34222273 = 9803 \cdot 3491$. Find all four solutions of $x^2 \equiv 19101358 \pmod{34222273}$.

Solution: First, find a square root mod each of the two prime factors, both of which are congruent to 3 (mod 4):

In[20]:=**PowerMod[19101358, (9803 + 1)/4, 9803]**

Out[20]= 3998

In[21]:=**PowerMod[19101358, (3491 + 1)/4, 3491]**

Out[21]= 1318

Therefore, the square roots are congruent to $\pm 3998 \pmod{9803}$ and $\pm 1318 \pmod{3491}$. There are four ways to combine these using the Chinese remainder theorem:

In[22]:=**ChineseRemainderTheorem**[{3998, 1318 }, {9803, 3491 }]

Out[22]= 43210

In[23]:=**ChineseRemainderTheorem**[{-3998, 1318 }, {9803, 3491 }]

Out[23]= 8397173

In[24]:=**ChineseRemainderTheorem**[{3998, -1318 }, {9803, 3491 }]

Out[24]= 25825100

In[25]:=**ChineseRemainderTheorem**[{-3998, -1318}, {9803, 3491}]

Out[25]= 34179063

These are the four desired square roots.

A.5   Examples for Chapter 6

Example 1. Suppose you need to find a large random prime of 50 digits. Here is one way. First, load the number theory package:

In[1]:=**<<NumberTheory'NumberTheoryFunctions'**

The function *NextPrime[x]* finds the next prime greater than x. The function *Random[Integer,{a,b}]* gives a random integer between a and b. Combining these, we can find a prime:

In[2]:=**NextPrime[Random[Integer, {10^49, 10^50 }]]**

Out[2]= 73050570031667109175215303340488313456708913284291

If we repeat this procedure, we should get another prime:

In[3]:=**NextPrime[Random[Integer, {10^49, 10^50 }]]**

Out[3]= 97476407694931303255724326040586144145341054568331

Example 2. Suppose you want to change the text *hellohowareyou* to numbers:

In[4]:=**num1["hellohowareyou"]**

Out[4]= 805121215081523011805251521

Note that we are now using *a=1, b=2, ..., z=26*, since otherwise *a*'s at the beginnings of messages would disappear. (A more efficient procedure would be to work in base 27, so the numerical form of the message would be $8 + 5 \cdot 27 + 12 \cdot 27^2 + \cdots + 21 \cdot 27^{13} = 8749522150238455495$. Note that this uses fewer digits.)

Now suppose you want to change it back to letters:

In[5]:=**alph1[80512121508152301180525 1521]**

Out[5]= `hellohowareyou`

Example 3. Encrypt the message *hi* using RSA with $n = 823091$ and $e = 17$.

Solution: First, change the message to numbers:

In[6]:=**num1["hi"]**

Out[6]= `809`

Now, raise it to the *e*th power mod *n*:

In[7]:=**PowerMod[%, 17, 823091]**

Out[7]= `596912`

Example 4. Decrypt the ciphertext in the previous problem.

Solution: First, we need to find the decryption exponent *d*. To do this, we need to find $\phi(823091)$. One way is as follows:

In[8]:=**EulerPhi[823091]**

Out[8]= `821184`

Another way is to factor *n* as $p \cdot q$ and then compute $(p - 1)(q - 1)$:

In[9]:=**FactorInteger[823091]**

Out[9]= `{ {659, 1 }, {1249, 1 } }`

In[10]:=**658*1248**

Out[10]= `821184`

Since $de \equiv 1 \pmod{\phi(n)}$, we compute the following (note that we are finding the inverse of *e* mod $\phi(n)$, not mod *n*):

In[11]:=**PowerMod[17, -1, 821184]**

Out[11]= `48305`

Therefore, $d = 48305$. To decrypt, raise the ciphertext to the *d*th power mod *n*:

In[12]:=**PowerMod[596912, 48305, 823091]**

Out[12]= `809`

Finally, change back to letters:

In[13]:=**alph1[809]**

Out[13]= `hi`

Example 5. Encrypt *hellohowareyou* using RSA with $n = 823091$ and $e = 17$.

Solution: First, change the plaintext to numbers:

In[14]:=**num1["hellohowareyou"]**

Out[14]= 8051212150815230118052515 21

Suppose we simply raised this to the *e*th power mod n:

In[15]:=**PowerMod[%, 17, 823091]**

Out[15]= 447613

If we decrypt (we know d from Example 4), we obtain

In[16]:=**PowerMod[%, 48305, 823091]**

Out[16]= 628883

This is not the original plaintext. The reason is that the plaintext is larger than n, so we have obtained the plaintext mod n:

In[17]:=**Mod[8051212150815230118052515 21, 823091]**

Out[17]= 628883

We need to break the plaintext into blocks, each less than n. In our case, we use three letters at a time:

$$80512 \quad 121508 \quad 152301 \quad 180525 \quad 1521$$

In[18]:=**PowerMod[80512, 17, 823091]**

Out[18]= 757396

In[19]:=**PowerMod[121508, 17, 823091]**

Out[19]= 164513

In[20]:=**PowerMod[152301, 17, 823091]**

Out[20]= 121217

In[21]:=**PowerMod[180525, 17, 823091]**

Out[21]= 594220

In[22]:=**PowerMod[1521, 17, 823091]**

Out[22]= 442163

The ciphertext is therefore 757396164513121217594220442163. Note that there is no reason to change this back to letters. In fact, it doesn't correspond to any text with letters.

Decrypt each block individually:

In[23]:=**PowerMod[757396, 48305, 823091]**

Out[23]= 80512

In[24]:=**PowerMod[164513, 48305, 823091]**

Out[24]= 121508

Etc.

We'll now do some examples with large numbers, namely the numbers in the RSA Challenge discussed in Section 6.5. These are stored under the names *rsan, rsae, rsap, rsaq*:

In[25]:=**rsan**

Out[25]=
11438162575788886766923577997614661201021829672124236256256184
29357069352457338978305971235639587050589890751475992900268
79543541

In[26]:=**rsae**

Out[26]= 9007

Example 6. Encrypt each of the messages *b, ba, bar, bard* using *rsan* and *rsae*.

In[27]:=**PowerMod[num1["b"], rsae, rsan]**

Out[27]=
70946758467612668598370164991550786182876331060685235410564704
11448678226171649720012215533234846201405328798758089926376
5142534

In[28]:=**PowerMod[num1["ba"], rsae, rsan]**

Out[28]=
35045130608975100325011709449871954273788204753948593060313697
69822762175980602796227053803156556477335203367178226130579
6158951

In[29]:=**PowerMod[num1["bar"], rsae, rsan]**

Out[29]=
44814512863855101076004530859492109342429531606607409070360543
40800084364598688040595310281831282258636258029878444115192
2606424

In[30]:=**PowerMod[num1["bard"], rsae, rsan]**

Out[30]=
2423807778511166642320286251209031739348521295905627078313499
1614256054323297179804928958073445752663026449873986877989329
909498

Observe that the ciphertexts are all the same length. There seems to be no easy way to determine the length of the corresponding plaintext.

Example 7. Using the factorization *rsan=rsap·rsaq*, find the decryption exponent for the RSA Challenge, and decrypt the ciphertext (see Section 6.5).
Solution: First we find the decryption exponent:

In[31]:=**rsad=PowerMod[rsae,-1,(rsap-1)*(rsaq-1)];**

Note that we use the final semicolon to avoid printing out the value. If you want to see the value of *rsad*, see Section 6.5, or don't use the semicolon. To decrypt the ciphertext, which is stored as *rsaci*, and change to letters:

In[32]:=**alph1[PowerMod[rsaci, rsad, rsan]]**

Out[32]=
the magic words are squeamish ossifrage

Example 8. Encrypt the message *rsaencryptsmessageswell* using *rsan* and *rsae*.

In[33]:= **PowerMod[num1["rsaencryptsmessageswell"], rsae, rsan]**

Out[33]=
9463942034900225931630582353924949641464096993400170972140435
2418271950654254365584906013966328817753539283112653197553130
781884

Example 9. Decrypt the preceding ciphertext.
    Solution: Fortunately, we know the decryption exponent *rsad*. Therefore, we compute

In[34]:=**PowerMod[%, rsad, rsan]**

Out[34]= 1819010514031825162019130519190107051923051212

In[35]:=**alph1[%]**

Out[35]= rsaencryptsmessageswell

Suppose we lose the final 4 of the ciphertext in transmission. Let's try to decrypt what's left (subtracting 4 and dividing by 10 is a mathematical way to remove the 4):

In[36]:=**PowerMod[(%%% - 4)/10, rsad, rsan]**

Out[36]=
47952999173195988664902352629525486409113633894375629846854 90
79705884123003734879696577942541171589569212679126284614944 75
682806

If we try to change this to letters, we get a long error message. A small error in the plaintext completely changes the decrypted message and usually produces garbage.

Example 10. Suppose we are told that $n = 11313771275590312567$ is the product of two primes and that $\phi(n) = 11313771187608744400$. Factor n.

Solution: We know (see Section 6.1) that p and q are the roots of $X^2 - (n - \phi(n) + 1)X + n$. Therefore, we compute

In[37]:=**Roots[X^2 -**
(11313771275590312567 - 11313771187608744400 + 1)*X +
11313771275590312567 == 0, X]

Out[37]= X == 128781017 || X == 87852787151

Therefore, $n = 128781017 \cdot 87852787151$. We also could have used the quadratic formula to find the roots.

Example 11. Suppose we know *rsae* and *rsad*. Use these to factor *rsan*.

Solution: We use the universal exponent factorization method from Section 6.4. First write $rsae \cdot rsad - 1 = 2^s m$ with m odd. One way to do this is first to compute $rsae \cdot rsad - 1$, then keep dividing by 2 until you get an odd number:

In[38]:=**rsae*rsad - 1**

Out[38]=
96103441961778226615691902335958383410985412905187833025064 46
04041155985575087352659156174898557342995131594680431086921 24
5830097664

In[39]:=**%/2**

Out[39]=
48051720980889113307845951167979191705492706452593916512532 23
02020577992787543676329578087449278671497565797340215543460 62
2915048832

In[40]:=**%/2**

Out[40]=
24025860490444556653922975583989595852746353226296958256266 11

5101028899639377183816478904372463933574878289867010777173031
1457524416

We continue this way for six more steps until we get

Out[46]=
37540407016319619771754649349983743519916176916088997275415 80
48453576556865268497132482880819748962107473279172043393328 61
16523819

This number is m. Now choose a random integer a. Hoping to be lucky, we
choose 13. As in the universal exponent factorization method, we compute

In[47]:=**PowerMod[13, %, rsan]**

Out[47]=
27574368507006530592243494868847161198423095707307805690569 83
96470301831098398623708005293380929847954901926435879608598 70
551239

Since this is not ± 1 (mod *rsan*), we successively square it until we get ± 1:

In[48]:=**PowerMod[%, 2, rsan]**

Out[48]=
48318960321928515580138476418723034554104099069940846225494 70
27766549964125829556360352661561086864311942985740758540375 12
277292

In[49]:=**PowerMod[%, 2, rsan]**

Out[49]=
78172814154877356579141928058754000021948787056483820917930 62
51152151818397420560132755219134875609447320735164877222738 75
579363

In[50]:=**PowerMod[%, 2, rsan]**

Out[50]=
42836191202508728742199299040582900202976222916017767167551 87
02165094445182394621863794705694420551013929922930822596017 38
228702

In[51]:=**PowerMod[%, 2, rsan]**

Out[51]= 1

Since the last number before the 1 was not ± 1 (mod *rsan*), we have an
example of $x \not\equiv \pm 1$ (mod *rsan*) with $x^2 \equiv 1$. Therefore, $\gcd(x - 1, rsan)$ is
a nontrivial factor of *rsan*:

In[52]:=**GCD[%% - 1, rsan]**

Out[52]=
3276913299326670954996198819083446141317764296799294253979828
8533

This is *rsaq*. The other factor is obtained by computing *rsan/rsaq*:

In[53]:=**rsan/%**

Out[53]=
3490529510847650949147849619903898133417764638493387843990820
577

This is *rsap*.

Example 12. Suppose you know that

$$150883475569451^2 \equiv 16887570532858^2 \pmod{205611444308117}.$$

Factor 205611444308117.
Solution: We use the Basic Principle of Section 6.3.

In[54]:=**GCD[150883475569451-16887570532858,205611444308117]**

Out[54]= 23495881

This gives one factor. The other is

In[55]:=**205611444308117/%**

Out[55]= 8750957

We can check that these factors are actually primes, so we can't factor any further:

In[56]:=**PrimeQ[%%]**

Out[56]= True

In[57]:=**PrimeQ[%%]**

Out[57]= True

Example 13. Factor $n = 3768755754263948555999989992897873239$ by the $p - 1$ method.

Solution: Let's choose our bound as $B = 100$, and let's take $a = 2$, so we compute $2^{100!} \pmod{n}$:

In[58]:= **PowerMod[2,Factorial[100],3768755754263948555999989999 2897873239]**

Out[58]= 3696766783019563319394221062511199512

Then we compute the gcd of $2^{100!} - 1$ and n:

In[59]:=**GCD[% - 1, 376875575426394855599989992897873239]**

Out[59]= 430553161739796481

This is a factor p. The other factor q is

In[60]:=**376875575426394855599989992897873239/%**

Out[60]= 875328783798732119

Let's see why this worked. The factorizations of $p-1$ and $q-1$ are

In[61]:=**FactorInteger[430553161739796481 - 1]**

Out[61]= { {2, 18 }, {3, 7 }, {5, 1 }, {7, 4 }, {11, 3 }, {47, 1 } }

In[62]:=**FactorInteger[875328783798732119 - 1]**

Out[62]= { {2, 1 }, {61, 1 }, {20357, 1 }, {39301, 1 }, {8967967, 1 }}

We see that 100! is a multiple of $p-1$, so $2^{100!} \equiv 1 \pmod{p}$. However, 100! is not a multiple of $q-1$, so it is likely that $2^{100!} \not\equiv 1 \pmod{q}$. Therefore, both $2^{100!} - 1$ and pq have p as a factor, but only pq has q as a factor. It follows that the gcd is p.

A.6   Examples for Chapter 8

Example 1. Suppose there are 23 people in a room. What is the probability that at least two have the same birthday?

   Solution: The probability that no two have the same birthday is $\prod_{i=1}^{22}(1 - i/365)$ (note that the product stops at $i = 22$, not $i = 23$). Subtracting from 1 gives the probability that at least two have the same birthday:

In[1]:= **1 - Product[1. - i/365, {i, 22}]**

Out[1]= 0.507297

Note that we used 1. in the product instead of 1 without the decimal point. If we had omitted the decimal point, the product would have been evaluated as a rational number (try it, you'll see).

Example 2. Suppose a lazy phone company employee assigns telephone numbers by choosing random seven-digit numbers. In a town with 10000 phones, what is the probability that two people receive the same number?

In[2]:= **1 - Product[1. - i/10^7, {i, 9999}]**

Out[2]= 0.99327

Note that the number of phones is about three times the square root of the number of possibilities. This means that we expect the probability to be high, which it is. From Section 8.4, we have the estimate that if there are around $\sqrt{2(\ln 2)10^7} \approx 3723$ phones, there should be a 50% chance of a match. Let's see how accurate this is:

In[3]:= **1 - Product[1. - i/10^7, i, 3722]**

Out[3]= 0.499895

A.7 Examples for Chapter 10

Example 1. Suppose we have a (5, 8) Shamir secret sharing scheme. Everything is mod the prime $p = 987541$. Five of the shares are

$$(9853, 853), (4421, 4387), (6543, 1234), (93293, 78428), (12398, 7563).$$

Find the secret.

Solution: One way: First, find the Lagrange interpolating polynomial through the five points:

In[1]:=**InterpolatingPolynomial[{ {9853, 853 }, {4421, 4387 }, {6543, 1234 }, {93293, 78428 }, {12398, 7563 } }, x]**

$$\text{Out[1]= } 853 + (-\frac{1767}{2716} + (+\frac{2406987}{9538347560} + (-\frac{8464915920541}{3130587195363428640000}$$

$$-\frac{495900372013464054337547(-93293 + x)}{1337886415109948765948822226797600000})(-6543 + x))(-4421 + x))$$

$$(-9853 + x)$$

Now evaluate at $x = 0$ to find the constant term (use $/.x-> 0$ to evaluate at $x = 0$):

In[2]:=**%/. x -> 0**

$$\text{Out[2]= } \frac{204484326154044983230114592433944282591}{222981069184991460991470377799600000}$$

We need to change this to an integer mod 987541, so we find the multiplicative inverse of the denominator:

In[3]:=**PowerMod[Denominator[%], -1, 987541]**

Out[3]= 509495

Now, multiply times the numerator to get the desired integer:

In[4]:=**Mod[Numerator[%%]*%, 987541]**

Out[4]= 678987

Therefore 678987 is the secret.

Here is another way. Set up the matrix equations as in the text and then solve for the coefficients of the polynomial mod 987541:

In[5]:=**Solve[{{{1, 9853, 9853^2, 9853^3, 9853^4}, {1, 4421, 4421^2, 4421^3, 4421^4 }, {1, 6543, 6543^2, 6543^3, 6543^4}, {1, 93293, 93293^2, 93293^3, 93293^4}, {1, 12398, 12398^2, 12398^3, 12398^4 }}.{{s0}, {s1}, {s2}, {s3}, {s4}} == {{853}, {4387}, {1234}, {78428}, {7563}}, Modulus == 987541}, Mode -> Modular]**

Out[5]= { {Modulus -> 987541, s0 -> 678987, s1 -> 14728, s2 -> 1651, s3 -> 574413, s4 -> 456741 } }

The constant term is 678987, which is the secret.

A.8   Examples for Chapter 11

Example 1. Here is a game you can play. It is essentially the simplified version of poker over the telephone from Section 11.2. There are five cards: ten, jack, queen, king, ace. They are shuffled and disguised by raising their numbers to a random exponent mod the prime 24691313099. You are supposed to guess which one is the ace. To start, pick a random exponent. We use the semicolon after *khide* so that we cannot cheat and see what value of k is being used.

In[1]:= **k = khide;**

Now, shuffle the disguised cards (their numbers are raised to the kth power mod p):

In[2]:= **shuffle**

Out[2]= {14001090567, 16098641856, 23340023892, 20919427041, 7768690848}

These are the five cards. None looks like the ace; that's because their numbers have been raised to powers mod the prime. Make a guess anyway. Let's see if you're correct.

In[3]:= **reveal[%]**

Out[3]= {ten, ace, queen, jack, king}

Let's play again:

In[4]:= **k = khide;**

In[5]:= **shuffle**

Out[5]= {13015921305, 14788966861, 23855418969, 22566749952, 8361552666}

Make your guess (note that the numbers are different because a different random exponent was used). Were you lucky?

In[6]:= **reveal[%]**

Out[6]= {ten, queen, ace, king, jack}

Perhaps you need some help. Let's play one more time:

In[7]:= **k = khide;**

In[8]:= **shuffle**

Out[8]= {13471751030, 20108480083, 8636729758, 14735216549, 11884022059}

We now ask for advice:

In[9]:= **advise[%]**

Out[9]= 3

We are advised that the third card is the ace. Let's see (note that %% is used to refer to the next to last output):

In[10]:= **reveal[%%]**

Out[10]= {jack, ten, ace, queen, king}

How does this work? Read the part on "How to Cheat" in Section 11.2. Note that if we raise the numbers for the cards to the $(p-1)/2$ power mod p, we get

In[11]:= **PowerMod[{200514, 10010311, 1721050514, 11091407, 10305}, (24691313099 - 1)/ 2, 24691313099]**

Out[11]= {1, 1, 1, 1, 24691313098}

Therefore, only the ace is a quadratic nonresidue mod p.

A.9 Examples for Chapter 15

Example 1. All of the elliptic curves we work with in this chapter are elliptic curves mod n. However, it is helpful use the graphs of elliptic curves with real numbers in order to visualize what is happening with the addition law, for example, even though such pictures do not exist mod n. Therefore, let's graph the elliptic curve $y^2 = x(x-1)(x+1)$.

First, load a graphics package:

In[1]:=<<Graphics'ImplicitPlot'

To graph the curve, we'll specify that $-1 \le x \le 3$:

In[2]:=ImplicitPlot[y^2 == x*(x - 1)*(x + 1), {x, -1, 3 }]

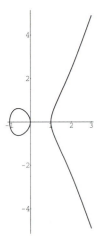

Graphics

Example 2. Add the points (1, 3) and (3, 5) on the elliptic curve $y^2 \equiv x^3 + 24x + 13 \pmod{29}$.

In[3]:=addell[{1, 3 }, {3, 5 }, 24, 13, 29]

Out[3]= {26, 1 }

You can check that the point (26, 1) is on the curve: $26^3 + 24 \cdot 26 + 13 \equiv 1^2 \pmod{29}$.

Example 3. Add (1, 3) to the point at infinity on the curve of the previous example.

In[4]:=addell[{1, 3 }, {"infinity", "infinity" }, 24, 13, 29]

Out[4]= {1, 3 }

As expected, adding the point at infinity to a point P returns the point P.

Example 4. Let $P = (1, 3)$ be a point on the elliptic curve $y^2 \equiv x^3 + 24x + 13 \pmod{29}$. Find $7P$.

In[5]:=multell[{1, 3 }, 7, 24, 13, 29]

Out[5]= {15, 6 }

Example 5. Find $k(1,3)$ for $k = 1, 2, 3, \ldots, 40$ on the curve of the previous example.

In[6]:=**multsell[{1, 3 }, 40, 24, 13, 29]**

Out[6]= {{1,3},{11,10},{23,28},{0,10},{19,7},{18,19},{15,6}, {20,24}, {4,12}, {4,17},{20,5},{15,23},{18,10},{19,22},{0,19}, {23,1}, {11,19},{1,26},{"infinity","infinity"},{1,3},{11,10}, {23,28},{0,10},{19,7}, {18,19},{15,6},{20,24},{4,12},{4,17}, {20,5},{15,23},{18,10},{19,22}, {0,19},{23,1},{11,19},{1,26}, {"infinity","infinity"},{1,3},{11,10}}

Notice how the points repeat after every 19 multiples.

Example 6. The previous four examples worked mod the prime 29. If we work mod a composite number, the situation at infinity becomes more complicated since we could be at infinity mod both factors or we could be at infinity mod one of the factors but not mod the other. Therefore, we stop the calculation if this last situation happens and we exhibit a factor. For example, let's try to compute $12P$, where $P = (1,3)$ is on the elliptic curve $y^2 \equiv x^3 - 5x + 13 \pmod{209}$:

In[7]:=**multell[{1, 3 }, 12, -5, 13, 11*19]**

Out[7]= {"factor=", 19 }

Now let's compute the successive multiples to see what happened along the way:

In[8]:=**multsell[{1, 3 }, 12, -5, 13, 11*19]**

Out[8]= {{1,3},{91,27},{118,133},{148,182},{20,35}, {"factor=", 19}}

When we computed $6P$, we ended up at infinity mod 19. Let's see what is happening mod the two prime factors of 209, namely 19 and 11:

In[9]:=**multsell[{1,3}, 12, -5, 13, 19]**

Out[9]= {{1,3},{15,8},{4,0},{15,11},{1,16}, {"infinity","infinity"}, {1,3},{15,8},{4,0},{15,11},{1,16}, {"infinity","infinity"}}

In[10]:=**multsell[{1, 3 }, 20, -5, 13, 11]**

Out[10]= {{1,3},{3,5},{8,1},{5,6},{9,2},{6,10},{2,0},{6,1}, {9,9}, {5,5},{8,10},{3,6},{1,8},{"infinity","infinity"},{1,3}, {3,5},{8,1},{5,6},{9,2},{6,10}}

After 6 steps, we were at infinity mod 19, but it takes 14 steps to reach infinity mod 11. To find $6P$, we needed to invert a number that was 0 mod

19 and nonzero mod 11. This couldn't be done, but it yielded the factor 19. This is the basis of the elliptic curve factorization method.

Example 7. Factor 193279 using elliptic curves.

Solution: First, we need to choose some random elliptic curves and a point on each curve. For example, let's take $P = (1, 2)$ and the elliptic curve

$$y^2 \equiv x^3 - 10x + b \pmod{193279}.$$

For P to lie on the curve, we take $b = 28$. We'll also take

$$
\begin{aligned}
y^2 &\equiv x^3 + 11x - 11, & P = (1, 1) \\
y^2 &\equiv x^3 + 17x - 14, & P = (1, 2).
\end{aligned}
$$

Now we compute multiples of the point P. We do the analog of the $p - 1$ method, so we choose a bound B, say $B = 12$, and compute $B!P$.

In[11]:= **multell[{2,4}, Factorial[12], -10, 28, 193279]**

Out[11]= {factor=, 347}

In[12]:= **multell[{1,1}, Factorial[12], 11, -11, 193279]**

Out[12]= {13862, 35249}

In[11]:= **multell[{1, 2}, Factorial[12], 17, -14, 193279]**

Out[11]= {factor=, 557}

Let's analyze in more detail what happened in these examples.

On the first curve, $266P$ ends up at infinity mod 557 and $35P$ is infinity mod 347. Since $266 = 2 \cdot 7 \cdot 19$, it has a prime factor larger than $B = 12$, so $B!P$ is not infinity mod 557. But 35 divides $B!$, so $B!P$ is infinity mod 347.

On the second curve, $356P = $ infinity mod 347 and $561P = $ infinity mod 557. Since $356 = 4 \cdot 89$ and $561 = 3 \cdot 11 \cdot 17$, we don't expect to find the factorization with this curve.

The third curve is a surprise. We have $331P = $ infinity mod 347 and $272P = $ infinity mod 557. Since 331 is prime and $272 = 16 \cdot 17$, we don't expect to find the factorization with this curve. However, by chance, an intermediate step in the calculation of $B!P$ yielded the factorization. Here's what happened. At one step, the program required adding the points (184993, 13462) and (20678, 150484). These two points are congruent mod 557 but not mod 347. Therefore, the slope of the line through these two points is defined mod 347 but is 0/0 mod 557. When we tried to find the multiplicative inverse of the denominator mod 193279, the gcd algorithm yielded the factor 557. This phenomenon is fairly rare.

Example 8. Here is how to produce the example of an elliptic curve ElGamal cryptosystem from Section 15.5. For more details, see the text. The elliptic curve is $y^2 \equiv x^3 + 3x + 45 \pmod{8831}$ and the point is $G = (4, 11)$. Alice's message is the point $P_m = (5, 1743)$.

Bob has chosen his secret random number $a_B = 3$ and has computed $a_b G$:

In[15]:=**multell[{4, 11}, 3, 3, 45, 8831]**

Out[15]= {413, 1808}

Bob publishes this point. Alice chooses the random number $k = 8$ and computes kG and $P_m + k(a_B G)$:

In[16]:=**multell[{4, 11}, 8, 3, 45, 8831]**

Out[16]= {5415, 6321}

In[17]:=**addell[{5, 1743}, multell[{413, 1808}, 8, 3, 45, 8831], 3, 45, 8831]**

Out[17]= {6626, 3576}

Alice sends (5415,6321) and (6626, 3576) to Bob, who multiplies the first of these point by a_B:

In[18]:=**multell[{5415, 6321}, 3, 3, 45, 8831]**

Out[18]= {673, 146}

Bob then subtracts the result from the last point Alice sends him. Note that he subtracts by adding the point with the second coordinate negated:

In[19]:=**addell[{6626, 3576}, {673, -146}, 3, 45, 8831]**

Out[19]= {5, 1743}

Bob has therefore received Alice's message.

Example 9. Let's reproduce the numbers in the example of a Diffie-Hellman key exchange from Section 15.5: The elliptic curve is $y^2 \equiv x^3 + x + 7206 \pmod{7211}$ and the point is $G = (3, 5)$. Alice chooses her secret $N_A = 12$ and Bob chooses his secret $N_B = 23$. Alice calculates

In[20]:=**multell[{3, 5}, 12, 1, 7206, 7211]**

Out[20]= {1794, 6375}

She sends (1794,6375) to Bob. Meanwhile, Bob calculates

In[21]:=**multell[{3, 5}, 23, 1, 7206, 7211]**

Out[21]= {3861, 1242}

and sends (3861,1242) to Alice. Alice multiplies what she receives by N_A and Bob multiplies what he receives by N_B:

In[22]:=**multell[{3861, 1242}, 12, 1, 7206, 7211]**

Out[22]= {1472, 2098}

In[23]:=**multell[{1794, 6375}, 23, 1, 7206, 7211]**

Out[23]= {1472, 2098}

Therefore, Alice and Bob have produced the same key.

Appendix B

Maple Examples

These computer examples are written in Maple. If you have Maple available, you should try some of them on your computer. If Maple is not available, it is still possible to read the examples. They provide examples for several of the concepts of this book. For information on getting started with Maple, see Section B.1. To download a Maple notebook that contains the necessary commands, go to

http://www.prenhall.com/washington

B.1   Getting Started with Maple

1. Download the Maple notebook math.mws that you find using the links starting at *http://www.prenhall.com/washington*

2. Open Maple (on a Unix machine, use the command `xmaple`; on most other systems, click on the Maple icon)), then open math.mws using the menu options under File on the command bar at the top of the Maple window. (Perhaps this is done automatically when you download it; it depends on your computer settings.)

3. With math.mws in the foreground, press the Enter or Return key on your keyboard. This will load the functions and packages needed for the following examples. Ignore any warning messages about names being redefined.

4. Go to the command bar at the top and click on File. Move the arrow down to New and click. A new notebook will appear on top of math.mws. However, all the commands of math.mws will still be working.

5. To give the new notebook a name, use the File command and scroll down to Save As.... Then save under some name with a .mws at the end.

6. You are now ready to use Maple. If you want to try something easy, type 1+2*3+4ˆ5; (don't forget the semicolon) and then press the Return/Enter key. The result 1031 should appear (it's $1 + 2 \cdot 3 + 4^5$).

7. Go to the Computer Examples in Section B.3. Try typing in some of the commands there. The outputs should be the same as those in the examples. Note that all commands end with a semicolon (alternatively, you can use a colon to suppress the output). Press the Return or Enter key to make Maple evaluate an expression.

8. If you want to delete part of your notebook, move the arrow to the black line at the left edge of the window and double click with the left button. The highlighted part can be deleted by pressing the Back Space key or by clicking on Edit on the top command bar then clicking on Cut on the menu that appears.

9. Save your notebook by clicking on File on the command bar, then clicking on Save on the menu that appears.

10. Print your notebook by clicking on File on the command bar, then clicking on Print on the menu that appears. (You will see the advantage of opening a new notebook in Step 4; if you didn't open one, then all the commands in math.mws will also be printed.)

11. If you make a mistake in typing in a command and get an error message, you can edit the command and hit Return or Enter to try again. You don't need to retype everything.

12. Look at the commands available through the command bar at the top. For example, Options, then Output Display, allows you to change the output format. In the examples, we have used the Standard Math Notation option.

13. If you are looking for help or a command to do something, try the Help menu on the command bar at the top. If you can guess the name of a function, there is another way. For example, to obtain information on gcd, type ?gcd (no semicolon) and Return or Enter.

B.2   Some Commands

The following are some Maple commands that are used in the examples. Some, such as phi, are built into Maple. Others, such as addell, are in the Maple notebook available at *http://www.prenhall.com/washington*

Each command is followed by a semicolon. If you want to suppress the output, use a colon instead.

The argument of a function is enclosed in round parentheses. Vectors are enclosed in square brackets. Entering `matrix(m,n,[a,b,c,...,z])` gives the $m \times n$ matrix with first row `a,b`, ... and last row `...z`. To multiply two matrices A and B, type `evalm(A&*B)`.

If you want to refer to the previous output, use %. The next to last output is %%, etc. Note that % refers to the most recent output, not to the last displayed line. If you will be referring to an output frequently, it might be better to name it. For example, `g:=phi(12345)` defines `g` to be the value of $\phi(12345)$. Note that when you are assigning a value to a variable in this way, you should use a colon before the equality sign. Leaving out the colon is a common cause of hard-to-find errors.

Exponentiation is written as `a^b`. However, we will need to use modular exponentiation with very large exponents. In that case, use `a&^b mod n`.

Some of the following commands require certain Maple packages to be loaded via the commands

`with(numtheory), with(linalg), with(plots), with(combinat)`

These are loaded when the math.mws notebook is loaded. However, if you want to use a command such as `nextprime` without loading the notebook, first type `with(numtheory):` to load the package (once for the whole session). Then you can use functions such as `nextprime`, `isprime`, etc. If you type `with(numtheory);` with a semicolon, you'll get a list of the functions in the package, too.

The following are some of the commands used in the examples. We list them here for easy reference. To see how to use them, look at the examples. We have used `txt` to refer to a string of letters. Such strings should be enclosed in quotes ("string").

`addell([x,y], [u,v], a, b, n)` finds the sum of the points (x,y) and (u,v) on the elliptic curve $y^2 \equiv x^3 + ax + b \pmod{n}$. The integer n should be odd.

`affinecrypt(txt,m,n)` is the affine encryption of `txt` using $mx + n$.

`allshifts(txt)` gives all 26 shifts of `txt`.

`chrem([a,b,...], [m,n,...])` gives a solution to the simultaneous congruences $x \equiv a \pmod{m}, x \equiv b \pmod{n}, \ldots$.

`choose(txt,m,n)` lists the characters in `txt` in positions congruent to n $\pmod{m}$.

`coinc(txt,n)` is the number of matches between `txt` and `txt` shifted by n.

`corr(v)` is the dot product of the vector v with the 26 shifts of the alphabet frequency vector.

`phi(n)` computes $\phi(n)$ (don't try very large values of n).

`igcdex(m,n,'x','y')` computes the gcd of m and n along with a solution of $mx + ny = \gcd$. To get x and y, type `x;y;` on this or a subsequent command line.

`ifactor(n)` factors n.

`frequency(txt)` lists the number of occurrences of each letter a through z in txt.

`gcd(m,n)` is the gcd of m and n.

`inverse(M)` finds the inverse of the matrix M.

`lfsr(c,k,n)` gives the sequence of n bits produced by the recurrence that has coefficients given by the vector c. The initial values of the bits are given by the vector k.

`lfsrlength(v,n)` tests the vector v of bits to see if it is generated by a recurrence of length at most n.

`lfsrsolve(v,n)` computes the coefficients of a recurrence, given a guess n for the length of the recurrence that generates the binary vector v.

`max(v)` is the largest element of the list v.

`a mod n` is the value of $a \pmod{n}$.

`multell([x,y], m, a, b, n)` computes m times the point (x, y) on the elliptic curve $y^2 \equiv x^3 + ax + b \pmod{n}$.

`multsell([x,y], m, a, b, n)` lists the first m multiples of the point (x, y) on the elliptic curve $y^2 \equiv x^3 + ax + b \pmod{n}$.

`nextprime(x)` gives the next prime $> x$.

`num2text(n)` changes a number n to letters. The successive pairs of digits must each be at most 26; *space* is 00, a is 01, z is 26.

`primroot(p)` finds a primitive root for the prime p.

`shift(txt,n)` shifts txt by n.

`text2num(txt)` changes txt to numbers, with space=00, a=01, ..., z=25.

`vigenere(txt,v)` gives the Vigenère encryption of txt using the vector v as the key.

`vigvec(txt,m,n)` gives the frequencies of the letters a through z in positions congruent to $n \pmod{m}$.

B.3 Examples for Chapter 2

Example 1. A shift cipher was used to obtain the ciphertext kddkmu. Decrypt it by trying all possibilities.

```
> allshifts("kddkmu");
```

```
"kddkmu"
"leelnv"
"mffmow"
"nggnpx"
"ohhoqy"
"piiprz"
"qjjqsa"
"rkkrtb"
"sllsuc"
"tmmtvd"
"unnuwe"
"voovxf"
"wppwyg"
"xqqxzh"
"yrryai"
"zsszbj"
"attack"
"buubdl"
"cvvcem"
"dwwdfn"
"exxego"
"fyyfhp"
"gzzgiq"
"haahjr"
"ibbiks"
"jccjlt"
```

As you can see, `attack` is the only word that occurs on this list, so that was the plaintext.

Example 2. Encrypt the plaintext message `cleopatra` using the affine function $7x + 8$:

```
> affinecrypt("cleopatra", 7, 8);
```

$$\text{"whkcjilxi"}$$

Example 3. The ciphertext `mzdvezc` was encrypted using the affine function $5x + 12$. Decrypt it.

   Solution: First, solve $y \equiv 5x + 12 \pmod{26}$ for x to obtain $x \equiv 5^{-1}(y - 12)$. We need to find the inverse of 5 (mod 26):

```
> 5&^(-1) mod 26;
```

$$21$$

Therefore, $x \equiv 21(y - 12) \equiv 21y - 12 \cdot 21$. To change $-12 \cdot 21$ to standard form:

```
> -12*21 mod 26;
```

$$8$$

Therefore, the decryption function is $x \equiv 21y + 8$. To decrypt the message:

```
> affinecrypt("mzdvezc", 21, 8);
```

$$\texttt{"anthony"}$$

In case you were wondering, the plaintext was encrypted as follows:

```
> affinecrypt("anthony", 5, 12);
```

$$\texttt{"mzdvezc"}$$

Example 4. Here is the example of a Vigenère cipher from the text. Let's see how to produce the data that was used in Section 2.3 to decrypt it. For convenience, we've already stored the ciphertext under the name vvhq.

```
> vvhq;
```

```
vvhqwvvrhmusgjgthkihtssejchlsfcbgvwcrlryqtfsvgahwkcuhwauglq
hnslrljshbltspisprdxljsveeghlqwkasskuwepwqtwvspgoelkcqyfnsv
wljsniqkgnrgybwlwgoviokhkazkqkxzgyhcecmeiujoqkwfwvefqhkijrc
lrlkbienqfrjljsdhgrhlsfqtwlauqrhwdmwlgusgikkflryvcwvspgpmlk
assjvoqxeggveyggzmljcxxljsvpaivwikvrdrygfrjljslveggveyggeia
puuisfpbtgnwwmuczrvtwglrwugumnczvile
```

Find the frequencies of the letters in the ciphertext:

```
> frequency(vvhq);
```

```
[ 8, 5, 12, 4, 15, 10, 27, 16, 13, 14, 17, 25, 7, 7, 5, 9, 14,
      17, 24, 8, 12, 22, 22, 5, 8, 5]
```

Let's compute the coincidences for shifts of 1, 2, 3, 4, 5, 6:

```
> coinc(vvhq,1);
```

$$14$$

```
> coinc(vvhq,2);
```

$$14$$

```
> coinc(vvhq,3);
```

$$16$$

```
> coinc(vvhq,4);
```

$$14$$

```
> coinc(vvhq,5);
```

$$24$$

```
> coinc(vvhq,6);
```

$$12$$

We conclude that the key length is probably 5. Let's look at the 1st, 6th, 11th, ... letters (namely, the letters in positions congruent to 1 mod 5):

```
> choose(vvhq, 5, 1);
```

"vvuttcccqgcunjtpjgkuqpknjkygkkgcjfqrkqjrqudukvpkvggjjivgjggp
fncwuce"

```
> frequency(%);
```

[0, 0, 7, 1, 1, 2, 9, 0, 1, 8, 8, 0, 0, 3, 0, 4, 5, 2, 0, 3,
6, 5, 1, 0, 1, 0]

To express this as a vector of frequencies:

```
> vigvec(vvhq, 5, 1);
```

[0., 0., .1044776119, .01492537313, .01492537313,
.02985074627, .1343283582, 0., .01492537313, .1194029851,
.1194029851, 0., 0., .04477611940, 0., .05970149254,
.07462686567, .02985074627, 0., .04477611940, .08955223881,
.07462686567, .01492537313, 0., .01492537313, 0.]

The dot products of this vector with the shifts of the alphabet frequency vector are computed as follows:

```
> corr(%);
```

```
    .02501492539,  .03910447762,  .07132835821,  .03882089552,
    .02749253732,  .03801492538,  .05120895523,  .03014925374,
    .03247761194,  .04302985074,  .03377611940,  .02985074628,
    .03426865672,  .04456716420,  .03555223882,  .04022388058,
    .04343283582,  .05017910450,  .03917910447,  .02958208957,
    .03262686569,  .03917910448,  .03655223881,  .03161194031,
    .04883582088,  .03494029848
```

The third entry is the maximum, but sometimes the largest entry is hard to locate. One way to find it is

```
> max(%);
```

$$.07132835821$$

Now it is easy to look through the list and find this number (it usually occurs only once). Since it occurs in the third position, the first shift for this Vigenère cipher is by 2, corresponding to the letter c. A procedure similar to the one just used (using `vigvec(vvhq, 5,2),...`, `vigvec(vvhq,5,5)`) shows that the other shifts are probably 14, 3, 4, 18. Let's check that we have the correct key by decrypting.

```
> vigenere(vvhq, -[2, 14, 3, 4, 18]);
```

```
    themethodusedforthepreparationandreadingofcodemessagesissim
    pleintheextremeandatthesametimeimpossibleoftranslationunles
    sthekeyisknowntheeasewithwhichthekeymaybechangedisanotherpo
    intinfavoroftheadoptionofthiscodebythosedesiringtotransmiti
    mportantmessageswithouttheslightestdangeroftheirmessagesbei
    ngreadbypoliticalorbusinessrivalsetc
```

For the record, the plaintext was originally encrypted by the command

```
> vigenere(%, [2, 14, 3, 4, 18]);
```

```
    vvhqwvvrhmusgjgthkihtssejchlsfcbgvwcrlryqtfsvgahwkcuhwauglq
    hnslrljshbltspisprdxljsveeghlqwkasskuwepwqtwvspgoelkcqyfnsv
    wljsniqkgnrgybwlwgoviokhkazkqkxzgyhcecmeiujoqkwfwvefqhkijrc
    lrlkbienqfrjljsdhgrhlsfqtwlauqrhwdmwlgusgikkflryvcwvspgpmlk
    assjvoqxeggveyggzmljcxxljsvpaivwikvrdrygfrjljslveggveyggeia
    puuisfpbtgnwwmuczrvtwglrwugumnczvile
```

Example 5. The ciphertext

$$22, 09, 00, 12, 03, 01, 10, 03, 04, 08, 01, 17$$

was encrypted using a Hill cipher with matrix

$$\begin{pmatrix} 1 & 2 & 3 \\ 4 & 5 & 6 \\ 7 & 8 & 10 \end{pmatrix}.$$

Decrypt it.

Solution: There are several ways to input a matrix. One way is the following. A 2×2 matrix $\begin{pmatrix} a & b \\ c & d \end{pmatrix}$ can be entered as `matrix(2,2,[a,b,c,d])`. Type `evalm(M&*N)` to multiply matrices M and N. Type `evalm(v&*M)` to multiply a vector v on the right by a matrix M.

Here is the encryption matrix.

```
> M:=matrix(3,3,[1,2,3,4,5,6,7,8,10]);
```

$$\begin{bmatrix} 1 & 2 & 3 \\ 4 & 5 & 6 \\ 7 & 8 & 10 \end{bmatrix}$$

We need to invert the matrix mod 26:

```
> invM:=map(x->x mod 26, inverse(M));
```

$$\begin{bmatrix} 8 & 16 & 1 \\ 8 & 21 & 24 \\ 1 & 24 & 1 \end{bmatrix}$$

The command `map(x->x mod 26, E)` takes each number in an expression E and reduces it mod 26.

This is the inverse of the matrix mod 26. We can check this as follows:

```
> M&*invM;
```

$$\begin{bmatrix} 27 & 130 & 52 \\ 78 & 313 & 130 \\ 130 & 520 & 209 \end{bmatrix}$$

```
> map(x->x mod 26, %);
```

$$\begin{bmatrix} 1 & 0 & 0 \\ 0 & 1 & 0 \\ 0 & 0 & 1 \end{bmatrix}$$

To decrypt, we break the ciphertext into blocks of three numbers and multiply each block on the right by the inverse matrix we just calculated:

```
> map(x->x mod 26, evalm([22,09,00]&*invM));
```

$$[14, \ 21, \ 4]$$

```
> map(x->x mod 26, evalm([12,03,01]&*invM26));
```

$$[17, \ 19, \ 7]$$

```
> map(x->x mod 26, evalm([10,03,04]&*invM26));
```

$$[4, \ 7, \ 8]$$

```
> map(x->x mod 26, evalm([08,01,17]&*invM26));
```

$$[11, \ 11, \ 23]$$

Therefore, the plaintext is 14, 21, 4, 17, 19, 7, 4, 7, 8, 11, 11, 23. Changing this back to letters, we obtain **overthehillx**. Note that the final x was appended to the plaintext in order to complete a block of three letters.

Example 6. Compute the first 50 terms of the recurrence

$$x_{n+5} \equiv x_n + x_{n+2} \pmod 2.$$

The initial values are $0, 1, 0, 0, 0$.

Solution: The vector of coefficients is $[1, 0, 1, 0, 0]$. The initial vector is $[0, 1, 0, 0, 0]$. Type

```
> lfsr([1, 0, 1, 0, 0], [0, 1, 0, 0, 0], 50);
[0, 1, 0, 0, 0, 0, 1, 0, 0, 1, 0, 1, 1, 0, 0, 1, 1, 1, 1, 1,
0, 0, 0, 1, 1, 0, 1, 1, 1, 0, 1, 0, 1, 0, 0, 0, 0, 1, 0, 0, 1,
0, 1, 1, 0, 0, 1, 1, 1, 1]
```

Example 7. Suppose the first 20 terms of an LFSR sequence are 1, 0, 1, 0, 1, 1, 1, 0, 0, 0, 0, 1, 1, 1, 0, 1, 0, 1, 0, 1. Find a recurrence that generates this sequence.

Solution: First, we find the length of the recurrence. The command lfsrlength(v, n) calculates the determinants mod 2 of the first n matrices that appear in the procedure in Section 2.11:

```
> lfsrlength([1, 0, 1, 0, 1, 1, 1, 0, 0, 0, 0, 1, 1, 1, 0, 1,
0, 1, 0, 1], 10);
```

$$[1, 1]$$
$$[2, 1]$$
$$[3, 0]$$
$$[4, 1]$$
$$[5, 0]$$
$$[6, 1]$$
$$[7, 0]$$
$$[8, 0]$$
$$[9, 0]$$
$$[10, 0]$$

The last nonzero determinant is the sixth one, so we guess that the recurrence has length 6. To find the coefficients:

```
> lfsrsolve([1, 0, 1, 0, 1, 1, 1, 0, 0, 0, 0, 1, 1, 1, 0, 1,
0, 1, 0, 1], 6);
```

$$[1, 0, 1, 1, 1, 0]$$

This gives the recurrence as

$$x_{n+6} \equiv x_n + x_{n+2} + x_{n+3} + x_{n+4} \pmod 2.$$

Example 8. The ciphertext 0, 1, 1, 0, 1, 0, 1, 0, 1, 0, 0, 1, 1, 0, 0, 0, 1, 0, 1, 0, 1, 0, 1, 0, 1, 0, 1, 0, 1, 0, 0, 1, 0, 0, 0, 1, 0, 1, 1, 0 was produced by adding the output of a LFSR onto the plaintext mod 2 (i.e., XOR the plaintext with the LFSR output). Suppose you know that the plaintext starts 1, 1, 1, 1, 1, 1, 0, 0, 0, 0, 0, 0, 1, 1, 1, 0, 0. Find the rest of the plaintext.

Solution: XOR the ciphertext with the known part of the plaintext to obtain the beginning of the LFSR output:

```
> [1, 1, 1, 1, 1, 1, 0, 0, 0, 0, 0, 0, 1, 1, 1, 0, 0]
  + [0, 1, 1, 0, 1, 0, 1, 0, 1, 0, 0, 1, 1, 0, 0, 0, 1] mod 2;
```

$$[1, 0, 0, 1, 0, 1, 1, 0, 1, 0, 0, 1, 0, 1, 1, 0, 1]$$

This is the beginning of the LFSR output. Now let's find the length of the recurrence.

```
> lfsrlength(%, 8);
```

$$[1, 1]$$
$$[2, 0]$$
$$[3, 1]$$
$$[4, 0]$$
$$[5, 1]$$
$$[6, 0]$$
$$[7, 0]$$
$$[8, 0]$$

We guess the length is 5. To find the coefficients of the recurrence:

```
> lfsrsolve(%%, 5);
```

$$[1, 1, 0, 0, 1]$$

Now we can generate the full output of the LFSR using the coefficients we just found plus the first five terms of the LFSR output:

```
> lfsr([1, 1, 0, 0, 1], [1, 0, 0, 1, 0], 40);
```

```
[1, 0, 0, 1, 0, 1, 1, 0, 1, 0, 0, 1, 0, 1, 1, 0, 1, 0, 0, 1,
0, 1, 1, 0, 1, 0, 0, 1, 0, 1, 1, 0, 1, 0, 0, 1, 0, 1, 1, 0]
```

When we XOR the LFSR output with the ciphertext, we get back the plaintext:

```
> % + [0, 1, 1, 0, 1, 0, 1, 0, 1, 0, 0, 1, 1, 0, 0, 0, 1, 0, 1,
0, 1, 0, 1, 0, 1, 0, 1, 0, 0, 1, 0, 0, 0, 1, 0, 1, 1, 0]
mod 2;
```

```
[1, 1, 1, 1, 1, 1, 0, 0, 0, 0, 0, 0, 1, 1, 1, 0, 0, 0, 1, 1,
1, 1, 0, 0, 0, 0, 1, 1, 1, 1, 1, 1, 1, 0, 0, 0, 0, 0, 0, 0]
```

This is the plaintext.

B.4   Examples for Chapter 3

Example 1. Find gcd(23456, 987654).

```
> gcd(23456, 987654);
```

$$2$$

Example 2. Solve $23456x + 987654y = 2$ in integers x, y.

```
igcdex(23456, 987654,'x','y');
```

$$2$$

```
> x;y;
```

$$-3158$$
$$75$$

This means that 2 is the gcd and $23456 \cdot (-3158) + 987654 \cdot 75 = 2$. (The command `igcdex` is for *integer gcd extended*. Maple also calculates gcd's for polynomials.) Variable names other than `'x'` and `'y'` can be used if these letters are going to be used elsewhere, for example, in a polynomial. We can also clear the value of x as follows:

```
> x:='x';
```

$$x:=x$$

Example 3. Compute $234 \cdot 456 \pmod{789}$.

```
> 234*456 mod 789;
```

$$189$$

Example 4. Compute $234567^{876543} \pmod{565656565}$.

```
> 234567&^876543 mod 565656565;
```

$$473011223$$

Example 5. Find the multiplicative inverse of $87878787 \pmod{9191919191}$.

```
> 87878787&^(-1) mod 9191919191;
```

$$7079995354$$

Example 6. Solve $7654x \equiv 2389 \pmod{65537}$.

Solution: Here is one way.

```
> solve(7654*x=2389,x) mod 65537;
```

$$43626$$

Here is another way.

```
> 2389/7654 mod 65537;
```

$$43626$$

Example 7. Find x with

$$x \equiv 2 \pmod{78}, \quad x \equiv 5 \pmod{97}, \quad x \equiv 1 \pmod{119}.$$

```
> chrem([2, 5, 1],[78, 97, 119]);
```

$$647480$$

We can check the answer:

```
> 647480 mod 78; 647480 mod 97; 647480 mod 119;
```

$$2$$
$$5$$
$$1$$

Example 8. Factor 123450 into primes.

```
> ifactor(123450);
```

$$(2)(3)(5)^2(823)$$

This means that $123450 = 2^1 3^1 5^2 823^1$.

Example 9. Evaluate $\phi(12345)$.

```
> phi(12345);
```

$$6576$$

Example 10. Find a primitive root for the prime 65537.

```
> primroot(65537);
```

$$3$$

Therefore, 3 is a primitive root for 65537.

Example 11. Find the inverse of the matrix $\begin{pmatrix} 13 & 12 & 35 \\ 41 & 53 & 62 \\ 71 & 68 & 10 \end{pmatrix}$ (mod 999).

Solution: First, invert the matrix without the mod, and then reduce the matrix mod 999:

```
> inverse(matrix(3,3,[13, 12, 35, 41, 53, 62, 71, 68, 10]));
```

$$\begin{bmatrix} \dfrac{3686}{34139} & -\dfrac{2260}{34139} & \dfrac{1111}{34139} \\[2mm] -\dfrac{3992}{34139} & \dfrac{2355}{34139} & -\dfrac{629}{34139} \\[2mm] \dfrac{975}{34139} & \dfrac{32}{34139} & -\dfrac{197}{34139} \end{bmatrix}$$

```
> map(x->x mod 999, %);
```

$$\begin{bmatrix} 772 & 472 & 965 \\ 641 & 516 & 851 \\ 150 & 133 & 149 \end{bmatrix}$$

This is the inverse matrix mod 999.

Example 12. Find a square root of 26951623672 mod the prime $p = 98573007539$.

Solution: Since $p \equiv 3 \pmod 4$, we can use the proposition of Section 3.9:

```
> 26951623672&^((98573007539 + 1)/4) mod 98573007539;
```

$$98338017685$$

The extra parentheses in the exponent are necessary; otherwise, the exponent would be taken as $98573007539 + 1$, and the result divided by 4. The other square root is minus the preceding one:

```
> -% mod 98573007539;
```

234989854

Example 13. Let $n = 34222273 = 9803 \cdot 3491$. Find all four solutions of $x^2 \equiv 19101358 \pmod{34222273}$.

Solution: First, find a square root mod each of the two prime factors, both of which are congruent to 3 (mod 4):

```
> 19101358&^((9803 + 1)/4) mod 9803;
```

3998

```
> 19101358&^((3491 + 1)/4) mod 3491;
```

1318

Therefore, the square roots are congruent to ± 3998 (mod 9803) and ± 1318 (mod 3491). There are four ways to combine these using the Chinese remainder theorem:

```
> chrem([3998, 1318],[9803, 3491]);
```

43210

```
> chrem([-3998, 1318],[9803, 3491]);
```

8397173

```
> chrem([3998, -1318],[9803, 3491]);
```

25825100

```
> chrem([-3998, -1318],[9803, 3491]);
```

34179063

These are the four desired square roots.

B.5   Examples for Chapter 6

Example 1. Suppose you need to find a large random prime of 50 digits. Here is one way. The function `nextprime` finds the next prime greater than x. The function `rand(a..b)()` gives a random integer between a and b. Combining these, we can find a prime:

```
> nextprime(rand(10^49..10^50]]());
```

        73050570031667109175215303340488313456708913284291

If we repeat this procedure, we should get another prime:

```
> nextprime(rand(10^49..10^50]]());
```

        97476407694931303255724326040586144145341054568331

Example 2. Suppose you want to change the text *hellohowareyou* to numbers:

```
> text2num("hellohowareyou");
```

            805121215081523011805251521

Note that we are now using $a = 1$, $b = 2$, ..., $z = 26$, since otherwise a's at the beginnings of messages would disappear. (A more efficient procedure would be to work in base 27, so the numerical form of the message would be $8 + 5 \cdot 27 + 12 \cdot 27^2 + \cdots + 21 \cdot 27^{13} = 87495221502384554951$. Note that this uses fewer digits.)

Now suppose you want to change it back to letters:

```
> num2text(805121215081523011805251521);
```

            "hellohowareyou"

Example 3. Encrypt the message `hi` using RSA with $n = 823091$ and $e = 17$.

Solution: First, change the message to numbers:

```
> text2num("hi");
```

Now, raise it to the *e*th power mod *n*:

```
> %&^17 mod 823091;
```

$$596912$$

Example 4. Decrypt the ciphertext in the previous problem.

Solution: First, we need to find the decryption exponent *d*. To do this, we need to find $\phi(823091)$. One way is

```
> phi(823091);
```

$$821184$$

Another way is to factor *n* as $p \cdot q$ and then compute $(p - 1)(q - 1)$:

```
> ifactor(823091);
```

$$(659)(1249)$$

```
> 658*1248
```

$$821184$$

Since $de \equiv 1 \pmod{\phi(n)}$, we compute the following (note that we are finding the inverse of *e* mod $\phi(n)$, not mod *n*):

```
> 17&^(-1) mod 821184;
```

$$48305$$

Therefore, $d = 48305$. To decrypt, raise the ciphertext to the *d*th power mod *n*:

```
> 596912&^48305 mod 823091;
```

$$809$$

Finally, change back to letters:

```
> num2text(809);
```

$$\texttt{"hi"}$$

Example 5. Encrypt `hellohowareyou` using RSA with $n = 823091$ and $e = 17$.

Solution: First, change the plaintext to numbers:

```
> text2num("hellohowareyou");
```

$$805121215081523011805251521$$

Suppose we simply raised this to the *e*th power mod *n*:

```
> %&^17 mod 823091);
```

$$447613$$

If we decrypt (we know *d* from Example 4), we obtain

```
> %&^48305 mod 823091;
```

$$628883$$

This is not the original plaintext. The reason is that the plaintext is larger than *n*, so we have obtained the plaintext mod *n*:

```
> 805121215081523011805251521 mod 823091;
```

$$628883$$

We need to break the plaintext into blocks, each less than *n*. In our case, we use three letters at a time:

$$80512 \quad 121508 \quad 152301 \quad 180525 \quad 1521$$

```
> 80512&^17 mod 823091;
```

$$757396$$

```
> 121508&^17 mod 823091;
```

$$164513$$

```
> 152301&^17 mod 823091;
```

121217

```
> 180525&^17 mod 823091;
```

594220

```
> 1521&^17 mod 823091;
```

442163

The ciphertext is therefore 757396164513121217594220442163. Note that there is no reason to change this back to letters. In fact, it doesn't correspond to any text with letters.

Decrypt each block individually:

```
> 757396&^48305 mod 823091;
```

80512

```
> 164513&^48305 mod 823091;
```

121508

etc.

We'll now do some examples with large numbers, namely the numbers in the RSA Challenge discussed in Section 6.5. These are stored under the names *rsan, rsae, rsap, rsaq*:

```
> rsan;
```

11438162575788886766923577997614661201021829672124236256256186
42935706935245733897830597123563958705058989075147599290026879
543541

```
> rsae;
```

9007

Example 6. Encrypt each of the messages `b`, `ba`, `bar`, `bard` using *rsan* and *rsae*.

```
> text2num("b")&^rsae mod rsan;
```
7094675846761266859837016499155078618287633106068523541056470
4114486782261716497200122155332348462014053287987580899263765
142534

```
> text2num("ba")&^rsae mod rsan;
```
3504513060897510032501170944987195427378820475394859306031369
7698227621759806027962270538031565564773352033671782261305796
158951

```
> text2num("bar")&^rsae mod rsan;
```
4481451286385510107600453085949210934242953160660740907036054
3408000843645986880405953102818312822586362580298784441151922
606424

```
> text2num("bard")&^rsae mod rsan;
```
2423807778511166642320286251209031739348521295905627078313499
1614256054323297179804928958073445752663026449873986877989329
909498

Observe that the ciphertexts are all the same length. There seems to be no easy way to determine the length of the corresponding plaintext.

Example 7. Using the factorization *rsan=rsap·rsaq*, find the decryption exponent for the RSA Challenge, and decrypt the ciphertext (see Section 6.5).

First we find the decryption exponent:

```
> rsad:=rsae&^(-1) mod((rsap-1)*(rsaq-1)):
```

Note that we use the final colon to avoid printing out the value. If you want to see the value of *rsad*, see Section 6.5, or don't use the semicolon. To decrypt the ciphertext, which is stored as *rsaci*, and change to letters:

```
> num2text(rsaci&^rsad mod rsan);
```

```
                "the magic words are squeamish ossifrage"
```

Example 8. Encrypt the message `rsaencryptsmessageswell` using *rsan* and *rsae*.

```
> text2num("rsaencryptsmessageswell")&^rsae mod rsan;
```

9463942034900225931630582353924949641464096993400170972140435
2418271950654254365584906013966328817753539283112653197553130
781884

Example 9. Decrypt the preceding ciphertext.

Solution: Fortunately, we know the decryption exponent *rsad*. Therefore, we compute

```
> %&^rsad mod rsan;
```

18190105140318251620191305191901070510051923051212

```
> num2text(%);
```

"rsaencryptsmessageswell"

Suppose we lose the final digit 4 of the ciphertext in transmission. Let's try
to decrypt what's left (subtracting 4 and dividing by 10 is a mathematical
way to remove the 4):

```
> (%%% - 4)/10)&^rsad mod rsan;
```

47952999173195988664902352629525486409113633894375629846854900
79705884123003734879696577942541171589569212679126284614944750
682806

If we try to change this to letters, we get a long error message. A small
error in the plaintext completely changes the decrypted message and usually
produces garbage.

Example 10. Suppose we are told that $n = 11313771275590312567$ is the
product of two primes and that $\phi(n) = 11313771187608744400$. Factor n.

Solution: We know (see Section 6.1) that p and q are the roots of $X^2 -
(n - \phi(n) + 1)X + n$. Therefore, we compute

```
> solve(x^2 -
(11313771275590312567 - 11313771187608744400 + 1)*x +
11313771275590312567, x);
```

87852787151, 128781017

Therefore, $n = 128781017 \cdot 87852787151$. We also could have used the
quadratic formula to find the roots.

Example 11. Suppose we know *rsae* and *rsad*. Use these to factor *rsan*.

Solution: We use the universal exponent factorization method from Section 6.4. First write $rsae \cdot rsad - 1 = 2^s m$ with m odd. One way to do this is first to compute $rsae \cdot rsad - 1$, and then keep dividing by 2 until you get an odd number:

```
> rsae*rsad - 1;
```

96103441961778226615691902335958383410985412905187833025064460
40411559855750873526591561748985573429951315946804310869212458
30097664

```
> %/2;
```

48051720980889113307845951167979191705492706452593916512532230
20205779927875436763295780874492786714975657973402155434606229
15048832

```
> %/2;
```

24025860490444556653922975583989595852746353226296958256266115
10102889963937718381647890437246393357487828986701077717303114
57524416

We continue this way for six more steps until we get

37540407016319619777175464934998374351991617691608899727541580
48453576556865268497132482880819748962107473279172043393328611
6523819

This number is m. Now choose a random integer a. Hoping to be lucky, we choose 13. As in the universal exponent factorization method, we compute

```
> 13&^% mod rsan;
```

27574368507006530592243494868847161198423095707307805690569839
64703018310983986237080052933809298479549019264358796085987055
1239

Since this is not $\pm 1 \pmod{rsan}$, we successively square it until we get ± 1:

```
> %&^2 mod rsan;
```

48318960321928515580138476418723034554104099069940846225494702
77665499641258295563603526615610868643119429857407585403751227
7292

```
> %&^2 mod rsan;
```

78172814154877356579141928058754000021948787056483820917930625
11521518183974205601327552191348756094473207351648772227387557
9363

```
> %&^2 mod rsan;
```
42836191202508728742199299040582900202976222916017767167551870
21650944451823946218637947056944205510139299229308225960173822
8702

```
> %&^2 mod rsan;
```

$$1$$

Since the last number before the 1 was not $\pm 1 \pmod{rsan}$, we have an example of $x \not\equiv \pm 1 \pmod{rsan}$ with $x^2 \equiv 1$. Therefore, $\gcd(x - 1, rsan)$ is a nontrivial factor of *rsan*:

```
> gcd(%% - 1, rsan);
```
32769132993266709549961988190834461413177642967992942539798288
533

This is *rsaq*. The other factor is obtained by computing *rsan/rsaq*:

```
rsan/%;
```
34905295108476509491478496199038981334177646384933878439908205
77

This is *rsap*.

Example 12. Suppose you know that

$$150883475569451^2 \equiv 16887570532858^2 \pmod{205611444308117}.$$

Factor 205611444308117.

    Solution: We use the Basic Principle of Section 6.3:

```
> gcd(150883475569451-16887570532858,205611444308117);
```

$$23495881$$

This gives one factor. The other is

```
> 205611444308117/%;
```

$$8750957$$

We can check that these factors are actually primes, so we can't factor any further:

```
> isprime(%%);
```

true

```
> isprime(%%);
```

true

Example 13. Factor $n = 376875575426394855599989992897873239$ by the $p - 1$ method.

Solution: Let's choose our bound as $B = 100$, and let's take $a = 2$, so we compute $2^{100!} \pmod{n}$:

```
> 2&^factorial(100)
mod 376875575426394855599989992897873239;
```

369676678301956331939422106251199512

Then we compute the gcd of $2^{100!} - 1$ and n:

```
> gcd(% - 1, 376875575426394855599989992897873239);
```

430553161739796481

This is a factor p. The other factor q is

```
> 376875575426394855599989992897873239/%;
```

875328783798732119

Let's see why this worked. The factorizations of $p - 1$ and $q - 1$ are

```
> ifactor(430553161739796481 - 1);
```

$(2)^{18}(3)^7(5)(7)^4(11)^3(47)$

```
> ifactor(875328783798732119 - 1);
```

$(2)(61)(8967967)(20357)(39301)$

We see that $100!$ is a multiple of $p - 1$, so $2^{100!} \equiv 1 \pmod{p}$. However, $100!$ is not a multiple of $q - 1$, so it is likely that $2^{100!} \not\equiv 1 \pmod{q}$. Therefore, both $2^{100!} - 1$ and pq have p as a factor, but only pq has q as a factor. It follows that the gcd is p.

B.6 Examples for Chapter 8

Example 1. Suppose there are 23 people in a room. What is the probability that at least two have the same birthday?

Solution: The probability that no two have the same birthday is $\prod_{i=1}^{22}(1 - i/365)$ (note that the product stops at $i = 22$, not $i = 23$). Subtracting from 1 gives the probability that at least two have the same birthday:

```
> 1-mult(1.-i/365, i=1..22);
```

$$.5072972344$$

Note that we used 1. in the product instead of 1 without the decimal point. If we had omitted the decimal point, the product would have been evaluated as a rational number (try it, you'll see).

Example 2. Suppose a lazy phone company employee assigns telephone numbers by choosing random seven-digit numbers. In a town with 10000 phones, what is the probability that two people receive the same number?

```
> 1-mult(1.-i/10^7, i=1..9999);
```

$$.9932699135$$

Note that the number of phones is about three times the square root of the number of possibilities. This means that we expect the probability to be high, which it is. From Section 8.4, we have the estimate that if there are around $\sqrt{2(\ln 2)10^7} \approx 3723$ phones, there should be a 50% chance of a match. Let's see how accurate this is:

```
> 1-mult(1.-i/10^7, i=1..3722);
```

$$.4998945410$$

B.7 Examples for Chapter 10

Example 1. Suppose we have a (5, 8) Shamir secret sharing scheme. Everything is mod the prime $p = 987541$. Five of the shares are

$$(9853, 853), (4421, 4387), (6543, 1234), (93293, 78428), (12398, 7563).$$

Find the secret.

Solution: One way: First, find the Lagrange interpolating polynomial through the five points:

```
> interp([9853,4421,6543,93293,12398],
[853,4387,1234,78428,7563],x);
```

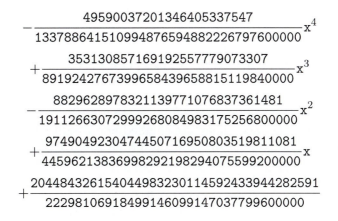

$$-\frac{49590037201346405337547}{133788641510994876594882226797600000}x^4$$

$$+\frac{35313085716919255777 9073307}{89192427673996584396588815119840000}x^3$$

$$-\frac{88296289783211397710768 37361481}{191126630729992680849831752568 00000}x^2$$

$$+\frac{97490492304744507169508035198 11081}{44596213836998292198294075599200000}x$$

$$+\frac{2044843261540449832301 14592433944282591}{222981069184991460991470377996 00000}$$

Now evaluate at $x = 0$ to find the constant term:

```
> eval(%,x=0);
```

$$\frac{204484326154044983230114592433944282591}{222981069184991460991470377996 00000}$$

We need to change this to an integer mod 987541:

```
> % mod 987541;
```

$$678987$$

Therefore, 678987 is the secret.

Here is another way. Set up the matrix equations as in the text and then solve for the coefficients of the polynomial mod 987541:

```
> map(x->x mod 987541,evalm(inverse(matrix(5,5,
[1,9853,9853^2,9853^3,9853^4,
1,4421,4421^2,4421^3,4421^4,
1,6543,6543^2,6543^3, 6543^4,
1, 93293, 93293^2,93293^3, 93293^4,
1, 12398, 12398^2,12398^3,12398^4]))
&*matrix(5,1,[853,4387,1234,78428,7563])));
```

$$\begin{bmatrix} 678987 \\ 14728 \\ 1651 \\ 574413 \\ 456741 \end{bmatrix}$$

The constant term is 678987, which is the secret.

B.8   Examples for Chapter 11

Example 1. Here is a game you can play. It is essentially the simplified version of poker over the telephone from Section 11.2. There are five cards: ten, jack, queen, king, ace. They are shuffled and disguised by raising their numbers to a random exponent mod the prime 24691313099. You are supposed to guess which one is the ace. To start, pick a random exponent. We use the colon after **khide()** so that we cannot cheat and see what value of k is being used.

```
> k:= khide():
```

Now, shuffle the disguised cards (their numbers are raised to the kth power mod p):

```
> shuffle(k);
```

> [14001090567, 16098641856, 23340023892, 20919427041,
>   7768690848]

These are the five cards. None looks like the ace; that's because their numbers have been raised to powers mod the prime. Make a guess anyway. Let's see if you're correct.

```
> reveal(%);
```

> ["ten", "ace", "queen", "jack", "king"]

Let's play again:

```
> k:= khide():
```

```
> shuffle(k);
```

> [13015921305, 14788966861, 23855418969, 22566749952,
>   8361552666]

Make your guess (note that the numbers are different because a different random exponent was used). Were you lucky?

```
> reveal(%);
```

$$["ten", "queen", "ace", "king", "jack"]$$

Perhaps you need some help. Let's play one more time:

```
> k:= khide():
> shuffle(k);
```

$$[13471751030, 20108480083, 8636729758, 14735216549,$$
$$11884022059]$$

We now ask for advice:

```
> advise(%);
```

$$3$$

We are advised that the third card is the ace. Let's see (recall that %% is used to refer to the next to last output):

```
> reveal(%%);
```

$$["jack", "ten", "ace", "queen", "king"]$$

How does this work? Read the part on "How to Cheat" in Section 11.2. Note that if we raise the numbers for the cards to the $(p-1)/2$ power mod p, we get

```
> map(x->x&^((24691313099-1)/2) mod 24691313099,
[200514, 10010311, 1721050514, 11091407, 10305]);
```

$$[1, 1, 1, 1, 24691313098]$$

Therefore, only the ace is a quadratic nonresidue mod p.

B.9   Examples for Chapter 15

Example 1. All of the elliptic curves we work with in this chapter are elliptic curves mod n. However, it is helpful use the graphs of elliptic curves with real numbers in order to visualize what is happening with the addition law, for example, even though such pictures do not exist mod n. Therefore, let's graph the elliptic curve $y^2 = x(x-1)(x+1)$. We'll specify that $-1 \leq x \leq 3$ and $-5 \leq y \leq 5$.

```
> implicitplot(y^2 = x*(x - 1)*(x + 1), x=-1..3,y=-5..5);
```

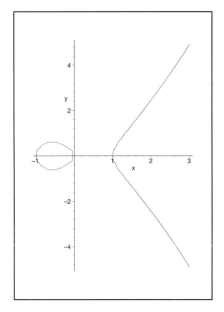

Example 2. Add the points (1, 3) and (3, 5) on the elliptic curve $y^2 \equiv x^3 + 24x + 13 \pmod{29}$.

```
> addell([1,3], [3,5], 24, 13, 29);
```

$$[26,1]$$

You can check that the point (26, 1) is on the curve: $26^3 + 24 \cdot 26 + 13 \equiv 1^2$ (mod 29).

Example 3. Add (1, 3) to the point at infinity on the curve of the previous example.

```
> addell([1,3], ["infinity","infinity" ], 24, 13, 29);
```

$$[1,3]$$

As expected, adding the point at infinity to a point P returns the point P.

Example 4. Let $P = (1,3)$ be a point on the elliptic curve $y^2 \equiv x^3 + 24x + 13 \pmod{29}$. Find $7P$.

```
> multell([1,3], 7, 24, 13, 29);
```

$$[15,6]$$

Example 5. Find $k(1,3)$ for $k = 1, 2, 3, \ldots, 40$ on the curve of the previous example.

```
> multsell([1,3], 40, 24, 13, 29);
[[1,3],[11,10],[23,28],[0,10],[19,7],[18,19],[15,6],[20,24],
[4,12],[4,17],[20,5],[15,23],[18,10],[19,22],[0,19],[23,1],
[11,19],[1,26],["infinity","infinity"],[1,3],[11,10],[23,28],
[0,10],[19,7],[18,19],[15,6],[20,24],[4,12],[4,17],[20,5],
[15,23],[18,10],[19,22],[0,19],[23,1],[11,19],[1,26],
["infinity","infinity"],[1,3],[11,10]]
```

Notice how the points repeat after every 19 multiples.

Example 6. The previous four examples worked mod the prime 29. If we work mod a composite number, the situation at infinity becomes more complicated since we could be at infinity mod both factors or we could be at infinity mod one of the factors but not mod the other. Therefore, we stop the calculation if this last situation happens and we exhibit a factor. For example, let's try to compute $12P$, where $P = (1,3)$ is on the elliptic curve $y^2 \equiv x^3 - 5x + 13 \pmod{209}$:

```
> multell([1,3], 12, -5, 13, 11*19);
```

$$["factor=",19]$$

Now let's compute the successive multiples to see what happened along the way:

```
> multsell([1,3], 12, -5, 13, 11*19);

[[1,3],[91,27],[118,133],[148,182],[20,35],["factor=",19]]
```

When we computed $6P$, we ended up at infinity mod 19. Let's see what is happening mod the two prime factors of 209, namely 19 and 11:

```
> multsell([1,3], 12, -5, 13, 19);
[[1,3],[15,8],[4,0],[15,11],[1,16],["infinity","infinity"],
[1,3],[15,8],[4,0],[15,11],[1,16],["infinity","infinity"]]

> multsell([1,3], 24, -5, 13, 11);
[[1,3],[3,5],[8,1],[5,6],[9,2],[6,10],[2,0],[6,1],[9,9],[5,5],
[8,10],[3,6],[1,8],["infinity","infinity"],[1,3],[3,5],[8,1],
[5, 6],[9, 2],[6,10],[2,0],[6,1],[9,9],[5,5]]
```

After six steps, we were at infinity mod 19, but it takes 14 steps to reach infinity mod 11. To find $6P$, we needed to invert a number that was 0 mod 19 and nonzero mod 11. This couldn't be done, but it yielded the factor 19. This is the basis of the elliptic curve factorization method.

Example 7. Factor 193279 using elliptic curves.

Solution: First, we need to choose some random elliptic curves and a point on each curve. For example, let's take $P = (2,4)$ and the elliptic curve

$$y^2 \equiv x^3 - 10x + b \pmod{193279}.$$

For P to lie on the curve, we take $b = 28$. We'll also take

$$
\begin{aligned}
y^2 &\equiv x^3 + 11x - 11, \quad P = (1,1) \\
y^2 &\equiv x^3 + 17x - 14, \quad P = (1,2).
\end{aligned}
$$

Now we compute multiples of the point P. We do the analog of the $p - 1$ method, so we choose a bound B, say $B = 12$, and compute $B!P$.

```
> multell([2,4], factorial(12), -10, 28, 193279);
```

$$["factor=",347]$$

```
> multell([1,1], factorial(12), 11, -11, 193279);
```

$$[13862,35249]$$

```
> multell([1,2], factorial(12), 17, -14, 193279);
```

$$["factor=",557]$$

Let's analyze in more detail what happened in these examples.

On the first curve, $266P$ ends up at infinity mod 557 and $35P$ is infinity mod 347. Since $266 = 2 \cdot 7 \cdot 19$, it has a prime factor larger than $B = 12$, so $B!P$ is not infinity mod 557. But 35 divides $B!$, so $B!P$ is infinity mod 347.

On the second curve, $356P =$ infinity mod 347 and $561P =$ infinity mod 557. Since $356 = 4 \cdot 89$ and $561 = 3 \cdot 11 \cdot 17$, we don't expect to find the factorization with this curve.

The third curve is a surprise. We have $331P =$ infinity mod 347 and $272P =$ infinity mod 557. Since 331 is prime and $272 = 16 \cdot 17$, we don't expect to find the factorization with this curve. However, by chance, an intermediate step in the calculation of $B!P$ yielded the factorization. Here's what happened. At one step, the program required adding the points (184993, 13462) and (20678, 150484). These two points are congruent mod 557 but not mod 347. Therefore, the slope of the line through these two points is defined mod 347 but is 0/0 mod 557. When we tried to find the multiplicative inverse of the denominator mod 193279, the gcd algorithm yielded the factor 557. This phenomenon is fairly rare.

Example 8. Here is how to produce the example of an elliptic curve ElGamal cryptosystem from Section 15.5. For more details, see the text. The elliptic curve is $y^2 \equiv x^3 + 3x + 45 \pmod{8831}$ and the point is $G = (4, 11)$. Alice's message is the point $P_m = (5, 1743)$.

Bob has chosen his secret random number $a_B = 3$ and has computed $a_b G$:

```
> multell([4,11], 3, 3, 45, 8831);
```

$$[413, 1808]$$

Bob publishes this point. Alice chooses the random number $k = 8$ and computes kG and $P_m + k(a_B G)$:

```
> multell([4,11], 8, 3, 45, 8831);
```

$$[5415, 6321]$$

```
> addell([5,1743],multell([413,1808],8,3,45,8831),3,45,8831);
```

$$[6626, 3576]$$

Alice sends (5415,6321) and (6626,3576) to Bob, who multiplies the first of these point by a_B:

```
> multell([5415,6321], 3, 3, 45, 8831);
```

$$[673,146]$$

Bob then subtracts the result from the last point Alice sends him. Note that he subtracts by adding the point with the second coordinate negated:

```
> addell([6626,3576], [673,-146], 3, 45, 8831);
```

$$[5,1743]$$

Bob has therefore received Alice's message.

Example 9. Let's reproduce the numbers in the example of a Diffie-Hellman key exchange from Section 15.5: The elliptic curve is $y^2 \equiv x^3 + x + 7206 \pmod{7211}$ and the point is $G = (3,5)$. Alice chooses her secret $N_A = 12$ and Bob chooses his secret $N_B = 23$. Alice calculates

```
> multell([3,5], 12, 1, 7206, 7211);
```

$$[1794,6375]$$

She sends (1794,6375) to Bob. Meanwhile, Bob calculates

```
multell([3,5], 23, 1, 7206, 7211);
```

$$[3861, 1242]$$

and sends (3861,1242) to Alice. Alice multiplies what she receives by N_A and Bob multiplies what he receives by N_B:

```
> multell([3861,1242], 12, 1, 7206, 7211);
```

$$[1472,2098]$$

```
> multell([1794,6375], 23, 1, 7206, 7211);
```

$$[1472,2098]$$

Therefore, Alice and Bob have produced the same key.

Appendix C

MATLAB Examples

These computer examples are written for MATLAB. If you have MAT-LAB available, you should try some of them on your computer. For information on getting started with MATLAB, see Section C.1. Several functions have been written to allow for experimentation with MATLAB. The MAT-LAB functions associated with this book are available at

$$http://www.prenhall.com/washington$$

We recommend that you create a directory or folder to store these files and download them to that directory or folder. One method for using these functions is to launch MATLAB from the directory where the files are stored, or launch MATLAB and change the current directory to where the files are stored. In some versions of MATLAB the working directory can be changed by changing the current directory on the command bar. Alternatively, one can add the path to that directory in the MATLAB path by using the *path* function or the Set Path option from the File menu on the command bar.

If MATLAB is not available, it is still possible to read the examples. They provide examples for several of the concepts presented in the book. Most of the examples used in the MATLAB appendix are similar to the examples in the Mathematica and Maple appendices. MATLAB, however, is limited in the size of the numbers it can handle. The maximum number that MATLAB can represent accurately is roughly 15 digits. The double precision used in MATLAB forces larger numbers to be approximated. We may, however, still use MATLAB for many of the examples used in this book.

It is possible to use Maple from within MATLAB. This requires that the Symbolic toolbox is available. The use of Maple from within MATLAB is not available on Student Editions of MATLAB and for that reason we have chosen to present functions that are native to MATLAB to avoid using the Symbolic toolbox.

A final note before we begin. It may be useful when doing the MATLAB exercises to change the formatting of your display. The command

```
>> format rat
```

sets the formatting to represent numbers using a fractional representation. This notation is particularly useful for representing large numbers. The conventional *short* format represents large numbers in scientific notation, which often doesn't display some of the least significant digits.

C.1   Getting Started with MATLAB

MATLAB is a programming language for performing technical computations. It is a powerful language that has become very popular and is rapidly becoming a standard instructional language for courses in mathematics, science, and engineering. MATLAB is available on most campuses, and many universities have site licenses allowing MATLAB to be installed on any machine on campus.

In order to launch MATLAB on a PC, double click on the MATLAB icon. If you want to run MATLAB on a Unix system, type *matlab* at the prompt. Upon launching MATLAB, you will see the MATLAB prompt:

```
>>
```

which indicates that MATLAB is waiting for a command for you to type in. When you wish to quit MATLAB, type *quit* at the command prompt.

MATLAB is able to do the basic arithmetic operations such as addition, subtraction, multiplication and division. These can be accomplished by the operators +, -, *, and /, respectively. In order to raise a number to a power, we use the operator ^. Let us look at an example:

If we type 2^7 + 125/5 at the prompt and press the *Enter* key

```
>> 2^7 + 125/5
```

then MATLAB will return the answer:

```
ans =
    153
```

Notice that in this example, MATLAB performed the exponentiation first, the division next, and then added the two results. The order of operations used in MATLAB is the one that we have grown up using. We can also use parentheses to change the order in which MATLAB calculates its quantities. The following example exhibits this:

```
>> 11*( (128/(9+7) - 2^(72/12)))

ans =
   -616
```

In these examples, MATLAB has called the result of the calculations *ans*, which is a variable that is used by MATLAB to store the output of a computation. It is possible to assign the result of a computation to a specific variable. For example,

```
>> spot=17

spot =
   17
```

assigns the value of 17 to the variable *spot*. It is possible to use variables in computations:

```
>> dog=11

dog =
   11
>> cat=7

cat =
   7
>> animals=dog+cat

animals =
   18
```

MATLAB also operates like an advanced scientific calculator since it has many functions available to it. For example, we can do the standard operation of taking a square root by using the *sqrt* function, as in the following example:

```
>> sqrt(1024)

ans =
   32
```

There are many other functions available. Some functions that will be useful for this book are *mod, factorial, factor, prod*, and *size*.

Help is available in MATLAB. If you are on a PC, you may either type *help* at the prompt, or pull down the Help menu. If you are on a Unix system, help is basically available by the same methods as those for the PC. However, if you are running a version of MATLAB before version 6.0, the pull-down menu may not be available to you. MATLAB also provides help from the command line by typing *help commandname*. For example, to get help on the function *mod*, which we shall be using a lot, type the following:

```
>> help mod
```

MATLAB has a collection of toolboxes available. The toolboxes consist of collections of functions that implement many application-specific tasks. For example, the Optimization toolbox provides a collection of functions that do linear and nonlinear optimization. Generally, not all toolboxes are available. However, for our purposes, this is not a problem since we will only need general MATLAB functions and have built our own functions to explore the number theory behind cryptography.

The basic data type used in MATLAB is the matrix. The MATLAB programming language has been written to use matrices and vectors as the most fundamental data type. This is natural since many mathematical and scientific problems lend themselves to using matrices and vectors.

Let us start by giving an example of how one enters a matrix in MATLAB. Suppose we wish to enter the matrix

$$A = \begin{bmatrix} 1 & 1 & 1 & 1 \\ 1 & 2 & 4 & 8 \\ 1 & 3 & 9 & 27 \\ 1 & 4 & 16 & 64 \end{bmatrix}$$

into MATLAB. To do this we type:

```
>> A = [1 1 1 1; 1 2 4 8; 1 3 9 27; 1 4 16 64]
```

at the prompt. MATLAB returns

```
A =
     1    1    1    1
     1    2    4    8
     1    3    9   27
     1    4   16   64
```

There are a few basic rules that are used when entering matrices or vectors. First, a vector or matrix is started by using a square bracket [and ended using a square bracket]. Next, blanks or commas separate the elements of a row. A semicolon is used to end each row. Finally, we may place a semicolon at the very end to prevent MATLAB from displaying the output of the command.

To define a row vector, use blanks or commas. For example,

```
>> x = [2, 4, 6, 8, 10, 12]

x =
    2    4    6    8    10    12
```

To define a column vector, use semicolons. For example,

```
>> y=[1;3;5;7]

y =
    1
    3
    5
    7
```

In order to access a particular element of y, put the desired index in parentheses. For example, $y(1) = 1$, $y(2) = 3$, and so on.

MATLAB provides a useful notation for addressing multiple elements at the same time. For example, to access the third, fourth, and fifth elements of x, we would type

```
>> x(3:5)

ans =
    6    8    10
```

The 3:5 tells MATLAB to start at 3 and count up to 5. To access every second element of x, you can do this by

```
>> x(1:2:6)

ans =
    2    6    10
```

We may do this for the array also. For example,

```
>> A(1:2:4,2:2:4)

ans =
    1    1
    3    27
```

The notation 1:n may also be used to define a variable. For example,

```
>> x=1:7
```

returns

```
x =
```

```
    1    2    3    4    5    6    7
```

MATLAB provides the *size* function to determine the dimensions of a vector or matrix variable. For example, if we want the dimensions of the matrix A that we entered earlier, then we would do

```
>> size(A)
```

```
ans =
    4    4
```

It is often necessary to display numbers in different formats. MATLAB provides several output formats for displaying the result of a computation. To find a list of formats available, type

```
>> help format
```

The *short* format is the default format and is very convenient for doing many computations. However, in this book, we will be representing long whole numbers, and the *short* format will cut off some of the trailing digits in a number. For example,

```
>> a=1234567899
```

```
a =
    1.2346e+009
```

Instead of using the *short* format, we shall use the *rational* format. To switch MATLAB to using the rational format, type

```
>> format rat
```

As an example, if we do the same example as before, we now get different results:

```
>> a=1234567899
```

```
a =
    1234567899
```

This format is also useful because it allows us to represent fractions in their fractional form, for example,

```
>> 111/323
```

```
ans =
    111/323
```

In many situations, it will be convenient to suppress the results of a computation. In order to have MATLAB suppress printing out the results of a command, a semicolon must follow the command. Also, multiple commands may be entered on the same line by separating them by a comma. For example,

```
>> dogs=11, cats=7; elephants=3, zebras=19;

dogs =
   11

elephants =
   3
```

returns the values for the variables *dogs* and *elephants* but does not display the values for *cats* and *zebras*.

MATLAB can also handle variables that are made of text. A string is treated as an array of characters. To assign a string to a variable, enclose the text with single quotes. For example,

```
>> txt='How are you today?'
```

returns

```
txt =
   How are you today?
```

A string has size much like a vector does. For example, the size of the variable txt is given by

```
>> size(txt)

ans =
   1   18
```

It is possible to edit the characters one by one. For example, the following command changes the first word of txt:

```
>> txt(1)='W'; txt(2)='h';txt(3)='o'

txt =
   Who are you today?
```

As you work in MATLAB, it will remember the commands you have entered as well as the values of the variables you have created. To scroll through your previous commands, press the up-arrow and down-arrow. In order to see the variables you have created, type *who* at the prompt. A similar command *whos* gives the variables, their size, and their type information.

Notes. 1. To use the commands that have been written for the examples, you should run MATLAB in the directory into which you have downloaded the file from the Web site *http://www.prenhall.com/washington*

2. Some of the examples and computer problems use long ciphertexts, etc. For convenience, these have been stored in the file ciphertexts.m, which can be loaded by typing *ciphertexts* at the prompt. The ciphertexts can then be referred to by their names. For example, see Computer Example 4 for Chapter 2.

C.2 Examples for Chapter 2

Example 1. A shift cipher was used to obtain the ciphertext `kddkmu`. Decrypt it by trying all possibilities.

```
>> allshift('kddkmu')
```

```
kddkmu
leelnv
mffmow
nggnpx
ohhoqy
piiprz
qjjqsa
rkkrtb
sllsuc
tmmtvd
unnuwe
voovxf
wppwyg
xqqxzh
yrryai
zsszbj
attack
buubdl
cvvcem
dwwdfn
exxego
fyyfhp
gzzgiq
haahjr
ibbiks
jccjlt
```

As you can see, `attack` is the only word that occurs on this list, so that was the plaintext.

Example 2. Encrypt the plaintext message `cleopatra` using the affine function $7x + 8$:

```
>> affinecrypt('cleopatra',7,8)

ans =


whkcjilxi
```

Example 3. The ciphertext `mzdvezc` was encrypted using the affine function $5x + 12$. Decrypt it.

Solution: First, solve $y \equiv 5x + 12 \pmod{26}$ for x to obtain $x \equiv 5^{-1}(y - 12)$. We need to find the inverse of 5 (mod 26):

```
>> powermod(5,-1,26)

ans =
    21
```

Therefore, $x \equiv 21(y - 12) \equiv 21y - 12 \cdot 21$. To change $-12 \cdot 21$ to standard form:

```
>> mod(-12*21,26)

ans =
    8
```

Therefore, the decryption function is $x \equiv 21y + 8$. To decrypt the message:

```
>> affinecrypt('mzdvezc',21,8)

ans =


anthony
```

In case you were wondering, the plaintext was encrypted as follows:

```
>> affinecrypt('anthony',5,12)

ans =


mzdvezc
```

Example 4. Here is the example of a Vigenère cipher from the text. Let's see how to produce the data that was used in Section 2.3 to decrypt the ciphertext. In the file ciphertexts.m, the ciphertext is stored under the name *vvhq*. If you haven't already done so, load the file ciphertexts.m:

`>> ciphertexts`

Now we can use the variable vvhq to obtain the ciphertext:

`>> vvhq`

```
vvhqwvvrhmusgjgthkihtssejchlsfcbgvwcrlryqtfsvgahwkcuhwauglq
hnslrljshbltspisprdxljsveeghlqwkasskuwepwqtwvspgoelkcqyfnsv
wljsniqkgnrgybwlwgoviokhkazkqkxzgyhcecmeiujoqkwfwvefqhkijrc
lrlkbienqfrjljsdhgrhlsfqtwlauqrhwdmwlgusgikkflryvcwvspgpmlk
assjvoqxeggveyggzmljcxxljsvpaivwikvrdrygfrjljslveggveyggeia
puuisfpbtgnwwmuczrvtwglrwugumnczvile
```

We now find the frequencies of the letters in the ciphertext. We use the function *frequency*. The *frequency* command was written to display automatically the letter and the count next to it. We therefore have put a semicolon at the end of the command to prevent MATLAB from displaying the count twice.

`>> fr=frequency(vvhq);`

a	8
b	5
c	12
d	4
e	15
f	10
g	27
h	16
i	13
j	14
k	17
l	25
m	7
n	7
o	5
p	9
q	14
r	17

```
s    24
t     8
u    12
v    22
w    22
x     5
y     8
z     5
```

Let's compute the coincidences for shifts of 1, 2, 3, 4, 5, 6:

```
>> coinc(vvhq,1)

ans =
    14

>> coinc(vvhq,2)

ans =
    14

>> coinc(vvhq,3)

ans =
    16

>> coinc(vvhq,4)

ans =
    14

>> coinc(vvhq,5)

ans =
    24

>> coinc(vvhq,6)

ans =
    12
```

We conclude that the key length is probably 5. Let's look at the 1st, 6th, 11th, ... letters (namely, the letters in positions congruent to 1 mod 5). The function *choose* will do this for us. The function *choose(txt,m,n)* extracts every letter from the string txt that has positions congruent to n mod m.

```
>> choose(vvhq,5,1)

ans =
```

```
vvuttcccqgcunjtpjgkuqpknjkygkkgcjfqrkqjrqudukvpkvggjjivgjgg
pfncwuce
```

We now do a frequency count of the preceding substring. To do this, we use the *frequency* function and use ans as input. In MATLAB, if a command is issued without declaring a variable for the result, MATLAB will put the output in the variable ans.

```
>> frequency(ans);
```

```
a    0
b    0
c    7
d    1
e    1
f    2
g    9
h    0
i    1
j    8
k    8
l    0
m    0
n    3
o    0
p    4
q    5
r    2
s    0
t    3
u    6
v    5
w    1
x    0
y    1
z    0
```

To express this as a vector of frequencies, we use the *vigvec* function. The *vigvec* function will not only display the frequency counts just shown, but will return a vector that contains the frequencies. In the following output, we have suppressed the table of frequency counts since they appear above and have reported the results in the *short* format.

```
>> vigvec(vvhq,5,1)

ans =
    0
    0
    0.1045
    0.0149
    0.0149
    0.0299
    0.1343
    0
    0.0149
    0.1194
    0.1194
    0
    0
    0.0448
    0
    0.0597
    0.0746
    0.0299
    0
    0.0448
    0.0896
    0.0746
    0.0149
    0
    0.0149
    0
```

The dot products of this vector with the shifts of the alphabet frequency vector are computed as follows:

```
>> corr(ans)

ans =
    0.0250
    0.0391
    0.0713
    0.0388
```

```
0.0275
0.0380
0.0512
0.0301
0.0325
0.0430
0.0338
0.0299
0.0343
0.0446
0.0356
0.0402
0.0434
0.0502
0.0392
0.0296
0.0326
0.0392
0.0366
0.0316
0.0488
0.0349
```

The third entry is the maximum, but sometimes the largest entry is hard to locate. One way to find it is

```
>> max(ans)
```

```
ans =
    0.0713
```

Now it is easy to look through the list and find this number (it usually occurs only once). Since it occurs in the third position, the first shift for this Vigenère cipher is by 2, corresponding to the letter *c*. A procedure similar to the one just used (using *vigvec(vvhq, 5,2)*,..., *vigvec(vvhq,5,5)*) shows that the other shifts are probably 14, 3, 4, 18. Let's check that we have the correct key by decrypting.

```
>> vigenere(vvhq,-[2,14,3,4,18])
```

```
ans =
```

```
themethodusedforthepreparationandreadingofcodemessagesissim
pleintheextremeandatthesametimeimpossibleoftranslationunles
```

```
sthekeyisknowntheeasewithwhichthekeymaybechangedisanotherpo
intinfavoroftheadoptionofthiscodebythosedesiringtotransmiti
mportantmessageswithouttheslightestdangeroftheirmessagesbei
ngreadbypoliticalorbusinessrivalsetc
```

For the record, the plaintext was originally encrypted by the command

```
>> vigenere(ans,[2,14,3,4,18])
```

```
ans =
```

```
vvhqwvvrhmusgjgthkihtssejchlsfcbgvwcrlryqtfsvgahwkcuhwauglq
hnslrljshbltspisprdxljsveeghlqwkasskuwepwqtwvspgoelkcqyfnsv
wljsniqkgnrgybwlwgoviokhkazkqkxzgyhcecmeiujoqkwfwvefqhkijrc
lrlkbienqfrjljsdhgrhlsfqtwlauqrhwdmwlgusgikkflryvcwvspgpmlk
assjvoqxeggvveyggzmljcxxljsvpaivwikvrdrygfrjljslveggveyggeia
puuisfpbtgnwwmuczrvtwglrwugumnczvile
```

Example 5. The ciphertext

$$22, 09, 00, 12, 03, 01, 10, 03, 04, 08, 01, 17$$

was encrypted using a Hill cipher with matrix

$$\begin{pmatrix} 1 & 2 & 3 \\ 4 & 5 & 6 \\ 7 & 8 & 10 \end{pmatrix}.$$

Decrypt it.

Solution: A matrix $\begin{pmatrix} a & b \\ c & d \end{pmatrix}$ is entered as $[a, b; c, d]$. Type $M * N$ to multiply matrices M and N. Type $v * M$ to multiply a vector v on the right by a matrix M.

First, we put the above matrix in the variable M.

```
>> M=[1 2 3; 4 5 6; 7 8 10]

   M =
      1    2    3
      4    5    6
      7    8   10
```

Next, we need to invert the matrix mod 26:

```
>> Minv=inv(M)
```

```
    Minv =
      -2/3      -4/3       1
      -2/3      11/3      -2
        1        -2        1
```

Since we are working mod 26, we can't stop with numbers like 2/3. We need to get rid of the denominators and reduce mod 26. To do so, we multiply by 3 to extract the numerators of the fractions, then multiply by the inverse of 3 mod 26 to put the "denominators" back in (see Section 3.3):

```
>> M1=(Minv*3)

M1 =
      -2      -4       3
      -2      11      -6
       3      -6       3

>> M2=round(mod(M1*9,26))

M2 =
       8      16       1
       8      21      24
       1      24       1
```

Note that we used the function *round* in calculating $M2$. This was done since MATLAB performs its calculations in floating point and calculating the inverse matrix $Minv$ produces numbers that are slightly different from whole numbers. The matrix $M2$ is the inverse of the matrix M mod 26. We can check this as follows:

```
>> mod(M2*M,26)

ans =
       1       0       0
       0       1       0
       0       0       1
```

To decrypt, we break the ciphertext into blocks of 3 numbers and multiply each block on the right by the inverse matrix we just calculated:

```
>> mod([22,9,0]*M2,26)

ans =
      14      21       4

>> mod([12,3,1]*M2,26)

ans =
      17      19       7
```

```
>> mod([10,3,4]*M2,26)
```

```
ans =
    4    7    8
```

```
>> mod([8,1,17]*M2,26)
```

```
ans =
    11    11    23
```

Therefore, the plaintext is 14, 21, 4, 17, 19, 7, 4, 7, 8, 11, 11, 23. This can be changed back to letters:

```
>> int2text([14 21 4 17 19 7 4 7 8 11 11 23])
```

```
ans =
```

```
overthehillx
```

Note that the final x was appended to the plaintext in order to complete a block of three letters.

Example 6. Compute the first 50 terms of the recurrence

$$x_{n+5} \equiv x_n + x_{n+2} \pmod 2.$$

The initial values are $0, 1, 0, 0, 0$.

Solution: The vector of coefficients is $\{1, 0, 1, 0, 0\}$. The initial vector is $\{0, 1, 0, 0, 0\}$. Type

```
>> lfsr([1 0 1 0 0],[0 1 0 0 0],50)
```

```
ans =
    Columns 1 through 12
      0    1    0    0    0    0    1    0    0    1    0    1
    Columns 13 through 24
      1    0    0    1    1    1    1    1    0    0    0    1
    Columns 25 through 36
      1    0    1    1    1    0    1    0    1    0    0    0
    Columns 37 through 48
      0    1    0    0    1    0    1    1    0    0    1    1
    Columns 49 through 50
      1    1
```

Example 7. Suppose the first 20 terms of an LFSR sequence are 1, 0, 1, 0, 1, 1, 1, 0, 0, 0, 0, 1, 1, 1, 0, 1, 0, 1, 0, 1. Find a recursion that generates this sequence.

Solution: First, we find a candidate for the length of the recurrence. The command *lfsrlength(v, n)* calculates the determinants mod 2 of the first n matrices that appear in the procedure described in Section 2.11 for the sequence v. Recall that the last nonzero determinant gives the length of the recurrence.

```
>> lfsrlength([1 0 1 0 1 1 1 0 0 0 0 1 1 1 0 1 0 1 0 1],10)
   Order   Determinant
     1          1
     2          1
     3          0
     4          1
     5          0
     6          1
     7          0
     8          0
     9          0
    10          0
```

The last nonzero determinant is the sixth one, so we guess that the recurrence has length 6. To find the coefficients:

```
>> lfsrsolve([1 0 1 0 1 1 1 0 0 0 0 1 1 1 0 1 0 1 0 1],6)

ans =
     1   0   1   1   1   0
```

This gives the recurrence as

$$x_{n+6} \equiv x_n + x_{n+2} + x_{n+3} + x_{n+4} \pmod 2.$$

Example 8. The ciphertext 0, 1, 1, 0, 1, 0, 1, 0, 1, 0, 0, 1, 1, 0, 0, 0, 1, 0, 1, 0, 1, 0, 1, 0, 1, 0, 1, 0, 1, 0, 0, 1, 0, 0, 0, 1, 0, 1, 1, 0 was produced by adding the output of a LFSR onto the plaintext mod 2 (i.e., XOR the plaintext with the LFSR output). Suppose you know that the plaintext starts 1, 1, 1, 1, 1, 1, 0, 0, 0, 0, 0, 0, 1, 1, 1, 0, 0. Find the rest of the plaintext.

Solution: XOR the ciphertext with the known part of the plaintext to obtain the beginning of the LFSR output:

```
>> x=mod([1 1 1 1 1 1 0 0 0 0 0 0 1 1 1 0 0]+[0 1 1 0 1 0 1 0
1 0 0 1 1 0 0 0 1],2)

x =
   Columns 1 through 12
     1   0   0   1   0   1   1   0   1   0   0   1
```

```
    Columns 13 through 17
      0   1   1   0   1
```

This is the beginning of the LFSR output. Now let's find the length of the recurrence:

```
>> lfsrlength(x,8)
    Order   Determinant
       1           1
       2           0
       3           1
       4           0
       5           1
       6           0
       7           0
       8           0
```

We guess the length is 5. To find the coefficients of the recurrence:

```
>> lfsrsolve(x,5)

ans =
     1   1   0   0   1
```

Now we can generate the full output of the LFSR using the coefficients we just found plus the first five terms of the LFSR output:

```
>> lfsr([1 1 0 0 1],[1 0 0 1 0],40)

ans =
    Columns 1 through 12
      1   0   0   1   0   1   1   0   1   0   0   1
    Columns 13 through 24
      0   1   1   0   1   0   0   1   0   1   1   0
    Columns 25 through 36
      1   0   0   1   0   1   1   0   1   0   0   1
    Columns 37 through 40
      0   1   1   0
```

When we XOR the LFSR output with the ciphertext, we get back the plaintext:

```
>> mod(ans+[0 1 1 0 1 0 1 0 1 0 0 1 1 0 0 0 1 0 1 0 1 0 1
0 1 0 1 0 0 1 0 0 0 1 0 1 1 0],2)

ans =
    Columns 1 through 12
```

```
    1   1   1   1   1   1   0   0   0   0   0   0
    Columns 13 through 24
    1   1   1   0   0   0   1   1   1   1   0   0
    Columns 25 through 36
    0   0   1   1   1   1   1   1   1   0   0   0
    Columns 37 through 40
    0   0   0   0
```

This is the plaintext.

C.3   Examples for Chapter 3

Example 1. Find gcd(23456, 987654).

```
>> gcd(23456,987654)

ans =
    2
```

Example 2. Solve $23456x + 987654y = 2$ in integers x, y.

```
>> [a,b,c]=gcd(23456,987654)

a =
    2

b =
    -3158

c =
    75
```

This means that 2 is the gcd and $23456 \cdot (-3158) + 987654 \cdot 75 = 2$.

Example 3. Compute $234 \cdot 456 \pmod{789}$.

```
>> mod(234*456,789)

ans =
    189
```

Example 4. Compute $234^{567} \pmod{9871}$.

```
>> powermod(234,567,9871)

ans =
    5334
```

Example 5. Find the multiplicative inverse of 8787 (mod 91919).

```
>> powermod(8787,-1,91919)
```

```
ans =
   71374
```

Example 6. Solve $7654x \equiv 2389 \pmod{65537}$.

Solution: To solve this problem, we follow the method described in Section 3.3. We calculate 7654^{-1} and then multiply it by 2389:

```
>> powermod(7654,-1,65537)
```

```
ans =
   54637
```

```
>> mod(ans*2389,65537)
```

```
ans =
   43626
```

Example 7. Find x with

$$x \equiv 2 \pmod{78}, \quad x \equiv 5 \pmod{97}, \quad x \equiv 1 \pmod{119}.$$

Solution: To solve the problem we use the function *crt*.

```
>> crt([2 5 1],[78 97 119])
```

```
ans =
   647480
```

We can check the answer:

```
>> mod(647480,[78 97 119])
```

```
ans =
   2   5   1
```

Example 8. Factor 123450 into primes.

```
>> factor(123450)
```

```
ans =
   2   3   5   5   823
```

This means that $123450 = 2^1 3^1 5^2 823^1$.

Example 9. Evaluate $\phi(12345)$.

```
>> eulerphi(12345)

ans =
   6576
```

Example 10. Find a primitive root for the prime 65537.

```
>> primitiveroot(65537)

ans =
   3
```

Therefore, 3 is a primitive root for 65537.

Example 11. Find the inverse of the matrix $\begin{pmatrix} 13 & 12 & 35 \\ 41 & 53 & 62 \\ 71 & 68 & 10 \end{pmatrix}$ (mod 999).

Solution: First, we enter the matrix as M.

```
>> M=[13 12 35; 41 53 62; 71 68 10];
```

Next, invert the matrix without the mod:

```
>> Minv=inv(M)

Minv =
    233/2158     -539/8142      103/3165
   -270/2309      139/2015      -40/2171
    209/7318      32/34139     -197/34139
```

We need to multiply by the determinant of M in order to clear the fractions out of the numbers in *Minv*. Then we need to multiply by the inverse of the determinant mod 999.

```
>> Mdet=det(M)

Mdet =
   -34139

>> powermod(Mdet,-1,999)

ans =
   589
```

The answer is given by

```
>> mod(Minv*589*Mdet,999)

ans =
```

$$\begin{array}{ccc} 772 & 472 & 965 \\ 641 & 516 & 851 \\ 150 & 133 & 149 \end{array}$$

Therefore, the inverse matrix mod 999 is $\begin{pmatrix} 772 & 472 & 965 \\ 641 & 516 & 851 \\ 150 & 133 & 149 \end{pmatrix}$.

In many cases, it is possible to determine by inspection the common denominator that must be removed. When this is not the case, note that the determinant of the original matrix will always work as a common denominator.

In this example, we have used the determinant of the matrix as the common denominator to remove. The determinant of the original matrix will always work as a common denominator.

Example 12. Find a square root of 29887 mod the prime $p = 32579$.

Solution: Since $p \equiv 3 \pmod 4$, we can use the proposition of Section 3.9:

```
>> powermod(29887,(32579+1)/4,32579)
```

```
ans =
    19237
```

The other square root is minus this one:

```
>> mod(-ans,32579)
```

```
ans =
    13342
```

Example 13. Let $n = 34222273 = 9803 \cdot 3491$. Find all four solutions of $x^2 \equiv 19101358 \pmod{34222273}$.

Solution: First, find a square root mod each of the two prime factors, both of which are congruent to 3 (mod 4):

```
>> powermod(19101358,(9803+1)/4,9803)
```

```
ans =
    3998
```

```
>> powermod(19101358,(3491+1)/4,3491)
```

```
ans =
    1318
```

Therefore, the square roots are congruent to ± 3998 (mod 9803) and ± 1318 (mod 3491). There are four ways to combine these using the Chinese remainder theorem:

```
>> crt([3998 1318],[9803 3491])

ans =
   43210

>> crt([-3998 1318],[9803 3491])

ans =
   8397173

>> crt([3998 -1318],[9803 3491])

ans =
   25825100

>> crt([-3998 -1318],[9803 3491])

ans =
   34179063
```

These are the four desired square roots.

C.4 Examples for Chapter 6

Example 1. As pointed out previously, MATLAB is limited in the size of the numbers it can handle. The maximum number that MATLAB can represent accurately is about 10^{15}. The double precision used in MATLAB forces larger numbers to be approximated. However, one can still use MATLAB to generate prime numbers less than 10^7. Two functions, *nextprime* and *randprime*, have been written to generate prime numbers. The function *nextprime* takes a number n as input and attempts to find the next prime after n. The function *randprime* takes a number n as input and attempts to find a random prime between 1 and n. Both of these functions use the Miller-Rabin test described in Chapter 6.

```
>> nextprime(346735)

ans =
   346739

>> randprime(888888)

ans =
   737309
```

Example 2. Suppose you want to change the text `hello` to numbers:

```
>> text2int1('hello')
```

```
ans =
   805121215
```

Note that we are now using $a = 1$, $b = 2$, ..., $z = 26$, since otherwise a's at the beginnings of messages would disappear. (A more efficient procedure would be to work in base 27, so the numerical form of the message would be $8 + 5 \cdot 27 + 12 \cdot 27^2 + 12 \cdot 27^3 + 15 \cdot 27^4 = 1497902$. Note that this uses fewer digits.) Now suppose you want to change it back to letters:

```
>> int2text1(805121215)
```

```
ans =
   hello
```

Example 3. Encrypt the message `hi` using RSA with $n = 823091$ and $e = 17$.
Solution: First, change the message to numbers:

```
>> text2int1('hi')
```

```
ans =
   809
```

Now, raise it to the eth power mod n:

```
>> powermod(ans,17,823091)
```

```
ans =
   596912
```

Example 4. Decrypt the ciphertext in the previous problem.
Solution: First, we need to find the decryption exponent d. To do this, we need to find $\phi(823091)$. One way is

```
>> eulerphi(823091)
```

```
ans =
   821184
```

Another way is to factor n as $p \cdot q$ and then compute $(p-1)(q-1)$:

```
>> factor(823091)
```

```
ans =
   659    1249
```

```
>> 658*1248
```

```
ans =
   821184
```

Since $de \equiv 1 \pmod{\phi(n)}$, we compute the following (note that we are finding the inverse of $e \bmod \phi(n)$, not mod n):

```
>> powermod(17,-1,821184)
```

```
ans =
   48305
```

Therefore, $d = 48305$. To decrypt, raise the ciphertext to the dth power mod n:

```
>> powermod(596912,48305,823091)
```

```
ans =
   809
```

Finally, change back to letters:

```
>> int2text1(ans)
```

```
ans =
   hi
```

Example 5. Encrypt sunshine using RSA with $n = 823091$ and $e = 17$.
   Solution: First, change the plaintext to numbers:

```
>> text2int1('sunshine')
```

```
ans =
   1921141908091405
```

Suppose we simply raised this to the eth power mod n:

```
>> powermod(ans,17,823091)
```

```
ans =
   640791
```

If we decrypt (we know d from Example 4), we obtain

```
>> powermod(ans,48305,823091)
```

```
ans =
   340339
```

This is not the original plaintext. The reason is that the plaintext is larger than n, so we have obtained the plaintext mod n:

```
>> mod(text2int1('sunshine'),823091)
```

ans =
   340339

We need to break the plaintext into blocks, each less than n. In our case, we use three letters at a time:

$$192114 \quad 190809 \quad 1405$$

```
>> powermod(192114,17,823091)
```

ans =
   686022

```
>> powermod(190809,17,823091)
```

ans =
   660591

```
>> powermod(1405,17,823091)
```

ans =
   702126

The ciphertext is therefore 686022660591702126. Note that there is no reason to change this back to letters. In fact, it doesn't correspond to any text with letters.

Decrypt each block individually:

```
>> powermod(686022,48305,823091)
```

ans =
   192114

```
>> powermod(660591,48305,823091)
```

ans =
   190809

ans =
   1405

Example 6. Encrypt the messages bat, cat, and hat using the RSA with the primes $p = 857$, $q = 683$, and the encryption exponent $e = 9007$.

Solution: First, we calculate enter the variables p, q, and e.

```
>> p=857; q= 683; e=9007;
```

To calculate n, we enter the command

```
>> n=p*q;
```

The ciphertexts are calculated by

```
>> powermod(text2int1('bat'),e,n)
```

```
ans =
   54984
```

```
>> powermod(text2int1('cat'),e,n)
```

```
ans =
   236057
```

```
>> powermod(text2int1('hat'),e,n)
```

```
ans =
   382934
```

Example 7. In the previous example, we had $e = 9007$ and $n = 585331$. For this choice of e and n, the corresponding decryption exponent is $d = 265743$. (How would you calculate this?) Let's use d and e to factor n.

Solution: We use the universal exponent factorization method from Section 6.4. First, we define $y = ed - 1$, and represent $y = 2^s m$. One way to do this is to first calculate y and then keep dividing by 2 until you get an odd number.

```
>> y=e*d-1
```

```
y =
   2393547200
```

```
>> y/2
```

```
ans =
   1196773600
```

```
>> ans/2
```

```
ans =
   598386800
```

We continue this way until we get 37399175. Let's define $m = 37399175$. Now choose a random integer a. Hoping to be lucky, we choose 13. As in the universal exponent factorization method, we compute

```
>> powermod(13,m,n)
```

```
ans =
   530690
```

Since this is not $\pm 1 \pmod{n}$, we successively square it until we get ± 1:

```
>> powermod(ans,2,n)

ans =
   450781

>> powermod(ans,2,n)

ans =
   1
```

Since the last number before the 1 was not $\pm 1 \pmod{n}$, we have an example of $x \not\equiv \pm 1 \pmod{n}$ with $x^2 \equiv 1$. Therefore, $\gcd(x - 1, n)$ is a nontrivial factor of n:

```
>> gcd(450781 - 1, n)

ans =
   683
```

This is the q factor. We can calculate the other factor by n/q.

```
>> n/ans

ans =
   857
```

Since MATLAB is not naturally capable of dealing with large numbers, we shall skip presenting the example of the RSA Challenge discussed in Section 6.5. We present the RSA challenge in the Mathematica and Maple computer examples.

For those readers who have the Symbolic toolbox, we now demonstrate how to perform some Maple commands from within MATLAB.

First, to calculate $234567^{876543} \pmod{565656565}$, type

```
>> maple('234567&^876543 mod 565656565')

ans =
   473011223
```

To calculate the nextprime after 574786324786343457, type

```
>> maple('nextprime(574786324786343457)')

ans =
   574786324786343459
```

For other useful Maple commands, we refer the reader to the Maple examples in Appendix B.

C.5 Examples for Chapter 8

Example 1. Suppose there are 23 people in a room. What is the probability that at least two have the same birthday?

Solution: The probability that no two have the same birthday is $\prod_{i=1}^{22}(1-i/365)$ (note that the product stops at $i = 22$, not $i = 23$). Subtracting from 1 gives the probability that at least two have the same birthday:

```
>> 1-prod( 1 - (1:22)/365)
```

```
ans =
    0.5073
```

Example 2. Suppose a lazy phone company employee assigns telephone numbers by choosing random seven-digit numbers. In a town with 10000 phones, what is the probability that two people receive the same number?

```
>> 1-prod( 1 - (1:9999)/10^7)
```

```
ans =
    0.9933
```

Note that the number of phones is about three times the square root of the number of possibilities. This means that we expect the probability to be high, which it is. From Section 8.4, we have the estimate that if there are around $\sqrt{2(\ln 2)10^7} \approx 3723$ phones, there should be a 50% chance of a match. Let's see how accurate this is:

```
>> 1-prod( 1 - (1:3722)/10^7)
```

```
ans =
    0.4999
```

C.6 Examples for Chapter 10

Example 1. Suppose we have a (5, 8) Shamir secret sharing scheme. Everything is mod the prime $p = 987541$. Five of the shares are

$$(9853, 853), (4421, 4387), (6543, 1234), (93293, 78428), (12398, 7563).$$

Find the secret.

Solution: The function *interppoly(x,f,m)* calculates the interpolating polynomial that passes through the points (x_j, f_j). The arithmetic is performed modulo m.

In order to use this function, we need to make a vector that contains the x values, and another vector that contains the share values. This can be done using the following two commands:

```
>> x=[9853 4421 6543 93293 12398];
```

```
>> s=[853 4387 1234 78428 7563];
```

Now we calculate the coefficients for the interpolating polynomial.

```
>> y=interppoly(x,s,987541)
```

```
y =
     678987    14728    1651    574413    456741
```

The first value corresponds to the constant term in the interpolating polynomial and is the secret value. Therefore, 678987 is the secret.

C.7 Examples for Chapter 11

Example 1. Here is a game you can play. It is essentially the simplified version of poker over the telephone from Section 11.2. There are five cards: `ten, jack, queen, king, ace`. We have chosen to abbreviate them by the following: ten, ace, que, jac, kin. They are shuffled and disguised by raising their numbers to a random exponent mod the prime 300649. You are supposed to guess which one is the ace.

First, the cards are entered in and converted to numerical values by the following steps:

```
>> cards=['ten';'ace';'que';'jac';'kin'];
```

```
>> cvals=text2int1(cards)
```

```
cvals =
     200514
     10305
     172105
     100103
     110914
```

Next, we pick a random exponent k that will be used in the hiding operation. We use the semicolon after *khide* so that we cannot cheat and see what value of k is being used.

```
>> p=300649;
```

```
>> k=khide(p);
```

Now, shuffle the disguised cards (their numbers are raised to the kth power mod p):

```
>> shufvals=shuffle(cvals,k,p)

shufvals =

    226536
    226058
    241033
    281258
    116809
```

These are the five cards. None looks like the ace; that's because their numbers have been raised to powers mod the prime. Make a guess anyway. Let's see if you're correct.

```
>> reveal(shufvals,k,p)

ans =

jac
que
ten
kin
ace
```

Let's play again:

```
>> k=khide(p);

>> shufvals=shuffle(cvals,k,p)

shufvals =

    117135
    144487
    108150
    266322
    264045
```

Make your guess (note that the numbers are different because a different random exponent was used). Were you lucky?

```
>> reveal(shufvals,k,p)

ans =
```

```
kin
jac
ten
que
ace
```

Perhaps you need some help. Let's play one more time:

```
>> k=khide(p);
```

```
>> shufvals=shuffle(cvals,k,p)
```

```
shufvals =

     108150
     144487
     266322
     264045
     117135
```

We now ask for advice:

```
>> advise(shufvals,p);
```

```
Ace Index:   4
```

We are advised that the fourth card is the ace. Let's see:

```
>> reveal(shufvals,k,p)
```

```
ans =

ten
jac
que
ace
kin
```

How does this work? Read the part on "How to Cheat" in Section 11.2. Note that if we raise the numbers for the cards to the $(p-1)/2$ power mod p, we get

```
>> powermod(cvals,(p-1)/2,p)
```

```
ans =
```

    1
  300648
    1
    1
    1

Therefore, only the ace is a quadratic nonresidue mod p.

C.8 Examples for Chapter 15

Example 1. We want to graph the elliptic curve $y^2 = x(x-1)(x+1)$.

First, we create a string v that will contain the equation we wish to graph.

```
>> v='y^2 - x*(x-1)*(x+1)';
```

Next we use the *ezplot* command to plot the elliptic curve.

```
>> ezplot(v,[-1,3,-5,5])
```

The plot appears in Figure C.1. The use of $[-1, 3, -5, 5]$ in the preceding command is to define the limits of the x-axis and y-axis in the plot.

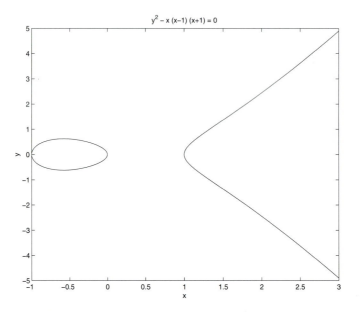

Figure C.1: Graph of the Elliptic Curve $y^2 = x(x-1)(x+1)$.

Example 2. Add the points (1,3) and (3,5) on the elliptic curve $y^2 \equiv x^3 + 24x + 13 \pmod{29}$.

```
>> addell([1,3],[3,5],24,13,29)

ans =
    26    1
```

You can check that the point (26,1) is on the curve: $26^3 + 24 \cdot 26 + 13 \equiv 1^2$ (mod 29).

Example 3. Add (1,3) to the point at infinity on the curve of the previous example.

```
>> addell([1,3],[inf,inf],24,13,29)

ans =
    1    3
```

As expected, adding the point at infinity to a point P returns the point P.

Example 4. Let $P = (1,3)$ be a point on the elliptic curve $y^2 \equiv x^3 + 24x + 13$ (mod 29). Find $7P$.

```
>> multell([1,3],7,24,13,29)

ans =
    15    6
```

Example 5. Find $k(1,3)$ for $k = 1, 2, 3, \ldots, 40$ on the curve of the previous example.

```
>> multsell([1,3],40,24,13,29)

ans =

     1     3
    11    10
    23    28
     0    10
    19     7
    18    19
    15     6
    20    24
     4    12
     4    17
    20     5
    15    23
    18    10
```

19	22
0	19
23	1
11	19
1	26
Inf	Inf
1	3
11	10
23	28
0	10
19	7
18	19
15	6
20	24
4	12
4	17
20	5
15	23
18	10
19	22
0	19
23	1
11	19
1	26
Inf	Inf
1	3
11	10

Notice how the points repeat after every 19 multiples.

Example 6. The previous four examples worked mod the prime 29. If we work mod a composite number, the situation at infinity becomes more complicated since we could be at infinity mod both factors or we could be at infinity mod one of the factors but not mod the other. Therefore, we stop the calculation if this last situation happens and we exhibit a factor. For example, let's try to compute $12P$, where $P = (1,3)$ is on the elliptic curve $y^2 \equiv x^3 - 5x + 13 \pmod{209}$:

```
>> multell([1,3],12,-5,13,11*19)
```

```
Elliptic Curve addition produced a factor of n, factor= 19
Multell found a factor of n and exited
```

```
ans =
     []
```

Now let's compute the successive multiples to see what happened along the way:

```
>> multsell([1,3],12,-5,13,11*19)
```

```
Elliptic Curve addition produced a factor of n, factor= 19
Multsell ended early since it found a factor
```

```
ans =
       1       3
      91      27
     118     133
     148     182
      20      35
```

When we computed $6P$, we ended up at infinity mod 19. Let's see what is happening mod the two prime factors of 209, namely 19 and 11:

```
>> multsell([1,3],20,-5,13,19)
```

```
ans =

       1       3
      15       8
       4       0
      15      11
       1      16
     Inf     Inf
       1       3
      15       8
       4       0
      15      11
       1      16
     Inf     Inf
       1       3
      15       8
       4       0
      15      11
       1      16
     Inf     Inf
       1       3
      15       8
```

```
>> multsell([1,3],20,-5,13,11)

ans =

     1     3
     3     5
     8     1
     5     6
     9     2
     6    10
     2     0
     6     1
     9     9
     5     5
     8    10
     3     6
     1     8
   Inf   Inf
     1     3
     3     5
     8     1
     5     6
     9     2
     6    10
```

After six steps, we were at infinity mod 19, but it takes 14 steps to reach infinity mod 11. To find $6P$, we needed to invert a number that was 0 mod 19 and nonzero mod 11. This couldn't be done, but it yielded the factor 19. This is the basis of the elliptic curve factorization method.

Example 7. Factor 193279 using elliptic curves.

Solution: First, we need to choose some random elliptic curves and a point on each curve. For example, let's take $P = (2, 4)$ and the elliptic curve

$$y^2 \equiv x^3 - 10x + b \pmod{193279}.$$

For P to lie on the curve, we take $b = 28$. We'll also take

$$
\begin{aligned}
y^2 &\equiv x^3 + 11x - 11, & P = (1, 1), \\
y^2 &\equiv x^3 + 17x - 14, & P = (1, 2).
\end{aligned}
$$

Now we compute multiples of the point P. We do the analog of the $p - 1$ method, so we choose a bound B, say $B = 12$, and compute $B!P$.

```
>> multell([2,4],factorial(12),-10,28,193279)
```

Elliptic Curve addition produced a factor of n, factor= 347
Multell found a factor of n and exited

```
ans =
    []
>> multell([1,1],factorial(12),11,-11,193279)

ans =
    13862    35249

>> multell([1,2],factorial(12),17,-14,193279)
```

Elliptic Curve addition produced a factor of n, factor= 557
Multell found a factor of n and exited

```
ans =
    []
```

Let's analyze in more detail what happened in these examples.

On the first curve, $266P$ ends up at infinity mod 557 and $35P$ is infinity mod 347. Since $272 = 2 \cdot 7 \cdot 9$, it has a prime factor larger than $B = 12$, so $B!P$ is not infinity mod 557. But 35 divides $B!$, so $B!P$ is infinity mod 347.

On the second curve, $356P = $ infinity mod 347, and $561P = $ infinity mod 557. Since $356 = 4 \cdot 89$ and $561 = 3 \cdot 11 \cdot 17$, we don't expect to find the factorization with this curve.

The third curve is a surprise. We have $331P = $ infinity mod 347 and $272P = $ infinity mod 557. Since 331 is prime and $272 = 16 \cdot 17$, we don't expect to find the factorization with this curve. However, by chance, an intermediate step in the calculation of $B!P$ yielded the factorization. Here's what happened. At an intermediate step in the calculation, the program required adding the points $(184993, 13462)$ and $(20678, 150484)$. These two points are congruent mod 557 but not mod 347. Therefore, the slope of the line through these two points is defined mod 347 but is $0/0$ mod 557. When we tried to find the multiplicative inverse of the denominator mod 193279, the gcd algorithm yielded the factor 557. This phenomenon is fairly rare.

Example 8. Here is how to produce the example of an elliptic curve ElGamal cryptosystem from Section 15.5. For more details, see the text. The elliptic curve is $y^2 \equiv x^3 + 3x + 45 \pmod{8831}$ and the point is $G = (4, 11)$. Alice's message is the point $P_m = (5, 1743)$.

Bob has chosen his secret random number $a_B = 3$ and has computed $a_b G$:

```
>> multell([4,11],3,3,45,8831)
```

```
ans =
    413    1808
```

Bob publishes this point. Alice chooses the random number $k = 8$ and computes kG and $P_m + k(a_B G)$:

```
>> multell([4,11],8,3,45,8831)

ans =
    5415    6321

>> addell([5,1743],multell([413,1808],8,3,45,8831),3,45,8831)

ans =
    6626    3576
```

Alice sends (5415,6321) and (6626, 3576) to Bob, who multiplies the first of these point by a_B:

```
>> multell([5415,6321],3,3,45,8831)

ans =
    673    146
```

Bob then subtracts the result from the last point Alice sends him. Note that he subtracts by adding the point with the second coordinate negated:

```
>> addell([6626,3576],[673,-146],3,45,8831)

ans =
    5    1743
```

Bob has therefore received Alice's message.

Example 9. Let's reproduce the numbers in the example of a Diffie-Hellman key exchange from Section 15.5: The elliptic curve is $y^2 \equiv x^3 + x + 7206 \pmod{7211}$ and the point is $G = (3,5)$. Alice chooses her secret $N_A = 12$ and Bob chooses his secret $N_B = 23$. Alice calculates

```
>> multell([3,5],12,1,7206,7211)

ans =
    1794    6375
```

She sends (1794,6375) to Bob. Meanwhile, Bob calculates

```
>> multell([3,5],23,1,7206,7211)

ans =
    3861    1242
```

and sends (3861,1242) to Alice. Alice multiplies what she receives by N_A and Bob multiplies what he receives by N_B:

```
>> multell([3861,1242],12,1,7206,7211)

ans =
    1472    2098

>> multell([1794,6375],23,1,7206,7211)

ans =
    1472    2098
```

Therefore, Alice and Bob have produced the same key.

Appendix D

Suggestions for Further Reading

For the history of cryptography, the best source by far is [Kahn].

For additional treatment of topics in the present book, and many other topics, see [Stinson], [Schneier], and [Menezes et al.]. These books also have extensive bibliographies.

An approach emphasizing algebraic methods in cryptography is given in [Koblitz].

A book oriented more toward protocols and practical network security is [Stallings].

The Internet, of course, contains a wealth of information about cryptographic issues. Also, the conference proceedings *CRYPTO, EUROCRYPT,* and *ASIACRYPT* (published in Springer-Verlag's Lecture Notes in Computer Science series) contain many interesting reports on recent developments.

Bibliography

[Atkins et al.]   D. Atkins, M. Graff, A. Lenstra, P. Leyland, "The magic words are squeamish ossifrage," *Advances in Cryptology — ASIACRYPT '94*, Lecture Notes in Computer Science 917, Springer-Verlag, 1995, pp. 263–277.

[Beker-Piper]   H. Beker and F. Piper, *Cipher Systems: The Protection of Communications*, Wiley-Interscience, 1982.

[Berlekamp]   E. R. Berlekamp, *Algebraic Coding Theory*, McGraw-Hill, 1968.

[Blake et al.]   I. Blake, G. Seroussi, N. Smart, *Elliptic Curves in Cryptography*, Cambridge University Press, 1999.

[Blom]   R. Blom, "An optimal class of symmetric key generation schemes," *Advances in Cryptology — EUROCRYPT'84*, Lecture Notes in Computer Science 209, Springer-Verlag, 1985, pp. 335–338.

[Boneh]   D. Boneh, "Twenty years of attacks on the RSA cryptosystem," *Amer. Math. Soc. Notices* 46 (1999), 203–213.

[Boneh et al.]   D. Boneh, G. Durfee, and Y. Frankel, "An attack on RSA given a fraction of the private key bits," *Advances in Cryptology — ASIACRYPT '98*, Lecture Notes in Computer Science 1514, Springer-Verlag, 1998, pp. 25–34.

[Brands]   S. Brands, "Untraceable off-line cash in wallets with observers," *Advances in Cryptology — CRYPTO'93*, Lecture Notes in Computer Science 773, Springer-Verlag, 1994, pp. 302–318.

[Campbell-Wiener]   K. Campbell and M. Wiener, "DES is not a group," *Advances in Cryptology — CRYPTO '92*, Lecture Notes in Computer Science 740, Springer-Verlag, 1993, pp. 512–520.

[Chabaud]   F. Chabaud, "On the security of some cryptosystems based on error-correcting codes," *Advances in Cryptology — EUROCRYPT'94*, Lecture Notes in Computer Science 950, Springer-Verlag, 1995, pp. 131–139.

[Cohen]   H. Cohen, *A Course in Computational Number Theory*, Springer-Verlag, 1993.

[Coppersmith1]   D. Coppersmith, "The Data Encryption Standard (DES) and its strength against attacks," *IBM Journal of Research and Development*, vol. 38, no. 3, May 1994, pp. 243–250.

[Coppersmith2]   D. Coppersmith, "Small solutions to polynomial equations, and low exponent RSA vulnerabilities," *J. Cryptology* 10 (1997), 233–260.

[Cover-Thomas]   T. Cover and J. Thomas, *Elements of Information Theory*, Wiley Series in Telecommunications, 1991.

[Crandall-Pomerance]   R. Crandall and C. Pomerance, *Prime Numbers, a Computational Perspective*, Springer-Telos, 2000.

[Damgård et al.]   I. Damgård, P. Landrock, and C. Pomerance, "Average case error estimates for the strong probable prime test," *Mathematics of Computation* 61 (1993), 177–194.

[Diffie-Hellman]   W. Diffie and M. Hellman, "New directions in cryptography," *IEEE Transactions in Information Theory*, 22 (1976), 644–654.

[Ekert-Joza]   A. Ekert and R. Jozsa, "Quantum computation and Shor's factoring algorithm," *Reviews of Modern Physics*, 68 (1996), 733–753.

[Fortune-Merritt]   S. Fortune and M. Merritt, "Poker Protocols," *Advances in Cryptology — CRYPTO'84*, Lecture Notes in Computer Science 196, Springer-Verlag, 1985, pp. 454–464.

[Gaines]   H. Gaines, *Cryptanalysis*, Dover Publications, 1956.

[Gallager]   R. G. Gallager, *Information Theory and Reliable Communication*, Wiley, 1969.

[Gilmore]   *Cracking DES: Secrets of Encryption Research, Wiretap Politics & Chip Design*, Electronic Frontier Foundation, J. Gilmore (editor), O'Reilly and Associates, 1998.

[Girault et al.]   M. Girault, R. Cohen, and M. Campana, "A generalized birthday attack," *Advances in Cryptology — EUROCRYPT'88*, Lecture Notes in Computer Science 330, Springer-Verlag, 1988, pp. 129–156.

[Golomb]   S. Golomb, *Shift Register Sequences*, 2nd ed., Aegean Park Press, 1982.

[Hughes et al.]   R.J. Hughes et al., "Quantum Cryptography over Underground Optical Fibers," *Advances in Cryptology — CRYPTO'96*, Lecture Notes in Computer Science 1109, Springer-Verlag, 1996, pp. 329–342.

[Kahn]   D. Kahn, *The Codebreakers*, 2nd ed., Scribner, 1996.

[Kilian-Rogaway]   J. Kilian and P. Rogaway, "How to protect DES against exhaustive key search (an analysis of DESX)," *J. Cryptology* 14 (2001), 17–35.

[Koblitz]   N. Koblitz, *Algebraic Aspects of Cryptography*, Springer-Verlag, 1998.

[Kocher]   P. Kocher, "Timing attacks on implementations of Diffie-Hellman, RSA, DSS, and other systems," *Advances in Cryptology — CRYPTO '96*, Lecture Notes in Computer Science 1109, Springer, 1996, pp. 104–113.

[Kozaczuk]   W. Kozaczuk, *Enigma: How the German Machine Cipher Was Broken, and How It Was Read by the Allies in World War Two*; edited and translated by Christopher Kasparek, Arms and Armour Press, London, 1984.

[Lin-Costello]   S. Lin and D. J. Costello, Jr., *Error Control Coding: Fundamentals and Applications*, Prentice Hall, 1983.

[MacWilliams-Sloane]   F. J. MacWilliams and N. J. A. Sloane, *The Theory of Error-Correcting Codes*, North-Holland, 1977.

[Matsui]   M. Matsui, "Linear cryptanalysis method for DES cipher," *Advances in Cryptology — EUROCRYPT'93*, Lecture Notes in Computer Science 765, Springer-Verlag, 1994, pp. 386–397.

[Menezes et al.]   A. Menezes, P. van Oorschot, and S. Vanstone, *Handbook of Applied Cryptography*, CRC Press, 1997.

[Merkle-Hellman]   R. Merkle and M. Hellman, "On the security of multiple encryption," *Communications of the ACM* 24 (1981), 465–467.

[Nelson-Gailly]   M. Nelson and J.-L. Gailly, *The Data Compression Book*, M&T Books, 1996.

[Okamoto-Ohta]   T. Okamoto and K. Ohta, "Universal electronic cash," *Advances in Cryptology — CRYPTO'91*, Lecture Notes in Computer Science 576, Springer-Verlag, 1992, pp. 324–337.

[Quisquater et al.]   J.-J. Quisquater and L. Guillou, "How to explain zero-knowledge protocols to your children," *Advances in Cryptology — CRYPTO '89*, Lecture Notes in Computer Science 435, Springer-Verlag, 1990, pp. 628–631.

[Rieffel-Polak]   E. Rieffel and W. Polak, "An Introduction to Quantum Computing for Non-Physicists," available at *xxx.lanl.gov/abs/quant-ph/9809016*.

[Schneier]   B. Schneier, *Applied Cryptography*, 2nd ed., John Wiley, 1996.

[Shannon1]   C. Shannon, "Communication theory of secrecy systems," *Bell Systems Technical Journal* 28 (1949), 656–715.

[Shannon2]   C. Shannon, "A mathematical theory of communication," *Bell Systems Technical Journal*, 27 (1948), 379–423, 623–656.

[Stallings]   W. Stallings, *Cryptography and Network Security: Principles and Practice*, 2nd ed., Prentice Hall, 1998.

[Stinson]   D. Stinson, *Cryptography: Theory and Practice*, CRC Press, 1995.

[Thompson]   T. Thompson, *From Error-Correcting Codes through Sphere Packings to Simple Groups*, Carus Mathematical Monographs, number 21, Mathematical Association of America, 1983.

[van der Lubbe]   J. van der Lubbe, *Basic Methods of Cryptography*, Cambridge University Press, 1998.

[van Oorschot-Wiener]   P. van Oorschot and M. Wiener, "A known-plaintext attack on two-key triple encryption," *Advances in Cryptology — EUROCRYPT '90*, Lecture Notes in Computer Science 473, Springer-Verlag, 1991, pp. 318–325.

[Welsh]   D. Welsh, *Codes and Cryptography*, Oxford, 1988.

[Wicker]   S. Wicker, *Error Control Systems for Digital Communication and Storage*, Prentice Hall, 1995.

[Wiener]   M. Wiener, "Cryptanalysis of short RSA secret exponents," *IEEE Trans. Inform. Theory*, 36 (1990), 553–558.

[Williams]   H. Williams, *Edouard Lucas and Primality Testing*, Wiley-Interscience, 1998.

Index

(n, M, d) code, 304
$GF(2^8)$, 88, 129
$GF(4)$, 84, 285, 344
$[n, k, d]$ code, 312
$\mathbf{Z}_p$, 86
$\oplus$, 44, 99
$\phi(n)$, 77
$p - 1$ method, 150, 281, 284, 393, 427
q-ary code, 301
$\mathcal{G}_{23}$, 325
$\mathcal{G}_{24}$, 321

addition law, 272, 276, 291
AddRoundKey, 128
ADFGX cipher, 31
Adleman, 137
Advanced Encryption Standard (AES),
    122, 127
affine cipher, 14, 267
Alice, 2
ASCII, 38
asymptotic bounds, 309
Athena, 242
Atkins, 154
attacks, 3
attacks on RSA, 142
authenticated key agreement, 238
authentication, 9, 29, 158
authenticity, 197
automatic teller machine, 228, 232

basic principle, 78, 145
Bayes's theorem, 252
BCH bound, 336
BCH codes, 335
Berlekamp, 348

Berson, 228
Biham, 98, 102
binary, 37
binary code, 301
birthday attack, 186–188, 194, 279,
    291
birthday paradox, 155, 186, 195
bit, 38
bit commitment, 173
Blakley secret sharing scheme, 213,
    217
Bletchley Park, 53
blind signature, 179
blind signature, restricted, 200, 206
block cipher, 33, 98
block code, 302
Blom key pre-distribution scheme, 240
Blum-Blum-Shub, 41
Bob, 2
bombes, 53
Boneh, 143
bounded storage, 40
bounds on codes, 305
Brands, 200
breaking DES, 118
brute force attack, 6, 136
burst errors, 345
byte, 38
ByteSub transformation, 128, 129

Caesar cipher, 13
Carmichael number, 92
certificate, 246
certification authority (CA), 246
chain rule, 256
challenge-response, 228

characteristic 2, 284

Chaum, 179, 183, 200

cheating, 224

check symbols, 314

Chinese remainder theorem, 72, 74, 94

chosen ciphertext attack, 4

chosen plaintext attack, 3

cipher block chaining (CBC), 33, 116

cipher feedback (CFB), 33, 117, 135

ciphers, 6

ciphertext, 2

ciphertext only attack, 3

Cliff, 243

Cocks, 138, 156

code, 301

code rate, 299, 304, 306

codes, 6

codeword, 296, 302

coding gain, 301

coding theory, 2, 295

coin, 202

collision-free, 182

composite, 60

computationally infeasible, 157, 158

conditional entropy, 256

conditional probability, 252

confidentiality, 9

confusion, 37

congruence, 66

continued fractions, 367, 368, 370

convolutional codes, 348

Coppersmith, 113, 114, 142

correct errors, 303

coset, 317

coset leader, 316, 317

cryptanalysis, 1

cryptography, 1

cryptology, 1

cyclic codes, 329

Daemen, 127

Data Encryption Standard (DES), 97, 107, 124, 237

decode, 301

degenerate curves, 283

DES Challenge, 120

DES Cracker, 120

designed distance, 339

DESX, 122

detect errors, 303

dictionary attack, 123

differential cryptanalysis, 102, 136

Diffie, 118, 137, 156, 239

Diffie-Hellman key exchange, 237, 238, 249, 288, 401, 436, 476

diffusion, 37, 136

digital cash, 199

digital signature, 10, 238, 289

Digital Signature Algorithm (DSA), 170, 190, 290, 292

digital signatures, 177

digram, 25, 30, 35, 263

Ding, 40

discrete logarithm, 90, 93, 165, 180, 188, 204, 223, 233, 234, 242, 278, 287

Disparition, La, 17

divides, 59

dot product, 21, 55, 300, 314, 318, 356

double encryption, 113, 122, 159, 161, 188

dual code, 318, 350

dual signature, 198

e-commerce, 196

electronic cash, 11, 199

electronic codebook (ECB), 33, 115

Electronic Frontier Foundation, 120

ElGamal cryptosystem, 159, 173, 287, 401, 435, 475

ElGamal signature, 179, 191–193, 289, 293

elliptic curve cryptosystems, 287

elliptic curves, 151, 272

elliptic integral, 273

Ellis, 138

encode, 301

Enigma, 49

entropy, 253, 254

entropy of English, 263
entropy rate, 269
equivalent codes, 305
error correcting codes, 295, 301
error correction, 29
Euclidean algorithm, 62, 63, 95, 370
Euler's ϕ-function, 77, 141
Euler's theorem, 77, 139
Eve, 2
everlasting security, 40
existential forgery, 192
expansion permutation, 108
exponent factorization method, 150, 361, 367
extended Euclidean algorithm, 65, 87

factor base, 152, 170
factoring, 149, 154, 280, 360
factorization records, 154
Feige-Fiat-Shamir identification, 231
Feistel system, 98, 99, 136
Fermat factorization, 149
Fermat's theorem, 76, 146
Feynman, 353
field, 84
finite field, 83, 129, 284, 285, 331
flipping coins, 219
football, 173
Fourier transform, 361, 365, 370
fractions, 71
fraud control, 204
frequencies of letters, 17, 24
frequency analysis, 24

Gadsby, 17
games, 11, 219
generating matrix, 313
generating polynomial, 332
Gilbert-Varshamov bound, 308, 311, 351
Golay code, 320
Goppa codes, 310, 346
Graff, 154
Grant, 243
greatest common divisor (gcd), 62, 95

group, 113
Guillou, 228

Hadamard code, 300, 311
Hamming bound, 307
Hamming code, 298, 311, 319, 350
Hamming distance, 302
Hamming sphere, 306
Hamming weight, 313
hash function, 182, 198, 232
Hasse's theorem, 278, 293, 294
Hellman, 119, 137, 156, 167
Hill cipher, 33
Holmes, Sherlock, 26
hot line, 40
Huffman codes, 258

IBM, 97, 127
identification scheme, 10, 231
independent, 252
index calculus, 170, 279
infinity, 272
information rate, 304
information symbols, 314
information theory, 250
initial permutation, 108, 113
integrity, 9, 197
intruder-in-the-middle, 238, 249
inverting matrices, 80
irreducible polynomial, 86
ISBN, 299, 349

Kerberos, 242
Kerckhoffs's principle, 4
ket, 356
key, 2
key agreement, 237
key distribution, 237, 241, 357
key establishment, 10, 236
key exchange, 288
key length, 6, 19, 272, 347
key permutation, 111
key pre-distribution, 239
key schedule, 131, 136
knapsack problem, 156

known plaintext attack, 3
Koblitz, 272, 279
Kocher, 143

Lagrange interpolation, 210, 211
Lenstra, A., 154
Lenstra, H.W., 272
Leyland, 154
linear code, 311, 312
linear congruential generator, 41
linear cryptanalysis, 107, 136
linear feedback shift register (LFSR), 42, 90
LUCIFER, 98

M.I.T., 242
Maple, 403
Mariner, 300
MARS, 127
Massey, 348
Mathematica, 372
MATLAB, 437
matrices, 80
Matsui, 107
Mauborgne, 38
Maurer, 40
McEliece cryptosystem, 159, 345
MD5, 185
MDS code, 306, 310
meet-in-the-middle attack, 122, 126, 188, 194
Menezes, 288
message digest, 182
message recovery scheme, 182
Miller, 272
Miller-Rabin primality test, 146, 163
minimum distance, 303
MixColumn transformation, 128, 130, 136
mod, 66
modes of operation, 115
modular exponentiation, 74, 93, 143, 191
Morse code, 258
multiplicative inverse, 69, 88, 132

National Bureau of Standards (NBS), 97, 119
National Institute of Standards and Technology (NIST)), 97, 119, 122, 127
National Security Agency (NSA), 55, 97, 118, 119
nearest neighbor decoding, 303
Newton interpolating polynomial, 217
non-repudiation, 9, 158
NP-complete, 317
number field sieve, 153

Ohta, 200
Okamoto, 200
one-time pad, 38, 261, 268
one-way function, 41, 123, 158, 166, 182
order, 92, 291

Painvin, 32
parity check, 296
parity check matrix, 314, 334
passwords, 123, 175
Peggy, 228
perfect code, 307, 350, 351
perfect secrecy, 260, 261
Pfitzmann, 183
plaintext, 2, 279
Playfair cipher, 30
Pohlig-Hellman algorithm, 167, 175, 191, 278, 293
point at infinity, 272
poker, 221
polarization, 354
Pollard, 150
preimage resistant, 182
Pretty Good Privacy (PGP), 247
primality testing, 145
prime, 60
prime number theorem, 60, 147, 193
primitive root, 79, 92
primitive root of unity, 336
probability, 251
pseudo-random bits, 40

pseudoprime, 146, 147
public key cryptography, 4, 137, 156
Public Key Infrastructure (PKI), 246

quadratic residue, 225, 226
quadratic sieve, 151
quantum computing, 359
quantum cryptography, 353, 357
quantum Fourier transform, 365
qubit, 357
Quisquater, 228

Różycki, 49
Rabin, 40, 94
random variable, 251
RC6, 127
recurrence relation, 43, 90
redundancy, 267
Reed-Solomon codes, 343
Rejewski, 49, 53
relatively prime, 62
repetition code, 296, 310
restricted blind signature, 200, 206
Rijmen, 127
Rijndael, 122, 127
Rivest, 122, 137, 185
root of unity, 336
rotor machines, 49
round constant, 131, 136
round key, 132
RoundKey addition, 131
RSA, 137, 138, 237
RSA challenge, 154
RSA signature, 156, 178
run length coding, 269

S-box, 100, 108, 112, 113, 130, 132,
    136
salt, 123
Scherbius, 49
Schnorr identification scheme, 235
secret sharing, 10, 208
secret splitting, 208
Secure Electronic Transaction, 197
Secure Hash Algorithm (SHA), 185

self-dual code, 318
Serge, 243
Serpent, 127
Shamir, 98, 102, 137
Shamir threshold scheme, 210
Shamir's three-pass protocol, 242
Shannon, 37, 250, 254, 258, 264, 265
shift cipher, 13
ShiftRow transformation, 128, 130, 136
Shor, 353, 359
Shor's algorithm, 359, 363
signature with appendix, 182
Singleton bound, 306
smooth, 282
sphere packing bound, 307
square roots, 73, 81, 94, 172, 219, 229,
    234
squeamish ossifrage, 155
Station-to-Station (STS) protocol, 237,
    238
strong pseudoprime, 146, 147, 163
strongly collision-free, 182
substitution cipher, 23, 267
symmetric key, 4, 158
syndrome, 316, 317
syndrome decoding, 317
systematic code, 314

ternary code, 301
threshold scheme, 209
ticket-granting service, 243
timing attacks, 143
Transmission Control Protocol (TCP),
    348
transport protocol, 241
trapdoor, 158
treaty verification, 156
Trent, 243
triangle inequality, 303
trigram, 35, 263
triple DES, 122, 126
triple encryption, 189
trust levels, 247
trusted authority, 232, 238, 239, 243
Turing, 53

two-dimensional parity code, 297
Twofish, 127

unicity distance, 267
universal exponent method, 141, 149,
        391, 425, 464
Unix, 124

van Heijst, 183
van Oorschot, 239
Vandermonde determinant, 210, 337
Vanstone, 288
variance, 144
Vernam, 38
Verser, 120
Victor, 228
Vigenère cipher, 16
Void, A, 18
Voyager, 320

weak key, 114, 125, 135
web of trust, 248
Wiener, 119, 142, 239
World War I, 6, 29
World War II, 4, 49, 53, 239

X.509, 248
XOR, 39

zero-knowledge, 228
Zimmerman, 247
Zygalski, 49